D0359743

SINATRA

SINATRA

Behind the Legend

J. RANDY TARABORRELLI

A BIRCH LANE PRESS BOOK
Published by Carol Publishing Group

A Birch Lane Press Book
Published by Carol Publishing Group
Birch Lane Press is a registered trademark of Carol Communications, Inc.

Editorial, sales and distribution, and rights and permissions inquiries should be addressed to Carol Publishing Group, 120 Enterprise Avenue, Secaucus, N.J. 07094

In Canada: Canadian Manda Group, One Atlantic Avenue, Suite 105, Toronto, Ontario M6K 3E7

Carol Publishing Group books may be purchased in bulk at special discounts for sales promotion, fund-raising, or educational purposes. Special editions can be created to specifications. For details, contact Special Sales Department, Carol Publishing Group, 120 Enterprise Avenue, Secaucus, N.J. 07094.

Manufactured in the United States of America
10 9 8 7 6 5 4 3 2 1

Library of Congress Cataloging-in-Publication Data

Taraborrelli, J. Randy.
    Sinatra : behind the legend / by J. Randy Taraborrelli.
       p.   cm.
    ISBN 1-55972-434-X (hc)
    1. Sinatra, Frank, 1915– . 2. Singers—United States—Biography.   I. Title.
    ML420.S565T37   1997
    782.42164′092—dc21
       [B]   97–27569
                                                                             CIP
                                                                             MN

For Rose Marie Taraborrelli

PREFACE

I t's easy to paint Francis Albert Sinatra with sweeping brush strokes. Great singer. Demanding boss. Loyal friend. Champion of causes. Friend of the famous. Confidant of the infamous. Generous, sometimes anonymous, benefactor. Unpredictable, loud-mouthed tough guy. Devoted son. Supportive parent. Womanizer.

All of that is true. Indeed, the public has always been able to find a side of Frank Sinatra to meet its expectations.

But those are just the obvious facts. One wonders about the rest of the story. What is it about this man that transformed him from what he was—just a kid with a voice and a dream from an Italian neighborhood in Hoboken, New Jersey—to what he became: the man with *the* voice, living the American Dream as an international star and arguably one of the most important cultural figures of the twentieth century? What was behind it all? When you closely examine the life and experiences of Frank Sinatra, what can be pinpointed as the driving force?

His intelligence as a singer as well as a sense of poetry and an innate homing instinct for the truth of the story, for implanting in the listener's heart the emotions and impact of a song and of a lyric, defined him professionally. Beyond that, his breath control, sense of phrasing—holding back, moving ahead of the beat, bridging lines and measures—and his ability to edit are all unparalleled. Most pop male singers after Sinatra were derivative of him, though certainly none of them had his impact on our culture.

His inestimable musical instincts would not have meant much to the world, though, if Sinatra were the kind of guy who just let life pass him by, who didn't have the guts to take on the world the way he did. This is a man who has truly *lived* his life; just about everything he did, he did with passion. For the sake of passion. In search of it. In the heat of it. In the moment of it. All of it. And this passion appeared in many forms in Sinatra's personal life: good living, good women, good sex—make that great living, great women, great sex—being chief among them.

Sinatra's story is one of triumph, but it is also one of immense sadness, for it begs the answers to certain questions that have been posed time and again not only in his life but in many of our own lives as well: How long

vii

can passion be sustained? What happens when it dies? How does one go about finding it again? Should one even try?

For decades Frank Sinatra searched and found, then lost and replaced, that almost overwhelming sense of ecstasy that he insisted must rule his life. For Sinatra, excess was never enough. A slave to his passions, he always wanted more, more, *more.* That kind of life would be interesting just on its face, but what makes it more fascinating—indeed, what makes this man even more compelling—is the way Frank divvied out the experience to us, his public, in bits and pieces, through his songs. We could be privy to all of it—the joy and misery of his life—if we just listened closely enough. Those weren't mere records he made; they were testaments to the way he was living at any given moment. It was in his music that his professional life and his personal experiences became one.

The lamentation about lost love, loneliness, and despair, the songs the saloon singer sings—"The End of a Love Affair," "One for My Baby," "Angel Eyes," and so many others—tell the story: Sinatra's story and sometimes our own. These are songs that search the soul and wrench the gut and touch a common chord of sorrow. He's nothing if not a poet, for only a poet could interpret his feelings and emotions—and yes, his passion—the way Sinatra has for so long.

He almost always knows exactly what songs are right for his voice, for his mood, for his life at the time. Sinatra's been there. His wives, Nancy Barbato, Ava Gardner, Mia Farrow, and Barbara Marx knew those highs, too. They soared with Frank and then plummeted with him, too. And the other women: Lana Turner, Marilyn Monroe, Lauren Bacall, and the rest. Frank took them there with him—to the moon, baby.

We, his listeners, have been there as well. Not with Frank, personally, though it certainly has sometimes seemed that way. That's how much this storyteller's tales have touched us. But if we've lived, *really* lived, we've been there.

Into our own lives often come those fleeting moments of passion. There are the big ones that make us soar to the heavens with abandon, like extraordinary sex, the kind that makes one's head spin and makes life seem worth living. And then there are the small ones that, even for just a moment, take one's breath away: a perfectly prepared meal when the pasta is just right; a fine glass of wine that warms the insides the way it was meant to. Even a moment of danger, of suspense (as long as it all turns out all right and we live to tell the tale over and over again), takes us there. Good living. The occasional self-indulgent vacation. The infrequent expensive gift that makes no economic sense whatsoever. It feels good when one splurges.

One Alan and Marilyn Bergman song asks the question "How Do You Keep the Music Playing?" Indeed, how can any man sustain from day to day that exhilarating feeling at the beginning of one of those memorable moments? What happens when the meal ends, the glass of wine empties, the orgasm subsides, or the bill shows up?

Most of us don't attempt to live our whole lives on clouds of euphoria, anyway, always looking for something bigger and better in life, never, ever, satisfied. For most of us the time comes when we settle into something deeper and, it could be argued, more meaningful. In the case of romance, it might be a relationship based on respect and admiration, common interests, shared history. If sex can last, more the better. The passion will probably dissipate.

We settle. Most of us do, anyway. It's not so bad, or at least not as bad as it sounds. It's easier that way. It makes more sense.

But not Frank Sinatra. He was inclined not to settle; he came from Italian immigrant stock that never settled (for if they had, they never would have made it to America) and from an influential mother who lived her whole high-flying life in search of power and excitement. But they, Frank's forebears, had common sense (most of them, anyway). They knew when to stop. Frank never did, and he had the fame and money and talent that made it possible for him to have it all, even when it wasn't such a good idea, even when he had had more than enough.

Was it worth it? This life lived always in constant pursuit of the next thrill, the wild ride that has been Frank Sinatra's life history. Was it worth it to him? Let's face it. He didn't do so badly, or as Frank might say, "You should be so lucky."

But was he ever really happy?

Only Frank himself could answer that question. If you asked him, he'd probably size you up, ponder the thought for a moment, and then say, "Hey, pal. Why don't you mind your own business?"

SINATRA

CHAPTER 1

Imagine a diamond in your hand. You hold it up to the light. Held one way, it reflects a clear and intense white, cold and unyielding. Turned another, it showers a myriad of rainbows filled with warmth and hope. Since there is no such thing as a perfectly cut stone, there are bound to be some flaws, some easily seen, others only apparent when viewed through a jeweler's loupe.

Frank Sinatra is like that diamond—brilliant on the surface, flawed beneath. Of course, it's those flaws, those hidden complexities, that make him human and reflect his story.

As in the life of every man, the intricacies of his nature can be traced back to where he came from and to those who came before him. For Frank Sinatra, it all started in Hoboken, New Jersey, where he was born and raised. Indeed, if one really wants to know about this man, one must travel from lower New York City across the Hudson River and into Hoboken, where Sinatra is a hero.

Everyone there seems to know someone who knew someone *else* who once knew, or still knows, Frank or his family. Every Italian bartender, delicatessen owner, dry cleaner, pizzeria worker, and thriftstore proprietor over the age of fifty seems to have a good Sinatra story, a juicy Sinatra rumor, or an inconsequential Sinatra anecdote about that time he or she ran into the man himself and rubbed shoulders with greatness. Unlike in other cities, where stories about hometown celebrities have to be pried out of reluctant townsfolk, in Hoboken the tales flow freely.

Indeed, the citizens of Hoboken talk about Sinatra with almost contagious emotion and enthusiasm. After all, he's Frank, Ol' Blue Eyes, the Chairman of the Board, the most famous person who ever came from those parts. They love him. They're proud of him. One can see it in their eyes when they speak of him, when they pull out of their wallets a dog-eared photograph taken "at Frankie's brilliant concert at the Latin Casino in Cherry Hill, New Jersey," or when they play that special Sinatra tune on the bar's jukebox, the one "I danced to at my wedding and my kid danced to at hers and her kid will dance to at his," the one that still brings tears to their eyes.

One would think that citizens of this quiet town would avoid prying questioners. After all, everyone knows Frank Sinatra is renowned for not

1

appreciating it when his privacy is invaded. But these people aren't afraid of Frank, in the accepted meaning of the word. Actually, they fear him the way they, mostly Italian-American Catholics, fear God. Be fair to him and he'll be fair in return. He wouldn't hurt them, not without good reason, anyway. He's one of them. They are a part of him.

It becomes clear when in Hoboken, a city whose Park Avenue library has a second-floor, glass-encased shrine to Sinatra filled with impressive memorabilia, that a Sinatra biographer has only to pick, choose, and separate those stories that seem to be accurate from the ones that have become just another part of Sinatra lore. Almost like oil and water, some stories separate themselves upon closer scrutiny. Others, however, take a bit more work to verify. These are the stories that have been repeated so often—handed down from one generation to another—that today no one can even remember whence they originated, let alone whether they're accurate.

All of it—the truth, the lies, the facts, the fiction—says something about the endurance of Sinatra's legend and the impact it has had on not only his people in Hoboken, but on our culture as a whole. One thing is certain: There are few in this country—maybe even in the world—as popular, as respected, as loved, and as feared as this man the people of Hoboken still call "Frankie."

In the late 1800s, Hoboken, New Jersey, a former resort area for the New York wealthy, was a run-down and destitute mile-square city. However, it was also a place of expectation and promise for many ambitious newcomers. With hope in their hearts, if not money in their pockets, they had come to the New World on crowded, rat-infested passenger liners and disease-ridden cargo ships. The Dutch, Swedes, Finns, English, Irish, and Scottish were all represented, and this was before 1700. The Germans and French Huguenots arrived by 1750.

The Irish came in 1845 because of the great Potato Famine in Ireland; many of them went into factories that were booming rather than return to the uncertainty of farming. The Germans arrived in 1848 after a revolution failed to produce a democracy. They were the most educated of the tide of immigrants and quickly became the aristocracy of the cities in which they settled.

By then, although there was still plenty of farmland left, New Jersey—sometimes called "the Foreign State" because it was home to so many immigrants—was rapidly becoming industrialized, a process that had started in 1830, when canals and railroads started to crisscross the state. Factories produced glass, iron, leather, oil, and munitions (Colt produced his revolver in New Jersey until he went bankrupt and moved to Connecticut), clothes, hats, coaches, cabinet ware, and chairs, among other things. From New York City, just across the river, came a steady supply of immigrants to work in these factories.

Although manufacturing brought prosperity to the state, it also resulted in a lack of zoning. In 1861 one enterprising developer, Charles K. Landis, envisioned Vineland, a planned business and industrial area to be run by New Englanders. But he needed labor to clear the woods and later raise crops for the residents. Landis considered the Italians hardworking and industrious, so he sent printed notices to Italian cities, extolling Vineland's wide streets, shady trees, and Mediterranean climate, none of which existed. So the Italians, the first group in New Jersey to actually be solicited for immigration, came to this land of transformation, a country they called *l'America*. Among them were John and Rosa Sinatra, born and raised in Agrigento, Sicily. After the birth of their son, Anthony Martin (Frank's father, Marty), they migrated to the United States and settled in working-class Hoboken, New Jersey.

In this town, they had heard, a person could reshape his life, embrace good fortune, and in the process, make previously unimaginable sums of money.

At least that was the dream.

The reality was that, with only so many available opportunities, life in America would be a constant struggle for many of its adoptive children; every day would pose a challenge to spirit and dignity as they attempted to find new ways to earn a living. The work was brow-sweating hard; newcomers toiled in poorly equipped factories or in menial jobs as street cleaners and garbage collectors. Some of the lucky ones became barbers, a tradition of self-employment that would be passed down from generation to generation of Italian Americans. After arriving from Sicily, John Sinatra, who obviously could not read or write English, supported his family by making pencils for the American Pencil Company. He earned eleven dollars a week.

Some immigrants would soon come to the conclusion that they may have been better off in their homeland. Defeated, many of them would return to their native lands; others of their lot would stay in the United States and lead sparse, desperate lives, cursing the day they had ever left the old country and the gods who had restricted their fortune.

However, some would make it. Some, like the Sinatras, would see the realization of their dreams. They would be the lucky ones, as would their children—and their children's children.

By 1910, New Jersey was the state with the most immigrants per square mile. The census that year showed that just under 40 percent of the population had native-born fathers and mothers. Hoboken was no exception. In fact, in one five-block section of West Hoboken lived Armenians, English, French, Germans, Greeks, Italians, Spanish, Turks, Syrians, Romanians, Poles, Russians, Chinese, Japanese, Austrians, Swiss, Jews, Belgians, and Dutch.

As each new group arrived, they were looked down upon by those that had already established themselves; often their own assimilated countrymen treated them with scorn. In Hoboken, since the Germans were the social elite, they could boast of several German-language newspapers, *biergartens,* and brass bands. (Their reign in Hoboken lasted until the beginning of World War I, in 1914, when their pro-German sympathies led several to be arrested as spies and many more to be kept under constant surveillance until the end of the war. During that time, the Irish ascended to the ruling class.)

Although most of the Irish were poor and had a reputation for being rowdy, they banded together and elected their own, controlling politics and police and governmental jobs and contracts.

The Italians were considered third on the rung of this social ladder. While the Germans and Irish lived in well-appointed homes, the Italians resided in broken-down tenements. Snubbed and ridiculed, they were looked upon as intellectually inferior. The downtown neighborhood in which they lived, Little Italy, was considered a ghetto by outsiders. But, like all races and ethnic groups, these Italian immigrants were a proud people, working to attain a better life for themselves and their families. Their heritage defined who they were and informed them with certain principles. They maintained their self-respect in spite of the existing class structure and, in turn, reared their children in Little Italy so that their personalities, too, were imbued with self-esteem and dignity.

Generally, the children were well behaved in Little Italy. Any parent could discipline any child. If a youngster misbehaved, he could get whacked by a neighbor or a stranger. That was completely acceptable. Often, writers give the wrong impression about Hoboken in books about Sinatra, making the city sound as if it were a living hell. But to its residents it was home. It was a better place than the old country, no matter how bad it may have been, because it was a place where children could have dreams. They didn't have money, but they had more. They had liberty; they had hope.

While youngsters were taught to respect themselves and their elders, they were also fighters. It was in their blood. Their tenacity and will to survive and succeed came naturally to them.

Certainly their parents and grandparents had to fight to survive; they were a daring, fearless people, which is how they got to America in the first place. A confident, assertive, and sometimes even combative nature seemed to be ingrained in just about every kid whose parents or grandparents had ever immigrated to Hoboken. So, as in every impoverished area, there were warring street gangs.

"It was a tough neighborhood," said Tina Donato, whose grandparents lived in Hoboken. "You had to have your wits about you. You had to walk around with eyes in the back of your head. But it had heart. So yes, appropriately enough, Frank Sinatra would be born into a place with great heart, a place of passion."

Frank Sinatra's parents, Marty and Dolly, were raised in a town of dissimilar personalities and cultures, so it is no surprise that they, too, were a study in contrasts.

"He was a very quiet man," Frank would recall of his mild-mannered father, Anthony Martin (Marty) Sinatra. "A lonely man. And shy. You could hear him wheezing. If he had an attack, a coughing spell, he'd disappear—find a hole in the wall somewhere and be outside before you knew it. But I adored him."

As a young man, blue-eyed, ruddy, and tattooed Marty Sinatra, who suffered from asthma and other breathing problems, distinguished himself as a prizefighter, boxing under the name "Marty O'Brien." (He and his parents believed that his life in Hoboken, dominated and controlled largely by the Irish and by Irish politicians, would be easier if he adopted an Irish name for professional bouts. O'Brien was the name of his manager. Later, when he quit boxing in 1926 after breaking his wrist, Sinatra would work as a boilermaker in a shipyard.)

Marty fell in love with the stunning and unusual-looking—given her ethnic background—blond, blue-eyed Natalie Catherine "Dolly" Garavente, daughter of Italian immigrants from Genoa. Dolly was brought to this country by her parents when she was two years old. She grew to be a comely, fair-skinned woman who was often mistaken for being Irish (and who, as an adult, would not be above using her non-Italian appearance to her advantage when doing business in the neighborhood or when "being Irish" suited her purposes.)

Their romance blossomed quickly, despite their dissimilarity. Whereas he was quiet, reflective, and brooding, she tended to be loud, impulsive, and fiery. A strong-minded and spirited woman, Dolly usually prevailed in any heated discussion between the two of them. Marty was ambitious (or he would not have been in her life at all, because she detested lazy men), but he was clearly more easygoing than was Dolly.

There were other differences as well.

Marty's family were grape growers in the old country, while Dolly's were educated lithographers. Whereas Marty was illiterate, Dolly had an elementary education. Marty's parents were not enthusiastic about the relationship. They didn't like Genoans; they felt that they were elitists. They wanted Marty to marry a Sicilian girl, someone "of your own kind." Dolly's parents were also not pleased. They, in turn, believed that Sicilians were of a lower class than Genoans.

The disapproval of the Sinatras and Garaventes shadowed the relation-

5

ship between Marty and Dolly in its early days, and it seemed that they would have no future together if they listened to their parents. Gradually, after many tears and arguments, Marty and Dolly discovered something they didn't think was possible: Their parents were wrong. Why should they limit their affections? Why should they focus on differences when they had so much in common? They had fun, they were in love. They also shared a core belief that life is what you make it, and they both wanted better lives.

Marty was reticent about how to proceed in his romance with Dolly. He wanted to wait, see if his parents could be swayed, give it some time. However, Dolly wholeheartedly disagreed. "Now is the time," she said. "Why wait? Life is short. I want to get married *now*."

Dolly was the type of person who became more determined to accomplish something when someone told her she couldn't or shouldn't. In fact, even as a young woman, she was never more infuriated than when someone tried to tell her what to do or how to live. Moreover, the mere fact that her parents disapproved of the relationship was an added incentive to Dolly. It made what she and Marty were doing even more exciting and romantic. She loved adventure, craved it, even.

So she convinced Marty that they should elope.

For Marty—a good son who wanted to please his parents, not defy them—eloping was difficult to do. Dolly felt the same way. However, she was more determined not to allow others to impose their prejudices on her.

Dolly and Marty eloped on February 14, Valentine's Day, in 1913, much to their parents' dismay and anger. They were married at City Hall in Jersey City.

To the senior Garaventes' and Sinatras' credit, they were willing to learn and change. A year later, by the time Dolly became pregnant with Frank, both families had come to terms with the marriage. At this time, rather than torment her parents, who felt strongly that she was "living in sin," she agreed to a church ceremony, performed before family members.

After their wedding, Marty and Dolly moved into a dilapidated four-story dwelling in the heart of Little Italy, at 415 Monroe Street in Hoboken, where eight other families resided.

In August 1914, World War I broke out in Europe. Though the United States was determined not to become involved, in three years the country would be sending troops overseas. Closer to home, on December 1, 1915, the forty-seventh annual convention of the New York State Women's Suffrage Association met at the Astor Hotel in the hope that 1916 would be the year women would get the vote. (However, that would not happen until 1920.) Meanwhile, *The Magic Flute* was playing at the Metropolitan Opera House in New York, and Ethel Barrymore was starring in *Our Mrs.*

McChesney at the Lyceum. *The Birth of a Nation,* D. W. Griffith's epic film, was advertised as the "Most Stupendous Dramatic Spectacle the Brain of Man Has Yet Visioned and Revealed." Also, for five dollars down and a promised payment of five dollars a month, a person could take home a Victrola and a stack of records, just in time for Christmas.

Into this world was born Frank Sinatra, in the middle of an East Coast snowstorm, to twenty-year-old Dolly Sinatra in her bedroom on Monroe Street. The building where the birth occurred was torn down years ago. Today a brick arch and gold-and-blue star on the sidewalk in front of a ramshackle establishment called Pinky's ("Everything and Anything: Wholesale and Retail") marks a hallowed spot in an otherwise battered and neglected part of town. Engraved within the star are the words "Francis Albert Sinatra. The Voice. Born here at 415 Monroe Street. December 12, 1915."

As has often been reported, it was a difficult breech birth; the doctors used forceps to deliver the large thirteen-and-a-half-pound baby from the ninety-two-pound woman. The infant nearly died during the delivery; in fact, the panicked doctor was dumbfounded by the child's survival. The baby was scarred on his ear, neck, and cheek—and his eardrum pierced—all by the clumsy use of forceps. Unfortunately, because of the troublesome birth and the damage it caused her own body, Dolly Sinatra would never be able to have another child.

In order to assist the infant in breathing, Dolly's mother, a capable midwife, held him under cold running water until his tiny, fragile lungs began to draw air. Kicking and screaming his way into the world, the baby would live. "They had set me aside in order to save my mother's life," Frank once explained. "And my grandmother had more sense than anyone in the room, as far as I was concerned. I have blessed that moment in her honor ever since because otherwise I wouldn't be here."

Dolly and her twenty-three-year-old husband, Marty, named their child Francis Sinatra. (Albert is not on the official birth certificate.)

With this young child—nicknamed "Frankie"—to support, Marty would eventually take a job as a fireman with the Hoboken Fire Department; Dolly would make candies at a store that produced chocolates.

Frank was baptized on April 2, 1916, at St. Francis Holy Roman Catholic Church. According to the records on the second floor of the Hoboken library and to many other accounts of Sinatra's life, he was given his name by accident.

As the story goes, Dolly and Martin had selected Frank Garrick, who worked for the *Jersey Observer,* to be the baby's godfather and Anna Gatto as godmother. Before the baptism, the priest asked Garrick his name. He answered "Frank." Then, when the child was baptized, the priest absentmindedly christened the baby Francis instead of Martin, the name he was supposed to be given.

Dolly was not present at the christening; rather, she was still home recovering from the birth, so she couldn't do anything about the error. And Marty did not bother to correct the priest. Thus, the boy ended up being named Francis Sinatra. Dolly didn't object, because she felt that her son's name would be a good link to his Irish—and potentially more powerful—godfather.

It's a good story that has been published and republished for decades. However, it doesn't appear to be true, for on the birth certificate that was filled out five days after Frank's birth (months prior to the baptism), it clearly says: Francis Senestro. In fact, the name "Francis" is practically the only thing the non-Italian who filled out the form got right. He misspelled Sinatra as well as "Garaventi" and listed Frank's father's country of birth as the United States rather than Italy.

Marty and Dolly unofficially gave their son the middle name Albert. On a corrected birth certificate twenty-three years after the original, Frank's name is recorded as Francis A. Sinastre. Again it was wrong.

The United States officially entered World War I on April 6, 1917. Shortly thereafter, American troops began arriving in Hoboken to board ships bound for France. Along with Newport News, Virginia, Hoboken was the center of ship movements for the duration of the conflict. The city would be under full military control until the Armistice. Soldiers guarded the piers and patrolled the streets looking for German sympathizers.

Meanwhile, President Woodrow Wilson shut down the city's 237 waterfront bars and introduced federal Prohibition to Hoboken, making it the first city in the country to experience it. However, it was difficult for the government to enforce Prohibition laws; local authorities would not cooperate. People wanted to drink alcohol, and there was a good deal of money generated by selling mixed drinks and beer. So northern New Jersey became a haven for anti-Prohibition activity. Soon, uòmini rispètti (men of respect) began infiltrating the neighborhood, manufacturing and distributing alcoholic beverages, while the officials, many of whom received kickbacks in the form of cash or favors, simply looked the other way.

An enterprising couple, Marty and Dolly Sinatra took advantage of this laissez-faire climate and opened their own saloon at Fourth and Jefferson Streets in Hoboken, "Marty O'Brien's." The bar was registered in Dolly's name because firemen were not permitted to own such establishments.

Prior to this time, Frank once remembered, his father used to aid bootleggers. "He was one of the tough guys," Sinatra said in a lecture at Yale Law School in the spring of 1986. "His job was to follow trucks with booze so that they weren't hijacked. I was only three or four, but I remember in the middle of the night I heard sounds, crying and wailing. I think my old man was a little slow, and he got hit on the head. Somebody opened up his head, and he came home and was bleeding all over the kitchen floor. My mother was hysterical. After that, he got out of that kind of business. They opened a saloon."

"Anytime we saw a drunk in the streets, we'd say that he was part of the MOB, meaning Marty O'Brien's pub," said Tony Macagnano, another boyhood friend of Frank's. "Us kids didn't go around there a lot. We were a little afraid of Marty. He was a grouchy kind of guy with a mad kisser on him. But he never said anything to hurt us. Dolly would have knocked him dead if he did. She was great, always laughing and joking and hollering, but Marty never said much. Just grunted a lot."

Because she owned a bar, Dolly and her husband befriended a number of *uòmini rispètti,* including Sicilian-born Waxey Gordon, a prominent underworld figure in the neighborhood. "They had a lot of shady friends because of the bar they ran," said one close friend. "Face it. *They owned a bar during Prohibition.* If you think they didn't have friends in the right places, you're kidding yourself."

As the establishment's barmaid, Dolly was the wisecracking, tough mother figure that many people in the neighborhood came to for honest advice. Also, if a person needed a job, he would appeal to Dolly. She was the one with connections. She knew everyone in town and could solve problems by calling in favors.

Helen Fiore Monteforte, who lived at 414 Monroe Street, across the street from the Sinatras, recalled Dolly: "She was a vivacious, beautiful, blue-eyed woman with light skin and strawberry blond hair. A real go-getter, she was constantly pushing to get her family ahead. She was a hell-raiser who would sing gaily and dance joyously right on the table at the famous Clam Broth House in Hoboken. She loved life, had tremendous charm, did a tremendous amount of public service work for the community without being paid. She could light the fire under anyone when she needed something to be accomplished."

Indeed, Dolly Sinatra was an enterprising, ambitious, and politically conscious woman who, in years to come, would become a Democratic committee woman. Using her gregarious, self-assured personality to her best advantage, she soon developed considerable political influence in Hoboken. For instance, she was often called upon by Irish politicians who needed Italian votes in Little Italy; she could be counted on to deliver at least six hundred votes from her neighborhood, which gave her influence most people simply did not possess. She had power, and she basked in it.

Well-spoken in the English language as well as in many Italian dialects, Dolly was an unusual woman, given the time and circumstances of her world. But she was not an easy lady to live with; she was judgmental, was known to have certain prejudices against the other "classes," and held firm to her beliefs. When she considered running for mayor, Marty was against the idea; he felt that the position would make her completely intolerable, that she would have too much power, and he wasn't sure how she would handle it.

Steve Capiello of Hoboken, who knew Dolly well, recalled: "She was ahead of her time. Unlike women of today, who speak of women's rights but do nothing about them, she was a woman of action. She supported me during the onset of my political career, and ultimately I was elected mayor of Hoboken. She could speak with a longshoreman's vocabulary if necessary, or be eloquent if she had to impress the political hierarchy in order to make a point.

"I came from a family of twelve and lived in a tenement house with three rooms and one bathroom," he added. "Because the bathroom was always occupied, we had a pot under the bed if someone had an urgent need. We called it the *piscerelle*. During one of my campaign rallies, Dolly sat beside me and was wearing a beautiful hat. Those hats were just as colorful as she was a person. I whispered in her ear, 'Dolly, that hat you have on looks just like a *piscerelle*.' She instantly took the hat off and screamed, 'You son of a bitch!' Then she hit me on the head with it."

Hoboken was not a pretty place. It was tough, and so, too, was Dolly, partly in response to her environment but also due to her nature and her ancestry. Generally, the daughters of women who had emigrated from Italy were not delicate; the boat trip taken by their mothers was no vacation cruise. Indeed, a woman had to have a toughness about her as well as a sense of enterprise and imagination just to embark on the journey to the Promised Land. Women who were dainty by nature would remain behind in Italy and enjoy safe, limited lives. Tough, ambitious women like Dolly's mother, Rosa Garavente, and Dolly herself hungered for more out of life. In fact, they felt they *deserved* more. In turn, they usually attracted men who were equally ambitious.

"Dolly had the roughest language of any female I've ever known," Doris Corrado, a Hoboken librarian, once said. "One time she walked into a party from pouring-down rain and the first thing she said when she got in the door was 'Holy Jesus! It's raining sweet peas and horseshit out there.' She was the devil! Her mouth dripped with honey one minute, and the next it was 'Fuck this' and 'Fuck that.' "

Much has been made in accounts of Frank Sinatra's life of the fact that Dolly Sinatra swore. Certainly Italian-American women like Dolly could seem vulgar to the outside world as they screamed at their kids, trying to get those "little bastards" into the kitchen to eat the homemade manicotti and meat balls before the sauce (which Dolly called "gravy") got cold. But that was just the way they were, the way they expressed affection, the way they lived their lives. Tough, bold, even profane, but capable of

10

great love, like Dolly Sinatra. She didn't have time to be cordial; she had things to do. Her friends and family loved her, and she loved them in return, which was enough for her. She was a powerful woman in every way and by far the greatest influence on Frank Sinatra's early life. She certainly dominated everyone around her, just as Frank would when he was her age. A son could not help but be influenced by such a mother.

So devoted was Dolly to her many pursuits outside the family home that from the ages of six to twelve Frank also had other influences—mostly female—in his upbringing. Much of his rearing in those six years came from his grandmother Rose and his aunts Mary and Rosalie. He has also said that he spent a great deal of time with "a kindly, old Jewish woman," who has only been identified by the name of Mrs. Golden, a woman he continued to visit until her death in the early 1950s.

Recalled his cousin John Tredy, "They [Dolly and Marty] didn't have too much time for Frankie. I think he was always underfoot. Frank was left to his own devices as a teenager; he rarely did homework. So he was rambunctious as a student; he skipped one entire year without his parents being any the wiser."

Other accounts of Frank Sinatra's childhood have painted him as being soft-spoken, extremely sensitive, a quiet child. It was said that his personality as a youngster more resembled his father's than his mother's. John Tredy has said, "He was a soft kind of boy. Like his father, Marty. Frankie was the quietest little boy."

His childhood friend Helen Fiore Monteforte described young Sinatra as "impeccably dressed, never disheveled. A fedora on. As a young boy, a fedora on. Even in the summertime."

Thoughtful and sensitive, he was sometimes taunted by other youngsters who resided in the tough neighborhood. "Prejudice is nothing new to me," Frank once said. "When I was a kid, I lived in a tough neighborhood. When somebody called me 'a dirty little guinea,' there was only one thing to do—break his head."

Not only was he ridiculed because of his ancestry, Frank was also singled out because of his appearance. They called him "Scarface," referring to scars that had been left from his birth. They often beat and bullied him. In some respects, Frank seemed like a misfit to the other boys by the time he attended David E. Rue Junior High in 1928, and his mother only made matters worse by dressing him in Little Lord Fauntleroy suits, handmade by her mother. He always had a lot of clothes, so many pants, in fact, that some people in the neighborhood called him "Slacksey O'Brien."

"We were walking down the street," one of his friends remembered, "and someone said, 'Hey, you little wop,' to Frank as he passed by. I said, 'Frank, just keep on walkin'.' And Frank said, 'I'm gonna walk all over that bastard's face, that's where I'm gonna walk.' And that was that, the fight was on. Frank got beat real bad. He wasn't much of a fighter, but not for lack of trying. Afterward, I said to him, 'Frankie, was it worth it? C'mon!' And he said, 'Hell yeah, it was worth it. He'll never call me a wop again.' Two days later, same thing, same guy. 'Hey, you little wop.' And the fight was on again, and Frank got beat up again.''

"'I'll never forget how it hurt when the kids called me a dago when I was a boy," he once said. "It's a scar that lasted a long time and which I have never quite forgotten. It isn't the kids' fault," he noted. "It's their parents. They would never learn to make racial and religious discriminations if they didn't hear that junk at home." He was always outspoken when he or his friends, no matter what their race, ethnic background, or appearance, were slurred. He would go on to speak out publicly for racial tolerance often and at times when it would be unpopular to do so.

Frank's father contributed to the often unexpected side of his son's character: his brooding pensiveness, his kindness, and his loyalty to friends. His near obsession with cleanliness, his unyielding stubbornness, and his legendary temper can be clearly traced to his mother. Sometimes young Frank would become so angry that his temper would simmer and then erupt and there would be nothing he could do about it.

For instance, he was so incensed about the scars of his birth that he somehow managed to track down the doctor who delivered him. Enraged, eleven-year-old Sinatra went to the doctor's home, determined to beat him up. Luckily, the doctor wasn't in.

"Hell, he was as scrappy as they come," said Joey D'Orazio—two years younger than Frank—who once lived in what he called Dolly's neighborhood.

"What's with this poor little Frankie crap? He was tough as nails. He was a wisecracking kid who talked back to his mother but had the greatest respect for her, as we all did for our mothers. She popped him upside his head and called him terrible names, but you didn't get offended by anything if you lived in Hoboken.

"Sure, he got beat up by some of the kids. I beat him up myself once, over what I don't even remember," said D'Orazio. "I just remember hitting him and knocking him to the ground, out cold. But he beat other kids up in return, the kids he could take on. They called him names, he called *other* kids names.

"He was a little dago—and I say that with love because I'm an old dago myself now—and like all the other little dagos in the neighborhood, he had a terrible temper. You could be shootin' marbles with him and he'd go off on you if he lost and take all your damn marbles from you, anyway.''

Frank grew up in a competitive society. Not only was each ethnic group battling for territorial control; in a manufacturing town like Hoboken, whenever there was a dip in the economy, everyone was affected. There was always competition for work; whom one knew was extremely important, especially for lucrative jobs controlled by politicians. A rivalry among most of the young men in Hoboken started with a competition for girls: who got the most prized ones and who got them fastest. Frank took this particular competition quite seriously.

"He had a fight with my dad over a girl once, and he screamed at my old man—scared the hell out of him, I was told—used words my old man had never even heard before, and he lived in the same neighborhood," said Tom Gianetti, the son of another childhood friend of Sinatra's, Rocky Gianetti.

Gianetti said that his father told him that when Frank was about thirteen, he would take girls "into the back alley" and become intimate with them. A sweet-talker, he could have any girl he wanted. If he had his way with a girl, however, she was his forever—at least as far as he was concerned.

From an early age Sinatra had a petulant, spoiled streak that dictated that if he didn't get his way, not only did he not want to be in the game, he didn't even want to know the other players. He was an only child in a culture and at a time when most people had large families. Children who have siblings usually learn about cooperation and sharing, about having to be reasonable. Not Frank. As an adult, he would always want it his way. If that wasn't possible, if he was crossed, he would simply disappear from the offender's life.

"My old man made the mistake of dating one of Frankie's girls about two years after he'd had her, and that's when they had the fight," said Gianetti. "Frank said, 'You broke my one rule. Don't go after any girl I had sex with.' He said terrible, terrible things to my father. What a mouth, what a temper. My old man said he was scared. Frankie was in his face like he was going to kill him, and he hadn't even seen this girl in two years. 'Think you're better than I am?' he was screaming. 'Think she liked it better? Well, think again. Think again.' After that, it was never the same between them.

"My old man would see Frankie walking down the street, and he'd say, 'Frankie boy, whatcha doing?' and Frankie would just stare straight ahead like he wasn't even there. My father would say, 'C'mon, Frank, don't be an idiot. It was just a broad.' Nothing. Just silence. He got that from Dolly," said Gianetti. "Dolly could write you off like you didn't exist if you pissed her off." Indeed, Frank never spoke to Rocky Gianetti again, ever.

"My son is just like me," Dolly once said in passing. "You cross him and he never forgets."

13

CHAPTER 2

Apparently, the desire to sing professionally came upon Frank Sinatra as gradually as adulthood. By 1930, when Sinatra enrolled in A. J. Demarest High School at Fourth and Garden, he had become addicted to the radio, which, as the primary source of American entertainment since 1922, introduced America to big-band music and to vocalists like Bing Crosby and Russ Columbo. The fifteen-year-old liked the way he sounded when he sang along with the popular singers during their live broadcasts. Young Frankie thought that perhaps he might want to sing for a living, too—unless something better presented itself.

He joined the school glee club. He sang at parties, for his friends, in school talent shows, and at other functions; in doing so, he received a warm response from his fellow students, which he enjoyed.

"He was singing here and there," said one relative. "But it wasn't like he had a burning desire. He was really just exploring his options. 'You wanna hear me sing?' he'd ask. And we'd say, 'Hell, no, Frankie. Let's play ball.' "

By 1930 the family had moved to a bigger, three-bedroom apartment in a much better neighborhood, at 703 Park Avenue in Hoboken. Actually, this home was less than a half mile away from the Sinatras' former residence on Monroe and Garden. In Hoboken at the time, a few yards could make a big difference in how one lived. The house was—and still is today—the biggest on the block. Whereas all the other row houses have three floors, this one, at the end of the street, at five floors, and with thirty-six panes (in two vertical columns of bow windows), facing the street, seems to tower over everything. It's impressive even today; back in 1930 it must have been a showplace.

"They were always moving up," said Steve Capiello. "These weren't your regular Hoboken folk. They were doing exciting things, making money, looking good, having a good life. When Frankie became a star, his press agent was saying he was a slum kid. I remember thinking to myself, Hey, if he was a slum kid, then what the hell was I? My family had no money, we had twelve kids under one roof, in three rooms, we were having it hard, but not the Sinatras."

Another childhood friend, Joe Lissa, remembered: "Being an only child made all the difference. Frank had more. He didn't have to share with brothers and sisters. He even had his own bedroom. None of the rest of us had half of what he had. He wore brand-new black-and-whites (shoes) that his mother bought him. He even had his own charge account at Geismer's department store."

The Sinatras and their neighbors often had good times in Hoboken. There were block parties during hot summer evenings when Dolly would show off her *braciola*.* Young Frank liked to play the popular ball games of the day with his pals—chink ball and penny ball—and no one could shoot marbles or flip baseball cards like Sinatra. If things became dull, he and his friends would take a train into "Fill-uff-e-ah" (Philadelphia) and eat hoagies,† even though they could be bought in Hoboken. "Gimmeya hoagie, hold da onions," Frank would say, always concerned about how his breath would affect his influence on the girls. Headed back home on the train, Frank and his buddies would stuff themselves full of Tastykakes, cupcakes that were—and still are—made only in Philadelphia.

Sometimes Frank and his buddies would borrow his dad's red Chrysler—when he was a teenager, he was the only one among his friends who had access to a car—and drive "down the shore" (the resort area of the eastern coastline) to "walk the boards" (the boardwalk) of "Lanic Cidy" (Atlantic City).

Other accounts of Sinatra's life have painted these years as sad, lonely, and pathetic. It would appear that they were not.

Frank Sinatra was not happy in high school. A difficult student, he often found himself in trouble; it's been reported that he quit after just forty-seven days. Frank has said he lasted longer than that, and records at the school are unclear. (Nancy Sinatra says that her father quit in his senior year.) At any rate, he did, in fact, leave high school one day, never to return. His parents were inconsolable about his decision, but he was as resolved about his life as they were about theirs. "My father was called into the principal's office for about the seven hundredth time," Frank used to joke. "And he said, 'Here's the diploma, now get him the hell out.'"

He took business classes at the Drake Business School for one semester and mulled over the idea of enrolling in the Stevens Institute of Technology, the oldest college of mechanical engineering in the country, which

---

* *Braciola* is an Italian meat treat rolled tight and securely tied with string, then marinated with a combination of secret spices before being browned and dropped into spaghetti sauce. Commonly called "brashoal" by Italian Americans, they're still one of Frank's favorite foods.

† A hoagie is a sandwich—or as Sinatra would have called it, "a sangwich"—made with fresh, thinly sliced lunch meats and provolone cheese on an Italian roll, stuffed with pickles, hot peppers, and just anything else edible that could be found behind the counter.

happened to be in Hoboken. However, the urge to sing professionally became more and more of an obsession. In fact, when his mother found pictures of Bing Crosby on his bedroom walls and questioned him about them, she learned that her only son was considering becoming an entertainer, not an engineer.

Dolly must have remembered that as a much younger child he had sung in the bar which she and Marty owned. But that was all in fun, to amuse the patrons—an extension of Dolly's humor. She probably never imagined that her son was serious about singing, even though she had heard about, but never attended, some of his glee club performances. When she realized that Frank was, in fact, truly mulling over the possibility of singing for a living, she did what any other Italian-American mother in Hoboken would do when informed that her dreams of a college education, or at least a steady job, for her son would probably not materialize: She threw a shoe at him.

Marty Sinatra proved to be just as challenging an opponent to Frank's ambitions. Frank's father was a hardworking immigrant who held fast to *la terra promessa*—the Promised Land—and to the upward mobility, the good life, that the American Dream had to offer. As a fireman for the Hoboken Fire Department, he didn't want to make a fortune. In fact, it was the Sicilian way, his own father had once explained, to have just a taste of the good life and then to build from there. *Fari vagnari u puzzi.* Wet their beaks is what Sicilians called it. Certainly they could do just that in this free country.

In an interview in 1985, Frank spoke of his father: "My father was a darling man, a quiet man," he said. "You know, he never touched me if I got in a jam. In spite of having been a professional boxer, he never laid a glove on me. My *mother* stayed in shape on me. She kept physically fit chasing me and whacking me around now and then."

In 1932, Martin and Dolly Sinatra continued to raise their standard of living by purchasing a three-story (plus cellar), four-bedroom house at 841 Garden Street in Hoboken for $13,400, quite a sum for the times. (Back then, folks used to call these "Father, Son, Holy Ghost" homes, to denote the three floors.) It was one of the most expensive properties in the county.

All of the homes on this street were, and still are, the same: seven to ten cement steps leading from the sidewalk to the front door, another entrance, at street level, to what is known as the cellar, where wine was often kept and where a second kitchen existed, and a "coal bin." Today this structure is just another house on a street of brick row homes, all joined together, all painted different colors. The houses are across the street from the Joseph E. Brandt Middle School.

* * *

"Jeet jet?" Frank would ask any visitor to the Sinatra home, which meant "Did you eat yet?" (The answer from anyone who knew his mother's reputation as a cook would be something along the lines of 'No, jue?' which meant 'No, did you?' ")

"Ma will make you something. Whaddya want?"

Dolly always had food on the stove or in the oven of her new kitchen, and no one could understand when she had time to prepare it.

"You'd walk in the door and sitting on the kitchen table would be a huge antipasto," remembered one relative, "with *pepperoncini*, olives, *giardinièra,* anchovies, and *prosciutti.* Or she would have hot *escarole* soup [chicken broth with escarole greens, vegetables, eggs, and small meatballs], which was something you never made except on holidays. You'd say, 'Dolly, when the hell did you have time to do this?' and she'd always say, 'Whaddya talkin' about? Time? You *make* the time. Now, eat.' "

Frank's father, Marty, took as much pride as his wife did in the Sinatras' new, gorgeously appointed, slightly ostentatious home, the result of hard work and sacrifice. So when Frank dropped out of high school and then announced that he had no intention of pursuing a higher education, Marty couldn't believe his audacity and what he viewed as his stupidity. Indeed, during these desperate times, when millions of unemployed Americans could not dream of college educations for their children, for young Frank to decline such an opportunity was, at least as far as Marty was concerned, unconscionable. He simply did not want his son to turn out the way he had; at least that's what he said.

In truth, there was nothing wrong with what Marty Sinatra had become. True, he couldn't read or write English—and Frank said once that he would never embarrass his father by reminding him of it or even mentioning it to him—but he was a hardworking, loving man. Like many parents, though, he wanted more for his kid than what he had achieved in his own life. Though one Sicilian proverb said, "Do not make your child better than you are," Marty didn't believe that at all and thought it was old-fashioned thinking. "A son's life should *always* make his father's life look bad," he would say.

Outraged at the prospect of his son turning out to be a "freeloader," Marty called young Frank a "quitter." Then, for years afterward, whenever Frank would change direction in his life, his old man would shout that demoralizing name out at him: "quitter." Perhaps Marty hoped that the derisive term would somehow spur his son on to a greater sense of responsibility. However, the word hurt Frank deeply. He would never forget it. "My old man stepped on my dream," he once bitterly put it.

"I ain't no quitter," Frank would scream at Marty.

"Don't raise your voice to your father," Dolly would shout before smacking Frank on the back of the head.

"But he called me a quitter."

17

"He's your father," Dolly would remind her son. "He can call you any goddamn thing he wants to call you. Now get outta here, you little son of a bitch."

Still, Marty's use of the term "quitter" did have the desired effect: It motivated Frank Sinatra. "I think it gave him incentive," said one relative, "to prove his old man wrong. Not an unusual story, but Frank's just the same."

In early 1932, to placate his father, sixteen-year-old Frank got a job in the Tietjen and Lang shipyards. Then he worked for Lyons and Carnaham in New York City, unloading crates of books. ("Do you know what a thrill it is to get a hernia for $62.50 a week lifting six-hundred-pound crates with another little guy and a hand truck?" Frank has joked.) Bored there, he took another job for the United Fruit Lines, working in the refrigeration units of transport ships. When Frank quit that job, saying that he was simply disgusted with manual labor, his father became disgusted again with the "quitter."

"You don't want to work," he told him one morning over breakfast, "then get the hell out. You want to be a bum, go somewhere else and be a bum." Marty told his son that his grandparents hadn't immigrated all the way to the United States "from It-lee [Italy]" just so that Frank could be a freeloader.

"I was shocked," Frank recalled. "I remember the moment. My father said to me, 'Why don't you get out of the house and go out on your own?' What he really said was *'Get out.'* And I think the egg was stuck in there about twenty minutes, and I couldn't swallow it. My mother, of course, was nearly in tears, but we agreed that it might be a good thing. I packed up a small case I had and came to New York."

Frank took a room in New York City, but the timing must have been wrong for him. He couldn't get work. He returned to Hoboken.

"You ready to go to work now, Mr. Smarty Pants?" Dolly wanted to know. "Mr. Big-Shot Singer." Then, after a beat, she would grin and ask, "So, you a star yet?"

Though opposed as they were to their son's aspirations to be a singer, deep down Dolly and Marty, like devoted parents, could not resist encouraging him. Other accounts of Sinatra's life stating that his parents were completely unsupportive of Frank's dream are simply inaccurate.

In fact, say her friends, by the time Frank got back from New York, his mother wanted him to sing almost as much as he did. However, this was Hoboken, not Hollywood. She didn't know how to assist her son.

"I had heard that it was on her mind, though," said Doris Sevanto, who was raised in Hoboken and was a friend of the Sinatras. "My mother once told me that Dolly was asking guys with clubs to give her kid a job, and Frankie worked in one club in Hoboken for a while. But that fell through when he had a fight with the proprietor. Dolly would say, 'You

18

know, that little son-of-a-bitch son of mine, he wants to sing. And he ain't bad. I think he might make it. But don't tell *him* that. He's already too big for his britches.' "

"The way most immigrant Italian parents were in Hoboken and in other cities at the time was that they supported their kids' goals in life, even when their kids were doing something they didn't like," said singer Tony Martin. "Sure, you tried to talk the kid out of it, you hit him, tried to knock reason into him, but then if he didn't listen and you did your best, you said, 'Fine. Now, what can I do to help?' "

Marty and Dolly Sinatra were parents who well understood, and could relate to, the notion of rebellion. After all, a sense of defiance had spurred their own parents to immigrate to the United States.

"So how could they not support their kids' dreams?" observed Tina Donato, who spent summers in Little Italy with her grandparents and who knew the Sinatras.

"Anyone who says they didn't, well, that's a person who doesn't understand one of the most important things about the Italian-American way of life. You don't knock down your kid, you build him up. At least that was the case with all the Italians I knew, and I know it was the case with Frankie's parents. Marty, well, he wanted something else for Frankie, but after he knew Frankie wanted to be a singer, he was in his corner, even if only secretly."

In fact, Dolly and Marty lent Frank the sixty-five dollars he needed to buy a portable public-address system and sheet-music arrangements so that he could work in local nightclubs. If he was going to do "this thing," as Dolly called it—be a performer—then he would have a distinct edge over the other young men in the neighborhood who were attempting to do the same "thing." Most of them did not have their own sound system and arrangements. The Sinatra parents made certain that Frank did.

"I started collecting orchestrations," Frank once explained. "Bands needed them. I had them. If the local orchestras wanted to use my arrangements, and they always did, because I had a large and up-to-the-minute collection, they had to take singer Sinatra, too. Nobody was cheated. The bands needed what they rented from me, and I got what I wanted, too. While I wasn't the best singer in the world, they weren't the best bands, either."

With his sound system and music, Frank, who was about seventeen by this time, started singing with small bands in clubs on weekends and evenings. His mother even helped him get bookings at Democratic Party meetings. He also performed at school dances. The more his parents and friends began to approve of his ambition, the more concrete Frank's plans became, until finally the idea of becoming a successful entertainer was a goal he now admitted that he hoped to realize.

He continually listened to Bing Crosby and tried to emulate that crooner's voice in the shower. However, he quickly decided that he wanted his own style, not Bing's. Too many other young men were, at the time, attempting to mimic Crosby's vocal stylings, or as Frank has said, "Boo-boo-booing like Bing," on such hits as "Just One More Chance" and "I've Found a Million-Dollar Baby (in a Five-and-Ten-Cent Store)."

Sinatra, whose voice was in a higher register than Bing's, anyway, said later that he was determined to be "a different kind of singer." Many years later, he would remember, "Bing was on top, and a bunch of us— Dick Todd, Bob Eberly, [Perry] Como, Dean Martin—were trying to break in. In occurred to me that maybe the world didn't need another Crosby. I decided to experiment a little and come up with something different. What I finally hit on was more the *bel canto* Italian school of singing. It was more difficult than Crosby's style, much more difficult."

His enthusiasm for singing was contagious. Dolly and Marty began to marvel at his talent. "When he would sing around the house, he was good, and we were, I don't know, surprised," his mother once said. And they were relieved to see him finally focus on a goal. Like the Italian-American sons of most of their Hoboken friends, their own kid wanted to *be somebody*, and, they decided, his way to recognition and success could very well be as an entertainer. It seemed a far-fetched idea. So did a lot of things that eventually occurred in their lives once they started making money in America.

The Sinatras were discovering that nothing was impossible in this golden land. Or as sociologists Glazer and Moynihan wrote in their book *Beyond The Melting Pot*, "The set of qualities that seems to distinguish Italian-Americans includes individuality, temperament and ambition . . . perhaps the ideal is the entertainer—to give him a name."

Certainly so many Italian-American young men, from different cities populated by immigrants across the country, had the same goal as did Frank. The names are now legendary: Dean Martin, Perry Como, Frankie Laine, Tony Bennett, Vic Damone, and many others, all Italian-American boys whose mothers probably threw shoes at them when first learning of their improbable aspirations. None, however, would ever be as famous or as successful—or as rich—as *the* Italian-American: Frank Sinatra.

"Yo! Waaas hup?" Frank wanted to know.

The young, brown-haired, brown-eyed girl looked up from her manicure and responded with a smile. "Nuttin'."

That's all it took. He was hers.

It was the summer of 1934 when eighteen-year-old Frank Sinatra met seventeen-year-old Nancy Rose Barbato, daughter of Mike Barbato, a plasterer from New Jersey. During his youth, Frank would often spend his summers with a favorite aunt, Mrs. Josephine Garavente Monaco—Aunt "Josie"—who owned a beach house in Long Branch, on the Jersey shore. Josephine, Dolly's sister, recalled, "He used to drive us crazy, playing the ukulele on the porch all the time. He would sit there and play, kind of lonesome. Then, one day, I noticed him talking to a pretty little dark-haired girl who was living across the street for the summer. She was Nancy."

Actually, Nancy Barbato was giving herself a manicure on the front porch of the home in which she was living for the summer with her father, Mike, and her aunt and uncle and their families when Frank approached her, his ukulele in hand.

"Yo. What about me?" he said. "I could use a manicure."

Frank was immediately attracted to this beautiful Italian-American girl. "We had a wonderful summer together. When it was over, I figured, well, that's it, it's over."

When the summer ended, Frank and Nancy went back to their respective homes, he to Hoboken and she to Jersey City, just one town away. However, the romance continued for the next four years. Frank would take the bus to visit and date her; Nancy would give him the fare if he didn't have it. Once, when he was broke, Nancy sent him one of her gloves and stuffed a dollar bill in each finger. They were romantic years. He would write poetry for her, and they would spend long hours listening to opera on the Victrola. They would go to the beach, walk the boards, and eat Creamsicles (vanilla ice cream on a stick, covered by orange ice) until they would both be sick to their stomachs. He would try to teach her how to play canasta, a complicated card game that involved melding sets of seven or more cards. But he wasn't very good at it himself, so they would spend more time laughing than playing.

During this time, Frank remembered, "I was singing for two dollars a night at club meetings. I sang at social clubs and at roadhouses, sometimes for nothing or for a sandwich or cigarettes—all night for three packs. But I worked on one basic theory," he recalled. "Stay alive. Get as much practice as you can."

Frank sensed that Nancy would be the kind of mate who would allow him to explore life as an entertainer. After discussing with her the reality that such a life offers few guarantees, he sensed that she understood.

"I'm goin' straight to the top," he warned her. "And I don't want no dame draggin' on my neck."

"I won't get in your way," she promised.

On September 8, 1935, nineteen-year-old Frank Sinatra got his first big break when he auditioned to appear on the popular *Major Bowes and His Original Amateur Hour*. Bowes's NBC radio show was broadcast live from the Capitol Theater in New York. (Bowes's program was launched on New York radio in 1934 and went national a year later.)

At the time of Frank's tryout, another act auditioned, a group calling themselves the Three Flashes—Fred "Tamby" Tamburro, Pat "Patty Prince" Principe, and James "Skelly" Petrozelli. It was either Bowes's idea to team Frank with this other act from Hoboken and call them the Hoboken Four or Dolly's, depending on which of the two accounts one wishes to believe. At any rate, when the quartet performed the Bing Crosby–Mills Brothers hit "Shine" on Bowes's show, they were a success. The host encouraged viewers to telephone a special number and vote for their favorites among the acts. The Hoboken Four generated a huge turnout of telephone calls voting for them. The amazing fact about Sinatra's first appearance on the *Amateur Hour* was that the voice was already in place. He didn't have an opportunity to show the intelligence or feeling yet, and he may not have known how to do that at this point, but the voice was already there. The group, with Frank on lead, would make several more appearances; Frank would also appear with them in two Major Bowes one-reel movie shorts directed by John Auer, *The Night Club* (in which he played a waiter) and *The Big Minstrel* (in which he played a singer in black face). He has never seen either film.

Frank recalled, laughing, "Bowes used to come on the air, and he used to say, 'The wheel of fortune spins, round and round she goes, where she stops, nobody knows.' That was the dullest opening I ever heard on any radio show. He was a pompous bum with a bulbous nose," he said of Major Bowes back in 1966 as part of his nightclub act, demonstrating an astonishing lack of gratitude. "He usta drink Green River [liquor]. He was a drunk, this guy. I don't know if you ever heard of Green River, but it takes the paint off your deck if you got a boat. Fifty-nine cents a gallon, baby."

Frank had his first opportunity to tour as a singer at about sixty-five dollars a week when Bowes asked him and the Hoboken Four to tour with one of Bowes's many amateur companies. This was a great opportunity for the young Sinatra, performing with sixteen other acts—tap dancers, jugglers, mouth organists, etc.—in front of enthusiastic audiences in different cities, honing his talent as a singer as well as his ability as a performer.

Frank Sinatra worked with the Hoboken Four for about three months, until the end of 1935, when the other three members began resenting all of the attention he received from audiences. It was difficult for Frank to hold himself back and try to blend in with a group. He couldn't help flirting with the women in the audience, winking at them, showing just a little more personality than the other fellows during performances.

With so much infighting taking place within the group—some of it actually physical—Frank, who had never intended to be in a group in the first place, decided to leave the act. "I had been thinking solo, solo, *solo*," Frank remembered. It had been a good experience, but he knew it was time to end it and move on. Besides, he missed his parents terribly (he'd been sending his mother letters and photographs from the road), as well as his girlfriend, Nancy.

Upon his return, though, Frank was greeted by his father's strong disapproval of the decision he'd made to leave the Hoboken Four. As far as Marty was concerned, his son had just "quit" another job.

A loud argument ensued during which father and son said things to one another that they would never forget. Marty's routine was the usual: His son would never amount to anything; he was a quitter. Frank sang the same refrain: His father didn't understand his ambitions. Why couldn't he be more supportive? Actually, Frank had become more angry now than hurt by Marty's attitude. In fact, he grew even more determined to prove his "old man" wrong. For her part, Dolly wanted peace. She was tired of the constant arguing between her husband and son. "The two of you are driving me nuts," she said. "Frankie wants to sing, Marty. Jesus Christ, let him sing, will ya?"

Just a few months later, back in Hoboken, Frank continued his career as a solo singer at the Rustic Cabin, a roadhouse in nearby Bergen County in Englewood Cliffs, New Jersey, two miles north of the George Washington Bridge.

Frank had met a tough song promoter named Hank Sanicola, who had taken on the unofficial job of managing Frank. Sanicola, also of Sicilian heritage, would be one of Sinatra's right-hand men for years to come; later, he would even play piano for him at times.

"I was always the strong arm," Sanicola, a former amateur boxer, once said. "I know how to fight. I used to step in and hit for Frank when they started ganging up on him in bars." "He's a great dag," Frank would say of Hank. (Frank used to call his buddies of Italian-American heritage the nickname "dag," a shortened version of "dago," which to Frank meant *paisano*.)

Sanicola booked a regular job at the Rustic Cabin for Sinatra, where he would make between fifteen and thirty dollars a week waiting tables and singing with the Harold Arden house band on WNEW in New York, broadcast throughout the tristate area.

"We had a blind piano player," Frank once recalled. "Completely blind, with a shiny, bald head. Between dance sets, I would push his little half piano around. We'd go from table to table, and he'd play and I'd sing. There was a dish out on the piano. People would put coins in the dish."

Frank almost didn't get the job, since Harold Arden didn't like him. Frank really wanted it, "but the bandleader doesn't like me," he complained to Dolly. Dolly told him that that was just fine. She didn't like the idea of his singing in a club all night, anyway.

"Frank just looked at me," she would recall in an interview many years later, "He took his dog, Girlie, in his arms and went up to his room. Then I heard him sobbing.

"I stood it for a couple of hours," she remembered, "and I suppose I realized then, maybe for the first time, what singing really meant to Frankie. So I got on the phone, and I called Harry Steeper, who was mayor of North Bergen, president of the New Jersey musicians union, and an assistant to James 'Little Caesar' Petrillo, president of the American Federation of Musicians. As fellow politicians, we used to do favors for one another. I said, 'What can we do? Frankie wants to sing at the Rustic Cabin, and the bandleader doesn't like him.' I told him what happened, and I asked him to see to it that Frankie got another tryout, and this time, I said, see to it that he gets the job.' "

Harry told Dolly that it was as good as a done deal. Frank got the job.

Helen Fiore Monteforte recalled that Dolly was so anxious that her son make a good impression at the Rustic Cabin, she "papered" the place with friends. She invited Helen's entire family and paid for everyone's tickets. "She was very generous, but also knew that the people present would benefit Frank at his shows."

"That's when it started for Frankie," said Joey D'Orazio, Sinatra's friend from Hoboken. "He knew he was gonna be a star then. We all went to the Cabin to see him. I mean, he was good, you know? He was no *Sinatra*, though. Not yet. I told him, 'Hey, Frankie, you ain't bad, but you could use some work.' And he was insulted. 'Fuck you and your whole family,' he said. 'If you can't pay a guy a decent compliment, don't be comin' round here. Whatcha think, I *need* to hear you tearin' me down?' Either you were with him, or you were against him; that was Frankie."

Frank once remembered the night Cole Porter showed up in the audience at the Rustic Cabin. "I had been so infatuated with his music, I couldn't believe he was sitting out there. I dedicated the next song, 'Night and Day' to Mr. Porter. However, I proceeded to forget all the words. I kept singing 'Night and Day' for fifteen bars. Many, many years later, I got to know Mr. Porter quite well. We were doing a film (*High Society*), and he called me aside and said, 'I don't know if you remember meeting me at some nightclub you were working.' I said, 'Oh, yeah.' And he said, 'So do I. That was about the worst performance I ever heard.' "

As well as working at the Rustic Cabin, Frank would commute back and forth between Hoboken and New York just to keep his finger on the pulse of what was going on in that city's nightlife. He would sneak into nightclubs to watch other popular entertainers and learn all he could from their acts. He would get himself booked on every radio show whose producers would let him sing. Anything to get ahead in show business. He was so determined to make it, he spent some of his hard-earned money on a voice-and-diction coach, who helped him lose his thick New Jersey accent. Throughout this entire time, Frank continued dating Nancy Barbato, who was supportive and understanding of his goals. She continually encouraged him and, say her friends, spent many hours bolstering his self-confidence.

For a while, Frank toyed with the idea of changing his name to Frankie Trent, in honor of his cousin, John Tredy, who died of tuberculosis at twenty-eight. (Tredy was the first professional entertainer in the family; he played the banjo in a group and sang.) He thought it would be wise to lose the ethnicity that might be attached to Sinatra and actually had some fliers printed up with the new name. However, his mother warned him that Marty would "kick his ass" if he changed his name. Later, Frank said, "Changing my name, man, that was the best thing I ever *didn't* do."

In early 1937, his cousin Ray helped Frank get a job on a fifteen-minute NBC radio program—a regular spot for the young singer—for seventy cents a week. "He'd do anything he could," said another cousin. "It didn't matter where, when, or for how much. If he could sing, he'd sing. And you know what? By the time he was twenty-one, he was getting to be good. Damn good. In fact, I told him, 'Frankie, man, you can sing.' And he said, 'No kiddin', you idiot. That's what I been tryin' to tell ya.' "

CHAPTER 3

For years, Dolly Sinatra had worked as a midwife, which was just another one of the many duties she had taken upon herself to perform in Hoboken. At this time, most babies in the United States were delivered by women who were not licensed doctors but were trained to assist in childbirth. As a midwife, she was often asked to perform abortions.

At the time that Dolly performed these abortions, she felt she was doing a service to the community. If an unmarried Italian-Catholic woman became pregnant, her entire life would be ruined because of social and religious conventions. To Dolly's way of thinking, she would perform the delicate operation in an effort to assist the hapless woman in putting back together the shattered pieces of her life. Some families in the neighborhood had as many as seven mouths to feed. An addition to such a family was often unwanted. Dolly would take care of it. In Dolly

Sinatra's eyes, nothing was an impossible situation, even an unwanted pregnancy. Like everything else in Dolly's world, it could be handled.

Dolly, a Catholic, was certainly breaking what was known by most Italian Catholics as "God's law" by performing abortions. However, the Sinatras were not very religious. They rarely attended church.

"There are things about organized religion which I resent," Frank would say years later. "Christ has been revered as the Prince of Peace, but more blood has been shed in his name than any other figure in history. You show me one step forward in the name of religion and I'll show you a hundred retrogressions."

"I got my own religion," Dolly told one friend. "I know what I'm doing. God knows what I'm doing. And God wouldn't have given me the idea to do it if he didn't want me doin' it."

"My mother was thirteen and pregnant," remembered Debra Stradella, whose mother lived in Hoboken at the time. "She told me that she didn't know what to do; she was scared that she would be ostracized. My grandmother called Dolly and said that her daughter needed help but that they could not afford to pay the, I think, twenty-five dollars. Dolly said they could pay three dollars a month until it was taken care of.

"My grandmother took my mother to Dolly's home on Garden Street. She had a table set up in her cellar. She came downstairs with a little black bag, and she did the abortion herself. My mother once told me that the whole thing took maybe fifteen minutes—it had to do with a wire clothes hanger—and that it was very, very painful and bloody. She used to tell us this story, and we would just cringe. But—I don't know—there was a certain pride, I guess, to know that Frank Sinatra's mother gave her an abortion. Isn't that sick?

"But Dolly was kind to my mother. She checked on her every week for a month, coming to her home and administering different medicines. She was like a savior, even though what she was doing was— Well, I guess it was wrong."

Indeed, some people in Hoboken did not approve of Dolly's activities, which were, no matter how they were viewed by her and her supporters, illegal.

"She was a criminal" is how one Hoboken resident puts it today. "Plain and simple. You can't glorify her. The woman performed illegal abortions. She shoulda been in jail."

There was trouble for Dolly in the summer of 1937. There had been complications to an abortion Dolly performed in her cellar. The patient had to be rushed to the hospital. She was in critical condition when she arrived and nearly died. Dolly was arrested, tried, convicted (of a felony), and put on probation for five years. Undaunted, she continued performing abortions even while on probation. In fact, she was arrested several more times after that incident. She was never jailed, though, perhaps because of her political connections.*

"I know that Dolly was ashamed when she was arrested, but angry as well," said the daughter of a friend of hers still living in Hoboken. "She honestly did not think she was doing anything wrong. She told my aunt, 'Jesus Christ, what is wrong with this town? What's the big deal? An abortion here, an abortion there. What's the problem?' I know that she and Frankie had a huge row about this. 'My mother's a goddamn abortionist. How does *that* look?' he said. 'How do you think that makes *me* feel.' I heard she slapped him. She was furious with him. She became passionate when talking about abortions. She thought she was doing the right thing, that there were too many hungry, unwanted kids in Hoboken."

That Dolly Sinatra was able to avoid jail after her arrest and still perform abortions in spite of her probation spoke of the power she wielded in her community. Today Hoboken residents who remember her—and the offspring of those who are no longer around—speak of her with awed fascination.

Not only was Dolly able to successfully defy legal, religious, and social conventions by operating, during Prohibition, an establishment that sold liquor; she also scoffed at the law by performing abortions.

In a culture and time when the man was the head of the family, Dolly had always played that role in the Sinatra household, and everyone who knew the Sinatras understood this to be a fact. There was never an indication that she went through the charade of pretending that Marty was really the boss and that she was just carrying out his wishes. With her well-recognized political clout, she was already a force to be reckoned within the neighborhood. By flouting legal and religious standards, she further demonstrated to any of the seventy thousand Hobokenites who took notice that she may well have been one of the most influential Italians, indeed one of the most powerful women, in the city. Just as her son would become years later, she was practically a *padrone*.

"People became scared to death of her," said another former Hoboken resident. "How did she do it? they wondered. She began to change from a woman who was beloved in the neighborhood to one who was greatly feared. They would point at her and whisper. And to her, well, that was fine. To her, that just meant they were paying attention. 'They think I'm a goddamn hero,' she would say proudly. 'Well, maybe I am.

* Today, in the Hudson County courthouse, there are no official records of Dolly Sinatra's arrest in Hoboken in the summer of 1937. It is whispered among certain residents that she was able to use her influence to have those records "misplaced." There is, however, a record documenting her arrest, this one on February 27, 1939, when Dolly was arraigned in Hudson Special Sessions Court for performing another illegal abortion. She pleaded no contest before Judge Lewis B. Eastmead.

Maybe I am.' It never occurred to her, however, that they may have been pointing because they thought she was a criminal. It was astonishing, really, what she got away with. However, Frank sometimes suffered as a result.''

When one of Frank's girlfriends at the time, Marion Brush Schrieber, tried to get Sinatra a job at a Friday night dance at Our Lady of Grace School, she remembered, ''the Irish Catholics wouldn't let him in because of the scandals involving his mother. They would have nothing to do with him. When he found this out, he went into one of his terrible moods,'' Schrieber recalled. ''He'd get real sullen and sour, and you couldn't get a word out of him. There were no tantrums. Just an ugly silence that could sometimes last for hours.''

Said the former Hoboken resident: ''It was hard on Frankie, but he loved his mother, and that was the end of it. She could do no wrong in his eyes, no matter what she did.

''Once, a guy came up to him in a bar and made a crack about his mom being an abortionist. He was drunk, or he never would have said it. Few people ever actually spoke ill of Dolly in public,'' she recalled, ''just secretly amongst themselves, in whispers. They were too intimidated by her to be open about any irreverence. Frankie was all over that guy, punching and kicking him. They had to pull Frankie off him.

''There was blood all over the floor. 'I don't give a shit what you say about me,' he said as they were throwing him out of the place, 'but don't ever, ever, *ever* talk about my ma. Ever!' ''

CHAPTER 4

By 1938, twenty-two-year-old Frank Sinatra was on what can only be described as an orgasmic quest. He was having intimate relationships with any woman who seemed even the least bit willing. He enjoyed each one and then couldn't wait for the next one. ''He had more broads around than you ever saw,'' said saxophonist Harry Schuchman, who helped Frank get his audition at the Rustic Cabin. ''I used to sit there and watch the gals with Frank and think, What do they see in him? He's such a skinny little guy.''

Joey D'Orazio said, ''The older he got, he didn't get any more good-looking. He was a skinny guy, ordinary looking, gawky, his Adam's apple protruded, and his ears stuck out, but he had more charisma and magnetism than anyone around. The broads—they swarmed all over him whenever he got offstage after a performance. He'd tie them to the bed and make love to them, man. They let him do that! No one did that kind of stuff in the thirties, no one I ever knew, anyway."

"All I know is that he could get all the tail he wanted," Fred Tamburro (of the Hoboken Four) once said. "This guy had an appetite for sex like no one I ever knew. He would screw a snake if he could hold it still long enough."

"He had sex on the brain," said Nancy Venturi, one woman who dated Frank at this time. "He would make love to anyone who came along, and furiously, as I remember it. There was something unusually intense about his lovemaking, at least it was with me. He was extremely erotic, so sexy, such an intense kisser. I'm an old woman now, but yes, I remember it, all of it."

"Jesus, Frankie, you sure like having sex, don't you?" Nancy recalled having asked him on their first date, just after he had finished pawing at her on her parents' couch.

Frank was taken aback. "Sex is something I can do myself, baby," he told her. "In fact, I do it every day, all by myself, you know, *that* kind of sex. What I want to do to you is make love to you. I wanna make love to you in a way that you'll never, ever forget. So c'mon, let Frankie in," he said as he unzipped her dress. "Let me love you, baby. Let Frankie in."

"Well, that just took my breath away," Nancy Venturi recalled. "Oh, my God, he had me. He really had me. This was 1938. Guys didn't talk like that back then. They didn't know how to romance a girl, but Frankie did. He was a cuddler, not a love-'em, leave-'em type. He'd stay the night, or at least slip out early in the morning, before my parents awakened. I felt loved, completely loved. I was thirteen, even though I looked, probably, eighteen. Still, what did I know?

"We made love five times. One night, just as he reached, you know, that moment, he whispered in my ear, 'Nancy, I love you.' I was thrilled until I found out he had a girlfriend named Nancy [Barbato]. I suddenly knew he had meant *her*, not me. So I called him and said we could never see each other again. I was getting so hooked on him, I was afraid I would get hurt. My, I can't believe how long ago that was. It seems like yesterday."

Frank's reaction to Nancy's telephone call?

"Okay. If that's the way you want it. See ya round, sweetheart," he said. "Oh, and think of me . . . the next time you have *that* kind of sex." Clearly, Frank was ready to move on, anyway, to the next conquest.

Three months later, Nancy Venturi thought she was pregnant. "I was very upset," she said. "I was just a kid. Frankie was the only boy I let touch me. And so I called him in tears and said, 'Oh, my God, Frankie, I think I'm pregnant.' He said, 'Oh, no. That ain't good.'"

"What are we gonna do?" Nancy asked, bewildered.

"I dunno. What do you want to do?" Frank said.

"Pray, I guess," she suggested. "Will you go to church with me?"

"If that's what you want, but I think we should think of something better," Frank answered. Then, almost as if it were a second thought, he said, "Maybe you're right. Maybe we should pray that Dolly doesn't beat the crap outta me."

Years later, Nancy recalled, "There's a church on Seventh and Jefferson. Frankie and I went there, and we knelt in front of the altar. And he closed his eyes, bowed his head, and said, 'God, you know what? If this girl here is pregnant, I'm in big trouble with Ma, and I don't need no aggravation right now. So c'mon, God, gimme a break, will ya? Make her not be pregnant. Okay? So, uh, thanks a lot, God, and . . . uh. That's it. So, amen, all right?'

"I turned to him and said, 'Frankie, what the heck kind of prayer is that?'

"And he got mad. He said, 'What the hell you want outta me, Nancy. Jesus Christ! That's the best fuckin' prayer I can come up with on such short notice. You're the one who dragged me down here, and you expect me to be a fuckin' priest? If you wanna add somethin', go 'head.' Then Frank motioned to the crucifix. 'I'm sure he's still listenin'.''

"Well, I thought a lightning bolt was going to strike us both down before we even got out of that church, the way he talked. I said, 'Let's just get outta here. Quick.' "

While Sinatra's prayer may not have been the most eloquent ever heard by the Almighty, it may have been effective just the same, because Nancy Venturi had what she called her "monthly" the next morning.

"I called Frankie and said, 'It worked. It worked. I ain't pregnant.' " she remembered, "And he said, 'Well, there you go, Nancy! Next time, don't be questioning my prayers.' We were about to hang up when he said, 'Oh, and if you need me to perform any other miracles, just call me.' "

According to some of his friends, Frank's charm was not his only asset when it came to catching girls.

Joey D'Orazio observed: "Not to be indelicate, but there was another factor in the action he got, and if you want to know the *real* Sinatra and what made him tick, you just gotta know that he is well equipped, if you know what I mean—hung like a horse, to be blunt—and the dames liked that. Soon the word got around that Sinatra would not let you down. He had the equipment to satisfy."

Some of Frank's childhood friends, and the sons of his friends, for these stories have since been passed down to another generation, say that Frank Sinatra was introduced to the ritual of communal display while in junior high school, which was when he realized he was "different" from other boys his age.

"He realized he had this big *schlong*, and at first he was self-conscious about it," said one of his boyhood friends, who asked not to be named because "who the hell talks about a thing like this. But then Frank started liking the fact that he was the biggest guy around. He got a certain respect, too, because of it. I gotta admit that it was something he used to his advantage."

In the competition for girls that was so important to Hoboken youth, Frank felt that his so-called manhood gave him an edge over other guys who may have been more muscular, better-looking, or even more intelligent. They didn't have what he had; at least most of them didn't. This focus on his sex organ may seem superficial to some, but for Frank it worked. It gave him what he felt he needed: self-confidence.

"Pal-y, no man's got what I got," he boasted to Joey D'Orazio. "And no man knows how to use it better."

In fact, Sinatra didn't mind being objectified by certain women who were interested in him merely because of what he had between his legs and not between his ears. They were sex objects to him, anyway. He decided that there was no reason that the feeling could not be mutual. He never wondered if perhaps he was lacking something in his psychological makeup that would make the size of his penis so material to him and be such a major factor in his self-confidence.

Nancy Venturi offers another suggestion to explain Frank's behavior. "I'm no shrink," she says, "but in talking to Frank, I felt that his sexual promiscuity was a cry for attention. He turned to strangers for the comfort and understanding that maybe he didn't receive from Dolly and Marty. After all, they were always so busy with other activities. He would often say that he felt that they had ignored him. He talked a lot about that. He definitely wanted to be patted on the back for his performance in bed, this is true."

Sinatra was never one to analyze his feelings, especially when he was a young man. Most young fellows of his time didn't wonder why they behaved the way they did, anyway.

"Look, I know what I'm doing. I ain't looking for any serious stuff," young Frank explained to another friend, Tom Raskin (whom Frank had met at the Park Avenue Athletic Club in Hoboken). "I got that with Nancy [Barbato]. I'm just looking to make it with as many women as I can. Why not? Gimme one good reason why not."

Raskin couldn't think of one. "Yeah, I guess you got a point, Frankie boy," he said. "Why not?"

"Exactly," Frank said.

"Oh, he was proud of it, all right," confirmed Nancy Venturi. "He would swing it around and call it 'Big Frankie.' It sounds ridiculous now, but back then— Well, it was ridiculous back then, too"—she laughed—"but that was Frankie. What can I say?"

The irony is that if it could be argued that the best lovers are not the ones with the biggest organs but, rather, those who are the best communicators, then Frank was that as well. She observed, "It really wasn't all about his penis, even though he may have thought it was. It was much more than that."

Most of Sinatra's dalliances were with women Nancy Barbato would not become aware of. He reasoned that these affairs had "nuttin' " to do with her. These were just girls he used for sex. He didn't care about them the way he cared about Nancy, the gal he truly loved. However, to limit himself to one woman was something young Sinatra simply could not imagine, or as his mother would say under different circumstances, "Life is too short."

"There's more to life than just Nancy," he explained to Joe D'Orazio, "and I gotta have it. We're animals. Face it, Joey boy. Fuckin' animals, each and every one of us, that's what we are, and we're damn proud of it, too."

Sinatra always had to have more than just routine in his life; he lived for the excitement of the hunt, for the moment of victory, when his animal desires were satiated. If it ended with his exploring new, fleshy curves in the sack, then all of the flirting and sweet-talking and cajoling he had done were well worth it. To him, it was a basic drive that simply had to be fulfilled. Besides singing, nothing was more important.

"What Nancy [Barbato] don't know ain't gonna hurt her," Frank would always say afterward.

In 1938, even though he was in a serious relationship with twenty-one-year-old Nancy Barbato, Frank began another with an attractive twenty-five-year-old brunet, Toni Francke (whose full name was Antoinette Della Penta Francke), from Lodi, New Jersey. Toni would definitely make her presence known. She felt more strongly about Frank than he did about her. To her, it wasn't just sex between them. Her fleshy curves were to be regarded more seriously.

"I love you, Frankie. I think we should get married," she told him.

"Whad'ya, crazy?" Frank wanted to know. "That ain't part of the deal, baby."

Rejected by Frank, Toni played the "scorned woman" routine to the hilt. She actually had him arrested on December 22, 1938, at the Rustic Cabin, after his midnight performance. The curious charge was "breach of promise." She claimed that Sinatra, "being then and there a single man over the age of eighteen years, under the promise of marriage, did then and there have sexual intercourse with the said complainant [on November 2 and 9] who was then and there a single female of good repute of chastity whereby she became pregnant."

32

Some of what Francke charged in her complaint, and in later interviews, seemed suspect to Sinatra's supporters. For instance, she said that when he was with her, "Frank didn't seem like he had been to bed with anyone before." That Sinatra could be a virgin in 1938 seemed farfetched, given his reputation in Hoboken.

She also claimed that he was mediocre in the sack; again contrary to what so many other women had reported. But then again, perhaps one woman's ecstasy is another's drudgery.

Francke further claimed that Frank Sinatra gave her a diamond ring, which also seemed unlikely, given the state of his finances. (He even got Nancy's engagement ring from his mother, and it's not conceivable that she would have given him another one for Toni.) Furthermore, she claimed in an interview that Frank told her he had to marry Nancy "or her father will kill me" because she was pregnant. ("So what?" she remembered telling him. "I was pregnant, and you didn't break your neck for me.") However, all of Sinatra's friends and associates who would discuss such a thing have insisted that Nancy Barbato was not pregnant at this time; she did not give birth to their first child until eighteen months after Toni Francke had Sinatra arrested.

The problem, though, was that Toni Francke had, as she charged, become pregnant and Frank wasn't able to perform one of his little "miracles" this time. Frank wasn't so certain it was his baby; anyway, he claimed that Francke had been with other men. However, as a result of his dalliance with Toni Francke, Sinatra had to spend sixteen hours in the Bergen County jail.

"Oh, yeah, he was pissed off," said Joey D'Orazio. "He was real pissed off. He called me up the next day and said, 'That broad is crazy. We went out for pasta fazule [*pasta e fagioli*, or pasta-and-bean soup], had a good time, went back to her place, and hit the sheets. So what? Next thing I know, this dame is tellin' me she's pregnant and I'm in the fuckin' slammer. Like I'm the only guy she ever did it with. I didn't even really have a good time with the dame.' "

The charges against Sinatra were dropped, though, when it was learned that Toni Francke was herself actually married at the time of her rendezvous with Frank Sinatra. (She had claimed in her complaint that she was "a single female of good repute of chastity.") Undaunted, Francke filed a new complaint on December 22 charging Frank Sinatra with having committed adultery. That complaint was also eventually dismissed.

"It was a big mess, Frank and this girl," said Salvatore Donato, an acquaintance of the Sinatra family's. "She ended up having a miscarriage in her third month. Nancy was crushed by the whole damn thing. There was a lot of screaming and hollering over that, let me tell you."

Toni Francke was probably one of Frank's first "groupies," though she would strongly object to that characterization. Simply put, she was some-one who just had to have him at any cost. Though she may have truly loved him, she must have known what she was getting herself into when she became intimate with him.

Sinatra, as he would with many other women in later years, treated Toni Francke in the heartless manner that would become his trademark with women in years to come. He simply cut her loose when he was done with her. In retaliation, Francke tormented not only Frank by having him arrested but also his flabbergasted parents, Dolly and Marty. She actually went to their home and became involved in a screaming brawl when Dolly refused to apologize for her son's callous behavior. Dolly had to lock her in the cellar, call the police, and have her arrested. (Charged with disorderly conduct, Toni Francke was given a suspended sentence.)

Of course, she wasn't the only woman with whom he was cavorting. She was just the one who became a problem. This unfortunate business with Toni Francke was a precursor of things to come for Frank and Nancy.

For twenty-three-year-old Frank, the local publicity he received was dreadful. "Songbird Held in Morals Charge" read the headline in the *Hudson Dispatch* on December 23, 1938. He was embarrassed, say his friends, but probably not as much as his parents, who were mortified.

"You've fucking disgraced all of us," Dolly, who, it would seem, had little room to talk, told Frank.

Dolly had already warned her son about Toni Francke. When Frank took his parents to Toni's home to meet her and her family over a maca-roni dinner, Dolly did not like Toni at all, mostly because she lived in Lodi, where, as far as Dolly was concerned, only the lowly resided. She called her "cheap trash." Frank could never take her disapproval seri-ously, though, because she had never approved of any of his girlfriends. (Also, Frank was never one to make distinctions about social class. It was a subject about which he and his mother constantly disagreed.)

Sinatra was outraged by the press coverage of what he thought was a private matter. This would be his first formal introduction to the media, and he didn't like it.

One friend noted, "He called up someone at the newspaper and said, 'I'm comin' down there, and I'm gonna beat your brains out, you hear me? I'm gonna kill you and anyone else who had anything to do with that article. And I ain't no fucking songbird, you idiot. A dame, now *that's* a songbird.' "

Despite his encounter with Toni Francke, Frank would be a man in search of his next sexual conquest for many decades to come, and he would continue to be angry with the media for just as many years for writing about it.

For Nancy, the ordeal was an even more sobering one. Even though Toni later claimed that she and Nancy had had a brawl at the Rustic

Cabin, Nancy insisted that a contretemps had never occurred and that she had no idea that Frank was being unfaithful to her until he was arrested. They were, by this time, engaged to be married. They had been intimate, and for Nancy, a Catholic, this was a major—and, at the time, unconventional—step in a relationship. She assumed that their love-making meant that she was special to Frank. However, his actions with another woman seemed to tell her otherwise.

Having so completely trusted him, when Nancy learned of the affair with Toni Francke, she was deeply hurt and disillusioned. When her own father had had affairs in the past, her mother had looked the other way. Nancy was determined, if only on a philosophical level, that this kind of behavior would not repeat itself in her own marriage. She and Frank had a number of emotional scenes regarding Toni Francke, and Nancy made him "swear to God" that he would never be unfaithful to her again.

"Was she the first woman you've been with since we've been together?" Nancy finally asked Frank through her tears.

"No," Frank said. "But she's the last."

Frank Sinatra did not want to lose Nancy Barbato. She was someone on whom he could truly depend; she had been very supportive of his aspirations even when it looked as though he would never make much money as a singer, even when his parents seemed to lose patience with his choice of career. He felt bad about the Toni Francke incident, although he also believed that it had nothing to do with Nancy. He assured her that such a thing would never again occur. He must have realized, however, that it would and that if it didn't he'd never be truly happy.

For her part, Nancy Barbato didn't know what to make of Frank's betrayal. Was this to be a habit with him? Would he ever be satisfied with just her? What was she getting herself into with this man? She considered breaking off the engagement. However, he was so gentle and sweet to her, and he seemed so genuinely contrite about what had happened between himself and the other woman, that she agreed to go through with the wedding plans.

They were wed on February 4, 1939, at Our Lady of Sorrow Church in Jersey City. Monsignor Monteleon performed a double-ring ceremony. Twenty-one-year-old Nancy wore a simple, full-length white taffeta gown with a deep neckline and short train. On her head she placed a coronet of white fabric trimmed with pearls, with a three-quarter-length veil. She wore white satin open-toed shoes. Twenty-three-year-old Frank appeared in a cutaway tuxedo with black-and-gray pinstriped pants and a matching silk tie. He wore a white flower in his lapel.

Nancy once remarked, "When the big day finally came, there were maybe fifty members of the family on each side of the aisle. Frank was in a cutaway tuxedo. I was wearing my sister's wedding dress, and the ring—a gold band with a cluster of diamonds—had been his mother's. I don't think I'd ever seen Frank so happy in his whole life."

Dolly encouraged her son's marriage to Nancy Barbato. She liked Nancy and, after the madness with Toni Francke, decided that Frank needed to settle down once and for all.

"She told my mother, 'Frankie found a girl I like,' said the daughter of a friend of Dolly's. "She's no whore, at least. So that's a good thing. Frankie's had too many goddamn whores. But this girl, Nancy, she'd better watch him. That little son of a bitch is gonna give her trouble."

"Yuze have a long life," Dolly said in a wine toast later at her home during a small reception for a few friends and family members. For a first course Dolly served *pasta e fagioli*, the meal Frank said got him in trouble with Toni Francke. He decided not to have any of it. Instead, he sat and waited for the homemade *gnocchi* (Italian potato dumplings). "Nobody makes *gnocchi* like Ma," he boasted. "I just hope she gives Nancy the recipe." (There was also a reception at Nancy's family's home on Arlington Avenue in Jersey City; wine and sandwiches were served.)

The newlyweds couldn't afford a honeymoon. They immediately moved into a small apartment in Jersey City, which they rented for forty-two dollars a month; it was completely furnished with wedding presents from relatives. Frank resumed his fledgling career, and Nancy went to work as a secretary at American Type Founders in Elizabeth, New Jersey.

"Frank Sinatra's life in the beginning was so normal," said his son, Frank junior, "that nobody would have guessed that this little Italian kid with the curly hair would become the giant, the monster, the great living legend."

By this time, February 1939, Frank Sinatra was twenty-three years old. Most certainly, without his wife's support it would have been difficult for Frank to continue in the entertainment business, where there are no guarantees of security. He probably would have made it without Nancy— he was that talented and that determined—but with a supportive wife at his side, Sinatra had the kind of morale booster he needed to face the rejection and disappointment so inherent in the career he had chosen to pursue. Nancy took a fifteen-dollar advance on her salary so that her husband could have publicity photos taken to give to trumpeter Harry James, who had recently left the Benny Goodman band to front his own ensemble.

Frank Sinatra felt certain that if he could get a job with James's band as a vocalist, his struggles would be over. (Frank had spent a short time with the Bob Chester band in early 1939, but not even Frank's closest followers can remember for how long, so it must not have made much of an impression on anyone. It was probably just a few performances at the New Yorker Hotel; Chester did, however, show up on Sinatra's official 1942 resumé.)

The big-band sound was purely American. The phenomenon of a male or female vocalist dreamily singing in front of a large band whose conductor—and not the singer—was really the star was an art form that was completely unique to America. Lasting roughly from the end of the Great Depression until the end of World War II, this exciting time in popular music generated some of the most memorable music in this country's history. Fronting a band was every struggling vocalist's great ambition. Sinatra had a friend give the photos to James, and soon after, James went to the Rustic Cabin to see Sinatra perform. Harry James was impressed with, as he later defined it, "Frank's way of talking a lyric."

James was auditioning vocalists at the Lincoln Hotel in New York. While all of the other singers were weighed down with stacks of arrangements, Frank showed up with nothing but a cocky grin on his face. He sauntered over to the piano player, told him what he wanted to sing and in what key, and then he sang. "They were auditioning a lot of people that day," said musician Arthur (Skeets) Herfurt, "but the musicians said that when they heard Sinatra, that was it. There was no doubt about it."

On June 30, 1939, Frank made his debut with the Harry James Band (also billed as Harry James and his Music Makers)—which itself was just three months old—at the Hippodrome Theater in Baltimore performing "Wishing" and "My Love for You." The band toured to enthusiastic audiences for the rest of the summer and into the fall. Frank would remember those days fondly.

"The kid's name is Sinatra," Harry James told one inquiring reporter.* "He considers himself the greatest vocalist in the business. Get that! No one's ever heard of him. He's never had a hit record. He looks like a wet rag. But he says he is the greatest. If he hears you compliment him," James said, perhaps only half-joking, "he'll demand a raise tonight."

Arranger Billy May, who would work on many of Sinatra's most memorable songs, met Frank at this time. He said: "I thought he was a good singer. But the musicians in Harry's band had the opinion that he was a smart-ass Italian kid."

"I was young and full of zip, zap, and zing," Frank remembered in 1965, "and I was also full of myself."

Night after night on the road—on trains, by automobile caravan, via buses—performing in small, dingy clubs or large halls with terrible acoustics, Frank, with his hair in a big pompadour, was never happier singing and being paid for it. Nancy went along on this early Harry James Band tour. Nancy and Frank were together around the clock, and they were blissful in their marriage. In fact, Nancy would one day reflect on these years as being the happiest in their relationship. As her husband per-

* James reportedly wanted to change Frank's name to Frankie Satin. Sinatra refused.

formed his love songs onstage in his dapper suit, she would watch dreamily from the wings. It was almost as if she were falling more in love with him with each performance. "He is so wonderful," she would say. "How did I get so lucky?"

Young women would wait for Frank after the show, hoping he would pay attention to them.

"I'm married," he would say. "My wife'll kill me if I even look at yuze."

There was little money. Sometimes nightclub owners didn't pay the full amount that had been promised. Band and crew ate fried onion sandwiches much of the time. Nancy would prepare an entire meal of hamburger, spinach, and mashed potatoes for four people (herself, Frank, and the band's arranger and drummer) with a dollar. If they could find some *capicola* (Italian ham) at a local butcher shop for "sangwiches," their day was made. They redeemed soda bottles for the return of cash deposits. It was a difficult time in many respects, but Frank and Nancy were happy just the same. When they learned that Nancy was pregnant, that news served to enhance their joy.

The year 1939 was also noteworthy, for it was then that Sinatra recorded his earliest songs, just ten commercially available recorded numbers (not counting alternate takes) with the Harry James Band, eight of which are believed to have been arranged by Andy Gibson, who had also worked with Duke Ellington and Count Basie.

On July 13, 1939, Frank recorded that first song with the Harry James orchestra in New York, where they were appearing at the time, at the Roseland Ballroom. The 78 rpm record, "From the Bottom of My Heart," backed by "Melancholy Mood," was issued on the Brunswick label. Then, on August 31, 1939, the Harry James Band recorded "All or Nothing at All," with a vocal refrain by Frank Sinatra.* It's a wonderful recording. In fact, Sinatra would go on to record the song three more times over the years, but the original version is the most effective rendition.

Sinatra recorded many memorable songs with James's band. On November 8, 1939, he recorded his last two with Harry James: "Ciribiribin," which was Harry James's theme song, and "Every Day of My Life." Artistically, Frank's association with the Harry James Band was a success. He greatly benefited from James's example in ways having to do with showmanship and artistry. Commercially, however, he wanted more.

---

* This recording was not released until the summer of 1940. At that time, it sold just eight thousand copies over many months; fifteen thousand was considered a hit at that time. It would generate greater sales for Frank—over a million copies, according to some estimates—when issued again in 1943, once "Sinatra" was a household name.

Business at the box office was sluggish. During one gig, at Victor Hugo's in Beverly Hills, the band was interrupted by the owner, who stopped the show in the middle of one of Frank's numbers, frustrated because so few people had shown up in the audience. The performers didn't even get paid for that engagement. Frank was ready to move on. While playing the Hotel Sherman in Chicago, the James band appeared in a benefit show for the musicians union with other popular bands at the time, including the Tommy Dorsey Orchestra, one of the most popular in the country. Dorsey, known at the time as "the Sentimental Gentleman of Swing,"* had his eye on Frank and wanted to hire him to replace the band's vocalist, Jack Leonard, at about seventy-five dollars a week, on a long-term contract. Frank was amazed, mostly because he had once auditioned for Dorsey with disastrous results. He had been so awed by Dorsey's presence at that tryout, he couldn't even sing. "I could only mouth air," he remembered. "Not a sound came out. It was terrible."

But that was then. Now Sinatra was different, more polished, experienced. He wanted the job; he had proved himself with Harry James. And with Nancy pregnant and the James band not doing well, Sinatra knew he had to leave Harry.

Luckily, Harry James was understanding of Sinatra's ambition, telling him that if he truly believed that the Dorsey band was a better opportunity, he should take advantage of it. Technically, he didn't have to let Frank go. Sinatra still had seventeen months on his contract. James later told radio interviewer Fred Hall, "Nancy was pregnant and we weren't even making enough money to pay Frank the seventy-five dollars he was supposed to get. So he wanted to go with Tommy Dorsey, and I said, 'Well, if we don't do any better in the next six months or so, try to get me on, too.'"

James always believed that Sinatra would be a star; there was never any question in his mind about it. He was gracious enough to let Sinatra go without a fuss, and for that Frank would always be grateful. (Frank was replaced in James's band by Dick Haymes.)

Still, it was difficult for Frank to leave the man who had given him his first break. He felt an allegiance to James, who had become like a brother to him. He recalled the final night with James's band, after the show at the Shea Theatre in Buffalo, New York, in January 1940: "The bus pulled out with the rest of the boys [on their way to the next tour stop, Hartford, Connecticut] at about half past midnight. I'd said goodbye to them all, and it was snowing, I remember. There was nobody around, and I stood alone with my suitcase in the snow and watched the taillights disappear.

---

* Tommy Dorsey's title was a variation on the 1932 Mitchell Parrish song "The Sentimental Gentleman From Georgia."

Then the tears started, and I tried to run after the bus. I figure to myself, I ain't never gonna make it. . . . There was such spirit and enthusiasm in that band. I hated leaving it."*

CHAPTER 5

The future looked bright for twenty-four-year-old Frank Sinatra as he took his place on the bandstand in front of Tommy Dorsey's orchestra in January 1940.† The band had already been in the midst of a tour; the group's manager sent Frank a ticket to join them. At this time, the Dorsey organization boasted a memorable lineup of musicians that included Buddy Rich, Bunny Berrigan, Joe Bushkin, and Ziggy Elman; arrangers such as Axel Stordahl, Paul Weston, and Sy Oliver; and singers Jo Stafford and the Pied Pipers, and now Frank Sinatra.

"It was like going from one school to another," Frank remembered. "I was really kind of frightened. I was nervous, but I faked a couple of tunes, and I knew the lyrics of some songs, so we did all right with the audience."

When Tommy Dorsey explained the preposterous terms of Frank's contract in a meeting with him prior to the Illinois engagement, Frank was stunned by the man's audacity. The deal Dorsey thought was equitable would mean that Sinatra would give up a third of his earnings for life, plus 10 percent for Tommy Dorsey's agent. A total of 43 percent of every dime Sinatra was to make for the rest of his career would go to Tommy Dorsey (after the original two-year term of their contract had expired, for

* Frank Sinatra and Harry James teamed up on July 19, 1951, at Columbia Records for three songs: "Castle Rock," "Deep Night," and "Farewell, Farewell to Love." They would also sometimes appear in concerts together in years to come, most notably at Caesars Palace in November 1968 and 1979. They appeared together on a John Denver special in 1976 and performed an excellent rendition of their song "All or Nothing at All." James died in July 1983 of lymphatic cancer. He worked up until a week before his death.

† Because it was so long ago, there is some discrepancy as to where Frank Sinatra actually joined the Dorsey orchestra. Dorsey's press agent, Jack Egan, and Sinatra's daughter Nancy insist it was in Indianapolis (at the Lyric Theatre on February 2). Dorsey's clarinetist, Johnny Mince, believes it was in Sheboygan, Wisconsin. Others, like Jo Stafford, say it was either Minneapolis or Milwaukee. In 1955, Frank himself said it was Baltimore, memorable to him because it had occurred after he played twenty-seven innings of softball with his bandmates.

which Sinatra would make seventy-five dollars a week, a sum that would soon be doubled).

Sinatra decided to accept Dorsey's terms, though he realized that the deal was a bad one. He wasn't thinking of any future ramifications it might have; he just wanted to sing and be famous. He also knew that Dorsey had tried out baritone Allan DeWitt for the position. Even though DeWitt did not work out, his audition served to remind Sinatra that there were other men in the business who might accept a terrible deal just for the opportunity to work with Dorsey. (Indeed, many young singers throughout the history of entertainment have signed deals as bad, but probably none worse.)

It wasn't an easy transition for Frank Sinatra—or for the other musicians—when he took over as the male singer with the Dorsey band. Because he was so cocky, the band disliked him immediately. Some of them mocked him by calling him "Lady Macbeth" because he was so obsessed with cleanliness.

Still, they were awed by his ability. Of Frank's first performance with the band, singer Jo Stafford (of the Pied Pipers, who joined the band about a month before Frank) said, "[Sinatra] was very young [with a] slim figure and more hair than he needed. We were all sitting back, like, 'Oh, yeah? Who are you?' Then he began to sing. Wow, I thought, This is an absolutely new, unique sound. Nobody had ever sounded like that. In those days, most male singers' biggest thing was to try and sound as much like Bing as possible. Well, he didn't sound anything like Bing. He didn't sound like anybody else that I had ever heard. I was mightily impressed."

The show would usually start with the band playing Dorsey's theme song, "I'm Getting Sentimental Over You," and then the hit "Marie." Then Dorsey would introduce Connie Haines for a number or two, followed by Jo Stafford and the Pied Pipers. After that, Ziggy Elman would do a trumpet solo, and then drummer Buddy Rich would, as they say, "take it home." Finally, Sinatra would sing a big number, such as "South of the Border." He would also do perky duets with Connie Haines, such as "Let's Get Away From It All" and "Oh, Look at Me Now." Of course, the show would vary over the years, and as Sinatra became more popular, he would be featured much more.

The band traveled by bus, as most did at the time. Those days were difficult but rewarding. "What can I say?" Frank reminisced. "For six months, the band gave me the cold shoulder—they loved Jack Leonard—until I proved myself. Finally, I did, and we became a unit. We worked damn hard, city after city. Just trying to get along, you know, learning about each other, learning about the road, trying to be entertaining. It was a good time. I missed my family, though. Missed Nancy. She was pregnant, so it was tough."

On February 1, 1940, Sinatra recorded his first two songs with Tommy Dorsey's band, "The Sky Fell Down" and "Too Romantic." Then it was back on the road, to Indiana, Michigan, New Jersey, and New York City. In New York the band appeared at the Paramount Theater (March 13–April 9).

On May 23, 1940, Frank, the Pied Pipers, and Tommy Dorsey and his orchestra recorded "I'll Never Smile Again."

With the war raging in Europe and threatening to involve the United States, this song seemed to typify the kind of rueful resignation that would soon envelop the world. The record, with a plaintive delivery by Sinatra and elegant harmony by the Pied Pipers, would become his first big hit: number one on *Billboard*'s charts for twelve consecutive weeks. Frank would go on to perform this classic song for the next forty years of his life, on television and in concert.* "I got ten dollars for recording it," said Connie Haines. "Frank got twenty-five."

Frank's career would never be the same after "I'll Never Smile Again." That record catapulted him to stardom and gave him top billing in the band, much to the chagrin of drummer Buddy Rich. In fact, a rivalry between the two erupted into physical altercations on more than one occasion. Because his ego was rising as fast as the record rose on the charts, Sinatra's relationship with the other band vocalist, Connie Haines, continued to deteriorate as well. He refused to share a mike with her—though he was forced to do so at times—calling her a "cornball" (because she was from the down-home South and not the more sophisticated New York). Ultimately, he found himself suspended for two weeks as a result of disagreements with her. Clearly, Sinatra—a man not given to compromise and cooperation—did not belong in a group environment. He never cared for either Rich or Haines and told his friends that he despised "the both of 'em."†

James's road manager, George H. "Bullets" Durgom, noted at the time, "This boy's going to be very big if Tommy doesn't kill him first. Tommy doesn't like Frankie stealing the show, and he doesn't like people who are temperamental, like himself."

Broadway columnist Earl Wilson, who wrote one of the best Sinatra

---

* Frank would also record this wonderful song for Capitol Records on May 14, 1959 (for the *No One Cares* album), and for Reprise on October 11, 1965 (available on *A Man and His Music*). There is also a recording of this song from April 23, 1940. However, it is not known whether or not that version of the song was actually issued. Sinatra historians insist it was not.

† In October 1944, though, when Frank Sinatra was famous, Buddy Rich went to visit him backstage at the Paramount Theater and mentioned that he wanted to start his own band. Frank wrote out a check for $40,000 and handed it to the startled drummer. "Good luck. This'll get you started," Frank said with a slap to Rich's back.

biographies in 1976, went to see Sinatra perform at this time at the Meadowbrook Ballroom in Meadowbrook, New Jersey. Afterward, Wilson interviewed the singer. Of the experience, he once remarked: "He spoke of his dreams and ambitions and said he was going to be the biggest star in the country. 'You'll see,' he said. Physically, he was less than impressive. The Sinatra frame was not only slender but fragile looking. The cheeks were hollow. He wore a bow tie, a thin wool sweater, and a dark suit. He seemed still a boy, and that added a charm to his cockiness. He had a lot of hair that straggled down the upper part of his right cheek, about to the bottom of his ear. He also had a spit curl. His hair, when he came offstage, was tousled looking. 'Sexy,' the girls said later."

On June 8, 1940, Nancy gave birth to the couple's first child, a girl named after the child's mother, at Margaret Hague Maternity Hospital in Jersey City. Her husband of eighteen months, Frank, was not at her side. "I was working the Hotel Astor in New York, I believe," Frank said later. "I hated missing that. I did. It was just a taste of things to come, man. When I think of all the family affairs and events I would miss over the years because I was on the road. But this was really the first one." (Tommy Dorsey had become such a mentor to Sinatra that Frank had chosen him to be the godfather of his firstborn.)

Later that month, NBC hired the band to replace Bob Hope on a summer-replacement variety show, Frank's first national radio exposure. Because the ratings were strong, the network began airing a Dorsey series, *Summer Pastime*, on Tuesday nights. It ran for three and a half months and further exposed Sinatra to a large viewing audience.

In an article he wrote for *Life* in 1965, Frank remembered that these days with the Dorsey band were some of the most influential on his singing style. Tommy didn't work much with him, he remembered, because most of his attention was on the band members. Left to his own devices, Sinatra absorbed everything around him, including the way Dorsey played trombone, and tried to integrate it into his artistry.

Dorsey could play a musical phrase as long as sixteen bars all the way through, it seemed, without taking a single breath. How the hell does he do that? Frank had wondered even before he joined the band. He knew that if he could sustain a note as long as that, he would be able to sing a song with much more dramatic impact. (Many singers ruined their songs by taking breaths in the wrong place, thereby interfering with the melody as well as the lyric's message.)

Sinatra would sit behind Dorsey on the bandstand and watch him closely, trying to see if he would sneak in a breath. Finally, after many dates, Sinatra realized that Dorsey had what he called "a sneak pinhole in the corner of his mouth." It wasn't an actual pinhole, of course, but rather a tiny place where Dorsey was sneaking in air. It was Frank's idea to make his voice work in the same way, not sounding like a specific instrument but "playing" the voice as if it *were* an instrument.

Frank realized that in order to do this—to sustain those notes in a seamless fashion—he would need extraordinary breath control. So he began an intense swimming regimen in public pools, which he would find in cities on the tour. As he took laps underwater, holding his breath, he would sing song lyrics in his head and approximate the time he would need to sustain certain notes. That it all looked so simple was just part of the magic. "It was easy," Frank said later. "It just wasn't simple."

When he was back in Hoboken, Sinatra would continue his training by running on the track at the Stevens Institute of Technology. He would run one lap and trot the next, singing to himself, holding notes, practicing.

"But that still wasn't the whole answer," Frank remembered. "I still had to learn to sneak a breath without being too obvious."

Indeed, it was easier for Tommy Dorsey to camouflage his breathing technique through his "pinhole" while he was playing the trombone because the mouthpiece covered his mouth. For Frank, this would mean more work, more training. Eventually, he tackled the task. Because his breath control had become so powerful, Frank was able to sing six bars— sometimes eight—without taking in air. Other singers were lucky to be able to sing two or four. Frank learned to sneak in air from the sides of his mouth, and no one was the wiser. It appeared that he could sing forever without taking a breath, holding notes longer than any of the competition. When he did decide to take that breath, he would do it in as dramatic a fashion as possible, effecting a gasp of anguish when he needed it, when it suited the lyric of the torch song being performed.

All of this training was a closely held trade secret at the time; Frank never explained any of it until years later, when he felt other singers could probably benefit from his experiences. In the 1940s, Sinatra understood that part of the magic of his art was to make it appear completely effortless.

Just as he intended, his breathing technique proved as crucial in the telling of his stories as it was in the delivery of his songs. He once explained to Arlene Francis, actress and *What's My Line* panelist. "It's important to know the proper manner in which to breathe at given points in a song, because otherwise what you're saying becomes choppy. For instance, there's a phrase in the song 'Fools Rush In' that says, 'Fools rush in where wise men never go / But wise men never fall in love / So how are they to know.' Now that should be one phrase," Sinatra said, "because it tells the story right there. But you'll hear somebody say, 'Fools rush in,' and breathe [right in the middle], 'Where wise men never go'—

breath. 'But wise men never fall in love . . .' But if you do it [in one breath], that's the point; you've told the whole story."

Of course, Sinatra's uncanny ability as a vocalist did not go unnoticed by even those in his profession. They knew he could do astonishing things with his voice; they just didn't know how he did them.

"I'd never heard a popular singer with such fluidity and style," songwriter Sammy Cahn once said. "Or one with his incredible breath control. Frank could hold a phrase until it took him into a sort of paroxysm. He actually gasped, and his whole being seemed to explode, to release itself. I'd never seen or heard anything like it."

Of Frank's stellar performance of "Ol' Man River," vibraphonist Emile Richards said: "He would hold his hands behind his back as if he were handcuffed, pull his shoulders forward, or his chest forward and his shoulders back, to get more air. He would go, 'Tote that barge / Lift that bale / Get a little drunk and you land in jail . . .' and without a pause for breath would go right into 'I get weary.' He would go that long without a breath and then still sing 'I get weary.' And by the time he got there, let me tell you, he was friggin' weary. It was so effective it gave me chills or made me cry every time."*

Simple, but not easy.

Frank even used a microphone and mike stand—standard equipment for amplification—in a way that was completely unique for the times. Most singers just stood woodenly in front of one and hoped that their voices would be carried to the rafters. Not Sinatra. "They never understood that a microphone is their instrument," Sinatra would say of the competition. "It's like they're part of an orchestra, but instead of playing a saxophone, they're playing a microphone."

Frank would tenderly hold the microphone stand like a considerate lover during romantic ballads or jerk it roughly if he felt he needed that kind of impact on a brassier number. He would back away from the mike when a dramatic note needed to soar to the heavens and echo, or step into it if he wanted the crowd to hear just the slightest sigh or breath. The girls would swoon in the audience when Frank was onstage, as much for his voice as for the unusual way he performed. The way Sinatra romanced a mike and mike stand was erotic and an important part of his appeal. He was just five feet ten and a half (maybe just five feet nine, depending on which family member is asked), 138 pounds, and with a 29-inch waist, but

---

* Some entertainers weren't as enthusiastic about Frank's success, like Al Jolson. When Sinatra met the competitive Jolson and went to shake his hand, Jolson pulled out a bank statement from his pocket and said, "Think you can do better than this, kid?" He wouldn't shake Frank's hand. Of course, Jolson is said to have had the biggest ego ever in show business; he treated just about everybody this way.

onstage, he somehow seemed like a passionate dynamo, especially when he quivered that lower lip. Paradoxically, he also seemed vulnerable, needy. The total package was irresistible.

Frank Sinatra invented the way he wanted to be, the way he saw himself, the way he wanted others to see him.

After the baby, Nancy, was born and her mother could no longer travel with Frank, the marriage began to weaken. Sinatra was busy with his career: his first movie for Paramount, in October 1940, *Las Vegas Nights,* for which he was paid a measly fifteen dollars a day just to be seen singing "I'll Never Smile Again," no acting; another engagement at the Paramount in New York in January 1941; his first of twenty-nine single releases with Dorsey, "Without a Song," recorded on January 20, 1941.

Of course, there were other women on the road. He would say, "I just can't help myself. This has nothing to do with Nancy. This is about me. What Nancy don't know won't hurt her."

Nancy knew.

Patti Demarest was a friend of Nancy's at this time; they lived in the same apartment complex on Bergen Avenue in Jersey City, New Jersey. She recalled: "Nancy came to my door one day in tears, the baby in her arms. I said, 'My goodness, what's the matter?' and she said, 'That son of a bitch is cheating on me again.' 'Again?' I asked, since this was the first I had heard of this. And she said, 'He's been cheating on me from the beginning.' "

Many of Frank's friends knew that his marriage was in trouble early on. "It must have been sometime in 1940," Sammy Cahn once said. "He was a restless soul even then. He told me how unhappy he was being a married man."

Joey D'Orazio, Frank's friend from Hoboken, said: "We were sitting at a bar in Hoboken. Frank had just gotten off the road, he was visiting his ma, and he was a big shot now. I wanted to know what it was like for him, you know? He said, 'Joey boy, a chump like you will *never* know what it's like for me, that's how fuckin' on top of the world I am.' I had to laugh. That was so typically Frank. Then he said, 'I can have any dame I want. That's the best part. They can't get enough of me. I snap my finger when I get off that stage, and they're at my feet, like puppies, man, lapping me up.' "

D'Orazio told Frank, "Man, you're a married man now. You can't be doing that."

Frank threw back a scotch and water and said, "Well, I can't help myself. What can I say?"

"Bullshit," Joey said. "You *can* help yourself."

Frank slammed his glass on the bar and looked Joey straight in the

46

eyes. "No," he said firmly. "I can't. Got that? I don't wanna. And I ain't gonna. So keep your goddamn mouth shut about it," he said, his tone suddenly threatening, " 'cause I don't want to hurt Nancy. I just don't want to sleep with her no more. It's got nothin' to do with her. It's no big deal."

"Frank, it *is* a big deal," Joey insisted.

"All right, I know it's a big deal. What d'ya think, I'm stupid?" Frank said as he threw some money on the bar. "How the hell can you understand what it's like for me? You and I, we live in different worlds now, ya bum."

Then he got up and stormed angrily out of the bar.

Frank would never discuss with Nancy whether he was still cheating on her. Perhaps he was beginning to view his desire for women as an uncontrollable addiction. As an alcoholic hides his drinking, Frank wanted to hide his affairs. "He knew she knew," said another friend of hers, "which made it worse."

Nancy still loved Frank. It wasn't easy, though, because he was so self-centered, wanting what he wanted without any thought given to the hurt it could cause her. At the same time, because he possessed enormous charm and was such a good lover on the occasional times when they were intimate, she attempted time and time again to overlook his faults.

For his part, it wasn't that Frank didn't love her. He did. However, he was bored. He wanted something—someone—else. Nancy longed for Frank to accept the typical domestic role of husband and father and help raise a family. However, when he wasn't at home in New Jersey with his wife and child, Frank led a fast-paced, glamorous life. When he was on tour, he actually could have anyone he wanted.

The hysteria Frank and the band caused on the road was surprising even to them. Something unusual had started to occur: Frank Sinatra had become a sensation.

"I think that my appeal was due to the fact that there hadn't been a troubadour around for ten or twenty years, from the time that Bing had broken in and went on to radio and movies," Frank said later. "And he, strangely enough, had appealed primarily to older people, middle-aged people. When I came on the scene and people began noticing me, I think the kids were looking for someone to cheer for. I began to realize that there must be something to all this commotion. I didn't know exactly what it was, but I figured I had something that must be important."

Tommy Dorsey was amazed by the reaction of the female audience members to Sinatra's performances. He knew for certain that he had struck gold when he signed this singer to that ridiculous contract. He once recalled: "I used to stand there on the bandstand so amazed I'd almost forget to take my solos. You could almost feel the excitement

47

coming up out of the crowds when that kid stood up to sing. Remember, he was no matinee idol. He was a skinny kid with big ears. And yet what he did to women was something awful."

"Maybe if I'm *more* of a woman," Nancy told Patti Demarest. "Maybe I can keep him at home. Maybe if I pray to God more. That could be it. Maybe I ain't praying to God enough."

"Oh, he'll come back," Patti told her. "But you *do* have to try to be better. Make him know that you're all he needs. Lose some weight, Nancy. Buy some new clothes. Get your hair done." ("That's how we used to think back then," Demarest—now in her seventies—said with a resigned chuckle.)

Divorce was not only against Nancy's Catholic faith; it was also universally frowned on in the 1930s and 1940s. It was not uncommon, however, for a man to take a mistress as well as a wife, an open secret that many people knew and that the wife usually attempted to ignore. In Nancy's case, she was willing to pretend ignorance as a way to preserve the marriage. But as the stories of her husband's infidelities kept finding their way to her, it became impossible for her not to acknowledge what was going on.

In October 1940, while in Los Angeles with the band, Sinatra met Alora Gooding, a blond actress. After a few passionate nights, Frank became convinced that she was the woman for him. Within a week, she moved into his suite at the Hollywood Plaza, which is where the band stayed when on the West Coast.

"He was crazy about her, really in love with her," said his friend Nick Sevano. "She was his first brush with glamour, and he was mad for her."

Finally, Frank confessed to his wife that he had fallen in love with another woman. To simply say she was hurt would understate the anguish she must have felt. Frank tried to convince her that his attraction to Gooding had nothing to do with her. It certainly didn't mean that their marriage was over. In fact, he should be commended for being honest with her, he said. "And if you're gonna penalize me now because I'm being honest, well, that ain't fair," he argued. "I'm trying my best here, Nancy. Why can't you see that?"

Frank's self-involved reasoning failed at first to mollify Nancy. However, in time, Nancy actually began to convince herself that her husband had a valid point. Maybe this relationship with Alora Gooding really had nothing to do with her, after all. As long as Frank continued to come back home to her and to little Nancy, perhaps whatever affairs he had while on the road with the band were simply none of her business.

Rather than give up on her marriage, then, Nancy attempted to accept Frank's sexual proclivities. She buried that part of herself that was hurt and betrayed while focusing on her daughter and feeding her emaciated-looking husband when he finally returned from Alora's arms.

Frank was making almost $15,000 a year—good money for the times. He was a good provider, Nancy told friends. He didn't beat her. He loved his daughter. "Okay, so maybe he has affairs. So what?" she said. She started reaching, trying to pinpoint whatever positive aspects of their relationship she could find. She would explain to friends that whenever she felt a twinge of pain or regret, she would quickly think about something else. She had to lose touch with her feelings. She knew it was the only way she, and her marriage, would survive.

Doris Sevanto said, "Nancy kept saying, 'It'll pass. It'll pass. I know what I'll do. I'll diet. I'll lose ten more pounds. He'll love me then. I've always just been too fat for Frankie, anyway. And I have a new recipe for gravy I think he'll love. It'll fatten him up. I am so worried about him.'

"There were a lot of women, Dolly told me. Teenagers, some of them. Actresses, singers, strippers, dancers, the gamut. Frank was shameless."

One evening, while Frank was away, Nancy received a disturbing telephone call from Alora Gooding, who informed her that she was pregnant with Frank's child. Nancy didn't know how to handle this revelation; she only discussed it with one female friend, who asked for anonymity rather than have Nancy know that—fifty-five years later—she had betrayed a confidence.

"She was crushed and desperate," the friend said. "We were young girls. I was eighteen myself. What did I know about this kind of behavior? How could I even begin to advise her? I liked her so much. She was so sweet. She'd do anything for you. I told her to go to a priest, maybe she could get an annulment. That was her plan, she said. She said she was finished with Frank, that he had gone too far. But first she wanted to talk to him. 'I want him to tell me himself. I want to hear it from his own mouth,' she said.

"When she did, of course, she told me he denied that the girl was pregnant. He became as hysterical as she was, sobbing and begging her for forgiveness. Then, a few days later, this girl—Alora—called Nancy to tell her the whole thing was a big mistake and that she was so sorry.

"I'm certain there's more to this story that I don't know—like whatever conversation Frankie had with Alora. All I know is that when I asked Nancy about it later, she said, 'Please, I would rather not discuss it, ever. It's all been taken care of.' I remember that her eyes were so sad. I always thought of her as the saddest person in the world."

CHAPTER 6

By the summer of 1941, twenty-five-year-old Frank Sinatra had become ubiquitous, on radio, on records, on movie theater stages, and in nightclubs. The band returned to the Paramount in New York at the end of August for another sold-out engagement. By this time, Frank was clearly its star attraction, and it began to make little sense that he even be a member of a band. The audience's reaction to him was so strong that he wanted to do more as a performer and not have to work within any kind of structure. He wanted to be a solo.

In December 1941 the Japanese attacked Pearl Harbor; the United States went to war. Sinatra had been rejected for military service with a 4-F classification because of a punctured eardrum, which, it's been said, he either suffered at birth or during a fight with another youngster. He tried to enlist several more times but was continually turned away.

Four years later, in 1945, Frank was suddenly called for reexamination by the draft board. By this time, his career was in high gear, and he really didn't want to go into the service. "I'm awfully upset right now," he told the press in Jersey City in front of Local Board 18. "I'm going to visit my New Jersey draft board to find out my Selective Service status." He was again rejected, causing a national debate over his status, mostly because he was such a high-profile entertainer and it was thought that he was receiving special treatment. Since he had been rejected, though, prior to his huge career upswing, it was clear that he had not received preferential treatment and that the controversy was just one that had been created by the media.

In January 1942, *Billboard* named Frank Sinatra top band vocalist. Sinatra had also moved Bing Crosby out of the top of the *Downbeat* popularity poll, which Crosby had occupied for six years. On January 19, Sinatra cut his first records without the band for RCA's Bluebird label. Dorsey wasn't thrilled about the prospect of Sinatra's working alone in the studio—with Dorsey's arranger, Axel Stordahl—but he knew that he needed to keep the young singer happy, and Frank was eager to do some recording work on his own. With a small, mellow band—no brass—he recorded "The

Night We Called It a Day," his first version of "Night and Day,"* "The Song Is You," and "The Lamplighter's Serenade." The songs sounded intimate and promising, even to the critical Sinatra ear. Bolstered by these recordings, especially by the way Hoagy Carmichael's "Lamplighter's Serenade" turned out, he began to sense that he would have a bigger career as a solo performer. He knew that he had to make his move.

He said in retrospect that he didn't want to be number one. "I knew that was Bing Crosby. But somebody had to be number two."

There was significant competition.

Onetime opera singer Russ Columbo, a strikingly handsome singer and actor, was thought by many to be heir apparent to Crosby, but his career ended tragically in a shooting accident in 1934. Other vocalists— Bob Eberly (with Jimmy Dorsey's band, Tommy's brother), Ray Eberle (Bob's brother, but with a different spelling, who later became Glenn Miller's star vocalist), and Perry Como (with Ted Weems)—were on their way up, as was Dick Haymes, Sinatra's replacement in Harry James's band, who was now doing concerts as well as working with Benny Goodman's band. Sinatra wanted to claim what he knew was his rightful place in the business.

"I'm gonna be the biggest singer in the business, as big as they come," he told Joey D'Orazio one day. It was a familiar refrain. He said the same thing to Sammy Cahn, among others. When Sammy Cahn agreed, telling him, "There is no way anything can get in your way," Sinatra was filled with an almost overwhelming sense of empowerment. "You *do* believe, then, don't you?" he said to Cahn, excitedly grabbing his arm. Certainly Sinatra believed in his own potential. He became excited when he was able to convince others, and with his prodigious talent, that wasn't difficult to do.

"Frank was making secret plans to strike out on his own," Hank Sanicola once said. "He wanted to be bigger, better. He didn't want to be Dorsey's boy any longer. Columbia Records was interested in him; an advance for Sinatra of roughly $350,000 was discussed. People were talking about him. None of this was anything Tommy [Dorsey] wanted to hear, though. He wanted his band members to stay with him for life."

Sinatra had learned a lot from Tommy Dorsey, just as he had from

---

* It's noteworthy that Sinatra would return again and again to the early numbers he'd sung over his recording career, and each new version presented new insights, reappraisals, and artistic growth. Much of the Capitol repertoire repeated that of Columbia, sometimes in similar arrangements, but the Capitol versions achieved a depth of artistry and feeling that those of Columbia only foreshadowed. Though much of Sinatra's recording repertoire consisted of remakes, in fact, he was never known as a remake artist. He could literally fashion new songs out of old ones, as he did with "Night and Day," which he recorded seven times between 1942 and 1977.

Harry James. From Dorsey, Sinatra began to fully understand that a vocalist doesn't necessarily have to sing a song the same way every time he performed it, though that is what most singers did. Dorsey taught Sinatra how to personalize a melody so that it was unique to the moment, yet familiar to the fans just the same. Along with Frank's growing ability to interpret a lyric as the mood struck so as to make each performance interesting to himself and to his audience, Dorsey's influence went a long way toward the final creation of Sinatra as a unique artist.

He had also made some fine records with Dorsey, including "Pale Moon," "Oh, Look at Me Now," "The One I Love," and "Blue Skies." However, it was time for him to move on.

In early 1942 twenty-six-year-old Frank told Tommy Dorsey that he was leaving the band in a year.

"Man, I'm ready to go. I want to leave the orchestra," Frank recalled telling him in a dressing room backstage in Washington while Dorsey was going over a musical composition.

Dorsey, always the taskmaster, looked at Sinatra with the indifference of a schoolteacher who had heard it all before from his students. "What for?" Tommy said. "You know you're doing great with the band, and we got a lot of arrangements for you."

"I know that, Tommy," Frank said. "But it's time for me to go out on my own."

"Well, I don't think so," Dorsey said, looking back down at his sheet music. "I don't think so at all." (Dorsey, of course, realized that Sinatra was arguably the best band vocalist in the business. He wasn't going to make his departure easy.)

Frank was unrelenting. "Well, I'm leaving," he said. "I just thought you should know. I think you might want to consider Dick Haymes. He's a helluva singer."

"Listen, you've got a contract," Tommy said, becoming angry.

"Well, I had one with Harry, too," Frank said naively. "And he took it and tore it up."

"I ain't Harry," Tommy shot back.

"I'm giving you a year's notice," Frank said before leaving. "This time next year, I'm leaving."

From that time on, Tommy Dorsey only spoke to Frank Sinatra when he absolutely had to. Frank wasn't concerned about Dorsey's attitude; he was busy planning his new career, contacting promoters, booking agents, and others in the entertainment industry that he knew would be able to assist him when the time was right. He was also taking diction classes with instructor John Quinlan in New York in an attempt to lose his New Jersey accent—a lost cause. However, he would learn to enunciate perfectly when performing. A driven man, Frank would do whatever he felt he had to do in order to make it in the competitive record business.

Through Tommy Dorsey's road manager, George H. "Bullets" Durgom, Frank would meet and befriend Emmanuel "Manie" Sachs," a recording executive from Columbia. Sachs, the head of Columbia's artists and repertory (A & R) division, believed he could make additional contacts for him in the industry and possibly even sign him to Columbia. At the time, Sinatra was still under contract to RCA because of his arrangement with Tommy Dorsey. Frank wanted to move ahead with his career now. To do so, he had to find a way out of his contract with Dorsey, especially when reminded that he would have to pay Dorsey a third of anything he earned as a result of that deal, which Sinatra called "a ratty piece of paper."

Matters were made worse for Tommy Dorsey because Sinatra intended to take arranger Axel Stordahl with him, paying him five times the $650 per month he was already earning with Dorsey, all of which alarmed Dorsey. Sinatra's allegiance to him was clearly nonexistent.

Finally, Dorsey let Sinatra leave, but the contract would remain in effect. He fully expected a third of Sinatra's income, plus 10 percent for Dorsey's agent. Frank decided he would deal with that issue later. The first order of business would be to leave the band before Dorsey changed his mind.

Frank Sinatra performed his last concert with Dorsey at the Circle Theater in Indianapolis on September 3, 1942. Sinatra introduced his replacement that evening, Dick Haymes, who would stay with Tommy Dorsey for only six months before embarking on his own solo career.

Many band singers, such as Ginny Simms, Ray Eberle, and Jack Leonard, failed to make the transition from dance band to center stage. That didn't worry Sinatra. After all, he realized that they were just vocalists who stood stiffly in front of bandstands. They did the best they could, but that wasn't enough to garner solo success. Sinatra knew, because he had made certain of it, that he was a romantic performer, an exciting entertainer as well as an adept singer.

Other than the fact that he could sing, like many other people, none of Frank Sinatra's skill resulted from happenstance. Frank had spent years trying to determine just how to excel at his craft and capture the public's imagination with all the proper tools, such as breath control, lyrical phrasing, elocution lessons, and even microphone techniques. Now it was time for those years of concentration to finally pay off. He was willing to take the gamble by leaving Tommy Dorsey because, quite simply, he knew he couldn't lose. He had earned the right to his success.

At this time, as fate would have it, Bob Weitman, manager of the Paramount Theater, saw Sinatra perform at a concert at the Mosque Theater in Newark on Frank's twenty-seventh birthday, December 12, 1942. He was impressed. He then asked Benny Goodman, the "King of Swing," if he minded having the singer on a bill with him and his band at the

Paramount at the end of December. Goodman's response: "Who the hell is Frank Sinatra?" Not many people would ask that question, though, after December 30, 1942.

Because employment was so high during the war, people had a lot of money, but because of the scarcity of things to buy, there was no place to spend it. Thus, movies flourished. People used them to escape the troubles of war. During the summer, air-conditioned theaters were often the only place to escape the heat. The downtown movie theaters were huge, with big, ornate lobbies decorated with mirrors and fancy chandeliers, plush padded seats, balconies, and uniformed ushers with flashlights to show patrons to their seats. Theaters opened at eight-thirty in the morning; because so many people worked swing and graveyard shifts during wartime, schedules were turned upside down, and there was always an audience available to fill the seats.

The program was often a double feature, plus shorts, like the Movietone News, which included a war report. Often theaters put on a live show, especially in the larger cities. In New York, for instance, the Radio City Music Hall featured the Rockettes, a precision tap-dancing chorus line. Big bands were often part of the show, as at the Paramount, where Frank—whenever he appeared—would do six, sometimes seven, shows a day.

"I went to rehearsal at seven-thirty in the morning," Frank said of opening day, "and looked at the [Paramount Theater] marquee, and it said, 'Extra Added Attraction: Frank Sinatra,' and I said, 'Wow!' "

The film playing at the Paramount was Bing Crosby's *Star-Spangled Rhythm,* which received top billing. Then, on the marquee, the Benny Goodman Band, up-and-coming vocalist Peggy Lee, pianist Jess Stacy, the BG Sextet, the Radio Rogues and Mike and Poke, and billed last and in small letters—Frank Sinatra.

He may have had last billing, but what an extraordinary debut this would turn out to be. In fact, the moment he was introduced (on opening night by Jack Benny), the young girls in the audience went crazy. They immediately started crying out: "Frankeeeeee, Frankeeeee." It was so sudden, this adulation, that everyone was taken by surprise.

"What the hell was that?" Benny Goodman asked no one in particular.

"Five thousand kids, stamping, yelling, screaming, applauding," Frank remembered. "I thought the roof would come off."

"I thought the goddamned building was going to cave in," Jack Benny said.

In fact, the audience—mostly comprised of teenage girls, who were known as "bobbysoxers" because of the white socks they wore*—simply

* The uniform of the day often was a sweater over a pleated knee-length skirt, white socks, and saddle shoes or penny loafers. After school and on weekends, skirts and

54

wouldn't leave after the show; they would attempt to stay through several performances, and the only way to get rid of them was for the theater's manager to screen the dullest films he could find, along with *Star-Spangled Rhythm,* between shows.

Frank Sinatra had become an "overnight sensation." Of course, it had taken three years. With the show a record-breaking success—and it would not be overstating it to say that this was because of Sinatra's contribution—the original two-week engagement was extended for two more months.

Frank was so grateful to his fans for their support, he had his assistant road manager, Richie Lisella, buy dozens of turkey sandwiches at Walgreen's for the girls who stayed in their seats all day long rather than risk losing them to newcomers. He never pandered to this audience, either. He sang intelligent, poignant love songs, though they were rarely heard over the din.

Although "Sinatramania," as it was dubbed by the press, did affect some older women and men of all ages, it was mostly the thirteen- to fifteen-year-old girls who became his biggest fans. What accounted for this phenomenon? One theory is that they were too young to have boyfriends. (Their older sisters did have beaus, many of whom were in the service.) Frank Sinatra became a handy love object. Even though they knew he was married and a father—on the children's birthdays there were enough gifts sent by fans to fill an orphanage—it made him safe because he was unattainable. On the other hand, even though he was an older married man, he was so thin and boyish looking, he could have been one of them.

"Psychologists have tried to go into the reasons why, with all sorts of theories," Frank said of the pandemonium he had caused. "It was the war years, and there was a great loneliness. I was the boy in every corner drugstore, the boy who'd gone off to war."

Then there was the business of the eyes. When Frank sang, he never looked off into space. His piercing blue eyes seemed to reach different members of the audience. It was something he did throughout his career, and it never failed to affect the women who came to see him. Each thought that he was singing to her alone. At a time when fathers were either off at war or working impossibly long hours and the girls were too young to have their own boyfriends, Frank became the number-one male in their lives. He was the ideal fantasy figure—vulnerable yet erotic flesh and blood. In truth, forbidden and even unattainable because he was married, older, and famous. Just to see him, to touch him, to have something to remember him by were enough.

---

sweaters were exchanged for dungarees (they're called jeans now), rolled up and worn to just over the ankles, along with a man's cotton or wool buffalo-checked shirt.

And they went to great lengths to do just that. In the winter, girls were known to dig up snow prints of his feet and take them home to their freezers. Ashes from his cigarettes were prized mementos. Hotel maids were bribed to let girls lie between his sheets before they made the bed in which he had slept. He had two thousand fan clubs.

Because of his success at the Paramount, Sinatra hired a new press agent, forty-one-year-old George Evans, who had been introduced to him by his friend Nick Sevano. Evans, an enthusiastic PR man, represented a host of celebrities who would go on to become show-business icons, including Lena Horne, Duke Ellington, and Dean Martin and Jerry Lewis. "Make me the biggest star there is," Sinatra told him. "Whatever it takes. I got the talent, now you do what you gotta do."

The first idea Evans had was to have one of his assistants, Marjorie Diven, hire a gaggle of girls to scream whenever Frank sang one of his romantic ballads. Each youngster was paid five dollars for her services. It was hardly necessary, though. The audience was so enthusiastic, they practically drowned out Evans's employees. To make Sinatra's performance even more interesting, Evans decided that some of the girls should faint during one of Frank's numbers. (Of course, only members of Sinatra's camp knew that these youngsters had been planted throughout the theater.) Much to Evans's amazement, thirty girls fainted one night. Only twelve had been hired. Then the girls started throwing their little brassieres onto the stage.

"Jesus Christ, can you believe how big I am?" Frank asked his pals backstage after one show. "Look at how high I'm flying."

Frank remembered those days in an interview years later. "I was everything," he said. "Happy? I don't know. I wasn't *un*happy, let's put it that way. I never had it so good. Sometimes I wonder whether anybody had it like I had it, before or since. It was the damnedest thing, wasn't it? But I was too busy ever to know whether I was happy or even to ask myself. I can't remember for a long time even taking time out to think."

"Frank was flying high, and we were proud of him," said a childhood friend. "He'd worked hard to get where he was, and he made sure we all knew it. We had a lot of laughs. He was the same ol' Frankie. I don't think he changed a bit. He was cocky, but hell, he was always cocky. But one thing was for sure: We liked him more when he was happy, and he was pretty damn happy during this time.

"He was spending money like crazy, I remember. He bought all of his pals from Hoboken watches and sweaters.* 'Anything you need, you come to me,' he said. 'And if your mother or father need something, you

---

* Frank's wardrobe had become quite impressive: fifty suits, two dozen sports coats, over a hundred pairs of dress pants, sixty pairs of shoes. His floppy bow ties, which became a trademark, were handmade by his wife, Nancy.

tell 'em to call me, too.' [Frank's salary went from $750 a week at the Paramount to $25,000.] I mean, he wasn't the kind of guy who ever forgot his buddies from the old neighborhood, you know?"

As a result of George Evans's ingenuity, no lull ever occurred in the crowd's hysterical participation; they were all *on* from the moment Frank hit the stage, instigated by Evans's few young charges. Then Evans took his responsibility to help turn Frank into a sensation a step further by giving away free tickets to other youngsters, just to be sure the house was packed. He contacted the press and made certain that photographers were present to document Sinatra's effect on the young people in his audiences. Soon all of New York—indeed, all of the country, for that matter—was reading and talking about the singer in the floppy bow tie that George Evans had dubbed "the Voice."*

Eventually, some of the youngsters Evans hired started, as he said later, "yapping," and rumors circulated that Sinatramania had been an orchestrated event. Via a press release Evans made a standing offer to donate $1,000 to the favorite charity of anyone who could prove that "a kid was given a ticket, a pass, a gift, or a gratuity of any kind in any shape or manner at all to go in and screech" at a Frank Sinatra concert. No money was donated.

Evans arranged press interviews, photo sessions, autograph parties, radio-station visits—whatever it took to spread the word that young Frank Sinatra had arrived. In press releases Evans rewrote Sinatra's history, lopping two years off Frank's age, having him "graduate" from high school, making him athletic and his parents native-born. Dolly was even transformed into a Red Cross nurse! (Eagerly, she played along with the hype. In fact, when Frank was rejected for military service, Dolly lamented to a reporter, "Oh, dear, Frankie wanted to get in so badly because he wanted to have our pictures taken together in uniform.")

Evans also passed the word that Frank was a slum kid, born into an impoverished family that struggled with financial woes in a gang-infested neighborhood. Frank was, for the most part, completely cooperative. George Evans's example taught him that a good story is a good story; it doesn't necessarily have to be true. Evans's successful campaign continued long after the Paramount engagement, and as far as many Sinatra historians are concerned, he is largely responsible for the wide scope of Sinatra's early fame. Of course, the fact that Frank Sinatra had been working for years to invent himself as a vocalist and entertainer helped significantly.

"Dolly was calling everyone she knew in Hoboken and bragging about

---

* Though Evans's friends credit him with nicknaming Sinatra the Voice, it has also been reported that the appellation actually came from Sinatra's agent, Harry Kilby, who dubbed Sinatra "the voice that thrills millions."

her kid," Joey D'Orazio remembered. "To hear her talk, he was the biggest thing since Moses. A bunch of us drove Dolly and Marty and some other family members to one show, and Frank asked me to bring Marty backstage afterwards. Frankie was extremely nervous. 'My old man never wanted me to sing,' he told me. 'What do you think he's gonna say now? You think he'll be proud, Joey boy?' I said, 'Jesus Christ, Frank, you're the hottest thing in show business. Of course he's proud.' Frank looked sad and said, 'I ain't so sure. You don't know my ol' man. This ain't his thing, this whole singing jazz. If it was up to him, I'd be workin' on the docks.'

"I got the feeling that a lot depended on Marty's reaction," D'Orazio continued. "Even though Frank was a star, I felt that if Marty didn't have the proper response, it would have ruined everything."

When Marty remained a bit quiet during the show, D'Orazio was concerned. "I can't hear a goddamn thing over the noise in this joint," the senior Sinatra complained during one ballad. "Is he any good or not? I can't hear him."

After Frank's final bows, Joey escorted Marty to the backstage door.

"It was madness there," D'Orazio said. "We couldn't get in. I remember that there was some kind of mix-up on the guest list. Frank's *paisano* Hank [Sanicola] forgot to put our name on it, and I was about to take Marty away rather than have him be embarrassed. Suddenly, Marty says to this big guy at the door, 'Hey, pal, that was my kid up there on that stage. I'm his ol' man, and if you don't let me back there, I'm gonna knock you out.' I was amazed. Marty was usually pretty quiet, but he really wanted to get backstage to see Frankie. 'Now where's Hank [Sanicola]? Get him out here.' For some reason, the guard was convinced, and he let us through."

Frank's small dressing room was cramped with excited well-wishers, but when Marty walked into the room all eyes seemed to turn toward him. It was as if everyone somehow knew that a significant moment was about to occur. "Hey, Pop," Frank greeted his father as he cut through the crowd and headed toward him.

"Well, whatd'ya think, Dad," he asked with a cautious smile.

"Who could hear?" Marty responded. "Nobody could hear anything. How do *you* hear what you're doing?"

Frank had to laugh. "So, I'm still a quitter? Or what?" Marty's eyes teared up.

"My son ain't no quitter," he said as he embraced Frank. "My son's a big shot."

"That I am," Frank said with a broad grin as he slapped his father on the back. "That I am."*

---

* Every Monday, for years, Marty Sinatra received a one hundred dollar check from "Sinatra Enterprises," mailed to the Hoboken Fire Department, where he worked—a

CHAPTER 7

or the most part, Frank Sinatra and his publicist, George Evans, completely agreed on their long-term goals for his burgeoning career. True, Frank's hotheadededness would often get the better of him; he was under a great deal of pressure and as a result was often disagreeable and unreasonable. "A real prick," George would say when describing Frank to intimates. "The worst kind there is, because not only does he have to prove you wrong, he has to make you agree that he just proved it."

Plagued by insomnia, Sinatra—always an erudite, socially conscious man—would read into the early hours of the morning. He would devour a wide variety of books. His particular interest was in the cause of racial tolerance. His favorites included *An American Dilemma* by Gunnar Myrdal; *The History of Bigotry in the United States* by Gustavus Myers, and the novel *Freedom Road* by Howard Fast.

Sinatra's voracious appetite for books, for being up on current events, for the how and why of life, may indeed be the major element in his singing that took him above everyone else. In an era of performers, he was an informed artist. Big difference.

In the morning, he was tired and irritable. By afternoon, he was giving everyone hell.

George Evans could deal with the irascible side of Sinatra's personality. He thought of it as a combination of artistic temperament and Italian stubbornness. The one problem he and Sinatra could not reconcile, however, was a more serious one: Frank's philandering.

"George had a meeting with Frank one afternoon in his office at 1775 Broadway—the first of many on the subject—and it turned into a screaming match," recalled Ted Hechtman, who was a New York friend of George Evans. "He told him flat out, 'You gotta stop with the dames.' And Frank was adamant. 'That ain't got nothin' to do with nothin.' That's my own private business, George. Keep your nose out of it.'

" 'But it *does* have to do with your career, Frankie,' George told him. 'If the word gets out that you're cheating on your wife, how do you think

---

secret gift from Frank to his father, "for him to do with whatever he wants, without Ma knowing," Frank explained to one friend with a wink.

those kids who're screaming about you and idolizing you are gonna feel about that? I'm tellin' ya, you could be ruined.'

" 'Well, it's *your* job to make sure it don't get out,' Frank insisted, raising his voice an octave. 'That's what I'm paying you for. And not only that, if it does get out, you're fired, you hear? You keep it out of the press, simple as that.'

" 'I can't guarantee that,' Evans said, angrily. 'Keep your trousers zipped, Frank. That's all I ask. What do want from me? Jesus Christ.'

"Frank screamed at him. 'Listen, pal, you do what you gotta do to keep it out of the papers, and I'll do what I gotta do to keep myself happy. 'Cause if I'm happy, I sing good. If I sing good, we *all* make money. You got that? Jesus Christ,' he said, exasperated, 'I don't gotta explain this to my own wife. Why am I talkin' to *you* about it? Now get the fuck out of here.'

" 'Hey, this is *my* goddamn office, Frankie,' " George reminded him. " '*You* get the fuck out.' "

Frank stormed off.

Happily, a month later, in 1943, Nancy Sinatra became pregnant again; that was one press release he was happy to give to the media. George Evans's worries were over—for about a week.

Ted Hechtman recalled: "Then Nancy called George—which would be the first of many calls like this one—and said that she couldn't find Frank and she needed him because little Nancy was sick with some baby illness.

"George made some calls and tracked Frank down at a seedy hotel outside Jersey City. Furious, he went down there and pounded on the door. When there was no answer, he just let himself in; the door was unlocked. No one was in the room, but George heard something going on in the bathroom. He walked in, and there was Frankie and this stripper whose name was—I'll never forget it as long as I live—Laura Lee Luango. She had the nickname 'Lips Luango.' Frank was caught in the act of doing what comes naturally to guys who are cheating on their wives.

" 'Frankie,' George blurted out, 'What about Nancy? You ever give her even a second thought? Jesus, look at you, with Lips Luango of all people!'

"And, as George told me, the dame burst out into tears and said, 'But I thought you said you and her was gettin' a divorce, Frankie. And that you and me, we was gettin' married. How could you *lie* to me after all we've meant to each other, and all?'

"And while Frank was scrambling around looking for a towel, he shouted, 'Shut the fuck up, why don't ya? Like I'm gonna marry a broad named Lips, anyway. Jesus Christ.' "

This particular woman gave Frank a gift he discovered a few weeks later: gonorrhea, a sexually transmitted disease. He was so angry with his "date," said his friends at this time, that he attempted to locate her to let her know that he was upset by his doctor's report. However, Lips Luango had disappeared without a trace. Moreover, says one of Frank's friends, "he couldn't be sure it was Lips who gave it to him, anyway."

As far as anyone knew, it was Frank's first experience with a venereal disease. He arranged for a doctor to give him a reusable glass hypodermic needle and medicine kit which he kept in his pocket at all times rather than take the chance that Nancy would find it in the medicine cabinet at home. Because Frank and Nancy were so seldom intimate, it is thought that she never knew of her husband's problem. However, George Evans did know, and he was appalled by his client's immature behavior.

Frank couldn't have cared less about Evans's opinion. He was still angry with him for breaking in on him and his paramour. When he and Frank discussed the health problem, according to intimates of Evans, Frank said, "Look, you keep your fucking nose out of my business." Then he threw a half-filled glass of Dubonnet at him.

"Your job is just to keep me in the papers. Stay out of my fuckin' life, George. Nancy's fine with what's going on."

Was she really?

Even before they were married, Nancy Barbato was one of Frank's staunchest supporters where his career was concerned. How many nights had he cried on her shoulder about Marty's bitter reaction to his aspirations? Then, when he was with Harry James's band, she went on the road with him, cooking for the band and again offering moral support when funds were low. She was the one who sewed the floppy bow ties that became his trademark, just another one of the small things she did to contribute to her husband's career. She also paid the bills and handled a myriad of financial concerns, including the task of trying to keep her husband from spending all of their money on gifts for friends once he became famous.

Now that her husband was a star, Nancy felt entitled to a share in some of the financial rewards he was beginning to reap. In a sense, Frank was partially correct; she *was* accepting, but not because she approved of Frank's behavior but, rather, because she had resigned herself to the fact that, as she bitterly put it to one friend, "My no-good husband is just going to do what he wants to do. I'll live with it."

"Nancy married Frank forever," said actress Esther Williams, who would become a friend of theirs in later years (when she appeared in the movie *Take Me Out to the Ball Game* with Sinatra). "I knew other Hollywood wives who would feel the same about their husbands. Jeanne Martin [Dean Martin's wife] and Patti Lewis [Jerry Lewis's] come to mind. These women were women who were with their men at the beginning of their big stardom, and they felt entitled to be wives forever. It simply didn't matter who else their men married or what they did or how they cheated."

"By the end of 1942, I think, the only reason Frank would ever be intimate with Nancy was to procreate," said Patti Demarest. "It was said—I think even by Frank in later years—that she became pregnant in an effort to save their marriage. I personally don't believe that. She wanted children because she wanted to be loved and needed by somebody, since she was not getting that from Frank. In fact, she began to resent him, not even want him anymore. He had changed her, made her bitter, made her sometimes even hate herself for the choices he was forcing her to make."

Indeed, without Frank, Nancy was an unmarried mother with no prospect of a well-paying job. With him, she was the wealthy wife of a major star. At the time, the choice seemed clear, if not easy.

The new year, 1943, began on a high note for twenty-seven-year-old Frank Sinatra. His career had taken off; he was featured on the cover of practically every show-business-related magazine. In January he was back at the Paramount, this time with Johnny Long's band, in another successful monthlong engagement there.

In February 1943 he became a regular (along with Beryl Davis and Eileen Barton) on radio on *Your Hit Parade,* sponsored by Lucky Strike cigarettes, whose motto was "LS/MFT. Lucky Strike Means Fine Tobacco."* (The cigarettes came in green packages, but when the green dye was needed for army uniforms, the packaging was changed to white. "Lucky Strike Greens have gone to war," the announcer would intone.)

The show, a countdown of the week's biggest hits, proved enormously popular. Also that month, Columbia Pictures released Sinatra's first film without the Dorsey band, *Reveille With Beverly* (in which Frank just had a cameo role singing "Night and Day"), starring future M-G-M costar, tap dancer Ann Miller (*On the Town*).

Early in the year, Frank and Nancy bought a seven-room home on Lawrence Avenue in Hasbrouck Heights, New Jersey, for about $25,000. Because there was no fence around the property, the home became a favorite stalking sight for Frank's eager fans. Indeed, the Sinatras soon grew used to having little privacy.

George Evans, Hank Sanicola, and others in his management-booking team realized that Sinatra's longevity depended on his appeal to a wider audience than just the youngsters who had caused such a sensation at the Paramount. They wanted him to play the Copacabana at 10 East Sixtieth Street in Manhattan, a new club that featured major adult-oriented performers, such as Jimmy Durante and Sophie Tucker. The Copa manager, Jules Podell, decided not to hire him, fearing he would not draw an adult crowd.

---

* Cigarettes were constantly in short supply for civilians. "Give me a pack of stoopies" became a jab at storekeepers who stooped under the counter to reach the packs they stashed for their favorite customers.

In late March 1943, Frank was booked into the Riobamba, a New York City nightclub on East Fifty-seventh Street. This important booking, for which he was paid only $750 a week, was made to solidify Sinatra's appeal to an older audience, the parents of the young bobby-soxers. Frank was furious when he learned he was billed as an "Extra Added Attraction"—in a show that headlined singer-comedienne Sheila Barrett, monologist Walter O'Keefe, and a bunch of chorus girls called the Russell Patterson Cover Girls—in a nightclub that was about to go out of business.

Except for perhaps Barrett and O'Keefe, who had never before in their careers been so ignored by an audience and eventually just walked off the gig and left Frank, the engagement at the Riobamba was a major success, standing room only. Sammy Cahn was there on opening night, and he recalled that "the audience was not [a bunch of] bobby-soxers. This was an adult, mature, sophisticated, two o'clock-in-the-morning Manhattan audience."

Earl Wilson reported: "Frank was in a dinner jacket, and he was wearing a wedding band. He had a small curl that fell almost over his right eye. With trembling lips—I don't know how he made them tremble, but I saw it—he sang 'She's Funny That Way' and 'Night and Day' and succeeded in bringing down the house. It was a wondrous night for all of us who felt we had a share in Frankie. The *New York Post*'s pop-music critic, Danny Richman, leaned over to me and said, 'He sends me.' "

After the engagement at the Riobamba, it seemed that Frank Sinatra could do no wrong, especially when his next engagement was at the Paramount in May. For this engagement he was paid $2,500 a week; his initial gig there, with Benny Goodman, earned him $150 a week. This success proved without a doubt that he still had the youngsters' allegiance as well as that of their parents. In June, Frank recorded his first sides at the Columbia studios, with the Bobby Tucker Singers. (Because of a long-running musicians' strike, Sinatra was forced to record nine songs a cappella, including, "You'll Never Know," "People Will Say We're in Love," and, most notably, "The Music Stopped.")

On August 12, 1943, Frank and his entourage, including Hank Sanicola and arranger Axel Stordahl, arrived in Pasadena, California. Frank was on the West Coast to appear as himself in *Higher and Higher*, his first acting role in a movie, and also at the Hollywood Bowl on August 14 in a series of concerts that served to lend him more credence as a respectable pop vocalist. Hysterical fans nearly caused a riot when Frank got off the train in Pasadena.

While in Los Angeles, Frank finally decided to confront Tommy Dorsey about the contract he had signed when he first began to sing for his band. Thirty-three and a third percent of his gross earnings to Dorsey? Forever? And another 10 percent for Dorsey's agent? "That's the most fucked-up thing I ever heard of," he told Hank Sanicola, who was now officially managing him. Sinatra was supposed to have been paying Dorsey from all engagements, including those at the Copa, Riobamba, and Paramount, but he was behind in his payments, much to Dorsey's indignation.

Bing Crosby suggested that he had better find a way out of the situation soon, before he started making millions. Frank agreed, and he actively pursued a strategy of trying to get out of that contract. He began giving press interviews claiming that Dorsey was cheating him out of money. Immediately, Sinatra's fans started a letter-writing campaign against Dorsey. Then press agent George Evans organized a campaign of Sinatra fans to picket Tommy Dorsey's opening at the Earle Theater in Philadelphia.

Sinatra and Dorsey sued each other.

In August 1943 attorneys for Sinatra and Dorsey attempted to work out a settlement whereby that contract would be canceled. It was not easy; Dorsey was unwilling to budge.

Emmanuel "Manie" Sachs, Frank's friend from Columbia Records, found a new attorney for Sinatra, Henry Jaffe, who also represented the American Federation of Radio Artists. Jaffe was able to use his connection with AFRA to convince Dorsey that if he continued to stand in Sinatra's way, he might have "just a little trouble" continuing his lucrative NBC radio broadcasts. Frank had been represented at this time by the Rockwell-O'Keefe agency, but he wanted to be with the bigger, more established MCA, which was interested in him. Finally, it was agreed that MCA would put up the money to get Frank out of his Dorsey deal. Dorsey was paid $60,000 ($25,000 of which came from Frank, who borrowed it from Manie Sachs). For its investment, MCA got the services of Sinatra, and agreed that it would split its commission on Sinatra with Rockwell-O'Keefe until 1948.

Sinatra had already signed with Columbia. "All or Nothing at All," the rerelease of the original Harry James recording, would become a major hit for him in 1943. It is remarkable that the original recording of "All or Nothing at All" (it would be recorded by Frank three more times, in 1961, 1966, and 1977) still sounds absolutely contemporary. It could have been recorded last week and be accepted as a new recording of a hallowed pop standard with a traditional big-band arrangement. Many later recordings of this song by other artists echoed the original James arrangement.

There were rumors that Sinatra had used underworld connections to convince Dorsey that he should release him from the contract. Specifically, the story was that New Jersey mobster Willie Moretti intervened on Sinatra's behalf—put a gun to Dorsey's head and forced him to release Sinatra from his contract. Moretti continually bragged that he had done this favor for Sinatra, until he was murdered gangland style in 1951.

Sinatra has insisted that the story is untrue and that he relied entirely on his legal team to extricate himself from the Dorsey contract.

"The truth is that Hank Sanicola had a couple buddies, not real underworld characters but just some frightening fellows that he and Sinatra both knew, threaten Dorsey that if he didn't let Frankie out of that contract, there'd be some big trouble," Joey D'Orazio recalled. "I know this because Sanicola called me up and asked me to fly to Los Angeles and go with this crew to Dorsey's office. I refused to do it, though. I had a wife and a kid, and I didn't want to end up in some Los Angeles jail if things got out of hand.

"But I know the hoodlums that went out there, because some of us hung out together, and when they got back, man, that's all they wanted to talk about. They told me that Sanicola didn't want Sinatra to know any of the details. 'Just take care of it,' he said. He didn't know for sure if it was necessary; they were close to ending it with Dorsey, anyway. 'He just needs a little nudge,' he told me.

"He always wanted Sinatra to be able to claim that he didn't know *nuttin'* about *nuttin'* if it all blew up. He was always protecting Sinatra, Sanicola was.*

"In the end, these characters told Dorsey that they'd break his arms, that he'd never play again, if he didn't just sign some legal papers and let Frankie out of that ridiculous contract. What a joke, threatening Tommy Dorsey, who was a tough bastard himself. He laughed in their faces and mocked them, saying, 'Oh, yeah, look at how scared I am. Tell Frank I'm scared to death. Then tell him I said, "Go to hell for sending his goons to beat me up." '

"The guys were stunned. Then Tommy said, 'I'll sign the goddamn papers, that's how sick I am of Frank Sinatra, the no good bum. The hell with him.'

"It wasn't much of an intimidation. In fact, one of the guys was so excited about meeting Tommy Dorsey, he had to be talked out of going back and asking the guy for his autograph after they left his office."

Betty Wilken is the daughter of Bea Wilken, a Los Angeles friend of Tommy Dorsey's wife, Pat Dane (who, along with her husband, also had quite the reputation as a rabble-rouser). She said: "My mother often told me that Dorsey was as difficult as they come, a very temperamental, argumentative person that you didn't want to cross. She also told me that Pat and Tommy hated Frankie for years because they felt he had sent his fellows to hurt Tommy. It was always said that Frank was lucky that Tommy hadn't killed all of his pals right there on the spot. He was that angry."

---

* "That son of a bitch will go down with the ship," Sinatra once said of his pal Hank Sanicola.

Dorsey was never happy about the way it ended with Sinatra; he felt that he had a gold mine in Sinatra's talent and he apparently wished to exploit Frank's gifts for the rest of his life—and the lives of his heirs as well. He didn't like losing. He later gave credence to Joey D'Orazio's version of how Sinatra extricated himself from the contract when he told *American Mercury* magazine in 1951 that during a breakdown in negotiations with Sinatra's attorneys, he was visited by three businesslike men who talked out of the sides of their mouths and ordered him to "sign or else."

"Well, I just hope you fall on your ass," he told Frank Sinatra when it was clear that indeed he *had* lost. Frank was too busy to care about Dorsey's bitterness; as soon as the contract with Dorsey was settled, Frank signed a seven-year deal with RKO to make movies, the first of which would be *Higher and Higher*.

Higher and Higher, with Jack Haley and Michele Morgan, marked Sinatra's acting debut, even though he portrayed himself in it. It was a showcase film in which he performed five songs, including "I Couldn't Sleep a Wink Last Night," nominated for an Academy Award. "It's hard to dislike a guy who seems so simple, friendly and natural, and Frankie seems that way on the screen because that's the way he is," wrote the critic for the *Hollywood Reporter*.

Tommy Dorsey died suddenly in his sleep in 1956. Though Sinatra and Dorsey never became close friends again, they did see each other from time to time and even worked together on a few occasions. Just months prior to his death, Dorsey and Sinatra appeared together at the Paramount Theater in New York. Sinatra also recorded an album in the sixties, *I Remember Tommy*, for Reprise, which paid tribute to Dorsey. Today he never tires of talking about the Tommy Dorsey days, both the good and the bad, and it would seem that Sinatra has special memories of those years despite the bitterness of the breakup.

Besides *Your Hit Parade*, Frank Sinatra starred in a number of CBS radio programs from late 1942 to 1945, including *Reflections, Broadway Band Box, Max Factor Presents Frank Sinatra, Old Gold Presents Songs by Sinatra* and *The Frank Sinatra Show*, which aired in 1944 as a fifteen-minute program and was revamped in 1945 as a half hour. He was a permanent fixture on radio, exposure that was also vitally important to his growth as a vocalist and popularity with audiences. One reason Sinatra did so much radio is that he could sing anything, from the most dramatic torch ballad to the silliest novelty, and make it all sound worthwhile. He was also a quick study and could do unfamiliar material with ease and credibility.

When, on October 1, 1943, Frank opened at the Waldorf-Astoria in New York, his mother, Dolly, was sitting ringside. She had gone to the show with a group of her friends from Hoboken, including Josephine

66

Barbone. Barbone's daughter, also named Josephine, recalled that her late mother often spoke of that night at the Waldorf.

"Frankie was making an important appearance, this one for adults, at the Wedgewood Room in the hotel," Barbone remembered, "and my mother said that Dolly was apparently a little overbearing. She went backstage afterward and refused to let Frank take any pictures unless she was at his side, smiling and posing. Apparently she was going to the different reporters, saying, 'You know, my son has broken just about every record that bastard Bing Crosby ever set. Write *that* down in your goddamn notepad.' And Frank had to keep telling her, 'Ma, you can't swear in front of the goddamn reporters. You gotta watch your mouth. This is the big time here. This ain't no fuckin' Hoboken press.' Dolly would say, 'Don't mouth off to me, Frankie. You're no star in my household.'

"But, oh, she was proud. She was her son's biggest supporter. And, as I understand it, she had already been able to parlay his success into her own popularity in Hoboken. She started going to supermarket openings, cutting the ribbon, as 'Frank Sinatra's Mother'—that sort of thing.* [Because of her son's celebrity—and, by extension, her own—Dolly was even recruited into St. Ann's Catholic Church as a member of the Rosary Club despite her history of performing abortions.]

On January 10, 1944, Nancy gave birth to her and Frank's second child—a son—at the Margaret Hague Maternity Hospital in Jersey City, New Jersey. Again, Frank could not be present for the birth, for he was in Los Angeles filming *Step Lively*. He was on the air in the middle of a radio broadcast at the moment Nancy actually gave birth. She and Frank had decided in advance that if it were a boy, the child would be named Franklin (after Franklin Delano Roosevelt) Wayne Emmanuel (after Manie Sachs) Sinatra, but he would go on to be known as Frank junior. In retrospect, the very popular photographs of Nancy in her hospital bed seem almost eerie. She appeared surrounded by press photographers, cradling the infant in her arms with a framed publicity photograph of her husband on her lap. Indeed, Sinatra really wasn't much more than a symbol in her life; he certainly wasn't much of a husband.†

Shortly after, Frank met the head of M-G-M, Louis B. Mayer, at a benefit for the Jewish Home for the Aged. Mayer was so impressed with Sinatra's performance of "Ol' Man River," he decided to put him under

---

* After this engagement, Dolly—still involved in the political arena—asked Frank to sing at a benefit for Vincent J. Murphy, the Democratic mayor of Newark, New Jersey, who was running for governor. Fifty thousand people greeted Sinatra when he arrived at Lincoln High School for the rally.

† Manie Sachs was chosen by Frank to be the child's godfather. At the christening, the priest balked at the idea of Sachs as godfather, since he was Jewish. He suggested that Sinatra find someone else. Incensed at what he felt was discrimination, Sinatra stormed out of the church.

contract to M-G-M, where, according to its slogan, there were "More Stars Than There Are in the Heavens." Sinatra would be in excellent company; some of the other contract players were Gene Kelly, Fred Astaire, Clark Gable, and Esther Williams. Frank would soon sign a $1.5-million, five-year contract with the studio, which, after some negotiation, preempted the RKO contract.* (George Evans then put out a press release claiming that Sinatra was "the highest-paid entertainer in the world," an item published by columnist Walter Winchell.)

A few months later, the Sinatras moved to Los Angeles.

"It's time to move the hell out of New Jersey," Frank told his wife, Nancy, who expressed some reluctance. At least on the East Coast she had friends she could rely on when she could not depend on her husband, which was a great deal of the time. In whom would she confide in California? Her husband's girlfriend, Alora Gooding?

Frank's mind was made up, however, and he went on to purchase Mary Astor's large Mediterranean-style estate at 10051 Valley Spring Lane in Toluca Lake, a Los Angeles suburb. Nancy would simply have to expand her horizons, George Evans advised her. Her husband was making over a million dollars a year now. He belonged in Los Angeles—M-G-M was there—and if she wanted to be supportive, she would have to go along with the plan. So the Sinatras traveled by train on the Twentieth Century Limited and the Super Chief from New York to Pasadena to begin their West Coast experience.

On June 15, 1944, Frank began work on his first M-G-M film under the new contract, in *Anchors Aweigh,* with Gene Kelly. The plot was simple. Kelly and Sinatra played the roles of sailors who get into mischief while on leave. The movie was considered juvenile, harmless fun when it was eventually released. It would turn into a big success.

During production Sinatra made waves. He became annoyed with the schedule at one point and told a reporter that he was thinking of quitting films because "most pictures stink, and the people in them, too." Jack Keller, who worked on the West Coast for Frank's publicist, George Evans, had to put out the flames Sinatra's statement caused by writing an apology for Frank and then getting it published in the newspaper.

As usual, Frank had to have his way, which meant he wanted Sammy Cahn to work with Jule Styne on the film, even though the film's producer, Joe Pasternak, and the studio didn't want Cahn. So there were the expected fireworks about that, too. In the end, a grateful Cahn got the job and did some extraordinary work, making Sinatra proud.

Frank then had a clash with producer Joe Pasternak over the viewing

---

* Sinatra made *Step Lively,* a remake of the Marx Brothers film *Room Service,* for RKO, with Gloria DeHaven.

of dailies. A daily is the industry's term for film shot on a particular day, which is often viewed by the director, cameramen, makeup artists, and other crew members to determine how the movie is progressing. M-G-M had a policy that actors were not to see dailies. It was Joe Pasternak's experience that no actor ever liked what he saw in a daily and that such dissatisfaction only caused trouble on the set. However, Sinatra wanted to see his dailies, and when told by Pasternak that he would not be viewing them, he became upset, and many arguments ensued. Finally, Pasternak relented and promised Frank that he would show him some of the more recent dailies in a private viewing. Sinatra must have been proud to see how much power he was able to exert over a studio like M-G-M, which was probably what the battle was really about.

When Sinatra showed up for the "private viewing" with six friends, Pasternak became enraged and refused to allow the group to see the footage. Frank quit the film, only to return a few days later. This type of unreasonable behavior, when reported by the media—and these stories were somehow *always* leaked to reporters—only served to make Sinatra appear to his public to be what, it could be argued, he really was: difficult.

In *Anchors Aweigh*, Kelly took the clumsy, inexperienced Sinatra under his wing and did what he could to transform him into a credible dancer. Sinatra did the best he could; however, as it turned out, his eyes betrayed him, not his feet. Those Sinatra baby-blues registered clear uncertainty and with each step seemed to ask, What's next? In fact, Gene Kelly joked to Frank that he "set dancing back twenty years."

The charm of Sinatra's performance in this film is that he is not an actor but a singer trying to act in his first big movie, and he lets the audience in on it. It's a bi-level, tongue-in-cheek performance in that regard. He continued this approach through several more films before finally making the transition to pure actor. Whether instinctual or planned, it was a brilliant maneuver.

The movie was hard work for Sinatra, emotionally as well as physically. He lost four pounds during the first week of rigorous rehearsal, which he could not afford to do, for he weighed only about 125 pounds. He wanted to make a good impression, and it frightened him that he was in a film that was perhaps beyond him. He was impatient with Kelly and wanted to cut many of the dance sequences. However, Kelly sensed that Sinatra could get through it if he persevered; in fact, Gene Kelly was so devoid of ego, he actually tailored the routines so that Sinatra looked good, even if that meant he, Kelly, couldn't show off as much as he might have wanted to do. "He's one of the reasons I became a star," Sinatra would later say.

On September 24, 1944, Frank enjoyed his White House experience when he visited President Roosevelt in the nation's capital with his pals

New York restaurateur Toots Shor and comic Rags Ragland (Phil Silvers's sidekick) and about twenty others. It was just an innocuous visit over cake and coffee, more a publicity gimmick for all concerned than designed to discuss anything of a substantive nature. At this time, there wasn't much Sinatra and FDR could have discussed, anyway.

"I was nervous," Toots Shor once recalled. "I kept thinking, A bum can go in and see the president? A crooner, a restaurant guy, and a burlesque comic can go call on the prez? I kept eating cake to keep myself busy. Sinatra did a Sinatra. He fainted."

Frank didn't faint, though he was nervous as well. "He was very nice," Frank said of the president. "I told him how well he looked. He kidded me about making the girls faint and asked me how I do it. I said I wished to hell I knew."

Frank also mentioned that he had voted for Roosevelt during the previous election and intended to do so again in November. He donated $7,500 to the Democratic campaign.

After the visit, Sinatra became excited by the idea of using his influence to sway votes for FDR. He appeared in radio commercials for the Roosevelt campaign and then spoke at Carnegie Hall about the president. "I said I was for Roosevelt because he was good for me and for my kids and my country," Sinatra recalled years later. "When I was through, I felt like a football player coming off the field—weak and dizzy and excited and everybody coming over to shake hands and pat me on the back."

George Evans and Hank Sanicola wanted Frank to move forward into a political arena in some way. This would actually be a courageous endeavor. Show-business personalities were reluctant to make their political preferences known in case any members of their audience disagreed with their stance. Most celebrities didn't want to take the chance of alienating anyone.

Evans and Sanicola had a meeting with Sinatra at his home to try to determine just how to proceed. Sinatra was certainly interested in politics. However, he was much more consumed by his career at this time than he was about being a Democrat.

"Well, let's just see where it takes us," Evans suggested. "I think you could be pretty influential."

"Who cares what a singer thinks about politics?" Hank Sanicola wanted to know.

"Don't let my mother hear you say that," Sinatra said with a grin.

"What, are you kidding me?" Evans laughed, for he himself was a liberal Democrat who had introduced Frank to many of his political friends. "*Everyone* cares what Sinatra thinks. Let's just wait and see what happens."

Indeed, after the White House visit, Frank's fans soon began wearing pins proclaiming *their* allegiance to FDR. Whether they had influence on their parents is debatable; however, Franklin D. Roosevelt won for an unprecedented third time in 1940 and a fourth in 1944, even though he was a sick man. (He died on April 12, 1945; Harry S. Truman, vice president and former senator from Missouri, then became president.)

One of Frank Sinatra's more memorable appearances occurred at the Paramount Theater, where he opened a three-week engagement on October 11, 1944. The movie playing at that time was *Our Hearts Were Young and Gay*. Besides Frank ("In Person, Paramount Theater's Greatest Discovery"), the other live performers were Eileen Barton, from *Your Hit Parade* radio program; impressionist Ollie O'Toole; dancers Pops and Louie; and Raymond Paige and his Stage Door Canteen Orchestra. The huge color, two-story-high artist's rendering of Sinatra's smiling face hoisted above the theater's entrance made it clear that Frank was the real attraction on this autumn day.

Youngsters started lining up for tickets at 4:30 A.M. By the time the theater, which seated thirty-six hundred, opened at 8:30 A.M.—Frank's first of five shows a day would take place at noon—it was filled to capacity. The problem arose when audience members refused to leave the theater; they stayed through performance after performance. Outside there were ten thousand people in line, six abreast. Another twenty thousand milled around Times Square, stopping traffic, trying to figure out what the commotion was about. Two hundred policemen were called from guard duty at the Columbus Day Parade, a few blocks away on Fifth Avenue. Those fans trying to get into the theater became boisterous and rowdy when the line did not move. A small riot broke out. "The worst mob scene in New York since nylons went on sale," joked one New York police officer..

By the time the melee was over, 421 police reserves, twenty radio cars, two emergency trucks, four lieutenants, six sergeants, two captains, two assistant chief inspectors, two inspectors, seventy patrolmen, fifty traffic cops, twelve mounted police, twenty policewomen, and two hundred detectives were involved. The ticket booth was destroyed, and nearby shop windows were broken. Because it was Columbus Day, the hysteria surrounding Frank's appearance was dubbed "the Columbus Day Riot" by the press. (In a *New York Times* interview the following morning, George H. Chatfield, a member of the board of education, said, "We don't want this thing to go on. We can't tolerate young people making a public display of losing their emotions.")

"Most of his fans are plain, lonely girls from lower-middle-class homes," noted E. J. Jahn Jr., of the *New Yorker*. "They are dazzled by the life Sinatra leads and wish they could share it. They insist that they love him, but they do not use the verb in its ordinary sense. As they apply it to him, it is synonymous with 'worship.' . . . "

Frank Sinatra was getting accustomed to this kind of melee developing whenever he made an appearance. Nothing surprised him anymore. He couldn't go out without bodyguards, he could no longer enjoy a meal in a restaurant, and when he went back to Hoboken to visit his parents, it was always a major event. "This is the way it's gonna be from now on," he cautioned his wife. "Better get used to it."

George Evans attempted to explain to Frank that they should think about the future. The adolescent bobby-soxers would grow up one day, and while some might remain Sinatra fans, others might attribute their interest in Sinatra to a childhood crush, one that they eventually had grown out of. In the end, Evans felt, their parents' interest—or lack of it—would make or break Frank's career. Certainly Sinatra's engagements for the older set—at clubs like the Riobamba and Waldorf-Astoria—seemed to be successful, so it was clear that Sinatra was developing an adult base. But there was still reason for concern.

It was incomprehensible to Frank that the teenagers who lavished such love and attention on him could ever lose interest. "You gotta be kiddin' me," he told one record-company executive during a career strategy meeting. "No one's ever been this hot. This is gonna last forever."

According to Ted Hechtman, after a recording session on December 19, 1944, in Hollywood, George Evans and his West Coast partner, Jack Keller, appeared to be concerned. Evans took off his spectacles and, while cleaning them, shook his head and said, "The kid won't listen."

"He's about to get his heart broke," Keller added.

One person in the Sinatra camp also understood Evans's concerns, and that was Sinatra's wife. Nancy and Frank argued constantly about the money he was spending. Never one to be prudent when it came to finances, Frank was buying clothing, household furnishings, and gifts for friends and family members. He took lavish vacations. He made risky investments that promised unreasonably lucrative payoffs, with no concern whatsoever for the future.

Nancy tried to be responsible for budgeting the household and professional finances. In fact, she had a philosophy of paying bills late because she felt that if she made a person wait for payment, he would work harder until he got it. However, Frank rarely listened to her advice. While she was amazed at how much money her husband was bringing in, she would be even more astonished at how much he spent—which was most of it. She and Hank Sanicola fretted about Sinatra's spending habits but would find that there was little they could do to control them.

"You're always worrying about the future," Frank told them. "Live for today. Live for now. Not tomorrow."

"There's not gonna be a tomorrow," Nancy told her husband, "if we don't start saving for it."

Frank laughed. What did Nancy know, anyway?

CHAPTER 8

In the years 1945 and 1946, in addition to making films at M-G-M, Frank Sinatra recorded some of his best and most memorable songs. In fact, much of the material recorded during this period would become Sinatra classics.

On January 29, 1945, twenty-nine-year-old Sinatra had what would turn out to be a historic day at the Columbia studios in sessions arranged by Axel Stordahl. Among the songs he recorded were "My Melancholy Baby," "Where or When," and "All the Things You Are" (with the Ken Lane Singers). During the course of the year he recorded more than forty songs; four of the 78 rpms released would make it into the Top Ten. In that period, some of his best work would include "I Should Care," "Put Your Dreams Away" (his closing theme song), "These Foolish Things," "Someone to Watch Over Me," and "I Have But One Heart."

It is difficult to consider the year 1945 in terms of Sinatra's noteworthy renditions, but surely the Oscar Hammerstein–Richard Rodgers song "If I Loved You" (from *Carousel*) is at the top of the list. Sinatra is at his yearning best on this inspired recording. His voice has never sounded so full-bodied and vibrant. He had created such a name for himself as a performer who made women swoon, it was easy to forget the talented vocalist he had become until one listened to this stellar performance.

A year later, on February 3, February 24, and March 10, Sinatra and Stordahl logged in with such songs as "All Through the Day," "Begin the Beguine," "They Say It's Wonderful," "That Old Black Magic," "How Deep Is the Ocean," and "Home on the Range." All told, there would be twelve recording sessions in 1945 and fifteen in 1946, producing a total of ninety songs, which would be compiled and released on a number of successful albums, like *The Voice* (his first 78 rpm album).

The Voice is considered by some popular-music historians to be the first "concept album." No singer before Sinatra—not even Bing Crosby—understood the potential of a record album as something more than just a collection of unrelated songs. Sinatra realized that the tunes could relate to one another and be sequenced in a way that would tell a complete, emotional story, as did the songs on *The Voice*. He would actually sit

73

down and plan an album song by song before recording it. This process could take weeks, but to Sinatra—and to his fans—it was worth it.

It was important to Sinatra that no one else, neither producer nor arranger, would have final say over the choice of songs that would ultimately be recorded. (Sometimes songwriters Jimmy Van Heusen and Sammy Cahn would offer suggestions, but Frank had veto power over any song.) Making Sinatra's efforts even more amazing in retrospect is that he was such a busy man. Not only did his personal life keep him occupied; professionally he was appearing in concerts, on radio programs, on television shows (later), and in movies.

In his most comprehensive book about Sinatra's music, *Sinatra! The Song Is You,* Sinatra historian Will Friedwald spoke to Alan Livingston, who would sign Frank to Capitol Records in 1953. Livingston explained, "If he was looking at songs, the lyric would be his first consideration. Frank wanted to know what that song said and whether it appealed to him or not. He said, 'I'll leave the music to somebody else. I pick the lyrics.' "

Once in the studio, Sinatra always took his recording sessions seriously. Unlike many artists who haphazardly recorded vocals at a producer's or arranger's direction and then anxiously awaited the song's release, Sinatra was involved in some way, even if unofficially, in nearly every aspect of the session, from the choosing of musicians to the fine-tuning of the arrangements. He had great appreciation for most music—jazz, classical, as well as pop—and understood it thoroughly, even if he could not read it. (He usually used the same men; they would be known in the industry as "Sinatra's Band." Race was never an issue for him, as it was for many artists at this time.)

Instinct was always important to Sinatra's success in the recording field. If the music or the recording didn't sound right to him, then it didn't matter if technically it was correct. "I'm not the kind of guy who does a lot of brain work about why or how," he once said. It had to *feel* right. Or, as he would say, it had to "swing."

Sinatra always told his producers to make sure they got the first performance on tape, as it would probably be the best. Anything after, he felt, suffered because he had expended so much commitment, energy, and concentration on that first take. Often he did many takes of a song, but those who have heard the alternates (and there is a thriving bootleg market that exists for Sinatra fans interested in these takes) say they are just as excellent as the version selected for release. (On many foreign album issues, alternate takes are used, and it is difficult to distinguish them from the selected take, the performance is so precise.)

Through the years, Sinatra worked only with orchestrators or arrangers who could interpret the music his way: Axel Stordahl, Nelson Riddle (who was actually an unknown in the business when he started with Sinatra but who would go on to do more than half of the 33 1/3 rpm albums), and other giants in that field whose names would become synonymous with Sinatra's success, like Billy May, Gordon Jenkins, Johnny Mandel, Neal Hefti, George Siravo, Robert Farnon, and Don Costa. Sinatra always knew which orchestrator worked best on which kind of song, and so he selected songs with the orchestrator in mind—and vice versa.

No orchestrator ever really challenged Sinatra, though they all supplied their input, which Sinatra welcomed. Gordon Jenkins once said that he would never question Frank's ideas because "I've never seen him wrong. Every suggestion that he's ever made to me has been an improvement." However, unlike some artists (for instance, Barbra Streisand), Sinatra was never a temperamental dictator in the recording studio. He knew that no singer can expect complete cooperation on future projects by alienating the best orchestrators in the business. Besides that, he was *anxious* for their involvement because, technically at least, they all knew far more than he did. He welcomed examples of their artistry and creativity as much as they delighted in his. In speaking of Sinatra sessions years later, practically all of them would sing his praises—and he, theirs. They would also note that Sinatra was never much for compliments; he seldom gave them, expecting those he hired to do their best, anyway, and he loathed receiving them, for they embarrassed him.

The key to Sinatra's success was that he understood his audience and what was expected of him. Even though he was well-read—books like Mary Fitch's socially conscious *One God* were a constant companion—he never flaunted his knowledge or acted in a way that would make him appear to be superior to his fans. In truth, he *was* one of them: an unpretentious guy from Hoboken who just happened to make it big. His wealth, his women, and his growing power were all really just the trappings of his success; they never put distance between himself and his audience, for his fans *wanted* him to be successful, and they, too, relished his success. As long as Frank Sinatra's music reflected a common human experience—pain, joy, heartbreak, or redemption—his fans were completely satisfied.

Of course, it's one thing to feel emotion about a song. It's quite another to make the audience *feel* that emotion. As Frank's Columbia producer Mitch Miller has pointed out, Frank understood how to take what he was feeling and make it believable in his voice. "The ability to bring all your talent together at a certain moment depends solely on craftsmanship," he noted. "You get a little tear in your voice, you put it there if the lyric calls for it—and little things like that."

For all of his hard work and dedication, Sinatra was *truly* finished with his recordings once he completed them. Just as in his personal life, he was always eager to jump to the next love conquest when he became bored with the last one. Professionally he was equally unsentimental. He doesn't remember many of the specifics of which session produced which classic song, seldom bothers to ruminate over his recording history, and would be hard-pressed to even name his favorite albums. (When pressed, he has picked *In the Wee Small Hours, Only the Lonely,* and, at a loss, "one of the jazz things with Billy May.")

While there was a certain amount of public relations wizardry connected to Frank's image as a heartthrob, no commercial manipulation was involved in his wide appeal and phenomenal success as a recording artist. He was doing what he enjoyed in a manner that was meaningful to him and to his audience.

During 1945, twenty-nine-year-old Frank Sinatra would immerse himself in the Hollywood social scene. He was thrilled to live in California and anxious to fit in; he became friendly with many of the town's most influential popular entertainers, such as Lauren Bacall and Humphrey Bogart, Jack Benny and Bing Crosby, who were more than happy to welcome him to their ranks. Restaurateurs Mike Romanoff, David Chasen, and Charlie Morrison became close friends. M-G-M producer Joe Pasternak traded gossip with Sinatra.

Along with his entrée among Hollywood's elite, Sinatra attracted women much different from Lips Luango of Jersey City. Actresses Lana Turner and Marilyn Maxwell were both interested in Frank and made their intentions clear. Frank had his pick of women, so he was in no rush; he pondered the tantalizing thought of affairs with both of them. As usual, his marriage seemed to be of little concern to him. "In the time that we were together [as friends] from 1945 to 1959, I never once saw him talk to her or touch her [Nancy] or relate to her in any way," said Phil Silvers's wife, Jo-Carroll Silvers.

Frank also met Ava Gardner in April 1945 at the Mocambo nightclub on the Sunset Strip. Ava, a ravishing twenty-two-year-old brunet film star, was married to Mickey Rooney at the time; Frank joked with her that had he met her before Rooney, he would most certainly have married her himself. Ava knew of Frank's reputation with women and wasn't impressed with the notion of being married to such a man. However, she couldn't help but be charmed by him just the same. Her smile was dazzling; Sinatra would keep her telephone number in his wallet "for future reference," he said with a wink.

In May 1945, Frank embarked on his first USO tour. He had been heavily criticized by some of the media for the draft status that had kept him out of the service, which, it would seem, he really could not do much about. George Evans decided that Sinatra could quiet the criticism by singing for the troops abroad. Unfortunately, by the time they were able to book a tour in Europe, the Germans had already surrendered to Gen. Dwight Eisenhower. However, the tour to North Africa and Italy went forward, with entertainer Phil Silvers—who taught Sinatra some comedy bits—dancer Betty Yeaton, and actress-singer Fay Mackenzie.

Before the tour began, the group was scheduled to have an audience with Pope Pius XII in Rome, which excited Sinatra. Such a visit seemed ironic to some observers, since Frank wasn't a particularly religious person and, it could be argued, his behavior in marriage was anything but Catholic in nature. Frank, though, felt it was appropriate. "Why the hell not?" he asked one confidant. "He's just a man, like me, with a better job, maybe. I ain't kissing his ring, though. I think that's goin' a little too far."

According to one relative, when Frank telephoned Dolly from New York before leaving for Rome to tell her that he was about to visit the pope, she gave him a list of suggestions she thought His Holiness might utilize, as she put it, "to clean up the whole goddamn church." Chief on the list was that abortions be sanctioned.

Frank, according to the source, was outraged at first. "You want me to tell the pope *that?*" he said, aghast. "I can't tell the pope that." Later, he found humor in his mother's suggestion and told everyone on the tour about it, saying, "Leave it to my own mother to get me kicked out of the Vatican."

While it seemed that Pope Pius XII had no idea who he was ("And what operas do you sing?" he asked him), Sinatra did manage to get a blessing from him in June 1945. He did not, however, mention the topic of abortions, though he did kiss the pope's ring of St. Peter.

Frank Sinatra, Phil Silvers, and company successfully toured abroad, singing for the troops for seven weeks. Unfortunately, when the group returned to the United States on July 6, 1945, Frank made some disparaging comments about the organization of USO tours ("Shoemakers in uniform run the entertainment division. Most of them had no experience in show business"), thereby causing another controversy. Defenders of the USO, such as writer Lee Mortimer, who was a protégé of Walter Winchell's, picked on Frank for embarking on a tour after the war was over, and the media focused much more on the controversy Sinatra's harsh words had caused than on any goodwill he might have spread on his tour. It was his own fault, however.

As George Evans had learned, one never knew what Sinatra was going to say or how the media would react—the story of Sinatra's life in the limelight. When *Anchors Aweigh* opened in August, it was a critical success, which served to make Sinatra an even bigger target for criticism. "They build you up, they tear you down," Frank said.

In truth, Sinatra did want to do his so-called fair share for his country, and if he couldn't serve overseas, he was determined to make an impact at home. He possessed a social concern for the youth of America when it really wasn't fashionable for entertainers to think that way. He realized that if he had the attention of America's youth, he should do something positive. To that end, he spoke at high school auditoriums and at youth centers across the country. Well-read himself, he wrote articles about juvenile delinquency, which George Evans had distributed to schools. He spoke to high school editors of newspapers about the problems he had with the press and also about race relations, encouraging students to be as tolerant as possible "if you want a better world for yourselves."

Sinatra also made an excellent, critically acclaimed, ten-minute-long film, *The House I Live In,** about religious and racial tolerance, in which he played himself. It was directed by Mervyn LeRoy, produced by Frank Ross, and written by Albert Maltz; all profits from this, his final RKO film, went to anti–juvenile delinquency programs and organizations.

In the film, Sinatra walks out of a studio after a recording session to have a cigarette. He comes across a bunch of kids hurling epithets at a Jewish boy. "Look, fellas," Frank tells the boys, "religions make no difference except to a Nazi or somebody as stupid." He says that he would be "a first-class fathead" if he were the type of person who would hate a man because of his ethnicity or religion. Then he sings the title song, a wonderful ballad written by Lewis Allan and Earl Robinson that was originally performed in a 1942 Broadway revue but which would go on to become one of Sinatra's signature songs.

A reporter from *Cue* magazine wrote, "The picture's message is tolerance. Its medium is song. And its protagonist is Frank Sinatra, who has, amazingly, grown within a few short years from a lovelorn microphone-hugging crooner to become one of filmdom's leading and most vocal battlers for a democratic way of life."

Frank Sinatra truly cared about these important issues; his interest was not just a matter of public relations, as has been reported elsewhere. In fact, in 1945 he went to Gary, Indiana, to help settle a four-day student strike at Froebel High School. The principal there had decided to integrate classes, and disgruntled white students had caused a riot—carousing and throwing bricks—and refused to return to classes until the new integration policy was changed.

A week earlier, Sinatra had spoken to an integrated class at a Harlem school, urging students to "act as neighborhood emissaries of racial goodwill." Afterward, he sang "Aren't You Glad You're You" from the Bing Crosby film *The Bells of St. Mary's.* The mayor of Gary, impressed by Sinatra's appearance in Harlem, called to ask whether he would speak to the students at Froebel.

When Frank walked onto the auditorium's stage at Froebel on November 1, he was met with boos, hisses, and catcalls from the forty-eight

* The film was awarded a special Academy Award from the Academy of Motion Picture Arts and Sciences on March 7, 1946.

hundred students and even some of their parents. This unkind reception continued for nearly two minutes while Sinatra stood center stage with his arms crossed, staring intently at the hecklers. Finally, the room quieted. Frank moved to the center microphone.

"I can lick any son of a bitch in this place," he said, his face grim.

He had their attention. Immediately, the place erupted in cheers.

"Aw right, Frankie. Go get 'em," one boy screamed out.

"We love you, Frankie. We love you, Frankie," a section of girls began chanting.

"I implore you to return to school," Frank said. "This is a bad deal, kids. It's not good for you, and it's not good for the city of Gary, which has done so much to help with the war for freedom the world over. Believe me, I know something about the business of racial intolerance. At eleven [years of age] I was called a 'dirty guinea' back home in New Jersey.

"We've all done it," he continued. "We've all used the words nigger or kike or mick or Polack or dago. Cut it out, kids. Go back to school. You've got to go back, because you don't want to be ashamed of your student body, your city, your country. . . . If President Roosevelt could do it with Churchill and Stalin, then the kids of America can work out their problems, too."

Frank then sang two songs, including "The House I Live In," before asking the youngsters to stand and repeat after him: "We will strive to work together to prove that the American way is the only fair and democratic way of life." Afterward, everyone sang the National Anthem.

Though Sinatra did not end the strike—it ended soon after, however—he was praised by many educational and religious organizations for his efforts.

Of course, there were special interest groups that were determined that someone like Sinatra, an Italian American from the streets of Hoboken who had made it big and who was such an ardent liberal, would not have such influence over the youth of America. For no reason, he was inexplicably branded a Communist by some members of the press. At this stage in his life—unlike at others, when similar accusations would be leveled because he would be in the wrong place at the wrong time—there wasn't a reason, even a misconstrued one, for the charge other than the fact that Sinatra had great empathy for the poor and homeless and felt that their problems should be solved in some fashion.

The Communist charge came suddenly and surprisingly when Gerald L. K. Smith, of the conservative America First party, testified before the House Un-American Activities Committee (HUAC) in January 1946 that Sinatra was acting "as a front" for Communist organizations. Smith, truly a voice for racism and anti-Semitism, had his own radio program at the time. He did not explain his comments about Sinatra or qualify them.

"That son of a bitch called me a Commie," Frank raged privately. "How can he do that?"

Indeed, Smith's accusation made no sense, yet it started a trend.

A short time later, Gerval T. Murphy, a director of the Catholic group the Knights of Columbus, said that Sinatra had demonstrated a penchant for communism by speaking "at a Red rally of sixteen thousand left-wingers." This was a ridiculous, spurious accusation. Actually, Sinatra—who called Murphy "a jerk"—spoke at a rally for the Veterans Committee of the Independent Citizens Committee of the Arts, Sciences and Professions. He called for the passage of legislation that would house veterans. Frank tried to set the record straight—"I don't like Communists either, and I'm not one"—but in a climate of such fears about communism, the charge stuck, much to Frank's dismay. Some of the parents of his young fans began voicing their concerns about Sinatra. Their concerns were based on unfounded allegations.

In the summer of 1946, Frank began another noteworthy affair with another contract player at M-G-M, twenty-four-year-old singer (with the Kay Kyser band) and actress Marilyn Maxwell (full name: Marvel Marilyn Maxwell). She was a stunning blonde from Iowa with an iridescent "movie star" smile who resembled Marilyn Monroe but had the humor of a Joan Blondell or even Mae West. "She was gorgeous, simply gorgeous," Frank's friend Nick Sevano recalled, "and they were crazy about each other."

Marilyn Maxwell had recently been divorced from actor John Conte, whom she married in 1944. When Nancy found out about Marilyn, she was more concerned than she had been about the other women. After all, this one was a movie star, not an extra or a stripper. She had long ago stopped trying to compete with Frank's women, but even if she wanted to, she felt she couldn't compete with the alluring Marilyn Maxwell.

Nancy asked some friends if now was the time for her to file for a divorce. Everyone, it would seem, told her that she should. But Nancy did not file.

She and Frank fought bitterly about Marilyn Maxwell just before he was scheduled to leave California for New York, where he was to film his next movie, It Happened in Brooklyn (with Kathryn Grayson, Peter Lawford, and Jimmy Durante). Frank wanted to meet Marilyn there and go out on the town with her, and when George Evans found about it, he sprang into action.

According to Ted Hechtman, "George didn't even bother talking to Frank about it. He called Marilyn and said, 'Listen, you got a morals clause in your studio contract that says you can't disgrace the studio by going out with a married man. You ain't never seen bad publicity like the kind you're gonna see if you go out on the town with Sinatra.' Since he was a publicist, poor Marilyn didn't know if that was a threat, a promise, or just a warning. So she didn't go. Of course, Frank was furious. He called George every name in the book for messing up his New York plans."

George Evans had his hands full with Frank Sinatra. "He's got more dollars than sense, let's face it," George told associates. He must have been happy that he won the Marilyn Maxwell struggle—at least for the moment—because his victories where Sinatra's public image was concerned were few.

Frank's problems with the media actually started two years earlier, in the spring of 1944, when a reporter, Lee Mortimer, who worked for the *New York Daily Mirror,* became Sinatra's archnemesis. He began to criticize Sinatra, calling him a coward for not enlisting, ignoring the fact that Frank had been rejected by the military. Sinatra's daughter Nancy later explained that her father believed that the problem with Mortimer really started because he sent a song to Sinatra that he had written in the hopes of having it recorded. Sinatra told him that the song was garbage, which may not have been the most delicate way to handle the prized work of an important reporter. Whatever the reason, Lee Mortimer would pursue Frank Sinatra aggressively.*

In 1946, columnist Louella Parsons chastised Frank for problems he was having on the set of *It Happened in Brooklyn.* The film was about a soldier returning to civilian life after the war, and in it Sinatra was to perform seven songs, including "Time After Time." He wanted the shooting schedule changed to accommodate his own career demands: a pinch-hitting stint at the Copa with Phil Silvers when Silvers's partner and costar Rags Ragland died,† an appearance on the *Burns and Allen Show* as a favor to that comedy team. Frank had problems with the script as well and wasn't interested in the movie, so it was not a priority to him. M-G-M took the position that he had repeatedly violated his contract and sent him a telegram telling him so.

The story was leaked to Parsons, who criticized Frank in her column and warned him that if he didn't change his ways, his M-G-M career could end as suddenly as it had begun. Frank resented Parsons's opinion and fired off a telegram to her which said, in part, "I'll begin by saying that if you care to make a bet I'll be glad to take your money that M-G-M and

---

* Another writer, columnist Westbrook Pegler, of the Hearst Syndicate, would so incense Sinatra that Sinatra actually trashed his own room at the Waldorf-Astoria during an engagement there (in November 1944), all in a fit over Pegler's comments about him in a New York newspaper.

† Rags Ragland died on August 20, 1946, with Sinatra and Silvers at his hospital bed. After his death, a gold lighter was found among his possessions, inscribed: "From Riches to Rags—Frank."

Frank Sinatra do not part company, permanently or otherwise. . . . In the future I'll appreciate your not wasting your breath on any lectures because when I feel I need one I'll seek advice from someone who either writes or tells the truth. You have my permission to print this if you so desire and clear up a great injustice."

Then Erskine Johnson, a Hollywood reporter, jumped on the Parsons's bandwagon with criticism of Frank. He, too, received a telegram from Sinatra: "Just continue to print lies about me, and my temper—not my temperament—will see that you get a belt in your vicious and stupid mouth."

There was not much George Evans could do; thirty-year-old Frank Sinatra was taking on the press, and unless he were going to start publishing his own newspaper so that he could print his defenses at his own whim, it would be a losing battle. Then, to make matters worse, Frank began an affair with one of the most highly paid actresses in the world, film star and twice-married-and-divorced Lana Turner.

A wealthy woman, the gorgeous twenty-six-year old blonde had a marvelous home in Bel-Air overlooking the Bel-Air Country Club and was truly living the lofty life of a star. That she had a three-year-old daughter, Cheryl Crane, the offspring of a brief marriage to restaurateur Steve Crane, did not impede her lifestyle. As she once recalled of this particular time, "Ciro's was a favorite haunt. I'd walk up the steps and through the glass door and pass the velvet rope that barred the less fortunates. And the headwaiter would spring forward—'Ah, Miss Turner'—and escort me in. I had a special table right by the stairs so I could watch the comings and goings. I'd head straight there, never glancing right or left.

"And then, when I was seated, I'd give the room a long casing, bowing to this one or blowing that one a kiss. Silly, I guess, but fun. . . . Everyone would stare, and you knew you were making an *entrance.* I'd usually dress in something clingy, black or white, sometimes gold, occasionally red. I'd wear diamonds and a fur of some kind draped over one shoulder. Often white fur, my favorite. Maybe ermine or silver fox. Or sable. I had beautiful sables. I'd have jewels in my hair, or flowers, and every hair in place."

When Frank saw *The Postman Always Rings Twice,* he could not resist Lana, who was tanned and gorgeous in white shorts, halter top, and matching turban. "I gotta have her," he said to one friend. "How can I *not?*" Frank obtained her phone number from a mutual friend and called her.

Lana was in love with dark and sexy thirty-three-year-old Tyrone Power, but the relationship was not going well. Although she and Frank were both busy with their careers and Lana was dating Power at the same time, they found time to be together.

"Lana certainly liked men," said actress Esther Williams, who was a friend of Turner's. "Her dressing room [at M-G-M] was right next to mine. The rest of us, we just had a couch, a coffee table, and a couple of chairs in our dressing rooms. But Lana—she had a king-size bed with pink satin sheets and a roomful of mirrors. When I saw all of this, I thought, Boy, it doesn't take an interior decorator to figure out what you like if you furnish your dressing room *this* way.

"But that's the way it was back then," Williams added. "Can't you imagine how it must have been in those dressing rooms at the end of the day when everybody's been so young and beautiful all day and touching and kissing? It's a miracle anybody ever kept their hands off of anybody."

"It was passionate intimacy and not much more," said Ted Hechtman. "George [Evans] was beside himself. This was all he needed. Frank didn't care. He was having one sexual explosion after another with one of the most desired women in films, and he wasn't about to stop."

Or as Esther Williams characterized the relationship: "Sex. Sex. Sex."

Frank was completely taken by Lana and said he'd never seen her brand of class before in any woman. He became so infatuated, he actually told Nancy he was moving out. "I'm with Lana now," he said, never thinking about the ramifications of his decision. He just jumped in with both feet, as he was wont to do. "But for how long?" teary-eyed Nancy wanted to know. "Who knows?" Frank said bluntly.

On October 5, 1946, Nancy telephoned George Evans to tell him that Frank wanted to move out of the house. "He wants his freedom without a divorce," she said. She was extremely distraught, for this was the first time Sinatra had actually wanted his independence to pursue another romantic interest.

That night, Frank and Lana attended a party hosted by Sonja Henie. The two danced all evening long, their romance suddenly becoming public. Then, according to Ben Hechtman and Esther Williams, Sinatra told George Evans that he intended to marry Lana Turner "as soon as Nancy gives me a divorce." It made no sense to any observer that Sinatra would suddenly want to marry Lana Turner. However it was part of his impulsive nature to do so. His desire also spoke volumes about his opinion of marriage and how lightly he took the concept.

After the Sonja Henie party, Sinatra took Lana Turner to a new duplex apartment in Hollywood which he had just rented two days earlier and furnished with $30,000 worth of antiques and furniture simply for the purpose of entertaining Lana there. (He already had an apartment in Hollywood but felt it wasn't glamorous enough for Turner, which is why he rented the new one.) However, Lana was not impressed. In fact, when she walked into Sinatra's new love nest, she looked around and said, "Who needs this *dump!* I'm not sleeping here."

"You're right, it *is* a dump," Frank said. Then he took Lana to the swanky Beverly Hills Hotel, where the two made love.

On October 6, George Evans had little choice but to announce that the Sinatras had separated. Calling it "a family squabble," he also noted that "there's no talk of divorce." He cautioned: "This is the first public battle they've ever had, and I don't think it's serious."

Frank then went to Palm Springs, where Lana owned a second home. He and Lana enjoyed dancing at the Chi Chi Club and didn't care who saw them there together. Afterward, Lana attempted to deny the affair and called Louella Parsons to say, "I am not in love with Frank, and he is not in love with me. I have never broken up a home. I just can't take these accusations." (Lana didn't mention that she was also dating Tyrone Power, which everyone in Hollywood knew that to be so, even though she continually denied it. At the time, Power was married to French star Annabella.)

Two weeks passed. During that time, Frank purchased a diamond bracelet for Lana. But he did not give it to her. "He had a change of heart about it," said one of his friends. "He thought it would send the wrong signal. He'd lost interest just that quickly."

Indeed, in that brief time, just as quickly as the flame had ignited for Frank, it had gone out. He had had his way with Lana—and she with him—and now, as far as Sinatra was concerned, it was over. Also, in the weeks after their first evening together, perhaps she wasn't quite what he had hoped she'd be.

At the end of October, Phil Silvers was performing at Slapsie Maxie's club in Hollywood. Frank joined him onstage in an impromptu moment that was actually a scripted part of Silvers's act. Nancy—who, it would seem, really would not let go, no matter the circumstances—showed up in the audience. When Frank started singing the number "Going Home," he became emotional. Phil, who knew that "these two kids belong together," walked him down to Nancy's table. She was crying. Frank put his arms around her; they embraced tightly, and the audience applauded the public reconciliation. The next day, Frank went home. (However, he did not give up the new bachelor apartment he began leasing in Hollywood, just in case.)

That morning, when Lana Turner awakened to a breakfast of eggs Benedict, which was served in bed, she picked up the morning newspaper from her silver tray and read the headline: "Frank Sinatra Back With Wife."

"What?" she screamed. "How dare he? *How dare he?*"

A maid who worked in the Turner home (who is now retired and living in Santa Fe, New Mexico and asked not to be named "because Cheryl would never understand") reported: "Oh, Miss Turner was so very upset. I heard a loud crash, and when I went into her room, I found that she had thrown her breakfast up against the wall. What a mess.

" 'Get in here,' she screamed at me. 'Clean this up. Now.'

"I didn't even know she cared about Frank Sinatra. I thought she was in love with Tyrone Power. I was very confused about the whole thing, none of which was my business, anyway. But while I was mopping up, she was pacing back and forth saying, 'That bastard Sinatra. That bastard Sinatra. I have never been so humiliated. I'll never forgive him for this. Doesn't he know who I am?'

"Later, I heard her on the telephone talking, I guess, to Sinatra and saying, 'For you to do this to me, a famous picture star, is unforgivable,' I remember that she said, 'I have an image to protect. *Nobody dumps Lana Turner, mister.*'"

According to Ted Hechtman, "George Evans told me that Sinatra had to have his telephone number changed because Lana Turner would not stop calling. She didn't want a reconciliation. All she wanted was for him to issue a statement to the effect that he was never really dating her and that anyone who had believed otherwise—who saw them together here and there and jumped to a wrong conclusion—was dead wrong."

Lana's continuous calls began to scare Nancy, who reportedly told Frank, "That woman is crazy. I'm telling you, Frank, she's crazy! She's gonna do something to us to get her revenge." Finally, Frank told George Evans, "Issue the goddamn statement. Who the hell cares? If it'll satisfy the dame . . ." But Evans refused to do it. It was too late, he decided. Why dredge up the notion of a Sinatra-Turner pairing just to quash the idea and save Lana's image?

Evans and Sinatra argued back and forth for weeks. Finally, Lana Turner just gave up.*

For the next few months, Frank Sinatra was the repentant husband. He bought Nancy a full-length ermine coat and muff; they went to New York together in November and were seen about town having a wonderful time. For Christmas he gave her an expensive three-strand pearl necklace. Nancy must have thought the marriage was going well, especially when she found a diamond bracelet in the glove compartment of the new Cadillac Frank had purchased for her. According to her daughter, Nancy, she assumed that the bracelet was just another expensive present from her generous husband. Rather than ruin the surprise, she put it back where she found it and decided to wait for him to present it to her. Then,

---

* An editor who worked at E. P. Dutton when Turner's memoirs, *The Lady, the Legend and the Truth*, were published in 1982 reports that an original draft of Turner's manuscript included the story of her affair with Sinatra just as it is reported on these pages. However, Turner decided to delete all references to the Sinatra affair, said the editor, because, as Lana put it, "I'm simply not going to give him the satisfaction. I know he can't wait to read about how devastated I was. Well, he's not going to. Not in this book."

at the Sinatras' annual New Year's party, at their home, she saw it again— on Marilyn Maxwell's wrist.

This was probably the bracelet Frank had purchased for Lana Turner but decided not to give to her. He had apparently begun privately dating Marilyn again during his public "reconciliation" with Nancy.

There were over two hundred guests at the party, but only a few witnessed the unfolding drama.

Nancy approached Marilyn in the living room and said in a controlled but angry voice, "I want you out of my house. Now, go! I mean it. Right now." Only a few people turned their heads after hearing the remark.

"Excuse me?" Marilyn asked, astonished. "I beg your pardon."

"Well, I . . . I . . . *I beg yours,*" Nancy said, clearly at a loss for words.

She pointed to the bracelet on Marilyn's wrist. "That belongs to me," she proclaimed. "And I want it back now. I've put up with a lot of crap in the last eight years of being married to that bum, and *I* deserve that goddamn bracelet."

Marilyn was so stunned that her mouth was agape. She began to unclasp the bracelet to present it to Nancy when Frank came over to the two women, put his arm around them, and then whispered something in Marilyn's ear.

Marilyn, her head held high and her walk proud, moved to a guest bedroom, where the coats were kept. In a few moments, she returned to the living room wearing a sumptuous white fur wrap and looking glamorous, even though she lacked a bit of her former sparkle. The bracelet was no longer on her wrist.

She almost bolted out the door but then seemed to harness enough courage to turn back to the partygoers. "It was never my intention," she projected regally, "to do anything this evening but spread good cheer. Sadly, that now seems impossible."

She whipped around to make her exit and yanked at the brass knob of the heavy front door. It swung open. Then she turned to face her audience one last time. "And now, my friends," she declared with all the decorum she could muster, "I simply must go." With that, she turned and entered the cold night air, leaving the door wide open. When a gust of wind blew into the house, a sequined-clad woman pulled the door closed and said, "Let's keep out the chill, shall we?"

The party continued as if nothing had occurred—but without Nancy, who had also disappeared from the festivities.

Indeed, even the most ardent Sinatra supporters, like Jule Styne (and his wife, Ethel) and Sammy Davis, both of whom remembered the story, were hard-pressed to defend Sinatra's behavior.

After most of the guests had departed, Nancy returned. She had changed from her red and green satin evening dress to a simple white silk robe. Her eyes were red. The guests who remained were all close friends and family members, about a dozen people, and perhaps she thought that she should join them for coffee, liqueurs, and dessert. But the sight of her husband laughing with Manie Sachs and his other buddies infuriated her. She may have wondered, Why is *he* so happy when *I'm* so miserable?

"How can you be so cruel and unfeeling?" she suddenly asked.

Everyone in the dining room froze.

"What have I ever done to you to make you treat me like this? I don't understand it. *What have I ever done?*"

Frank rolled his eyes. "Oh, boy, there you go again, Nancy. What have I done? What have I done?" he said, mocking her tone. "You, you, you. Jesus Christ, what about *me?* You think this is easy for me? You think I like the way I am? Well, I don't, Nancy," he said, stunning his friends, all of whom, by now, probably wanted to leave as quickly as they could gather their coats.

"I don't like myself at all. Alright?" he continued. "You happy now? That make you happy? That make your day, Nancy?"

Nancy was speechless. Frank was not. "What is it?" he challenged her, his face just inches from her own. "You don't have enough jewels? You don't have enough money? We don't live a good life? I don't work hard enough? I don't kill myself enough for this family? I ain't a big enough success? What is it? You tell me? Why embarrass me in front of our friends?"

Nancy burst into tears and left the room.

"Alright," Frank said to the guests. "Everybody out. Out. Out. Out! Happy fucking New Year's. Now get the hell out. The show's over."*

CHAPTER 9

One of the most enduring rumors about Frank Sinatra is that he is involved with the Mafia. The first stories of this nature began to circulate after Sinatra's attorneys and agents extricated him from the unreasonable Tommy Dorsey contract. Afterward, because it was so well known that Dorsey was adamant about not releasing Sinatra, it had been rumored that Sinatra had his underworld friends intervene on his behalf. (Of course, the motley crew from Hoboken who, at Hank Sanicola's di-

---

* Marilyn Maxwell died as a result of high blood pressure and a pulmonary ailment in 1972. She was just forty-nine. Frank Sinatra was an honorary pallbearer at her funeral.

rection, did so on Sinatra's behalf could hardly be considered dangerous gangsters.) However, the most lurid and long-lasting stories connecting Sinatra to the mob started years after the Dorsey contract was settled. They actually began in 1947.

Frank Sinatra would always claim that the reason he was picked on by certain members of the press and accused of being a friend of the Mafia's was due to his Italian-American heritage, because his name ends in a vowel. He and his family have labeled the charges "discrimination." Their position is understandable and perhaps at least partly accurate. But why, one might wonder, is it that other Italian Americans, such as Vic Damone, Perry Como, even Al Pacino (who actually went on to play a Godfather in the series of films by that name) are not similarly persecuted because of their vowel-ending last names?

Frank and his family have also said that many of the nightclubs in the forties and fifties were run by gangsters, and that if a person wanted to work in show business then he or she had to do business with the underworld. All true.

However, there is more of an explanation for the fact that Frank's reputation has been so sullied over the years than just his name and the particulars of the profession he chose. In fact, he was guilty of poor judgment when it came to the people with whom he socialized when he *wasn't* working.

In January 1947, thirty-one-year-old Frank was asked by Joe Fischetti, a buddy he had known from Hoboken since 1938 (and cousin and heir of Al Capone's), if he would like to meet the boss of the Cosa Nostra crime syndicate Lucky Luciano. Thirty-nine-year-old Luciano, who had been in exile in Havana since late October 1946, was living the good life in a spacious estate in the exclusive Miramar suburb, among the other estates and yacht clubs of affluent Cubans and resident Americans.

At this time, Luciano was planning the first full-scale confab of American underworld leaders since a Chicago gathering in 1932, which would be held on the upper floors of the Hotel Nacional in Havana, a busy mecca for gamblers. There were certain decisions to be made—one of which had to do with Luciano's determination to be, as he once put it, "the boss of bosses," *capo de tutti capi,* head of the American underworld—and each delegate would have a vote about pressing underworld matters. During the convention, there would be banquets, meetings, and parties of the Mafia and its allies, all off-limits to the other guests of the Hotel Nacional.

At the beginning of the year 1947, the delegates—all known by the FBI to be members of the syndicate and recognized gangsters—began to show up in Havana for this conference of big shots. Frank Costello, Augie Pisano, Mike Miranda, Joe Adonis, Tommy "Three Fingers" Brown Lucchese, Joe Profaci, Willie Moretti, Giuseppe [Joe "the Fat Man"]

Magliocco, Albert "the Executioner" Anastasia, and Joe "Bananas" Bonanno arrived from New York and New Jersey. Santo Trafficante came from Florida; Carlos Marcello, from New Orleans. Tony Accardo, the head of the Chicago underworld, came with Rocco and Charlie "Trigger Happy" Fischetti (Joe's brothers). Two other noteworthy delegates would also be present; however, they would not be able to vote on important matters because they were Jewish: "Dandy Phil" Kastel and Meyer Lansky.

As soon as each "businessman" arrived, he would first go to Luciano's villa and pay homage to him by reaffirming that Luciano was, indeed, the "Big Cheese," the guy who made all of the important decisions about who got "rubbed out" and about who made money by engaging in illegal activities. Then, after his preeminence was acknowledged by these minions, each man would give him an envelope stuffed with cash—$150,000 in all—which Luciano used to buy points in the casino at the Nacional. Upon the conclusion of such bowing and scraping, the delegates were dispatched to the Hotel Nacional, where thirty-six opulently appointed suites had been reserved for them. Luciano would join them there later, upon the adjournment of the first general meeting of the council of the *Unione Sicilano* in ten years.

The plan Joe Fischetti proposed to Frank was that Frank and Nancy meet him in Miami for a February vacation, after which Frank and Joe, Charlie, and Rocky Fischetti would go to Havana and meet Lucky Luciano. (Joe was the best-looking, most charismatic of the Fischettis, though the FBI called him "the least intelligent and least aggressive.") Frank couldn't wait to go. In his old Hoboken neighborhood, thugs like Luciano were revered by the underdogs of the neighborhood, the Italians. He wanted to know what made a guy like Lucky Luciano tick, and he was excited about the opportunity to socialize with such a dangerous character.

So, on January 31, 1947, Frank applied for a gun permit and made plans to go to Havana with the Fischetti brothers. He did not—as least from all available evidence—realize that he was going to be attending an underworld confab, nor, apparently, did he realize that he was being used as a "cover" for that conference in order to give it an air of legitimacy. Frank thought he was going to Havana just to meet Luciano, but unbeknownst to him, Luciano was telling people that his friends from across the country were coming to Havana to meet Sinatra! Or as Luciano's autobiographer Martin A. Gosch *(The Last Testament of Lucky Luciano)* explained, "If anyone asked, there was an outward reason for such a gathering. It was to honor an Italian boy from New Jersey named Frank Sinatra, the crooner who had become the idol of the nation's bobby-sox set."

On February 11, Frank and the Fischettis flew to Havana and checked into the Hotel Nacional. In a few days, Frank came to a startling realization: He was surrounded by a bunch of known criminals, all of whom wanted his autograph.

None of Frank's friends would talk on the record about his visit to Havana. However, they remember it well based on what Sinatra told them privately years later. From all indications, it would appear that Frank took a walk on the wild side and found it to be a little wilder than he expected. At least in his view, once he was there it was too late to do anything about it. He had too much pride to leave and believed that he would look like a "punk" if he did so, and so he decided: What the hell. I'm here and might as well have some fun. He stayed, had a good time, gambled at the casino, went to the races and to a party with Luciano, and never gave a second thought as to how all of this would appear to his public, and to his critics, when his presence in Havana became known (which, given his stature in the entertainment business, was inevitable).

Many years later, mobster Joseph "Doc" Stacher—also present at the confab and the man who controlled all the jukeboxes in Newark—once recalled Sinatra's visit to Cuba: "The Italians among us were very proud of Frank. They always told me they had spent a lot of money helping him in his career, ever since he was with Tommy Dorsey's band. Lucky Luciano was very fond of Sinatra's singing."

To Martin A. Gosch, Lucky Luciano confided: "Frank was a good kid and we was all proud of him, the way he made it to the top . . . a skinny kid from around Hoboken with a terrific voice and one hundred percent Italian. He used to sing around the joints there, and all the guys liked him.

"When the time came when some dough was needed to put Frank across with the public, they put it up. He had a job workin' for Tommy Dorsey's band, and he was gettin' about a hundred and fifty bucks a week, but he needed publicity, clothes, different kinds of special music things, and they all cost quite a bit of money—I think it was about fifty or sixty grand. I okayed the money, and it come out of the fund, even though some guys put up a little extra on a personal basis. It all helped him become a big star, and he was just showin' his appreciation by comin' down to Havana to say hello to me."

Luciano's words would seem to be verification of the underworld's influence on Sinatra's early career. But can they be believed? Is crime lord Lucky Luciano a credible source for information about Frank Sinatra, or anybody else for that matter? Certainly it should at least be remembered that whenever a person becomes famous and powerful—like Sinatra—it often happens that everyone who can, and is inclined to do so, will try to claim responsibility for that fame (especially, it would seem, a bunch of posturing gangsters trying to act like big shots at a mafioso convention). Indeed, Sinatra's global fame has been so great over the years, many people have wanted to share in his mystique.

Certainly if any of the "boys" helped Frank Sinatra when he was with Tommy Dorsey's band, it was news to Frank and to anyone who knew him well. Ted Hechtman says, "Fifty thousand? That's what Luciano claims to be responsible for? Well, that makes no sense. Sinatra had friends with money, like Axel [Stordahl]. He would never go to the mob with a favor like that if he needed money, which he didn't at the time. He was not stupid—impulsive and unthinking, yes, but not stupid. Anyway, this was before he was having the big money problems, *before* the big fall from grace and financial distress of the 1950s."

Hechtman adds, "And his act, well, it wasn't like he had this big production going on with fancy costumes and dancers. He wore one of the same three tuxedos every night.

"And publicity? Before George Evans came into his life, the only publicity Sinatra ever got was whatever Tommy would let him have and whatever Frankie would generate for himself by hounding reporters.

"Song arrangements? Those were Tommy's arrangements.

"The whole thing is a bunch of crap from gangsters trying to make themselves look important."*

True or not, that Luciano took credit for Sinatra's career in his memoirs is precisely the kind of information that has fueled sinister stories about Sinatra over the years. It's not so much that, as the Sinatra family has persistently argued, his Italian last name ends in a vowel as it is that Sinatra often allowed himself to be in the wrong place at the wrong time with the wrong kinds of people. Then, as a result of such poor judgment on his part, reports would inevitably surface from not only the press but also from principal players, like Lucky Luciano, forcing the public to make a decision as to whom to believe: Luciano or Sinatra, big-time mobster or big-time singer. Of course, Sinatra's detractors are inclined to believe Luciano and his ilk, while Sinatra's fans believe him. The rest of the public can only wonder. None of this would have happened at all had "starstruck" Frank Sinatra exercised common sense and not gone to Havana in the first place to hang out with a gang of notorious hoodlums.

Many years later, Frank attempted to explain his presence in Havana this way: He happened to run into Joe Fischetti when he was performing in Miami for a Damon Runyon Cancer Fund benefit. The two spoke and realized that, quite by coincidence, they were both headed for Havana for a vacation. When he got there—he didn't say whom he went with—he

---

* It could be argued that Hechtman's reasoning does not address the publicity, clothing, and musical arrangements necessary for Sinatra's appearances, club dates, and recordings made by him while still under contract to Dorsey but not sanctioned by him.

was having a drink and met a large group of men and women. He was then invited to dinner with them, and while he was sitting at the table talking, it occurred to him that one of the diners was Lucky Luciano. "It suddenly struck me," Sinatra said, "that I was laying myself open to criticism by remaining at the table, but I could think of no way to leave the table without creating a scene." Then, as Frank explained, he ran into Luciano again at the Hotel Nacional's casino, "had a quick drink, and excused myself. Those were the only times I have ever seen Luciano in my life." A good story but not true.

Even Luciano admitted that Sinatra did nothing illegal while in Havana. "I don't wanna give the idea that he was ever asked to do somethin' illegal, by me or by anybody else that I know about" he said. "He gave out a few presents to different guys, like a gold cigarette case, a watch, that kind of thing, but that was it. As for me, the guy was always number-one okay."

Years later, in early 1961, Lucky Luciano was planning a movie about his years in exile, with a screenplay written by Martin Gosch. Though Luciano wanted to flatter himself by having Cary Grant play him in the film, Gosch had a better idea: Dean Martin. Gosch did not know Martin, however, and wondered how they would go about getting the script to him. "Don't worry about that," Luciano told him. "I'll take care of it." Luciano then airmailed a copy of the 175-page script to Frank Sinatra and asked him to present it to Dean Martin. When Sinatra did so, Martin turned it down, saying he did not like the implications of his playing such a character in a film.

When George Evans learned of Sinatra's whereabouts, he could not believe it. Says Ted Hechtman, "He almost had a heart attack. He started hyperventilating. He saw Frank's career come tumbling down before his eyes. 'That son of a bitch is crazy,' he said. 'He doesn't give a second thought to common sense. Why would he go? *Why?*' He flew down there and had a big fight with Frank over the whole thing. I understand that Frank told him, 'Look, I'm playing with the big boys down here. Don't ruin it for me. I ain't doing nothing but having fun. These guys are great.' When George returned, he said, 'That's it. His career is ruined. And it's his own fucking fault.' "

Afterward, Sinatra went to Mexico City to join his wife for a holiday together. He tried to ignore the fact that he had made a huge blunder, but the media would not allow it.

Robert Ruark, a Scripps-Howard newspaper columnist, wrote a blistering attack on Sinatra, calling him a hypocrite for, on the one hand, presenting himself as "the self-confessed savior of the country's small fry," yet, on the other, wanting to "mob up with the likes of Lucky Luciano." Ruark, of course, was correct in his harsh assessment, though he went too far in another editorial in which he called Luciano

"Frankie's boyfriend." George Evans was also partially right. The shadow of his visit to Havana would always loom large; his critics would always think the worst of him because of it.

In time, Ruark and Lee Mortimer—and later, FBI investigators, based on their published reports—claimed that Frank Sinatra was carrying $2 million (in small bills!) in a briefcase he brought with him, all of which he was going to give to Luciano. One of his friends countered, "If you think Sinatra was going to give a deported drug dealer two million bucks, you're nuts. If you think he would walk around with a briefcase full of that much cash in 1947, forget it! I know what he had in that briefcase. Clean underwear. That's what he always carried with him. He was such a damn clean freak. Clean underwear worth about fifty bucks." (Moreover, if Sinatra ended up giving Luciano $2 million, he got gypped because all of the delegates combined only came up with $150,000 for their boss. How did Sinatra end up getting stuck with a $2-million tab?)

About a week after Frank left him, Lucky Luciano was arrested by Cuban officials for a crime he said he did not commit, then sent back to Italy. His arrest generated international publicity, especially when Sinatra's name was linked with Luciano's, again causing much speculation as to the connection between them. (Many years later, in 1972, a troop of police raided Luciano's penthouse in Rome and seized some of his belongings. A gold lighter was later found among Luciano's possessions, inscribed to "To my dear pal, Charlie, from his friend, Frank Sinatra.")

"Any report that I fraternized with goons and racketeers is a vicious lie," Frank said, furious with the coverage he was receiving, especially from Robert Ruark. "I was brought up to shake a man's hand when I am introduced to him, without first investigating his past."

It must have been difficult for Frank's chief nemesis in the press, "Amusements/Arts Editor" of the *Mirror*, Lee Mortimer, to resist jumping into the fray. He wrote about Sinatra's befriending "cheap hoodlums," gave his current picture, *It Happened in Brooklyn*, a terrible review, and then jeopardized his own credibility by adding that Sinatra's fans were "imbecilic, moronic, screemie-meemie autograph kids."

Frank had known for some time that he was being investigated by the FBI; he had a difficult time securing a passport for his USO trip with Phil Silvers for that very reason. The FBI took accusations that anyone in show business was a Communist very seriously in the 1940s. Though Frank wasn't a Communist, he realized that there was little he could do about the government's investigation. In actuality, he didn't care. "Let 'em do whatever they want," he said. "I ain't guilty."

However, after Sinatra's Havana escapade, the FBI began looking into Frank's association with unsavory underworld characters, and it used as one of its chief sources of information, and at times misinformation, Frank's enemy Lee Mortimer. Frank had suspected that Mortimer was providing "information" about him to the FBI, but he could never be sure. However, years later, when FBI documents regarding Sinatra were released under the Freedom of Information Act, it would be revealed that Mortimer was indeed a primary source of information for data compiled by the FBI's associate Director Clyde Tolson. For instance, Mortimer was the one responsible for the story about Sinatra's bringing to Havana millions "in small bills" to lay at the throne of Luciano. This anecdote remains in the FBI records as fact, not rumor.

Indeed, the persistent problem with the reams of FBI documents, often referred to in accounts of Frank Sinatra's ties to the underworld in the forties, is that many of them state as unequivocal facts the stories and anecdotes that Lee Mortimer—not always the most reliable journalist— had not confirmed. Mortimer and Tolson were simply exchanging gossip about Sinatra.

By this time, 1947, Frank Sinatra had become tired of Mortimer's vitriolic attacks. Moreover, he was convinced that Mortimer was participating in the FBI investigation. Through a mutual friend, violinist Joe Candullo, Sinatra sent him a message: "If you don't quit knocking me and my fans, I'm gonna knock your brains out."

"I'm not afraid of him," Mortimer told Candullo. "I'm not going to quit writing about him. Tell that to him and his cheap hoodlums."

"He's digging into my life, fine," Sinatra told George Evans. "I'm digging into his. I think he's a faggot. Find out everything you can about that."

George protested. He said he was not a private investigator, he was a publicist. He had to have a working relationship with this particular columnist; Sinatra was not his only client. Furthermore, he thought Sinatra's idea was mean-spirited and would lead to more trouble.

"Sinatra became enraged," said Ted Hechtman. "He came barging into the office one day and started pulling books off the shelves and clearing things off George's desk, onto the floor. 'Guess what I just found out,' he said. 'The guy's a fucking faggot,' he said of Lee Mortimer. 'I found a guy whose dick he sucked. How can he write these things about me when he's got his own secrets? I can't believe it.' "

"Frank, that's not true," George Evans said, alarmed by the mess he was causing. "Knock it off, Frank."

(The thrice-married Mortimer was not known to be gay. However, his cozying up to Clyde Tolson, known to be Hoover's homosexual lover, did raise a few eyebrows, including, perhaps, Sinatra's.)

"It is true," Frank said, throwing a glass pitcher of water to the floor. "I just talked to the guy. They did it last week. *I just talked to the guy.*"

Frank stopped his tirade, grabbed George Evans by the collar, and pulled him close. Lowering his voice and trying to become calm, he said, "Look, we can pay this guy some money to come out with the story that

Lee Mortimer sucked his dick. That'll show the bastard. How do you think he'll like *that?*"

"I'm not doing it, Frank," said Evans. "Just forget it."

Sinatra let go of Evans's collar, pushed him back, and stormed out of the office.

"That was a terrible day," Ted Hechtman said. "George was sure Frank was going off the deep end."

On April 8, 1947, Sinatra accosted Mortimer at Ciro's in Hollywood, called him "a fucking homosexual," and then decked him. As three of Frank's "hangers-on," fellows he always liked, who acted as bodyguards, held down the hapless, skinny reporter, Frank punched away, calling him names and screaming at him, "Next time I see you, I'll kill you, you degenerate."

"Okay, I hit him," Frank told the press later. "I'm all mixed up. I'm sorry that it happened, but I was raised in a tough neighborhood where you had to fight at the drop of a hat, and I couldn't help myself." Frank also said Mortimer started the fight by calling him a "little dago bastard," which, of course, Mortimer denied doing.

Lee Mortimer had Sinatra arrested and charged with assault and battery, as a result of which Frank's gun permit was revoked. Bail was set at $500, which, embarrassingly enough, Frank didn't happen to have in his pocket when he was arrested. It was raised by his pals.

Mortimer also sued him for $25,000. The suit was settled the day before it was set to go to trial. Louis B. Mayer was disgusted with Frank Sinatra's histrionics and demanded that Sinatra settle publicly with Mortimer by giving the reporter $9,000, which he did. The court also ordered Sinatra to apologize to Mortimer. The charges were then dropped.

In her book about her father, *Frank Sinatra—An American Legend,* Nancy Sinatra provided some insight into the Sinatra family's understandably biased feelings about Lee Mortimer when she wrote, "This was the guy who began the 50-year smear that cost Dad some important jobs and caused the family so much heartache." Nancy, her father's daughter in many ways, to wit, in her general disdain for the media, writes as if Frank had nothing to do with the feud. However, whenever a personality is the subject of great scandal, it is usually due, at least in part, to that entertainer's own lack of good judgment, in this case Frank Sinatra's fraternizing with dangerous hoods, thereby giving the press something about which to speculate.

In reference to the alleged ethnic remark uttered by Lee Mortimer, Nancy wrote that "some applauded my father for teaching Mortimer a lesson he deserved." In fact, however, the district attorney's office concluded later that no slur was made and that Sinatra had been an unprovoked attacker. Furthermore, when he settled the case on June 4, Frank admitted that he had actually been told by an acquaintance that Mortimer made the slur, that he hadn't heard it himself, and that he then believed that Mortimer hadn't called him a dago, after all. He also said there was "probably no reason" for him to have struck the writer. Though he was forced to make an apology, it's difficult to believe that Frank Sinatra would have gone that far—made those kinds of self-incriminating statements—unless they were true. He was nobody's patsy, not even Louis B. Mayer's.

George Evans tried to salvage Sinatra's image by having him grovel to Louella Parsons ("I know I did many things I shouldn't have, things I'm sorry for"), but it was too late. Much of the public had made up its mind about Frank Sinatra: Not only did he socialize with murderers and drug kingpins; he beat up skinny, defenseless reporters in Hollywood nightclubs because they wrote about him. "Why doesn't Frankie just hang himself and get it over with," George Evans asked one of his friends. " 'Cause he's killing himself, anyway."

In the spring of 1947, as part of Evans's campaign to resurrect Frank's public image, he had Sinatra write "An Open Letter" to his fans, which was written on an M-G-M studio letterhead and published in many magazines and newspapers. The long letter, signed "Gratefully yours, Frank Sinatra," thanked his fans for supporting him throughout the time that he was "called a Red and the intimate chum of Lucky Luciano. Not a word of that happens to be true," he wrote. "And thousands of you, in every city and town where these cowardly attacks on my character were published, threatened to quit reading these newspapers unless they played fair with me. Thanks to you the attacks ceased."

In fact, the "attacks" would continue for years to come, for as long as Frank Sinatra would continue to live his life in a devil-may-care manner that would provide reporters with sensational and controversial stories to write about. Indeed, in September 1947, Hearst writer Westbrook Pegler wrote about Frank's association with a wide array of gangsters—all of whom he did know and with whom he had socialized—including Bugsy Siegel, Joe Adonis, and Frank Costello. Then, for good measure, Pegler reminded readers who weren't aware of it that Sinatra was arrested on a morals charge in 1938, when Toni Francke became pregnant by him. [In Sinatra's defense, Ed Sullivan wrote that the attack was unfair, that the matter had been settled years ago.] Frank would never be able to live down his past no matter how much he may have wanted to or how successful he would become.

In May 1947, Frank appeared at the Capitol Theater in New York, where he had his original success with Major Bowes in 1935. It was at this engagement that he may have had an epiphany.

For years now, Sinatra had been living his life on the edge of rebellion, in a selfish daze, both personally and professionally.

In fact, there were so many incidents of unreasonable temperament on

Sinatra's part, that most people had lost track. It didn't seem to matter that he was still making excellent records and that people were still purchasing them. His image had been tainted. The final bad publicity grew out of his trip to Havana, where he met Lucky Luciano, and the incident with Lee Mortimer.

Back in 1945, when Frank Sinatra played the Paramount Theater, he was mobbed by so many fans, he couldn't even leave the theater for dinner. "No one's ever been this hot," he boasted at the time. "This is gonna last forever. . . ."

Three years later, when Frank walked to the stage door after a tepid reception of his opening night at the Capitol Theater, he found only a few fans waiting for him.

"This ain't good," Frank reportedly told George Evans the next day at a backstage meeting with members of the Sinatra entourage and his wife, Nancy, who had accompanied him. "Pay some kids. Get them in here. What's the matter with you?"

"Frankie, lemme ask you something," Evans began. "You think you can do anything you want to do? Think you can say anything you want to say? Think you can tell everyone to go to hell? Well, right here is where you start paying, buddy boy. 'Cause I couldn't *pay* people to cheer for you right now. So what do you say to that?"

Frank didn't have much to say. He turned to Nancy.

She didn't have much to say, either.

CHAPTER 10

By 1948, having turned thirty-two, Frank Sinatra was spending much less time with his family at the Toluca Lake estate. With their third child due in June, Nancy wanted her husband to be at home more. She knew, however, that this was an unrealistic desire. Instead, Frank leased an apartment in Sunset Towers in Hollywood, where he, Jimmy Van Heusen, Sammy Cahn, and other buddies could drink long into the night. When they learned that film star Ava Gardner lived in a nearby apartment building, they would drunkenly call from the balcony, "Ava, can you hear us? Ava, we know you're in there." Eventually, she would come to the window and wave, which was all the encouragement Frank needed.

Ava was an exquisite-looking woman, her skin flawless, her hair dark and luxurious, and her shapely figure the envy of many women. She would walk into a room, her green eyes flashing, and everyone would take notice. Like Lana Turner, Marilyn Maxwell, and the other women to whom Sinatra was most recently attracted, Ava exuded a smoldering sensuality that translated into star quality on the screen. In her private life, she was—to use a term that today describes self-involved, temperamental stars—a diva. She knew how to conduct her professional career ("I like only reflected light on my face and a small spotlight under my chin," she once told cameraman George Folsey) and her personal life ("I like my men compliant," she told Lana Turner). Spoiled, temperamental, selfish, and a real challenge to a man's masculinity and authority, she was as seductive as any woman Sinatra had met. She also had a refreshing down-to-earth side when around close friends and enjoyed kicking off her shoes, getting comfortable on a couch, and being casual.

Her good friend and fellow M-G-M contract player Esther Williams said, "I knew Ava so well. She was flash and dash. That's an elusive combination in somebody so beautiful, and Frank was vulnerable to it. But you never really own a person like that, even as a friend. You just rent a person like that for a little while. Ava was like beer. You never really own beer, you just rent it."

Frank Sinatra had first been captivated by Ava Gardner when he was singing with Tommy Dorsey. After seeing her posing on the cover of the December 1944 issue of *Photoplay* (for which she was bare-shouldered and wore an expensive-looking emerald necklace), Sinatra was enchanted. (The caption on the cover photo read: "She's sexational!") "Stop drooling, Frankie baby," a friend said. "You like what you see, don't you?" Frank responded, "You bet your ass I do. And you wanna know something? I'm gonna marry that broad."

Frank and Ava saw each other throughout the late 1940s at M-G-M and RKO and also at a few Hollywood nightclubs, like the Mocambo, during the time she was married to Mickey Rooney.

In early 1948, Frank asked Ava out on a date for drinks and dinner. Although she knew that Frank was married, she agreed to go out with him because, as she remembered it, "he was handsome, with his thin, boyish face, the bright blue eyes, and this incredible grin. He sure was attractive. Very attractive. What else could I do?"

After talking to her, Frank may have realized that he and Ava seemed to have a great deal in common. In fact, there was something magical about what happened on that first date. They drank quite a bit, which was not surprising, and, the drinks released their inhibitions, which made it easy to confide in one another.

Ava had once said that she felt insecure about her North Carolina background, the way she was raised, the poverty that surrounded her on the farm on which she lived. She once recalled that she wore the same coat and sweater for four years. She purposely alienated people before they were able to get close enough to her to expose what she felt were her shortcomings.

"I loved Ava," said Esther Williams, "but she always thought of herself as poor white trash. She had a terrible inferiority complex, though I never understood how she could have when she looked at that perfection in the mirror. Marilyn [Monroe] had it, too. She couldn't even get out of the dressing room for fear that somebody would find fault with her performance. They were alike in that respect."

Ava was very sensitive. She was, however, reluctant to reveal that side of herself, fearing that doing so would bring people closer to her; afraid that they would eventually hurt her, she always wanted them as far away as possible. Like Frank, though, she was not an intensely analytical person. "Deep down," she would say, "I'm pretty superficial."

They both worked hard to achieve the success they enjoyed. They seemed to understand each other, even though they really didn't know one another. They could feel a sexual magnetism between them. Frank would tell friends that he was so drawn to Ava, "it made me feel like she had put something in my drink." He couldn't wait to take her to bed, he said. In fact, they almost—but not quite—ended the evening just that way. Ava's conscience suddenly bothered her; she felt it was "cheap and wrong"—at least for now.

Professionally, 1948 would not be a good year for Frank. In March he recorded "It Only Happens When I Dance With You," and "A Fella With an Umbrella" (first performed by Peter Lawford in the film *Easter Parade*), two of only ten songs he would record the entire year.

March was also the month RKO released *The Miracle of the Bells*. It was Frank's first nonmusical role. Remembering that his singing rival Bing Crosby had won an Academy Award playing a priest in *Going My Way* (1944), Frank hoped he would be as fortunate in this film as "Father Paul." George Evans wanted Frank to play a priest to help his image, which had been so battered in recent years. Producer Jesse L. Lasky consulted the Catholic church hierarchy to make sure that they would not object to Frank's playing the role, and Evans then announced that Sinatra would donate his entire salary of $100,000 to the church. Opposite Fred MacMurray, Alida Valli, and Lee J. Cobb, Frank acquitted himself nicely as an understanding man of the cloth and sang one a cappella song in the process ("Ever Homeward"). When finally released, the movie received mostly negative reviews, and Frank was disappointed.

Wrote the critic for *Time*, "Frank, looking rather flea-bitten as the priest, acts properly humble, or perhaps ashamed."

Frank was so unhappy with the reviews, he wanted nothing more to do with the picture and was reluctant to even promote it. Even costarring with Fred MacMurray and Rudy Vallee in the *Lux Radio Theater*'s adaptation of *The Miracle of the Bells* on May 31 didn't help matters; it, too, was panned.

The frustration was getting to him. His concerts were drawing fewer fans, and people seemed to be losing interest in him. The only thing to cheer him at this time was the birth of daughter Christina (Tina) at Cedars of Lebanon Hospital on June 20, 1948. ("Dad talked Mom into having another child, Tina recalled.) The baby was born on Father's Day, and this was the only time Sinatra was in town for the birth of any of his children. He drove Nancy to the hospital at two in the morning. "He went through red lights and had a good time," she once said.

"Mom went into labor while she and Dad were playing charades with friends," Tina recalled, "and when my father returned from the hospital in the predawn hours, he pantomimed my arrival to their anxious guests. I was definitely born into show business."

From July 18 to October 24, Frank worked on *Take Me Out to the Ball Game* for M-G-M, another musical with Gene Kelly. They played song-and-dance partners who played baseball on a team during the summer. When finally released in March 1949, the movie would fare better at the box office than his last film, *The Kissing Bandit* (1948).

This film was notable for Esther Williams's valiant—and successful—attempt to get through a nonswimming, comedy and dancing role. She said that she was hired for the film because "Judy Garland didn't show up for rehearsals, so they fired her. I couldn't believe they would do that to her. Then Junie [June] Allyson, their next choice, got pregnant. So they looked on the M-G-M list to see who wasn't working and picked me."

Esther Williams recalled: "There was the little kid in Frank where he loved to stay out and party, and the producers were going to let him go because he was always late to the set. But I understood Frank. He was just living his life. At that time in Hollywood, you could be on time, you could even get there at five o'clock in the morning, like Barbara Stanwyck always did, and sit down and talk to the crew. But you gotta figure that anyone who did that was a really lonely person, and that wasn't Frank. Anyway, he was such a natural actor and so well prepared, what difference did it make if he came in at noon?

"When I was introduced to him, my knees went weak," she remembered, "because it was really *the* Frank Sinatra. The way he sang was so, so real to me and so different from others. He didn't just sing a song; he owned it. Not that I had a crush on him, but you see, talent is very attractive, very compelling. He was too short for me. I'm five feet eight. I got scoliosis just trying to be the same height as Frank and Gene for the dance scenes. But when he sang to me in the movie, I felt like his biggest fan in that moment. Here he was, singing to me. What a wonderful moment for my memory book."

Despite the enthusiasm of fans like Esther Williams, by the end of the year, Frank would confide to friends, like Manie Sachs, that he felt washed up.

Sammy Davis Jr. recalled that late in 1948 he saw thirty-two-year-old Frank in New York. "Frank was walking down Broadway with no hat on and his collar up, and not a soul was paying attention to him. This was the man who, only a few years before, had tied up traffic all over Times Square. Now the same man was walking down the same street, and nobody gave a damn."

Things continued on a downward spiral through 1949.

When Frank Sinatra learned that *Downbeat* listed him as the number-five male singer, he became even more depressed. It was the first time he had not been in the top three spots since the late 1930s. Throughout the year, songs sung by Sinatra, such as "Some Enchanted Evening" and "Bali Ha'i" were poorly received by the public and negatively reviewed by critics. Still, Sinatra maintained the opulent lifestyle he so enjoyed by purchasing a three-acre estate for $250,000 at 320 Carolwood Drive in West Los Angeles during the summer. The property had a pool, a badminton court, and a citrus orchard. He did not, however, keep up with his taxes. That would cause serious problems.

Frank Sinatra Jr. recalled, "Our home on Carolwood Drive was the most wonderful of estates, situated on beautiful grounds. Nancy and I were, by this time, school age. And I can still remember the smiles on my parents' faces on those mornings when the two of us would burst into their room, usually at the crack of dawn, and jump on their bed to awaken them."

The year ended on a hopeful note with the film *On the Town*, a fun-filled movie costarring Sinatra, with Gene Kelly (together for the third time). The film, the first musical to be shot entirely on location in New York, was notable for its exteriors. It was a romantic comedy about what happens when sailors meet girls during shore leave, a simple premise but one that brought forth great performances by Sinatra, Kelly, Betty Garrett, Ann Miller, and Vera-Ellen. Sailor Sinatra dazzled with his dancing, and the film was well-received. Sinatra was quickly becoming a realist, however. One good film did not a comeback make—especially when M-G-M decided to relegate him to second billing under Gene Kelly.

Frank was depressed. He was telling friends that he felt he needed a reason to get up in the morning. Though he felt that his marriage was unsatisfying, he and Nancy had another child. That addition to the family made little sense even to their closest friends; to Frank, it made no sense at all, even though he loved Christina dearly. The other women in his life no longer interested him, either. He was becoming bored. Another man might have settled into his marriage, learned more about his long-suffering spouse, and found common ground on which to build and sustain a relationship. Not Frank. He wanted thrills, especially during these days when his career wasn't providing them for him.

Enter, again, Ava Gardner.

While in Palm Springs for a party in 1949, Frank ran into Ava. The sparks started flying.

"I suppose we were rushing things a little the last time we met," he said, smiling.

"*You* were rushing things," she countered.

"Let's start again," Frank offered eagerly.

Ava said, "We drank, we laughed, we talked, and we fell in love."

They had another date in Hollywood shortly thereafter. This time, Ava wanted to know about Sinatra's marriage. He told her it was over but that he was committed to his children. That was all she needed to hear. That night, they made love, and as Ava remembered it, "Oh, God, it was magic. We became lovers forever—eternally."

Ava Lavinia Gardner was born on Christmas Eve in 1922 in the small farming community of Grabtown, North Carolina, located about eight miles from the rural town of Smithfield, in Johnston County. This sleepy, impoverished community—with no electricity and unpaved, always muddy roads—was about as far away from the life of a movie star as one could get.

Named after her dad's sister, Ava was the last of seven children born to southern sharecropper and tobacco farmer Jonas Bailey Gardner and his wife, Mary Elizabeth, who was often called Molly.

William Godfrey, a friend of Ava's formerly from Grabtown, recalled, "She worked in the tobacco fields, I remember, but she couldn't wait to make her mark on the world in some way. She flailed around for a bit in the early days. She went to business school for a while after graduation, as I recall. She seemed to know, though, that whatever it was she was destined for, it was going to be big."

When Ava was growing up, young men were afraid to date her because of her wild, explosive temper. Her friends recall the time she caught a boy she was dating kissing another girl. She berated him, slapped him and kicked him. As one friend put it, "You didn't cross Ava."

At the age of eighteen, Ava went to New York to visit her sister Beatrice ("Bappie"), now married to a photographer named Larry Tarr (who worked for the family-owned business, Tarr Photographic Studios). After he took her picture, just as a lark, and displayed it in his shop, it was seen by an errand boy who worked in the law department of Loews, Inc. The errand boy wanted Ava's telephone number so that he could call her for a date and used his tenuous connection with M-G-M (since M-G-M and Loew's were affiliated) to try to attain it. He told Larry Tarr that he believed M-G-M would be interested in Ava. He didn't get her phone number; Tarr refused to give it to him. However, Tarr did take the pictures to M-G-M. So struck were the M-G-M talent scouts by Ava's stunning, full-lipped, green-eyed beauty that they suggested she submit to a screen test. Louis B. Mayer was immediately enchanted by the test and by Ava. Miraculously, Ava Gardner was on her way to superstardom when she finally moved to Hollywood a year later, at the age of nineteen.

"I didn't know anything about anything," she recalled, "but part of me had no doubt I would end up a movie queen."

Although her southern accent was so thick that many people at M-G-M didn't have the vaguest idea what she was saying when she spoke, Mayer signed her to a seven-year contract and assigned her to studio voice coach Lillian Burns. It would be four more years, though—years filled with bit parts and small roles—before M-G-M began grooming her to be a movie star, giving her etiquette lessons, changing her hair and makeup constantly in search of just the right look, and attempting to teach her a few other things as well—like how to act.

According to all accounts, even as a major film star, Ava was insecure about her ability as an actress. She had often said that her greatest fear was that she would be "found out," that her true self would be revealed. "I'm a fucking fraud," she'd say to intimates, "and I live in fear of being discovered." (Between 1941, when she first arrived in Hollywood, and 1946, Ava would appear in seventeen films, many on loan-out to RKO and Universal, for which M-G-M exacted heavy fees.)

"Maybe her insecurity is what made her so attractive on film," speculated her business manager (from 1962 until her death in 1990), Jess Morgan. "That insecurity of hers haunted her for her entire life and, in her personal life, made her act in ways that could be construed as completely unreasonable. You had to learn how to handle Ava. If she saw that you were weak, she'd go after you and run right over you."

Ava Gardner had two brief marriages, one in 1942 to a man who was, arguably, the biggest star at the time, actor Mickey Rooney, which lasted fourteen months, and another in 1945 to bandleader Artie Shaw, which lasted two years. Both were unhappy unions.

Ava also had a turbulent relationship with Howard Hughes, whom she described as "cold and ruthless, although with me he was always gentle and concerned." She claimed that they never became intimate.

According to her friends, Artie Shaw treated her badly, though he was also the true love of her life, not Frank Sinatra, as has been assumed over the years. (Ava wanted to have Shaw's child. She never wanted Sinatra's.) However, she moved on with her life after her second marriage ended, though she never got over the way Shaw treated her. She said that he was emotionally abusive to her, always putting her down, making her feel worthless, and in effect validating those feelings of inadequacy that had colored her entire life.

"You know, I don't trust love anymore," she told her friend Arlene Dahl after her two failed marriages. "If a man knows you love him, he'll take advantage of you and treat you badly."

"She was shy, insecure, uncertain with people," said Jess Morgan. "She could be skeptical and suspicious of people. But she was a straight shooter. She'd give it to you straight. If you had her loyalty and trust, you had it completely. You had to understand her, and you couldn't be bamboozled by her. If you were afraid of her, you were finished."

On December 8, 1949, Ava Gardner and Frank Sinatra were said to have bumped into each other in the lobby of the Ziegfield Theater in New York when both attended the opening of the Broadway musical *Gentlemen Prefer Blondes*. It was during this impromptu meeting, according to Sinatra legend, that they first became attracted to one another, or as Ava's friend Ruth Rosenthal-Schechter put it, "an overpowering attraction. The next day, their meeting was the talk of New York."

Actually, Frank and Ava went to the premiere together with another couple, whom they invited as a cover for their presence. Not only were they together at the premiere, they were staying together at the swanky Hampshire House in New York in Manie Sach's suite. Ava broke off a relationship with actor Howard Duff as soon as Frank came into her life, and by the end of 1949, their romance was blossoming, even though Ava would later say that she felt it was "cheap and wrong."

Frank may have gotten a lift in his life from his romance with Ava Gardner, but George Evans was more depressed than ever.

"How many more women, Frank?" he wanted to know. "What's it gonna take?"

George Evans telephoned Robert Harris, a publicist who was representing Ava at this time. According to Harris, Evans said, "Frank and Ava, that's bad news."

"For who?" Harris wanted to know.

"For Frank."

"Yeah, but not for Ava," said Harris. "The publicity can only help her."

"But it's gonna ruin Frank," Evans said.

"Well," Harris concluded, "I don't work for Frank, now, do I?"

Later, a defeated Evans told Earl Wilson, "I can't do it anymore. You know how much I've talked to him about the girls. The public knows about the trouble with Nancy and the other dames, and it doesn't like him anymore."

Of course, George Evans's concerns mattered little to Frank. He had his mind on something else now.

"All of my life, being a singer was the most important thing in the world," he told Ava Gardner at the end of 1949. "Now you're all I want."

CHAPTER 11

Frank Sinatra's recording and film career may have been in the doldrums by 1950, but a volatile affair with tempestuous, unpredictable film star Ava Gardner kept him in the public eye, and in a manner that would often be less than ideal.

During a time that was much more conservative in terms of the acceptability of illicit sex and extramarital affairs, Ava Gardner was somewhat of an anomaly. She was certainly not opposed to having affairs with married men; she'd had them in the past, most notably with Robert Taylor when he was married to Barbara Stanwyck, and now she set her sights on Frank Sinatra, reasoning that "there's no rhyme or reason to a love affair." True to the contradictory side of Ava, however, what she demanded from any man in her life was complete loyalty and fidelity. In fact, she said, she respected and longed for the kind of fulfilling marriage enjoyed by her own parents.

Two weeks after the *Gentlemen Prefer Blondes* date, Frank and Ava spent time together in Palm Springs, clubbing into the wee hours of the morning. The extraordinary passion that burned between them was undeniable. It fused them together in a magical—and as it would turn out—damaging way. Her friends say that Ava felt an urge to, as one put it, "save Frank. She wanted to mother him. He was like a lost kid, but oh, so cocky."

It would seem that as charmed by Sinatra's debonair attitude as she was, she was equally fascinated by his sexual prowess. "He can go for hours and hours," she said at the time. For his part, Frank told friends that he saw Ava as a temptress; he couldn't resist her despite his marital commitment—or whatever was left of it—to Nancy.

However, at the beginning of the affair, he was hopelessly romantic. For instance, Frank drove her to the home she and her sister were leasing in Palm Springs, she once recalled, and pulled over to the side of the road so that he could serenade her under one of the palm trees. A private concert by Sinatra. What girl would not be touched by such a romantic moment?

The next day, she found that she was thrilled by his dangerous side as well when the two of them drove through Palm Springs in Frank's Cadillac and fired bullets out of the car from .38 revolvers. Unfortunately, they not only hit some streetlights and store windows in their dangerous game, they nicked a passerby and as a result were promptly arrested. It cost almost $20,000 for Sinatra to keep the incident out of the news: $2,000 for the arresting officers, $2,000 to repair the damage to city property, $10,000 to hide the records of the man who had been grazed by one of the bullets, and $5,000 for the Indio, California, chief of police. (Frank's public relations men went to Palm Springs to take care of all of the expensive transactions on his behalf.)

Ava was a fun-loving, wild girl who courted trouble. She could swear like a New York cabdriver, yet she was also sexy and could even be demure when she wanted to project that image. It's easy to see why Frank Sinatra was attracted to her. They were both the kind of Hollywood stars who enjoyed being up all night, drinking, partying, and then sharing intimacies and secrets in a booze-induced haze. They both loved Italian food and watching the televised boxing bouts.

He was tender to her, but he knew how to push her buttons, and she most certainly knew how to push his. They would learn how to zero in on each other's insecurities and then use them against each other in fierce battle.

Some of her friends did try to warn her about Frank, but Ava would not listen. On one occasion, Lana Turner spotted Ava across a crowded room at a cocktail party in Beverly Hills. Lana politely excused herself from conversation and headed toward the powder room. Along the way there she gained eye contact with Ava and, with a quick tilt of the head, summoned her to a pow wow.

Once Ava had joined her in the ladies' room, Lana began her lecture while cosmetics were being reapplied. She left out few details while documenting the events of her own affair with Frank and how it had ended. "Not a single big female star hasn't cried on his cock," she told Ava. According to what Ava later told friends, Lana said that Frank was a real "son of a bitch" for the way he had acted, and she wanted to warn Ava about him. Finally, Lana took a look at herself and realized she was done. She snapped her purse shut and concluded, "To think he could do *that* to a woman like *me.*"

"I told Lana gently that Frank and I were in love," Ava would later recall, "and that this time he was really going to leave Nancy for good. If I'm in love, I want to get married; that's my fundamentalist Protestant background. If he wanted me, there could be no compromise on that issue."

Ava's emotions were running wild by this time, and no ladies'-room therapy session with Lana Turner was going to slow things down for her. She was "mad" for him, Ava kept insisting, and while it bothered her at first, she was no longer concerned about his legal commitment to Nancy. For her, one woman's husband was another woman's fantasy.

By 1950, not only was Frank Sinatra's recording career in trouble, so was his voice. One Columbia recording engineer remembered, "He couldn't sing anymore, plain and simple. The songs were there; the voice was not. Because he was failing, he was miserable about it."

In January, Frank performed his first concert in two years, in Hartford, Connecticut. Though record sales were slow, it was clear that the public was still interested in him: these shows generated his biggest take ever: $18,267 for two days.

Also at this time, Sinatra and his press agent of nine years, George Evans, tried to smooth over some of the disagreements that had led to Sinatra's dismissing Evans late in the previous year, after that nasty shooting incident in Palm Springs. Sinatra had been incensed with Evans for constantly insisting that he end the relationship with Gardner. "It's bound to get out," Evans told him. "And when it does, it's gonna ruin you."

"I'm already ruined," Frank said before firing Evans. "So what do I care?"

That Ava Gardner apparently did not much like Evans contributed to Frank's decision to let him go. It seemed to many observers that she did not want anyone around Frank who had known him prior to her involvement with him and who could exert any influence over him where she was concerned. A self-preservationist, she apparently felt that she had to employ a certain amount of strategy if she were to get what she really wanted; namely, Frank Sinatra. Because he was already so emotionally vulnerable, she felt that he might be susceptible to any differing opinion, especially if it came from someone he trusted.

Ava was only trying to protect her own interests, it could be argued, but alienating all of Frank's confidants would prove to be a challenge for her because a great many people knew and cared about him and few of them—if any at all—were supportive of her. Besides, as time would prove, she had completely underestimated Frank's resolve, at least where his deep feelings about her were concerned.

"No one wanted to discuss that aspect of it," said Dick Moran, who, as a starstruck teenager, worked with Evans as a junior publicist in 1948 and 1949, "and it's never really been addressed in other accounts of Sinatra's life, but I know that what happened was that Ava pushed Frank into getting rid of this guy [Evans]. I overheard her one day in the office discussing George with Frank."

Moran remembered that Ava had a vodka and tonic in one hand and a lit cigarette in the other. She sat on a stool in a corner with her legs crossed, her body erect, and her head tilted back in a glamorous pose. She was ready for her close-up.

"You know, I just have to ask you, Frank," she said. "How is it that this guy, a fucking lowly publicist who works for you, tells *you* what to do, tells *you* who to see, tells *you* who to date? Forgive me if I seem presumptuous, but I simply have to know. I've never seen anything quite like it."

Sinatra studied her. He was unaccustomed to women taking that tone with him. Making it worse, she had a habit of blowing little smoke rings, which irritated Frank. ("If you're gonna smoke, just smoke," he'd tell her. "It ain't art, baby. It's just a fucking cigarette.")

"Get some backbone, Frank," she continued. "Tell this guy to scram. I know a lot of publicists better than this one. I can find you someone who will do his job, *publicity,* and *that's it.*"

Frank walked toward her, put his own cigarette to his lips, and inhaled. Then a thick plume of smoke was delivered point-blank in Ava's face.

"Look, I'll deal with it my *own* way, sweetheart," he said.

Ava, having lost the showdown, chose to exit the cloud—and the room. As she did, she passed Dick Moran, who had been waiting just outside the door for the tension to subside. He remembered that her perfume, as she walked by, reminded him of rose petals in an ashtray.

When Frank ended the successful business alliance with George Evans, many in his circle felt that he had made a big mistake. Up until this time, Evans had done a truly masterful job of choreographing Frank's career.

All of the nasty business of the past involving Frank's affairs with other women had occurred during an extremely puritanical era, the 1950s, when overt sexuality was completely taboo and extramarital sex was wholly unacceptable to most people. But Frank didn't care about the moral concerns of "most people;" he was thirty-four years old, driven by his own hormonal urges, and he felt free to do in his private life whatever he wanted to do. He cared nothing about the mores of the time.

Said George Evans's eldest son, Phil, "I'd say there were no more than two or three consecutive nights when there wasn't a phone call of some kind—Nancy crying or Frank in a jam, or Lana or Ava or somebody."

It seemed that Frank was linked with a different actress every week in the gossip columns. Some of the reports were accurate; others were not. Understandably, Nancy was disturbed by all of them and would often telephone Evans to determine whether he had planted a certain item to generate publicity for her husband or the affair in question was really true. George constantly found himself in a difficult position, especially at those times when he knew Frank was having a little fling. He had befriended Nancy over the years and in fact tried to glamorize her, hoping that perhaps if she were more like the type to whom Sinatra was attracted, then the marriage would survive. So, at George's suggestion, Nancy had a nose job and her teeth capped.

It didn't matter. Frank still saw other women. In order to placate Nancy, or maybe to make matters easier for her, George would sometimes suggest to Frank that he buy his wife a present. In the end, poor George would be the one to take Nancy shopping.

As much as Evans had tried, there was no reasoning with Frank where Ava Gardner was concerned. George could see that the road ahead was going to be a difficult one for both of them in terms of what would occur to Frank's image once the affair became public. (And, he felt, that would be just a matter of time.) However, Frank disagreed with him about that, which resulted in a parting of the ways between the two men. When Frank fired George, it was loud and rancorous.

One morning in early January 1950, Sinatra and Evans were joined by entertainer Lena Horne in the upstairs lounge of the Copacabana in New York. Evans wanted to work through his differences with Sinatra and hoped that Horne would act as an intermediary. So with Horne perched on a bar stool between them and sipping a soft drink, the two men aired their grievances over prenoontime shots.

Horne, also a client of Evans's, tried to convince Frank that his many affairs with other women were in poor taste considering the fact that he was a married man with a family. Ironically, Lena was a friend of Ava's. They were both M-G-M contract players and had often commiserated about the men in their lives. However, even Lena realized that Frank's image would suffer from an affair with Ava and that Ava's would be damaged as well. She probably also knew Ava well enough to know that, if encouraged, she would be relentless in her pursuit of Frank Sinatra. So Lena tried to convince Sinatra that George Evans was right and that he should "come to his senses."

Frank didn't want to hear any of that, especially from a complete outsider. In fact, according to one witness to the meeting, Frank told Lena, "Butt out, sister. Who the hell asked you for your opinion?" Then he threw some money down on the bar and took off, muttering obscenities under his breath. As he left the lounge, Lena was heard to say, "What does Ava see in him? Please, won't someone explain it to me, because I swear to God, I just don't understand it."

Obviously, George Evans was not rehired after that meeting at the Copa. This was a difficult decision to make, Frank would say many years later, and one that he would eventually regret. However, if Evans would not support Frank's relationship with Ava Gardner, Frank couldn't imagine how they could work together in the future. She was just that important to him. Either you were with him or against him where she was concerned.

Evans, feeling understandably wounded and abandoned, then made a dreadful prediction to Earl Wilson: "Frank is through. A year from now, you won't hear anything about him. He'll be dead professionally. I've been around the country, looking and listening. They're not going to see his pictures. They're not buying his records. They don't care for Frank Sinatra anymore. You know how much I talked to him about the girls. The public knows about the trouble with Nancy now, and the other dames, and it doesn't like him anymore."

At this time, early 1951, Frank was booked at the new Shamrock Hotel in Houston, Texas, which would open its doors on January 28. Frank arrived with his friend songwriter Jimmy Van Heusen. But while changing planes in El Paso, they learned that George Evans had died suddenly of a heart attack at the age of forty-eight. He had been completely distraught about what Frank's friends called "the Ava business" and had even become involved in a loud, blood pressure–raising fight with a reporter about it.

"He's making a terrible, terrible mistake," George said privately of Frank the night before he died, "and he doesn't know what he's doing."

Perhaps it all was too much for him, this "Ava business." At least that's what his friends decided when they buried him.

Dick Moran said: "To be honest, it ate away at him that Frank let him go like that, and over a broad no less. He just could not get over it. He kept saying, 'I can't believe it. I can't believe Frank would do that to me. I got rid of all the other dames; I just couldn't get rid of this one. *She* fucking got rid of *me*.' The night he died, he called me and told me that he'd tried to telephone Frank but that he couldn't get through. He said, 'You know, I just gotta get through to him. I don't care if I'm working for him or not. I gotta talk some sense into him.'

"Then he was gone."

When Frank Sinatra learned of George's death, he immediately grabbed a plane for New York so that he could attend the funeral at the Park West Chapel on Manhattan's West Side. Of course, as expected by those who knew him best, Frank blamed himself for Evans's death. "If I hadn't been such an ass, the way I handled my life, he probably would still be alive," Frank said at the time. "But I gotta live my life. What can I do? George couldn't handle it, I guess. But I feel bad about it. I feel real bad."

Over the years, Frank would never let himself think much about Evans and what had happened. If someone else brought it up in conversation, he would change the subject. On some level, it seemed, he knew that he was guilty of something. He just didn't want to analyze the matter more closely. He didn't want to know.

Ava rarely mentioned the name George Evans to anyone.

It would seem that a troublesome period for Frank was getting tougher. At this same time, he had made some unkind remarks about singer and actress Ginny Simms, M-G-M boss L. B. Mayer's companion,

110

with whom Mayer was said to have had a romantic relationship. As it happened, Mayer had recently been injured in a fall from a horse. However, Frank joked that he hadn't fallen off a horse at all. "He fell off of Ginny Simms." When he told the joke—which wasn't really that funny, since Simms was a vital talent and a dignified person—to Gene Kelly, Kelly called him a "stupid dago bastard" and asked him when he was going to "learn to keep [his] mouth shut." Kelly knew that if Mayer heard that gag, he would be upset. Kelly was right.

Mayer called Sinatra into his office.

Sinatra said, "Mayer was a very difficult man who was completely devoid of a sense of humor. Three days after I made that joke, he wanted to see me. I didn't know he had heard it. So I'm sitting there, and he's almost in tears, and he says, 'I love you like my son. I never had a son.' And I'm thinking, Jesus Christ, he's gonna give me the whole studio. Then he said, 'I hear you tell a funny story about me and Ginny Simms.' My face dropped. I knew I was sunk."

Mayer told Sinatra, "I want you to leave this studio here, and I don't ever want you to come back again."*

"That's why I say he had no sense of humor," Sinatra recalled.

Years later, in a speech at Yale University in 1986, Frank said, "If I had stayed at that studio, I never would have made *From Here to Eternity*, because M-G-M had a policy of never lending an actor to any other studio." Then he added, with a grin, "So when Mayer fell off Ginny Simms, well, that made my whole career." (Of course, Sinatra was not being truthful here. M-G-M often lent out its actors to other studios, and Sinatra must have known it.)

Frank Sinatra's contract was terminated a full year before it was due to expire. Frank regretted what he had said and again uttered those words for which he'd become known among members of his inner circle: "When am I ever gonna learn?"

He was paid $85,000 when the contract was terminated, but he would rather have had the contract.

Also complicating Frank's life and career at this time was the resignation of Manie Sachs, a staunch Sinatra ally, from Columbia Records. His replacement, Mitch Miller, would prove to be less successful in finding material for Frank and much of the material Frank would record would not be considered suitable by fans and critics alike.

Miller, who would go on to great success with singers such as Tony

---

* In 1951, after twenty-seven years as head of M-G-M, Mayer was fired by the board of directors of Loew's, Inc., M-G-M's parent company. And Sinatra did, indeed, "come back again" to M-G-M five years later in *Meet Me in Las Vegas*, albeit in an unbilled guest appearance, and in *High Society*, billed third (after Bing Crosby and Grace Kelly).

Bennett and Rosemary Clooney, didn't know what to do with Sinatra.

"Came the age of Millerism," Sinatra said years later when discussing his career. "Mind you, I'll admit he's a great musician, but I can't go along with him. Instead of a real interest in the lyrics or the melody, all Miller cared about was gimmicks. One day he said to me, 'Frank, we're going to make a record with a washboard.' I looked at him and said, 'Mitch, you're kidding.' But he wasn't. I refused to do it."

One novelty song, in particular, was a tune Frank felt was most responsible for ruining his career. It was called "Mama Will Bark," a silly duet—on which Miller made him bark—with a blond female comedienne-singer named Dagmar, once a fixture as Jack Paar's verbal sparring partner when he hosted *The Tonight Show.* "I guess it sold," he said later, "but the only good it did me was with the dogs."

Actually, Frank's career was in its decline long before Mitch Miller arrived at Columbia Records. Moreover, according to his contract, Frank had approval over all of his material, so he did not have to record anything he didn't want to record, not even that silly "Mama Will Bark" song. If, after recording the song, he was unhappy, it would not be released. "All he had to do was say the word and the session was just canned," said Mitch Miller. "He had complete power."

Years later, when Mitch Miller met Frank in a Las Vegas hotel, Miller tried to make peace with Frank, saying, "C'mon. Let's let bygones be bygones." Frank wasn't interested. "Fuck off," he said as he turned his back on Miller and walked away.

Frank had canceled the first couple of days of his engagement at the Shamrock Hotel in order to attend George Evans's funeral. He finally went to Houston to begin work. A surprise visitor was already there to meet him.

Ava.

It has been previously reported in other accounts of Sinatra's life that Frank had invited Ava to join him in Houston. That is not true. Headstrong and foolhardy, she surprised him, and he wasn't thrilled about it, either. He knew that her presence there was simply asking for trouble—the press would surely spot them wherever they went—but it was too late to do anything about it.

About a week later, Frank and Ava were at a dinner party at Vincento's Sorrentino Italian restaurant hosted by the mayor of Houston when trouble started. Photographer Ed Schisser, of the *Houston Post* asked to take their picture. Frank told him to "get lost," and it looked as if fisticuffs were about to break out. (Ava later said that at the sight of the photographer Frank "reacted as if he'd found a live cobra in his salad.") The owner of the restaurant, Tony Vallone, defused what looked like a big fight in the making. The next day, news of Sinatra's having angrily confronted the photographer made all of the news wires.

Nancy, Frank's wife, did not know what to make of this affair of her husband's. For years she had suffered through his philandering. She did what she could to hold the marriage together, for Frank always came back to her. However, this time it was different. This time Frank wanted out of the marriage for good. He was serious, he told her, about Ava. He didn't want to hurt her, he said, but the fact remained that he loved another woman. In fact, nothing in his life meant as much to him. Nancy was shattered by Frank's declaration of love for Ava. She slapped him, kicked him out of the house, and had all of the locks changed.

"She still thought that this affair was like all of the others," said a friend of hers. "She never dreamed that it was really over for her and Frank. She loved him so much, she would have been willing to overlook this affair, as she tried to do all of the others. The public, though, was beginning to think of her as a sap. That hurt. It hurt Frank, too."

On February 15, 1950, gossip columnist Hedda Hopper reported that the couple had separated the previous morning, Valentine's Day. As a devout Catholic, Nancy could not immediately divorce Frank, nor did she wish to. Without George Evans to intervene, she had no idea how to handle her husband. A separation, she thought, would give Sinatra time to get Ava out of his system. A distraught Nancy told Hedda that life with Frank had become "most unhappy and almost unbearable. We have therefore separated. I have requested my attorney to work out a property settlement, but I do not contemplate divorce proceedings in the foreseeable future." Nancy admitted that this was the couple's third separation. ("Really?" Ava said to a friend. "The son of a bitch never told me *that.*") "He's done it before, and I suppose he'll do it again," Nancy said of Frank's blatant philandering. Nancy added that the decision to separate had been her own.

The reaction of the press, and public, to this news was decidedly negative for both Frank and Ava. Frank was perceived as a dishonest womanizer; Ava, as a hussy, a home wrecker. Movie magazines, the fifties version of today's supermarket tabloids, trumpeted sensational, and often inaccurate, details of Frank's affair with "the other woman" and of Nancy's complete and utter devastation.

"The shit really hit the fan," Ava Gardner would have to admit years later. "In the next few weeks, I received scores of letters accusing me of being a scarlet woman and worse. The Legion of Decency threatened to ban my movies, and Catholic priests found the time to write me accusatory letters. I even read that the Sisters of Mary and Joseph asked their students at St. Paul the Apostle School in Los Angeles to pray for Frank's poor wife. I didn't understand then, and still don't, why there should be this prurient mass hysteria about a male and a female climbing into bed and doing what comes naturally."

Ava's Metro boss, Louis B. Mayer, joined the fray in being outraged about the affair and, citing a standard morals clause in her studio contract, complained bitterly to Ava about it and threatened action against her. Her contract stipulated that she was to act "with due regard to public conventions and morals" and that she must not "do or commit any act or thing that will degrade her in society, or bring her into public hatred, contempt, scorn or ridicule, that will tend to shock, insult, or offend the community in general." (If she was photographed in a nightclub while smoking, studio executives would order the offending cigarette to be airbrushed away!) Ava had said that she thought the morals clause was "worth a few laughs." It meant nothing to her. In fact, Mayer's meddling in her life only served to further infuriate her and induce her—and Frank, for that matter—to embrace the notion that an extramarital affair was just the headache Mayer deserved from the two of them.

Ava Gardner's feelings about Frank's marriage to Nancy were simple: "If he was happy with her, he would have stayed with her. But he wasn't, which is how I got 'im," she told friends.

It could probably be argued that Ava Gardner—now dubbed "Hurricane Ava" by some reporters because she had been blamed for having wreaked devastation on Sinatra's family—was an intensely selfish woman. However, she had never had a happy marriage, nor had she any children (which is probably why she so often complained to friends, "Why do his kids always have to come first?"). Quite simply, she could not relate to Nancy Sinatra in any way, and she had no patience for whatever Nancy was enduring at this trying time in her life. Certainly Ava would never have been one to find herself in the same position. In fact, if her husband wanted out of a marriage, she would be more than eager to let him go, she had told friends. "Why would a woman want a man who doesn't want her," she asked, truly mystified by Nancy's unequivocal loyalty, "and why would she be devastated to have him out of her life? I would say, 'Good riddance.' " She was tough, all right—so tough that Jimmy Van Heusen started calling Ava Gardner "the Man."

In March 1950, Frank Sinatra was booked into the Copacabana in New York City. Ava, who had, by now, stepped up her demand that a Sinatra divorce be finalized so that he could get on with his life with her, accompanied him to Manhattan, sharing a suite with him at the Hampshire House. Ava and her sister, Bappie, stayed in one bedroom; Frank, in the other. Reporter Earl Wilson wanted an interview with Ava to discuss the situation with Frank and Nancy, but she begged off, saying that she had the flu. Instead, she issued a written statement: "The main reason I am in New York is because I am on my way to make a picture. The main reason

Frankie is here is because he is scheduled to open at the Copacabana. Inasmuch as Frank is officially separated from his wife, I believe I have a right to be seen with him. However, since he is still officially married, I believe it would be in the worst possible taste to discuss future plans. One thing I am sure of is that Frank's plans to leave Nancy came into his life long before I did."

Frank approved of Ava's statement, and added, "The fact that I have had a few dates with her means nothing. Why shouldn't I have dates? I'm separated from my wife. I don't intend to sit home alone."

The Copa engagement was pivotal for Sinatra in that it was his first nightclub appearance in five years. The stress in his life was making itself known in his voice. It was husky and hoarse; at times he could barely sing a note. That he was usually up all night, drinking and smoking, only made matters worse where his vocal ability was concerned. The workload was horrific. He did three shows a night at the Copa, and five radio shows a week; recording sessions dominated his schedule as well. Toward the end of the engagement, Frank was also booked to appear at the Capitol Theater for matinee performances; he needed the work—and the money. Because he was nervous about his ability and tense about the prospect of facing a tough New York audience, he had to be treated with sedatives by doctors.

Jimmy Silvani is a cousin of Al Silvani's, who was one of Sinatra's bodyguards. Jimmy, who also worked as a bodyguard for Sinatra when he was assigned to the singer by the Fontainebleau Hotel in Miami, was backstage for this Copa engagement. He said: "Sinatra practically collapsed before that first show at the Copa. He kept saying, 'My career is over. I'm fucking washed up, and now I have to go out and face those people—the same goddamn people who aren't buying my records, who aren't seeing my movies.'

"He was taking a lot of pills at this time, pills to get up, pills to relax, pills to go to sleep. One crack of light in a room and he couldn't sleep, so he always had to have these heavy drapes everywhere we went. Today he would definitely have checked into Betty Ford; that's how screwed up he was with these pills. Back then, though, people just stayed screwed up.

"At one point that night at the Copa, he just sat in front of the dressingroom mirror and stared at himself, mumbling, 'You can do this, Frank. You can do this, pal. Just go on out there and do this.' He was trying to psych himself up. I felt badly for him. Ava came into the dressing room, and man, what a looker she was! She had on a white dress, looked great, with a kind of smile that could light up a stage."

Silvani's relative remembered that Ava stood behind Frank. Looking straight at their image in the mirror, she said, "Francis Albert Sinatra, you are the greatest goddamned entertainer who ever walked the face of this earth. I believe in you. I love you. And I salute you." With that, she raised her glass of champagne to their reflection. "Now I want you to get on out there, Francis, and prove me right."

Frank said, "I'm gonna do it, baby. I'm gonna do it for you." Then he got up and turned to face her. Smiling at him broadly, she melted into his arms. Frank kissed her passionately.

When Frank left the dressing room, an employee noticed a telegram lying on the dressing table: "Best of luck on your opening night. Love, Nancy."

When Frank Sinatra walked onto the stage opening night, March twenty-eighth, he appeared pale and seemed weak not only vocally but physically. From the beginning, the audience was not enthusiastic about his performance and seemed more interested in talking among themselves than in watching Sinatra or in listening to the Voice. At one point, Frank was forced to ask one noisy group, "Am I speaking too loud for you ladies?" Then, after a few more songs that seemed to fall on deaf ears, he was reduced to pleading, "This is my opening night. C'mon, give me a break."

"Oh, it was heartbreaking, all right," Ava would later recall. "Those bastards, they wouldn't cut him a break. He was trying so hard. Fucking New Yorkers. They're a tough crowd."

(It's often been reported that matters got dicey for the otherwise supportive Ava during Frank's rendition of "Nancy." Some distracted audience members, who probably thought Frank was singing the song for his wife rather than for his daughter [for whom it was written], began pointing at Ava and whispering. Supposedly, she left the club, furious with Frank for not having the sense to delete that song from his repertoire when he knew she would be in the audience. However, according to Ava and to many of her friends, this incident never happened. Frank and Ava had plenty of explosive disagreements during that New York engagement, but that particular song was never the subject of any of them.)

The reviews of the Copa engagement were, for the most part, critical of Frank's performance. The critic for the *Herald Tribune* wrote, "Whether temporarily or otherwise, the music that used to hypnotize the bobby-soxers—whatever happened to them anyway, thank goodness?—is gone from the throat. Vocally, there isn't quite the same old black magic there used to be when Mr. Sinatra wrenched 'Night and Day' from his sapling frame and thousands swooned."

"When Frank read the reviews, he was furious with those writers," Ava later told her New York socialite friend Mary LaSalle-Thomas, who later worked for Ava as a secretary (1950–52). "Ava said that in a real huff he had called one reporter from the *Herald Tribune* and challenged him about his opinion of the show. She was out shopping and when she came back to the suite, she heard Frank screaming at the top of his lungs at this guy on the telephone. She said that she heard him say something like

'You wouldn't know a good performance if it bit you in the ass. Why do you have to get so goddamn personal, anyway? I can take the criticism, but you ruin it by getting so personal.' "

According to LaSalle-Thomas, after some more swearing, Frank slammed the telephone down, pulled the wire out of the wall, and threw the phone across the room. It smashed into a corner and produced a deep hole in the wall. Ava was angry at Frank's tantrum, but not so annoyed that she didn't want to join in the fun. She picked the telephone up and hurled it out the window. Then the two lovebirds leaned out the window and watched in horror as the telephone narrowly missed the head of a passerby down below.

"I don't know why she did that," said LaSalle-Thomas, "except that she was probably just that angry with him. She never understood why he took on the press.

"Once I heard her tell Frank, 'Just smile when you see a photographer, be nice when asked for a quote, grin and bear it all, and lead your life like a star. There's enough ugliness in the world,' she said. 'We're responsible for the beautiful part.'

"I also heard her say, 'What the hell is wrong with being a star? *What is it?* Are we not paid enough in this fucking business to be criticized by assholes who don't know what they're talking about?' But, of course, Frank would never listen. He would just go to the medicine cabinet and get some more pills. He was on so many different prescriptions at that time, for his throat, for his back, for his head, to sleep—*especially* to sleep—he was practically an addict."

Frank was surly for the entire engagement. His accompanist and conductor, Skitch Henderson, remembered: "The understatement of the year would be to say that he was difficult." According to Henderson, Sinatra was annoyed that he couldn't get a hit, yet a group of harmonica players called the Harmonicats, which Sinatra thought of as a witless ensemble, had a mllion seller with a song called "Peg o' My Heart." One night when the band was off-key, Sinatra turned to Henderson and muttered, "If I'd tried a little harder, maybe I could have gotten the Harmonicats to back me." Later, Henderson said, "That cut me deeper than anything that had ever been said to me."

It was during this engagement at the Copacabana in New York that one of Frank's much-reported suicide attempts occurred. There have been many accounts of this episode, but this is what really happened:

Frank and Ava had another of their now-infamous quarrels over dinner when Ava decided that during the main course Frank had started flirting with the waitress. As it often happened, they began screaming at one another, and Ava stormed off. Annoyed at him and at herself, she went back to the Hampshire House. When she got there, she telephoned her ex-husband, Artie Shaw, who lived in New York. They had remained friends, and she wanted to pour her heart out to him about her relationship with Frank. So he invited her to his apartment to share a drink with him and his then girlfriend, Ruth Cosgrove (later Mrs. Milton Berle). On her way to Artie's, right before Ava walked out the door—just to make matters even more interesting—she left her telephone book open to the page with Artie's address on it.

Frank was jealous of Artie Shaw and did not like Ava socializing with him. Whenever he couldn't find Ava, he feared that she was with Artie and promised anyone who would listen that he would "kill the both of 'em, I swear it." (For his part, Shaw once said of Frank: "There's a lot of vindictiveness in Frank, a lot of hatred there.") Frank must have sensed that Ava still had some feeling for Artie; after all, she had confided that she had once been deeply in love with him. (In fact, years later, she would say that of all of her husbands—Frank included—the one she most admired was Artie Shaw, whom she called "an exceptional man.")

She was only at Artie's for twenty minutes when Frank showed up, accompanied by his friend and manager, Hank Sanicola. Sinatra took one look around the room and saw Ava sitting in a chair with a drink in her hand and looking self-satisfied. Their eyes met. (She would say later that she could see the hurt in Frank's.) Seemingly defeated, he walked right out the door without saying a word. About a half hour later, Ava and Ruth exchanged angry words about something, the details of which no one now seems to recall, and then Ava departed and caught a taxicab back to the Hampshire House.

By the time Ava returned to the suite, she knew that Bappie was in their room, asleep. She didn't want to wake her. Frank was in his room asleep, she thought. So, feeling a little inebriated, Ava just sank into the couch in the living room and began to sleep it off. Suddenly, she was awakened by the startling ring of the telephone. It was Frank, calling from the bedroom.

"I can't stand it any longer," he said in a voice dripping with desperation. "I'm going to kill myself. Now."

Then he fired two shots.

Ava screamed, dropped the phone, and ran across the living room and into Frank's bedroom. She was understandably panicked, terrified, even. When she burst into Frank's room, she saw him lying on the bed. The gun was still smoking. "*Oh, my God.*" Ava threw herself onto Frank's body, sobbing hysterically. Then Frank's eyes opened, and they met Ava's. For a moment, the two lovers stared at one another. He was alive? What was going on here? Frank smirked and said, "Oh, hello, Ava. And how are *you?*"

Sinatra had faked the whole thing, firing the shots through a pillow and into the mattress. Actor Tom Drake was also staying at the hotel, and he recalled: "The corridor was full of police, firemen, you never saw anything like it." In the end, Frank managed to convince the police that the whole thing must have been a hoax, because, clearly, no gunfire had occurred in his room. "Frank's denials could have won him an Oscar," Ava recalled. Ava later said that one of Sinatra's entourage removed the pillow and mattress with bullet holes and replaced them.

Frank felt enormously guilty about what he had put Ava through that night at the Hampshire House. "It was a cheap shot," he said to Hank Sanicola, though he didn't intend his statement to contain such obvious irony. "I think I'm slipping. Man, this dame has gotten to me so much, I'm out of control. How could I have done that? What the hell was I thinking?"

Frank said that he was unable to concentrate on his career or his voice. "This love I feel for her, it's sapping me of everything I got. I got no energy left for anything. What is this spell she has me under?"

Hank Sanicola, according to a close friend of his, warned Frank that if he wasn't careful, "this Ava broad is gonna be the death of you, either her or the pills. You can't control this kind of passion," he told Sinatra. "This woman has you so fucked up, you'll do anything in the world to be with her. Is the sex that good, Frank? Is it?"

According to Sanicola's friend, who witnessed this scene at a recording studio in New York, Frank just shook his head, sadly. "I love her," he said. "Goddamn me for it. I know I'm gonna burn in hell for what I've done to Nancy and the kids. But I love Ava. I adore everything about her, and I just want her to feel that way about me. It's killing me." Then he turned to Hank and said seriously, "Little by little, man, I'm dying."

CHAPTER 12

On March 26, 1950, Ava Gardner left the United States to film a movie (*Pandora and the Flying Dutchman* with James Mason), first in London and then in Spain. By this time, she later said, she was the one who needed a breather, from Frank Sinatra and from the emotional theatrics inherent in their relationship. The opportunity for time away from him was one she said she welcomed.

While in Spain, though, Ava became somewhat infatuated with the dashing Spanish matador-turned-actor thirty-four-year-old Mario Cabre, who was playing Juan Montalvo, her bullfighter-lover in the film. Though he had acted in just a few films, he was an enormously popular, good-looking actor who had made as much a name for himself by escorting beautiful actresses about Spain as he had for any limited ability he may have had as an actor. Ava was captivated by his charming personality as well as his swarthy Latin good looks and brash conceit. As Ava later put it, "A single girl will do what a single girl must do." In short order, she began a brief affair with the dashing Mario. "After one of those romantic, star-filled, dance-filled, booze-filled Spanish nights, I woke up to find myself in bed with him," she would later confess.

"Well, that was typically Ava," said Mary LaSalle-Thomas. "What she had with Mario was no reflection on her feelings for Francis. She was simply crazy about him, of course. This tryst with the bullfighter was strictly a matter of sex and had nothing to do with Frankie." Gardner's feelings were nothing if not an interesting echo of Sinatra's when it came to explaining his own dalliances and how they related to his wife, Nancy. "She was very masculine in the way she looked at these things, actually," said LaSalle-Thomas. "She would say, 'Men treat women like dirt. Well, I sometimes treat men the same way. So, go ahead, sue me.' "

The fling with Mario Cabre was not a relationship that Ava Gardner took seriously. It was just a respite from the mad world of Frank Sinatra, an uncomplicated but heated little affair with a sexy actor who somehow managed to satisfy her in the boudoir. Also, according to her friends, Ava hoped that her actions with Mario would make Frank jealous enough to once and for all end his marriage to Nancy and make a commitment to her.

Cabre did what he could, however, to use the affair to generate publicity in the hopes of advancing his career. "I am in love with her," he said in a prepared statement. "This is pure love. The first time I saw her, I felt something that was not normal. . . ." He said he was using his Spanish-English dictionary to compose his statements so that they could be understood "by an international audience."

Hearing rumors that Ava was possibly involved with another man and not being able to do anything about it was making Frank irritable and anxious. Phone connections to Spain were impossible, and he couldn't just pick up and leave New York to follow her. The Copacabana engagement was an important one; he was under a lot of pressure to prove himself. Because of the continuing problems with his throat, brought on by stress, his reckless lifestyle, and the rigors of three shows a night, he needed all of his resolve to get through it. Adding to his problems was the house band, which did not perform up to Sinatra's standards: to be as close to perfect as possible.

He had decided to try to sleep without the help of sleeping pills. It didn't work. "I can't sleep no matter what I do," he complained. "There's nothing more frustrating. I gotta sleep." So instead of pills, he would drink himself unconscious. By the time he was ready to go onstage at night, he was in terrible shape, dizzy and off balance.

On April 26, 1950, he had more trouble than usual with his voice during the dinner show; his voice cracked, embarrassingly enough, during "Bali Ha'i." Afterward, one of Frank's doctors told him to cancel the third show, but Frank was determined to sing. He had heard that Lee Mortimer, the Hearst reporter with whom he had a longtime feud, had made a wager that Sinatra would not finish the engagement. The third show went on at 2:30 A.M. Frank strolled to the microphone. As always, he was impeccably dressed: black tuxedo with satin lapels, a floppy bow tie, shoes so highly shined that the spotlights were reflected in them. He was thin, gaunt, and pale.

He walked on to applause, which he acknowledged with the megawatt Sinatra smile. It's been reported in the past that he never sang at all during that third show. Not true. The first number was "I Have But One Heart," which he dedicated to Ava after he finished it. The audience responded enthusiastically. However, his voice started to falter on the second song, "It All Depends on You," and when he reached for a high note, it left him completely. He was stunned. No matter what he had done before, the booze, the brawls, the broads, his voice had never failed him. Now, just when things were finally starting to look up, when he was back at the Copa—Why now?

He clutched at the microphone. He tried to sing again. He felt a trickle in the corner of his mouth. Thinking it was saliva, he wiped it away with his white handkerchief. It was blood. Later, it would be diagnosed as a submucosal throat hemorrhage, but that was later. If he had fallen writhing to the floor, someone would have rushed to his aid. As it was, no one knew what to do.

"I was never so panic-stricken in my whole life," he would later recall. "I remember looking at the audience. There was absolute silence—stunning, absolute silence. Finally, I whispered to the audience, 'Good night,' and walked off the floor."

"I thought for a fleeting moment that it was a joke," said his conductor, Skitch Henderson. "The color drained out of my face as I saw the panic in his. It became so quiet, so intensely quiet in the club. Like they were watching a man walk off a cliff."

Billy Eckstine took Sinatra's place for the rest of that ill-fated Copa engagement. However, when Eckstine collapsed at the end of the week from nervous exhaustion, Frank decided that "the goddamn place must be jinxed or something."

On May 10, 1950, Sinatra canceled an engagement at the Chez Paree in Chicago rather than take any more chances with his voice. As it was, the doctors said it could be as long as two months before he would sing

121

again. So he went to Miami to bask in the sun and figure out what his next move should be. While he was there, Nancy kept telephoning him to express her concern. He refused to take her calls, saying, "If she's so goddamn concerned about me, why won't she give me the divorce?" Every time he would raise his voice, however, his staff members would hover around him and plead with him not to speak. (He was supposed to communicate by writing on pads of paper.)

He was thirty-four years old and his career was in complete chaos: the movies, the records, now the voice, all gone. Frank said that he didn't know how he could take another breath if he couldn't sing, but he felt in his heart that if he had Ava in his corner, he'd be able to survive anything. At this time, in Miami, he desperately wanted to hear her voice, her laugh, but Louis B. Mayer was having her calls blocked so that she would not be distracted by anyone, especially her possessive and temperamental boyfriend. This made it impossible for Frank to get through to her. Frustrated, he knew what he had to do. He made arrangements to charter a plane to Spain.

Luckily, by the time Frank arrived in Barcelona, on May 11, Mario Cabre was miles away, in Gerona, filming a series of scenes for the movie. Ava suspected that the movie's director, Albert Lewin, purposely sent Cabre away on location shots when he overheard Cabre say that he would start trouble with Frank if they came face-to-face in Spain.

Sinatra rented a car at the airport and drove sixty miles north along the Catalan coast to the Sea Gull Inn, where he and Ava planned to rendezvous, in the resort town of S'Agaró. Their reunion was a happy one, especially when Frank gave Ava a $10,000 emerald necklace, which he had wrapped in toilet paper and stuffed in his back pocket; he was thrilled to hold her in his arms once again. He also presented her with a case of her favorite soft drink, Coca-Cola, a gesture she found charming and amusing until she realized that he was taking sleeping pills with the soft drink because he had heard that it made them work faster in a person's system.

He looked dreadful. Weighing less than 130 pounds, he was pale and weak and clearly in a drug-induced daze. The two then drove to Tossa de Mar, to the La Bastida estate, where they both had adjoining haciendas.

As the press hounded him and Ava at the estate, he was barely able to fight off their enthusiasm. "Let 'em do whatever the hell they want," he told Ava wearily. "I'm too fucking sick to care."

For most of the six days Frank was in Spain, he was sick. When he and Ava went tuna fishing, Ava, concerned about the fact that Frank could not sleep without his pills, threw a prescription bottle she found in his jacket overboard. He jumped in after it and almost drowned. He had to be rescued by the boat's captain. When Ava finally got him back to the estate, he was in no shape for the confrontation that occurred when he came across another newspaper article with a photograph of Ava and Mario Cabre on the doorstep of his hacienda. He had wanted a showdown with her about this man, anyway. That was why he really came. However, he barely had the energy for it. According to what Ava told her long-time friend Lucille Wellman, Frank grabbed her and shook her violently.

"Please, why are you doing this?" he asked as he throttled her. "Don't you know how I feel about you? Don't you know what you're doing to me, lady? Help me. Help *us,*" he pleaded with her. Exhausted, addicted, and emotionally spent, it was as if he simply couldn't take any more. He released his hold on her and, with tears streaming down his face, said, "I'm begging you, Ava. Look at me, here. Jesus, can't you see how I feel?"

Frank had done for Ava what he was not wont to do with many people: He had pleaded with her to acknowledge his feelings, his pain and suffering. Ava responded in the same callous, insensitive manner in which he had treated so many women who had come before her. "Oh, you're a fine one to talk," she said in a tone so dismissive it must have sounded familiar to him. "You've got me, you've got Nancy, and who knows who else you have on the side? Fuck off, buddy. Don't sing me your sad song. I'm not interested anymore."

"I only go back to Nancy to see the kids," Frank argued weakly. "What's with you and this . . . this . . . *greaseball?*"

Though Ava insisted to Frank that she and Mario Cabre were "just friends," Frank didn't believe her. Ava was incensed by his persistence; she didn't like being challenged, especially when she was lying.

It must have been impossible for Frank to imagine that he was being treated this way by a "dame." And whether he realized it or not, Ava had just underscored what would become the theme of their entire relationship: He needed her more than she needed him.

The next day, Mario Cabre gave an interview in Madrid in which he again proclaimed his undying love for Señorita Ava, "the woman I love with all the strength in my soul," he said. "Twice I have been gored by bulls. But Ava—she has hit me harder than any bull, in the heart."

Of course, that article spurred another fight between Ava and Frank, during which she told him *she* was worn out by the strain—the highs and lows—of their combative relationship. "I simply just can't do it anymore," she told him. "I just want you to leave me alone. Go home and get a divorce. And if you can't, then fuck you, Francis. Fuck you, you hear me?"

Sinatra left Barcelona twenty-four hours earlier than he planned to, feeling completely betrayed. He decided to go to Paris and have some fun there with his friend Jimmy Van Heusen.

"I'm tired of all the publicity Ava and I are getting about seeing each other," he told the ever-present media at the airport in Barcelona.

Meanwhile, on the day Frank left, Mario and Ava were filming a scene for the movie in front of a mob of extras and tourists when Cabre suddenly opened his shirt and proclaimed, "This is where a bull gored me yesterday. I was distracted by my feeling for Ava. I think of her day and night." That night, according to reporters, the two were "reunited for dinner." One of her friends said, "Ava took Cabre into her bedroom and was intimate with him for many long hours. She was so sick of Frank and what she had just been through with him that Mario was a welcome relief. Afterward, she kicked the Spanish caballero out of her room and said, 'Adios, muchacho.'"

In Paris, Sinatra complained to Van Heusen, "I'm willing to leave my wife and kids for this dame, and she treats me like *this?* Nancy won't give me a divorce, man. She's Catholic. She's Italian. What can I do?"

A couple of days after he arrived in Paris, Sinatra was startled in the middle of the night by a knock on the door of his hotel room. It was Ava. Saying that she missed him terribly, she removed all of her clothes in an impromptu striptease, slipped into his bed, and made love to him as if he were the only man on the planet. The next day, before he had even awakened, she stole out of the room and departed for London, where she was to finish the *Dutchman* film.

When he awakened, Sinatra probably didn't know what had hit him. It was as if Ava just stopped by to make sure he was still interested in her.

By the time he and Jimmy Van Heusen returned to the United States, Frank had made up his mind that he was finished with Ava and vowed to not telephone her. His buddy agreed that this decision was the best one he had made in a long time. "Move on, Frank," said Van Heusen. "No dame is worth what she's putting you through."

On May 23, loaded with gifts for his children, Frank spent the night at his Los Angeles home with Nancy and the children. It was a difficult visit. Every time he went back there, he gave Nancy renewed hope that they would have a future together. Then, when he left, she was heartbroken all over again. Of the visit, he told reporters: "Nancy and I had a long talk. We've never had anything but kind words. We're always friendly. But there's no reconciliation."

Frank's separation from Ava did not last long. They simply could not stay apart. It was torturous for them to be together but worse for them when they were not. This was not love, their friends told them. This was obsession. On the West Coast, they rented a cottage in Laguna Beach, California, for more lovemaking and emotional terrorizing.

With Sinatra's voice restored as a result of strong throat medication he had begun taking while in Los Angeles, Frank was scheduled for an engagement at the London Palladium. On July 10, 1950, he flew to London, where—by coincidence—Ava Gardner was filming "pickup" [insert] shots for *Pandora*. Frank moved into an expensive apartment in Berkeley Square, where he would stay for the next two months.

The Palladium engagement would turn out to be successful. Ava was seen front row, center, and was simply amazed—and relieved—to find that the audience of teenagers responded to him in much the same way the youth in the States used to react back in the good ol' days. While sipping tea onstage to soothe his throat, Frank performed a concert of classics that included "Embraceable You" and "I've Got a Crush on You."

" 'I can be happy, I can be sad,' " he sang, looking in Ava's direction. " 'It all depends on you.' " Tears welled in his eyes, and a pained expression played on his stress-lined face, a face that now seemed so much older than its thirty-four years. For Frank, every song was about Ava. Every *moment* was about Ava.

A reporter for the *Musical Express* wrote, "I watched mass hysteria. Was it wonderful? Decidedly so, for this man Sinatra is a superb performer and a great artist. He has his audience spellbound."

Frank was in a jolly mood as a result of the strong reception in London and also because the British press seemed to be of the opinion that his romance with Ava was not of national concern. In fact, little was reported about it, and Frank was relieved not to have to contend with the media every time he and Ava ventured outdoors.

In September 1950, Frank Sinatra and Ava Gardner returned to New York and continued their affair in a very open, public manner. They attended the Joe Louis–Ezzard Charles world-heavyweight-championship bout at Yankee Stadium, where they were photographed, all smiles and arm in arm. At this same time, on September 28, 1950, Nancy made an appearance at Santa Monica's Superior Court in her bid for a legal separation and separate maintenance.

Shaking and sobbing and practically being held up by her sister Julie Barbato, Nancy tried to plead her case to Judge Orlando Rhodes. Her marriage was clearly over, she said. "On numerous occasions, he would go to Palm Springs for weekends without me," she said of Sinatra through her tears. "He also stayed several days at a time. This happened many times. When we had guests, he would go off by himself and not feel like talking. This made me terribly nervous and upset." Several times, the proceedings had to be halted so that Nancy could compose herself. She seemed to be close to a breakdown.

Nancy was granted, first, $2,750 a month in temporary support. She had estimated that Frank's 1949 income had been $93,740 and assessed the value of their community property at $750,000.

Ava was thrilled that the divorce seemed on its way to becoming a reality, or as she put it to one friend, "All I want is for Nancy to come to her senses and live her life so that I can live mine. Is that so selfish? No," Ava reasoned. "I don't think it is. I just don't. Can't she just go on with her life, for Christ's sake?"

Frank was having such a difficult time with his career, he couldn't possibly make those court-appointed monthly payments to Nancy. He even had to borrow money from Columbia Records to pay back taxes. "He was so humiliated by what was happening in his life, he could barely look some of his friends straight in the eye," his daughter Nancy once said.

He told Ava, "Look, I won't have enough bucks to buy you a pair of nylons once they're through with me."

At this time, Ava was determined to meet Frank's parents. Unfortunately, he had not spoken to them in some time. They had both been distressed about the affair with Ava, and their outspoken feelings had caused a rift in their relationship with their son. Even though Dolly had no love for Nancy, because of her refusal to give Frank his freedom, she believed that Frank should have officially divorced her before taking on a new lover in such a public way. Marty agreed.

Headstrong Ava, however, would make prolonged estrangement between parents and son impossible. She continually pushed for a meeting with the Sinatras and would not abandon the idea. Actually, Ava's tough self-assured nature had always reminded Frank of his mother, and he anticipated that they would be great friends. That was certainly Ava's hope as well. Frank said he would arrange a meeting, but when he started to balk, Ava brazenly picked up the telephone and called the Sinatras herself. The next thing Frank knew, Ava had managed to get the two of them invited to Dolly and Marty's small, three-story Hoboken home for dinner. Her hope was that she would be able to ingratiate herself with them.

Ava and Dolly got alone well when they finally met. Dolly had more in common with Ava in terms of temperment and personality than she did with Frank's wife, Nancy. She enjoyed Ava's ribald sense of humor and quickly approved of the affair, which made it easier for Frank to continue the relationship.

While Dolly was won over, Marty was angry about what Frank was doing and tried to discourage it. Father and son engaged in loud disagreement about the affair in the kitchen while Ava was visiting with Dolly in the living room. "Your marriage is supposed to be the most important thing in your life," Marty told Frank. 'Where's your head?' "

Frank felt unhappy about letting his father down, but in the end he knew that he had to be true to his heart. "I want Ava now" he told Marty, words that would become a battle cry of Frank's for some time to come.

Ava had overheard some of the father-son debate, but she wasn't overly concerned about it. Later, she said, 'Well, at least I have the mother on

126

my side, and she's the powerful one in that family. I could see that right away. Perhaps I'll have to work on the old man a little. But I don't think he can change Francis's mind about anything.' "

In October 1950, Ava Gardner returned to Hollywood to film the M-G-M film version of the Hammerstein and Kern musical *Show Boat.* Meanwhile, Frank Sinatra had begun working on his own television series, *The Frank Sinatra Show* on CBS, from nine to ten P.M. on Saturday nights. It was a major break for Frank when the show went on the air (on October 7, 1950). The ratings were never strong, but the show did manage to struggle along for a couple of years. Meanwhile, at the same time, Frank starred in a weekly CBS radio program, *"Meet Frank Sinatra,* on Sunday afternoons, which also was short-lived. He was doing everything he could to keep his name and talent in the public eye, but to no avail.

The year ended as badly as it began when, in December 1950, Frank learned that he was going to be secretly questioned about his Mafia connections by Joseph Nellis, an attorney for Sen. Estes Kefauver's(D-Tenn.) Special Committee to Investigate Crime in Interstate Commerce. These investigations, which would be televised to the nation, really marked the first time the American public would begin to focus on organized crime in this country. Up until this point, most Americans got their information about the underworld from fictional books and films, and many people simply didn't believe that the Mafia even existed. Now that there was official congressional scrutiny into underworld activities, many mobsters were being put on notice—as were their friends in the entertainment community—that, as Frank Costello once put it, "maybe things are gonna get a little tense round here."

Frank was nervous about the prospect of being questioned by the committee. "I don't have anything to say," he complained. "I know a lot of people, but so what?"

Lucille Wellman remembered: "Ava told me that Frank was afraid that he was going to be ruined once and for all by this questioning. Things were already going badly, and now this thing was about to occur. It was like a nail in the coffin.

"Ava told me that she said to him, 'You made your bed, Francis. Now you gotta sleep in it. If you'd never started with these hoods, you wouldn't be in this mess today.' Ava hated those men, and they were always around, she said.

"Once, she and I were in a nightclub with Frank when one of those mobsters—I suspected he was a mobster, but, really, I couldn't know except by the way Ava glared at him—came over to the table and sat down with them. A second later, a photographer came by and snapped a photo of us. As soon as she saw the flash of the bulb, Ava bolted up and grabbed the camera out of the photographer's hands. She then very calmly opened it—I was amazed at how easily she did that—pulled out the film, put it in her purse, and then handed the camera back to him. The photographer just walked away as if it was the most natural thing in the world. Ava sat down, and we all went on with our delightful evening."

Senator Kefauver, in an attempt to explain to his millions of viewers the way the Mafia worked, told a television audience that "the Mafia is a shadowy international organization that lurks behind much of America's organized criminal activity. It is an organization about which none of its members, on fear of death, will talk. In fact, some of the witnesses called before us, who we had good reason to believe could tell us about the Mafia, sought to dismiss it as a sort of fairy tale or legend that children hear in Sicily, where the Mafia originated. The Mafia, however, is no fairy tale. It is ominously real, and it has scarred the face of America with almost every conceivable type of criminal violence, including murder, traffic in narcotics, smuggling, extortion, white slavery, kidnapping, and labor racketeering."

At the time, though, no one knew that Frank Sinatra was being interrogated because he was questioned in secrecy in Nellis's Rockefeller Center office at four in the morning (on March 1, 1951). If it had been revealed that Sinatra was being questioned, it certainly would have further damaged his already tainted reputation.

Based on a transcript of the meeting, Nellis seemed to feel that he was about to pin Frank down on a number of important issues regarding his relationships with certain questionable personalities. In the end, though, the questioning amounted to nothing more than an admission of the obvious: Frank Sinatra did, in fact, know a whole lot of gangsters—names like Joe Fischetti, Frank Costello, Joe Adonis, Benjamin "Bugsy" Siegel, and Lucky Luciano came up—but nothing more. At one point, a nervous Frank asked Nellis, "You're not going to put me on television and ruin me just because I know a lot of people, are you?" Nellis responded that the decision would be made by Senator Kefauver. Later in the two-hour session, the attorney asked Frank why he was so involved with unsavory underworld characters. Frank answered, "Well, hell, you go into show business, you meet a lot of people. And you don't know who they are or what they do."

Even though Nellis would later say that he felt Frank Sinatra was lying, that the singer had more than just a passing acquaintance with the characters discussed, he decided (within hours of the questioning) not to recommend that the singer be called to testify. It seemed that there was really nothing Frank could, or would, add to the public record. Either he really had no business connections with the mobsters in question, or he was an adept liar. The file on Sinatra was closed, and other vocalists, like Dean Martin, were also taken off Nellis's list. Certainly, if Estes Kefauver were to begin dragging in for questioning all the singers who had worked in clubs run by gangsters, the hearings would have looked a great deal more like *The Ed Sullivan Show* than a serious congressional investigation.

CHAPTER 13

In 1951, Frank Sinatra, now thirty-five years old, was still as captivated by Ava Gardner as he had ever been. As always, Frank didn't speak much of his despair publicly, but he didn't have to. His music said it all.

On March 27, 1951, Frank gave one of his most emotional performances in the studio when he recorded "I'm a Fool to Want You." This session marked a defining moment in the development of Sinatra's interpretative skills. The anguish he felt as a result of his tumultuous relationship with Ava is clear with every note in this recording (which was not a hit and remains obscure except to the most diehard Sinatra aficionados). In fact, so overcome by grief was Sinatra when he tried to record it, he left the studio in tears. He had to return later to complete the song.

"That was one of the finest recordings he ever made," observed his daughter Nancy. "It's enough to tear your heart into pieces, it's so beautiful. As a matter of fact, we played it on Thanksgiving night (1996) at his house. We were sitting at the table listening to it in the background, and he said, " 'My God. That's good.' "

"I'm a Fool to Want You" is Sinatra at his most expressive. He cowrote the song with Jack Wolf and Joel Herron. Frank would rerecord it for Capital Records six years later; although it was a stunning performance, it didn't have the same emotional intensity as the original.

Despite Frank's obviously sincere emotions for Ava Gardner, his wife Nancy, from whom he was now legally separated, still held on to some hope that her husband would return to her and the family. "He still loves me," she maintained. "In my heart, I believe that."

On some level, Frank Sinatra's friends and associates have maintained, Frank felt tremendously guilty about what he had done to Nancy. One evening, according to what Nancy told a close friend, Frank was at the house visiting the children when she presented him with a photo album. In it, Nancy had compiled pictures of herself and the family throughout the years. She had spent hours poring over these photographs. "Funny how good the past looks when you don't have a future," she had said.

"If you can still leave here after looking through this book, then I'll know that you really don't care about any of us any longer," she told her estranged husband. He opened it and glanced at the first couple of pages—photos of their wedding carefully arranged so as to be chronological, pictures of his children as infants—and then closed the album. Tears came to his eyes. The emotional manipulation was more than he could take. He threw the album onto the couch and left.

"How is it that *I'm* such a villain just because I want to keep my family together?" a weeping Nancy Sinatra screamed after her husband as he drove off.

At about this time, Frank Sinatra filmed a new movie, *Meet Danny Wilson,* for Universal, with Shelley Winters. The script seemed strangely patterned after what the public and press had conceived as Frank's life. In the film, he portrays a shady nightclub singer who is involved with the underworld. Frank would do anything for a break, even exploit the image of himself that he despised and said was untrue.

He was happy to have some work (he was paid $25,000), but as always these days, he found himself completely distracted by his personal life. That Frank and Shelley Winters grew to despise each other during the course of filming (she called him a "skinny, no-talent, stupid Hoboken bastard") only served to make matters worse. The only reason Shelley even finished the film with Frank was because his estranged wife called her and begged her to; otherwise, Frank wouldn't get the $25,000 and "me and my kids are going to be on the street because we can't make the mortgage payment." In the movie, Frank plays a brash but likable young crooner—typecasting, no doubt, but effective just the same because Sinatra's portrayal is wonderful. He once said it was the first film role "I could really sink my teeth into." Though the film was unsuccessful at the box office, it showcased some memorable songs, including "All of Me," "She's Funny That Way," "You're a Sweetheart," and "I've Got a Crush on You."

Another film released in 1951, *Double Dynamite,* a comedy caper and romp costarring Jane Russell and Groucho Marx, was a disaster. It was originally entitled "It's Only Money" when filmed a year or so earlier but was shelved by RKO until 1951 because it was so poor.

Steve Stoliar, Groucho Marx's former secretary, said, "Sinatra still kept the star attitude through filming, even though it looked like he was finished. Groucho told me Sinatra was often late to the set, stuck in his dressing room going over racing forms. Groucho went up to him finally and said, 'If you're late one more time, you're going to have to act opposite yourself, because I'm not going to show up here.' Sinatra was on time after that."

On July 17, 1951, Ava and Frank attended the premiere of *Show Boat* at the Egyptian Theater in Hollywood. Ava never looked more glamorous, wearing an emerald green and black satin and lace evening gown courtesy of the M-G-M costume designer Irene. A striking diamond necklace, an expensive gift from Frank to commemorate the occasion, gracefully adorned her neck. Famed Hollywood stylist Sydney Guilaroff did her hair. From the expression on his face, Frank was clearly proud to be the escort of the woman who was described by one television reporter present as "a true Hollywood vision."

"It gives me a great pleasure and pride to be able to escort Ava to a public premiere," Frank said happily. "I've cared for a long, long time. I'm very much in love with her and it's wonderful to know we can be seen together without hurting anyone. There's no ill feeling about it anywhere—with anyone."

As the glamorous, romantic couple exited a stretch limousine and walked down the red carpet to the theater, devoted fans screamed out their names in unison: "Frankie!" "Ava!" "Frankie!" "Ava!" Flashbulbs popped all about. It was a mad scene, but so exhilarating. A party was planned later at Romanoff's, but the couple bowed out because Frank had to be at work early the next morning, at RKO on the set of *Meet Danny Wilson.*

Reviews for Ava's performance in *Show Boat* were, for the most part, raves. Now her career was truly in high gear, whereas Frank's was still struggling along.

Ava was exhausted from filming a movie (*Lone Star,* with Clark Gable) and said she needed to get away from it all. She loved Mexico, everything from the art to the food, the booze to the men. "We decided to go far away for a desperately needed vacation in Mexico [on August 4, 1951]. We thought we could sneak in a little bit of peace and quiet. Not a chance," she said. "The chaos started at the Los Angeles Airport when reporters and photographers filled the tarmac and even crowded the steps of the plane, treating our departure like a goddamn presidential visit."

Upon their return from Mexico, Frank announced that he and Ava were officially engaged to be married, even though his divorce from Nancy was not final. This incensed Nancy, who still hoped her husband would return to her. However, Frank was apparently sending her a message through the media: "It's over."

On August 11, Frank was booked at the Riverside Inn and Casino in Reno, Nevada, marking his first appearance in a casino in the state of Nevada. While there, Frank decided to establish a Nevada residency so that *he* could file for divorce there; he was tired of waiting for Nancy to come through with hers. His filing involved his having to stay in Nevada for five weeks.

It had been Ava's idea that Frank take matters into his own hands. She was determined to move things along and was, by this time, completely fed up with Nancy's obvious delaying tactics. Though Frank went along with Ava's plan, his friends say he was beginning to feel that Ava was much too pushy. "She won't let up on this divorce business," he complained to Hank Sanicola. "I want it as bad as she does, but she's making me crazy. Jesus Christ, she won't let up."

Over the Labor Day weekend, Frank, Ava, and Hank Sanicola and his wife, Paula, went to Lake Tahoe; they stayed at the Cal-Neva Lodge. What happened there has been widely examined in stories and books about Frank Sinatra, but the reasons behind what occurred were never accurately reported.

On the evening of August 31, 1951, Frank and Ava had another terrible fight after a pleasant dinner at the Christmas Tree Restaurant with his friend and manager Hank Sanicola and his wife. Ava would say later, "We had both drunk too much, and Frank made an offhand remark that hurt me so deeply that I decided to go back to Los Angeles."

Her friend, Lucille Wellman, elaborated. "Actually, the fight started because, after dinner, Ava drunkenly confessed that she and that Spanish bullfighter [Mario Cabre] really *did* have an affair. Who knows why she did that? Just to throw it in Frank's face, I guess. I never understood it. Then the fight continued about relationships and commitment, which went down a path that found them arguing about Nancy.

"She said some things that hurt Frank. For instance, she told him, 'If you ever treat me the way you treated your wife, I'll cut your balls off.' And he said something like 'What are you talking about?' and then Ava went at him, detailing how he had left Nancy for another woman and how he had abandoned his own children. She recounted all of it as if she hadn't even been involved, as if she weren't the other woman. Her insensitivity made Frank crazy. He called Ava a whore and told her that she was really the one responsible for all of the pain and misery.

"Ava was madder than hell and said she was leaving. Frank said she would be sorry if she did. She ignored that threat, and the next thing he knew, she was in a car driving all the way back to Los Angeles, sipping bourbon all the way. That's what the fight was really about, though no one had ever wanted to admit it publicly, not even Ava when she wrote her memoirs."

After that argument, Frank went back to the lodge and apparently started stewing over the sorry state of his affairs: a career that had taken a nosedive, a wife whose heart he had broken, children who missed their father, and the sometimes insensitive but always intoxicating woman for whom he had risked it all. It was too much to bear, and in a moment of desperation he took an overdose of sleeping pills. His longtime valet,

George Jacobs (who worked for him from 1953 to 1969), found Frank and called in a physician, Dr. John Wesley Field, to attend to him. Frantically, Hank Sanicola telephoned Ava, who had just gotten back to her home in Pacific Palisades, "exhausted, hung over, and miserable," as she recalled.

"Quick, get back here, Frank took an overdose," Hank told Ava.

Remembering what had occurred in New York with the simulated suicide attempt, Ava was hesitant to run to Frank's side. Still, she got on a plane and returned to Nevada.

When Ava got to Frank's room, she found him lying on the bed, surrounded by a gaggle of overly concerned staff members and sycophantic hangers-on. Gazing up at her with innocent blue eyes, he feigned an exhausted, overwrought demeanor. "Oh, Ava," he said weakly. "I thought you'd gone."

Lucille Wellman says, "Oh, please, he never intended to kill himself. Ava said they didn't even have to pump his stomach. He hadn't taken enough pills for that. It was just a grand attempt to get attention from everyone around him and from Ava as well. And it worked."

"I wanted to punch him, I really did," Ava would later admit. "I wanted to punch him as much as I'd ever wanted to punch anybody."

The next day, Frank's "suicide attempt" was front-page headlines. He denied all of it. "I've never heard anything so damn wild and ridiculous," he stormed at one reporter. "This would be a hell of a time to do away with myself. I did not try to commit suicide. I just had a bellyache. What will you guys think of next to write about me?"

There must have been a part of Ava Gardner that was flattered by Frank's melodrama. After all, here was one of the most popular entertainers in the country (even though his career was on a downslide, he was still a controversial celebrity) in effect telling her through his actions that his life meant nothing without her complete attention. Certainly suicide was the most desperate move Sinatra could make to guarantee Ava's continued interest in him. His actions most certainly had to give Gardner—described by her friends as an insecure woman—an ego boost, just in knowing that she was Frank Sinatra's very lifeline, his only reason for living.

"That was definitely part of it," said Lucille Wellman. "It was hard for her not to be at least a little impressed by his sensational gestures."

On the other hand, as flattered as she might have been, Ava was also scared—not only for Frank but for herself as well. As she told her friend Mary LaSalle-Thomas, "Francis is dying inside because his career is over and his life is shit. I don't know what to do for him. I love him like crazy, Mary, I do. But am I the one to handle all of this?" she asked. "Am I up for the job?" She answered her own question: "No, I just don't think so."

133

"Francis is crying out for help. But who's gonna help me?" she asked rhetorically. "Who's there for *me*? And what if it doesn't work out between us? Am I going to be responsible for the death of Frank Sinatra? Do I want that on my conscience for the rest of my life?"

After Frank's six-week residency in Nevada was completed, he was able to officially file for divorce there, which he planned to do on September 19. However, when Nancy heard what he was about to do, she was hurt by what she perceived as his impatience and lashed out at him. She contested the divorce, which was unexpected. Since she had already filed, Frank reasoned, why would she object to *his* filing? The reason was that she was angry that he was so anxious for the marriage to end and now she was becoming vindictive.

Nancy's attorney informed Frank that the property settlement on which they had earlier agreed was no longer acceptable because Frank was now about $50,000 behind in his payments.

"What the hell is she doing?" Frank asked. "Where's all this coming from? She usta be so sweet."

Frank went ahead and filed for the divorce, anyway, but then Nancy obtained a levy against an office building Sinatra owned at 177 S. Robertson Boulevard in Beverly Hills in order to collect the payments due her.

"You gotta be kiddin' me," Frank said to a group of reporters when he was told that news. "Nancy wouldn't do that? Would she? Tell me she wouldn't."

Things got worse when Frank's own attorneys, those representing him in his divorce, jumped on the bandwagon with Nancy before all of Frank's assets were completely attached by her. They sued Frank for $12,250 in legal fees, securing their own lien against the Beverly Hills building and on Frank's home as well.

"My own team turning against me," Frank said. "Finks!"

By this time, Sinatra was completely annoyed by this legal wrangling, and he told his new attorneys to give Nancy whatever she wanted. Frank couldn't fight her. He simply didn't have the strength or the moral resolve. So he signed an agreement to pay her all of the money he owed, and more, if she would just, once and for all, finalize a California divorce. Nancy reluctantly agreed; she probably couldn't think of any more stalling tactics.

Finally, when both Sinatras were completely spent by what they had put each other through, the attorneys moved ahead with the legalities.

Tina Sinatra wryly observed that she regrets that her parents didn't stay married, "but I also think they might have killed each other if they had."

* * *

In truth, in some respects the ongoing drama was perhaps as emotionally draining for Ava as it was for Frank and Nancy. On September 26 she was rushed to St. John's Hospital after having reportedly collapsed from a viral infection and low blood pressure. Forced to cancel an appearance with Bing Crosby on Bob Hope's radio show, and the rest of her schedule as well, Ava lay in the hospital for weeks. Making matters worse for her was that Frank could not be at her side because he had prior commitments in New York.

Immediately, rumors circulated that Ava had actually had an abortion, and when these lurid stories got back to Frank in New York, he became suspicious. One friend of Frank's reports that Frank telephoned Ava's doctor, William Weber Smith, to push for information about her condition. When told that the physician would not discuss Ava with him, Frank slammed the telephone down. He then called some of his pals in Los Angeles to ask them to "nose around" and learn what they could about the reason for Ava's hospitalization. Of course, when Ava later heard of Frank's instructions to his friends, she became enraged and telephoned him herself. "She gave him an earful," said Frank's friend, "and threatened to call off the marriage if he didn't trust her. She said she would never, ever, have an abortion without telling him about it." (Ava's words would come back to haunt her in about a year.)

The next day, Frank telephoned Nancy. She cried, once again saying that she might change her mind about the divorce, after all. Overcome by loneliness and fear, she was in great despair. That much was clear. But how much longer could Frank allow her to procrastinate? The clock was ticking. What if Ava were to leave him? As far as he was concerned, she was all he had.

Frank Sinatra had always been an intensely proud man. To have to be so reliant on the capricious nature of these two women, to have his very existence shaped by their unpredictable emotions and impulsive decisions, was unbearable to him.

Making matters worse, his career continued its downward spiral. If anything, Frank had been a careerist, at all costs. A driven, directed person, the realization of more than certain show business goals was important to him: it gave his entire life a sense of purpose. After having reached the pinnacle of success in a business in which so few thrive, losing it all had laid waste to his ego.

Understandably, after so many disappointments in the last few years and so many rejections by the entertainment industry, he felt he would never again be able to attain the kind of success he had so relished in the early years of his career. Back then, he hungered for it and went after it with almost fanatical determination, and finally he tasted it. When he did, he loved it—passionately. "Let me tell you one thing," he said. "There ain't nothin' like success, baby."

135

His life, once overflowing with the grand emotions and vital juices of his existence, now seemed empty. He had to wonder if it was even worthwhile now. In other words, what was the point of being a has-been? What pride was there in *that* for a man like Frank Sinatra?

Over time, desperate thoughts and unanswerable questions began to invade Sinatra's mind, jeopardize his common sense, and compromise the fighter instinct that had always been an integral aspect of his personality. As difficult as it was for his friends to believe, considering the powerful way he had lived his life up until this point, Frank Sinatra had become apathetic. "If I don't live another month, hey, fine with me," he told Ava at one point. She never believed he would kill himself, though. No one did, really. After all, the phony suicide attempts had convinced most people that he was not serious about ending his life. They were, however, cries for help, for attention.

"But something had changed in 1951," said one close associate. "He was ready to die. He was truly, truly tired," said his friend. "Tired of being alone. Tired of fighting for love, career, life. He said, 'Why does it all have to be so hard? Why can't I get a break?' Imagine Frank Sinatra saying that: *'Why can't I get a break?'*"

While in New York, Frank Sinatra stayed at the apartment of his close friend, Manie Sachs. (Sachs was someone on whom Sinatra could always depend. When he died of leukemia in February 1958, Frank was desolated. "When I holler for help, he ain't gonna be there anymore," he sobbed.)

One evening, Sinatra went out alone and had too much to drink. He could always count on Jack Daniels, if on no one else. Afterward, he walked back to Sachs's elegant apartment and, he would later remember, poured himself yet another drink. Then he put a cigarette into his mouth, went into the bathroom for some sleeping pills, and shuffled absentmindedly into the kitchen. Turning on the gas oven, he bent over one of the burners to light the cigarette that dangled from his mouth. While in that position, he couldn't help but smell the gas as it seeped from the stove. He inhaled deeply. It smelled good. It smelled like death. Frank Sinatra must have decided in that split second that death was good, because he turned the gas up all the way. Then he turned on the other burners. As the noxious fumes coursed from the oven, Sinatra pulled up a chair and sat in front of it. He inhaled deeply. At long last, peace, he must have thought as he drifted off.

The next thing he knew, he was being jostled back to life by a frantic Manie Sachs. Had he arrived just a few minutes later, it would have been too late. This was no phony suicide attempt. Sinatra wanted to die.

"Damn you," Manie said, clenching his teeth. "Damn you, Frank. How could you do this? How could you do it?"

"I'm sorry, I'm sorry," Frank mumbled as he came out of his stupor. "That was stupid. That was real stupid."

"He would have died for sure," Manie Sachs said later. "He wanted out. He wanted to go. Imagine the entertainment world without Frank Sinatra. It would have been a very different place, that's for sure. This man was in trouble."

Apparently, Ava Gardner never learned about the suicide attempt. Frank had insisted that it be kept from her. She never mentioned it to any of her friends or associates and didn't write about it in her candid autobiography. Frank was ashamed; he felt weak. He promised Manie Sachs that he would never try anything like that again and agreed to consider consulting a psychiatrist, even though, as he put it, "I know what the guy's gonna say. I know what's wrong. So why pay someone to tell me what I already know?"

Finally, exhausted and drained, Nancy Sinatra decided to go ahead with the divorce. "Regretfully, I am putting aside religious and personal considerations and agreeing to give Frank the freedom he has so earnestly requested," said Nancy in a statement. "This is what Frank wants. . . ."

The Sinatra divorce was granted on October 31, 1951, in Santa Monica, while Frank and Ava were in New York.

Nancy, who did not mention Ava in the divorce papers, would receive one-third of Sinatra's gross income on the first $150,000; 10 percent of the next $150,000; and a smaller percentage thereafter (but never less than $1,000 dollars a month for the rest of her life). She was also awarded custody of the couple's three children, the home in Holmby Hills, part interest in the Sinatra Music Corporation, furnishings, furs, jewelry, and a 1950 Cadillac. Frank kept the home in Palm Springs, with its swimming pool, his 1949 Cadillac convertible, 1947 four-wheel-drive Jeep, bank accounts, oil interests in Austin County, Texas, and all rights to, and royalties for his musical compositions and recordings. The couple agreed to sign over to Frank's parents the Hoboken home he had bought for them.

"She took her pound of flesh from him and then some," Ava said of Nancy's settlement with Frank.

A day later, Frank and Ava obtained a marriage license.

"Whatcha gonna get each other for a wedding present?" one reporter asked them during one of the public outings, where, as always, they were descended upon by the media. "Boxing gloves?"

Even Ava had to laugh at that one.

"Will it be a white wedding dress, Miss Gardner?" a photographer asked sarcastically.

At that, her smile froze. Incensed, Frank shoved the photographer as hard as he could. As the lensman fell backward and hit the pavement, the couple raced away, got into a limousine, and sped off into the night.

A couple of days later, Frank took Ava to his parents' home to celebrate the upcoming wedding.

"Hey, where's the bar?" Ava wanted to know as soon as she and Frank walked through the door. "I need a drink." She was joking, of course (about the bar but certainly not about the drink).

"We got no bar," Marty said icily. "But I will get you a drink."

"I don't even know the names of some of the things we had," Ava said of the spectacular Italian feast which Dolly had prepared. "Chicken like you've never tasted in your life, some wonderful little meat thing rolled in dough, and just about every Italian goody you can imagine."

It was at this meal, though, that Dolly took a second look at Ava and didn't like what she saw.

One of Frank's cousins, who was not at the dinner but came later for *cannolis*, said, "I remember it like it was yesterday, and we're talking some thirty-five years ago. We were sitting around the table eating dessert and having after-dinner drinks. Everyone was having a good time. The booze had been flowing all night, so Ava was in good spirits."

Then, according to the cousin, Frank and Marty (who had never approved of the way Frank handled the situation with Nancy) began talking about Frank's first wife, Nancy.

"You know, Pop, I do feel badly about how it ended with Nancy," Frank said in all sincerity, "but that's the way it goes. As Ma would say, 'You gotta do what you gotta do.' I just hope she's okay. I don't know what else I coulda done."

"Oh, fuck that," Ava suddenly exclaimed in a loud, exasperated voice.

After a collective gasp from everyone at the table, an unfazed Ava began to tear into Frank. "Jesus Christ, Francis, will you please stop it?" she yelled at him. "She got what she wanted, didn't she? She got the money, didn't she? So would you please just stop it? I can't take it anymore. I just can't take hearing another word about your poor, poor Nancy.'"

After a beat, Dolly glared at Ava, slammed both hands on the table, rose, and walked out of the room. Marty dutifully followed. Then, loudly enough for everyone present to hear, Dolly bristled to Marty, "How dare she talk to my son like that? Who does she think she is? I won't have it. Not in my home, I won't. And certainly not at the dinner table."

"Marty didn't say much; he rarely said much to Dolly," said Sinatra's cousin. "There was no way he could stand up to her or even express an opinion. Dolly couldn't have cared less about Nancy by this time; in fact, she loathed her for what she felt she'd put Frankie through. But she did not appreciate the way Ava had spoken to her son, especially at the dinner table, which was the most sacred place in that Italian home."

Frank was angry with Ava for humiliating him in his parents' home. "Get your coat; we're leaving," he told her. Impatiently, he assisted her with her jacket. She jerked all about as he forced her arms into the sleeves.

"Ouch, you're hurting me, Francis," she said, *"Stop it."*

"Twelve years, Ava," he reminded her, paying no attention to any pain he may have caused her. "That's a twelve-year relationship we're talkin' about. Jesus Christ. Have some compassion, why don't you? What's wrong with you? You don't have a heart; that's what's wrong. You ain't got a heart."

Then, as he hustled her out of there, Frank added, "And another thing. When you're my wife, you'll learn to behave yourself at the dinner table if it's the last fucking thing I ever teach you."

Ava had tears running down her cheeks when she left; clearly, she was hurt by Frank's harsh words. She didn't say a word in her defense.

"So, I don't care what you've read in books and magazines over the years," the Sinatra cousin observed. "Dolly Sinatra did not like Ava Gardner from that moment on. She may have put up a front, she may have said complimentary things, but as far as she was concerned, Ava had committed a cardinal sin: She had treated her son like dirt."

Frank and Ava were to be married on November 7, 1951, at the home of Manie Sachs's brother, Lester, in Philadelphia.

However, the night before the wedding, a handwritten letter was delivered to Ava. It was from a woman who claimed that she had been having an affair with Frank. She provided sordid details that, to Ava, seemed all too convincing. The affair had been going on for months, the writer claimed, and right under Ava's nose. Ava had been a fool, claimed the woman, for ever having believed in Frank Sinatra.

How could Ava go through with the wedding now? She felt that she couldn't marry Frank, at least not until she determined the accuracy of the letter she had just received. So she called off the wedding and hurled her engagement ring—a six-carat emerald stone in platinum with pear-shaped diamonds—out the window of the Hampshire House, where they were staying in New York. (It was never found.)

Frank was inconsolable. He swore that the letter writer was a fake, "a fucking phony," and he simply could not fathom that after all they had been through together, Ava would be inclined to take as gospel the word of an anonymous accuser. Ava's sister, Bappie, talked to her throughout the night to convince her that she really should not place so much importance on a nameless letter. In the end, Ava relented.

It had snowed hard in the Midwest the day before. By Wednesday,

November 7, 1951, the storm had reached Philadelphia in the form of a cold, driving rain. Small-craft warnings were being posted all along the East Coast. A page 1 story in the *New York Times* that morning was about Eva Peron resting comfortably after an operation for an undisclosed ailment. But in the home of Lester Sachs, in the upscale Germantown suburb of Philadelphia, nobody cared about what was going on in the outside world. The twenty or so invited guests were attending the wedding of Frank Sinatra and Ava Gardner.

A crowd of reporters and photographers huddled miserably outside in the rain. Although Sinatra's career was on the skids, he still attracted the media. "The one thing he could do to keep his name in the news," Sammy Davis once observed, "was to constantly be pissed [because] the press was interested in him. Deep down, though, he had to know he was lucky they still cared. Let's face it . . ."

Frank and Ava arrived from New York in a rented, chauffeured Cadillac. Sinatra refused to surrender his privacy on this day, as if he ever really had any. His first reaction upon seeing the contingent of reporters was to lash out. "How did you creeps know we were here? I don't want no circus. I swear, I'll knock any guy on his can who tries to get in."

Then he barged into the house, slamming the door. Encountering a written request inside from photographers to pose for pictures, he promptly reopened the door and shouted out, 'Okay, who sent the note? Which one?' He pointed a finger at first one, then another. 'Did you? Did you? You're not going to get any pictures. You'll get shots from the commercial photographer when he gets around to it." When one photographer said he'd like to take his own picture, Frank fixed him with a steely gaze and snarled, "I'll betcha fifty dollars you don't. And another fifty dollars that if you even point your camera at me, I'll knock you on your ear."

That commercial photographer was Irving Haberman, and four of his pictures of the beaming newlyweds would appear in the November 19 issue of *Life* magazine. Pictures of the other guests did not appear. They included Frank's parents; Bappie; Mr. and Mrs. Isaac Levy; Hank Sanicola; Frank's partner, Ben Barton; his conductor, Alex Stordahl, and wife, singer June Hutton; music arranger Dick Jones; and Manie Sachs, vice president of RCA.

Although Manie Sachs was supposed to give the bride away, the bride almost got away from him. Ava was nervous. She had been waiting for this day for a long time, and after the fight the night before, she must have been wondering if something else might occur to interrupt her happiness. She had been drinking a lot of champagne to calm herself. She could hear Dick Jones trying his best with the "Wedding March," but the piano was hopelessly off-key.

Ava was a woman who preferred going barefoot, but now she was wearing satin pumps dyed to match her wedding dress. As she walked down the stairs, gripping tightly Manie's arm, she felt herself slipping, and Manie started to stumble with her. Ava had visions of both of them landing in a heap at the bottom of the stairs—hardly an auspicious way to begin a marriage.

Always a stunning woman, Ava was dazzling on her wedding day. Her dress was designed by Howard Greer, the Paris-trained couturier for such stars as Irene Dunne, Joan Crawford, Ginger Rogers, Rita Hayworth, and Katharine Hepburn. Greer believed in making a woman look sexy; Ava was no exception. The strapless top of her wedding dress was pink taffeta over a high-waisted mauve marquisette cocktail-length skirt. Deferring to modesty, she wore a sheer mauve marquisette bolero edged with the same pink taffeta as the top. Her jewelry consisted of a double-stranded pearl choker and pearl-and-diamond teardrop earrings.

She was so breathtaking that no one could take their eyes off her, certainly not Frank. Wearing a navy suit with a slim light gray tie, a white silk shirt, and a white boutonniere in his left lapel, he waited beside Judge José (Joseph) Sloane of the Common Pleas Court of Germantown, who was to perform the ceremony. Ava handed her white orchid spray to her matron of honor, June Hutton, as she approached the judge.

The ceremony was brief. They exchanged simple, thin platinum bands. Ava, wearing stiletto-heeled shoes, was almost as tall as Frank. They looked into each other's eyes the whole time, mechanically repeating their vows, almost absentmindedly putting the slim, unadorned platinum bands on each other's fingers. So lost were they in their own enchantment that when the judge pronounced them man and wife, they did not move.

"You may kiss your bride, Mr. Sinatra," Judge Sloane said.

It was as though he had not spoken.

"Mr. Sinatra," the judge repeated. "Your bride." He tapped Frank on the shoulder and pointed to Ava. "You may kiss her now."

With an embarrassed grin, Frank put his hands on her shoulders and gently pulled her toward him. His lips brushed her for an instant.

"I love you," she whispered.

"Of course you do," he said with a grin.

She smiled and shook her head at him as if to say, You never cease to amaze me, Francis Albert Sinatra. Then Ava hugged her new in-laws, Dolly and Martin Sinatra.

The guests broke into applause. The champagne corks popped. Mr. and Mrs. Frank Sinatra were about to begin a marriage even more tumultuous and passionate than their courtship.

CHAPTER 14

W e finally did it," Ava Gardner said in a telephone call to her friend Lucille Wellman from the ritzy Hotel Nacional in Cuba, where she and Frank Sinatra were honeymooning for a couple of days. (They had chartered a plane from Philadelphia to Miami, then on to Havana.)

"Congratulations," said her Los Angeles friend. "Are you happy?"

"Well, Frank's a wonderful man. It's just that what it took to get us here has been so exhausting," Ava responded.

"You didn't answer my question," her friend said, pushing.

Ava hesitated. "Well," she began, carefully, "let's just say I'm not *un-happy.*"

"How's the honeymoon going?" Lucille asked.

"Great, considering I paid for the whole goddamn thing," Ava said.

The marriage was off to a rocky start, Ava told Lucille. Frank's wedding gift to his wife was a sapphire blue mink cape stole. She presented him with an expensive gold locket with a St. Francis medal on one side, a St. Christopher on the other, and a photograph of her as well. But the battles continued to rage.

"We've already had fifteen fights—and that's just today," she said, only half-joking. "He's under a lot of pressure. I'm just not the patient, understanding type. You know that. I mean, I *try* to be," she added. "But that's just not me."

Fifteen minutes after she hung up, Ava called her friend back. "Listen," she said, "I know I can trust you, but don't ever, ever, mention to anyone that I paid for the honeymoon. Frank would kill me. So promise me."

"I promise," her friend vowed. (In fact, Lucille Wellman would keep that promise for forty-three years.)

The year 1952 saw thirty-six-year-old Frank Sinatra's professional downward slide continue. Frank's old-style recordings—lush arrangements of songs with romantic lyrics—simply weren't working anymore. In 1952 he would record only four sides for Columbia, three of which he cut on January 7: "I Hear a Rhapsody," "I Could Write a Book," and "Walkin' in the Sunshine." Later in the month, he appeared as a guest on the *Martin and Lewis Show.*

Meanwhile, the year just limped along: Frank's film *Meet Danny Wilson* was released on February 8, 1952, to mediocre reviews; he returned to the Paramount Theater in New York on March 26 for an engagement with Frank Fontane, Buddy Rich, and June Hutton, but the bobby-soxers who had once adored him there had grown up, and the engagement was a box-office disaster. When he performed at the Chez Paree in Chicago, only 150 people were seated in the nightclub, which seated twelve hundred. Ava, who was with Frank, tried to keep his spirits up, but he was angry.

In April the two were seen at Johnnie Ray's opening at the Copa. Frank was annoyed that the audience's reaction to Ray was much more enthusiastic than it had been for him a month earlier at the Paramount. When asked what he thought of Ray's performance, he told Earl Wilson, "I'd love to tell you, but my wife won't let me."

"I'm really washed up," he later told Ava in front of another writer, who scribbled down their whole conversation on a notepad. "I oughta just face it. The public is finished with me. I had my time. I had my day in the sun."

"Over my dead body," she said. "No one with your talent is ever washed up. This is just a bad time. Trust me. I happen to specialize in good luck," she added. "Rub my ass. It'll give you good luck, too."

Frank forced a halfhearted smile, then softly rubbed Ava's derriere.

"You know that I love you, don't you?" he told her.

"Of course you do," she said.

However, despite any moral support he may have received from Ava, there were still struggles ahead for Sinatra. In June 1952 he was officially dropped by Columbia Records as well as by his talent agency, MCA. With his movies and records doing so poorly, it was not a surprise. Making matters worse for Frank's ego, though, was that Ava's career was flourishing. M-G-M was about to offer her a ten-year contract for twelve movies at $100,000 per film. However, she wasn't completely selfish; she wanted to assist her husband, if at all possible. In fact, in an attempt to help him, she had a "Frank Sinatra clause" written into her studio contract which said, basically, that if the studio made a film she was planning called *St. Louis Woman*, it would "agree that we will employ Frank Sinatra to appear" in it. If that film was not made, "we agree at some time prior to the expiration of her contract, we will do a picture in which Frank Sinatra would appear."

Riding on his wife's coattails in such a blatant manner was the ultimate humiliation for Frank Sinatra. He had never been so low. Frank and Ava argued bitterly whenever she ventured an opinion about the state of his affairs; she felt that he had alienated the powerful press by his treatment of the media over the years and that his own behavior was largely responsible for the problems he was now experiencing. "And the fact that you've been a jerk to so many other people hasn't helped, either," she told him. "Fine," Frank said. "Kick me when I'm down, why don't ya?" She was only trying to be helpful, but in truth there wasn't much she could do.

Meanwhile, much to Frank's dismay, Ava began work on a new film for 20th Century–Fox, *The Snows of Kilimanjaro*, the story of a mortally wounded big-game hunter who, in a camp at the base of Mount Kilimanjaro, recalls the story of his life. Ernest Hemingway, author of the original story, had personally asked Darryl Zanuck to cast Ava in the role of the lost twenties girl Cynthia, with whom the game hunter (Gregory Peck) is in love. (M-G-M had lent Ava to Fox for this film.)

Screen writer Casey Robinson (whose credits had included *Now, Voyager* and *Dark Victory*) recalled, "I asked her if she wanted to play it [the role]. She said, 'I'm interested, very interested.' She paused and walked away. 'But I have a problem, a very great problem. My husband doesn't want me to play it. Frankie's against it.''

Ava explained to Robinson that Frank was so depressed about his life, he felt that he needed her to accompany him to New York, where he had a few nightclub engagements. "His agents were having difficulty booking him into top nightspots," she recalled, "and he was having to play saloons and dates that were way beneath him, and feeling that way, it was really important to him that his wife be by his side." Robinson conferred with the film's director (Henry King) and decided to propose that they shoot all of Ava's part on the 20th Century–Fox back lot in just ten days.

However, he never let Ava alone to do her work. He called her every day on the set, recalled Robinson, "making her life pretty darn miserable. I hated the little bastard." Because of unforeseen scheduling problems, it was decided that the production team had no choice: It would have to exceed the ten-day limit by just one day. When King and Robinson reluctantly told Ava what was about to occur, she became hysterical. She knew how Frank would respond, and she was right: He was furious with her when she telephoned him with the news. They had another terrible fight, and he hung up on her. She was so angry, she could hardly work. "God knows how we got through that last day," said Robinson. "But it was the right role for her, and it launched her as a very great international star."

Ava was now a star, and it appeared that Frank's career was over. What was he to do? He needed a vehicle. Sinatra had been in the movie business long enough to realize that often an artist has to secure his own property—whether a record deal or a film contract—and then exploit it for all it's worth. While logic had told most people that Frank's time was over, he knew that all he needed was a break. However, no one was handing Frank Sinatra anything at this time. Thus, if he were to be saved, he'd have to do it himself. Either he could sit at home and lament the fact that his wife was a major film star and he was not, or he could finally do something about it.

"I was a has-been," he remembered, "wondering what happened to all the friends who grew invisible when the music stopped, finding out fast how tough it is to borrow money when you're all washed up. My only collateral was a dream. A dream to end my nightmare. And what a dream it was. It began when I read an absolutely fascinating book written by a giant, James Jones. More than a book," he said, "it was a portrait of people I knew, understood, and could feel, and in it I saw myself as clearly as I see myself every morning when I shave."

Sinatra was referring to James Jones's first novel, the bestselling *From Here to Eternity*, which had been published in 1951. Jones's 430,000-word, 850-page book had not only been critically acclaimed, it also was considered revolutionary because of its strong criticism of the U.S. Army. Jones's story is based on his own experiences in the infantry just before Pearl Harbor. In it, the lead character, Robert E. Lee Prewitt, a boxer in civilian life, leaves the ring after blinding an opponent. He joins the army. Because of his previous experience as a fighter, his commanding officer wants him to go back into the ring and fight for the coveted division championship. Prewitt refuses, and as a result is subjected to "the treatment"—a brutal combination of mental and physical abuse. The only man to stand by him is Pvt. Angelo Maggio, streetwise and cocky. However, because he is considered a disciplinary problem (and also because of his loyalty to Prewitt), Maggio is eventually thrown into the stockade. Toward the end of the story, he is beaten to death by Fatso Judson, the sadistic sergeant in charge of the stockade. Then, driven to a murderous rage, Prewitt kills Judson in a knife fight and escapes to be with his prostitute-girlfriend. When the Japanese attack on December 7, 1941, he tries to return to his company. As he nears the base, he is killed by an MP.

The novel won the prestigious National Book Award for fiction and was on the top of the bestseller list for months. But it would prove to be an enormous challenge to write a screenplay based on this work. The novel is over 800 pages long, its language strong and graphic. At a time when all films had to adhere to the Production Code, which oversaw movie morality, it would also be hard to work around the fact that the two main women characters in the book were a prostitute and a captain's wife who commits adultery with many enlisted men. Finally, with its brutal portrayal of the plight of enlisted men, *From Here to Eternity* presented the army in an unfavorable light at a time when most Americans did not question their government. In the 1940s and 1950s it was virtually impos-

145

sible to produce a military film without help from the Pentagon. Military equipment was too expensive to duplicate; the only way to use authentic government matériel was to cooperate with the government.

Two studios had considered and turned the book down before Harry Cohn of Columbia Studios bought it in 1951. Screenwriter Daniel Taradash managed to compress the material into a 161-page working script while being true to the novel's themes. The film's producer, Buddy Adler, a former lieutenant colonel in the Signal Corps and husband of blond film star Anita Louise, was assigned to deal with the army's many objections. By toning down some of the brutality, Adler was able to obtain their cooperation.

When Sinatra heard that the novel was being made into a film by Columbia, he knew that he was perfect for the character of Angelo Maggio, the scrappy Italian-American soldier from the streets of Brooklyn. This part would give him a dramatic break from the musicals in which he'd previously appeared, and he felt strongly that the role would revitalize his career.

"I know if I can get this part, I can hit a home run," he told Ava. "I grew up with a hundred Maggios in my neighborhood. I *am* Maggio."

Montgomery Clift had been cast in the coveted role of Prewitt, the unregimented Regular Army soldier. Joan Crawford would have been the commanding officer's wife, Karen Holmes, had she not insisted on having her own wardrobe designers. She was replaced by Deborah Kerr, who worked hard with a voice coach to lose her British accent. Other major roles were assigned to Burt Lancaster, as Warden, the first sergeant who manages his company with saintly dedication while having an affair with Kerr's character, and Donna Reed, as Alma, Prewitt's girlfriend. (Ernest Borgnine would also appear in the film as the cruel Fatso Judson, the man who kills Maggio. Borgnine was such a fan of Sinatra's—"my idol, my everything,"—that he actually had named his daughter "Nancy" after Frank's song.) Still to be cast was Maggio.

Ava, wanting to be of assistance, offered to use any influence she might have to persuade Harry Cohn to cast her husband in the film. However, Frank wanted her to stay out of it. If he was to get this part, he told her, it would be on his own and by his own merit. In actuality, though, he had recruited practically everyone he knew who also knew Harry Cohn to bombard Cohn with requests that he consider Sinatra for this part. He also sent telegrams to Cohn and to the film's director, Fred Zinnemann, signed "Maggio."

Ava felt that if her husband had this role, perhaps it would take some strain off their marriage. So she defied Frank's orders—a course of action which had, by now, come naturally to her—and met with Cohn's wife, Joan, to see what she could do to secure the role for her out-of-work

146

husband. "Just have him test Frank," she asked Joan. "Please. He really needs this role."

However, Sinatra had already met with Cohn over lunch about this particular job, and Cohn had made it clear that he was not interested, even when Frank offered to do the role for a thousand dollars a week, which was a big reduction in fee, since he had previously been paid as much as $150,000 per film. "You're out of your fucking mind," he told Frank. As far as Cohn was concerned, Frank Sinatra was a singer, not an actor. In fact, he told Frank that he didn't think he had ever made a good movie. (It must have been difficult for Sinatra to hold his temper, but he probably knew he had to do just that if he wanted the part.)

Meanwhile, Ava continued politicking for Frank. A friend of hers, Paul Clemens, who lived in a guest house on the estate of Harry and Joan Cohn, invited Ava for dinner with the Cohns. Over dinner, Ava started in on Harry Cohn. "You know who's right for that part of Maggio, don't you?" she said. "That son-of-a-bitch husband of mine, that's who. Let me tell you something," she said, according to Earl Wilson. "If you don't give him this role, he'll kill himself." She wasn't kidding.

Eventually, Harry Cohn and the film's director, Fred Zinnemann (*High Noon* and *The Member of the Wedding*), began to buckle under so much pressure. Cohn telephoned Sinatra and said he might screen-test him for the role, and if he decided to do so, he'd be back in touch. Meanwhile, he asked Frank to "call off the dogs, and Ava, too."

Now it would just be a matter of time before a decision would be made.

On September 17, 1952, Frank recorded his last side for Columbia Records in New York, "Why Try to Change Me Now?" Composed by Cy Coleman and arranged by Percy Faith, this pensive song was another that spoke to the essence of Frank's emotions at this time. Ed O'Brien and Robert Wilson said it best in their book *Sinatra 101—The 101 Best Recordings and the Stories Behind Them*: "Gone was the innocent, naive singer of the previous decade. Burned by love, the singer is able to convey the darkness, the sadness, and the cynicism that would characterize much of his work in the years to come." Like "I'm a Fool to Want You," this song is another obscure Sinatra song that didn't mean much to anyone (except for writer, producer, and artist) at the time, but like a fine wine that ages well, as the years have gone by, it has become a true gem. (He would record the song again for Capitol in March 1959.)

Meanwhile, the "Battling Sinatras," as some members of the press had dubbed them, continued with their tumultuous marriage. While the Sinatra-Ava bouts had become, by 1952, the stuff of show-business legend, one in particular is still talked about today among Sinatra fans.

The battle started in October 1952, just before Ava left for Africa to film her movie *Mogambo*. Frank and Ava, at their home in Los Angeles, had a loud conflict about something that had occurred earlier over dinner with friends.

Later, Ava soaked in a luxurious bubble bath while drinking a vodka gimlet. She was trying to collect herself. However, Frank broke the sanctity of her private moment by bursting in on her in the bathroom. "And one more thing . . . ," he began, trying to continue the fight.

Ava became indignant. She hated to be seen with her clothes off. (In fact, Ava once said that with each of her three husbands, "it took me several drinks and a lot of courage to appear disrobed in front of them. And I hate intrusions when I have my clothes off.")

"Get out! Get out!" she shrieked. Frank angrily left, but not before delivering a classic parting shot: "Okay, fine, then. If that's the way you want it. I'm leaving. And if you wanna know where I am, *I'm in Palm Springs fucking Lana Turner.*"

Ava had to laugh. She knew a great line when she heard one, and seldom had she heard one better.

However, when the new Mrs. Sinatra began pondering the notion that her husband may have been serious and then remembered that Lana was, in fact, at the Sinatra home in Palm Springs (borrowing the residence at 1147 Alejo and staying there with her manager, Ben Cole), she became concerned. She telephoned her sister, Bappie, and convinced her that the two of them should go to Palm Springs and "catch Frank in the act."

So the Gardner sisters made the drive from Los Angeles to Palm Springs and arrived in the middle of the night to find Lana and Ben relaxing, Bloody Marys in hand. Frank was nowhere to be found.

Lana had had her cook prepare a roasting pan filled with fried chicken, spare ribs, and "the most delightful little Cobb salad you've ever seen." So the four of them—Lana, Ben, Ava, and Bappie—enjoyed a sumptuous candlelit meal. Then the drinks started flowing once again. Soon they were in a giddy, vodka-induced haze. Or as Lana's and Ava's good friend Esther Williams put it, "Drinking, drinking, and drinking and smoking, smoking, and smoking and laughing and having a wonderful time because they were so goddamn young and so goddamn gorgeous."

Suddenly, in walked—or rather, burst—Frank Sinatra. According to one of Ava's friends, Frank entered just in time to hear Ava say, "Oh, *please.* Let me tell you, he is the biggest goddamn womanizer in the world."

Of course, Frank, perhaps allowing his guilty conscience to get the best of him, assumed that he was the subject of their discussion. (Actually, as it was later learned, they weren't even talking about Frank. Lana was infatuated with actor Fernando Lamas, and Ava was trying to convince her that *he* was a philanderer, not Frank.")

"*Aaaaah,* Frank!" Ava said when she saw him. Her voice was slurred, and her common sense had clearly deserted her. "I thought you were going to be down here . . . *fucking Lana.*"

"Oh, yeah? Give me a break," Frank shot back. "I wouldn't touch that broad if you paid me."

He was so incensed, Ava would later remember, because it appeared that his ex-girlfriend and his wife were having "a fine old time," boozing it up at his home, drinking his best vodka, and probably—he decided— "cutting me up behind my back."

Poor Lana—ordinarily a tough-skinned woman but now suddenly a delicate flower—ran off in tears, her feelings hurt by Frank's words. ("Believe me, she'd had worse things said about her in Hollywood," a friend of hers later noted.)

"Now look at what you've done to Lana," Ava said. "You made her cry, you fucking brute."

"Out of my house," Frank screamed. "Out! Out! All of you."

From there the fight between Frank and Ava escalated until the two of them began throwing all of Ava's belongings—clothes, cosmetics, books, records, "and every other goddamn odd and end I had," she recalled— out of the house and into the driveway. They had caused such an uproar that the neighbors summoned the police. Once Ava was out of the house, Frank ran upstairs to the bathroom, found a douche bag, filled it with water, then ran down and back outside. He then poured the cold water over Ava's head and said, "Have a good time in Africa, bitch."

Police officers arrived to find Frank with both his hands around Ava's waist, trying to pry her off a doorknob so he could throw her back out of the house after she had tried to reenter to fetch a towel.

The next day, the brouhaha was in all the newspapers; "Frankie Throws Ava Out" trumpeted the *New York Post.* Ava was finished with Frank, she said. "It's over."

Frank was desolated by the whole incident, and after spending the night in the bathroom throwing up (a side effect of the vaccinations he had been taking in order to accompany Ava to Africa), he talked to writer Earl Wilson and begged him to print an apology in his New York column. Wilson did, in an article entitled "Frank Ready to Surrender; Wants Ava Back, Any Terms."*

Mack Miller, one of the publicists who had replaced George Evans, had also inherited all of Evans's problems with Sinatra and Gardner. "I told Frank that if he didn't stop fighting with Ava and the press, I'd have to give him up," Miller said. "I told him he wasn't worth what he was paying

---

* The Palm Springs fight fueled rumors that Frank had actually found Ava and Lana being intimate with one another at his home, a story that was oft repeated in fan magazines and other Sinatra biographies over the years. It would seem, however, that there is no truth to this tale.

if this kind of thing continued. What pleased me to no end is that Ava backed me up one hundred percent. She told Frank he'd have to straighten out."

Stewart Granger, costar with Ava in *Bhowani Junction* (in 1956), once recalled: "Ava invited us to go to the Ambassador Hotel, where Frank was singing. We went to pick them up and there were screams and shouts and things banging against things, and out came Ava saying, 'I'm not going anywhere with that son of a bitch.' So Frank took off in a rush and went ahead without us, and then we followed. And the whole time in the car, she was saying, 'He's impossible, that stupid son of a bitch. And he's not that great a singer, anyway.' Finally, we arrived at the Ambassador and on came Frank, and he started to sing. He sang right to her. And floods of tears just came from Ava. I turned to her and said, 'I thought you said you hated him.' And she said, 'Oh, no, he's wonderful,' with the tears pouring down her face. 'Look at him,' she said, crying. 'Just look at him.' Crazy. They adored each other."

On November 7, 1952, Frank and Ava left for Africa, where Ava was scheduled to film *Mogambo*.* Frank wasn't keen on the idea of his wife going to Africa with Clark Gable—her costar in the film, along with Grace Kelly—and since he really had nothing else to do—he still hadn't heard whether or not he would be able to audition for the role of Maggio in *From Here to Eternity*—he decided to accompany her.

"He's going with me," Ava told the press of her husband. "He's going to do some theaters around Nairobi. . . ." As if Sinatra hadn't sunk as low as he could in the public's eye, now his wife had it that he was to play "some theaters around Nairobi."

The Sinatras celebrated their first wedding anniversary en route to Africa on a Stratocruiser. (Frank gave Ava a beautiful diamond ring, which he charged to her account.) While in Nairobi, he spent his time reading books while Ava worked.

"Frank was her little helper," said Joseph Godfrey, employed on the film as a costume assistant to designer Helen Rose. "It was sad. She was a slave driver, to be honest. Sometimes you just wanted to smack her. But, my god, she was so young and beautiful, she could get away with any behavior."

"Get me a drink, baby, will ya?" pampered Ava would ask when she was done with a shot. "A Manhattan, straight up with a cherry, sure sounds good right about now.

---

* Lana Turner was originally offered the role of Eloise "Honey Bear" Kelly, stranded in an African jungle compound with Vic Marswell, played by Clark Gable. It went to Ava when Lana declined.

"And rub my back, won't you?

"And fetch my script, huh, sweetie?"

Frank, his face an expressionless mask, would say, "Sure, why not?" Could he sink any lower? He was depressed and low-key. Nearly everyone noticed that he was hardly the tough guy the press had been writing about for years. Rather, he seemed quiet, defeated.

On tough days, Ava wanted five different kinds of sherbet—blackberry, raspberry, lime, cherry, and orange—as a treat. She liked them served in pretty oval scoops on a white plate, and with tiny wild strawberries, if possible. ("But if you can't get the strawberries, then I guess I'll just have to live without them.")

"Do you know how hard it is to find *sherbet* in this goddamn jungle?" Frank wanted to know.

"Oh, I know, Frank," she said wearily. "Just call someone in London and have it shipped in. And see if you can get those dainty little butter cookies, too. I just love those."

"All right. All right."

"He needed a lift," recalled Bea Lowry, makeup artist Colin Garde's assistant on the film. "I know Miss Gardner was concerned. She called Harry Cohn from Nairobi. I heard the conversation myself. She was angry with him, and she said, 'Jesus Christ, you know Frank is right for this part. Please, I am begging you. Give him this role. He can't take it anymore. *I* can't take it anymore.' I believe he hung up on her because she slammed the phone down onto the receiver and said to me, 'Bea, remind me to hate that man as soon as I have a free minute. Right now, I am *much* too busy.' "

Little said that Gardner then fixed her with an imperious look and added, "That man should be worshiping at my throne. How *dare* he hang up on me." Then she broke out in robust laughter.

The weather was sweltering hot, the daytime temperature as high as 130 degrees, and Ava was unhappy for most of the shoot. She hated sleeping in a tent with mosquitoes swarming everywhere and ants crawling up her legs; she was sick to her stomach most of the time and felt woefully inadequate as an actress working opposite the legendary Gable. Because she was under such stress, she just wanted the filming to end. Moreover, Ava didn't get along with the film's director, John Ford (*The Grapes of Wrath; Tobacco Road*); in fact, she embarrassed him when he introduced her to the British governor and his wife. But he deserved it. "Ava, why don't you tell the governor what you see in this one-hundred-twenty-pound runt you're married to," he said. "Well," Ava responded, "there's only ten pounds of Frank, but there's one hundred and ten pounds of cock."

Making matters worse, she discovered while in Africa that she was pregnant.

151

Previously, in November 1951, Ava gave an interview to Marie Torre of the *New York World Telegram and Sun* and expressed her desire to have children. "Maybe we'll start thinking about a family," she said. "I love large families. When I was younger, I used to think about how wonderful it would be to have four sons. I'm twenty-eight now. It's too late for such a large family. So I think I can be happy with two, maybe three, kids."

However, she had apparently changed her mind.

Ava would write in her autobiography many years later that she hadn't told Frank about the pregnancy. Even Nancy Sinatra's authorized biography of her father notes that Frank was not aware of it. But many of Ava's close friends insist that she did, in fact, tell him she was pregnant while they were in Africa and that the baby was a point of contention between the couple.

Frank was elated about the baby. Ava, however, was not. She had no maternal instincts whatsoever, even though she often tried to convince herself otherwise. Frank suggested that she quit work on the film for the sake of the pregnancy but his pleas fell on deaf ears. During one fight, he decided that the unspoken issue between them was actually that Ava, as a rising star, was embarrassed to be carrying the child of a "has-been."

However, that was not the case. As Ava wrote in her autobiography, "I felt that unless you were prepared to devote practically all your time to your child in its early years, it was unfair to the baby. If a child is unwanted—and somehow they know that—it is handicapped from the time it is born." Moreover, M-G-M had a penalty clause in her contract that said that her salary would be cut off if she had a baby. She was the breadwinner in that family, she reasoned. Without her income, what would they do?

Before they were able to reach a decision about the baby, however, Frank received a telegram from his new agent, Burt Allenberg, of the William Morris Agency, telling him that Cohn had agreed to screen-test him for *From Here to Eternity*. What might have been a jubilant moment for the couple was ruined, however, by the fact that Ava clearly did not want to have his child. He had to leave on the next plane back to the States and hoped that they would be able to work matters out between them when the filming was completed. Then, as if to lower Frank's morale even further, his financial circumstances forced him to ask Ava to pay for the plane ticket back to the States. He was just that broke.

Standing there before her, his head lowered, Frank Sinatra had to agree to Ava Gardner's suggestion that he charge his ticket to her studio account. It was as if the gods, showing a complete absence of mercy, had somehow plotted to ruin Frank Sinatra's life, strip him of all of his pride, and leave him with nothing but degradation.

By the time he left Africa, Sinatra was practically a broken man. However, he still had whatever it is that makes a man believe that he has a chance if he can just catch that one lucky break. When Frank Sinatra arrived in Hollywood, California, he was ready for his close-up and for that one chance.

Ava had mixed feelings about Frank's opportunity to appear in *From Here to Eternity*. Another friend of hers, actress Nancy LaPierre, who had known Ava since their early days together in New York, explained: "On the one hand, she had worked for this behind the scenes and wanted Frank to get the role. But she also realized that he was so perfect for it, he would get it. Then, when he didn't need her, when he was back on top, what would that do for their marriage? She knew that he wouldn't put up with her if he wasn't so down and out. She had the whole thing played out in her mind already, and she knew that their marriage would not survive his imminent success. So she made a decision about the baby, and her mind was made up. She wanted to have an abortion."

The film's director, John Ford, tried to talk her out of aborting the baby. "Ava, you are married to a Catholic, and this is going to hurt Frank tremendously when he finds out. I'll protect you if the fact that you're having a baby starts to show," he told her. "I'll arrange the scenes; I'll arrange the shots. We'll wrap your part up as quickly as we can. Nothing will show. Please go ahead and have the child."

She cast him a withering look and said, "No, this is not the time. I'm not ready."

Ford capitulated and, along with some M-G-M higher-ups, arranged for his star to go to London for the procedure on November 23, 1952. Ava left Africa with her publicist and the wife of cameraman Robert Surtees at her side and checked into the Savoy Hotel. From there, she went to a private nursing home, where she had the abortion. Afterward, she gave an interview to a reporter for *Look* magazine to discuss her ideal marriage to Frank. That reporter only revealed to his closest friends that he did the interview with Gardner while sitting on the edge of her bed in the abortion clinic. (In the article, he said she had dysentery.)

Meanwhile, Frank Sinatra's screen test had gone well. In fact, when the film's producer, Buddy Adler, who originally did not want Frank in the film, gave him the script for the scenes he was to play, Frank handed it back to him and said he already knew it. He had memorized it, having read it so many times. He was ready. During the test, Frank improvised the saloon scene in which Maggio shakes dice and then casts them across a pool table. Frank used olives instead of dice. "That one scene, that one moment of ingenuity, won him the role as far as I was concerned," said Fred Zinnemann a couple of years before his death in March 1997. But that one gimmick wasn't all there was to Frank's performance. In fact, according to all accounts, it was a commanding audition in every sense, part realistic, part theatrical, filled with as many showy gestures and as much real artistry as an actor can squeeze into fifteen minutes. As written, the role was dark and intense, and Sinatra, a desperate actor and even more desperate man, gave it all he had.

Buddy Adler recalled: "I didn't think he had a chance [of getting the role] and didn't even go down to the soundstage for the test. But I got a call from Fred Zinnemann, telling me, 'You'd better come down here; you'll see something unbelievable; I already have it in the camera. I'm not using film this time. But I want you to see it. Frank thought he was making another take, and he was terrific. I thought to myself, If he's like that in the movie, it's a sure Academy Award.'"

There was nothing left to do now but to wait for a decision.

Meanwhile, Frank was told that Ava had collapsed and had been sent to a hospital in London. In a prepared statement, her publicist announced that she had a tropical infection and was suffering from anemia. Concerned, Frank telephoned her at the Savoy, and she assured him that she was fine, as was the baby.

According to her friends, when Frank got back to Africa at Christmastime, Ava finally confessed to him the real reason she had been in the hospital. "I was pregnant, and now I'm not, and I'm glad," she told him.

At first, Frank thought that she had suffered a miscarriage. When he learned that she had had an abortion, he couldn't believe it. He demanded to know how she could have done such a thing. She refused, though, to allow him to make her feel guilty about her decision. It was *her* baby, *her* body, *her* choice, she told him. According to all accounts, this news was more than Frank Sinatra could bear. That the woman he loved more than anything in the world would betray him like this—would abort his child, and without even first giving him the opportunity to change her mind—broke his heart. Ava, however, had no time to pick up the pieces. She was dressed and on her way out when her husband had arrived so suddenly, and she intended to go to a party either with him or without him.

"Stay with me," he begged her. "I need you now more than ever."

Either Ava couldn't bear to discuss with Frank what she had done or simply wasn't interested in doing so and thereby becoming locked in the same old quarrels, because as she later told friends, she left him behind with tears in his eyes.

On the way out, as Ava once remembered it, she paused for a moment and reconsidered what she was doing to the man she loved. Then she looked at Sinatra and said, 'Don't hate me, Frank. Just don't hate me. I couldn't take that."

"Too late," Frank said sadly. "Too goddamn late."

154

CHAPTER 15

By December 25, 1952, Frank Sinatra and Ava Gardner had apparently reconciled enough to celebrate her thirtieth birthday, and Christmas, in Africa.

It would seem that few people on the set of *Mogambo* knew of the trouble between Frank Sinatra and Ava Gardner at the time. Privately, a wedge had developed between them as a result of Ava's having terminated her pregnancy. "It was never the same after that," Hank Sanicola once said. "He never got over it. He never discussed it, either. The only thing he ever said to me about it was 'I shoulda beaten her fuckin' brains out for what she did to me and the baby, but I loved her too much. Any other dame, I swear to Christ, she would be dead now.' That was his Sicilian pride speaking. It was tough for him to think she did it her way instead of his.

"For years, it was just assumed by everyone, even his family, that Frank didn't know about that baby," said Sinatra's friend. "Then, when Ava's memoirs came out in the early 1990s, and even *she* wrote that he didn't know, that beefed up the line of thought that she had done it all without his knowledge. He *did* know, though. And it ate him up. It killed him inside."

The question remains: Why would Ava write in her memoirs that Frank was in the dark about the pregnancy and the abortion if that was not the case?

"Perhaps she was so embarrassed by what she had done," Lucille Wellman speculated, "that she wanted it to at least appear that she had not discussed it with him, that it was a decision she made on her own. I guess she felt that the truth—that he knew she was pregnant and she had the abortion behind his back—was somehow worse. I don't pretend to understand this logic. Then, to confuse things even more, she made up *another* story, and it's become part of Sinatra history, that she got pregnant *again* within a month. This time, she wrote in her book, she told Frank about it and that she went ahead and had another abortion he was opposed to. As far as I know, this did not happen. I don't know what that was all about for her, why she wrote that."

Ava wrote in her memoirs: "The silliest, stupidest and most natural thing happened: I got pregnant again. This time, Frank did know, and he was delighted. Yet, despite Frank's feelings, I reached the same decision about my second pregnancy as I had my first." Ava wrote that she decided to have another abortion, without telling Frank, but that this time he found out about it—though too late—and was at the nursing home in Wimbledon when she awakened after the procedure. "As long as I live, I'll never forget waking up after the operation and seeing Frank sitting next to my bed with tears in his eyes," she wrote. "But I think I was right. I still think I was right."

Even Nancy Sinatra, in her authorized biography of her father, repeated Ava's story. But it seems that most people who knew Ava back then, and Frank Sinatra as well, agree that she was never pregnant a second time.

"What the hell was that lie all about?" said one of Frank's closest friends, a relative who would speak only if given anonymity. "Frank told me specifically that she was pregnant once and only once. So we don't know what she was talking about in her book. 'Musta been some other pregnancy and some other guy named Frank at Wimbledon,' Frank told me when the book came out, ' 'cause it wasn't me.' "

Ava's friends don't know what Ava's motivation was when she wrote about a second pregnancy in her book, however they doubt that it ever happened. Indeed, how could it have? The timing makes no sense. The first pregnancy was terminated at the end of November. Then she was pregnant again, knew about it, and had another abortion within a month? Impossible.*

By the end of the year, Frank Sinatra was certain that another actor, his friend Eli Wallach, had gotten the role he so wanted in *From Here to Eternity*. "When I heard that Eli Wallach had tested for it, I said, 'Forget it,' " Sinatra remembered. "He's a seasoned actor and a fine, fine performer." But then "I got the call," he said. "They decided that I had the part [at a salary of just one thousand dollars a week]. "I woulda done it for nothing," Frank said, "because it was something I really understood."

"I'll show them bastards," Frank said excitedly after he hung up with the studio. "They'll be glad they finally cast me. This role is *mine*."

There are four versions of how Sinatra won the part over Eli Wallach. One is that Wallach asked for too high a salary. The second is that Wallach turned down the part because he had a prior commitment to a Broadway play. The third—and probably the most accurate—is that Sinatra had been right for the part: physically, ethnically, and emotionally he

*When interviewed for this work, Ava's manager, Jess Morgan, said that Gardner's memoirs, published after her 1990 death, were based on her notes, tapes, and rough drafts. It's possible, then, that a mistake was made in the editing, given the fact that Ava was not able to check her book for accuracy.

was Maggio. It showed up on the test. Both Cohn and Zinnemann had recognized it immediately. Then there's the fourth—and the most popular—belief: that the mob somehow helped Frank get the role. Many people believe that the underworld gave Frank a helping hand in putting his career back on track.

So widespread was this belief—really one of the enduring rumors about Frank Sinatra—that when Mario Puzo's book *The Godfather* was published in 1969 (and later made into a movie), most people were certain that the character of down-on-his-luck singer Johnny Fontane was inspired by Frank Sinatra. It's easy to see why.

In Puzo's story, singer Fontane is Don Vito Corleone's beloved godson. However, the two men hadn't seen each other for two years; Corleone was angry because Fontane had left his wife and children for a sensational actress who treated him badly. When Fontane shows up to sing at Corleone's daughter's wedding, the two men reconcile, and Johnny shares his problems with the older man. He's sorry, he says, that he left his first wife. He misses his children, and his second marriage is hell. His voice is shot; he's finished as a singer. Now he wants a particular acting role desperately, a part he thinks is made for him and will be his comeback, one he has no hope of getting because Jack Woltz, the head of the studio, hates him.

Don Corleone tells Johnny to stay with him for a month; at the end of that time, he will have the part. Fontane is dubious; Woltz is close to J. Edgar Hoover, head of the FBI. There's no way Corleone can get to him.

"He's a businessman," Corleone replies. "I'll make him an offer he can't refuse."

Corleone sends Tom Hagen, his consigliere, to Hollywood to meet with Woltz. Woltz listens and refuses to give the role to Fontane. He will do anything he can to hurt Fontane's career because Fontane had an affair with his girlfriend. Woltz is very possessive of what is important to him: his girlfriend, his studio, his films, his ostentatious way of life, and especially his latest acquisition: a $600,000 racehorse which he says he will use for breeding.

When Hagen returns to New York, Corleone is not surprised at Woltz's refusal. He has his own ways of dealing with people who do not do his bidding. Several days later, Jack Woltz awakens to find the severed head of his prize horse at the foot of his bed. That afternoon, Johnny Fontane gets a call from the producer to report for filming the next Monday. The coveted part is his, and he will later win an Oscar for a stellar performance.

When *The Godfather* was published—it stayed on the bestseller list for sixty-seven weeks—the public immediately saw that very many aspects of the Fontane character mirrored Sinatra's life: his temper, his marital history, his connection with the underworld, his desire for the role after

157

his singing career was in trouble, and his winning the Oscar for it. They assumed that he got the role of Maggio through the Mafia.

Did Sinatra sleep with Cohn's girlfriend? Sinatra's prowess with women was well known. Women threw themselves at him whether he was married or single; they apparently made him offers *he* couldn't refuse. It's possible, but certainly not documented, that he and Cohn shared the same woman.

One fact is generally acknowledged, however: Cohn never owned a racehorse.

Mario Puzo, who hadn't known a real gangster when he wrote the book, which was originally called "Mafia," confirmed that the horse's head was complete fiction. He said that he had thought up the idea based on Sicilian folklore that a man's favorite animal is killed by his enemy and hung up as a warning. (In the film, they used a real horse's head, from a rendering plant in New Jersey.) In fact, Puzo and everyone connected with the picture—the first to ever take in a million dollars a day—steadfastly denied any story-line connection to Frank's Sinatra's life and career. (Still, as Dean Martin once said with a gleam in his eye, "One never knows, do one.")

Frank was annoyed by Mario Puzo's work. After hearing about the Fontane character, he had his attorneys demand that Puzo allow him to read the manuscript prior to publication. Puzo refused. After the book was published, Sinatra was enraged by the similarities to his own life.

"The public doesn't know the difference," Frank told one of his attorneys. "They think this is me."

"It practically *is* you Frank," suggested the attorney. " 'cept for the mob stuff, I mean."

Frank glared at the attorney.

"This joker is making a fortune off a bastardized version of my life story," he complained, "and I think we should sue him for every fuckin' penny he's got." When told he would never prevail in a lawsuit against Puzo, Sinatra seethed. "Look, if I ever see this guy, I'll make sure he knows you can't just steal a man's life and make money from it."

Frank almost had that opportunity at Elaine's in New York after the book was published. Puzo was at a table; Frank was at the bar. The owner, Elaine, asked Puzo if he wanted to meet Sinatra. Puzo said that he would; he was a big fan. Frank, perhaps trying to avoid a scene as much as he may have wanted to have one, said, "Not interested."

A year later, while Puzo was working on the script of the movie, he was at a private birthday party at Chasen's in Beverly Hills. Frank was also present in the restaurant, seated at a table eating dinner. The host of the party dragged an apprehensive Puzo to Sinatra's table and, intruding on Sinatra's meal with his close friend Jilly Rizzo and some acquaintances, said, "I'd like you to meet my good friend Mario Puzo."

"I don't think so," Frank said, not looking up from his marinated trout.

"Listen, it wasn't my idea," an embarrassed Puzo said apologetically as he left the table.

Mario Puzo meant that it had not been his idea to intrude on Frank Sinatra's dinner. Frank thought that Puzo meant it had not been his idea to write the character of Johnny Fontane in *The Godfather*.

"I thought Frank was gonna kill him," Rizzo recalled later.

"Time has mercifully dimmed the humiliation of what followed," Puzo recalled. "Sinatra started to shout abuse. I remember that, contrary to his reputation, he did not use foul language at all. The worst thing he called me was a pimp. He said that if it wasn't that I was so much older than he, he would beat the hell out of me. [Puzo is five years younger than Sinatra.] Sinatra kept up his abuse, and I kept staring at him. He kept staring down at his plate, yelling. He never looked up."

Finally, a humiliated Puzo walked away from the table and out of the restaurant. The last thing he remembers of that evening is Frank shouting out after him, "Choke. Go ahead and choke."*

Upon completion of the filming of the interiors in Hollywood, shooting for *From Here to Eternity* started in Hawaii on March 2, 1953. All of the exteriors were filmed at the exact locations described in the novel: Schofield Barracks, the Royal Hawaiian Hotel, Waikiki Beach, Diamond Head, and the Waialea Golf Course. Harry Cohn sent cast and crew to the islands with a strict budget regarding money and time. The chartered plane arrived at 5:00 A.M on March 2. By the time the plane landed, Frank and Montgomery Clift were so drunk, Burt Lancaster said later, "They were *gone*. Deborah [Kerr] and I had to wake them up. This is the way they arrived, and Harry Cohn is down there with the press and everything."

During filming, director Fred Zinnemann was surrounded by actors with many different temperaments.

"It wasn't easy," he said. "But then again, it was never easy. No film is easy." Burt Lancaster was protective of Deborah Kerr in her role of the adulterous wife, a 180-degree change from her usual noble characters. But with Zinnemann, Lancaster was argumentative and difficult, trying to get the director to change his lines the way Lancaster felt they should be written. Clift made no secret of the fact he considered Lancaster "a big bag of wind."

---

* In *Frank Sinatra—My Father*, Nancy Sinatra stoked the coals of intrigue about this subject when she wrote: "[Puzo] creates a character who was owned by the mob. The press and some of the public assumed the character had to be Frank Sinatra. Well, my father is a character, all right, and the Mario Puzo fiction is based on facts. But the facts pertain to another performer."

Later, Fred Zinnemann would say that Sinatra was easy to work with "ninety percent of the time." He did not elaborate about the other 10 percent of the time, but when asked about that comment later in 1996, he said, "What I meant was that Sinatra was really no problem at all and that we only had disagreements ten percent of the time we worked together. With other actors, you were lucky to have forty percent cooperation. Frank was very giving, very eager. He was troubled. He had a dark side; that was definitely true. He drank much too much. He must have been an alcoholic; he simply *must* have been. Though, I have to say, he was never a falling-down drunk. He just became very, very ugly when he drank. He brooded. But I felt that whatever he was going through in his personal life somehow added dimension and depth to his performance. He imbued the role with his life experience at the time, whatever it was, and that was clear to anyone watching. He was a pleasure to work with and to watch as he worked."

The scenes between Frank Sinatra and Montgomery Clift were challenging. As soon as Clift knew he was going to play Prewitt, he took boxing and trumpet lessons and also learned how to march in close-order drill so that he could appear as authentic as possible on film. He rehearsed before every scene, encouraging retakes because he discovered different nuances with each take. The intensity that Clift brought to the role had a positive effect on the other actors: They became better in their own parts because he set such high standards for himself. Frank, however, was known as one-shot Sinatra. By the third take, he was bored, and he showed it.

"As a singer, yeah, I rehearse and plan exactly where I'm going. But as an actor, no, I can't do that," he once explained. "To me, acting is reacting. If you set it up right, you can almost go without knowing every line. But if you're not set up right, if the guy you're acting with doesn't know what he's doing, forget it, the whole thing's a mess. If I rehearse to death, I lose the spontaneity I think works for me. So, yeah, it's a problem for me sometimes working with a guy, or girl, who has to go over something fifty times before they get it right. I wanna climb the wall. I wanna say, 'Jesus Christ, just do it and let's move on.' With Montgomery, though, I had to be patient, because I knew that if I watched this guy, I'd learn something. We had a mutual-admiration thing goin' there."

Montgomery Clift had been a longtime fan of Frank Sinatra's. He felt that Sinatra had many attributes that he himself lacked. It was more than Frank's superb musical ability that fascinated Clift. Inhibited and timid, Clift admired Sinatra's freewheeling ways. For Sinatra's part, he was impressed by Clift's devotion to acting. So when Clift offered to help him, he jumped at the chance. In many ways, Clift took Sinatra to a place he had never before been as an actor. He made him look deep into the role and taught him to *experience* a part rather than just react to what the other actors were doing.

Author James Jones was usually on the set and often joined the two of them—Sinatra and Clift—after the day's work. And what a sad trio they were.

Frank would try to reach Ava on the telephone, always a nearly impossible task. As Burt Lancaster put it, "In those days in Spain, if you lived next door to your friends, you couldn't get them on the telephone, let alone try to get them on the phone from Hawaii. He never got through. Not one night."

James Jones was unhappy because he felt that the movie script was not being true to the book.

Montgomery Clift was secretly wrestling with his sexual identification.

The three of them would break out a couple of bottles and drink away their misery until, night after night, they passed out cold. Sometimes Burt Lancaster would gather them up, take them to their rooms, and get them undressed and into bed. Frank was able to compose himself for the next day's shooting; Monty was not always so fortunate. There were times when he had to be pumped full of coffee just to do a scene.

Zinnemann was generally easygoing; there weren't many problems. However, when the last scene of the movie had to be shot, a night scene in which Maggio is drunk and Prewitt is afraid the MPs will catch him, Sinatra decided that the two men should be sitting down rather than standing up. When Zinnemann said they would do the scene as written, Sinatra got so angry and obnoxious that Buddy Adler put in a hurried call to Harry Cohn, who was dining at the Royal Hawaiian Hotel with General O'Daniel, the commander of the entire Pacific Air Force. Just as Zinnemann was negotiating with Sinatra that they would shoot it sitting down *after* they did it standing up, an air force limousine came roaring onto the set. Out jumped Cohn in his white dinner jacket. He started shouting that no actor should dare to tell the director what to do, that they would shoot the scene as written or else he would shut the whole production down immediately. Without waiting for an answer, he marched to the limousine and got in. He drove off as quickly as he had arrived. The scene was shot as written.

From Here to Eternity was completed in forty-one days. Now it would be just a matter of time before the public, and critics, would determine whether or not the film—and Frank Sinatra—would be a success.

With the movie done, a priority for thirty-seven-year-old Frank Sinatra was to get his recording career back on track. While it is difficult to imagine today, back in 1953 Frank Sinatra simply could not secure a record deal. His contract with Columbia had expired at the end of the previous year, and that company showed no interest in renewing it.

Sinatra's good friend Manie Sachs, in a top-level position at RCA at the time, attempted to sell Sinatra to that label by calling a meeting of just about every top executive and saying, "He's available. We need to sign him up. What can we do?" A few days later, Sachs got back the word: "Manie, we can't do it. There's nothing we can do with Sinatra." Frank Sinatra Jr. later remembered, "Manie said it was the hardest thing he ever had to tell my dad. 'The guys don't think they can move you,' he told him. 'I could force it and get you on the label with us. But I'd rather you went somewhere else than have you come on with these guys who think, in all honesty, they can't do it.' Pop assured Manie he understood."

Other record companies were also approached, but there was simply no interest in Sinatra. Finally, executives at Capitol Records expressed some modest interest in Frank and offered him a terrible one-year deal that called for no advance against royalties. All arranging, copying, and musicians costs were to be incurred by Frank. This was the kind of contract that would be offered when record-company executives had practically no faith at all in the artist. Still, in order for Capitol to offer even this shabby deal, three of Frank's supporters had to push for it: Axel Stordahl (husband of Capitol recording artist June Hutton) asked Glenn Wallachs (president of the label) for a favor in signing Sinatra, as did Dick Jones (who had played piano for Frank's wedding to Ava) and Dave Dexter, Capitol's jazz producer and a big fan of Frank's, who, ironically enough, would be rejected by Frank as a producer of his music because he had written some critical reviews of Sinatra's music for *Downbeat* magazine.

Frank's first recording date for Capitol was in April 1953. Producer Voyle Gilmore wanted to team Frank immediately with trumpeter Billy May as arranger, but since May was with his band in Florida, he wasn't able to make the date. So Heinie Beau substituted for him and arranged Frank's session, "Lean Baby," on April 2 so as to be reminiscent of May's style. Also, Axel Stordahl arranged "I'm Walking Behind You" for that same session. For Frank's April 30 sessions, Gilmore recruited thirty-one-year-old Nelson Riddle (former trombonist-arranger for Tommy Dorsey and arranger of the classic "Mona Lisa" for Nat King Cole) to arrange "I Love You" and "South of the Border." Other tunes were also recorded at this time, including the marvelously optimistic "I've Got the World on a String" (which Frank would often use as an opening number in his act), and the contemplative ballad "Don't Worry About Me," both arranged by Riddle. Now they were on to something magical; Riddle had injected new life into Sinatra's sound.

Any Frank Sinatra aficionado will concur that Nelson Riddle would go on to be the primary architect of Sinatra's swinging sound of the fifties at Capitol. Said Riddle of Sinatra, "There's no one like him. Frank not only encourages you to adventure, but he has such a keen appreciation of achievement that you are impelled to knock yourself out for him. It's not only that his intuitions as to tempo, phrasing, and even figuration are amazingly right but that his taste is so impeccable."

On May 2, Frank recorded "My One and Only Love," another wonderful Nelson Riddle arrangement, their third together. This is a hidden treasure, an obscure song but a favorite among his fans, that truly demonstrates Frank Sinatra's stunning ability as a balladeer. The depth of Sinatra's vocal range and the breadth of his emotional commitment to a song to which he could easily relate are again in full display on this recording.*

"Working with him was always a challenge," Riddle said of Sinatra. "And there were times when the going got rough. Never a relaxed man, as Nat Cole was, for example, he was a perfectionist who drove himself and everybody around him relentlessly. You always approached him with a feeling of uneasiness," Riddle admitted, "not only because he was demanding and unpredictable but because his reactions were so violent. But all of these tensions disappeared if you came through for him. I can't help thinking of him with a certain sadness. This man is a giant. Not that there aren't other good singers around. But he has the imagination and scope of the rarest." Riddle, who collaborated with Sinatra on more than ninety recording sessions, also mentioned that Sinatra was not one to give praise to producers and arrangers after successful sessions. "He'd never give out compliments," he said. "He just isn't built to give out compliments. He expects your best." (Nelson Riddle died in 1985.)

Ironically enough, considering the circumstances of his signing with the company, many Sinatra historians still feel that the albums that resulted from Frank's next seven years at Capitol are among his best and most memorable recordings. Whereas Columbia nurtured the smooth balladeer, at Capitol would be born the cool, swinging Sinatra, thanks to producer Voyle Gilmore and arranger-conductor Nelson Riddle. (Sinatra's fans reverently refer to this period of time, 1953–61, as "the Capitol Years.") Not to say that Frank didn't also record some of his greatest ballads during this period, because he certainly did. But there was something different about Frank now. At Columbia, he was a phenomenon. At Capitol—where time, place, and circumstance, not to mention personal experience, all played a big hand in Frank's stunning evolution as an artist—he would become a very serious singer who would go on to carefully choose his material. And, to be succinct about it, he just *sounded* better.

* Sinatra considered "My One and Only Love" one of the most difficult songs to sing. Many other singers who attempted it had to fudge over the notes. The song didn't become well known until Joni James recorded it three years later for an album, and she did make all of the notes. Why Sinatra's ravishing single went so unnoticed is a mystery.

"Nelson began to pump a little more power into the sound," Frank Sinatra Jr. once observed. "Instead of sounding like that silky-smooth crooner of the forties, now Pop was putting more energy into it, belting a little more. His voice lowered, too, got better, lost some of its sweetness. His whole attitude was becoming a little more hip now. The curly-haired, bow-tied image was gone. Now there was the long tie and the hat."

Sinatra was thrilled with his first collaborations with Nelson Riddle and, after the April 30 sessions, went throughout the studio shaking the hands of the musicians and slapping them on the back, telling them, "I'm back, baby. I'm back."

In early May 1953, Frank embarked on a three-month tour of Europe with Ava, who now signed autographs "Ava Sinatra," at his side. Audience reaction to Sinatra was enthusiastic, and things seemed to be on an upswing for him. The word had begun to filter through the media that Sinatra would soon be making a huge comeback, that the film he had just completed, *From Here to Eternity*, was going to put him back on top. So there was a renewed interest in him as a performer. Plus, the material he had recorded at Capitol thus far had also injected new life into his career. Professionally, things looked good. Personally, however, the marriage was still a challenge for both participants.

CHAPTER 16

From Here to Eternity opened at the Capitol Theater on Broadway in New York on August 5. Harry Cohn decreed that there would be no grand opening with stars, limousines, and interviews. The movie opened with no more fanfare than one full-page ad in the *New York Times,* signed by Harry Cohn, president of Columbia, urging people to see it. Incredible as it may seem, the lines were so long on opening night—advance word of mouth about the film had been so positive—that the theater management added another show at 1.00 A.M to accommodate anxious ticket buyers. Shortly thereafter, the Capitol Theater was showing *From Here to Eternity* around the clock. They closed for a short time in the early-morning hours so that the janitors could clean the place out.

Frank was amazed at the public and critical reaction to the film. "I knew it was a good movie," he said, "and I sensed that I was good in it. But the way the people reacted to it, well, I never expected all of that. I was grateful."

"He called me up, and I hadn't heard from him in a couple of years," said Joey D'Orazio, his friend from Hoboken. "And he said, 'Hey, man, you gotta go see me in this fucking picture. I'm fucking *great* in this picture.' I said, 'Frankie, I already seen it, and you were great.' 'I know it, man,' he told me. 'I know it.'

"He was just so goddamn happy. He said, 'I'm back. This is my fuckin' comeback.' And I said, 'Frankie, you never left.' He laughed and said, 'You know what? There are a lot of bastards out there, Joey, who thought I was down. But I'm proving them wrong now, ain't I? Goddamn! Ain't I doing it? And I ain't even *singing* in this picture.'"*

By September 1953, Frank's film was a critical and popular sensation, and his career was showing definite signs of revitalization. Not so his marriage.

"There was always tension," said their good friend artist Paul Clemens. "My wife and I spent a weekend with them in Palm Springs. It was fun but lots of tension. I remember we went to the Racquet Club and Frank stopped at the bar. There were people milling around, and among them were attractive girls who were pleased to meet Frank. Well, Ava took about five or six minutes of this, and all of a sudden she said, 'I'm leaving.' When Ava said, 'I'm leaving,' that was an open-ended itinerary, because she was a woman of means and temperament. She could mean back to the house or into L.A. or London or Acapulco. So I said, 'I'll drive you home,' Not merely to see that she got home but also so that we knew where she was going. When I returned to the Racquet Club and told Frank what I did, he said, 'Good thinking.' "

That month—September—Sinatra appeared at the Riviera in Englewood, New Jersey. It was a sold-out engagement due to Sinatra's growing popularity as a result of *From Here to Eternity*.

According to Joey Bishop, who was Sinatra's opening act: "Frank had seen me at the Latin Quarter in New York City, liked my act, and asked me to open for him. There were eleven hundred people in the audience opening night, and I wanted to make a good impression. I was a little nervous. So I'm saying, 'Good evening, ladies and gentlemen,' and all of a sudden the man I am looking at dead center, ringside, is suddenly on my right side. And the guy who was at my left is suddenly sitting dead center. And I'm thinking, What the hell is going on? The room is spinning! Then I see Frank in the wings with his thumb to his forehead and waving the rest of his fingers at me. Turns out it was a revolving stage, and I didn't know it. Frank was back there pushing the button that made it

* Curiously, in May 1953, Sinatra recorded a song entitled "From Here to Eternity" for Capitol, obviously anticipating the success of the film having that title. In today's film market, the song would doubtless be used under the opening and closing credits.

turn. And then he said to the audience on a backstage mike, 'Place your bets, folks, 'cause I don't think he's comin' around again.' "

Eddie Fisher remembered Frank's opening at the Riviera this way: "[It was] one of the greatest performances I've ever seen. He couldn't sing a wrong note, couldn't make a wrong move. It was electrifying. There was only one empty seat on that opening night—the one reserved for Ava."

Oddly enough, it was Dolly Sinatra who forged a reconciliation between Frank and Ava.

As Ava's friend Lucille Wellman remembered it, Dolly telephoned Ava in New York at the Hampshire House, where she was staying. She used the excuse that she wanted to give her the recipe for *pizzelles** that Ava had been asking for. Then she got to the point. "Look, you and I know that I am not happy about the way it's going with you and my son. This marriage is a goddamn disaster. Frank's on sleeping pills, he's drinking, he's in trouble. Now, do you want to stay married to him or what? Because he's miserable, and something has to be done."

Ava cried and said that, yes, she wished things could work out, but now she believed that Frank was having an affair with Donna Reed, who had costarred with him in *From Here to Eternity.* "Rubbish," Dolly said. Then she invited Ava to the Sinatra home in Weehawken where they now lived; she also invited Frank without telling him that Ava would be present.

When Frank arrived—in between shows at the Riviera—Ava was sitting on the couch. Sinatra took one look at her and bolted. Dolly ran after him, saying, "Francis, get back here right now, damn it. Don't you dare leave my house like that."

Frank turned around and, like a little lamb, meekly went back into the living room. Dolly then acted as therapist and made the two lovebirds apologize for whatever it was that they were fighting about. After about a half hour of conciliation, they kissed and made up. On the way out, Ava turned to Dolly and said, "Mama, be sure to send me your bill."

That night, Ava went back to the Hampshire House, while Frank returned to the club for his second show. He told her to wait up for him, and she did. However, after that show, he and his buddies went barhopping. He didn't get back to Ava's suite until four in the morning, which caused another fight between them. "He is so goddamn inconsiderate," Ava told one friend. "I don't know if he wants this marriage to work or not."

The next night, Ava went to Sinatra's show. She sat with Eddie Fisher in the audience.

A *Journal-American* story that next day reviewed the show: "The Voice

---

* A flat, circular-shaped, crispy Italian pastry made with batter in a so-called *pizzelle* iron. "Look, Ava, you gotta make 'em thinner," Dolly used to tell her. "The thinner the better."

unleashed a torrent of sound at the sultry Ava. Emotion poured from him like molten lava as he piled the decibels ceiling high. He sang twenty-four songs with scarcely a pause for breath. The customers, except those completely numbed by the moving reconciliation [with Ava], loved it. Never before in the history of nightclubs had an artist been so generous with his voice."

While the audience enjoyed Sinatra's performance, it would seem that Ava was not impressed.

Eddie Fisher said, "Ava didn't seem to care. Her head was lowered, her hair fell over her face, and she never bothered to look up from her glass."

The night after that, Frank was in low spirits despite—and, oddly, even *because* of the crowd's strong reaction. He was moody; his behavior, erratic. Eddie Fisher remembered that on this evening Sinatra was introduced to tumultuous applause, cheers, and whistles, with women screaming out: "Frankie! Frankie! Frankie!" It was like old times; only Sinatra didn't want to hear it. He just wanted to perform his set and get off that stage. He stood at the footlights waiting for the commotion to cease so that he could begin singing his opening number. When the audience would not quiet down despite his requests that they do so, he called out, "Waiter, menu." The crowd thought he was joking as he looked at the menu, ordered a rare steak, a salad, and a baked potato and then said, "Good night, ladies and gentleman." Then he walked off the stage. The audience was stunned, especially so because he did not return.

On October 2, Ava's *Mogambo* premiered in New York, and the Sinatras attended the festivities at Radio City Music Hall. The next day, they flew back to Hollywood and fought on the plane all the way. "When he was down and out, he was sweet," she told a friend. "But now that he's successful again, he's become his old arrogant self." In about a week Ava went to the Palm Springs home to rest, while Frank was off to Las Vegas to prepare for a singing engagement at the Sands, which would commence on October 19. He was disappointed that Ava would not join him for opening night. "I can't eat. I can't sleep. I love her," Frank told gossip columnist Louella Parsons from Las Vegas. She responded by saying, "You should be telling that to Ava, not to me."

Marilyn Lewis (Cain, at the time) was a switchboard operator at the Sands Hotel at that time. She says that she only worked for four weeks in a temporary position there and that one of those weeks was during this Sinatra appearance. "I couldn't believe my luck," she said, "to be working there during a Sinatra engagement and to have the chance to speak to him as his operator, even though he didn't know who I was. Well, I was thrilled to death.

"The thing I most remember is Mr. Sinatra placing countless phone calls to a Palm Springs number that I assumed was his home. One evening, before he retired, he told me that he should not be disturbed unless his wife called. Well, she did call at about three in the morning. Then I have to assume that they either kept getting disconnected or she was hanging up on him, because for the next three hours he must have called her back at least twenty times.

"Then, at one point in all of that, she called and said, 'Connect me to Mr. Sinatra's room.' Because I had instructions not to connect anyone unless it was his wife, I politely asked, 'Who's calling, please?' And she screamed at me, 'You know damn well who this is. This is his fucking wife. Now get him on the line.' Startled, I said, 'Yes, Mrs. Sinatra,' and she said, 'Miss Gardner. My name is Miss Gardner. Now get him on the line.' She was upset, to put it lightly.' "

Lucille Wellman remembered that Ava had told her that she heard that Frank was "shacking up in his room" at the Sands with a Copa girl. " 'If it had been a major star, then fine,' " Ava reasoned. " 'I could deal with it. I could even compete with it if I chose to. But a showgirl! How dare he? How dare he fuck a showgirl when he can have *me*.' Their sex life was in trouble, anyway. Ava said she hadn't had an orgasm in months with Frank. I don't know why. . . ."

Then, when Ava telephoned her husband in Las Vegas to check on the rumor, she heard a woman's voice in the background.

"That's when the fight started," Lucille Wellman said. "She was sure then that Frank was cheating on her. I told her that perhaps it was room service. And she said, 'At three in the morning the only room service he's getting is between his legs, believe me. I know my son of a bitch of a husband.' She made up her mind then and there that the marriage was over. She told him on the telephone that she was filing."

An astonishing memo from Sands hotel and casino manager Jack Entratter addressed to "Front Desk Personnel," and dated October 25, 1953, seemed to sum up the status of the Sinatras' marriage. The memo, found among the Sands Papers housed at the University of Nevada at Las Vegas, states: "As per Mr. Frank Sinatra's instruction, his wife, Ava Gardner Sinatra, is hereby barred from the premises of the Sands Hotel for the remainder of Mr. Sinatra's engagement here. If Mrs. Sinatra attempts to check into the hotel, she should be referred to this office. Under no circumstances is Mrs. Sinatra to have any contact with Frank Sinatra. Therefore, no telephone calls from Mrs. Sinatra should be connected to Mr. Sinatra's suite. Furthermore, as per Mr. Sinatra, all media inquiries regarding the status of the Sinatra marriage should be directed to the office of [publicity director] Al Guzman without comment."

Howard Strickling, M-G-M's chief publicist, issued a statement on October 27, 1953, announcing that Ava Gardner and Frank Sinatra had separated and "the separation is final and Miss Gardner will seek a divorce."

Ironically, as much as they had grown to despise the media in recent years, Frank and Ava used reporters to explain their positions in the marital dispute. Frank telephoned New York columnist Earl Wilson and told him, "If it took seventy-five years to get a divorce, there wouldn't be any other woman."

Then Ava called Wilson and, while sobbing on the phone, said, "Frank doesn't love me. He would rather go out with some other girl, almost any other girl. Maybe if I had been willing to share Frank with other women, we could have been happier."

Her personal hairstylist, Sydney Guilaroff, said, "Ava was not the tough woman she portrayed herself as having been. I doubt that even Frank knew how vulnerable she was, because she practically never let him see that side of her."

The night after the divorce was announced, Guilaroff was watching the evening news when he was startled by the doorbell. When he opened the door, he found Ava. Clearly shaken, she said, "I've got to talk to someone." He moved to hug her, but she backed off onto the front lawn. She started sobbing, and from her obvious tremor, Sydney recalled, he feared the worst.

"Is Frank okay?" he asked.

She took a deep breath and let out a long sigh. Her mouth hung open, and suddenly the glamour that she had always worn so well seemed to vanish. She embraced him, and with her chin on his shoulder, she whispered, "I thought I could do it, but I can't talk about it, any of it."

He shook her free, looked into her eyes, and said firmly, "Please come inside."

She gathered herself as best she could. "No, no. I'd just break down, and that's what I'm trying not to do."

Thinking it best that she be left alone, he went back into the house. For hours, he kept a vigil, peering out his front window, only to find Ava Gardner still on his lawn, pacing back and forth, awash in moonlight. Well after midnight, he turned in. Finally, the roar of her car's ignition awakened him. He watched as she drove off into the night

Many years later, he would recall, "There was a sorrow in Ava that evening that I never thought her capable of. She was best as the life of the party, but somehow something had gone awry. I remember thinking, If only certain gossip columnists who always thought the worst of her could see this lost woman. Most certainly they would have shown a bit more compassion. It was that moving a sight."

Two days after the announcement concerning the status of his marriage to Ava Gardner was made, Frank Sinatra appeared before the Nevada Tax Commission. As it happened, a few months earlier he had applied for the purchase of a 2-percent interest in the Sands Hotel in Las Vegas. There was a great deal of discussion among the members of the commission about the fact that Frank still owed the government $70,000 of a $160,000 levy. In fact, one commissioner argued that the $54,000 Sinatra was using to buy into the Sands should be applied to his tax debt. However, Frank had been diligent in paying his back taxes, a thousand dollars off the top of what he was paid for each singing engagement. He had already paid $90,000 of the debt. Because they felt he was acting in good faith, the commission would eventually vote six to one in Frank's favor, even though there was considerable concern about Frank's connections to the Mafia.

The fact, though, was that the Sands was practically run by mobsters, anyway, because it was easy to "skim" from the take, lie about gross receipts, and only report to the Internal Revenue Service (IRS) whatever was left. Moreover, because it was not required then that cash transactions be reported to the IRS, Las Vegas quickly became a haven for underworld activity. Mobsters were welcome in Las Vegas as guests of the hotels and friends of many of the stars who performed there. Some of the entertainers, like Frank, always knew with whom they were dealing when they played Las Vegas and made "connections" there for other business opportunities. Others, like Sammy Davis Jr., just did their job and asked no questions.

Frank's interest in the Sands—which, in time, would grow to 9 percent—would prove to be invaluable to him financially. It was a wise investment that would make him a millionaire many times over in the next couple of years. Eventually, he would become vice president of the Sands Corporation. For him, it was a combination of business and pleasure, because, above all, Frank liked to gamble. It was one of his passions. Both of his parents were gamblers; he would say that "it's in my blood." He would be given thousands of dollars a night in credit by the Sands with which to gamble. If he won, great! The winnings were his. If he didn't win, so what? He never paid back the original investment, anyway. Who wouldn't enjoy gambling with those kinds of guidelines? He loved the game of baccarat and would lose up to $50,000 a night playing that game. "It's just money," he once told Dean Martin. "You make it, you lose it, you make it back. That's life."

There were a number of significant Sinatra recording sessions for Capitol in the winter of 1953.

One of the most noteworthy sessions, on November 5, 1953, is the classic Sinatra interpretation of Rodgers and Hart's "My Funny Valentine," arranged by Nelson Riddle. Originally composed for the Broadway musical *Babes in Arms* in 1937 (and sung by Mitzi Green), "My Funny

Valentine" is perhaps the finest of all love songs by Richard Rodgers and Lorenz Hart. Frank's sentimental, graceful delivery is unforgettable, and he would go on to perform this song in nightclubs and concert halls for the next forty-some years. In fact, "Valentine" was just one of the many amazing songs Frank recorded on November 5 and 6, for the ten-inch Capitol eight-song album *Songs for Young Lovers* and Frank's *Swing Easy* (which was also originally a ten-inch but was later issued as a twelve-inch album): "A Foggy Day," "They Can't Take That Away From Me," "Like Someone in Love," "I Get a Kick Out of You," and "Little Girl Blue."

Much has been made of *Songs for Young Lovers* being the first true concept LP. But, on Capitol, Nat Cole had done the similar *Songs for Two in Love,* and on M-G-M, Joni James had done a true story-in-song concept album, *Let There Be Love.* Furthermore, albums had been established as a medium for standards, and Capitol was issuing albums with similar contents, cover art, and concepts prior to *Songs for Young Lovers.* Beyond that, for his album Sinatra basically took songs he was doing in person and had the introductions added to them. So all that has been written about *Songs for Young Lovers* emerging from confusion about just what to do with an LP isn't accurate. The album was a smash not because the idea was anything new but because Sinatra and the arrangements bordered on the unbelievable in their sheer excellence and taste.

There was a world-weariness, an adult sadness, about Sinatra's voice now. This was a man who had been around the block a few times. He knew about love. He knew about heartbreak. One could hear the sorrow in his voice. "It was Ava who did that to him, who taught him how to sing a torch song," Nelson Riddle would observe years later. "That's how he learned. She was the greatest love of his life, and he lost her."

A little more than a week after those brilliant sessions, Frank flew to New York prior to an engagement at the Chase Hotel in St. Louis. When staying with his close friend Jimmy Van Heusen on Fifty-seventh Street, Frank always made sure he was surrounded by people. He never wanted to be alone. All night long, friends would appear and be held hostage; Sinatra wouldn't let them leave. It would be this way for many years to come: three A.M., four A.M., five A.M, six A.M. Sinatra's party would still be jumping.

"Everybody have a little more gasoline," Frank would say as he poured the whiskey. "But I wanna go home, Frank. I'm tired, man." someone would plead. "You ain't goin' nowhere, Charley," Sinatra would insist. "Now, break out them there cards. And who's gonna go out and get more of them glazed crullers." Finally, at seven A.M., Frank would have enough. "All right, you bums, now get the hell out. I'm going to bed." When everyone was gone, Frank would find himself alone. "That there's when the demons start comin' out," he once said.

One night at Jimmy Van Heusen's, on November 18, 1953, when Frank Sinatra couldn't find anyone to keep him company, he became despondent. Chain-smoking in the kitchen, wearing his white pajamas, he couldn't make a decision: Should he get drunk? Or should he just kill himself and get the whole goddamn thing over with. Jack Daniels or the Grim Reaper. Opting for the latter, he slashed his wrists.

Van Heusen came home to find a bleeding, disoriented Frank Sinatra standing in his kitchen. "I don't wanna get blood on my pajamas, Jimmy. But I can't stop the bleeding." Jimmy rushed his friend to Mt. Sinai Hospital.

The incident was kept quiet by Van Heusen and Frank's other friends.* However, someone did tell Nancy, Frank's first wife. She telephoned Frank in the hospital, but he refused to speak to her. Later, Nancy would say that, from this moment on, every time her telephone rang, she would feel a chill: Had Frank finally been successful in ending his life? Ava never learned of the latest misadventure. Again, Frank was too ashamed to tell her, and he ordered that no one else relay the news to her. He complained that he could no longer satisfy Ava in bed and that she made him feel like "less than a man."

On December 8 and 9, 1953, Frank Sinatra, who was about to turn thirty-eight, was in the recording studio again, now looking worse than ever as a result of the stress in his life. He and Ava were separated, and though she had not filed for divorce, it seemed that they would never reconcile.

"It was all Mondays" is how he remembered this time. He was down to about 118 pounds. He had just gotten out of the hospital after the slashed-wrist episode. How amazing, then, that he was recording such memorable music, including the plaintive and, clearly, heartfelt "Why Should I Cry Over You" and the classic "Young at Heart." What a memorable, wistful performance Frank delivered on the latter. "You can laugh when your dreams fall apart at the seams," he sang hopefully. "Young at Heart" had been turned down by a number of artists, including Nat King Cole. Jimmy Van Heusen convinced Sinatra to record the song, and it was a fortuitous move for him, for the song would take Frank to new heights of success when finally released a month later. Part of the magic of the Sinatra recordings was their simplicity. "Young at Heart" is an example. It's a straightforward, uncluttered, lilting performance. It goes right to the heart of both the song and the listener.

* * *

* Jimmy Van Heusen always had Frank's undying loyalty; he once canceled an entire tour of Australia just because the airline could not provide a last-minute berth for Van Heusen.

At Christmastime, Ava was in Italy filming a movie, *The Barefoot Contessa*. Frank telephoned her in Rome and told her that he wanted to be with her for the holidays and to celebrate her thirty-first birthday. She didn't tell him not to come, but she didn't seem too happy about the idea, either.

When Frank arrived, armed with expensive gifts for Ava, he found that she had already left London for the Madrid home of film executive Frank Grant. So he followed her there, and they spent Christmas together.

Frank wanted to work on improving the relationship; however, Ava was finished with it, and with him as well. Finally, she felt that she had to be honest with her estranged husband. Her friend Nancy LaPierre remembered: "Ava sat him down, and she said something like 'Look, I am in love with a bullfighter now. You gotta get over me, baby.' "

In fact, Ava was having an affair with a slim, handsome Spanish bullfighter named Luis Miguel Dominguin. Perhaps the dalliance meant nothing to her, like the one she'd once had with Mario Cabre. But to Frank it meant everything.

"She couldn't help herself," said a good friend of hers and an M-G-M Hollywood actress herself. "Ava was, by this time, a nymphomaniac. Deep in her heart she lacked self-esteem. She was a textbook case, a girl who couldn't get enough sex. And why? Due to the fact that she doesn't feel she deserves to be satisfied. But still, she could fuck all night long, hoping for one. And Frank, with his male pride and that lovely genitalia of his, nearly broke his back trying to satisfy her. He couldn't, though. So poor Ava was always looking for someone who could."

Ava would say later that Frank became so enraged at her confession, he completely trashed the room in which she was staying at Grant's home. He threw the television set out the window. He shattered all of the crystal. He threw lamps against the walls, turned over tables, and hurled expensively framed photographs all about, sending small, dangerous shards of glass into the air like missiles and causing a terrified Ava to run for cover.

"She told me that she was scared to death that he was going to kill her," said Nancy LaPierre.

"Stop it, baby, please," Ava pleaded with him.

However, Frank didn't stop until the room was a complete shambles. Then, as he walked out the door, he peeled off a few dollars from a wad of money, threw them at her, and said, "This is for the damage, sweetheart. And, oh, by the way, if you ever call me baby again, I'll rip your tongue right out of your fucking mouth, you bitch."

Then Sinatra took a cab to the airport, got on a plane, and went to Rome for a few days.

"A downcast and lonely-looking Frank Sinatra sneaked out of Rome this afternoon on a New York–bound plane after a five-day attempt to win back his wife," wrote Reynolds Packard of the *New York Daily News* at the end of Sinatra's European trip.

"That's it," Frank reportedly told Jimmy Van Heusen when he returned to the States. "That's gotta be it. What else can I do? I gotta move on. This broad is gonna kill me. Who the fuck does she think she is? I swear to you, no woman will ever do this to me again, because I'll never let another woman—another person—get that close to me again."

Meanwhile, Ava was finding it tough going in Spain with her new paramour Dominguin, who had lost interest. Said her friend Esther Williams, "Luis was so handsome, and Ava was crazy about him. He was having a party, a big afternoon barbecue, and in came Ava, crashing the party, being loud and happy. It was very embarrassing for Luis. He came to me and said, 'Is she your friend?' and I said, 'Yes, Luis, but I am not going to ask her to leave.' He said, 'Well, she's gotta get out of here.' And I said, 'Sweetheart, *you're* the one who stands in front of two-ton animals [a reference to his being a matador]; you tell her yourself.'"

The year 1954 began on a bleak note.

Frank Sinatra didn't want to be alone. He was afraid of what he would do to himself.

"He had given up something so special to him," observed Esther Williams. "The mother and constant friend that Nancy was—he gave that up for Ava and her free spirit. She *was* the Barefoot Contessa. She just couldn't get through the night without dancing it away. And when you dance the night away with a band of Gypsies, they're still going to be there in the morning, and with the empty bottles of booze under the couch. The thought of all of that just drove poor Frank crazy."

He was now seeing a psychiatrist, Dr. Ralph H. "Romy" Greenson, the brother-in-law of Milton "Mickey" Rudin, who became Sinatra's lawyer when the singer signed with the William Morris Agency. When Frank returned from Italy, he asked his friend Jule Styne to move into the five-bedroom apartment he owned on Wilshire Boulevard.

In a 1986 interview, Styne recalled, "He was down. He was really in bad shape. The Ava thing, you know? He called me up and said, 'Man, I know I can't make it alone. I need someone to hang out with, to stay with me.' I liked Frank. I wanted to help him out. So I said, 'Yeah, I'll be your roommate.'

"He moved me into the place. I had been staying at the Beverly Hills Hotel. The first thing I noticed when I got to Sinatra's were the framed pictures of Ava all over the place. He had a virtual art gallery of Ava pictures, each one softly lit. I said to him, 'Jesus Christ, Frank, you can't go on like this. This woman is not a saint. She's just a woman, and a woman who has ruined your life.' And I went to reach for one of the pictures, and he almost broke my arm off grabbing me. 'Don't touch

174

that,' he told me. 'Don't ever touch any picture of her as long as you're living in this house.' "

Styne, the brilliant composer of *Gypsy* and *Funny Girl*, added, "Frank used to sing these songs around the house, these sad, sad songs like 'Nevertheless.' You know, 'Maybe I'll live a life of regret, but nevertheless I'm in love with you. . . .' And that voice—it was just such an amazing kind of instrument. I mean, even in the shower Frank Sinatra was a great singer. I would stand outside the bathroom door and just listen to this man's voice, with all that tremendous heartbreak and pain in it, and I would say to myself, What I'm hearing right now should be recorded. This is an award-winning performance.

"And the man never slept. Never," Styne remembered. "He would be up all night, drinking booze—way, way too much brandy—calling friends at all hours, begging people to come over. He would engage me in long conversations about music until finally I would say, 'Jeez, Frank, I gotta go to sleep.' He'd say, 'Fine. Go to sleep, ya bum.' Next morning, I would wake up, and there's this guy, Frank, sitting in the same chair he was in when I went to bed, staring up at the ceiling, an empty bottle of brandy on the floor next to him."

Styne lived with Sinatra for eight months before he was asked to leave. As it happened, Frank was hurt because he felt Styne had betrayed him by telling not only friends but reporters as well what it was like to live with the star. He openly discussed Frank's heartbreak and depression. (In another interview Styne said, "At four o'clock in the morning, I hear him calling someone on the telephone. It's his first wife, Nancy. I hear him say, 'You're the only one who understands me.' Then he paces up and down some more and maybe reads, and he doesn't fall asleep until the sun comes up.") Surely he must have known that this breach of trust would not sit well with Sinatra, but Styne acted completely surprised when he came home one day to find a note from Frank that said, "I'd appreciate it if you'd leave."

Later, according to Jule Styne, he would ask for forgiveness. The two had known each other for years, after all. (Styne recalled that in 1943, when he first met Sinatra at the Riobamba in New York—Sinatra's first engagement geared toward an adult crowd—Frank gave him a gold Cartier identification bracelet that was inscribed: "To Jule, Who Knew Me When. Frankie.")

"Hey, Frank buddy come on, I'm begging you, man," he pleaded.

"Good," said Frank. "I'll remember you that way. Now get the fuck away from me, you fucking traitor."

It would be five years before the two men would speak again.

During this time, Marilyn Monroe's divorce from Joe DiMaggio was finalized. Lena Pepitone, her secretary, has remembered that Marilyn went to live with Sinatra for a while so that she could regain her emotional bearings. It's difficult to determine when Frank and Marilyn first met, though some point to a meal at Romanoff's in 1954. During the final weeks of 1953, Marilyn had rejected a script (*Pink Tights,* a remake of Betty Grable's 1943 movie *Coney Island*) that would have teamed her with Sinatra, causing her to be put on suspension by Fox. (She called that script "cheap, exploitive.") However, she had always been a fan of Sinatra's. Joey Bishop recalled the time Marilyn went to see Frank at the Copacabana, "sometime in the fifties."

"I'm doing my act, and in the middle of it in comes Marilyn Monroe walking into the room like she owns the joint," Bishop remembered. "Of course, I lost the crowd. Who's gonna pay attention to me when Marilyn Monroe walks in? There wasn't an empty seat in the house, so they pulled a single chair up for her to sit in and stuck it ringside, about four feet away from me. I looked down at her and I said, 'Marilyn, I thought I told you to wait in the truck.' "

Now the two consoled each other over their losses: Frank's over Ava and Marilyn's over DiMaggio. They were both still in love with their estranged spouses, so for a time there was nothing sexual going on between them. They were just sharing a vast, common loneliness. Frank wasn't interested in anything more, though it was difficult for his friends to fathom that he had one of the most beautiful and sought after movie stars living in his apartment with him and was not intimate with her.

As it happened, Marilyn had a habit of not wearing clothes. She simply did not like wearing them and would rather be naked. Her friends and staff were used to seeing her *au naturel.* It was not a surprise to find her in that state, and she liked to surprise visitors by suddenly materializing in a room with nothing on but that beautiful Monroe smile. When she stayed with Frank during this time, she did not change that behavior.

One morning, according to one friend of Sinatra's, he awakened, went into the kitchen wearing just his shorts, and found Marilyn standing in front of the open refrigerator with her small finger in her mouth, trying to decide between orange juice and grapefruit. She was naked. "Oh, Frankie," she said, probably feigning embarrassment, "I didn't know *you* got up so early."

"That was the end of anything platonic between the two of them," reported Sinatra's friend.

"He told me that he took her right there in the kitchen, up against the closed refrigerator. 'Man,' he told me, 'I never had sex like that. She is one fantastic woman.' This was the beginning of a long affair between them, one that lasted until she died in 1962. Frank loved her, he really did. He absolutely couldn't get enough of her."

Frank thought Marilyn was intelligent, witty, sexy, and exciting. "Marilyn was like a shooting star," observed Esther Williams, "and you

176

couldn't help but be fascinated by her journey. While you knew she was going to crash and burn, you didn't know how. However, you knew it was going to be a merry ride."

The only reason Sinatra wouldn't allow himself to become more serious about Marilyn, he had said, was because he was so wracked with pain about Ava. It was much too soon. Also, he would never end up with another actress. He had made that promise to himself.

He and Marilyn fought from time to time. Once, she almost absent-mindedly walked naked into a poker game he was having with friends, which infuriated him. ("Get your fat ass back in your room," he told her.) However, he could never stay angry at Marilyn for long. He truly loved her—though he was not *in* love with her—and he understood her frailties. She was often weak and delicate, and he usually despised those traits in a woman. He would never allow any of his women the luxury of vulnerability, but with Marilyn it was different. She was special.

After that poker-game incident, Sinatra went back into her room after his friends departed, as Marilyn later remembered it, "kissed me on the cheek, and made me feel like a million. From then on I always dressed up for him, whether or not anyone was coming over."

After Marilyn moved out of Frank's apartment, he embarked on a romantic relationship with an eighteen-year-old actress, the soft and curvy pinup girl and trick-shot golf pro Jeanne Carmen, who would later become a neighbor and—as she would claim and others would contest— a friend of Marilyn Monroe's. The charismatic, sexy Carmen, from Paragould, Arkansas, appeared in a dozen low-budget motion pictures and television programs. Though not a major star, she, like most actresses, aspired to be one. At the time she met Frank, the five-foot-six, 123-pound, 36-26-36 pinup girl, recently divorced from an opera singer, was also dating gangster Johnny Roselli.

"Frank had just left Ava Gardner," she recalled. "At that point, I had brown hair like Ava, we were both about the same weight and height. He told me that my breasts were larger than hers, and he liked that." Everything Carmen did, she said, reminded him of Ava. "Whenever I kicked my shoes off, he would say I reminded him of her, because apparently she liked to go barefoot."

"I remember that one," said Ava's friend Lucille Wellman, "the Carmen girl, because someone, and I don't know who—it might even have been her—sent a picture of her to Ava and said that she was Frank's new love. In the picture she was quite glamorous and looked much like Ava. Ava told me, 'Look at this, Frank is settling for pale imitations because he can't have the real thing.' "

"We had a tumultuous time together," Jeanne Carmen remembered. "He was torching for Ava, so he wasn't being Mr. Personality of the Year. Always moping around; occasionally, he would just cry like a baby over her right in front of me. Now, I'm not into a guy crying on my shoulder, so this was annoying.

"Then he would say, 'C'mon, let's go to bed.' And we would go to bed, and he would start pleading with me, 'Hold me. Hold me.' He would just sob. I was too young to understand or to empathize, unfortunately. I would think, Oh, no. How do I get out of here? He's going to keep me awake all night long with this crying."

Jeanne Carmen says she was torn by the vast disparity in the personality of Sinatra as heard on record and the one that truly existed. She said that she would sit at home and play his romantic music on the record player and think to herself, Oh, my God, I have to run over there and be with him. I need him. I want him.

Carmen would jump into her car and drive over to Sinatra's Wilshire Boulevard apartment, where she would find Frank in a deep funk, "a moping bore," as she put it. On weekends, she would drive to Palm Springs to be with him in the home he owned there, "Once I got there I would end up thinking, Oh, my God, I can't take another weekend of *this.*"

Ava Gardner did not apply for her divorce from Frank Sinatra until 1954. The proceedings would take three years to finalize because the couple kept vacillating about how to proceed with their relationship. When Earl Wilson asked Ava Gardner about the divorce proceedings in July 1957, it just happened to be the day she had signed the final decree. Her face froze when she was asked about specifics, and the icy expression on her face indicated that she was glad the whole matter was behind her. "I just signed the bloody thing, and I couldn't care less."

The grounds for Ava's Mexican divorce were "desertion." Her attorney, Raul de Villafrance, claimed that "for no legal reason" Sinatra walked out of the home he and Ava shared "for more than six months." Frank didn't bother to contest it. To him, it was all too ridiculous.

After it was all over—almost six years of marital discord and turmoil—there seemed to be nothing left for them to do but go on with their respective lives—not only Frank Sinatra and Ava Gardner but also Frank's first wife, Nancy Sinatra.

Frank would never really get over Ava. "Maybe one day, in some lifetime, we'll be together," he told his daughter Nancy. There would be many reconciliations over the years, but in the end Sinatra and Gardner would never end up together.

After the separation from her third husband, Frank, Ava began spending more time in Spain, a country for which she had great affection. When mutual friends would visit her there, she would always ask an endless series of questions about Sinatra. However, she would say that she had grown weary of their constant battling and that she now preferred European men "because they're such smooth sweet-talkers and their tempers are at least predictable."

Ava seemed to have survived her divorce with great and typical aplomb. Earl Wilson once told an anecdote about the time he and his wife were entertained by Ava and her boyfriend, Luis Miguel Dominguin, during the time that the Sinatra's divorce was pending. Characteristically hospitable, Ava suggested that Miguel get them a drink. "Get a piece of ice," she told him. Then, with a wicked laugh, she added, "A piece of *ice*. That's not the same as a piece of *ass*. He's trying to learn English," she explained. (By the time the divorce was granted, in 1957, Luis was out of Ava's life and Italian comedian and actor Walter Chiari—the Danny Kaye of Italy—was in it. When Frank heard that Ava might actually marry Chiari, he became so upset, he pulled all of the expensive drapes down from the curtain rods in his home. In the end, Ava would never marry again.

Meanwhile, Nancy Sinatra, Frank's first wife, never imagined that the intense feelings she and Frank shared, which were based on what she perceived as esteem and respect as well as passion, would ever come to an end. She was left to rebuild her life over the rubble of a marriage she thought was indestructible. "It pays not to care," she told one friend as she tried to recover from the emotional battering she had taken at the hands of Frank and Ava. "It's better if you don't have your soul on the line."

However, by sheer willpower as well as the love and caring of her three children to support her, Nancy Sinatra did eventually recover from her husband's betrayal. In time she became grateful for having known the deep and complete love she shared with him. In fact, as the years passed, she regained the elegance and bearing that had made her so attractive to Frank in the first place.

Nancy Sinatra's achievement in becoming a respected, elegant member of Hollywood society cannot be overstressed. Abandoned wives of stars are rarely heard from again, but Nancy established for herself a remarkable identity of class and worth. Her origins have been totally forgotten, and she bears no resemblance to the girl Frank married. She has remained a popular fixture in show-business circles, the friend and confidante of many celebrities and so-called industry movers and shakers. Her reputation has always been spotless, and the affection for her in Hollywood is that of a bona fide star, even though she has never been in show business.

Nancy would also never marry again. When one friend asked her why she never wed, she reponded, "After Sinatra?"—which could probably be taken a number of ways.

* * *

In truth, besides clearly following her heart, she knew she could only remain who she was—"a Sinatra." In fact, some of her acquaintances say that she often refers to herself as "Mrs. Frank Sinatra" and insists that others—store clerks, waiters and waitresses, reporters—do the same, even forty years after the divorce. However, when contacted to comment for this book, Nancy said that while she is obviously still "Nancy Sinatra" by virtue of the fact that she never remarried, "I have never referred to myself as Mrs. Frank Sinatra after the divorce because, frankly, I wasn't. He had several others after me. Many people might say that they still consider me 'Mrs. Frank Sinatra' and think of me in that way, but that's just their opinion. I know who I am. I have always known who I was."*

It could be argued Nancy has every right to remain a Sinatra. She believed in Frank, encouraged him, and, her supporters have insisted, even lent him money in the early days so that he would not have to work at a job and could instead concentrate on his career. Nancy, however, insists, "I never lent Frank money, or at least not to my memory." When reminded that she once put dollar bills in gloves and gave them to him, she laughed. "That wasn't a loan, it was a gift, *of ten dollars*. I think he earned it."

She also bore his three children, was—and is—an exemplary mother, and did not alienate him from them even after he betrayed her with Ava Gardner. She continued to be a part of his life whenever he needed her. "It was not difficult to do that," she said. "Not difficult at all. I felt it was my responsibility, as a mother, as a woman."

More important, though, Nancy Sinatra never bad-mouthed her ex-husband in public, even though she had many opportunities to do so over the years with reporters who have wanted "the real story" from her. "All I can say is that he was my first love, and I would never betray him," she concluded. "Never."

* Perhaps the power of the Sinatra name was demonstrated by Nancy Sinatra Sr. when she had difficulty contacting Cathy Griffin, the author's chief researcher. Chagrinned that Griffin's telephone number is unlisted, Mrs. Sinatra obtained it by speaking to a supervisor at the telephone company. Indeed, a person would be hard-pressed to persuade a telephone company employee to reveal an unlisted number, unless, of course, the enquirer's name is Sinatra!

Frank's parents, Marty and Dolly Sinatra, on their wedding day, circa 1915. This second ceremony was attended by their families, the first having taken place on Valentine's Day, 1913, when they eloped. (Archive Photos)

Francis Albert Sinatra was never a particularly religious youngster, but he did receive his First Holy Communion at about the age of seven, circa 1922. (Archive Photos)

Sinatra was always cool, even at the age of fifteen. "When I was a kid, I lived in a tough neighborhood," he said. "When somebody called me 'a dirty little guinea,' there was only one thing to do—break his head." (Archive Photos)

(Below) In 1935, nineteen-year-old Frank Sinatra (far right) was a member of the Hoboken Four, seen here with Major Bowes (in background), who named the group and featured them on his popular radio show. The other members were Fred Tamburro, James Petrozelli, and Patty Principe. (Archive Photos)

Sinatra with Harry James at the Hollywood Canteen in California. (CBS Photo Archive/Archive Photos)

(Below) Frank married Nancy Barbato on February 4, 1939. He insisted to his pals that his constant philandering "ain't got anything to do with her." (Courtesy of the Academy of Motion Picture Arts and Sciences/Paragon

(Top left) Sinatra with Buddy Rich and Tommy Dorsey. "I hope you fall on your ass," Dorsey told Sinatra when he left the band to strike out on his own in 1942. (Metronome/ Archive Photos)

(Middle left) Frank's father, Marty, called his son a "loser" —until he became famous. (Paragon Photo Vaults)

(Bottom left) "So, Mr. Big Shot Singer," Dolly would say to her son, Frank, "Are you a star yet?" (Paragon Photo Vaults)

(Opposite) Frank became a bobby-soxer sensation in the 1940s when he played the Paramount in New York. "Nobody's ever been a bigger star then me," he bragged. "This'll never end." (Archive Photos)
(Inset opposite, The Kobal Collection)

Young Frank enjoying breakfast and catching up on entertainment-industry news. (Courtesy of the Academy of Motion Picture Arts and Sciences/Paragon Photo Vaults)

Frank and Nancy and their children, Nancy, infant Tina, and Frank Jr. (Brown Brothers)

Frank almost left his wife, Nancy, for actress Lana Turner in 1946; she learned that he changed his mind when she read about it in the newspaper. "For you to do this to me, a famous picture star, is unforgivable," she screamed at him. *"Nobody dumps Lana Turner, mister."* (Archive Photos)

In 1947, Frank led a softball team called the Swooners in games against other celebrity teams. Ava Gardner *(center)* and Marilyn Maxwell *(right)* were two of the team's cheerleaders. Off the field, Frank hit home runs with both women, even though he was a married man. (Darlene Hammond)

Frank and Ava on their wedding day, November 7, 1951. When asked how she enjoyed the honeymoon, Ava responded "Great. Considering I paid for the whole goddamn thing." (Photofest)

(Inset) Frank accompanied Ava to the premiere of her film *Show Boat*. "Part of me had no doubt I would end up a movie queen," said Ava. "Deep down, I'm pretty superficial." (Paragon Photo Vaults)

CHAPTER 17

March 1954. What a splendid month this would prove to be for Frank Sinatra. His song "Young at Heart" was number one on *Your Hit Parade* and would become his first Top Five hit in eight years. He was named Most Popular Vocalist of the Year by a *Downbeat* poll. He was back on top, especially later, when his first two Capitol albums, *Songs for Young Lovers* and *Swing Easy*, became successful. Frank was named top male vocalist by *Billboard, Downbeat,* and *Metronome,* and by the end of the year it would be difficult to remember that just a short time earlier no record company was even interested in Frank Sinatra.

Frank's comeback was completed when he attended the Academy Awards ceremony on March 25, 1954. He was ecstatic about having been nominated in the Best Supporting Actor category for his performance in *From Here to Eternity*. His competition was Eddie Albert (*Roman Holiday*), Brandon de Wilde (*Shane*), Jack Palance (*Shane*), and Robert Strauss (*Stalag 17*). Although he was rumored to be the favorite, he was wise enough to know that nothing was certain. Certainly the nomination served to validate his own judgment about the role of Maggio. He knew all along he was right for it when everyone else, except Ava, thought he was insane.

For any actor, there's nothing more prestigious than an Academy Award. Although the thirteen-and-a-half-inch statue weighs only eight and a half pounds and is only gold-plated, it is literally worth its weight in pure gold in terms of advancing an actor's career. The year prior to these festivities, 1953, was the first year the awards were televised. (Prior to that, and beginning in 1931, they had been broadcast over radio.) The ceremonies were held in both New York and Los Angeles, with cameras in both locations. On March 25, Frank Sinatra sat close to the back on the left side of the Pantages Theater, one of twenty-eight hundred people, at twelve dollars a seat, attending the Academy Awards ceremonies. Beside him sat his fourteen-year-old daughter Nancy, and beside her, his ten-year-old son, Frankie. That day had been Nancy senior's birthday, and she had invited him to dinner, at which they gave Frank a small gold medallion. On one side was a bust of St. Genesius, the patron saint of actors. On the other was a miniature Oscar in bas relief. The inscription read: "Dad, all our love, from here to eternity."

Of the awards presentation, Frank junior recalled, "I was a young boy, of course, wearing my first pair of long pants, with very little understanding of the purpose of this event. I knew that something important was going on that night because all through the previous year I had been hearing about my father's performance in *From Here to Eternity*. As the evening progressed, I forgot the crowds of cheering people and thought only that I was getting very sleepy. But when [actress] Mercedes McCambridge announced Frank Sinatra as the winner, the audience in the theater gave a cheer and broke into spontaneous applause. The theater went crazy. Men and women cheered, tears flowed from the faces that had suddenly turned to where we were seated. My father slowly rose from his chair and began to walk to the stage, the greatest walk of his life, to receive his Oscar. On his face was a smile I will remember forever."

Frank, wearing a natty, well-tailored dark suit, clasped the Oscar and for a moment didn't know what to say. He was that stunned.

"Ladies and gentleman," he finally began. "I'm deeply thrilled and very moved. And I really, really don't know what to say because this is a whole new kind of thing, you know? I'm a song-and-dance-type." Members of the audience chuckled at the irony of his statement, for it was precisely that sentiment that nearly prevented him from getting the role in the first place. "I'd just like to say, however," he joked, "that they're doing a whole lot of songs here tonight, but nobody asked me [to sing]. I love you, though. Thank you very much. I'm absolutely thrilled."

Frank junior recalled: "When Dad, carrying his trophy, returned to Nancy and me in the audience, Donna Reed spoke to us in a loud whisper. *'Oh, let me just touch it,'* she said, and she placed her hand on the gold statue. Then, just a few minutes later, *her* name was called as the winner of Best Supporting Actress for the same film. I can still see the smile on her face. . . ."

In all, the film won eight of the thirteen Academy Awards for which it had been nominated, including one for Best Picture, which tied the record for wins, previously set in 1939 by *Gone With the Wind*. *Variety* reported Frank's win as "the greatest comeback in theater history."

How astonishing, in retrospect, that Frank Sinatra, basically known as a vocalist, would make one of the most dramatic comebacks in entertainment history as an actor.

According to her friends, when Ava heard about Frank's win, she cried tears of joy. She was going to call him to offer personal congratulations, but she feared that the sound of her voice would ruin the moment for him. By this time, she thought, he probably hated her. Instead, she sent a telegram.

As Ava would later admit, she felt oddly displaced, for she knew that Frank was celebrating his win with Nancy. After all, Ava had been so instrumental in getting the role for Frank, she wanted to be with him to share in his victory, but that wasn't possible. She herself had been nominated for a Best Actress Academy Award for her role in *Mogambo*. Ironically, she was the loser this time; Frank was the winner.

"Talk about being 'born again,' " Frank would later recall of the post-Oscar bash at his apartment on Wilshire Boulevard (where Nancy served, among other dishes, pasta and sardines with wild fennel). "I couldn't even share it with another human being. I ducked the party, lost the crowds, and took a walk. Just me and Oscar. I think I relived my entire life as I walked up and down the streets of Beverly Hills. I started the decade as 'the man least likely' and closed it out as a grateful human being given a second shot at life."

Unfortunately, it turned out to be less of a rebirth than Frank may have needed, since much of his personal behavior did not change for the better. Of winning the Academy Award, Frank concluded, "It's a moment. Like the first time you hit a guy . . . and he goes down."

On the evening of November 5, 1954, Frank Sinatra became involved in the oft-told drama of the so-called Wrong Door Raid. The events that led up to the raid and the subsequent investigation have been reported numerous times, and in excruciating detail, because of reams of sworn testimony from which to cull the reports.

Simply stated, Frank Sinatra, Joe DiMaggio—who was attempting to collect evidence to use against his estranged wife, Marilyn Monroe, in their divorce—and a small group of men were accused of breaking into a West Hollywood apartment in which Marilyn was supposedly having a lesbian affair. Unfortunately for the men—and perhaps fortunately for Monroe and Hal Schaeffer, her vocal coach at 20th Century–Fox, who actually *were* having a rendezvous in an apartment just above the one raided—they broke into the wrong apartment, practically frightening its occupant into a heart attack as they burst into her bedroom and started taking pictures of her in bed as she shrieked. (The woman whose apartment had accidentally been broken into, thirty-seven-year-old Florence Kotz, later sued Sinatra and DiMaggio for $200,000 and settled out of court four years later for $7,500.)

Ironically, the controversy that exploded years later wasn't because of the raid itself but as a result of a retrospective report about it in *Confidential*. In February 1957 the sensational magazine published a story entitled "The Real Reason for Marilyn Monroe's Divorce From Joe DiMaggio." The California State Senate Investigating Committee began a probe to determine just how these kinds of stories about celebrities were leaked to scandal publications and what the practices of certain unethical private detectives had to do with any of it. As part of the investigation, Frank was called to testify about his participation in the raid.*

---

* The manner by which he was served with the subpoena was more interesting than the case itself: Three policeman broke into his home while he was sleeping, sneaked

Frank Sinatra was furious about being dragged into any investigation by the media. He despised publications like *Confidential* and could not have cared less how its reporters gathered their information. Though he wanted nothing to do with any of it, he was still compelled to testify.

Under oath, Frank swore that he had only driven Joe DiMaggio to the scene of the break-in, where they then met two private detectives who had been hired by DiMaggio to keep Marilyn under surveillance. Frank claimed that while he stood by his car, DiMaggio, Billy Karen (maître d' of the Villa Capri restaurant in Los Angeles), Hank Sanicola, and the two private investigators broke into the wrong apartment.

DiMaggio later insisted that he didn't break into the apartment at all. In fact, all of the principal players would eventually deny any involvement.

There was even testimony that one of the private detectives, who claimed to have been beaten up by some of Frank's cronies, feared even further physical reprisals from Sinatra. Because of conflicting testimony, a grand jury convened, and Frank was forced to testify again. The investigation made headlines for months in 1957. In the end, *Confidential* magazine was cleared of any wrongdoing, and it was ruled that the magazine was "quite zealous in checking out and documenting their reports to the public. . . . As well, the activities of detectives [engaged by the magazine] were well within the rigorous code of regulations prescribed by the state for their business."

Years later, Marilyn Monroe told writer George Carpozi, "Frank Sinatra got a raw deal in that raid, but he wasn't exactly doing a nice thing for me, was he?"

In November 1954, Sammy Davis performed with his family act, the Will Mastin Trio, at the Old Frontier Hotel in Las Vegas. During that engagement, he was involved in an automobile accident. He lost his left eye as a result of his head smashing into the pointed cone in the center of the steering wheel. A horrified Sammy woke up in a hospital room in San Bernadino, California, covered with bandages above the nose. He was lucky to be alive, he was told.

After a few days, when the bandages were removed, Sammy began wondering why his friend Frank had not visited him. He became even more concerned when his father brought into the room a copy of *Confidential* magazine with the headline "What Makes Ava Gardner Run for

---

into his bedroom, awakened him by shining a flashlight in his eyes, and then handed the subpoena to him. Frank was incensed, and with good reason. "*I'm* the fucking one who got raided," he said when he threatened to sue the police department. He never did. He later said that the officers were lucky he was asleep when they broke into his residence, "or I might have gotten a gun."

Sammy Davis Jr." It was a completely fabricated story about a romance between Sammy and Ava (as if Sammy would ever have taken such a chance with Sinatra's friendship). Sammy was frantic. What if Frank saw this? Even if he felt that the story was untrue, he might still have a doubt or two. And what about Ava? How would she react? As if Davis didn't have enough to worry about at this time, he telephoned Ava's publicist from the hospital to find out if there had been any repercussions from the article. He was told that Ava had decided to simply ignore the story. However, there was no word from Frank's camp. For the next few days, Sammy had to sweat it out and wonder what Sinatra's reaction to the story would be and why he had not sent even a telegram, let alone flowers, to the hospital.

Then, one afternoon soon after, Sammy was being examined by a doctor when an excited nurse came into his room. "It's Frank Sinatra," she said breathlessly. "He's on his way up." The buzz through the hospital was palpable as doctors and nurses crammed the hallway to get a glimpse of the star. When Frank strutted into Sammy's room, tossed his hat onto a chair, and lit a cigarette, Sammy was never so happy to see another person. "You're gonna be all right," Frank declared with a grin. (Later, Sammy said Frank acted as if "he'd just gotten the word from upstairs.") Not only was Frank not upset about the *Confidential* piece; he even arranged for Sammy to stay at his home in Palm Springs during his recuperation. "So what else is new?" he finally said of the magazine story when Sammy pushed for a reaction to it. "Forget it, Charley. You don't even have to mention it."

Sammy confessed to Frank that he feared his career was now over. "Who wants a one-eyed entertainer?" he asked.

Frank said, "Relax, man. You're gonna be bigger than ever. Trust me. The public likes a good comeback story. Take it from me."

"But how am I gonna dance if I can't keep my balance?" Sammy asked, feeling hopeless about the future. "If I can't dance, Frank, I don't even want to live, man. I've worked so goddamn hard to get here, and look where I've ended up. How'd this happen, man. How'd this happen to *me?*"

He started to sob.

Sammy would later recall that Frank hugged him tightly and kissed him on the neck. Then he held his face in his hands with more affection than he'd ever seen from a man.

"You're gonna be fine," Frank whispered urgently. "Charley, you gotta be strong. You'll come outta this thing bigger than ever. You're alive, man. *You're alive.*"

The next day, Sammy held a press conference in his room.

When one of the swarm of reporters and photographers that had congregated around his bed asked about Sinatra's reaction to the *Confidential*

185

story, Sammy became misty-eyed. "Frank believes that if you have a friend then he's your friend and you believe in him, and that's it," Sammy said. "If he'd thought about me to the contrary, he just wouldn't have shown [yesterday]."

Four months later, Sammy Davis was back onstage, at Ciro's in Hollywood, and Frank Sinatra was the man who introduced him to an enthusiastic crowd of celebrities, such as Cary Grant, Lauren Bacall, Humphry Bogart, Edward G. Robinson, Jimmy Cagney, and Spencer Tracy. When Sammy walked out, they stood and cheered, shouting, "Bravo," and whistling, all proud to see one of their own survive what should have been certain death.

In 1954 and through the end of 1955, Frank—the Comeback Kid—made a number of successful films, including *Suddenly* (in which he played a coldhearted killer, to terrific reviews); *Young at Heart* (as an out-of-work songwriter in this marvelous musical re-make, opposite Doris Day,* of the John Garfield movie *Four Daughters*); *Not as a Stranger* (as a dedicated doctor, with Olivia de Havilland and Robert Mitchum); and *The Tender Trap* (as a ladies' man and actor's agent, opposite Debbie Reynolds). One role Frank wanted badly was that of Terry Malloy in *On the Waterfront*. He lost that one to Marlon Brando.

Also this year, Frank starred as Nathan Detroit—proprietor of "the world's oldest established permanent floating crap game"—in the film version of the Broadway sensation, *Guys and Dolls*, which had a smashing score by Frank Loesser. He had wanted to play Sky Masterson, the role portrayed by Marlon Brando, and always believed that the film would have been better if they had switched parts (since the Masterson role was more a singing part). The film was a box-office success just the same. (In years to come, Frank would record the Masterson song "Luck Be a Lady Tonight.") As all film historians know, Sinatra and Brando feuded on the set; there was no love lost between those two. Sinatra said of Brando, "He's the most overrated actor in the world." And of Sinatra, Brando observed, "When he dies and goes to heaven, the first thing he'll do will be to find God and yell at him for making him bald."

---

* Doris Day and Sinatra had worked compatibly together as early as 1949 when both were Columbia recording artists, dueting on "Let's Take an Old-Fashioned Walk," from Irving Berlin's Broadway musical *Miss Liberty*. But on this film they had a number of disagreements on everything—from how the movie should end to the constant presence on the set of her Svengali husband, Marty Melcher, and the schedule of filming: She liked to start early; he, late in the day. In the end, though, they became friends again when, after a sniffling scene, someone tossed a box of Kleenex at Doris. When it hit her in the forehead, Frank became incensed and hollered at the pitcher, "What's the matter with you? You don't ever throw things at a lady! Understand?" Even today, Doris says she often thinks of Sinatra whenever she reaches for a Kleenex.

In February 1955, Frank recorded one of his best albums, the ever-memorable *In the Wee Small Hours*. This was a double ten-inch set that was almost immediately issued as a twelve-inch album. The long-playing record opened up new possibilities for Sinatra. Previously, Frank's ability to create a certain mood with his music was limited to the three-minute span of single recordings. The advent of the "long play" allowed Frank to create a mood—whether depressing, with torch songs (or, as writer Steven Petkov called it, "suicide music"), or upbeat, with swinging numbers—by recording a series of thematically similar songs.

Most albums of the time contained a hodgepodge of material—ballads and upbeat songs, with no thematic line. Many of Frank's best albums were concept albums, especially at Capitol, where he did more than a dozen of them—like the aforementioned *In the Wee Small Hours*, which was a collection of love-gone-bad songs, or "Ava Songs." As music critic Pete Welding noted, "Ava Gardner may have left scars, but as happens so often with great artists, personal pain translated into artistic achievement."

Among the most noteworthy performances was Cole Porter's "What Is This Thing Called Love?" Frank made arranger Nelson Riddle's evening difficult when they recorded it. At his request, the tempo was changed, the chart was rearranged, and the composition was shortened, but in the end, after twenty-one takes, Frank got exactly what he wanted. "When Your Lover Has Gone" is Sinatra at his most evocative, and the lyrics said it all for Sinatra at this time in his life: "At break of dawn, there is no sunrise, / when your lover has gone. . . ."

"I Get Along Without You Very Well" is arguably one of his most sober ballad performances. Like all the songs in this moody collection, it speaks volumes for the melancholy Frank. It's as intense and true a performance as any he has committed to disc. "Glad to Be Unhappy" is a delicate, heartfelt performance of the Rodgers and Hart classic. "In the Wee Small Hours of the Morning," the heavyhearted title track of the album, was originally intended for Nat King Cole, and "Mood Indigo," a bluesy reading of the wonderful Duke Ellington number, was said to have been a personal favorite of the Duke's in 1968. Sinatra and Ellington would record a marvelous album together entitled *Francis A. & Edward K.*

In August, Frank recorded songs that were to be used in the film *Carousel*, in which he was to star as Billy Bigelow for 20th Century–Fox. A problem developed, though, when Frank learned that he would have to film the entire movie twice: once in standard 35-mm Cinemascope and then again in the 55-mm wide-screen process. This was a surprise that was not a part of the original deal. Sinatra told the producers that he wasn't about to film a movie twice for one fee. He quit the production and was replaced by Gordon MacRae. (Later, during production, technicians

187

found that they could convert the film, thereby making it possible to use only one camera after the first two weeks of filming.)

In August 1955, Frank found himself on the cover of *Time* magazine. The report called him "just about the hottest item in show business today" and said, "Four months shy of forty, he is well away on a second career that promises to be, if anything, more brilliant than the first."

At the end of 1955, *The Man With the Golden Arm* was released. Many consider this to be Sinatra's finest moment as an actor. In the black-and-white film, he portrayed the tragic Frankie Machine, a heroin-addicted, golden-armed poker dealer and would-be drummer. He wanted the part badly after reading sixty pages of the Nelson Algren book on which the movie is based and started making phone calls. For Sinatra, the filming was hard work; arduous twelve-hour days.

In the climax of the movie, Sinatra's character goes through a hair-raising drug withdrawal. Director Otto Preminger thought that the scene would be too difficult for Sinatra and suggested a great many rehearsals and the possibility of retakes. Frank had never been much for rehearsal when working on a film, and retakes were out of the question unless someone *else* flubbed a line. (*He* rarely did.) For Sinatra, a sense of immediacy was the key to his success as an actor. He knew just how he wanted to play that difficult scene. "I did some research on my part," he remembered, "and for about forty seconds, through a peephole, I was allowed to see what happens to people when they try to kick heroin cold turkey— a youngster climbing a wall. It was the most frightening thing I've ever seen. I never want to see that again. Never."

While filming that challenging scene, Frank told Preminger to keep the cameras rolling. "You'll get what you want," he said. "Trust me." Then, with no rehearsal whatsoever, the extremely grueling scene was shot in one take. Most Sinatra historians feel that next to the scene in *From Here to Eternity* in which Maggio dies, the drug-withdrawal scene in *Golden Arm* is Sinatra the actor at his best. When the film was finally released, ticket buyers and critics alike praised Frank's work. Arthur Knight in the *Saturday Review* summed it up best when he wrote that Sinatra's performance was "virtuoso."

"I wish I had some formal dramatic training," he would once observe, "but I never had enough time. Once we begin shooting, I rarely open the script. I feel that you don't have to go by the script verbatim. If two good actors in a scene listen intently to what the other is saying, they'll answer each other intelligently. Actors who go only by the lines never seem to be listening to the other actor, so the scene comes out on the screen as if you can see the wheels going around in their heads."

Frank's work in *The Man With the Golden Arm* would earn him an Oscar nomination for Best Actor. Sinatra believed that he did a convincing job in the film and said, "I felt if I ever deserved a prize, it should've been for that picture, because I did the finest work I ever did in my life on that film." Though he didn't win the Oscar (Ernest Borgnine did, for *Marty*), the film remains a testament to his brilliant, transcendent skill as an actor.

CHAPTER 18

In December 1955, Frank Sinatra turned forty years old, a milestone in any person's life. His work, particularly his recordings, suggested a man who had finally grown up, an adult who had somehow—and rather miraculously, it could be argued—survived a reckless youth and irresponsible love life. His voice had only gotten better, enriched and emboldened by time and experience. In fact, he had actually become the embodiment of the songs he would help to make famous over these last few years. "If the song is a lament at the loss of love," he once said, "I get an ache in my gut, I feel the loss myself, and I cry out the loneliness, the hurt, and the pain that I feel. I know what the cat who wrote the song is trying to say. I've been there and back. I guess the audience feels it along with me."

While his recordings seemed effortless, they weren't. Music was still a challenge to him; recording an album required intense concentration. Acting? Well, that was easy. Sinatra just *did* that, and it was often superlative; he was a one-take wonder capable of expressing great gentleness, compassion, and even humor onscreen in a natural, yet always compelling, manner. Indeed, Sinatra always communicated much of his hard-lived personal experience with his work, both in the recording studio and in front of the movie camera, and he was respected for it, which was important to him. All the jokers who had insisted that he was finished at the age of thirty-five—well, by the time he turned forty, they knew better. He had proved them wrong. Indeed, Frank Sinatra, at forty, was living the life of the consummate artist, of show-business royalty of the highest order, or as writer Pete Hamill put it, "a full-blown American legend." But the question remained: Was he happy?

To paraphrase Ava Gardner on her 1951 honeymoon with Frank Sinatra, let's just say he wasn't *un*happy.

Sinatra started the year 1956 back in the recording studio cutting the *Songs for Swingin' Lovers* album with Nelson Riddle. (This would be a year of great music for Sinatra; sixty-three recordings in all.) This extremely popular album, considered his finest by some critics, contains what many Sinatra fans feel is the greatest single recording of his entire career, his rendition of Cole Porter's "I've Got You Under My Skin." It took twenty-two takes to finish the song, which had to do with getting the orchestration and orchestral dynamics down right, not Sinatra.

Sinatra historian Ed O'Brien wrote in *Sinatra 101—The 101 Best Recordings and the Stories Behind Them*: "The driving sound of the brass section, featuring trombonist Milt Bernhart, combined with Sinatra's rhythmic cadence, is a transcendent moment in the history of popular music . . . often imitated but never equaled."

Ironically, "I've Got You Under My Skin" was added to *Songs for Swingin' Lovers* at the last minute. Sinatra telephoned Nelson Riddle at his home in Malibu in the middle of the night to tell him that they needed a few more tunes for the album. The next day, on the way to the studio, Riddle scored "Skin" in the backseat of his car while his wife drove. The arrangement was so superb that after the musicians rehearsed it for the first time in the studio, they gave Riddle a standing ovation. (Frank and Nelson rerecorded the song for Reprise in April 1963.)

Whether working with Nelson Riddle, Billy May, or Gordon Jenkins, Sinatra—who, ironically, cannot read music—always surrounded himself with the best of everything in the studio: arrangers, producers, musicians, engineers. Not only is he talented in his own right, he learned early on in his career something many artists of his stature never figure out ever: *other* people have imagination and vision, too. What's really fascinating is that despite the input of various composers, lyricists, arrangers, band members, and all of the other recording personnel, Sinatra's records still come across as intensely personal statements. Moreover, his private complexities and, arguably, the often poor choices he made in his personal life notwithstanding, Frank has always made sound choices when it comes to his art.

"There's one thing Sinatra has, especially when it comes to music: taste," observed his son, Frank junior. "In picking arrangers, in picking songs. Some people are very good singers and pick the dumbest goddamn songs in the world. Other people are bad singers and pick the greatest songs you ever heard in your life. Pop has both the taste to pick it and the tools to cut it."

Also in January 1956, Sinatra formed a film-production company, Kent Productions, which would develop his own movie projects. (The Sinatra western *Johnny Concho,* in which he played the cowardly brother of a famous gunman who of course redeems himself by the end of the film, would be the first film produced by Frank for the new company.) Later in the year, Frank would star in M-G-M's musical comedy *High Society,* a successful remake of *The Philadelphia Story* (1940), which had starred Katharine Hepburn as a society girl about to be married for the second time, Cary Grant as her ex-husband who interrupts the wedding, and Jimmy Stewart, who won an Oscar for his role as the reporter who falls in love with her in vain. Now, sixteen years later, *High Society* arrived in Technicolor and with music. Princess-to-be (in real life) Grace Kelly, in her last movie role, is the society girl, Bing Crosby is her ex-husband, and Sinatra is the reporter. Louis "Satchmo" Armstrong helps out with the tunes. Cole Porter's score includes, "Well, Did You Evah?" "You're Sensational," and "True Love."

About a year or so earlier, Frank Sinatra had thought it might be interesting to date Grace Kelly, with whom he had struck up a friendship in Africa when Ava filmed *Mogambo* there. Terence Gibb, a friend of the Kelly family from Philadelphia, remembered: "Grace got a phone call one day from Frank saying, 'Gracie'—he always called her that, she told me, until the day she died—'you know, I have always dug you, and I think we should get to know each other better.' Grace was flattered and said, 'Well, let me think about it. But I can tell you now, the answer is yes, yes, *yes*.' She could be quite the flirt."

At the time, Grace was having a very public affair with the handsome fashion designer Oleg Cassini, who was once married to the stunning doe-eyed film star Gene Tierney. She was very much in love and wanted to marry him, even though her family was opposed to the relationship. Still, according to Gibb, she was always secretly fascinated by Frank. She asked Cassini if he would mind if she went out on one date with Sinatra. "Just one little date; it'll mean nothing," she said. Of course, he said he did mind. She went, anyway.

Gibb said, "She told me that after one date with Frank, she knew that she could never have a relationship with the guy. She said he was all over her, trying to kiss her, man-handling her in a way that was unacceptable to her. Maybe that was the way you handled Ava, but that wasn't the way with Grace at all. You had to approach her differently, more romantically. You couldn't man-handle her the way Frank was used to doing with his chicks. She told me, 'Frank could be a wonderful mate if he'd just treat a lady like a lady.' "

"Grace said that Frank was inebriated when he picked her up and that this was a turn-off to her. Then, over a dinner of oysters ('Cocktail sauce! Whatsa matter with you, Gracie? You don't put *cocktail sauce* on oysters'), he started sobbing, telling her how much Ava had hurt him. He asked Grace if she could telephone Ava and talk some sense into her. Clearly, Frank wanted Ava to know that he and Grace had been on a date, probably hoping it would make Ava jealous. Grace refused.

"The next day, Frank telephoned Grace to apologize. He said he

191

didn't know what had gotten into him except, as he put it, 'way too much Jack Daniels.' He was truly contrite, she said. And he asked if he could take her out again and make it up to her. Laughing, she said, "Frank, I wouldn't date you again if you were the last man on earth, and even then I'd try to find someone else.'

"Grace always liked Frank very much," her friend said. "She rarely told this story to anyone because she knew he was going through a tough phase at the time. She always wanted to protect him. So that was an anecdote that wasn't much told."

On April 4, 5, and 9, 1956, Frank recorded more memorable music, including "Everything Happens to Me" and "With Every Breath I Take" (both recorded for the Top Ten album *Close to You,* with the Hollywood String Quartet). Then, later in the month, he found himself in Spain for four months filming *The Pride and the Passion* with Cary Grant and Sophia Loren, which had something to do with the moving of a giant cannon across war-torn Spain by a band of Spanish resistance fighters.

At the time he was making *The Pride and the Passion,* Sinatra was having an affair with twenty-four-year-old singer Peggy Connolly, who was with him in Spain and proved to be more of an annoyance than anything else. Ava Gardner lived in Spain, and anytime Frank could sneak off to see her, he would, even if that meant sending Peggy on a shopping spree just to keep her occupied.

Producer and director Stanley Kramer said, "When Sinatra walks into a room, tension walks in beside him. You don't always know why, but if he's tense, he spreads it. When we were shooting *The Pride and the Passion* in Spain, he was impatient. Frank is a tremendously talented man, facile and fast, which is good for him but not always good for the other actors.

"He worked hard and insisted on doing a lot of things you'd normally expect a star would want a double to perform. He ran through explosions and fires. He often started scenes as though he didn't quite know what was going on. It seemed like a palpable case of lack of preparedness, but after a couple of minutes he was going like a high-precision machine.

"He didn't want to wait or rehearse. He didn't want to wait around while crowd scenes were being set up. He wanted his work all done to-gether. He was very unhappy. He couldn't stand it; he wanted to break loose. Eventually, for the sake of harmony, we shot all of his scenes to-gether, and he left early. The rest of the cast acquiesced because of the tension."

Of Sinatra's need to get the job done and move on, Vincente Minnelli, who later directed him in *Some Came Running* (1958), once said, "There are great advantages when you work with Frank. If you can get the com-pany into Frank's fast tempo, enthusiasm, and pace, there are fewer shooting days, and you spend less money. It's very tough on Frank when he's on location. Once, he told me, 'This is something I can't help. I have to go. No one seems to be able to help me with it—doctors, no one.'"*

At this time, actor Humphrey Bogart had a tight-knit group of friends, which he and his wife Betty "Lauren" Bacall had dubbed the Rat Pack. Sinatra—who had been named "Pack Master"—Dean Martin, Peter Lawford, Sammy Davis, Judy Garland and her husband, Sid Luft, David Niven and his wife, Hjordis, and other stars who lived in the ritzy Holmby Hills area of Los Angeles were all a part of the so-called Pack at various times.

This Rat Pack was really just a social group of antiestablishment celebrities who enjoyed drinking, carousing, and getting into mischief together. "We admire ourselves and don't care for anyone else," Bogart said of the Rat Pack, only half-joking. They hated "squares," and anyone they found to be pretentious would be met with their wrath.

Once, Irving "Swifty" Lazar, the famous literary agent and the so-called recording secretary of the Pack, bought a Rolls-Royce and offered a ride one evening to Frank, Dean, and Judy. Proud of the automobile and its pristine state, he simply couldn't stop bragging about it. As Lazar drove the stars about town, they busied themselves with their own project: They built a nice fire in the backseat. It would take Lazar years to forgive them. This was typical of the kinds of pranks in which these celebrities engaged just to, as Frank once put it, "let off a little steam."

The Packers loved Sinatra's sense of style, his cool "habits," and his extravagant lifestyle, which is why he was named Pack Master. They marveled about his one hundred suits and fifty pairs of shoes, the fact that he carried only one-hundred-dollar bills; anything smaller just didn't matter in Sinatra's world. They were amazed by the brutal way he treated his minions and called upon him for advice, what with good help being so hard to find and all. Your chef overcooked your hamburger? Take it off the plate and throw it at him. That was Frank's way. ("Dumb jerk should know how I like my hamburgers by now, all the money I pay him.") Your personal assistant fouled up the day's schedule? Throw an ashtray at him. Again, Frank's way. ("Dumb jerk should know I hate to be late, all the money I pay him.")

And what about that confounding sense of humor? A friend wired him for money he said he needed to "bail out an overdue hotel bill," and Frank sent him a parachute and $30,000—fake money. (Then, the next day, he paid the man's hotel tab.)

And this was also a guy who really knew how to stage a bar brawl. He'd start a fight with some "joker," and then, when things would get rough as

* Of *Some Came Running*, Minnelli also remembered: "In the story, Frank is supposed to be killed in the end. But he suggested that Shirley [MacLaine] be killed instead, adding more weight to her part and, naturally, giving her much more importance as a star.

the room erupted in a free-for-all, he'd have his buddy Hank Sanicola, one of his managers and also a former fighter, and one or two of his other pals kick everyone's ass while he slipped out and waited in the car outside. ("I ain't gettin' my hands dirty on those finks," he'd explain.) Of course, as everyone well knew, sometimes Frank couldn't resist throwing a punch himself. Once, in a small nightclub, Frank suddenly got up and punched the guy sitting next to him in the mouth. The place exploded in fisticuffs. Afterward, as Frank was nursing a cut under his eye, one of his buddies asked, "Now what the hell was that about?" Frank responded, "The guy called me a dirty Jew. I don't mind the Jew part. But nobody calls *me* dirty."

His pals recognized that Frank's rowdy exploits—the wild fights in particular—did little to dampen the enthusiasm his fans felt for him. Michael Ventura, who published a novel in 1996, *The Death of Frank Sinatra*, remembered: "I'm Sicilian on both sides of my family, and if you grew up Sicilian in New York, Sinatra was a part of your family. He was the most famous Italian, except for some baseball stars. He was held up to me by my father, who would say, 'See him. He can punch anybody in the eye and get away with it.' "

Indeed, Frank Sinatra's temper and the resulting repercussions only served to *enhance* his image and add more luster to his celebrity. He was even more admired by his public for his displays of rage, especially if the press constantly derided him about such outbursts. He spoke for his fans. He did what many of them longed to do in their own lives but didn't dare; he didn't take crap from anyone. He fought back for the person who hated his boss but couldn't do anything about it for fear of losing his or her job; the person treated rudely by a waiter but who could only retaliate by leaving a meager tip; the person whose foot was stepped on in an elevator but who could only mumble something angrily incoherent instead of giving the offender a good poke. He was the kind of man many people wanted to emulate but couldn't *possibly* be like because they were stuck in day-to-day, mundane lives ruled by civility and manners and timid deference to power, while he— Well, he was Frank Sinatra. The Man.

Frank was a rebel even to his show-business peers. In fact, all of the Rat Packers, led by Pack Master Sinatra, were celebrities who loathed being told what to do but who often had to submit to a movie studio's will just the same because of contracts or protocol. Frank knew how to do that in style as well. For instance, when RKO asked him to attend the premiere of *Meet Danny Wilson* in San Francisco, Sinatra didn't want to go. However, when forced to do so, he fixed it so that the studio would be sorry.

First, he ordered eighty-eight Manhattans for his three-man entourage and charged them to the studio. (None of the glasses was empty when room service came by the next morning to clean up. Not one.)

He went to the premiere.

Afterward, he took a party of twenty people to four expensive nightclubs and later entertained them in his suite through the early-morning hours with gumbo and booze, all of which was charged to the studio. (He kept sending the spicy gumbo—shrimp, sausage, and crab meat—back to the kitchen, complaining that it wasn't thick enough to stand a spoon in.) At 4:00 A.M., he decided he wanted a piano delivered to his room, which required waking the manager of a musical-instruments store and paying a truck driver triple time to deliver it, which was charged to the studio. Nobody played the piano. Nobody even knew how to play.

The next morning, he and his buddies—all hung over—staggered into the best men's shop in the city and, at Frank's direction, bought anything they wanted: sweaters, slacks, suit jackets, ties. The studio got the bill. And that afternoon, when the weather was too foggy for a flight back to Palm Springs, Sinatra demanded—and got—a chauffeur-driven limousine, stocked with rare wines from one of San Francisco's best restaurants, for him and his friends, courtesy of RKO.

Afterward, back at Sinatra's home, he and his pals devoured some of the shrimp they'd brought back from San Francisco. "Guess that'll show them scabs at RKO," Frank said as he pulled away the shell from a steamed prawn and then tore off its head.

He also had heart. He was particularly sympathetic to the victims of automobile accidents. For instance, when he found out that a young girl (the niece of a music publisher) had been paralyzed in a car mishap and was a fan of his, he went to the hospital and sat with her for hours, talking to her even though she could not respond.

When Lee Remick's husband, Bill Colleram (who had directed a television special for Frank), was in a car crash, Remick and her mother flew to Los Angeles and stayed at the Beverly Hills Hotel for a week until she was finally told that he would live. When they checked out, they learned that Sinatra had paid the hotel tab; she could not remember ever having met Frank Sinatra.

Such stories could fill volumes, there are so many. That was—is still—Frank Sinatra, Pack Leader. He could be your most hated enemy or your Good Samaritan, your most treasured lover or your tormentor, your most troublesome pain in the ass or your best buddy in the world, but as Sammy Davis once put it, "Whatever he was, he was, above all else, *cool.* He was our leader. Nobody did it like Frank. Nobody dared."

CHAPTER 19

In 1956, Frank Sinatra had romances with three distinctive stars: Judy Garland, Kim Novak, and Lauren Bacall.

Judy Garland, who had been dubbed a vice president of the Rat Pack because of her bright, caustic wit, was unfortunately always in and out of hospitals over the years. Suicide attempts, drug overdoses, alcohol abuse, and a myriad of calamities constantly befell her, all of which have been chronicled in many Garland biographies. Sinatra felt about Garland the way he would feel about Marilyn Monroe in years to come. He was annoyed at her for her weaknesses, though he did feel a certain amount of pity for the fact that she was never able to overcome them. Whenever Judy was in the hospital for one reason or another, Frank would often send flowers. He would fly in all of her friends to her bedside.

Sometimes he would be so sweet to her, even close friends were amazed. For instance, when, at the age of thirty-three, she had a baby on March 28, 1955, Frank went to the hospital to lend support; he brought Lauren Bacall with him. In true Sinatra fashion, he hired a caterer to bring in food for all of those friends and family members waiting in the lobby for the arrival of Judy's baby. Then Frank gave her a small stuffed animal as she was being taken out of the delivery room after the rather difficult birth of her son, Joey.

Later, though, Frank would watch in dismay as Judy abused her body. He sometimes showed nothing but contempt for her, making her feel bad about herself. He couldn't help himself, though. He was revolted by the self-destructive way she lived her life, perhaps because it was, at least in some ways, such a reflection of his own.

Despite those feelings, he would still be intimate with her from time to time. Why? Frank would probably have answered, Why not? She was interesting, complex, and talented beyond all reason (and he had great admiration for her ability as an entertainer). Did he make love to her periodically over the years? Yes, he did. However, it would probably be fair to say that he did not have much respect for her. They did, however, remain friends until she died at the age of forty-seven in 1969. (Frank even offered to pay for her funeral, but daughter Liza Minnelli graciously declined his offer.)

After Frank and Ava broke up, Judy had actually convinced herself that he might be the man for her. She began telling friends that they might marry.

When Frank heard about her announcement, according to one of his associates, he telephoned her and said, "I don't go for broads who are into the sauce like you are. Get clean and we'll see what we'll see." That promise of sorts did little to spur Judy onto any kind of permanent recovery.

Over the years—before, during, and after their respective marriages—Frank made a habit of making dates with her and then not showing up. He would promise to return phone calls and then disappear from her life for weeks. To most men, Judy Garland was a much-celebrated star. To Frank, she was just another dame. He played with her feelings. Said one of his associates, "He was a dog. She was his chew toy."

Judy Garland once called Sinatra's behavior toward her "pretty repulsive." She also said (in 1956), "You have to take Frankie as he is. When you invite him to a party, he may be an hour late, or he may not show at all. He gets involved and forgets even to telephone." Their connection lasted for years, but Judy Garland would never make it onto the list of important relationships in Frank's life. Lauren Bacall would fare better in the sense that, for a time, she did have Sinatra's affections, though she would eventually wish that had not been the case.

Frank had great admiration and respect for Bacall's husband, Humphrey Bogart. Bogie, just fifty-six years of age, was already considered by most observers the elder statesman of Hollywood actors. He and Frank had long, fascinating conversations over the years about everything from moviemaking to art to books; they had a great deal in common. Bogie considered Sinatra a close friend, and the reverse was certainly true; Frank once sent a workman to the Bogart home and had an expensive hi-fi system installed in it without even telling the Bogarts. "Frank's a hell of a guy," Bogie said. "If he could only stay away from the broads and devote some time to develop himself as an actor, he'd be one of the best in the business."

In February 1956, when Humphrey Bogart was diagnosed with cancer of the esophagus, Frank was a constant and reassuring companion, cheering his pal onto what he prayed would be an eventual full recovery. Unfortunately, Bogie would have less than a year to live. During this dreadful time, Bogie's thirty-one-year-old fourth wife, Lauren Bacall (born Betty Joan Perske in New York City), began to cry on Frank's shoulder. He was there for her, as she was for him. She spent hours talking to him about Ava and listening as Frank complained about the way Gardner had treated him. Before they knew what was happening, they were feeling an attraction toward one another. "When he's with you, he adores you," Bacall once said (in 1956). "But don't let that boyish quality fool you. You may get the idea that he wants to lean on you, but actually he wants to be boss."

Bogie had long suspected that Frank was interested in his vivacious, beautiful wife, and he wasn't happy about it. He knew, though, that nothing intimate would ever occur, at least as long as he was around to stop it from happening. Now that he was ill, however, there was nothing he could do to prevent a romance from blossoming between the woman who meant everything to him and the man he called a friend.

"He was somewhat jealous of Frank," Lauren Bacall once recalled of her husband. "Partly because he knew I loved being with him, partly because he thought Frank was in love with me, and partly because our physical life together, which had always ranked high, had less than flourished with his illness."

Frank and Lauren were discreet about their ardor. Most people who were acquainted with them back at the time feel that Bogie never knew of the romance. It became an urgent matter among his friends, then, to make certain that Bogie never learned what was going on between his wife and Sinatra.

"It was no secret to any of us," said playwright Ketti Frings, a friend who often visited Bogart during the actor's illness. "Everybody knew about Betty and Frank. We just hoped Bogie wouldn't find out. That would have been more killing than the cancer."

Ethel Anniston was an assistant of Bacall's at this time. She says she was hired by Sinatra to "keep an eye on Mrs. Bogart, make sure she got her rest, took certain medications." Anniston did not live in the Bogart home at 2707 Benedict Canyon Drive in Los Angeles but, rather, "popped in and out just to make sure Mrs. Bogart was all right and then report everything I noted back to Mr. Sinatra, who cared deeply about her." (She was paid $175 a week by Sinatra.)

"If a romance happened between Mrs. Bogart and Mr. Sinatra—which I believe did occur—it wasn't the sneaky betrayal it has been portrayed as having been in the past. They were brought together by the pain, suffering, and anxiety that resulted from Mr. Bogart's illness. It was the thing they had in common."

Lauren Bacall was a vibrant young woman brimming with energy and spunk. She would say privately that she had certain needs that her desperately ill husband could no longer satisfy—emotionally as well as sexually—and that Frank Sinatra was there for her in an unconditionally supportive way. In fact, she was so devastated by Bogie's illness, say her associates, she simply could not handle the ordeal on her own. The radiation treatments, the sicknesses, and the gradual and merciless debilitation of this once robust man were all too much for her to take.

"She would most certainly have cracked up if she had to be alone to deal with it; she was that unprepared for this terrible thing that was happening to her husband," said Ethel Anniston.

"I could not think in terms of Bogie not living," Lauren Bacall would later recall. "It was just totally unacceptable."

To say that Lauren Bacall deserted her husband for Frank Sinatra or that Sinatra callously betrayed his dying friend is to paint the experience with too broad a brush stroke. It could be argued that if they did have an affair, as people close to them seem to suspect, then what they shared was wrong (at least based on most reasonable standards of morality, especially given the era). However, to whatever degree Bacall and Sinatra were involved during the final months of Bogie's life, it was important to both of them. Frank represented to Lauren wholeness and vitality at a time when her life was filled with nothing but sickness and despair. She was accustomed to being around a certain energy and zest for life; she had always been surrounded by spontaneity and exuberance while she was with Bogie. Her husband and Sinatra were most certainly cut from the same cloth. They both lived each moment with gusto. So did Lauren Bacall.

"Hmm. I think I'd like strawberry shortcake for breakfast today," she decided one morning upon rising. Her wish always Frank's command, he sent one of his minions to Orange County, California (an hour from Beverly Hills), to purchase sweet, locally grown strawberries. "None of that store-bought crap for my girl," he said.

According to her friends, Lauren Bacall was—despite the romance with Frank—still devoted to Humphrey Bogart, her husband of almost eleven and a half years. "Whatever was going on with Sinatra had absolutely no bearing on her deep feelings for her husband," said Ethel Anniston. "Besides, Sinatra was also dating Kim Novak at the same time, so things were complicated on many levels."

Indeed, Frank was seeing the blonde Novak from time to time, one of his costars from 1955's *The Man With the Golden Arm*, and 1957's *Pal Joey*. Despite her great beauty and intelligence, Novak was just another in a string of post-Ava romances that Sinatra did not take seriously. He had helped the insecure Novak as an actress on the set of *Golden Arm*, giving her confidence in herself that would help make her one of the biggest movie stars of her time.

Novak was a sweet girl, sexy and with a winning personality. She had also been tormented over the years by Columbia studio head Harry Cohn, who always claimed credit for having "made" her a star. In fact, he did take a plain-looking brunet girl from the Chicago suburbs and transform her into a blond bombshell. He taught her how to speak, walk, dress, and act like a star.

Unfortunately, she paid a dear price for her fame. Cohn constantly had her under surveillance and refused to allow her to live her own life and have her own romances (falling in love was out of the question) for fear that she would cause a scandal that would jeopardize his substantial investment in her career as a movie queen. "I made her, and I can break her," he liked to say. Frank always felt that Kim was too nice for the industry in which she worked and feared that Cohn's machinations would one day destroy her.

Sinatra and Novak were occasional lovers, though she continues to deny it to this day. To actually be in a serious relationship with her was not a consideration for Frank, however. On a superficial level, he thought she wore too much makeup, and that was always a turnoff to Frank. "I think women—generally—have enough beauty without doing the circus-tent-type thing," he said. More important, he simply wasn't attracted to women who were constantly in peril, always the victim. If a woman wasn't strong, like Dolly and Ava, she wasn't for Frank. Frank Sinatra hated weakness in himself; therefore, he would never allow it in others, men or women. Like Judy before her and Marilyn Monroe later on, Kim Novak reflected something back to Sinatra about himself that he didn't want to see, ever.

On January 14, 1957, three weeks after his fifty-seventh birthday, Humphrey Bogart died. Frank, who was performing at the Copacabana in New York, canceled five shows, saying he was too devastated to perform. Jerry Lewis substituted for him in some shows; Sammy Davis, in others. Frank did not, however, attend the funeral. Many reporters over the years have indicated that Sinatra probably felt too guilty about the affair he was having with Bogie's wife to attend the funeral. In truth, at this time Sinatra rarely attended the funerals of people he cared about. He considered funeral services morbid displays and had said that he preferred to remember his friends as having been surrounded by laughter rather than tears.

"I don't believe that either Frank Sinatra or Miss Bacall felt the least bit guilty about the affair," said Ethel Anniston. "Miss Bacall once said that Frank was taking care of her while her husband was indisposed and she was taking care of him after the terrible marriage to Ava Gardner. That's how they looked at it. I think there would have been tremendous guilt if they thought Mr. Bogart knew what was happening, but since he didn't, there was not."

After Bogart's death, Sinatra and Bacall continued their romance publicly, attending film premieres, dinners, and other Hollywood functions together. "At all of his small dinner parties, I was his hostess," she would later remember. "People were watching with interest. It seemed to everyone that we were crazy about each other, that we were a great pair."

Bacall fell hard for Sinatra, but Frank was more tentative with his emotions where she was concerned. To her credit, Lauren was also someone who would never back off from a good fight, and Frank did like noisy fireworks now and then in a relationship. Even though Lauren would always insist that she was not a confrontational person, she actually loved to be challenged, especially by strong men. It excited her.

She and Frank fought about everything from the weather to her clothes, his choice of friends and her spending habits.

They also bickered about her chain-smoking. Frank—a chain-smoker himself—hated it when his women smoked. "Women who smoke from the moment they open their eyes until they put out the light at night—that drives me batty," he said. "It's unfeminine and dangerous—burn up the whole damn house, you know?"

And his flirting, not to mention the fact that he could walk into a room and have any woman he wanted, was a constant source of irritation to her.

"I am a star," she once told him, according to Ethel Anniston. "And let me tell you something, Frank Sinatra, if that's not good enough for you, then *fuck you*."

In February 1957, Hearst Broadway columnist Dorothy Kilgallen, for whom Frank Sinatra had always had nothing but disdain because of the way she reported stories about him and his friends, wrote a six-part series entitled "The Real Frank Sinatra Story," which, she said, included "heretofore unpublished episodes in Frankie's life." Actually, Kilgallen had been a thorn in Sinatra's side for years. When he moved, she published his New York address. When he moved again, she published his *new* address. When he saw her in a nightclub wearing a pair of sunglasses, he walked over to her table and dropped a dollar bill into her cup of coffee, saying, "I always figured she was blind."

Actually, most of what Kilgallen wrote about Sinatra in her series was true—she was an adept reporter—but accuracy wasn't the point. As far as Sinatra was concerned, she had attacked him mercilessly. She reported that the women in his life were "starlets who never got past first base in Hollywood, assorted models and vocalists, and chorus girls now lost in the ghosts of floor shows past. Others belonged to the classification most gently described as tawdry."

After the series was published in the *Journal-American*, he sent her a tombstone with her name on it—a frightening gesture.

Onstage at the Copa—and later in shows across the country—between his songs "Young at Heart" and "The Second Time Around," he worked a routine into his act that described Dorothy Kilgallen as very unattractive. He said she had a face like a chipmunk. Her profile looked like one of his car keys. "Dorothy Kilgallen isn't here tonight," he said at the Copa. "I guess she's out shopping for a new chin." (Sinatra actually coined the phrase "chinless wonder" in reference to Kilgallen.) "The town where she came from, they had a beauty contest when she was seventeen years old," he said. "And nobody won. There was a poor little Chinese kid standing there, and they gave him the cup because he was better lookin' than the broads in the line."

Reporter Nick Lapole of the *Journal-American* saw the show and heard Sinatra's comments at the Copa: "There was a lot of laughing from his entourage and from the people in the audience that she had been rough on." Sinatra did change the way the public perceived this extremely popular, high-profile columnist and CBS television personality. (She was a regular on *What's My Line?*) Mail sent to CBS never before focused on her appearance until Sinatra denigrated it as part of his routine. Her friends say that the insecure Kilgallen was completely shattered by Sinatra's criticism and the effect it had on the public's perception of her. He had found a way to cut her to shreds, and things would never be the same for her. Once, she went to a Broadway opening with record producer Ben Bagley. She must have felt beautiful and glamorous until a stranger came right up to her, nose to nose, and said, "Hi ya, chinless." Bagley said, "I was stunned. Even as her escort, it was like being hit in the face. Dorothy's hand began to tremble."

The vendetta went on for years.

In 1961, in fact, Frank so embarrassed himself in front of an audience at the Sands in Las Vegas by devoting twenty minutes of his act to putdowns of Kilgallen's looks that Vegas critic Ralph Pearl mentioned it in his televised review of the show. "You should be the last guy in the world to attack the lady in such a lowly, unethical manner no matter what she said about you," Pearl declared. "After all, Frank, a Rock Hudson you ain't, by any stretch of the imagination."

Sinatra was watching Pearl on TV while reclining in a lounge chair at the Sands Hotel Health Club. He was so angry, he picked up a pot of coffee and hurled it at the television set. Then he made a few telephone calls and barred the reporter from the Sands. It would be four years before the writer was allowed back into the hotel.

When Dorothy Kilgallen died in November 1965, Frank was given the news while eating a dinner of curried oysters and champagne sauce with friends. "Too bad," he said. Then, after a beat, he added, "Well, I guess this means I'll have to change my act."

It's startling, in retrospect, just how busy and productive Frank Sinatra was in the middle of the 1950s with memorable record albums and noteworthy movies. By this time, it was estimated, he was making about $4 million a year. Considering his schedule, it was amazing that he found the time to host his own television series of big-budgeted one-hour musicals and half-hour dramas for ABC-TV, *The Frank Sinatra Show,* which aired in 1957. (This would be his last TV series. Frank was never fond of making television appearances and always seemed ill at ease with the cue cards and TelePrompTers used in TV studios.)

In 1957, Sinatra recorded an astonishing fifty-seven new songs, but probably none are more significant than "Witchcraft" and "All The Way." "Witchcraft," recorded on May 20, would go on to become a huge hit for Sinatra in 1958 and receive a Grammy nomination. "All The Way," with lyrics by Sammy Cahn for the film *The Joker Is Wild,* recorded on August 13, 1957, is one of Frank's bestselling singles. It was on the charts for thirty weeks and went on to win the 1957 Academy Award for Best Song. (Frank played comedian Joe E. Lewis in the film.)

This was also the year of Frank's classic concept albums, *A Swingin' Affair* and *Come Fly With Me* (his first outing with arranger Billy May, which would soar to number one on the sales charts). Sinatra also issued *Where Are You?*—an album of romantic ballads in a musical collaboration with the multitalented Gordon Jenkins.*

There was also Sinatra's premiere Christmas album, *A Jolly Christmas With Frank Sinatra.* For sheer artistry, taste, sense of pacing, and atmosphere, *A Jolly Christmas* is untouchable. Great cover art, too. Capitol typically couldn't leave it alone and reissued it with a bland cover as *The Sinatra Christmas Album.*

Today a popular recording artist like Michael Jackson releases one album every four or five years. Back in the fifties, though, Frank Sinatra's output—four or five, sometimes more, albums a year—was not unusual.

In 1957 *Pal Joey,* with Kim Novak and Rita Hayworth, was released. Sinatra played the title role, the tenderhearted Joey Evans, which Gene Kelly originated on Broadway—"the only role I've dreamed of doing for many years besides Private Maggio." It's easy to see why Sinatra would feel comfortable in the role. His character alternates between being a heel and a nice guy while pursued by two beautiful women who are opposites in personality. A singer in a San Francisco nightclub, Sinatra is chased by all the chorus girls except Kim Novak, who rejects his advances. The club plays a benefit at the home of a wealthy widow, Rita Hayworth, who falls in love with Sinatra and offers to set him up in his own nightclub, Chez Joey. However, when she realizes that he loves Novak and wants to make her a star, Hayworth issues an ultimatum: If Sinatra wants Chez Joey, he can have it, as long as he drops Novak. When Sinatra

---

* *Where Are You?* was recorded in stereo but released only in mono. Several decades later, it finally appeared in stereo, stunningly recorded.

refuses, he demonstrates to Novak that he really does love her. Novak reconsiders; no woman could refuse a man who makes such a sacrifice to show his love.

A popular story about the film has to do with its billing. Harry Cohn was concerned about how Sinatra would want the film billed; he didn't want any arguments with Frank, who by this time was not the kind of star with whom anyone wanted to disagree. They had a meeting. "We talked things out," Frank once remembered, "and I saw an uneasy look on Harry's face. I don't like frightened people. And I don't like being frightened myself. So I asked, 'What's the trouble? If it's billing,' I said, 'it's okay to make it Hayworth, Sinatra, and Novak. I don't mind being in the middle of that sandwich.' Man, were they relieved." (The soundtrack of *Pal Joey*, an outstanding album, included some wonderful Rodgers and Hart songs, such as "I Didn't Know What Time It Was," "There's a Small Hotel," "I Could Write a Book," and "The Lady Is a Tramp")

George Sidney, who directed Sinatra in *Pal Joey* (as well as in *Anchors Aweigh*), observed of Sinatra, "If he only wanted one or two takes, what's wrong with that? Horowitz played an hour and a half in concerts without going back and correcting a note or a passage he thought he could do better. He was a natural personality. No matter what he played, he was always Frank Sinatra, just as Clark Gable and Spencer Tracy were always themselves. His secret was complete concentration on what he was doing. There were no heights he couldn't reach, not much he couldn't do if he put his mind to it."

Despite a personal life that would keep most mortals completely preoccupied, Sinatra's career continued to soar in 1958 and 1959.

The year 1958 is best remembered by Sinatra's fans for his album *Frank Sinatra Sings Only the Lonely*, an album of torch songs that Frank considered his best work. Arranged by Nelson Riddle, the album contains some of Frank's finest saloon songs, such as "Angel Eyes (the quintessential story of a loser at the game of love); "Guess I'll Hang My Tears Out to Dry," "Blues in the Night," and the title track, "Only the Lonely," such a fine ballad that it prompted one reviewer to ask the question "Was Sinatra invented for the ballad, or was the ballad invented for him?" This album, which his son, Frank junior, has called "the greatest blues album ever made," remained at number one for many months and is still one of Frank's biggest sellers in the reissued CD format. (When Frank performed these songs in concert, he would sometimes introduce them as songs about men who have been done wrong by women. "Shake hands with a vice president of the club," he would say.)

Author Robin Douglas-Home (*Sinatra*) once described a Sinatra recording session he had the privilege of attending, a date when Frank was recording a song whose lyrics were intensely personal. "I saw complete and utter involvement with the song he was singing—involvement so close that one might feel he was in the throes of composing both tune and lyrics as he went along. He was putting so much into that song, giving off so much of himself, that it drained my own energy just to watch him . . . left me so limp that I felt I had actually been living through some serious emotional crisis."

Also noteworthy in 1958 was *Come Dance With Me,* a swing album arranged by Billy May. (It won Grammy Awards in 1959 for Album of the Year and Best Male Vocal.) The next year saw the release of the *Look to Your Heart*—not a true album but a collection of singles—and *No One Cares,* two more Top Ten twelve-inch releases. (It's interesting to note that Sinatra always took great care to sequence the songs properly on his albums, especially on his concept albums, a job most often left to record-company personnel. For instance, on the melancholy *No One Cares* album, when listened in consecutive order, each song moves the story forward. As Frank explained, "Why did no one care? Because there's a 'Cottage for Sale,' that's why—so it had to be track two. That song's the saddest ever written. It depicts the complete breakup of a home."

Nelson Riddle is on the cover of *No One Cares,* among the crowd at the bar, though it's Gordon Jenkins who arranged the album.

Sinatra loved Gordon Jenkins's work, said it was like being wrapped up and floating in a musical womb. Jenkins's sighing strings, long and languishing phrases, and classically based arrangements brought the best out in Sinatra, as it did with Nat King Cole and Judy Garland, with whom Jenkins also recorded historic albums. From bucolic Webster Groves, Missouri, a suburb of St. Louis, Jenkins was a New York City transplant and frequently wrote songs, suites, and albums about the Big Apple. Later, he moved to California and did the same there. His wife, Beverly Mahr Jenkins, was a background singer in great demand.

Of course, there were plenty of films released during these years as well.

He played a crippled World War II infantry lieutenant, costarring with Tony Curtis and Natalie Wood, in *Kings Go Forth;* a disillusioned war veteran with Dean Martin and Shirley MacLaine in *Some Came Running;* with Eleanor Parker and Edward G. Robinson, a careless dreamer and widower trying to raise his ten-year-old son in Frank Capra's comedy with dramatic overtones *A Hole in the Head;* and an army captain fighting the Japanese in World War II Burma in *Never So Few,* with Gina Lollobrigida. In 1959, Sinatra recorded the optimistic "High Hopes" for *A Hole in the Head,* which would win the Academy Award for Best Song that year.

On *The Frank Sinatra Timex Special,* which would air later in the year (October 19, 1959, with Bing Crosby, Mitzi Gaynor, and Dean Martin),

Frank performed this song in a fun segment with forty youngsters. Wearing a black tuxedo with a satin lapel and sitting in the center of a lively group of eager, energetic boys and girls in their play clothes and party dresses—all of whom provided slightly off-key background vocals—Frank never seemed more at ease on a television broadcast. His rapport with those youngsters was charming; he was like a favorite uncle entertaining at a birthday party. "I got that side of me, yeah," he once told a reporter, laughing. His sense of self-deprecating humor was always key to his charm. "I can be one helluva sweet guy. Just ask anyone under the age of twelve."

CHAPTER 20

By early 1958, Lauren Bacall was very much in love with Frank Sinatra and constantly suggested the notion of marriage to him. "My friends were worried I'd be hurt," she recalled, "that he wasn't good enough, couldn't be counted on for a lifetime. But just then it was going so smoothly. I was the center of his life, for a moment."

For his part, Frank began to bask in the warmth of Lauren Bacall's devotion and attention. After all, at least *she* was there. Ava was not. He tried to convince himself that he now wanted to be with Lauren Bacall, that Ava Gardner no longer mattered to him. And think of the sweet revenge against Ava that would be exacted if he were to end up married to another exquisite, even younger, star, and so soon after their divorce. He was drinking heavily, as always, and his friends say that he was constantly in a lonely funk. So he proposed marriage to thirty-three-year-old Bacall on March 11, 1958, about a year and a half after his divorce from Ava was finalized.

Lauren accepted Frank's proposal immediately. She was amazed that he had finally asked, and elated as well, as evidenced by the fact that she immediately began signing autographs "Betty Sinatra."

"My dependence on Frank became greater and greater," she would say. "It wasn't planned. It simply was."

What happened next has been told often but never completely explained.

On March 12, the day after their engagement was official, Frank departed for Miami. That night, Bacall—ecstatic about the wedding plans they had discussed and feeling that her future would once again have meaning and purpose—went to a party given by Zsa Zsa Gabor for Noël Coward at the Gabor home. Accompanying her was agent Swifty Lazar. Louella Parsons, another guest, asked Lauren if it were true that she and Frank were going to marry. Lauren has said that she refused to say and that she dashed off to the ladies' room rather than be grilled by the persistent Parsons. She would insist that Lazar was the one who confirmed the engagement. However, Parsons reported the next morning that Lauren had, in fact, "finally admitted that he [Sinatra] had asked her to marry him. She was beaming with happiness."

Lauren Bacall knew the next morning, when it was published, that this kind of publicity was not good; Frank would assume that she had made an important announcement unilaterally and wouldn't like it at all. She knew she had ripped the lid off a Pandora's box, she just didn't know what would result from it.

When Sinatra did not return her phone calls, she became more concerned. His behavior had been erratic in recent months; sometimes he seemed content in the relationship and at other times uncomfortable. As she later put it, "[He was] adoring one day, remote the next," which is why she was so astonished when he proposed marriage. When Lauren finally reached Frank, he was angry with her. "Why did you do it?" he asked her. She didn't do "it," she explained. Swifty Lazar did "it."

Frank said, "I haven't been able to leave my room for days; the press are everywhere. We'll have to lay low for a while, not see each other." They were to go to Chicago on March 25 to attend a Sugar Ray Robinson fight. That would have to be canceled, Frank said. They would also cancel their trip on the twenty-sixth to New York, where Lauren was to be at his side when he received the Boys Town of Italy Award, which was the reason he would not be able to perform his nominated hit "All the Way" at the Academy Awards that year, and their plans to attend a policeman's benefit in Palm Springs on March 27.

Her heart sinking, Lauren Bacall reluctantly agreed.

And that was the last time she ever heard from Frank Sinatra.

Two weeks later, Frank was in Las Vegas opening an engagement at the Sands. Meanwhile, Dean Martin was appearing at the Cocoanut Grove in Los Angeles. Lauren Bacall was at Martin's opening. When asked about Frank, she told a reporter, "Do me a favor. Never mention me again in the same breath with Frank Sinatra."

The media reported that a problem had developed in their romance when Frank signed on to appear in the film *Paris by Night* with Brigitte Bardot. It was said that Bacall was jealous of Bardot. Then, Brigitte, who was always a fairly adept public-relations strategist herself, jumped into the fray by saying, "Miss Bacall is no fool. If I were she, I would [object]. Sinatra and I together will make interesting chemistry. It is in the contract," she said ridiculously enough, "that Miss Bacall is not allowed to come with him while he makes the picture. You see, I am no fool, either."

Of course, Brigitte Bardot had nothing to do with what happened between Frank and Lauren. In fact, Frank had never even agreed to appear in a picture with her.

The sad truth was that Frank had dumped Lauren, and he didn't even have the courtesy to tell her. How he could have done such a thing to her was beyond the comprehension of anyone who knew and cared about her. That he could just drop out of her life was incomprehensible to her and her friends. But not to Frank's. They'd seen similar behavior from him many times in the past.

Didn't Frank Sinatra know how much Lauren Bacall had grown to depend on him? Of course he did.

If there was one thing Frank Sinatra completely understood, it was the concept of desperate obsession. After all, Ava Gardner had once been everything to him. Without her, his life meant nothing, at least in his view. Quite simply, he now did not want to be regarded as that important and central a figure in anyone else's life, ever, especially if it was someone about whom he truly cared. Perhaps it could be said that he loved Lauren Bacall too much to marry her.

It would seem that Frank's mother, Dolly, influenced her son's decision to end his relationship with Lauren Bacall, and partly for her own reasons. Doris Sevanto remembered: "Frank and Dolly were fighting at this time. She used to make him so mad, he would slam the phone down and burst into tears. He would call and ask for advice, and when she would give it, he would whine at her: 'Mama, why are you always butting into my life.' It was a typical dependent-Italian-son–domineering-Italian-mother relationship. She had so much power over him, it's not surprising that he felt that women were to be conquered. I think that was the story of all of his romances.

"Anyway, Dolly was never that happy when Frank was involved with a woman more powerful than she was. That's one of the reasons she disliked Ava. Too strong. Too masculine. *She* wanted to be the most powerful woman in his life. So when Dolly heard that Frankie was going to marry Betty—someone she knew was a ball-buster—she called him in Miami and told him he was biting off more than he would be able to chew.

" 'The two of them, they're wounded,' she said later of Frank and Betty Bacall. 'One is worse than the other. They don't need to be together. What kind of marriage is that? It's based on tears: his for Ava, hers for Bogie. And not only that,' she said, getting to the real point, 'that woman is gonna run his life. And no one runs my son's life. But me.' "

For Frank Sinatra, the decision to leave Bacall was not a casual one, as has been reported. There was a great deal of angst about it, "a lot of going back and forth," as Doris Sevanto put it. In fact, Frank also telephoned his ex-wife, Nancy, who was adamant—perhaps for her own reasons—that Frank break off the engagement, that it was too soon for him to marry another woman.

Neither Dolly nor Nancy Sinatra suggested that Frank break up with Lauren the way he did. While his motives may have been unselfish, his actions were heartless. He took the cowardly way out of the romance and avoided dealing with any painful ramifications of an appropriate ending to this long relationship. One moment he was there, making love to her, confiding past hurts in her, sharing his life with her. Then, the next moment, he was gone, as if he had never even existed, as if they'd never met. It all seemed inexplicable, but as one writer once said of Frank, "You might as well try to analyze electricity."

"I couldn't deal with this," Lauren Bacall would recall. "There was no way to understand it. We had been such friends for so long, how could he drop the curtain like this? I was under a permanent cloud then—trying to excuse him to others, pretending I understood—but others had seen this behavior before. No one just drops someone without discussion. It was such a shock. . . . I spent night after night in tears."

It's been said by both Ethel Anniston and M-G-M hairstylist Sydney Guilaroff that after Frank dropped out of sight, Lauren Bacall—depressed and anxious—confided in a few friends that a romance with Sinatra had actually begun prior to Bogart's death. Perhaps she now felt guilty about any possible indiscretion, especially when she realized that she had taken such a chance for nothing more than what turned out to be a fling, at least for Frank.

"And I believe that this is what put the nail in the coffin where Frank was concerned," said Ethel Anniston. "They had a deal, a love vow, so to speak, that never, ever, was the origin of their romance to be revealed to anyone. Mr. Sinatra was embarrassed by it because he truly cared about Mr. Bogart and he simply didn't want it to be known. Mrs. Bogart agreed at the time that it was best for all concerned. But after the breakup, she was so upset, she slipped and told a few people, and this got back to Mr. Sinatra. When he found out that she had betrayed him, well, that was the end of her. She was dead in his life. Thank goodness she had her children [Stephen, ten, and Leslie, six, at this time] or she never would have survived."

In years to come, when the two of them would see each other at a social function, Sinatra would completely ignore Bacall. Once, she found herself face-to-face with him after a concert, and he looked at her as if she weren't even there. "Not a flicker of recognition" is how she remembered the moment. Helpless in the face of his cruelty, she felt completely diminished as a woman, as a person. She needed him in an almost crippling way. "I felt sick. My humiliation was indescribable."

CHAPTER 21

By 1960, no entertainer was more controversial or more popular than forty-four-year-old Frank Sinatra. Despite the growing prevalence of rock and roll as well as British popular music, Sinatra still managed to maintain a premiere status in the world of show business.

However, this was a difficult period for Sinatra as he attempted to extricate himself from his Capitol recording contract. In fact, there would be no new Sinatra product between September 1959 and May 1960. That eight-month lag, by today's standards, could hardly be considered cause for concern. (Artists go years without product these days.) Back in the fifties, however, Frank's fans had become accustomed to the release of albums every couple of months. Single issues were always on the market as well.

Frank felt that Capitol Records was restricting the way he recorded his music. Basically, he wanted to do it his way—select his own tunes, record at the times when he wanted to, schedule his releases when he felt they should be in the stores, and even spearhead the careers of other recording artists—and he couldn't as long as he was working for a label he did not own.

Also, Frank sincerely felt that he had been artistically stifled at Capitol. He felt Capitol did only three types of albums: slow and sad, up-tempo and happy, and collections of singles. In fact, that's all he did, except for *Come Fly With Me,* a number-one album.

The lag in recording releases to the public resulted from Sinatra's wanting to deny Capitol product. Finally, he capitulated and worked out an agreement by which he would finish his term at Capitol and start Reprise concurrently. (Many people assumed his later work with Capitol, ending with *Point of No Return,* an album arranged by Axel Stordahl, came from the can, but it was new.)

While the time without recorded product was alarming to some of his fans, they were heartened by the fact that Sinatra never stopped performing in concert halls and nightclubs.

Sinatra had always enjoyed appearing in Las Vegas more than anywhere else. He had made his Las Vegas debut at the Desert Inn back in September 1951, when there were only four hotels on the Strip. By 1960, though, the Strip was a virtual mecca of colorful lights, high-rise hotels, and noisy casinos. The entertainment in Las Vegas at this time was always the best in the business: Danny Thomas, Jerry Lewis, Lena Horne, Red Skelton—the list was endless. Because Frank's friends and relatives would all make their way to Las Vegas to see him work there, the good times really never ended for anyone in his circle during an engagement in the desert. The gambling. The "dames." The audiences. For Frank, it was all completely irresistible. "He goes and goes and goes and never stops until he's completely done in," said Red Norvo, his part-time accompanist. "But to see him *really* go, you've got to see him in Vegas."

On January 26, 1960, the marquee in front of the Sands Hotel in Las Vegas looked like a Who's Who of contemporary show business: Frank Sinatra, Dean Martin, Sammy Davis Jr., Peter Lawford, and Joey Bishop. By this time, Frank was a co-owner of the Sands, and a 6 percent share in the hotel (each point worth close to $100,000). He had unlimited credit with the hotel, for Jack Entratter, the corporate president, had ordered that the management tear up his IOUs just because having Sinatra in the casino always made for big business, especially when he was joined by his pals Martin, Davis, Lawford, and Bishop. They were called the Rat Pack by some in the media, the Clan by others.

Frank felt that the media-inspired moniker "the Clan" was going too far in describing the relationship between himself and his performing pals. "He wasn't happy about that name," Joey Bishop* remembered, "because even though it wasn't with a K, it still had racist connotations, and out of respect for Sammy, I think, Frank didn't want it. The Rat Pack was okay with him, but he really liked the Summit."

In fact, Frank preferred to refer to himself and his buddies—Martin, Davis, Lawford, and Bishop—as the Summit. (At this time, Eisenhower, Khrushchev, and de Gaulle were planning a summit conference in Paris. Frank said that he and his pals would have their own "summit conference of cool"; thus, the name the Summit.) All of them—Frank, Dean, Sammy, Peter, and Joey—were in the midst of making the silly film *Ocean's 11* for Frank's Dorchester Productions, in association with Warner Bros. This film, shot in Las Vegas, was the first of four mediocre movies they would do together. The schedule was grueling, and their lifestyle made it even tougher on them. After each performance was over, at two in the morning, they would drink the rest of the night away, partying with "dames," "broads," and "dolls" until the sun came up. Then, somehow, they would manage to be in front of the cameras at dawn for work on the film. Afterward, they'd sleep for a couple of hours and then begin again.

* During an interview for this book, Joey Bishop joked, "Another reporter said to me recently, 'There's only you and Frank left from the Rat Pack.' And I said, '*Shhh.* Be quiet. Frank's got connections.'"

(*Ocean's 11,* a comedy-drama about Danny Ocean's [Sinatra's] recruiting of a bunch of former military buddies to rob five major Las Vegas casinos simultaneously on New Year's Eve, would premiere at the Freemont Theater in Las Vegas on August 3, 1960, and on Broadway at the Capitol Theater. Sammy Davis displayed the most credible acting ability among the Rat Pack. At the Capitol, the movie would break attendance records set seven years earlier by *From Here to Eternity.* Though the movie was generally panned, ticket sales were strong; it went on to make money for Sinatra's production company.)

Showtime was at 8:00 P.M.

"Let's start the action," Frank would say to his pals as the orchestra played the overture and they prepared to take the stage. While standing in the wings, each would smoke a cigarette and then guzzle a final swig out of a bottle of Jack Daniels. Then the Summit performers would slap each other on the back as each bounced onto the stage to an enthusiastic Las Vegas welcome.

Las Vegas was never the place to see the Rat Pack if one wanted to actually hear them sing. In other cities, the performances were of a high caliber; each gentleman had the opportunity to sing a separate set of hits and standards before the finale, when all would gather onstage for scripted and unscripted comedy and a few jointly performed songs. In Las Vegas, all they did was clown, much more concerned about entertaining each other with juvenile humor and "inside" wisecracks than they were about singing.

The running comedic themes had to do with Dean always being inebriated, all of them indulging in a great deal of sex with women, and Sinatra being involved with the Mafia. Some of it was insufferably silly; at one point during the show, for instance, Sammy would smash a cake in Joey's face, typical of their raucous, adolescent humor. Sometimes one of the performers would manage to squeeze a complete song into the merriment, but then one of the other fellows would inject himself into the big number with a joke or a prank.

For instance, the lights would go to soft blue as Frank began softly crooning "When I was seventeen . . ." This promised to be a great moment, a Sinatra classic—"It Was a Very Good Year"—in the offing. But then, from the wings, the audience heard Dean complete the sentence by shouting, ". . . you were a pain in the ass." The intrusion generated big laughs but killed the moment—and the song with it. Later, when Sinatra and the audience finally quieted down and the master vocalist began the ballad again, it was spellbinding until near the end of the number, when he sang "When I was thirty-five . . ." and Dean again shouted out from behind a curtain, ". . . you were *still* a pain in the ass."

"Do you know how boring four weeks two times a night can be?"

explained Joey Bishop, who wrote most of the act. "That's why we just had to have fun. We couldn't wait to go on out there and do the show. Spontaneity was the key to our fun. When the show was over, Frank always said to the audience, 'If you liked it, give a little credit for the hub of the wheel.' I always thought that was nice of him."

In truth, none of the singers was in good voice, anyway, when they performed in Las Vegas. No singer's vocal chords could hold up under the pressure of the schedule Frank, Dean, and Sammy maintained (Peter and Joey did little singing, thankfully)—the booze, the smoking, the late hours. The men would spend an hour in the steam room every day, as if the hot steam would somehow magically restore their vocal cords and stamina. It didn't.*

Only once—to anyone's memory, anyway—did the shenanigans get out of hand onstage, and that was the night Joey Bishop walked off. Frank and Dean, in an improvisational routine, started calling each other "dag." Even though Frank had used the phrase "dag" for years as a short version of "dago" when he was bonding with fellow Italian Americans, Joey—who had recently been lauded for his defense of Italian Americans on *The Jack Paar Show*—became offended and left. Later, when Frank asked him why he had done that, Joey said, "Hey, Frank, you ever think about how you're gonna feel when you leave the stage and somebody calls you a dag. You're not gonna like it, and if you argue about it, the other guy's gonna say, 'Hey, what's your problem? I heard you say it yourself onstage.' I don't know how to act out there when you start that stuff. Am I supposed to think it's camaraderie? I'm sorry, but I can't stand on that stage when you're doing dago jokes." Frank agreed, and neither he nor the rest of the fellows used the word onstage again.

"If you tell Frank something and you're right," said Joey Bishop, "then you were home free. The key to our relationship was trust. He trusted me. We all trusted each other."

It can be said, though, that the fellows didn't always offer Sammy Davis the same consideration when it came to ethnic concerns. Historically, most people who have written about the Rat Pack, including Nancy Sinatra, make note of the cracks about Davis's color and how, while "a little rough," they were acceptable "because of what they knew was in their hearts." In retrospect, much of it does not seem funny.

For instance, all of the fellows wore white robes with their names stitched in back for their daily steam-room ritual. One day, Sammy went into the steam-room and couldn't find his robe. When he asked about the missing garment, he was informed by the attendant that Frank had ordered a new one for him. Then the attendant reached under a counter

* Joey Bishop joked: "The first time I saw Frank Sinatra nude in the steam room, he became my idol. Ten minutes later, Sammy Davis came in, and I became *his* idol."

and presented Sammy with a brown robe, along with brown towels and brown soap. "Mr. Sinatra said you can no longer use the white towel or the white soap," said the attendant solemnly. Then Frank and his buddies came from behind a curtain, and everyone laughed at Sammy's reaction.

Or, while onstage and with the lights low, Frank would say to Sammy, "You better keep smiling, Sammy, so we can see where you are."

When Sammy did his Sinatra impression of "All the Way," Frank would say, "He's just, excuse the expression, a carbon copy."

Or, during some other shows, Dean would pick up Sammy and say, "I want to thank the NAACP for this wonderful trophy." (Joey Bishop explained, "When I wrote that bit, it was supposed to be 'I want to thank the B'nai B'rith for this award, referring to the fact that Sammy had recently converted to Judaism. But Dean couldn't remember the words B'nai B'rith. He blew it every night until he finally changed it to NAACP.")

Later, Dean said to Sammy, "I'll dance wit ya, I'll sing wit ya, I'll swim wit ya, I'll cut the lawn wit ya, I'll go to bar mitzvahs wit ya. But don't touch me." (Sammy, stomping his feet hysterically, would practically roll on the floor while laughing at these jokes.)

Sinatra's dedication to racial equality went back years, all the way to his Hoboken childhood, when he himself felt the sting of prejudice because of his own ethnicity. People still remember that when Sinatra first began singing "Ol' Man River" back in the forties, he was careful to replace the line "Darkies all work on the Mississippi" with "Here we all work on the Mississippi." (After he made that lyrical change, most other performers followed suit whenever they sang the Kern-Hammerstein song in concert.)

In years to come, Sinatra opened up many doors for Sammy Davis, especially in Las Vegas, where he demanded that Sammy be allowed to perform in certain hotels and be paid what other stars were paid. But did that give him and his Caucasian friends the right to joke about Sammy's race? Indeed, Sinatra historians have always been baffled by his, and the other Rat Packers', seemingly complete disregard for the ideal of racial tolerance during their shows in the early sixties.

As Sammy himself once put it, "For the times, yeah, the jokes were offensive. But, man, look at the company I was keeping. I had to put up with it. I loved those guys, and I know they loved me. But, yeah, it wasn't right. I didn't like it a lot of the time. Sometimes I had to wonder, Are these cats for real or what? I had to bite my tongue a lot."

Their mediocre performances, potentially racist and hammy routines, aside, there was definitely something tantalizing about these handsome, robust, and talented men in their impeccably tailored, expensive suits— white shirts crisp and new, ties well chosen—all on one stage together.

Ringsiders could smell the strong scent of cologne, the favorite brand the fellows would liberally slap on their faces and necks in the dressing room.

Shirley MacLaine—at twenty-five—was considered the Rat Pack's mascot because she was a "dame" they allowed to hang out with them and, according to her, with whom they were never intimate. (MacLaine starred with Sinatra in the 1958 film *Some Came Running* and received an Academy Award nomination for her work.)

She best described the way the Rat Packers looked when she wrote about watching Frank and Dean get ready for a night on the town in her memoirs—*My Lucky Stars—A Hollywood Memoir.** "What got me were their hats. They wore wide-brimmed hats right out of the racetrack number from *Guys and Dolls*. Their shoes were uncommonly polished and I was certain their socks didn't smell. Underneath it all, I sensed their underwear was as white and fresh as soft, newly fallen snow."

Not only did they look charming, their presence together suggested something exciting and even dangerous. After all, these entertainers were considered by much of the public to be troublemakers, always on the edge of revolt, engaging in unlawful acts most people would never countenance. So, for some ticket buyers, there was a certain thrill in the thought that after the show any one of them could be arrested for disturbing the peace or beating up some hapless photographer. They always had a sense of humor about their reputations, often referring to Sinatra as their "hoodlum leader."

The Sands was sold out during this January 1960 engagement, as it was whenever the Rat Pack performed there. Celebrities were scattered among the audience every night to see the action, including Milton Berle, Bob Hope, Red Skelton, Shirley MacLaine, and even John F. Kennedy. Also, the performances were tremendously lucrative for the performers: Frank and Dean both owned a piece of the Sands's Copa Room, so they would earn between $75,000 and $100,000 a week when the Rat Pack played Las Vegas. The rest of the guys made about $25,000 a week.

Sen. John F. Kennedy, running for president at the time, was a big fan of the Rat Pack's, especially Frank. As Peter Lawford's brother-in-law (Lawford married into the powerful Irish-American Kennedy dynasty in 1955 when he wed JFK's younger sister Patricia), he had front-row-seat entrée to the Las Vegas festivities on February 7, 1960. He was on the campaign trail and en route from Oregon to Texas on the *Caroline,* his private plane, with about a half-dozen reporters when he decided to accept Sinatra's invitation and stop off in Las Vegas.

Sinatra became immersed in Kennedy's presidential campaign in 1959,

---

* Even though she was generally complimentary to him, when Shirley MacLaine's book was published in 1995, Frank Sinatra said of it, "It's amazing what a broad will do for a buck."

when it was first decided that Kennedy would be a candidate. Sinatra committed himself to John Kennedy because he respected his politics. They had become friends,* and he wanted to see him in the White House. Jack's father, Joseph, the ambassador, was primarily responsible for campaign strategy. "We're going to sell Jack like cornflakes," he had boasted.

In the summer of 1959, Frank Sinatra and Peter Lawford flew to Palm Beach, Florida, to visit with Joseph Kennedy, who had said he wanted their assistance in the campaign. Joe Kennedy had always been fascinated by show-business personalities and understood the power that celebrities could wield to influence the masses. He owned a film-production company in the 1920s, which eventually evolved into a part of the once-powerful RKO and under Howard Hughes would become one of the most profitable Hollywood studios of its day. It was during that time that the married Joseph Kennedy began a much-publicized romance with film star Gloria Swanson.

Lawford once remembered: "Joe Kennedy ran the campaign from an outdoor enclosure next to the swimming pool. He called it 'the bullpen.' There was no roof on the structure. Inside were a telephone and a deck chair. Joe spent his mornings on the telephone barking orders at frightened minions and employees. What seemed off about the arrangement was that he made the calls in the nude, which was the reason for the enclosure."

Joseph Kennedy told Frank that he wanted him to begin outlining plans for concerts to raise money for the campaign. He also wanted Sinatra to network with his influential friends in show business and secure their support for Kennedy. He asked Sinatra to record a theme song for the campaign as well, and they settled on a reworking of Frank's song "High Hopes." There would probably be other favors in the future, he told Frank. Sinatra was eager to help.

John Kennedy always looked forward to socializing with Sinatra, to whom he was introduced by Peter Lawford, because he liked Frank's wild antics, exciting women, show-business excesses, and Hollywood gossip. Kennedy's interest in the entertainment industry can be traced back to 1945, when he spent much of his free time in Hollywood, socializing with glamorous stars, in particular, Gene Tierney. When Peter Lawford married his sister and the two purchased a home in Santa Monica, Kennedy became an even more regular visitor and was anxious to see Sinatra in Las Vegas in January 1960. Blair Clark, who worked for CBS Radio, said, "We

---

* Kennedy had spent the weekend of November 6 and 7, 1959, at Sinatra's home in Palm Springs after a Los Angeles fund-raiser. Afterward, Frank had a plaque mounted on the door with the inscription "John F. Kennedy slept here November 6 and 7, 1960." Sinatra got the year wrong on the plaque!

all figured, How bad can it be to catch Sinatra at the Sands? We were seated at Sinatra's table, and people kept coming and going, jumping up and sitting down. There were all these bimbos and showgirls standing around."

Sexual activity was always high on the list of priorities for Sinatra and all of his pals whenever they played Las Vegas (except for Joey Bishop, who was happily married, and still is, to the same woman). Certainly, none of them could resist the charms and temptations of a shapely show-girl, and with the passing of years, the stories have almost become legendary.

One former Las Vegas showgirl, Betty Rose Lehman, now a thrice-divorced grandmother living outside Las Vegas, revealed: "Sammy was the one who really recruited girls for the Rat Pack. He would have some-one in his organization call up all of the hotels and say, 'Send me your best showgirls. The fellas are lookin' for some fun.' All of us girls, from all the hotels, would all go to the Sands and wait in a private lounge for the guys to get offstage. They always had terrific food and lots of booze. Then, when they were ready, we would go off with them—three with Dean, three with Sammy, and so on. Frank sometimes ended up with four or five.

"I admit that I had intimate relations with Sinatra once with two other women. He wasn't what we had heard he would be, the great lover, you know? He was sort of disappointing, in fact. I expect, though, that this was because he was so completely drunk. The strangest thing happened, though, when I put my hands through his hair and this black, inklike substance came off on them. He explained that he'd had the back of his head painted with something to hide his bald spot during a performance and he forgot to wash it off."

"It was well known that Frank could have his pick of the women, especially the extras on his movie sets," said Evelyn Moriarity, who worked as a stand-in for Marilyn Monroe in her films. "However, I hap-pen to know of a time he didn't get his way," she said, laughing. "When he was doing *Ocean's Eleven,* he would often finish out his workday by picking up an extra to take back to his hotel room. One day, he saw this particular extra he liked and commanded her to go to his room. 'Here's the key. Now, go on up there and wait for me.' When she didn't show, he was so upset he did everything he could to get her fired. But he couldn't . . . because she was the casting director's wife! Afterward, she said, 'I actually might have gone to bed with him, because, after all, he *is* Frank Sinatra. But how dare he order me to his room?'"

Most of the time, though, Frank scored with the "dames." His suite was always filled with voluptuous female performers and prostitutes. He was single, relatively young at forty-four, and saw no reason why he shouldn't have as much of a swinging time as possible, because, as he put it to Lena Samuels, an African-American woman who worked as a secretary to Sammy Davis on the set of *Ocean's 11* and was also a Sands showgirl (called a "Copa Girl" after the Copa Room, where Sinatra and the rest worked), "How many more years have I got? I ain't gonna be the one looking back wishing I had done this or that. I'm doing it all now while I can still do it, while I'm young. Now, take your clothes off," Frank instructed her, "and fly me to the moon, baby. Let me play among your stars."

"I swear to you," recalled Lena Samuels, "that's what he told me, 'Let me play among your stars.' I had to laugh. He was so corny, but they all were, those guys. Of course I was intimate with him. I was eighteen. He was irresistible to me.

"The thing I remember is that he was the best kisser in the world. He was paranoid about his breath and kept asking me if I smelled cigarettes or liquor on him. He was considerate. You know that thing you read in romance novels about being ravished with kisses, having your breath taken away and all that nonsense, well, that was the way I felt with him.

"The other thing is that because he was such a complete brute on the set, I thought he'd be the same way in the bedroom. He wasn't. He was loving and considerate, but it bothered me that he was swigging from a bottle of Jack Daniels at the same time he was making love to me. Then he wouldn't kiss me again until he brushed his teeth and gargled with mouthwash.

"After we finished, we were having a smoke in bed, and I said to him, 'Why is it that you're such a bastard out there [on the set] and such a sweetheart in here?' He said, 'Because if I was a bastard in here, you wouldn't come back for more, now, would you?' Then he asked me, 'Who's bigger, me or Sam?' He knew I'd been intimate with Sammy Davis, just once. I answered, 'Oh, *you* are, Frank. You're *much* bigger.' He absolutely loved hearing that. He laughed his head off and said, 'Of course I am. And that takes care of another racial stereotype, doesn't it?' Then he got up and went to take a shower, which was the first time I noticed his naked body in the daylight. I must say, he had a great ass for a skinny guy; he really did."

Lena Samuels thought that what she and Sinatra shared in the bedroom had afforded her special privileges with him. So the next day, on the movie set, she went over to him on the set and whispered seductively in his ear, "See ya after work, sweetheart?" Then she rubbed against him. Outraged, Sinatra pulled her aside and began to holler at her, "Are you crazy? Don't you fuckin' flirt with me. *I* flirt. The dame doesn't flirt." Then, as he was walking away, he turned and said, "And by the way, Lena, the answer to your question is 'Hell, yeah.' "

Dawn Lindner Lewis, who still lives in Las Vegas today, was a showgirl at the Stardust Hotel in Las Vegas during this time. She remembered:

"You always knew when Frank Sinatra was in town, because there was a buzz, an electrical charge, and you could feel it throughout the whole city. All of the girls from the hotels were vying for an invitation to the Sands when word got out that the handsome young senator from Massachusetts, Kennedy, was there. Jack Kennedy was so gorgeous, all the girls wanted to meet him."

Dawn had met Dean Martin a month earlier, in January 1959, when he appeared at the Sands. One of his assistants had told her to give him a call whenever Dean was in town if she ever wanted to say hello to him. On the night that Senator Kennedy attended a Rat Pack show, Lewis found herself in an opulently appointed suite with the Pack and with about twenty other women. What she observed there, however, not only offended her but forever changed her image of these celebrities.

She remembered that Frank, Dean, and Sammy acted as if they were spoiled high school boys, squirting champagne over each other and stripping the tops off some of the women present. Frank went to each topless woman and buried his head in her bosom while making lewd noises. Dean took Polaroid photographs for posterity. They snapped brassieres at one another, and at one point Dean wore one on his head, as if it were a hat, and pranced around the room; then the men went into one of the bedrooms with a group of the women, all of whom seemed to be delighted.

Shirley MacLaine had similar observations about such immature humor: "They were primitive children, and their reactions to things, adolescent. They put crackers in each other's beds and dumped spaghetti on new tuxedos. They would grab an ice cube from a drink and thrust it in the hand of a formally dressed fan and ask him to skate around on it."

Eventually, Dawn Lindner Lewis remembered, Frank—"a gaunt, wiry little thing"—emerged from the bedroom wearing only a skimpy white terry-cloth towel. She was seated in a corner, enjoying a cocktail, when Sinatra pointed at her and said, "So, doll, I guess you're all mine."

"You make me sick," she told him before throwing her drink in his face. "I don't know what came over me," she said years later. "I was just so suddenly repulsed by the whole thing."

Frank was enraged. He screamed at her, "Jesus Christ, get the fuck outta here. *Scram.* What'd you come in here for if you didn't want to do it?"

At that moment, Peter Lawford came into the room and grabbed Frank by the shoulders, saying, "Calm down, Frank. She's leaving; she's leaving. Don't worry about it. C'mon, man. Forget it. Don't worry. Don't get yourself all riled up. We're havin' fun, ain't we, pal-y?"

As Lawford escorted Lewis out of the suite, she remembered, he seemed frightened "that Sinatra was going to go over the deep end and start hurting people." Out in the hallway, Lawford sent another busty blonde—a Copa Girl—in to take Dawn Lewis's place. "Sweetheart, go on in there and make Frank forget what just happened," he told her. She did as he suggested.

Apparently, Frank could also be rather territorial about his one-night stands, at least according to one close business associate and friend of Peter Lawford's. When Frank and Lawford's associate were staying at the Savoy Hotel in New York, Frank hired two high-priced call girls to be intimate with him. After he was finished with them, Lawford's associate took one of them to his suite, where he also had sex with her. In the middle of their rendezvous, there was a loud banging on the door. It was Frank. "Open this goddamn door," he said. 'No, Frank, I'm in bed,' said Lawford's associate. Frank continued to pound on the door, screaming as loudly as he could. Then, after twenty minutes of silence, Sinatra suddenly burst into the suite. He had paid a hotel engineer to take the door off its hinges!

"When he barged into the room, I was scared to death," said Lawford's associate. "I didn't know what he was going to do. He grabbed the broad right out of my bed and said, 'Don't you *ever* do that again, do you hear me.' As he was dragging her down the hallway back to his room, he was shouting at her at the top of his lungs, 'Whatsa matter wit' you,' until a giant of a man, eight feet tall at least, came out of his room and said, 'Hey, you, shut da fuck up!' at which point Frank quickly ducked into his room."

That same associate tells of the time matters got out of hand with a prostitute in Sinatra's suite at the Fontainebleau Hotel one night in November 1958 when Sinatra was filming a movie in Miami. Hosting a wild party for his friends, including Peter Lawford, Sammy Davis, and Joe E. Lewis, Sinatra invited a bevy of high-priced hookers he had hired for "entertainment" to his suite. (He posted a sign on the door that said: Through These Portals Pass the World's Nicest Broads.)

At about four A.M., Frank ordered two of the women—a small, thin brunet and a tall, busty blond—to go into the bedroom and strip. They obliged and came back into the living room wearing only bras, panties, and garter belts. Frank said, 'Okay, so entertain us, dolls." As the brunet tried to balance a drink on her head and dance about the room, the blonde stood motionless. Frank went over and whispered a lewd suggestion in her ear. The poor girl must have had a sudden attack of propriety because she became insulted, called Frank a "goddamn wop" and retreated into the bedroom to put her clothes back on.

A furious Sinatra went after her. After a loud exchange of words, there was an alarming crash. The other partygoers ran into the bedroom only to find Frank Sinatra lying on the bed on his back with the hooker sitting on top of him, repeatedly hitting him on the head with a stiletto-heeled shoe.

"Get this bitch off me," he screamed at the astonished onlookers. *"Get her off me!"*

At the hospital, later, the doctor who was stitching his forehead asked Frank, "So what are you doing down here in Florida, anyway?"

Sinatra said, "Making a movie."

The doctor asked, "Oh, yeah, what's it called."

With a groan, Sinatra answered, *"A Hole in the Head."**

In Las Vegas, during the Rat Pack's engagement at the Sands, Frank Sinatra gave John F. Kennedy a "present": a twenty-five-year-old, raven-haired Irish beauty named Judith Campbell (later Campbell Exner), with whom Sinatra had once had an intimate relationship.†

Much has been said and reported about Judith Campbell and her connection to Sinatra and Kennedy. Most of it has been contradictory and even inaccurate, leaving everyone but the most devoted Kennedy historian and archivist in the dark about exactly who this person is and where she fits into the puzzle of Kennedy's life. Simply put, for the uninitiated, the Judith Campbell Exner saga began when she met Kennedy on February 7 at Sinatra's table. The next day, Kennedy and Campbell had wine and lunch on the patio of Sinatra's suite at the Sands. A month later, on March 7, the day before the New Hampshire primary, the two began a romantic entanglement that would last for at least the next two years (until spring 1962). Telephone records indicate that she called Jack seventy times at the White House during that time. They also had, she claims, at least twenty private lunches at the White House in 1961, not to mention a four-day stay at the Plaza Hotel in New York as well as private encounters in Los Angeles, Chicago, and Palm Beach.

Some find Exner's claims preposterous. Milt Ebbins, a close friend of Peter Lawford's who was well-acquainted with John Kennedy, said, "Jack was one of the sharpest men in the world. Judith's claims make no sense. You mean to tell me he took her to the *White House?* He wasn't crazy. He did some stupid things but never anything *that* stupid." Still, Campbell's claims are bolstered by the fact that her name does appear on the White House registry numerous times during the period that she says she was there.

Meanwhile, Sinatra, who seemed to somehow always be at the center of everyone's lives, also introduced Judith to mob chieftain Sam Giancana (as "Sam Flood," his alias) within about six weeks of her having begun

---

* *A Hole in the Head*, produced and directed by Frank Capra, was released in 1959 and costarred Edward G. Robinson, Eleanor Parker, Thelma Ritter, Carolyn Jones, and Keenan Wynn.

† Campbell would later explain that the reason she and Frank Sinatra stopped dating was because he requested that she participate in a *ménage à trois* at his home one evening. She was not interested and said he was "too kinky" for her. They did, however, remain friends.

the affair with Kennedy. It's been reported many times over the years, and has become part of Exner folklore, that she was romantically involved with the president of the United States and Sam Giancana at the same time. Today she insists that this was not true. In fact, she now maintains that she was *never* romantically involved with Sam Giancana, even though she wrote in her autobiography *My Story* that they did have an affair. She now says that he was just a close friend with whom she was intimate only one time. (Nothing makes her angrier, she says, than to be called a "Mafia mistress.")

At the age of twenty-six, she insists, she found herself acting as a messenger between Giancana and Kennedy, delivering documents and money from the White House to the mobster in satchels and manila envelopes. The documents are thought to have had something to do with a secret plot to get rid of Fidel Castro at a time of worsening relations with Cuba. Exner says that Kennedy didn't trust the CIA to eliminate Castro, he wanted to deal with the mob directly on that matter.

Though her stories about the Kennedys and the mob have been anything but consistent over the years, Judith has nonetheless carved out her own niche in American popular history, first with her own 1977 autobiography *My Story*. When Frank Sinatra first heard that Exner was writing her memoirs, he quipped, "Hell hath no fury like a hustler with a literary agent."

What is most fascinating about *My Story* is that it is an autobiography that has now been completely disavowed by the subject, who says she felt unable to write the truth because of threats and intimidation. She says she would never have come forward at all with her affair with Kennedy when she did (in 1975) except that if she hadn't, the story would have come out, anyway, as a result of ongoing hearings into organized crime, and it would have been distorted in the process. Even more surprising, perhaps, is that many members of the press are forgiving of Judith Campbell Exner and believe her when she says that she has changed her story over the years not because she has embellished it but because she now feels free, with the passage of time, to give more details.

Judith Exner is, from all accounts, an amiable, well-intentioned woman who seemed to always be in either the right place at the wrong time or the wrong place at the right time, depending on one's view of it. After her book, with subsequent press interviews, she continued to reveal more about her romance with Kennedy and association with Giancana. "The only mistake I made," Exner, sixty-three in 1997, now insists, "is that I fell in love with a married man."

That Frank Sinatra could share Judith Campbell with John F. Kennedy seemed to make him feel closer to the senator; for Frank, it was practically a ritualistic bonding experience. In fact, Peter Lawford once said—and it's been quoted *ad nauseam* in other accounts of these people's lives, but is still a good line—that "Frank was Jack's pimp. It sounds terrible now, but then it was really a lot of fun," he said. Frank was never certain how far it had gone between Kennedy and Exner. He made the assumption, knowing Kennedy's reputation, that he and Exner were intimate, but he did not know for certain the full scope of their relationship. Contrary to what is often thought of Jack and Frank, they did not often discuss their personal lives with one another. Except for an occasional drunken orgy, Kennedy kept his distance.

One former Kennedy aide put it this way: "None of these Kennedy and Sinatra accounts over the years has ever gotten it right about Jack and Frank and this supposedly close relationship they shared. The fact is that while Kennedy liked Sinatra, he was always extremely concerned about him. It wasn't just Bobby who was apprehensive about Frank's image. Jack thought Sinatra was crude and vulgar and had no scruples whatsoever.

"We were discussing Frank one day and all that he was doing for the campaign, and Jack said to a group of us, 'Look, make no mistake about it. Sinatra's a thug. Let's face it. Let's be aware of it and then let's try to use him to our advantage.' But Jack knew that if Sinatra made one wrong move, he [Kennedy] would be finished due to his close association with him. And if he ever forgot that, Bobby was there to remind him."

According to this source, John Kennedy once quipped, "Every night before I go to bed, I pray to God that I don't wake up and read in the newspaper that Frank Sinatra has been arrested again, at least not until after I'm elected."

CHAPTER 22

The Summit engagement at the Sands Hotel in Las Vegas ended on February 16, 1960. The Rat Pack then took a train to Los Angeles, where they finished *Ocean's Eleven*. After that, it was back in the studio for Frank on March 3, 1960, to cut the *Nice 'n' Easy* album with the Nelson Riddle Orchestra. First up during that recording session was the Johnny Mercer song "Dream." While singing the song during a first take, Sinatra was taken aback by a high note. "Jesus," he told Nelson Riddle, "that's a high mother." He tried again on the second take. Still, he wasn't satisfied with the way he had attacked that note. "Next tune," he said abruptly.

When Sinatra went home for the evening, Nelson Riddle stayed up through the night and composed a new orchestration for "Dream," which Frank recorded the next evening. Also that evening, Frank cut another rendition—his second—of the classic, romantic "I've Got a Crush on You." (Frank performed this song in concert for decades, and another version of the song was included in Sinatra's 1993 *Duets* album, with Barbra Streisand.)

Nice 'n' Easy was a comeback album for Sinatra at Reprise artistically and commercially. Originally, it didn't even have his name on the cover. The public was so starved for Sinatra that the album shot to number one. It was an easygoing, relaxed, unambitious project, artistically right on the nose for the moment, tremendously charming and engaging. One shining aspect, among many, of the album was Sinatra's amazing talent for selecting the right songs and sequencing them in just the right way to achieve the best results. *Nice 'n' Easy* was music for a basement club or an afternoon on the patio. It was played constantly on jukeboxes.

For the rest of the year, Frank Sinatra and John F. Kennedy continued their friendship and—according to FBI records, if they can be believed—swapped women in New York, Palm Springs, and Las Vegas. It's true that Kennedy did seem to marvel at Sinatra's womanizing. In fact, Judith Exner has said that whenever she would visit Jack at the White House, she was always inundated with questions about Frank. "Almost immediately, Jack started pumping me for gossip, most of it directed at Frank," she said. "What was Frank doing? Was it true that he was seeing Janet Leigh? We always went through the same routine." (Since Leigh was costarring with Sinatra at this time in *The Manchurian Candidate*, JFK's question seems logical.)

Frank Sinatra felt that Kennedy was the right candidate for the White House. Not only did he respect his politics; he was excited by the notion of having a pal in the White House. Always a devoted Democrat ("I've been campaigning for Democrats ever since I marched in a parade for Al Smith when I was a twelve-year-old kid," he liked to say), Frank would campaign tirelessly for Kennedy, raising money by performing at concerts, calling in favors, and as one associate put it, "by just being Frank."

For instance, Frank arranged a secret meeting between "Old Joe"—Joseph P. Kennedy, father of John Fitzgerald and U.S. ambassador to England during World War II—and Teamsters vice president Harold J. Gibbons to discuss hard feelings caused by Bobby's investigation of mobster involvement in labor unions and to possibly get the union's endorsement of the Kennedy-Johnson ticket. While the Teamsters Union never did endorse that ticket, mobster Sam Giancana contributed money from the Teamsters pension fund to the campaign.

Joseph Kennedy also asked Frank Sinatra to talk to Sam Giancana about swinging some votes his son's way in West Virginia, where Jack had to win the primary in order to get the Democratic nomination. A strong anti-Catholic sentiment prevailed among voters there (and no Catholic had ever been elected president before).

Frank was reluctant to talk to Sam Giancana about this problem. He didn't want the Kennedys to think he was so closely aligned to the underworld that they could use him as an intermediary. In fact, he was insulted by the intimation. However, Sinatra could not turn down the opportunity to do a favor for the Kennedys. So, one day on a golf range, Frank did talk to Sam about the Kennedys' problem in West Virginia. Then, as a personal favor to Frank, Sam sent Paul "Skinny" D'Amato to West Virginia.

Paul D'Amato, a mutual friend of Sinatra's and Giancana's, owned the popular 500 Club in Atlantic City. According to FBI files and other official accounts, he had strong ties to the Mafia. He used his influence with sheriffs who gambled illegally in Greenbriar County to encourage the coal miners' unions, and anyone else with whom they had influence in the West Virginia area, to vote for the Kennedy ticket. It's entirely possible that Kennedy would have had the support of West Virginia's coal miners' unions anyway, because Joseph Kennedy also enlisted the support of Franklin D. Roosevelt Jr., who sent many thousands of letters to voters. FDR junior's father, President Roosevelt, was greatly respected in West Virginia because he had given coal miners the right to organize in the first place. Joseph Kennedy was shrewd enough to realize that many West Virginians would vote for the candidate who was the favorite of FDR's son.

In the end, the joint efforts of D'Amato and Roosevelt resulted in 120,000 votes, which helped Kennedy win that state.

Giancana didn't care about Roosevelt's participation; he felt that what he and Skinny D'Amato had done was what really captured the state. It was a favor Sam Giancana would not let Frank Sinatra, or the Kennedys, forget.

Sam Giancana—Chicago's Mafia boss—with his Cuban cigars, sharkskin suits, flashy automobiles, and violent reputation, was a dark, dangerous character. He and Frank had met a few years earlier in Miami at the Fontainebleau. Frank was with Ava at the time, and she disliked Sam immediately. She knew trouble when she saw it. However, Frank became friendly with Sam (who had fourteen aliases and nicknames but was mostly known as "Mooney Giancana," "Momo Salvatore," "Dr. Goldberg," "Mr. Morris," "Sam Flood," and "Moe") and gave him a gaudy star-sapphire pinkie ring as a gift, which was just what this man needed to complete the stereotypical image of a gangster. "See this ring," Sam told his younger brother, Chuck. "Frank gave me this ring. I'm his fucking hero, man. The guy's got a big mouth sometimes. But he's a stand-up guy. Too good for the lousy scum out in Hollywood."

Sam Giancana had been a suspect in three different murder cases before he reached his twentieth birthday. He'd done time for burglary and was rejected as unfit for military service by his wartime draft board because, according to FBI documents, he had "strong antisocial trends and a psychopathic personality."

By 1960, it has been reported, Giancana had ordered the murders of over 600 people. It has also been reported that he also had a financial interest in the Riviera, Desert Inn, and Stardust Hotels in Las Vegas.

Sam Giancana was the kind of mobster all the others admired, one who didn't think twice about ordering a killing but still had a tender spot when it came to the dames. Just ask the lovely Phyllis McGuire, Sam's girlfriend and the lead singer of the McGuire Sisters trio.

In 1960, Phyllis was a slender and attractive, sometimes blonde, sometimes brunet, all-American girl singer. With an infectious smile and wide-ranging vocal talent, she and her sisters—who had been regulars on the *Arthur Godfrey and His Friends Show*—enjoyed a long string of hit records, including "Sugartime," "Sincerely," and "May You Always." She met Sam in 1958.

She was standing in as a celebrity blackjack dealer when Giancana wagered $500 at her dollar table. At the time, she was dating comic Dan Rowan of the comic team Rowan & Martin. "None of us knew who he was," she said of Sam. "I knew him as Sam Flood. I didn't know for many months that his name wasn't Flood." (Sam Flood was the name Giancana used whenever he checked into a Las Vegas hotel, for the FBI didn't take kindly to his frequenting Las Vegas casinos.) When she was finally told by friends that Giancana was a leading underworld figure, she refused to accept it.

"I just knew that I liked the man," she said in retrospect. "His wife had passed away, and he was very nice to me. And if he had done all those things they said he did, I wondered why in God's name he was in the street and not in jail."

Perhaps Phyllis McGuire might have had a clue about Sam Giancana's real personality, though, when he had Dan Rowan's room put under taped surveillance in order to demonstrate to her that entertainers make lousy boyfriends. Rowan was at least smart enough to back off. He went to Phyllis and said, "If someone that powerful is after you, I don't stand a chance. I'll be in the bottom of Lake Mead if I don't cool this."

Though she was intelligent enough to make it in a cutthroat record industry, some observers couldn't help but feel that naïveté took on new meaning when applied to Phyllis McGuire. A great many people would disagree with Phyllis's generous assessment of Sam Giancana, particularly the families whose fathers, sons, and brothers were hung on meat hooks or tortured with blowtorches at Sam's order. Sam's brother, Chuck, once noted. "[Mooney] never liked women who were smart enough to ask intelligent questions."

As well as his varied interests in mob businesses across the country,

Sam controlled all of the underworld activity in Chicago: Protection, extortion, bookmaking, and the numbers were all a part of Sam Giancana's Chicago kingdom. He would make at least $50 million a year on these various enterprises. Her talent was singing, not thinking.

Tommy DiBella, related by marriage to a powerful Philadelphia Mafia family, was a personal friend of Giancana's. He has never before given an interview. As he so delicately put it, "I was always afraid I'd be misquoted; then I'd have to shove the book up the writer's ass, and I woulda hated having to do that." Now, at the age of eighty, he recalls, "I gotta tell you, Sam was a charming guy. He could have any girl he wanted, and blondes were his favorite. And as a buddy, well, it was hard not to like him. He'd do anything for a pal.

"I was at his home once when the phone rang, and it was Sinatra. Frank apparently was having a problem with a reporter who was on his ass about something. It was a big deal to Frank, and Sam said he would take care of it. He kept saying, 'Frank, stop ya whinin'. I'll deal with it. It's a nonissue.' He would say that all the time: 'It's a nonissue.' He hung up the phone, called one of his pals, and said, 'So-and-so at such and such newspaper is giving Sinatra a hard time. Pay him a visit, will ya? Give him a little headache.' [That's another thing he used to say when ordering some kind of retaliation: 'Give him a little headache.'] 'I promised Frank I'd take care of it.' That's how it was with those two: a favor here, a favor there."

They were also wise guys, said Phyllis McGuire of Sam and Frank. "They were always playing pranks. It was like college-initiation stuff. They'd throw cherry bombs into a barroom, and everybody would jump. They thought that was the most hilarious thing to do, to scare their friends. I thought it was so immature."

Dean Martin said of Sam, "He was an okay guy for a murderer. He would call me up, say, Hey, I need you to do a concert, or something, and I would go. Why? 'Cause the money was good, and you didn't want to turn the guy down. He didn't like me much," Martin allowed. "I don't know why. Didn't care."

Dean said that accounts of Sinatra's life implying that he and the other Rat Packers performed gratis for Sam Giancana were inaccurate. "Sam would never have asked us to perform for free; he always paid top dollar," said Martin. He also said that he never worked for free unless Sinatra asked him to, which he did on occasion.

Frank Sinatra had worked for Sam Giancana over the years in many nightclubs. In fact, Sam had given Frank work in the lean fifties when no one else would hire him, so Frank was grateful to him for that. Also, Sinatra seemed to enjoy the fact that people were frightened of him just because they were so intimidated by his association with Sam. So he made certain that everyone with whom he had business dealings understood that he and Sam were close. "It doesn't hurt," he explained to Dean. "There's nothing wrong with secondhand intimidation."

For his part, Sam Giancana felt that being associated with Frank Sinatra brought him a degree of respectability, and so he maintained a good rapport with the singer.

Tommy DiBella said, "Sam always made sure people knew that he and Frank—who he called the Parrot sometimes—were pals. If he was trying to impress a broad, for instance, he would say, 'I'm gonna take you over to Frank's mother's house for dinner.' And she would say, 'Frank who?' Sam would smile that weasel smile of his and say, 'Sinatra, baby, he's a close pal.' And then she was his in the sack. It wasn't enough that he was worth fifty mil or that he was a top gangster, he was Frank's friend, and that was always good for a lay.

"Sam had a sensitive side, though, that people didn't know about, hard as that might be to believe," said DiBella.

"For instance [in January 1962] Sam Giancana had just what he was looking for—a way to bring down the Kennedys—fall right into his lap, and he decided not to use it because he was trying to be a nice guy to Judy Exner."

The "gift" referred to by Tommy DiBella was not publicly revealed until the highly regarded entertainment reporter Liz Smith broke the story in December 1996. Afterward, Judith Campbell Exner was interviewed by Sylvia Chase on the ABC-TV program *20/20*, and told a national viewing audience that she became pregnant with Kennedy's child during her last White House rendezvous with him in December 1962. Kennedy offered the option of her having the child. However, she felt that under the circumstances she had no choice but to have an abortion, illegal at that time. Overcome by Catholic guilt because of her affair with Kennedy and now the two-months-long pregnancy, Exner was in great emotional turmoil.

"He [Kennedy] said, Well, do you think Sam [Giancana] can help us? Would you ask Sam? Would you mind asking? I said, 'I don't know,' " Exner remembered. "I called Sam, and I told him, 'Jack and I are both coming to you for help.' And he said, 'First, let me ask you something.' He said. 'Do you want to keep the baby?' I said, I couldn't. He said, 'Let me ask you something else. Will you marry me?' And I just fell apart. I said, 'Sam, you don't want to marry me,' and he said, 'Well you deserve to be asked.'

"I was so needy and so alone that I really did fall into his arms," said Exner, "and that was the one time we were intimate, the one and only time." Judith knew that Sam was dating Phyllis McGuire and that there was no hope that she could have a relationship with him. She wasn't in love with him, anyway. Sam Giancana arranged for her to have the abortion at Grant Hospital in Chicago—now known as Columbia-Grant—on January 26, 1962.

"I know that Judy's story is true because Sam told me about it at the time," said Tommy DiBella. "He said, 'I'm helping the kid out. She got knocked up by Kennedy.' But he didn't use it against Kennedy, which was amazing. I said to him, 'Jesus Christ, you got this great thing on Jack. Why not use it? And he said, 'I ain't gonna hurt Judy. This would ruin her. She'd never get over it.' So there you go. Sam Giancana did have a soft side, I guess."

An associate of Sinatra's, who asked for anonymity because he still has a close, long-standing association with the Sinatra family, said, "This I know because I was in the room when it went down: Sam called Frank and said something like 'You'll never guess who's pregnant? Judy.' Frank said, 'So what? Big deal. Probably ain't the first time.' Sam told him that it was Jack's baby, I guess, because then Frank said, 'You gotta be fucking kidding me. That fucking idiot' [referring to Kennedy]. 'How'd he let *that* happen? Jesus Christ. Just what this country needs, a little bastard Kennedy runnin' round. This can't be good.'

"Then there was a lot of discussion about whether or not it was really Jack's kid, as Judy had claimed. Frank said, 'Why is everyone just gonna believe *her*? I don't get it. That kid could belong to *a lot* of different guys. After all, Judy ain't no barn burner [Sinatra-speak for "classy woman"].'* Finally, Frank told Sam, 'I don't think I wanna know anything more about this. In fact, I wanna forget you ever told me.' Then he hung up, turned to me, and he said, 'This whole thing is a big fuckin' joke. I got enough problems. Why are people always trying to get me involved in theirs? I ain't gettin' involved in that one. Count me out.' "

Sinatra's relationship with the Kennedys fell into jeopardy in March 1960 when he decided to hire Albert Maltz to write a screenplay for *The Execution of Private Slovik*, the story of the only U.S. soldier since the Civil War to be executed for desertion, which Sinatra planned to produce and direct. Maltz had been the writer of Sinatra's Oscar-winning *The House I Live In*, but since that time he had been imprisoned, fined, and blacklisted, as one of the Hollywood Ten, for refusing to cooperate with the House Un-American Activities Committee. Maltz moved to Mexico in 1951, which is where Sinatra found him. He hadn't been able to work on a film since 1948. Sinatra, like a few other Hollywood celebrities, such as Otto Preminger and Kirk Douglas, felt strongly that not only was Maltz's blacklisting unfair but that *any* blacklisting was unconscionable and that Maltz was the man to write the screenplay.

---

* Judith Exner insists that she was not intimate with any other man the entire time she was dating John Kennedy, "not ever, the whole time."

A huge controversy resulted. Newspaper editorials across the country either endorsed or decried—mostly the latter—Sinatra's bold attempt to break the blacklist. At one point, actor John Wayne said, "I wonder how Sinatra's crony Senator John Kennedy feels about him hiring such a man. I'd like to know his attitude because he's the one who is making plans to run the administrative government of our country."

Sinatra became angry at Wayne and bought a full-page advertisement in *Variety* defending his decision and saying, "This type of partisan politics is hitting below the belt. I make movies. I do not ask the advice of Senator Kennedy on whom I should hire. Senator Kennedy does not ask me how he should vote in the Senate . . . In my role as picture maker, I have—in my opinion—hired the best man to do the job."

None of this controversy made Joseph Kennedy happy, especially when told by Cardinals Spellman (in New York) and Cushing (in Boston) that Sinatra's support of Maltz could do damage to his son's career among Catholics. The ambassador telephoned Sinatra and told him he would have to choose: Maltz or the Kennedys. Begrudgingly, Frank chose the Kennedys; he paid Maltz $75,000, which was the entire amount he had promised to compensate him for his work. "In view of the reaction of my family, my friends, and the American public, I have instructed my attorneys to make a settlement with Albert Maltz and to inform him that he will not write the screenplay for *The Execution of Private Slovik.*"

Sinatra never produced *The Execution of Private Slovik.* However, the story did make it onto television in 1974 as a movie starring Martin Sheen, with a script by Richard Levinson and William Link.

With the Maltz affair behind him, Frank Sinatra continued his diligent campaign for Kennedy with performances and donations and also by hiring a private investigator to see what kind of dirt he could dig up on Richard Nixon, which, as it would turn out, was not much. (He learned that Nixon had been a patient of psychiatrist Dr. Arnold Hutschnecker and gave the information to Bobby Kennedy to use if he chose to. He chose not to.) During much of the campaign, Kennedy's campaign motorcade was preceded by a sound truck that played a recording of Sinatra's "High Hopes," with new lyrics by Sammy Cahn, extolling the virtues of the JFK campaign. This was one of the favors that Joseph Kennedy had asked for in his 1959 meeting with Sinatra. ("Everyone is voting for Jack / 'Cause he's got what all the rest lack/Everyone wants to back Jack / Jack is on the right track / 'Cause he's got high hopes . . .")

Whatever Frank could do for the campaign, he would do, no matter how big or small. Imaginatively, he unofficially renamed the Rat Pack the Jack Pack and started singing about "that old Jack magic." He gave concerts, made personal appearances, and raised money.

Of a total of 1,520 delegates, Kennedy had 700 guaranteed by July, when the Democratic National Convention was to take place. He only needed 61 more votes to win a first-ballot nomination.

On July 10, the night before opening ceremonies of the Democratic National Convention, Frank Sinatra worked behind the scenes of a gala fund-raiser, a hundred-dollar-a-plate dinner at the Beverly Hilton in Beverly Hills, attended by twenty-eight hundred people. Many of Frank's celebrity friends, such as Angie Dickinson, Shirley MacLaine, Peter Lawford, and Judy Garland sat at the head of the table with Jack Kennedy. (Jacqueline stayed behind in Hyannis Port because she was six months pregnant and had a history of medical problems associated with her pregnancies.) Because it was so well attended, the gala required two ballrooms. Sinatra, Garland, Davis, and Mort Sahl performed in both. Later, Frank beamed as he sat at the table with Democratic candidates Stuart Symington, Adlai Stevenson, and Lyndon Johnson. As everyone watched, Frank would go over to Jack and whisper something in his ear, causing Jack to nod vigorously. Then Jack would whisper in Frank's ear, and Frank would laugh heartily.

The next day, the Jack Pack, along with Janet Leigh and Tony Curtis, performed "The Star-Spangled Banner" to open the Democratic convention for a hundred thousand people at the Los Angeles Memorial Sports Arena and coliseum. At the beginning of the song, some ringside racist hecklers from the Mississippi delegation began berating Sammy Davis. "Don't let them get to you, those dirty sons of bitches," Frank told Sammy. But it was more than Sammy could bear; he became so distraught by their jeers that he left and didn't attend the convention.

It could be said that no one else stood a chance of securing the nomination, the enthusiasm for Jack Kennedy was so strong. The Kennedy nomination was guaranteed when Wyoming gave its fifteen votes to him. As the crowd cheered and waved flags and Kennedy banners, a jubilant Frank Sinatra told Peter Lawford, "We're on our way to the White House, buddy boy. We're on our way . . ."

CHAPTER 23

By the fall of 1960, the Kennedys were beginning to reconsider Sinatra's involvement in the presidential campaign. John F. Kennedy had been deluged with mail from people who felt that his relationship with Sinatra was not wise due to the singer's controversial reputation. There was also pressure from Kennedy's friends and advisers. Too many unanswered questions loomed where Sinatra was concerned, they argued, primarily about the extent of his involvement with mobster Sam Giancana. It was ironic that this association between Sinatra and Giancana was now a concern of the Kennedy brothers; both knew that their father had asked Sinatra to solicit Giancana's involvement in the West Virginia primary. This was not public information, however, and now that the primary had been won, the Kennedys seemed anxious to distance themselves from Sinatra, Giancana, and any other characters they felt were unsavory *before* JFK got into the White House.

Robert Kennedy suggested that he and his brother begin to consider damage control in regard to John's association with Sinatra. John had to agree. In fact, at his suggestion, Robert had his staff check to see how many photographs existed of his brother and Frank posing together at various parties with women. John decided that he wanted them found and destroyed. Robert went a step further and also demanded the negatives. To that end, a representative from Robert Kennedy's office contacted Frank Sinatra's and requested that any photographs or negatives that could prove to be embarrassing be sent to the White House immediately. Of course, Frank was not going to be cooperative in this regard and, lying, said that no such photographs existed.

John F. Kennedy tried to distance himself from Frank Sinatra after he won the nomination. Dorothy Kilgallen quoted Kennedy as saying, "He's no friend of mine. He's just a friend of Pat's [his sister] and Peter Lawford's." Of course, Kilgallen wasn't about to let Kennedy get away with that. She wrote, "Last week, the Democratic candidate for the presidency was guest of honor at a private little dinner given by Frank. No reason why he shouldn't, of course, but why try to kid the press?"

Another reason John F. Kennedy was distancing himself from Frank was that Jacqueline so disliked him. She thought he was ill-mannered and unrefined, and from the stories she had heard about the way he treated women, she deduced that he was someone she did not want in her social circle. "I am disgusted by him" is how she put it to a White House aide. "I just don't want him in the White House. I don't think Jack should associate with him in any way."

Peter Lawford once said that he and Jack joked about "stuffing Frank into a body bag and dragging him around to the side door so the gardeners could bring him in like a bag of refuse and Jackie wouldn't see him."

One Kennedy aide said, "I happened to be with Jack one day in a limousine with two other people and with Jacqueline. Jack said, in a very nonchalant manner, 'You know, we really owe a great debt of gratitude to Frank Sinatra. We should do something for him, don't you think?' And Jackie snapped back, 'Maybe we should buy him a book?' We all looked at her quizzically. 'A book of etiquette,' she continued. 'Maybe he'll learn some manners.' Nobody said a word after that. It was very uncomfortable. Jack quickly changed the subject. Then, about five minutes later, as if Jack hadn't changed the subject, Jacqueline said, 'You know, I really don't like that man.' She was still stewing over Sinatra. Jack just ignored her and started reading a newspaper."

No one was happier than Frank Sinatra when John F. Kennedy finally won the election over Richard Nixon by a narrow victory on November 8, 1960. He was proud to have a man he considered a friend in the top White House position.

Former Kennedy aide Dave Powers once remarked, "I heard President Kennedy say to Peter Lawford how helpful Sinatra had been to him. You know, Nevada and New Mexico were the only western states President Kennedy carried, and Sinatra helped him carry Nevada."

Even though the Kennedys were concerned about Sinatra and the public's reaction to their relationship with him, they continued to waffle where he was concerned. Privately, they had begun distancing themselves from Sinatra. Publicly, they demonstrated support for him. Pierre Salinger, Kennedy's press secretary, wrote one irate voter in Cincinnati, "I do not think it is an issue whether you like or do not like Mr. Sinatra. It is a fact that he and his friends helped the Democratic Party raise $1.3 million to help clear the deficit from the 1960 campaign. His help was welcome."

On November 13, 1960, Sammy Davis Jr. married Mai Britt, a Swedish actress, in Las Vegas. As has been widely reported, the wedding had been scheduled to take place prior to the election, but it was delayed because Joseph Kennedy was concerned about the fact that Davis was so linked with Sinatra in the public consciousness and his bride was white. He feared that this interracial marriage would somehow reflect poorly on the Kennedys. Frank was to be Sammy's best man, and he had made it clear that he didn't care what anyone thought of it. Frank never evaluated anyone by the color of his or her skin and would vigorously challenge anyone in his circle who did.

"If you don't know the guy on the other side of the world, love him, anyway, because he's just like you," Frank said in an interview at this time when asked about racial tolerance. "He has the same dreams, the same hopes, the same fears. It's one world, pal. We're all neighbors. But didn't somebody once go up onto a mountain long ago and say the same thing to the world?"

The civil-rights movement was still a couple of years off, however. Frank, like a lot of broad-minded people at the time, had to accept the fact that there were racists in this country who strenuously, and sometimes violently, objected to the notion of interracial dating, let alone interracial marriage. After all he had done to assist in John F. Kennedy's election, it made no sense to allow a damaging scandal to develop so soon before the election. Robert Kennedy asked Frank to talk to Sammy about postponing the ceremony, but before he had a chance to do so, Sammy offered to do just that. He knew the score, and he wanted to save Frank the embarrassment.

"To be honest with you, I think that this is when Frank was really starting to get pissed at the Kennedys," said Sammy Davis in retrospect. "Now his political ambitions for Jack were beginning to interfere with his personal friendships with us, and that was no good. Frank was a loyal friend, man. They didn't come no better. You didn't mess with that unless you were the fucking president of the United States, in which case you got to mess with whoever you wanted to mess with."

Matters got worse, though, when Frank and Peter Lawford were asked to produce and star in John Kennedy's preinaugural ball. White House planners told Frank that Sammy was not to attend because of the public fervor that had, just as predicted, occurred over his marriage. There seemed to be nothing Frank could do to convince the White House that Sammy should be allowed to perform; in fact, he couldn't even get in touch with John F. Kennedy to discuss it with him. Kennedy ducked his calls.

"Sammy loves Jack," Sinatra told a White House aide. "You just can't allow this to happen."

However, Sammy's affection for John F. Kennedy did not matter at this point. Davis would not be attending the festivities. Frank was so upset about this turn of events that he wasn't even able to make the call to Sammy himself to tell him the news; he had Peter Lawford do it. (Lawford, it would seem, always did everybody else's dirty work; he seemed to specialize—and not willingly—in telling people things they didn't want to hear.)

The White House was well aware of the fact that Frank was hurt and felt completely betrayed by Kennedy. That Jack would not discuss the matter with Sinatra personally only served to underscore the fact that the friendship Sinatra thought he had with the president had its limits. Frank called one White House aide (who was interviewed for this book but who asked for anonymity) demanding that he find a way for him to talk to Kennedy. He refused, knowing that Kennedy didn't want to discuss the Davis matter with him. Sinatra said, 'Fucking Jack owes me, man. He doesn't know how much he owes me. I am fucking responsible for getting him in the White House. And now *this*?'

"I tried to tell him, 'No, Frank, it's not Jack. It's Bobby. Bobby's the one responsible,'" said the Kennedy aide.

"But Frank was adamant that it was Jack's fault. 'Fuck, fuck, fuck, *fuck,'* he screamed at me. 'I cannot believe this. How can Jack do this to Charley? Just the fact that he's a buddy of mine should be enough for Jack to call an end to this.'"

No doubt Frank was finally seeing the light. He didn't have as much influence on Kennedy as he thought he had and even deserved. Kennedy was a politician and, as such, a pragmatist who was not about to allow emotions to get in the way of his career. That Sinatra didn't realize this fact about his "buddy" earlier only served to demonstrate his lack of experience and knowledge of the political world, not to mention his utter naïveté about men from powerful political families.

Sammy Davis was not invited to attend, or perform, at the ball. In fact, Frank and Sammy never bothered to discuss the matter. It was understood between them that there was nothing that could have been done.

On December 12, 1960, his forty-fifth birthday, Sinatra was in the midst of another film, *The Devil at 4 O'Clock*, with Spencer Tracy, in which Sinatra played a convict from Jersey City. He and actors Bernie Hamilton and Gregoire Aslan, also playing convicts, end up on a remote South Pacific island on their way to a prison in Tahiti. There they meet a Roman Catholic priest [Tracy], who is hated by the natives because his leper hospital threatens the tourist trade. When a volcano jeopardizes the village, the three convicts become heroes by rescuing the leprous youngsters. Meanwhile, in the midst of all of the action, Sinatra finds time to fall in love with a blind nurse, played by Barbara Luna. It's an exhausting movie to watch.

It had been a hell of a year for Frank. He was making about $20 million a year through his film and TV production companies (Essex, Kent, and Dorchester), four music-publishing companies, his gambling interests in Las Vegas and Lake Tahoe, radio partnerships, and his many real estate holdings.

The year culminated with Frank's decision to start his own record label, Reprise, even though his contract with Capitol still had two more years to go. After he announced the formation of Reprise, Frank told the media that he was "a new, happier, emancipated Sinatra, untrammeled, unfettered, unconfined."

Sinatra was bursting with concepts for a tribute to Tommy Dorsey, a string album, a concert album—so many ideas. How strange, then, that when he finally did get Reprise going, he started with two albums indistinguishable from his Capitol work (*Ring-a-Ding-Ding!* released in 1961 and *Swing Along With Me* in 1962), except they weren't nearly as good.

However, Sinatra thoroughly enjoyed owning his own label; each recording session was an event for him. Often musicians would actually stand and cheer after they cut a track because his enthusiasm was so contagious. The *Ring-a-Ding-Ding!* album provides a great deal of fun, if not eventful listening. Produced by Felix Slatkin and arranged by Johnny Mandel, the album featured the title track (somehow Jimmy Van Heusen and Sammy Cahn were actually able to come up with a memorable song using that title!), "Be Careful It's My Heart," "A Fine Romance," "Let's Face the Music and Dance," and "Zing Went the Strings of My Heart."

The problem, as it would evolve in years to come, was that while the Reprise albums were superb, not one of them ever quite approached the matchless quality of the Capitol work. At the time, Sinatra was publicly critical of Capitol, especially after a legal battle when Frank's former label began releasing product to compete with Reprise.* But Sinatra had one blind spot many artists have. He needed other people to rub up against; he needed feedback. When an artist does it all himself, something ends up missing. At Capitol, the reins worked *for* him, not against him. Left to his own devices at Reprise, Sinatra would bring forth many fine ideas, but none would be burnished to the point of the Capitol work. As for the many remakes of Capitol work he did at Reprise, much of it did not equal the Capitol versions, just the reverse of the Columbia-Capitol remakes. And, significantly, he couldn't resist playing with the material, as he did in adding a hip "And don't tell your mama" to "Come Fly With Me," and such. Such self-indulgence was new for him and not always appealing.

In 1961 and 1962, Sinatra would record a plethora of material for Reprise. In May 1961 alone, Sinatra recorded twenty-four songs, to be used on two albums, *Sinatra Swings*† (arranged by Billy May) and *I Remember Tommy* (arranged by Sy Oliver). The *Tommy* album is a tribute to Tommy Dorsey, and on it can be found some of Sinatra's most evocative singing, especially "I'm Getting Sentimental Over You," "I'll be Seeing You," and "Imagination." It is fascinating—and says a lot about Sinatra—that he would want to salute Dorsey on vinyl given the bad blood that had developed between them. However, the music and its legacy was more important to Sinatra than any bad feelings that existed between him and his former mentor so many years earlier. He feels that it's one of his best works. It is.

---

* For all his bad feelings about Capitol, Sinatra gave his best until the end. The final album of new material, *Point of No Return,* is memorable in all ways, for Axel Stordahl truly rose to the occasion. But the recording quality was a mystery—muddy, muted, as if it had a web spread over it. Decades later, when the album was rereleased, it was pristine.

† *Sinatra Swings* was originally entitled "Swing Along With Me," but the title had to be changed after Capitol filed an injunction claiming it was too close to their own Sinatra album *Come Swing With Me.*

Also in 1961 (November), Frank would record the unforgettable *Sinatra and Strings* album, produced by Neal Hefti amd Skip Martin. Don Costa's striking arrangements of "Come Rain or Come Shine," "Stardust," and an extraordinary rerecording of Sinatra's hit "All or Nothing at All" make this album a standout—unique in that the sound is, by Sinatra's design, more lush and grandiose (with over fifty musicians in the orchestra) than on previous outings.

What is considered by some to be his most emotionally complex album would be recorded in January 1962, *All Alone*. In her book about her father, Nancy Sinatra writes: "If you have this album and haven't thought about it for a long time, play it now. It's one of the best." (Nancy also notes that the emotional "When I Lost You" was recorded on the day Sinatra had been a pallbearer for Ernie Kovacs.)

All Alone originally was conceived as an album to be called "Come Waltz With Me," and a title song was written and recorded. However, after the album was finished, Sinatra realized that he had another Gordon Jenkins masterpiece and changed the concept. Steve Lawrence eventually recorded the song and used it as a title for an album. It didn't make much of a splash. Sinatra had realized that the great public was not out there looking for a waltz album. They were waiting for another "lonely" album.

Other memorable songs recorded during this two-year span would include "I Get A Kick Out of You." "Love Is Just Around the Corner," "At Long Last Love," and "I'm Beginning to See the Light" (all for the excellent *Sinatra and Swingin' Brass* album) and "London by Night" and "A Nightingale Sang in Berkeley Square" (for the *Great Songs from Great Britain* album, which was recorded during Sinatra's record-breaking European tour in the summer of 1962 but not released in the United States).

On January 6, 1961, John F. Kennedy sent his private plane, the *Caroline*, for Frank Sinatra and Peter Lawford so that they could spend the next two weeks planning the preinaugural gala in Washington. According to his daughter Nancy, in what has to be one of the most astonishing cases of Frank doing it "his way," "Dad wasn't fazed by the news that Laurence Olivier and Ethel Merman couldn't make the date because they were appearing on Broadway in *Becket* and *Gypsy*, respectively. He bought all of the seats and closed the shows for that night in both theaters."

Drawing on a long list of his friends, Sinatra assembled a stellar cast for the gala, some of whom flew long distances to take part. Participants included Olivier and Merman, Leonard Bernstein, Sidney Poitier, Anthony Quinn, Joey Bishop, Louis Prima, Keely Smith, Juliet Prowse, Helen Traubel, Ella Fitzgerald, Gene Kelly, Nat King Cole, Milton Berle, and, of course, Sinatra.

John Kennedy, Lyndon Johnson, and Eleanor Roosevelt were scheduled to give speeches.

Prior to the festivities, Frank hosted a black-tie reception for the cast, the Kennedys, and the Johnsons in the Statler-Hilton's South American suite. Murray Kempton, of the *New York Post,* attended the party and wrote, "All these people, the Sinatras, Nat Coles, Gene Kellys—the most inescapably valuable collection of flesh this side of the register of maharanis—sons of immigrant or second-class citizens of not so long ago. They are in their wealth, their authority, their craft, the heirs of the Roosevelt revolution."

Kempton could not have said the same thing about John Kennedy himself. Sinatra certainly identified with Kennedy—both liberal Democrats growing up with at least one parent deeply involved in politics, both Catholics, both womanizers, both the subjects of prejudice at one time or another, both overcoming odds to get to the top. He considered Kennedy a friend, and rightly so. Sinatra, whose loyalty to friends sometimes bordered on the fanatical, had done a lot to help Kennedy get elected: raising money, enlisting top entertainers to do the same, and even recruiting Giancana and D'Amato to swing 120,000 West Virginian votes by influencing coal miners' unions and other powerful political organizations there. Tonight he basked in the glow of Kennedy's victory. In fact, both men had worked hard, paid their dues, and made it. They were living the American Dream.

Like Frank Sinatra, Jacqueline Kennedy also had an obsession with detail and being in control. She had plans that were to cover every aspect of the inauguration. The one thing she couldn't control, however, was the weather. Although it does snow in Washington, the city never seemed prepared for anything more than flurries; schools and government offices would close early, and highways would be jammed. On January 19, almost eight inches of snow fell on Washington, D.C. Endless confusion in an already crowded city was caused when snow vehicles failed to appear. Mrs. Kennedy had arranged to have buses pick up people at their hotels to transport them to the preinauguration party, but those plans were ruined when the buses did not show up because of the storm. As a result, hotel lobbies became jammed with women in mink and men in dinner jackets, all trying, with no success, to get cabs to take them to the National Guard Armory.

The snow was so heavy that even the Kennedys were caught in a traffic jam and did not arrive until about ten, an hour after the event was scheduled to start. By then, only about three thousand of the expected twelve thousand guests had arrived. Financially, it didn't matter, because all of the seats had been paid for in advance: There were forty boxes for ten at $10,000 each; Ed Pauley, California oilman, and Joseph P. Kennedy, the president's father, each bought a box. Members of the general public could purchase tickets for $100 a seat.

Matthew McCloskey, treasurer of the Democratic National Committee, would later announce that the evening would gross the party approximately $1,400,000. That stunning achievement would have meant nothing to Sinatra at the time, though, because the Kennedys had not yet arrived and he was frantic that they might not show up at all. When he heard after ten that their car was pulling up to the door, he rushed into the swirling snow to personally escort them inside. Taking Jacqueline by her white-gloved hand, he led her into the raised presidential box.

No matter how many other people were in a room, no matter what else was happening at the time, whenever Jacqueline Kennedy entered, she commanded every eye. That night was no exception. Her Oleg Cassini gown was of white double satin with elbow-length sleeves, princess-shaped bodice, and a two-part, bell-shaped skirt. Stunning in its simplicity, its only decoration was a rosette of the same satin at her left waist. She wore long white kid gloves. Her diamond-and-sapphire earrings perfectly matched her necklace. Regardless of how many stars were performing onstage, it would seem that Jacqueline Kennedy was the real star that evening.

The gala got off to a rousing start at 10:40 P.M. when Leonard Bernstein raised his baton for the fanfare and "The Stars and Stripes Forever." Mahalia Jackson sang the national anthem. Even though Ethel Merman had campaigned for Nixon, all was forgiven when she sang "Everything's Coming Up Roses." Frank Sinatra's reworded "That Old Jack Magic" drew hearty applause from the presidential box. Although the audience may have been small, it did not lack enthusiasm.

People were still cheering the performers when John Kennedy took the stage. "I'm proud to be a Democrat," he said, "because since the time of Thomas Jefferson, the Democratic Party has been identified with the pursuit of excellence, and we saw excellence tonight. The happy relationship between the arts and politics which has characterized our long history I think reached culmination tonight.

"I know we're all indebted to a great friend, Frank Sinatra. Long before he could sing, he used to poll a Democratic precinct back in New Jersey. That precinct has grown to cover a country. But long after he has ceased to sing, he is going to be standing up and speaking for the Democratic Party, and I thank him on behalf of all of you tonight. You cannot imagine the work he has done to make this show a success."

Frank Sinatra has said that he wanted the preinaugural gala to be "the greatest show ever." He had achieved his dream. In retrospect, January 19, 1961, was probably one of the happiest nights of his life.

CHAPTER 24

For Frank Sinatra, the year 1961 was in full ring-a-ding swing.

On January 27, he, Dean, and Sammy—and Jan Murray, substituting for Joey Bishop—performed a benefit concert at Carnegie Hall for Dr. Martin Luther King's Southern Christian Leadership Conference. Ticket sales were slow for this engagement, so much so that Dorothy Kilgallen reported, "Anyone would assume that the Sinatra name would be a guarantee of a packed house. But apparently it hasn't happened because Sammy Davis Jr. has been reduced to writing letters to his best friends for help." In the end, though, the hall was packed with concertgoers who paid more, in some cases, than $100 a ticket. Clearly, though, at least based on the audience's weak response to the show, the Rat Pack had a mostly white—not African-American—following. They fared much better immediately following the Carnegie Hall show when the Rat Pack was back in Las Vegas at the Sands for two weeks in February.

From February 28 through March 13, Frank spent two weeks at the Fontainebleau Hotel in Miami Beach. He still loved performing in front of an audience. Onstage is where he felt the most comfortable and in control. To him, the best way to express himself and his emotions was through a song. An appreciative audience—an audience who *got it*, who understood it, all of it—meant the world to him. Most certainly, the sight of Frank Sinatra wearing a tuxedo on a stage illuminated by a soft blue light thrilled ticket buyers whatever the controversy currently raging.

To Frank's loyal public, his talent has always been all that mattered, not the salacious particulars of his personal life. This is why he has been so famous, so revered, for so long—because of his great ability as a performer, the way he relates to each song, and the way he communicates with his audience. It was not because he supposedly has had mob connections, not because of his tempestuous love life or his wicked temper, but because, as his son Frankie so aptly put it, "nobody was ever as *cool* as Frank Sinatra, and nobody could ever please an audience more."

One thrill of any Sinatra performance was that he did not replicate the records. He always created anew on the spot. He also varied his shows. Most singers did exactly the same songs in exactly the same order. Sinatra, however, needed variety and challenge and did the extra work necessary to achieve it.

"Most of what has been written about me is one big blur," Frank said at this time, "but I do remember being described in one simple word that I agree with: 'honest.' That says it as I feel it. Whatever else has been said about me personally is unimportant. When I sing, I believe. I'm honest. If you want to get an audience with you, there's only one way. You have to reach out to them with total honesty and humility. When you don't reach out to the audience, nothing happens. You can be the most artistically perfect performer in the world, but an audience is like a broad: If you're indifferent, it's Endsville."

Besides the amazing voice and personalized phrasing, Sinatra has always been a most gracious, charming performer. His banter with an audience—natural and easy—is so ingratiating, so personal, he is irresistible. "You'd always leave a Sinatra concert feeling like you made direct contact with him," his son Frankie once said. "That's his goal. He wants to reach every person in the audience." In 1961, Frank was—just as he had been for decades—the ultimate showman (at least when he wasn't surrounded by his Rat Pack buddies, who—when together on stage—were always seemingly more interested in horseplay than they were in music.)

"Given the choice, more than anything else I'd rather sing with people in front of me," Frank said during one of his television specials during this time. "See, I love to see 'em sitting out there, because when they're sitting, they're not coming up to get me. Yup, people. Nice, smiling, receptive, unarmed people. Because when all is said and done," Frank continued, "whether a performer is all by himself in a recording studio or facing a lonely camera on an empty soundstage, it's the people he's trying to reach. And it's the people what make ya. And if you're not doing your proper work, it's the people who're gonna break ya."

In late 1960, the president appointed as attorney general his thirty-five-year-old brother Robert. Sam Giancana later said that as far as he was concerned, this was a sucker punch he had not expected. He felt that the only reason Kennedy had given his brother that powerful position was because he wanted Robert to, as he put it, "clear away all markers." In other words, as he told his brother, Chuck—who wrote a book about his brother entitled *Double Cross*—he believed that Jack wanted Bobby to eradicate the underworld figures who had helped JFK get elected, thereby alleviating any future problems that might arise in terms of returned favors—and do it all under the guise of "a war on organized crime."

Of course, Sam Giancana was just egotistical enough to believe that everything the Kennedys were doing in terms of their efforts against the underworld was planned with him, and only him, in mind. The fact is that organized crime was being investigated by the Senate and Bobby Kennedy before the 1960 election. In fact, Bobby's first investigations of Jimmy Hoffa occurred while he served as majority counsel to the Kefauver Committee.

It is true, however, that when Bobby became attorney general, he turned the heat up and was eager to attack organized crime on all levels and in all cities once and for all. Determined to eradicate *all* underworld activity from the United States, not just Giancana and his cronies, Robert Kennedy demanded that J. Edgar Hoover mobilize all of the FBI's resources for that purpose. Kennedy even recruited the Internal Revenue Service to step up its pursuit of syndicate figures suspected of tax evasion. Moreover, he had recently appointed a committee to compile a list of men to be investigated and prosecuted, and some of them were Sinatra's closest friends, like Giancana, Mickey Cohen, and Johnny Roselli. But some were not, like Jimmy Hoffa and Roy Cohn, neither of whom had any markers with the Kennedys, or Sinatra for that matter.

Though not directed solely at him, none of this was good news for Sam Giancana or for any of his associates who had become rich and powerful as a result of their "work." Moreover, Sam did have certain favors he had planned to ask of the Kennedys in the near future, and he expected his wishes to be granted because of his involvement in the successful West Virginia primary.

Over the next two and a half years, Sam Giancana would wage a war against the Kennedys and try to involve Frank Sinatra in his scheme to "bring them down." He told his younger brother, Chuck, that he was determined to one day hit the brothers where he knew they were weakest—between their legs. In fact, Chuck has claimed that his brother told him that he'd been instrumental in surreptitiously arranging sexual encounters between the Kennedys and various unwitting women, ranging from prostitutes to well-known celebrities. He also had the Kennedys secretly photographed while in compromising positions with these women. He intended to use these photographs to blackmail the brothers and to eventually ruin them. Chuck says that when Sam told him all of this, it seemed unthinkable. However, Sam Giancana had a special talent for the unthinkable.

"I've got enough dirt on Jack Kennedy and his lousy old man to ruin ten politicians' careers," Sam told his brother. "I've got pictures, tape recordings, film, you name it, all safe and sound in a safe-deposit box. The American public would be real happy to see their president being serviced by three women, and one of 'em a shine [slang for African American] to boot. Yeah, if I ever need an ace, here's the key," he told Chuck as he showed him the small gold key to the safe deposit box.

Because he believed that John F. Kennedy trusted Frank Sinatra, Sam asked Frank to introduce the Kennedys to various women for his treacherous purposes, and Frank did what he was told. Did Frank know what was going on? Did he know of Sam's plan?

"To tell you the truth, Frank doesn't know for sure what I'm up to," a snickering Sam Giancana reportedly told Chuck. "He thinks I just want to make the Kennedys happy."

Was Sam Giancana delusional? Did he actually think he could get away with all of these plans?

"How can I answer those questions about Sam?" asked his friend Tommy DiBella. "He wanted to be king. Whether he was doing all the things he said he was doing or just showboating—like everyone did in those days—it's hard to say. You gotta remember that this was a time when gangsters were all trying to outdo each other, trying to bring down this politician, own that territory, whatever. It was a lot of bullshit."

Of course, the most logical reason to believe that all of Giancana's threats were bluster is that he never produced anything. No tapes. No photos. Nothing. Ever.

At this time, March 1961, Sam Giancana visited Frank Sinatra at the Fontainebleau in Miami. He needed a favor. He wanted Robert Kennedy to back off from his investigation of Sam's friends, and he wanted Frank Sinatra to talk to Bobby's father, Joseph, about the possibility of Bobby's agreeing to do just that. Just as Frank was not happy when Joseph asked him to discuss with Sam the Kennedys' problem in West Virginia, he was unhappy about Giancana's request. Still, though, Frank could not resist the temptation to act like a "big shot" in front of Sam Giancana. According to a wiretapped phone conversation between Giancana and Johnny Roselli (taped on December 6, 1961), Frank had said to Sam, while they were in Florida, "Don't worry about it. If I can't talk to the old man [Joseph Kennedy], I'm gonna talk to the man [Jack Kennedy]."

Giancana was probably delighted. As far as he was concerned, he and Frank Sinatra had just made a deal.

This "deal" would come back to haunt Frank in eight months, when, in August 1961, Joseph Kennedy contacted Frank, saying that he wanted to thank him for his participation in the election, for helping swing the West Virginia primary, and for his work on the inauguration gala. He said that his son Jack wanted to entertain him at the White House and that he was invited after that to Hyannis Port, the family's compound. Frank was elated. But then Sam Giancana took some of the pleasure out of the moment.

Tommy DiBella, who heard a tape recording of a telephone conversation between Sam and Frank, made by Giancana, remembered: "Sam Giancana, having heard that the Parrot [Frank] was going to be with the Kennedys, called Frank and said, 'Hey, pal, don't forget about me.' Frank stalled and said something like 'Well, I'll see what I can do. But, you know, I, uh, I can't make no promises. I mean, you know . . .' Well, Sam just exploded,'' said DiBella. '' 'You *already* promised me, Frank,' he said. 'Now deliver or you'll be sorry. Jesus Christ. *You're* the one always sayin' a deal is a deal.' ''

According to DiBella, Sinatra didn't like being threatened. He lost his temper and said to Sam, ''Man, don't ruin this for me. I worked *hard* for this honor. Now, *fuck you*, Sam, if you ain't gonna give me a break here. Fuck you, hear me? I ain't scared of you, pal. If you think I am, well, you're an idiot. In fact, you're a bigger idiot than you think *I* am.''

Sam hung up on him.

''This was not good,'' said Tommy DiBella. ''This was not good at all. Frank must've been crazy to have said those things.''

Frank didn't seem concerned about Giancana's anger. In fact, he thoroughly enjoyed his White House visit on September 23, 1961. Dave Powers, a presidential aide, recalled: ''I still remember how he showed the White House maître d' how to make Bloody Marys with his own fantastic special recipe. He sat on the balcony sipping his drink and looking out at the sun streaming in and the wonderful view of Washington. He turned to me and said, 'Dave, all the work I did for Jack. Sitting here like this makes it all worthwhile.' ''

The next day, Frank flew to Hyannis Port with Pat Lawford and Ted Kennedy on one of the Kennedys' planes. The day after that, Frank, the president, and other friends and family members went cruising for three and a half hours off Cape Cod on the *Honey Fitz.*

One Kennedy aide said, ''I wasn't on that trip, but I remember the reaction to it. Jack was a little cold to Sinatra, I heard. He was long past the buddy-buddy phase. But I also heard that Sinatra didn't notice, or maybe didn't care. He was in his glory. He was also pushing for Peter [Lawford] to talk to Bobby Kennedy about laying off of Giancana. Lawford did talk to Bobby and was told to mind his own business. Bobby was going after Sam with a vengeance, and he certainly wasn't going to meet with Frank about any of it.''

When Lawford told Sinatra that he was not able to get a meeting for him with Bobby, he probably expected Sinatra to blow up. Frank always blamed Peter whenever he wasn't able to come through for him on a Kennedy-related favor. But this time Frank said, ''Oh, well . . . Hey, pal, you tried.'' If he seemed relieved, that's because he was.

One Sinatra confidant explained, ''The last thing Frankie wanted was to speak to Bobby about Giancana. Forget it. He told me, 'I ain't gonna jeopardize my relationship with the Kennedys for this goddamn punk mobster. What do I look like? Do I look like some kinda moron? I don't care if Sam's hacked off. Fuck Sam.' ''

Tommy DiBella said, "The way I heard it, when he got back, Frank lied and told Mooney [Sam Giancana] that he and Bobby *had* talked. Maybe they talked about the weather, maybe they talked about how pretty the water looked, but one thing I know they didn't talk about was Sam Giancana.

"Yet Frank said, 'Yeah, Mo [sometimes he called him that], I wrote your name down, and I said, 'This is my buddy boy. I just want you to know that,' and he claimed Bobby nodded in recognition that he wouldn't fuck with Sam. But that was pure bullshit, and Sam sensed it. He just knew on some gut level that Frank was a lying son of a bitch. He was pissed at Frank—I mean, really pissed—but he didn't say nothing at that point. He just kept quiet. But Frank knew damn well that Sam was pissed off at him."

Indeed, transcripts of federal wiretaps from December 6, 1961, reflect the essence of DiBella's memory.

Giancana and his California associate Johnny Roselli were speaking on the telephone that day when Roselli told Giancana that Frank "says he's got an idea that you're mad at him."

Giancana responded by saying, "He just has a guilty conscience. I never said nothing."

Roselli also told Giancana of a meeting with Sinatra at his home in Palm Springs after the cruise with the Kennedys: "He [Frank] says: 'Johnny, I took Sam's name and wrote it down and told Bobby, 'This is my buddy, this is what I want you to know, Bob.' "

Giancana responded, "It's a lot of shit. Why lie to me? I haven't got that coming."

Roselli agreed. "If he can't deliver," he said of Frank's efforts to intercede with the Kennedys on behalf of Giancana, "I want him to tell me, 'John, the load's too heavy.' "

"That's right," Giancana said. "At least then you know how to work. You won't let your guard down."

Later, Sam concluded of Frank, "When he says he's gonna do a guy a little favor, I don't give a shit how long it takes. He's got to give you a little favor."

Accounts of Frank Sinatra's relationship with the Kennedys have always been inaccurate in that historians and biographers over the years have observed that Frank simply had no influence over Joseph, John, and Robert Kennedy where Sam Giancana was concerned, no matter how hard he tried. It's true that Frank didn't have any influence over the Kennedys, but it's also true that at least where Giancana was concerned, *he never tried.*

Frank may have implied that he would intervene, he may have even promised he was going to do so, and as he did in Hyannis Port, he may

245

have even halfheartedly asked someone else, like Lawford, to start a dialogue. However, any attempts by Frank Sinatra at assisting Sam Giancana in this regard were always indifferent.

Tommy DiBella said, "Frank took this position where the mob was concerned: *Fuck you.*"

Nicolas D'Amato, a former member of the so-called Philadelphia Mafia family (who says that he is not related to well-known reputed underworld figure Paul "Skinny" D'Amato), observed: "Sinatra was an idiot for playing both sides of the field like that. Playing Mooney for a sucker? What, are you kidding me? If he wasn't so fucking talented, he never woulda gotten away with being such a fink. With the boys, when you let 'em down, you got hit; whether it was your fault or not, you got hit; whether you could control it or not, you got hit.

"And to lie to Sam? Forget it. I can't think of anyone else who would've continued to breathe air after telling a story like the one Frank told to Sam."

Tommy DiBella adds, "One time I asked Sam why he let the so-called Parrot get away with so much shit, and Sam said, 'What can I do? *What?* Beat him up? Have him killed? He's one of the most famous men on the planet and I'm gonna be the one to do him in? I ain't crazy.' So you might say Sinatra had something on Sam and the rest of the mobsters who may have been pissed off at him. He was too goddamn famous to touch.

"Another time, Sam told me, 'You know something? I thought I'd have the little fucker's throat slit, just enough to have his vocal chords damaged so he can't sing anymore. Then, that night, I'm [making love to] Phyllis, playing Sinatra songs in the background, and the whole time I'm thinking to myself, Christ, how can I silence that voice? It's the most beautiful sound in the world. Frank's lucky he's got it. It saved his life.' "

Simply put, Frank Sinatra was probably one of the few men in the country capable of screwing with the mob and getting away with it. Now, *that's* power. Or as Dean Martin once put it, "Only Frank could get away with the shit he got away with. Only Frank. Anyone else woulda been dead. . . ."

Sinatra practically spat in Giancana's face, making promises, breaking them, acting cool, being a big shot, berating him behind his back, befriending him when it was convenient, and then denouncing him when that was appropriate.

"He treated Sam Giancana like he was one of his dames," said Tommy DiBella. "In fact, he treated him worse than a dame, because at least his dames got wined and dined after he screwed them."

The word had started to leak out that Sinatra had a special relationship with the underworld. None of Sinatra's associates—Dean Martin, Sammy

Davis, Joey Bishop, even Peter Lawford—seemed to know the specifics. (They didn't *want* to know.) They only knew that Frank Sinatra was bigger than the mob, that he never did what he said he was going to do for the "boys" but was still around despite that.

Outside his immediate circle, he was a feared person, someone people looked upon with awe, much the way Hoboken townsfolk reacted toward his mother, a woman who defied legal, religious, and societal convention. That he rubbed shoulders with gangsters actually imbued him with a certain glamour. Now, more than ever, when he walked into a room, he had a presence. Indeed, the word spread, from the big shots all the way down to the lower echelons of show business. Marilyn Monroe's stand-in, Evelyn Moriarty, said, "Sinatra was a horrible man. Dangerous. He wielded a lot of power. There was a perception by almost everyone in Hollywood that Frank Sinatra had ties to the mob. You just didn't cross him."

"I noticed that no matter who was in a room, when Frank entered it, he became the focus," Mia Farrow wrote in her memoirs, *What Falls Away*. "And no one was ever really at ease with him, no matter who they were or how charming he was, because there was something about him that made people uncomfortable."

Stories and rumors about Frank Sinatra abounded; people thought—and still do today—that he was one of the key men behind the Mafia. Even Kennedy's cabinet was whispering about it. Dave Powers said, "Let's face it. The mob made Sinatra. But he had outgrown them."

In fact, though, it would appear that the mob never did much for Sinatra, and Sinatra never did much for the mob—not that anyone has ever been able to document, anyway, and many have attempted to do just that—except for the occasional concert. "Big deal," he used to say privately. "Throw 'em a bone. Sing for 'em now and then if that's what they want. I sing every night, anyway. What's the difference? Long as it keeps those mobsters happy . . ."

Indeed, when Sam Giancana associate Johnny Formosa suggested (in another FBI wiretapped conversation) that Giancana "take out" Sinatra, Giancana wasn't interested.

"Let's show 'em," Formosa pushed. "Let's show those asshole Hollywood fruitcakes that they can't get away with it as if nothing's happened. Let's hit [kill] Sinatra. Or I could whack out a couple of those other guys. [Peter] Lawford and that [Dean] Martin, and I could take the nigger [Sammy Davis Jr.] and put his other eye out."

Giancana said, "No. I've got other plans for them."

A better-thought-out, better-orchestrated "hit"? Not quite.

In fact, the only orchestrated plan Sam Giancana had in mind was one with strings and horns that would be backing Frank and his pals at the

Villa Venice, a new nightclub he planned to open in Chicago, as they sang their own hits. Their talent, it would seem, was the power that *all* of the Rat Pack, not just Frank Sinatra, had over the mob.

CHAPTER 25

Not much has been written over the years about the relationship Frank Sinatra shared with Marilyn Monroe. In fact, it was serious and based not only on Frank's sense of compassion where Monroe was concerned but also shared interests. Though Sinatra was not a particularly reflective person, he was still attracted to creative people, literature, poetry, and the arts. So was Marilyn. However, the two of them always felt somehow oddly disconnected from their cultural pursuits. Because of their lack of education, they were never able to engage in the kind of reflection that would have produced true depth in them. Both on the same level of appreciation and understanding of culture, they spent hours discussing books, art, and politics. They seemed to understand each other perfectly.

"She and Frank both cared about civil rights," said Patricia Newcomb, who was Marilyn's publicist and friend at the time of her death. "They both cared about the underdog. She was a serious person who wanted to learn as much as she could about everything. Frank was the same way. They shared a lot of common ground."

Of course, by early 1962, forty-six-year-old Sinatra and thirty-five-year-old Monroe had known each other for at least eight years. She and her former husband, Joe DiMaggio, had been friendly with Sinatra, who had been involved in DiMaggio's "Wrong Door Raid." After their marriages ended, Marilyn's to DiMaggio and Frank's to Ava Gardner, the two took solace in each other's company and had been intimate on a number of occasions at the end of the fifties. They continued seeing each other from time to time over the years, even during her marriage to Arthur Miller, from whom she officially separated at the end of 1960.*

* In August 1960, Sinatra invited the cast of *The Misfits* to the Cal-Neva Lodge to see him perform. Miller was there with Monroe. Frank and Marilyn slipped away for private conversations, and she confided in him about her marital woes. However, Sinatra told friends that they were not intimate with one another at that time because, he said, he didn't want to exploit her feelings. "She is already nuts about me," he explained boastfully.

Apparently, after Marilyn and Arthur Miller split, he got custody of their basset hound, Hugo. It's been written in many accounts of Marilyn's life that Frank Sinatra gave her a small white French poodle which she loved and called "my baby, mine and Frankie's."

"Actually, I gave her the dog," said Patricia Newcomb. "I bought it from Natalie Wood's mother [Newcomb also represented Natalie Wood], who was raising poodles. I gave it to Marilyn when she checked out of the hospital [Manhattan Polyclinic, where she was treated for gall-bladder and digestive problems in June 1961] and said, 'Now, you'll never be alone again.' And she said, 'I think I'll call him Maf-Honey. That was the dog's full name: Maf-Honey. She meant it short for Mafia in honor of Frank, or as a joke, I should say."

Marilyn's childhood had been a painful one. Her father was unknown to her, and her mother was committed to a mental institution. She grew up in a series of orphanages and foster homes, all the while dreaming of the day she would be loved and admired. Because she eventually found love and acceptance only through her physical appearance, every move Marilyn Monroe made in her professional and personal life was geared toward making people desire her. She polished this skill well, using her beauty as a lure and her vulnerability as a hook. Her clothes were often designed to show off every curve of her body. Her hair was unnaturally blond, her lips the deepest red, yet she always managed to project utter innocence and femininity—a paradox that resulted in an incandescent, sexual glow so exciting that it would never really be equaled, although often imitated.

By the early sixties, the mixture of pain and beauty, vulnerability and allure, that was Marilyn's persona had transformed her into one of Hollywood's greatest stars, desired by some of the most important men of her generation. The way she moved, spoke, and looked made people want to reach out to her, protect her, be a part of her life. Frank Sinatra was no exception.

While Frank had romantic feelings for Marilyn, his relationship with her was not one to which he could become committed. No one could take Ava Gardner's place in his heart. Moreover, Marilyn Monroe had her own entanglements. She was still in love with her ex-husband Joe DiMaggio after having engaged in an intimate relationship with John F. Kennedy. By February 1962 she was supposedly involved romantically with Robert Kennedy, an affair that is said to have started when Robert was dispatched by John to end *his* relationship with her.

It might be assumed by some of his public that Frank Sinatra knew everything that was going on in the lives of everyone in his circle just because he wielded so much power and seemed to be at the center of all the action. He wasn't God, however. He was just Sinatra.* He could never get the story straight from Marilyn as to the extent of her relationships with the Kennedys. She was giddy and evasive whenever he asked her about them. Given to wild mood swings, she was either deeply despondent and unwilling to talk or tremendously elated and—in her mind, anyway—had no reason to examine her depression.

Besides the secondhand information everyone else in his circle had also heard, Frank Sinatra didn't know much more about Marilyn and the Kennedys than anyone else at the time. He and Robert Kennedy were not friendly; he wasn't about to ask him to define his relationship with Monroe.

It should be noted that author Donald Spoto, while researching his well-documented book *Marilyn Monroe: The Biography*, found practically no concrete evidence to support the notion that Robert Kennedy and Marilyn Monroe had an affair. Still, the rumors persist today, as they did in 1962.

"If Marilyn and Bobby were involved, it was very, very gently orchestrated," said Milt Ebbins, Peter Lawford's close friend and the executive president of ChrisLaw Productions (which produced a number of films and also the popular *Patty Duke Show* for television). "I was Peter's closest friend. He told me everything. Things that will never be revealed. He never told me about Bobby and Marilyn, and he told me things that would have been considered much more confidential than that. I'd been to his house a hundred times, at parties with Jack and Bobby, and never saw Marilyn. Wouldn't you think she'd be there? I don't say it couldn't have happened [an affair with Bobby], but I say that I doubt it."

Ebbins added, "Marilyn Monroe was not a slut. What kind of character do these people think she had, trading one brother in for another. It's preposterous."

It was an example of Frank's paradoxical personality that he would even have a romantic interest in Marilyn Monroe. As with Judy Garland before her, he often told Marilyn that her self-destructive nature and dependency on alcohol and pills bothered him. It would seem, though, that this was because he had let both vices affect his own life over the years. He, too, had been self-destructive, and he simply didn't want to be reminded of that fact.

He had also repeatedly said that he never again wanted to be in a relationship with a woman in show business, insisting that he didn't want to share his women with their careers. However, Marilyn was nothing if not a Hollywood star.

* A funny joke about Sinatra in the sixties, told in nightclubs by comedians, was "He thinks he's God. In fact, he's the only guy who calls Dial-A-Prayer and asks if there are any messages."

Also, Sinatra certainly didn't want to be involved with anyone who would be considered weak or vulnerable. Women like Marilyn were usually too much trouble for him. He liked "dames" with more inner strength and self-reliance, like Ava Gardner and Dolly Sinatra, both of whom represented to him his ideal of the total woman. He often didn't have the patience necessary to deal with someone as conflicted as Monroe. For instance, at one gathering at his home, Marilyn started telling sad stories to the guests, only to be cut off by Frank, who chided her, saying, "Look, Norma Jean, we don't want to hear it. Toughen up, baby, or get the hell out. I ain't no baby-sitter."

Generally, though, Sinatra was kind, not mean, to Marilyn, and she appreciated that about him and had strong feelings for him because of it. Because she felt that she really wasn't worthy of love—especially when she was in her mid-thirties and began agonizing about aging—she seemed to attract men who would use her and then discard her. Frank didn't do that to her.

Indeed, just when it was thought that Frank Sinatra had definite preferences in women—and in life, for that matter—he would do just the opposite. Certainly for him to have Marilyn Monroe as an important fixture in his life was nothing if not a demonstration of an impulsive, unpredictable nature.

Renowned makeup artist George Masters recalled of his days working for Monroe, "I would arrive at noon, and she'd still be in bed. Then she'd get up and start staggering around, groggy, and put on a Sinatra record. Then she would flop back in bed and tell me to keep changing the records. Always Sinatra records. Nothing else. I would stay there changing Sinatra records or talking to her, trying to bring her around."

In fact, Sinatra and Marilyn Monroe had been closely linked since at least 1961.

After a brief stay at the Payne Whitney Psychiatric Clinic in New York (in February 1961), Marilyn wanted to spend some time in Los Angeles; Frank generously offered her his home in Bel-Air. When she accepted, he was excited. She had not been well, and he was anxious to see how she was faring. Then, at the last moment, she changed her mind and decided to stay elsewhere. She and Joe DiMaggio had enjoyed an intimate vacation in Redington Beach, Florida, in March, and perhaps she had decided not to complicate her life by staying at Sinatra's home. (DiMaggio and Sinatra had not been friendly since 1954's Wrong Door Raid.)

In June 1961, Frank invited Marilyn Monroe to Las Vegas. He was appearing at the Sands and was also planning a party for Dean Martin's forty-fourth birthday (on June 7).

From the Sands interdepartmental correspondence between Jack Entratter, president, and Al Guzman, publicity director, and Al Freeman, advertising and promotional director, it can be gleaned that there was a great deal of preparation for the Dean Martin party, some of it having to do with Monroe and Sinatra. Apparently, Sinatra was determined to conceal his relationship with Monroe from the public and, at least according to Jim White, who was a close colleague of Sinatra's friend Jilly Rizzo, from Joe DiMaggio too. "He didn't want Joe to get pissed off," said Whiting. " 'I don't need the aggravation,' he used to say, 'unless me and Marilyn are gonna be serious about this thing, and I think she ain't.' "

Many reporters knew of the romance, anyway, but as one journalist put, "Back then you didn't write everything you knew. Not like today."

One memo, from Entratter to Guzman and Freeman, dated June 5, 1961, states: "Please be advised that under no circumstances is any backstage photographer permitted to photograph Mr. Sinatra and Miss Marilyn Monroe together at the cocktail reception to follow the performance on June 7. Any photographer who attempts to do so will be permanently barred from the hotel. Be advised that this is not only a Sands requirement, it is a requirement of Mr. Sinatra's and, as such, will be absolutely enforced. Thank you."

Another memo, from Entratter to "All Concerned," dated June 6, 1961, states: "Marilyn Monroe will be Mr. Sinatra's guest. It is Mr. Frank Sinatra's intention that Miss Monroe be accorded the utmost privacy during her brief stay here at the Sands. She will be registered in Mr. Sinatra's suite. Under no circumstances is she or Mr. Sinatra to be disturbed by telephone calls or visitors before two p.m."

President Kennedy's sisters Pat Lawford and Jean Smith were present for the Las Vegas opening night, as were Elizabeth Taylor and her then husband Eddie Fisher. And Dean and Jeanne Martin, with whom Monroe sat. Ultrablond, ultradrunk, and spilling out of a low-cut dress, Marilyn was *on* that night, and when Marilyn was on, she was like electricity switched on high voltage, giving off a powerful, seductive heat.

"She was beautiful, a vision with a great smile, lots of teased blond hair, and a dress that was so low cut you couldn't take your eyes off her bosom. However, she was quite inebriated," said a Las Vegas photojournalist, who—along with a photographer for Wide World Photos—was one of the few reporters granted access to the opening-night party in Sinatra's suite. (Now retired, he said, "Don't use my name, because I don't need any more headaches from Sinatra.")

"At the party, I remember Marilyn whining, 'Oh, Frankie, c'mon, let's make out for the photographers. I love you, Frankie. I want the whole world to know.' I remember that she was standing behind him and had her hands around his waist, almost as if she was leaning on him for support."

When Frank pulled away rather than be photographed with her, Marilyn almost lost her balance. He gave her a concerned look and told one of his bodyguards, "Keep an eye on her. I don't like the way she's wobblin'. Let me know if she faints or something."

The reporter recalled: "Marilyn still wanted a picture taken with Frank. She sidled over to him like a kitten and motioned my photographer with her index finger, indicating that he should take the shot while Sinatra wasn't looking. She was very playful, coy.

"Just as my photographer was about to take the picture, Frank's bodyguard grabbed the camera. He gave it to Frank and whispered something in his ear. Then Frank walked to where we were standing and hissed, 'Next time you try that, I'll crack your skull open with this goddamn camera, the both of ya.' I remember that he talked out of the corner of his mouth, like an uneducated hustler or gangster.

"At that moment, Marilyn Monroe came over and said, 'Frankie, I'm gonna throw up,' He looked alarmed and said, 'When?' and she said, 'Now. Right now. I mean it, Frankie.' He said, 'Oh, Jesus Christ, Marilyn, not again.' And he got her out of there quick."

Elizabeth Taylor, who happened to be standing right next to the reporter, observed the entire scene. Taylor turned to the photojournalist (who recalled that the alcohol on her breath was so strong that he found himself backing away from her reflexively) and said, "Oh, my God, that Marilyn Monroe is a mess, isn't she? How she keeps her beauty, I'll never know. She simply shouldn't drink if she can't hold her liquor. Now, me," she said, sounding somewhat triumphant, "I know how to hold *my* liquor."

Then Taylor flashed her famous violet eyes, threw back a martini, and laughed giddily.

When she saw that the reporter had written her comment down on his notepad, Elizabeth grabbed the pad out of his hand, smacked him playfully on the back of the head with it, and said, "Now, *that* was strictly off the record, buster."

A couple of months later (August 1961), Marilyn and Frank entertained guests on Sinatra's yacht. Prior to their leaving Frank's home for the boat, Jeanne Martin recalled Frank as having asked her to help get Marilyn dressed. She was too disoriented from all of the pills she was taking to do so herself. Frank was fed up with Marilyn on the yacht and, remembered one of his former associates, "couldn't wait to get her off that boat. She was giving him a hard time, pressuring him to marry her, taking a lot of drugs and drinking. Frank told me, 'I swear to Christ, I was ready to throw her right off that fucking boat.' Instead, he called one of his assistants at the end of the trip, when they were ashore, and had her taken away."

When that associate asked Sinatra if he was going to stop seeing Monroe, he said, "By now I woulda cut any other dame loose. But this one—I just can't do it."

253

Another acquaintance of Frank's, Jimmy Whiting, recalled: "Marilyn was real dependent on Frank. There were many late-night phone calls to him. She used to say, 'If I have any problem in the world about anything, there's only one person I know can help: Frankie.' Frank's feeling was Hey, if I can help out the dame, I will. She's a good kid."

"Frank was going through this whole impotency trip at this time also. Way too much sauce [liquor]. The booze was completely ruining his sex life. He was getting too old to drink like that and then expect to also perform in the sack with the dames. He was frustrated by it because one thing Sinatra always prided himself on was his ability to satisfy a woman."

Marilyn cured Sinatra of his impotency, at least for a while. She said that she didn't care how long it took; she was determined that he was going to perform in bed with her. They were innovative sexually. For instance, they began sharing intimacies outdoors. Sinatra had never done that before Monroe, and it excited him. According to Sinatra's friends, he and Monroe engaged in sexual activity at night on the roof of the Sands Hotel, above the Las Vegas strip.

Interestingly, a memo dated May 30, 1959, from Jack Entratter to the hotel's security staff reads: "Please be advised that Mr. Frank Sinatra is permitted twenty-four-hour access to the roof of the Sands Hotel. Mr. Sinatra will use his own discretion in choosing to entertain any guest on those premises. Thank you."

On occasion, Sinatra and Monroe also engaged in group sex. "The one time I know of involved Marilyn and some other dame, a colored girl, and Frank," said Jimmy Whiting. "That didn't work out because the dame and Marilyn started going at it; Frank got pissed off and kicked them both out. Generally, though, it was good sex for him. Frank was his old self."

Marilyn and Frank had an argument, however, when she drunkenly confessed to him that while she was attempting to cure him of his impotency, she had been "faking it," not achieving sexual satisfaction herself. Frank was upset about that revelation and said, "Jesus Christ, if I can't satisfy her, then what the hell am I doing with her? Why'd she even have to tell me that? Did I have to know that? Hell, no." (While Frank took Marilyn's confession as an affront to his masculinity, others who knew her well said that she rarely felt satisfaction during sexual relations and that this problem was the result of certain psychological issues that had plagued her for years.)

Jimmy Whiting recalled, "So Sinatra got real depressed and started calling prostitutes left and right, getting them to come over to try to satisfy him, paying—no exaggeration—thousands and thousands of bucks on whores, one after the other, all colors, all shapes, all sizes. He was looking for that one magic whore, the one who could make him feel young again, you know? Marilyn was the only one I know of at this time who could do it, and she was no whore. Frank always said, 'That lady ain't no tramp. She's a *lady*.' "

"For a while, starting in 1961, it was bad, this impotency thing," concluded Whiting. "I believe it went on for another few years, until he met Mia [Farrow]. Still, Frank wouldn't stop drinking, even after a doctor ordered him to do so. He said, 'If I gotta choose between gettin' my bird up and gettin' loaded, hey, fuck it, I'm gettin' loaded.' "

Marilyn's secretary and confidante, Lena Pepitone, who, along with cowriter William Stadiem, wrote a book entitled *Marilyn Monroe—Confidential* in 1979, claims that by September 1961, Marilyn was certain that Frank was going to ask her to marry him. "He's almost ready," Marilyn told her hopefully. When asked about Joe DiMaggio, the man Monroe had said she never stopped loving even after their divorce, Marilyn said, "He'll never marry me again. Never. He loves me, but we can't agree about [my career]. Frankie wouldn't expect me to be a housewife. We can both have our careers. It'll be perfect.' Then, according to Pepitone, Marilyn crossed the fingers of both hands. "Let me be lucky just once," she wished, her eyes closed tightly.

Lena Pepitone's credibility has been called into question by a number of Marilyn Monroe historians over the years. Like Judith Exner's book, Pepitone's must also be read with a certain amount of suspicion. For instance, that she wrote that Marilyn thought Frank would allow her to continue with her career after they married demonstrates either how little Marilyn knew about Frank or how little Lena knew about him when she was writing her book. Frank was adamant that he would never have another wife in show business, not after what he'd gone through with Ava.

However, since Pepitone wrote in such detail about Frank and Marilyn, it would be imprudent to disregard all of it. In fact, in analyzing her stories, kernels of truth can be found throughout. For instance, Pepitone writes of the time Frank escorted Marilyn to a Hollywood party in September 1961. According to Pepitone, she was in New York when Monroe called her from Los Angeles. She asked her to bring with her a $3,000 sequined, emerald evening gown designed for Marilyn in New York. She wanted to wear it to the gala. Pepitone claims that she then flew first-class to Los Angeles with the dress in tow.

Norman Mailer in his book *Marilyn* seems to corroborate this aspect of Pepitone's story. In his book, published by Grosset & Dunlap in 1972—seven years *before* Pepitone's Simon & Schuster work—he writes: "She [Marilyn] even phones New York in great excitement. She is having a gala evening out with Sinatra. Although she has bought two dresses at Magnin's, she needs a particular dress from New York. The maid, Lena Pepitone, flies out first class to bring the dress, but in the interim, Marilyn has found another."

Pepitone wrote that Monroe reserved a suite for her at the Beverly Wilshire Hotel. "Because Marilyn was so thrilled that she and Frank Sinatra were growing closer every day," she wrote, "I was sure that she didn't need anyone else around to disrupt the romantic atmosphere she was trying to create."

The next evening, Frank arrived at Marilyn's apartment wearing a tuxedo. "I opened the door for him," Lena Pepitone remembered, "but before we could introduce ourselves, Marilyn flew into the room like an exotic tropical bird. Frank's face lit up. He was clearly thrilled by the way she looked."

"Frankie!" Pepitone's recalls Marilyn exclaiming as she embraced him. The two kissed passionately. They stopped for a moment so that each could admire the other's appearance, and then Frank asked Marilyn to close her eyes. When she did, according to Pepitone's recollection, he reached into the breast pocket of his jacket and pulled out a small box with emerald earrings in it. He pinned them on Marilyn's ears.

"Then they kissed again," Lena Pepitone remembered, "so passionately this time that I was embarrassed to be standing by. "(When Frank told Marilyn that the earrings cost him $35,000, Pepitone wrote, "she nearly fainted. The kissing began again.")

However, Evelyn Moriarty (whose memory has proved to be consistent over the years) says, "I know for a fact that Frank Sinatra did give Marilyn those earrings, but he gave them to her on her birthday. Marilyn didn't care for earrings very much. She thought jewelry took away from her looks." If Moriarity's recollection is true, it would seem that Sinatra would have given Marilyn those earrings in Las Vegas when she was there with him for Dean Martin's birthday on June 7, 1961, less than a week after her own.

Back to Lena Pepitone's story:

Two limousines then took the Sinatra-Monroe party to the gathering: one for Pepitone and another assistant of Marilyn's; the other for Frank and Marilyn. A wonderful evening was had by all, Pepitone reports. At the end of the evening, Marilyn and Frank went back to Frank's home together.

Pepitone is also challenged about this aspect of her story by chroniclers of Marilyn Monroe's life. Because Pepitone described the event as "a benefit on Sunset Boulevard . . . [with] nearly every star in Hollywood there," some have speculated that the gala she speaks of was the Golden Globe Awards. However, they were held not in September but on March 16, 1961, at the Beverly Hilton Hotel on Wilshire Boulevard. It seems impossible that Nancy Sinatra, in her chronological diary of her father, *Frank Sinatra—An American Legend,* would have neglected to mention that he took Marilyn to *any* awards that year.

"I know for a fact that Frank and Marilyn saw a lot of each other in

September of 1961," said Jimmy Whiting. "They spent a lot of nights together at his home. He did give her the earrings, and he gave her other gifts as well. They took bubble baths together. She would hold her breath and go down on him under the bubbles; not to be indelicate, but that's what she did. Frank dug it. He used to say, 'If Marilyn Monroe is ever found drowned, you'll know why. She's so good, I don't want to let her up for air.'

"I know they went out a lot, but I don't know about the event in question. I tend to doubt it occurred.

"Frank's whole thing was that he did *not* want to be photographed with Marilyn. That was a rule of his. So I doubt he would go to such a big deal function with her, where there would be photographers. Makes no sense."

Unfortunately, it would seem that only three people can truly corroborate Pepitone's memory of that evening: Lena herself; Marilyn, who's gone; and Frank, who's not talking.

By the beginning of 1962, Marilyn Monroe seemed so desperate, so emotionally needy, that even Frank—usually not the most thoughtful man when it came to a woman's emotional needs—had become concerned for her welfare. "I'm afraid she's gonna do somethin' to herself," he said to Jilly Rizzo. "She reminds me of myself when I was at my worst. That ain't good." (By this time, Frank and Marilyn were sharing the same psychiatrist, Dr, Ralph Greenson, Mickey Rudin's brother-in-law.)

Jimmy Whiting related: "She was in love with Joe DiMaggio. She refused to stop with the drugs. Frank was worried that maybe she was a lost cause; he kinda threw his hands up in the air and said there wasn't much he could do if she won't help herself. 'She wants to kill herself,' he said. 'I been there. I just don't know what to do about her.'

"He was busy with *The Manchurian Candidate* film, and that was important to him and took a lot of energy. He said it was his toughest role. I remember him saying, 'I'm too old for this shit, all this anxiety, all this memorization.' He said that all of those speeches in that film were driving him crazy. He couldn't sleep at night, he said, with all those words running through his head."

The Manchurian Candidate, based on the book by Richard Condon, with Laurence Harvey in the title role, and also Janet Leigh and Angela Lansbury, would turn out to be one of Sinatra's finest movies. In it he portrayed a former prisoner of war who became embroiled in a Communist-inspired assassination plot. His excellent performance compared favorably to those he gave in *From Here to Eternity* and *The Man With the Golden Arm.* "I think it's a damn good film," Frank has observed. "The screenplay was wonderful, and it was based on one of the most interesting books I've ever read. Larry Harvey was a consummate, powerful actor. He had great strength."

In February 1962, Frank Sinatra announced that he was going to marry twenty-six-year-old, blue-eyed dancer-singer-actress Juliet Prowse, whom he had met in August 1959 and had been dating for the last ten months. Most people were dumbfounded by the relationship; the two never seemed to have much in common, and it seemed to Sinatra intimates that, if anything, their romance was a publicity stunt for Prowse.

While promoting his third memoir, *Why Me?*, Sammy Davis said that he thought the engagement to Prowse may have been Frank's way of putting some distance between himself and Marilyn Monroe. "Marilyn was a sweetheart, but Frank had his hands full with her. Next thing I knew, I get a call from him telling me he's involved with Juliet Prowse, gonna marry her. And, to me, it was like my phony marriage to Loray White. I had my reasons and figured he had his. I called him and asked him about it, and he slammed the phone down. So I figured, Hey, this ain't none of my business, anyway. But I do think it had to do with Marilyn in some way; maybe trying to break from her a little."

(On January 10, 1958, Davis married dancer Loray White, though, as he remembered it, he was not in love with her. He felt pressured to do so, however, because he was dating Kim Novak at the time, and the interracial relationship had so angered egomaniacal and racist studio head Harry Cohn that, Davis said, Cohn put a contract out on his life. [Novak's agent, Al Melnick, once confirmed, "Harry called a highly placed attorney, a man with the mob, and he arranged serious action against Sammy."] While Davis was appearing at the Sands in early January 1958, Sinatra warned him that he should not go back to Los Angeles until, as he remembered it, "I straightened things out with Cohn." Drunk on Jack Daniels and despondent over the way racism had so affected his life, Davis married the African American Loray White just to get out of a tight jam with Harry Cohn and the mob. The marriage lasted two months.)

"It's true that this was a strange and brief fling," said Beatrice King of the Sinatra-Prowse union. King is a former Copa Girl who was a close friend of the late Miss Prowse's in 1962. "Frank was pissed off with a dancer [Barrie Chase] who had walked out on the film *Can-Can,* which Sinatra was doing with Shirley MacLaine. He couldn't believe that this practically unknown dancer would walk out on one of his films. He said something like 'Whoever comes into this picture replacing that dame, I'm gonna make famous. This is the favor I'm gonna do her.'*

"So in came Juliet, who was really unknown at the time, originally from South Africa. He romanced her a little. I know he gave her a $10,000 pearl necklace because I saw it with my own eyes. Soon after, they were engaged. I think Michael Romanoff hosted an engagement party for

---

* Barrie Chase is remembered today mainly as having been plucked from obscurity by Fred Astaire as his dancing partner in three landmark television specials.

them at his restaurant [Romanoff's]. Frank gave her a five-carat diamond. But when I asked Juliet about Frank after the engagement, she told me, 'Oh, please, don't be silly. We'll never marry,' and when I asked why, she said, 'Frank's not serious about this, and neither am I. This is just for fun.' That's what she told me. I had no idea what she meant.

"He met her parents, she met his, and all of this for a publicity stunt? But I thought, Well, this *is* Hollywood, isn't it? He was doing her a favor. I guess there's no telling what kinds of favors she was doing for him. Her heart belonged to her manager [Eddie Goldtone], though. She loved him, not Frank."

After the "engagement" was announced, Juliet told the press, "He [Sinatra] doesn't want me to work. But I do. After working this long and this hard for a career, I'd hate to give it up." Meanwhile, Prowse's manager began negotiating a new contract with 20th Century–Fox, just based on all the publicity Prowse received from the association with Sinatra.

When asked about Juliet's comments, Frank told another reporter, "She's not going to do any work. I'd rather not have it."

And as for that deal with 20th Century–Fox? Frank said he expected her to "just walk away from it."

Though an amiable person, Prowse was anything but easygoing. She was an aggressive career strategist who was not about to give up the spotlight. Frank always knew that about her. In 1962 one movie studio executive said of her, "Prowse is a cocky, arrogant kid who's been bumming around this business since she was twelve years old. Nothing is going to stand in her way."

If the purpose of the "engagement" was to encourage people to be interested in Juliet Prowse, it worked. After she and Sinatra were viewed as a couple, she became a major star.

When Marilyn Monroe heard the news of Frank's engagement, she went to the apartment of a neighbor, Gloria Lovell, Sinatra's secretary. The two stayed up all night long, commiserating about the mistake they believed Frank was making. However, Marilyn was reportedly showing her housekeeper photographs of herself and Frank on the yacht cruise they hosted, and she said that she would not be giving him copies because "I've already given him enough."

The Prowse-Sinatra union lasted just a short time. Supposedly, Juliet called it off. "Talk about short engagements," Johnny Carson said. "Frank has had longer engagements in Las Vegas."

A story has been published repeatedly—even in Nancy Sinatra's authorized biography of her father—that Juliet telephoned Frank to tell him that she had changed her mind. However, Frank reportedly said, 'Too late, baby,' and hung up on her.

"Juliet told me that no such thing had ever happened," said her friend Beatrice King. "She told me that they parted friends after the stunt served its purpose and helped advance her career and secured her contract at 20th [Century–Fox]. Anything to the contrary was, she said, simply inaccurate."

For public consumption, however, Prowse, who went on to a successful career in theater and films, was sticking to her public story.

"At first I was broken up about it [the canceled wedding] because I was in love with Frank," she told a reporter two years later. "But it was only a temporary feeling. I found that absence does not make the heart grow fonder. I think marriage would be a very good thing for Frank but not with me. He's a lonely man, and a happy marriage would snap him out of it."

In March 1962, while Frank was making another appearance at the Fontainebleau in Miami (where he was joined by the Summit during the last three nights), he taped a television special for ABC—his fourth and last for Timex—with guests Sammy Davis, Peter Lawford (whom Sammy laughingly referred to as "Charlie Snob" before singing a special-material number based on *The King and I*'s "Shall We Dance"), Joey Bishop, daughter Nancy Sinatra (sporting a short haircut and conservative white skirt and looking nothing at all like the sex bomb she'd become in just a few years), and special guest Elvis Presley, who had just returned to civilian life after two years in the army. In fact, the show was called *Frank Sinatra's Welcome Home Party for Elvis Presley*.

Frank actually had no interest in Elvis Presley.

"His kind of music is deplorable," he said at the time, "a rancid-smelling aphrodisiac." It was nothing personal against Elvis; Frank hated all rock-and-roll music—said it was "sung, played, and written for the most part by cretinous goons"—and made sure everyone in his life knew it. For instance, his son, Frankie, once brought home a record by the Rolling Stones, just out of curiosity, since no rock and roll was ever played in the Sinatra household. Frankie put the album on the turntable, and according to one former Sinatra employee, "Frank senior went nuts. He said, 'Who told you you could put those bums on.' He went to the stereo, took the record off the turntable, and broke it over his knee. Then he hurled one half of the record one way and the other half another way. Frankie just shrugged and went to his room. Frank had strong opinions about rock and roll. He hated anything that took attention away from himself. Moreover, he thought it was just bad music."

Whatever Sinatra thought of Presley and rock and roll, he was shrewd enough to realize that Presley's return from the army was such big news that his first appearance would generate huge ratings for the special. Elvis was paid $100,000 by Frank to make the ten-minute appearance. Colonel Parker, Elvis's manager—in an unintentional tip of the hat to George Evans's tricks back in the forties with Sinatra at the Paramount—made

Young Sinatra, in the
mid-forties. (Photofest)

Sinatra and Gene Kelly in
M-G-M's *Anchors Aweigh*,
1945. (The Kobal
Collection)

Young Frank taking a doughnut break backstage. (Archive Photos)

Happy Holidays from
Sinatra, early fifties.
(Paragon Photo Vaults)

Swinging Frank, the Capitol Years, in the fifties. (Archive Photos)

The Rat Pack—Dean Martin, Sammy Davis, Peter Lawford, and Frank Sinatra—in the 1962 movie *Sergeant's Three*. (Photofest)

Firm Frank: "Toughen up baby or get the hell out," he told Marilyn Monroe. "I ain't no baby-sitter." (Photofest)

Sinatra with Steve Lawrence and Eydie Gormé on the "Diamond Jubilee Tour" in 1990. (DMI Photos)

Frank and his wife, Barbara, on the town. (DMI Photos)

Getting older, but still cool. (Photofest)

Even at the end, in his final concerts, there was no separating the singer from the meaning of the songs he sang. (Carlo Mastrodonato) certain that three hundred girls from Presley's fan club were present in the audience to guarantee a strong audience response to him.

After Elvis, who appeared constrained wearing an ill-fitting tuxedo, did a couple of numbers ("Fame and Fortune," "Stuck on You"), Frank joined him onstage. "I'll tell ya what we'll do," Frank said, taking charge and treating Elvis rather dismissively. "You do 'Witchcraft,' and I'll do one of those others . . ." (which meant that Elvis would sing one of Sinatra's songs and Sinatra would sing one of Presley's). They really had no chemistry, these two performers, but historically this meeting of two pop-culture icons is considered a classic moment by both Sinatra and Presley enthusiasts.

Longtime Presley associate Marty Lacker reported: "Elvis didn't like the thrust of the show. I think he thought they were making fun of him, the way Steve Allen did when he had him sing to a basset hound. But he said, 'Man, to my face they couldn't do enough for me. They were totally different from what I heard.' But knowing those people, I'm sure they were different behind his back. Mia Farrow told Elvis one time that Frank couldn't stand being in the same room with him."

In retrospect, the most noteworthy part of that broadcast really had nothing to do with Elvis and everything to do with the Man himself, Frank. At one point during the hour-long broadcast, Frank—wearing an exquisitely tailored dark suit and black bow tie—walked to center stage and casually lit a cigarette. Taking a puff, he looked at it intently as the orchestra swelled behind him. Then, tilting his head back, he began the first few notes of a lovely rendition of composer Allie Wrubel's "Gone With the Wind," from Sinatra's pensive *Only the Lonely* album.

This was a natural-feeling performance, so simple and elegant. Through it, Frank demonstrated once again what a masterful communicator he was as he conveyed the sadness of the song ("yesterdays kisses are still on my lips") in such a direct, easy manner. At one point in the song, Frank paused and casually let out a small cough. This was Sinatra at his heartbreaking, aching best. Then, at the end of the song, he took a final puff and lowered his head sadly.

In an interview at this time, Frank beautifully articulated his ability to communicate a song when he said, "I don't know what other singers feel when they articulate lyrics, but being an eighteen-karat manic-depressive and having lived a life of violent emotional contradictions, I have an overacute capacity for sadness as well as elation. I know what the cat who wrote the song is trying to say. I guess I've been there—and back.

"I get an audience involved, personally involved in a song, because I'm involved myself," he explained. "It's not something I do deliberately. I can't help myself. If the song is a lament at the loss of love, I get an ache in my gut, I feel the loss myself, and I cry out the loneliness, the hurt and the pain I feel."

Though what was happening onstage with Frank and Elvis was exciting to their fans, it would seem that what had happened the night before back at the Fontainebleau Hotel, where the Rat Pack was staying as well as performing, was also entertaining. Joey Bishop remembered that after the final show he went back to his fifteenth-floor suite at about three in the morning, only to find a young woman on his balcony, threatening to jump unless she could meet Frank Sinatra. (She had paid the bellhop twenty dollars for access to Bishop's room: "Mine was the only room he'd let her into for twenty bucks. What was I s'posed to make of *that*?")

"Please don't jump," Joey said to the lady. "Wait a second. I'll get Frank and bring him back here. Just don't jump before I get back."

Joey ran to Frank's suite and found Joe DiMaggio in the living room playing gin rummy with a friend.

"Jesus, this is a life-or-death emergency," an excited Joey said as he bolted into the room. "Where the hell's Frank? See, there's this girl, and she's gonna jump off my balcony unless she meets him."

"Too goddamn bad," DiMaggio said, unimpressed. "Frank's busy. He's in the bedroom with Juliet [Prowse]. He can't be disturbed."

As Bishop and DiMaggio argued, Frank came out of the bedroom, wondering what the disturbance was about.

Bishop said, "When I told him what was happening, he said, 'Okay, you tell that girl that I'm coming. Go back and tell her that Frank's coming and not to jump.' I took off. Frank then put on a white robe, grabbed a publicity picture of himself from a stack on the table and a beautiful box of chocolates, and then ran over to my suite. He went out to the balcony and said to the girl, 'What's going on out here, sweetheart? Are you here all alone?' By now she was crying hysterically. She said her parents were in town with her. 'Well, look, let's get back inside,' Frank said. He talked to her, calmed her down—she seemed real disturbed—and said, 'Tell you what. You and your parents will be my special guests for the first show tomorrow night.' Sure enough, the next night, she and her folks were sitting at the first table, and this same girl was smiling and laughing like she didn't have a care in the world."

Later in the spring, Elvis Presley began dating Juliet Prowse, just after her engagement to Frank was broken. There have been reports over the years that Sinatra was angry with Presley for dating Prowse, but that simply was not the case. Sinatra was not in love with Juliet; their engagement had been a calculated publicity stunt, and he didn't care whom she dated even while they were "engaged" as long as she was discreet and didn't embarrass him.

"She wants to fuck Elvis Presley, fine. Let her," Sinatra told one associate. "But she's gonna be real disappointed, going from me to him. Ha!"

Presley's longtime associate Lamar Fike said, "[The Presley film] *G.I.*

Blues was where Elvis got involved with Juliet Prowse, his costar. She was just a little too smart for him, so he dumped her ass. Part of the attraction with Juliet was that she was Sinatra's girlfriend. Frank visited her on the set one day. Then he came by Elvis's dressing room to say hello. But Elvis was never paranoid about Frank, or afraid of him, either."

By this time (late 1961, early 1962), Sam Giancana and his pals were still stewing over the way Frank Sinatra continued to waffle on promises.

"He's got big ideas, Frank does, about being ambassador or something. You know, Pierre Salinger [Kennedy's press secretary] and them guys. They don't want him. They treat him like a whore. You fuck them, you pay them, and they're through," Johnny Roselli said in a FBI wiretapped telephone conversation with Sam (on December 4, 1961).

The ongoing FBI investigations of Sam Giancana (and other mobsters, such as Roselli, Carlos Marcello, Mickey Cohen, and Jimmy Hoffa) and, by virtue of Giancana's association with him, Sinatra as well, continued. Giancana was a dangerous man. Many people suffered because of his illegal activities. However, Frank didn't take any of it seriously. He knew he could handle Giancana. After all, he was still alive, wasn't he?

However, Sinatra finally paid the price as a result of his relationship with Giancana in March 1962. As has been widely reported since that time, John F. Kennedy was due to stay at the Sinatra home while on the West Coast that month (March 24–26, 1962). His wife, Jacqueline, had plans to be in India and Pakistan at the time, so Jack was anxious to have some fun with his Hollywood pals. Sinatra greatly anticipated the visit, spending hundreds of thousand of dollars in completely renovating his home on the grounds of the Tamarisk Country Club in Palm Springs (with the exception of his bedroom), adding guest quarters for the Secret Service. ("I think he's got it in his head he wants to be ambassador to Italy," Sam Giancana told his brother Chuck.)

Demonstrating that excess is never enough when it came to extravagance, he also built a fifty-by-fifty-foot asphalt heliport. Frank had it built with the Federal Aviation Administration's approval, but when a dozen neighbors became upset about it, some of them began looking up the permits, and it was discovered that Frank had failed to obtain one. When Frank finally applied for one, he was turned down by the Riverside County Planning Commission on the grounds that helicopter flights from Frank's estate would endanger nearby homes. "Now what am I supposed to do with this goddamn heliport," Frank raged to his representative at the hearing, Bruce Ramer. Ramer could only shrug his shoulders.

In February 1962, Robert Kennedy's initial investigation of the underworld was completed and a report was compiled by the Justice Department. In part, it said:

Sinatra has had a long and wide association with hoodlums and racketeers which seems to be continuing. The nature of Sinatra's work may, on occasion, bring him into contact with underworld figures, but this cannot account for his friendship and/or financial involvement with people such as Joe and Rocco Fischetti, cousins of Al Capone; Paul Emilio D'Amato, John Formosa, and Sam Giancana, all of whom are on our list of racketeers. No other entertainer appears to be mentioned nearly so frequently with racketeers. Available information indicates not only that Sinatra is associated with each of the above-named racketeers, but that they apparently maintain contact with one another. This indicates a possible community of interest involving Sinatra and racketeers in Illinois, Indiana, New Jersey, Florida and Nevada.

Thomas Calabrino, a former Philadelphia "business associate" of John Formosa's, recalled: "This is a long time ago, but I believe that Joe was the one who clued in Frank about that report. Frank was upset about it. John called me from Frank's house in Palm Springs and said, 'I think Frank's gonna make Bobby Kennedy's life miserable.' I said, 'Whatdya mean?' He said he told him about the report, and Frank was so angry he threw a bottle of wine through the television set. Frank said, 'Goddamn that Bobby Kennedy. I'm gonna get 'im. I swear to God. If he wasn't Jack's brother, I'd strangle that little bastard.'

"Then, from how I understood it, he was so drunk he stripped off all of his clothes right there in the living room, like a crazy man, and ran down the hall stark naked, and into the bathroom, where he jumped into a cold shower. Go figure. John told me once that Frank would take three and four showers a day when he was nervous or upset. It was one of his strange habits. . . ."

Matters became even darker for Frank Sinatra when (on February 27, 1962), FBI agents reported to J. Edgar Hoover that they had discovered, in an investigation of Las Vegas mobsters, that Judith Campbell Exner, Sam Giancana's girlfriend, was also sleeping with John F. Kennedy. Better late than never, it might be said of revealing news that had been known and discussed for some time in the Kennedy camp. Hoover then put to work the proverbial arithmetic of two plus two and realized that Sinatra was the one who introduced all of these players to one another. When Bobby Kennedy told his brother about this—certainly none of which was a surprise to him, but the fact that it was known by the FBI was news—he told Robert to make a decision about his visit to Sinatra's home. Bobby canceled it, reasoning that it made no sense for the president of the United States to stay with Frank Sinatra under the circumstances. It was decided that Jack would stay at Bing Crosby's home—a Republican!— instead.

Peter Lawford was chosen by Robert Kennedy to break the news to Sinatra, a task which Lawford dreaded having to do. The one thing Lawford—who had known Frank since April 1944, when they met at a party for Henry Ford II, hosted by Louis B. Mayer—did not want to do was to incur Sinatra's wrath. He well remembered what happened the last time Frank was angry at him.

Back in 1953, after Frank's divorce from Ava Gardner, Peter and his friend Milt Ebbins had the poor judgment to have drinks with Ava and her sister, Bappie, at a club in Beverly Hills. They were only together for about an hour, but that was enough time for gossip columnist Louella Parsons to sniff out a story. (As it happened, Lawford once dated Gardner back in the mid-forties, years before she even knew Frank Sinatra.)

The next day, when Parsons reported the "date" Lawford and Gardner had and hinted that it could be the rekindling of an old romance, Sinatra became incensed at Lawford. One of his "buddy boys" dating his ex-wife? That was not going to occur. Not in Sinatra's world, anyway.

Peter Lawford, in a February 1976 interview with ace reporter Steve Dunleavy, remembered what happened next: "I was in bed at three in the morning, and the telephone rings. Then comes a voice at the other end of the telephone, like something out of a Mario Puzo novel: 'What's this about you and Ava? Listen, you creep. You wanna stay healthy? I'll have your legs broken, ya bum. If I hear anything more about this thing with Ava, you've had it.' "

Frank Sinatra didn't speak to Peter Lawford for about five years after that incident regarding Ava. Who knows why Lawford even allowed a reconciliation with Sinatra (which occurred in 1959 in Monaco after a benefit show sponsored by Princess Grace) after such completely unreasonable behavior? Sinatra's pals tolerated him because, as Dean Martin put it, "when it was good, it was so good, you had to be there. He was a loyal friend as long as he felt you were being loyal to him. But when it was bad between you and Frank, it was piss-poor bad."

Lawford used to tell the story of what happened one New Year's Eve after he and Frank reconciled. Peter and his wife, Pat, had dinner with Robert Wagner and Natalie Wood at Romanoff's in Beverly Hills. Afterward, Frank asked the two couples to spend New Year's with him in Palm Springs. But the two women were tired and didn't want to take the two-hour drive to the desert. They wanted to leave the next morning.

"This, of course, did not fit in with Frank's plans," Lawford said, "and he left in a huff." Frank went back to his home and took all of the clothes that Peter and Pat kept in a closet there and threw them into the pool.

In another Lawford-Sinatra story, this one reported by Kitty Kelley in her Sinatra biography, Lawford was quoted as saying, "One time at a party in Palm Springs, he got so mad at a girl that he slammed her through a plate-glass window. There was shattered glass and blood everywhere and the girl's arm was nearly severed from her body. Frank paid her off later and the whole thing was hushed up."

Nancy Sinatra Jr. explained: "I had never heard this story before. When I asked my father if it was true, he told me what really happened. His story was independently corroborated by pianist Joey Bushkin. A woman who came to the house with one of Frank's friends was extremely drunk and created a scene inside Dad's house. Her escort was told, 'Get her out of here,' which he did, but she became unruly, pulled away from him, and fell through the window *into* the house. My father paid her hospital bills because it was his house and his responsibility. He even drove her to the hospital."

Now Peter had to tell Frank that John F. Kennedy would be staying at the home of Bing Crosby. Even though Peter told Frank that the decision was based on the fact that Crosby's home was better suited for a presidential visit in terms of security, Frank knew that the real explanation had to do with Frank's association with Sam Giancana.

It was useless for Peter to try to lie. After all, just a few months earlier, there had been a party at Peter's home attended by, among many, Frank, Bobby Kennedy, and Marilyn Monroe. Robert Kennedy pulled Sinatra aside at that gathering and told him that he needed to back off, that the president would only be hurt by Sinatra's ongoing association with Giancana. In other words, it was time for Frank to choose between the Kennedys and Giancana, and Bobby would just as soon Sinatra choose Giancana than have to have him so closely linked with his own family.

Frank tried to be polite, but he was determined that Bobby should not tell him what to do.

In frustration, Robert Kennedy even threatened that if his brother continued associating with Sinatra, he (Robert) would be forced to resign; that's how exasperated he was by the whole matter. That the attorney general of the United States would resign over Frank Sinatra must have served only to make Sinatra feel more powerful, more important, more invincible. It certainly didn't encourage him to stop associating with John F. Kennedy or with Sam Giancana.

Now, though, Robert Kennedy had exacted his revenge on Sinatra and taken from him one of the things he most treasured: the ability to say that the president, his buddy, had stayed at his home. He was hurt and angry. Unfortunately, he took his anger out on the messenger: Peter Lawford.

"If you can't be loyal to me, then the hell with you," he told Peter.

Peter had never felt more helpless. He was a relative by marriage to the Kennedys. What could he do?

"I'm married to 'em, Frank," he tried to explain. "My hands are tied."

Sinatra blew up and kicked Lawford out of his home, thereby ending their friendship forever.

Tommy DiBella says, "Of course, Frank was being completely unreasonable. Even Sam—when he was told about this incident—laughed his ass off. 'Why the fuck would the president stay with Sinatra? He ain't crazy.' But Frank had these illusions that his home would be Jack's home away from home when he was on the West Coast, what with the heliport, the [two-bedroom] cottage guest houses he built for the Secret Service, and the phone lines to Washington, and all of that nonsense. It was ridiculous. Sam used to laugh about it. He thought Frank was an idiot."

Most observers felt that Sinatra should have known better than to think that John Kennedy would be able to stay at his home in the midst of so many sensitive and controversial investigations. For Frank to end his relationship with Peter Lawford over this matter seemed unreasonable. After all, what pull did Peter Lawford have with Kennedy? None. Or, as Tommy DiBella put it, "Sinatra had no influence on the Kennedys either. And you didn't see Sam end his relationship with Frank for that reason, did you?"

Peter Lawford told Kitty Kelley that after his meeting with Frank, Frank telephoned Bobby Kennedy and called him "every name in the book."

That didn't happen. "The problem was that Frank couldn't talk to *anyone* about it. Joe Kennedy had had a stroke, so he was out of the picture. Jack was unavailable, on purpose. And Bobby simply wouldn't take his calls. The Kennedys' behavior only reinforced the fact that they were not close friends of Sinatra's. Frank couldn't even get them on the phone to talk about what had happened! "He was pissed," said a long-time associate. "He was throwing things, had a big Sinatra tantrum. It was a bad scene."

To this day the Sinatras refuse to admit that the reason Jack Kennedy did not stay at the Sinatra home was because of Frank's ties with Sam Giancana. In her authorized biography of her father, Nancy Sinatra wrote: "My father's place was open all around, but Bing Crosby's was back up against a mountain and was ideal for their purposes." Nancy says that even Robert Kennedy was adamant that his brother should stay at the Sinatra home but that the Secret Service wouldn't hear of it. In the end, she wrote, Jack phoned Frank from Bing's.

Because of the news that Peter had been forced to deliver, Frank decided that Peter's loyalty to the Kennedys was greater than his loyalty to him. So, as had been Frank's way with so many people in the past, he cut Peter out of his life—again. He removed him from the two upcoming Rat Pack films, *Robin and the 7 Hoods* and *4 For Texas,* and never took his calls or saw him again.

There probably aren't many people who can hold a grudge like Sinatra. In fact, twenty years later, Peter and his wife went to Las Vegas to see a performance by Sinatra at the Sands. When word filtered back to Frank that Peter was in the audience, he dispatched two security guards to

267

remove Peter from the premises. "Mr. Sinatra refuses to perform," Lawford was politely told, "until you are gone."*

Sammy Davis, who had nothing to do with any of the drama, remembered in an interview with this writer: "The thing was this: Frank was hurt. We talked about it a couple of times. He thought it was chickenshit, the whole goddamn thing. And for the president to stay at Bing's, well, that looked to Frank like a slap in the face. A Republican! In other words, it looked to Frank like Kennedy was saying, 'I'd rather stay *anywhere* than with you.' I think Frank felt that the whole thing was designed to humiliate him, and you know what, pal? I fucking agree. I do. The way Frank helped the Kennedys, man, that whole thing they did was *cold*."

After that incident, though Sinatra cut Peter Lawford out of his life, he still kept John Kennedy in it, even though Kennedy didn't seem to want to be there.

On June 4, 1962, more than two months after the visit to Crosby's, Kennedy wrote to Sinatra thanking him "for the floral rocking chair that you thoughtfully sent me on my birthday."

An August 28, 1962, telegram from Frank mentioned a film that Kennedy had urged him to make: "United Artists representatives will contact you regarding Manchurian Candidate. Print will be available any hour, day or night, for reviewing by the President."

CHAPTER 26

In the summer of 1962, Frank Sinatra embarked on a record-shattering concert tour of Europe—called the World Tour for Children—during which he visited children's hospitals and youth centers in Hong Kong (where he donated $95,000 for children's charities); Israel (where he established the Frank Sinatra International Youth Center for Arab and Jewish Children); Greece (where he was awarded the Athens Medal of

---

* In February 1968, Sinatra was annoyed with columnist Earl Wilson—always his staunchest supporter—because of some items he had written which Sinatra misinterpreted. When Wilson and his wife went to Miami to see Sinatra perform at the Fontainebleau, they got the news from the hotel's publicist, Harold Gardner: "Frank says he won't go on if you're in the room." Reported Wilson, "I surrendered to Sinatra's decree in what was one of the saddest moments of my career. I cannot describe the shame I felt. The dejection and the hurt of rejection." It would be seven years before Wilson was allowed back into a Sinatra performance and permitted to speak to him, and even then—just as always seemed to be the case—the matter was not discussed.

Honor); Rome, Geneva, Madrid, and London (where he had a successful concert at Royal Albert Hall and visited the Children's Home for the Blind); Paris (where he dedicated the Sinatra Wing of the Summer Home of the St. Jean de Dieu for Crippled Boys at Bruyères le Chatel); and Monaco. In ten weeks, Sinatra personally financed thirty concerts and raised more than a million dollars.

Frank was deeply affected by the World Tour for Children. Upon his return, he said that visiting and attempting to comfort so many ill and crippled children filled him with a deeper sense of compassion than he'd known before. Perhaps this is one of the reasons he felt so strongly that something needed to be done to help Marilyn Monroe, whom he always called "the kid," his close friend and off-and-on romantic partner. Her life was in terrible turmoil by the time he returned to the United States.

After the departure of Juliet Prowse, Frank and Marilyn picked up where they left off and resumed dating. Playwright Garson Kanin said that he had heard that Frank offered a million dollars for the rights to remake the film *Born Yesterday,* to star himself, with Marilyn in the Judy Holliday role. "He wanted to help her," said Kanin. "He was finally reaching out to help her."

"There's no doubt that Frank was in love with Marilyn," recalled Milt Ebbins. Ebbins remembered how Marilyn unwittingly interfered with Sinatra's plans to attend a luncheon with President Kennedy at the White House. The invitation had come when Peter Lawford tried to get back into Sinatra's good graces after Kennedy had stayed at Bing Crosby's, rather than Sinatra's, home. Lawford and Ebbins persuaded Jack Kennedy to entertain Sinatra for lunch during a time when Jackie was out of town. Jackie did not want Sinatra near the White House.

Kennedy hired an Italian chef from New York to prepare fettuccine Alfredo, veal piccata, a salad, and an elaborate ice cream dessert. Ebbins arranged to have Sinatra picked up at Dulles International Airport and taken to the White House.

"The afternoon of the luncheon, I got a telephone call from Sinatra's secretary, Gloria Lovell," Milt Ebbins recalled, "telling me that he had a cold or the flu and couldn't make it. I couldn't believe it. I said, 'Gloria, please, he's gotta come. You don't turn down lunch with the president because you have a cold.' She said he wasn't coming. When I told Jack, he was completely unaffected. 'Fine,' he said. 'More food for us.' "

Later, Ebbins learned from Sinatra and Lovell that the real problem had to do with Marilyn. She had been staying at Sinatra's home for the weekend but had gone shopping and never returned. Not only was he worried for her safety, he was also jealous of her whereabouts.

"It was as if he was saying, 'To hell with the president's lunch,' " said Ebbins. "For Frank to break an engagement with the president of the United States—and I can assure you how badly he wanted to go there—

was a major thing for him. He was hung up on this girl [Marilyn]. It was very serious for him."

Retrospectively, it is widely believed that her film career had lost its momentum. However, that was not the case. Although her more recent movies had not been as successful as the earlier ones, Marilyn had just renegotiated with 20th Century–Fox to complete two more pictures for them. After having been fired from the set of the first one—*Something's Gotta Give*—she was, shortly thereafter, rehired to complete it when the studio realized that no actress could replace her. Then, as a vote of confidence, the studio offered her another film as well, *What a Way to Go* (which was intended as a vehicle that would costar Sinatra. In fact, the negotiations were handled by Mickey Rudin, the attorney Monroe and Sinatra shared).

For these two films, Monroe would have been paid a total of $1 million—more money than she'd ever earned before for making a movie. She had also reportedly signed a deal with an Italian production company to star in four movies in Italy and was to be paid $11 million at contract signing. Although her career was apparently on the upswing again, it would seem that she was not faring so well in affairs of the heart.

Because this time in Marilyn Monroe's life has been the subject of such great debate, speculation, and innuendo, it remains difficult to sort through all of the nonsense—a job better left, perhaps, to Marilyn Monroe biographers.

It would seem, though, that by 1962 the affair between Monroe and President Kennedy had ended badly. According to the legend, when Robert Kennedy was sent by his brother to end the romance with Monroe for him, Robert and Marilyn then became attracted to one another. Those who believe that this liaison actually happened say that the relationship quickly grew more serious and that Bobby had even proposed marriage to Marilyn. However, by August 1962, Robert was also trying to end the affair with Monroe after having been advised that even a hint of a romance with a Hollywood love goddess would seriously jeopardize his political ambitions.

Patricia Newcomb said of writers who have reported Bobby's proposal of marriage to Marilyn, "Are they *crazy*? I knew Bobby very well, better than Marilyn did in a lot of ways. However, you didn't even have to know him well to know that he would never have left Ethel. And with all of those children? Come on. I think she [Monroe] may have come on to him, but I don't believe anything happened between them; just from the little things he said to me about her, I don't think so."

On July 27–29, a full week before Marilyn Monroe's death, Monroe went to the Cal-Neva Lodge, which Sinatra had purchased a part interest in a few years earlier, at the behest of either Peter Lawford or Frank Sinatra, depending on which source one believes.

The Cal-Neva, located exactly on the Califonia-Nevada border, boasted a beautiful show room (where the same performers who frequented Las Vegas—Frank's friends, for the most part—appeared), an enormous dining room, plus about twenty furnished cottages that cost about fifty dollars a day. The luxurious gambling casinos were located on the Nevada side of the compound. It was advertised as "Heaven in the High Sierras." (According to FBI documents, Frank owned the largest interest in the Cal-Neva, 36.6 percent.)

Nancy Sinatra recalled: "Dad liked Cal-Neva because it was unpretentious but glamorous, homey but exciting. He had the final say on every employee, choosing people who were honest and hardworking and who would turn the lodge into a wonderful getaway destination. He reveled in the fun of hotel, casino, and stage ownership, throwing countless parties, even chartering planes to fly in friends, such as Lucille Ball, to share his enjoyment at ringside."

Frank put Marilyn in Chalet 52, one of the quarters he reserved for special guests. Mae Shoopman, then a cashier at the lodge, recalls: "She wasn't well. She kept herself disguised pretty much with a black scarf."

One longtime Sinatra associate, who is still with him today, remembered: "Frank called Jilly and said that he wanted Marilyn at Cal-Neva so he could keep an eye on her, because he'd heard that she had had an abortion in the last couple of weeks. He didn't know whose kid it had been—his, Bobby's, Jack's—and he wanted to find out what was going on.

"But then when Frank confronted her at Cal-Neva and asked her if it were true that she had been pregnant, she denied it, and he believed her.* He had deep feelings for her, which is why she was there. Lawford was with her. However, Sinatra ignored him and refused to have anything to do with him. The only reason he even allowed him on the premises was because he felt Lawford could help Marilyn, that she trusted him. He was willing to suppress his animosity for Peter if it meant helping Marilyn. He told me, 'I care about this woman more than she cares about herself.' I think she reminded him of what he had been with Ava, self-destructive."

It has been reported by some authors, and hotly contested by others, that while at Cal-Neva, Marilyn took an accidental overdose of sleeping pills. It was true that because she had been taking barbiturates for so long, more than ten years, her body was practically immune to them and she had to take triple doses—with vodka—in order for them to work.

---

* In Anthony Summers's book, *Goddess*, private investigator Fred Otash is quoted as saying, "An American doctor went down to Tijuana to do it, which made Marilyn safe medically and made the doctor safe from U.S law." Peter Harry Brown and Patte B. Barham, in their book *Marilyn—The Last Take*, quote numerous reliable sources as saying that Monroe had an abortion, and probably at Cedars of Lebanon in Los Angeles.

(She had always suffered from severe insomnia and nightmares. Without pills, she simply could not sleep—something she and Sinatra also had in common.)

Ted Stephens worked in the kitchen at the lodge: "All I know is this: We got this call from Peter Lawford. 'We need coffee in Chalet 52,' he screamed into the phone, then hung up. He sounded frantic. No less than two minutes passed and it was Mr. Sinatra on the phone screaming, 'Where's that goddamn coffee?' I learned later that they were in 52, walking Marilyn around, trying to get her to wake up."

Jim Whiting recalled: "Jilly told me she was drunk and had some kind of reaction to the booze. She was having stomach problems then, gall-bladder problems, and the booze was having a bad effect on her digestion. 'Sinat' [Rizzo and a few others sometimes called Sinatra 'Sinat'] was pissed at her for drinking so much, for letting herself go with the booze and pills. She was screwed up, yeah, drinking, taking lots and lots of pills."

Mickey Rudin added, "Frank is a very, very compassionate person. He brought Marilyn to Cal-Neva to give her a little fun, a little relief from her problems. If she was upset during the time, well, she could have a crisis over what she was having for lunch, she was that emotional and high-strung. She could have had an *imagined* crisis."

True to the conflicting stories that always surround Monroe, some Sinatra employees at Cal-Neva remember a sad, stricken Marilyn with a babushka around her head and dark glasses, while others remember a calm, composed—if not subdued—Monroe walking the grounds pensively.

Joe Langford, a Sinatra security employee at Cal-Neva who now lives in New Mexico, said, "Mr. Sinatra wanted a special meal prepared for her—lots of food, a steak, potatoes, a cheesecake. He went to the kitchen and gave a menu for every day she was to be there. I know that the meal was sent to her chalet. Mr. Lawford answered the door in Marilyn's room. The waiter never saw her. Then the tray was back in the kitchen about two hours later. The only thing that had been eaten was the cheesecake, and someone said that Mr. Sinatra had eaten that."

Langford added: "When Frank saw Marilyn, he was alarmed at how depressed she seemed. He was on the phone to her psychiatrist [presumably Dr. Ralph Greenson] screaming at him, saying, 'What the hell kind of treatment are you giving her? She's a fucking mess. What the hell is she paying you for? Why isn't she in a sanitarium, or something?' "*

There was a story that Sinatra took photographs of Monroe at this time. After a film processor saw the photos, he suggested that Sinatra

---

* Dr. Ralph Greenson was being paid $1,400 per month—half the fee he charged other patients—for what amounted to at least fifty-two hours of therapy a month.

burn them; that's how sickly she looked. Supposedly he did just that. However, Delores Swann, a friend of Nancy Sinatra's—Frank's first wife—insists that at least one photo survived: "I know for a fact, because I saw it in his home, that Frank has a photo of himself and Marilyn taken that weekend. He told me, 'That was taken the week before she died. Whenever I look at it, I want to cry.' He said, 'She was a beautiful woman, wasn't she? But she was weak,' Frank said. 'She was so goddamn weak.' He loved her a great deal; I'm sure of it."

Sinatra was annoyed during the entire time Marilyn Monroe was at Cal-Neva because Joe DiMaggio had shown up. It is not known if he had surprised Marilyn or if she knew he was going to be there. Referring to DiMaggio, Frank said to Joe Langford, "If the guy don't want her, why doesn't he leave her the fuck alone. He's just making things worse here."

DiMaggio did not stay at Cal-Neva. Apparently, he could not make a reservation. He stayed at the Silver Crest Motor Hotel.

Harry Hall, a friend of DiMaggio's, told Monroe biographer Anthony Summers, "He [Joe] was very upset. She went up there. They gave her pills. They had sex parties, and Joe thought—because at that time he was a friend of Sinatra's—it should never have happened. I don't think Joe ever talked to Frank again. He felt he should have had more respect for Joe. He should've left her alone."

The FBI believed that Monroe and Sam Giancana were intimate at Cal-Neva. William Roemer, a former FBI agent, insists that one of the FBI's wiretaps confirmed that Giancana and Monroe had sexual relations. "Sam was gleeful that he was one up on the Kennedys," said Roemer, "that he was the last one to sleep with her."

However, Milt Ebbins disagreed, saying: "Let me tell you about Frank Sinatra: Sinatra does not pass his women around unless he's finished with them, and he wasn't finished with Marilyn. He builds a picket fence around them so high, they can't get out. He wanted to marry her; I know it. He wouldn't have allowed half the things people have been saying happened at Cal-Neva—sex parties with Giancana and all that nonsense—to have actually occurred."

"No way," said Giancana's friend Tommy DiBella when asked if he thought Sam had had an intimate relationship with Marilyn Monroe. "And I'll tell you why: because he knew how Sinatra felt about her, and Sam never screwed with another man's girl. He thought Monroe and Sinatra were engaged to be married—at least that's what he told me—and that it just hadn't been announced yet. He said, 'Sinatra's nuts to marry that dame, but I heard he's gonna. She's crazy. She's a dope addict. She'll bring any man down.' Screwing her right under Sinatra's nose at Cal-Neva? No way."

Of course, as years pass, more and more people claim to have been involved in some way with Marilyn and the Kennedys, which is why the possibility that she was intimate with Sam Giancana is difficult for some Monroe aficionados and historians to believe despite Roemer's claim of a wiretap and a book written by Sam Giancana's brother, Chuck, *Double Cross*, which also alleges that the tryst occurred. No one witnessed the sexual encounter between the mobster and movie star—or at least that person has not yet come forward with his or her book—and since both are gone, the truth will probably never be known. Antoinette Giancana, Chuck's niece and Sam's daughter, disputes the allegations: "I knew my father's taste in women. Marilyn was too wiry, too active, for him. I don't believe it." Indeed, Monroe fans refer to the final days of her life as "the lost weekend," because no one really knows what happened at Cal-Neva during that time.

Unsure of public opinion, trying to complete a film with a troubled production schedule, ever fearful of her encroaching age, and maybe even passed between—then ultimately rejected by—the two Kennedys, from whom she had sought salvation, Marilyn Monroe was found dead at her Los Angeles home on August 5, 1962. What led to her demise will probably never be known. She left behind so many rumors and so much gossip that, over the last thirty-six years, an endless series of sensational theories and fantastic scenarios have been generated about her death. Or as Mickey Rudin put it, "In death, Marilyn was as defenseless as she was in life. She couldn't prevent these things from being said about her, and she couldn't answer them. She was gone."

Marilyn Monroe was a deeply depressed woman who abused drugs and alcohol. Those facts are undisputed. It seems to many, though, to judge from information uncovered in recent years, that there was some sort of massive cover-up after her death and that this subterfuge somehow involved many of her last relationships. However, most of the particulars of her death, and of who—if anyone—was involved in it, are pure speculation. At least it is known that Frank Sinatra was not present when she died and was not involved in her demise.

However, according to some Sinatra intimates interviewed for this book, he actually did consider marrying her just weeks prior to her death. It should be remembered that Sinatra often made impulsive, irrational decisions to marry women, such as Lana Turner and, many years later, even Jacqueline Onassis. It didn't mean he was in love with them as much as he was infatuated. In the case of Marilyn Monroe, however, it would seem that his intentions were honorable.

One close associate of Sinatra's who worked with him for over thirty years and is a close, personal friend of his (who also worked for Marilyn Monroe) insists that Sinatra considered marrying Marilyn in an effort to save her from herself.

"He felt that if she were his wife, everyone else would back off, give her some space, and allow her to get herself together," said the source. " 'No one will mess with her if she's Mrs. Frank Sinatra,' he said. 'No one would dare.' He's the most compassionate man I know, and he would definitely have done this for Marilyn; he cared about her that much.

"One day he came into my office and talked it over with me, asked me for my advice. I told him I thought he was coming from a good place, but that marrying Marilyn could pose a future problem. She was so desperate and needy, if he had married her and it went sour—as I felt sure it would—I knew that she'd go off the deep end and self-destruct and that he would feel responsible for that. Also, historically, I didn't think it was such a good idea that it be one day written that Marilyn Monroe killed herself over a bad marriage to Frank Sinatra. I admit that, while he was thinking of her well-being, I was thinking of his."

It didn't seem, though, that Sinatra's friend and adviser had convinced him not to proceed with his plans, because before he left the office, Sinatra said, 'Look, I'm gonna want to marry her in Europe, not here in the States. I don't want to have to deal with Joe [DiMaggio] on this thing. So I want you to look into it," he instructed. "See how this can work, where the best place would be to do it quietly, without a big deal. No photographers. No press."

Alarmed, Sinatra's confidant asked, "Frank, what does this mean? Are you gonna do this thing? And how the hell can you marry Marilyn Monroe and expect the press not to find out about it [in advance]?"

Very calmly, Sinatra responded, "Look, don't go losing your head over this thing. Let's just consider this a project in development, something we're looking into, like a picture [a film]. I'm gonna talk to her about it. And then we'll see what happens."

Added the source, "I'll bet that had Marilyn lived, Frank would have married her within the year. I don't know that it would have saved her, but it couldn't have turned out much worse than it did, I guess. After she was gone, he told me that he regretted not having gone through with it. He was angry at me for having tried to talk him out of it and wouldn't speak to me for a few weeks."

"I think he might have married Marilyn if he had had the chance, and that's my personal opinion" said Milt Ebbins. "He loved her, and he would have done anything to save her. I think he propsed to her. I do. The problem was that Marilyn was not in love with Sinatra."

Jim Whiting added, "All I know is what Jilly told me, because I never saw 'Sinat' and Marilyn together. Jilly said, 'Yeah, Frank wanted to marry the broad. He asked her, and she said no.' She was still hung up on DiMaggio and had just had a little reconciliation with him. She hoped they would get together, so she turned Frank down. Too bad."

"Don't underestimate the compassion of Frank Sinatra," warned his longtime attorney Mickey Rudin.

Certainly if Frank Sinatra had married Marilyn Monroe, her fate might have been different. He has always demonstrated fierce loyalty and a protective nature with all of his ex-wives—Nancy and Ava by 1962, and later, Mia Farrow. He never abandoned them, nor did he allow anyone to hurt them. In the end, he might not have been able to save Marilyn Monroe—the seeds of her self-destruction and dysfunction had been planted long before he was in her life and no doubt go all the way back to her sad, torturous childhood—but he certainly would have tried.

Frank Sinatra said he was "deeply saddened" by the news of Marilyn's death, especially when he learned that she was playing his music at the time she died. His valet, George Jacobs, has remembered that "Frank was in shock for weeks after Marilyn died, distraught."

About two months after her death, Frank wanted to know more about what happened to Marilyn Monroe. He had certain associates investigate the matter, and he didn't like what he was hearing when they began reporting back to him. "You know what" he finally said. "I don't think I need to know what happened, after all. What's the point? It's not gonna bring her back, is it?" Frank dropped his personal investigation after seven weeks.

When Frank went to Westwood Memorial Park for the funeral, he was greeted by the news that a deeply grieving Joe DiMaggio had given guards specific instructions to keep him, and most everyone else closely connected to Marilyn, including the Kennedys, away. He blamed them all for her death.

It must have been difficult for Frank to even attempt to go to the funeral. He hated those kinds of ceremonies and, at the time, rarely attended them. It was a testament to his affection for Marilyn that he would even try. He left quietly and didn't make a scene. Later, of Joe DiMaggio, he said to one associate, "That son of a bitch, to deprive me of paying my last respects. I'll never forgive him for that, not for as long as I live. I loved her, too," Frank said. "No one can ever say I didn't love her, too."

Jimmy Whiting recalled a conversation Frank had with Marilyn that Sinatra then relayed to Jilly Rizzo. Sinatra was in Monroe's chalet at Cal-Neva the weekend before her death, trying to encourage her to start anew—the way he had a number of times—and to live her life fully.

"Why bother? I'm not going to be here too much longer," Marilyn reportedly told him.

"What are you talking about?" he asked her.

"I'll be gone soon," she concluded sadly. "But don't worry, Frankie," she offered. "I'll be seeing you . . . in your dreams."

CHAPTER 27

The FBI's ongoing investigation of mob boss Sam Giancana continued through the end of 1962. In fact, nearly everyone Sam knew, including Frank Sinatra, was now under surveillance. Sam Giancana even knew the names of FBI agents who tailed him—Marshall Rutland, Ralph Hill, and William Roemer—and would wave at them when he caught them spying on him.

Dean Martin, who called these investigations of the fifties and sixties "stupid cops-and-robbers games," said, "The FBI was bugging people's rooms and following them around, looking for shit that wasn't there, making everyone paranoid, and spending millions of dollars to document when anyone who knew Sam went to the grocery store."

Of the constant surveillance, Phyllis McGuire remembers Sam telling her, "Relax. Just think what protection we have."

On October 31, 1962, Sam Giancana opened his own nightclub, the Villa Venice, outside Chicago, in Wheeling, Illinois. It was said that Giancana's idea was to bring in top name performers who would attract high rollers. They would later be steered to what was alleged to be an illegal gambling establishment nearby called Quonset Hut. Giancana wasn't exactly subtle about his intentions; he provided free shuttle service to the Hut.

"Sam spent a fortune [$250,000, according to published reports] redecorating this place, trying to make it a glamorous nightclub," remembered Tommy DiBella. "Another guy—a man by the name of Leo Olson—was the guy on the deed of sale, the official owner, but everyone knew this was Mooney's place. Sam wanted Eddie Fisher to open the club [on October 31, 1962], but there was a problem because Fisher was booked at another place at the same time [the Desert Inn, in Las Vegas]. So Sam called Frank and said, 'Look, I know he's booked elsewhere, but I need him. Take care of it, will ya?' And of course Frank did whatever needed to be done—who knows what *that* was?—and Eddie appeared at Villa Venice."

Eddie Fisher said, "I was singing at the Latin Casino when I got the call from Frank in August 1962. "It was the day Marilyn Monroe was found dead, and he was very upset. He said he wanted me to open for him at a club called the Villa Venice in Chicago. I said, 'Frank, I can't do it. I've been working too hard. I'm too tired to go to Chicago.' That wasn't good enough for Sinatra. He persisted until I said, 'All right. But I'm supposed to go back to the Desert Inn after I close at the Winter Garden. If you can get me out of that, I'll come to Chicago.' I thought I had the perfect excuse. Sinatra owned a piece of the Sands, one of the Desert Inn's chief competitors, and I was certain there was no way the Desert Inn would let me go. But somehow Frank arranged it, and now I had to go to Chicago."

During Fisher's engagement there, three FBI agents came to visit him in his hotel room to ask him questions about Sam Giancana as well as why he was performing at the Villa Venice. "Because a friend asked me to do him a favor," Fisher explained. "I was paid next to nothing and even got stuck with a huge hotel bill at the Ambassador East. Doing favors for friends can be very expensive."

Eddie Fisher was followed by Sammy Davis, Dean Martin, and Frank Sinatra in separate engagements and then in a joint one as the Summit. It would seem, at least according to FBI wiretaps, that all of these performers appeared without a fee, even though Dean Martin would, years later, deny ever having performed free of charge for Giancana. (Chuck Giancana would concur, claiming that the Rat Packers were paid $75,000 each because "Mooney had an unwritten policy of always paying the people who worked for him, entertainers included. He didn't want to feel obligated.")

When interviewed by the FBI and asked if he was performing for Giancana, Sammy Davis got a little rattled and said, "Baby, let me say this. I got one eye, and that one eye sees a lot of things that my brain tells me I shouldn't talk about. Because my brain says that if I do, my one eye might not be seeing anything after a while."

Sammy had good reason to keep his mouth shut. According to sources close to Giancana, Sammy owed the mobster $20,000, which he had borrowed from him to pay for jewelry. When Chuck Giancana and George Unger, Giancana's New York associate, met with Sammy backstage at an Atlantic City nightclub to collect, Sammy almost had a heart attack, he was so scared. "The name Giancana was as good as any bullet ever invented," said Chuck with a chuckle. Poor Sammy did pay his debt.

The Villa Venice's entertainment policy didn't last very long—apparently by design. By the end of the month, Sam Giancana had reportedly made three million in unreported, tax-free dollars. Then the Quonset Hut closed, and all future performances were canceled at the Villa Venice. "It was a sucker trap set by Sam, plain and simple," Peter Lawford once said, "and Frank lent himself and Dean and Sammy and Eddie Fisher as bait to bring in the high rollers while Sam and the boys fleeced them. I guess it was either that or die."

"It wasn't like that at all," said Tommy DiBella. "There were no threats made against these guys. Frank Sinatra recruited them as a favor to Sam. Frank didn't ask questions. He was told to do something, and he did it, like a good little boy. Then his friends were told by him, and they did it, like good little boys. No one wanted to know the answers, so no one asked the questions. That was always the best policy."

The year 1963 would prove to be difficult for forty-seven-year-old Frank Sinatra. In fact, his personal life and his family's sense of security would be challenged by year's end.

A number of albums were released in 1963, but the best of the lot is the superb *Sinatra-Basie: An Historic Musical First,* the first of two albums teaming Sinatra and Basie. (The second was *It Might as Well Be Swing,* issued in August 1964.)

Have any two guys ever looked *cooler* than Frank and the Count on the cover of this album? Frank is pictured in his tailored suit and dress hat, tie clip perfectly in place behind a maroon polka-dot tie. Count Basie wears a black dinner jacket, a green button-down shirt, and a jaunty yachting cap. In the photo, they are smiling good-naturedly, and with good reason, for this album is indeed a lot of fun. Basie's band swings through numbers like "Pennies From Heaven," "Nice Work If You Can Get It," and "I'm Gonna Sit Right Down and Write Myself a Letter," as Frank gives some of his best and most freewheeling performances throughout. It all sounds improvised—which, of course, it isn't—lending to the entire album the buoyant feeling of a live performance.

In January, Frank flew to New Jersey to host his parents' fiftieth wedding anniversary party. At this time, Frank sold his parents' modest three-story home to a Hoboken truck firm owner and bought them a new one: a split-level ranch house in Fort Lee with a remote view of the Hudson River. (He purchased the home under the name of "O'Brien," which was the name used by his father, who once fought in the ring as Marty O'Brien.) Dolly was proud of her son's present and annoyed when one press account noted that Frank had paid $50,000 for the home. She asked friends to telephone the newspaper and make the correction: The house had actually cost her son $60,000.

Once a beautiful strawberry blonde, Dolly was now a round-faced brunet. She and her son were as close as ever, though they did have their disagreements. "He's my love, my life," she told one friend of the son who gave her a $25,000 diamond bracelet as another anniversary present.

In February 1963, Frank recorded the excellent album *The Concert Sinatra* in Los Angeles, a collection of Broadway classics. All eleven songs, including "Lost in the Stars," "Bewitched," and "This Nearly Was Mine," were recorded on Stage 7 at the Samuel Goldwyn Studios, giving the album a full acoustical sound. Nelson Riddle said, "I never saw Frank so businesslike and concentrated as he was for *The Concert Sinatra.*" ("I

Have Dreamed," from *The Concert Sinatra,* is considered by Sinatra purists one of his best vocal performances at Reprise. Backed by a seventy-three piece orchestra, Sinatra delivers an emotional, heartwrenching reading of the Oscar Hammerstein–Richard Rodgers number from the 1951 Broadway musical *The King and I.*)

By the end of February, Frank had finished work on the film *Come Blow Your Horn* with Lee J. Cobb and Jill St. John. Frank played a womanizer in the movie; frankly, the best thing about it is the optimistic, swinging title song, which can be found on Sinatra's *Softly, As I Leave You* album. (The film was released, though, to strong, positive reviews in June 1963.)

Frank began a brief affair with beautiful redheaded actress Jill St. John* and had his private jet flying her to and from singing engagements. Though he took her "home" to meet Dolly—who cooked her one of her enormous Italian meals—the Sinatra and St. John dalliance resulted in nothing much more than publicity for both of them.

In March he appeared on a Bob Hope special, and then Frank hosted the Academy Awards. In May another film went into production: *4 For Texas,* with Dean as Frank's sidekick in a silly western comedy. Frank's schedule was always full. "I don't know how he did it," Dean Martin, who also had a busy schedule, said. "Then, again, I don't know how I did it. In fact, I don't even *remember* doing it."

Also in February 1963, *Playboy* published an in-depth interview with Sinatra, which raised a few eyebrows because of his views on politics and religion. Frank wanted a strong piece from Playboy and said he wouldn't sit down with the writer unless he promised to "talk turkey, not trivia." Frank had been interviewed on the set of *Come Blow Your Horn,* in his Dual-Ghia automobile en route home from the studio and during breaks at a Reprise recording session during the recent Count Basie dates; he spent a week with the writer. When the journalist asked Frank a broad question about the "beliefs that move and shape your life," Frank became impatient. The question was just too vague. "Look, pal, is this going to be an ocean cruise," he wanted to know, "or a quick sail around the harbor? I believe in a thousand things, and I'm curious about a million more. Be more specific."

For starters, Frank revealed that he did not believe in organized religion. "I'm not unmindful of man's seeming need for faith," he allowed. "I'm for anything that gets you through the night, be it prayer, tranquilizers, or a bottle of Jack Daniels."

He added, "Over twenty-five thousand organized religions flourish on this planet, but the followers of each think all the others are miserably misguided and evil as well."

* St. John had been married to Lance Reventlow, son of Woolworth heiress Barbara Hutton. She would become Robert Wagner's wife after the death of Natalie Wood.

This is not to say that Frank Sinatra was an atheist. Quite the contrary. He simply did not believe in a capricious or mean-minded, distant God. "I believe that God *knows* what each of us wants and needs. It's not necessary for us to make it to church on Sunday to reach him. You can reach him anyplace. And if that sounds heretical, my source is pretty good: Matthew, five to seven, 'the Sermon on the Mount.' "

On July 25, 1963, Frank Sinatra recorded another one of those classic "swing" Sinatra numbers, "Luck Be a Lady." With words and music by Frank Loesser, this song was written in 1950 for the Broadway musical *Guys and Dolls*. (Marlon Brando sang the song rather weakly in the 1955 film version.) In his recorded version, Frank's voice is full and strong, his delivery exhilarating. Clearly, this is one of his favorite numbers. His singing is sensational; the orchestra sounds fantastic.*

During the summer of 1963, Frank Sinatra, forty-seven, and Ava Gardner, forty, attempted to pick up where they had left off. It had been seven years since their divorce, and she was still the only woman who could really get to Frank and to whom he had always been completely vulnerable. When he performed "I've Got You Under My Skin," Ava was the "dame" for whom he was singing.

Jess Morgan became Ava's business manager in 1962 and would keep that position until her death in 1990. He remembered: "Ava felt as strongly about Frank as he did about her. She used to talk about him all the time. I was in her apartment in London many times, and often when I would walk in, she'd have one of Frank's records on. She'd say, 'That's my ol' man. What d'ya think? You like my ol' man?' Clearly, she had a certain spot in her heart for Frank. I heard the good and bad about it over almost thirty years, the times she railed about Frank and the times she praised him."

As much as he cared about her, Frank knew it would never work with Ava. Their combative romance had demonstrated their utter incompatibility time and time again over the years. After each breakup, Frank would vow never to see her again. Then—months, even years, later— when he would see her at a party or at some other social function, his eyes would meet hers across a roomful of people. Suddenly, Ava, with the luminous green eyes and the disarming, iridescent smile, would be the only woman in the room; everyone else would simply vanish. "I can't give up on us," he would insist. "I *won't* give up on us."

* A brilliant live performance of this song is available on the videotape of *A Man and His Music II*, Frank's 1966 television special. It's Sinatra in all of his swaggering glory in front of a full, lively orchestra in a memorable trilogy of performances, including "That's Life" and "My Kind of Town." Also, Frank recorded "Luck Be a Lady" again on July 9, 1993, for Duets II. It's found on the album as a duet with Chrissie Hyde.

This obsession Frank Sinatra felt for Ava Gardner tormented him for years. Was Ava equally obsessed? She most certainly loved Frank, but she simply didn't have that hunger, that preoccupation, for him that he always had for her. However, she was always a rather insecure woman whose relationships with men had, for the most part, not been fulfilling to her. So the constant attention by someone like Frank Sinatra—a wealthy, powerful, handsome celebrity—would sweep her away time and time again.

In the summer of 1963, Ava moved many of her belongings into Frank's New York apartment. Frank told pals, "She's back, and I'm the happiest man in the world." His euphoria lasted about a month. Then the fights started, with the running themes of discontent repeating themselves: her jealousy, his possessiveness, her career, his mobster friends.

"These creeps are going to bring you down," she warned him at one gathering at Jilly's in New York during this reconciliation. (Jilly's was a bar-restaurant owned by Sinatra's pal Jilly Rizzo on West 52nd Street.) Witnesses remember her as having said, "One of these fucking days, Francis, you are going to end up at the bottom of some river somewhere wearing cement shoes. And I'll be damned if I'm gonna end up down there with you, you stupid frigging wop."

"To be honest, Ava was scared to death just being around him," said one of her New York friends. "She felt that at any moment there would be gunfire and she would fall dead in his arms. In fact, she told me that the only place she ever felt safe with Frank was when they were at his parents' home, because she knew that no one would touch them there. Dolly cooked a big Italian meal for her and Frank and another woman in June of '63."

The "other woman" Ava's assistant refers to was Phyllis McGuire, Sam Giancana's girlfriend.

"Ava told me that she pulled Phyllis aside and said, 'Tell me something, aren't you scared to death of these people you hang around with?' and Phyllis—all wide-eyed and innocent—said, 'Why, no. Whatever are you talking about?' Ava said, 'Sister, you'd better watch out. That innocent act doesn't work for me, and it's not gonna work for the FBI either.' I could just see it: Phyllis was probably just left standing there with her mouth wide open."*

One evening in New York, according to Tommy DiBella and others, Frank and Ava were at Jilly's with a group of people. Ava, wearing an impeccably cut black-and-white-checked dress, which showed off her shapely figure to its best advantage, had never looked more alluring. Sinatra, too, was dapper in a chalk-striped suit, with starched white shirt

---

* It would seem that Phyllis McGuire finally came to her senses. Dominick Dunne tells the story of going to visit her at her home in Las Vegas decades after the above incident. "A guy with a machine gun answered the door."

collar and cuffs. Around his neck was a striking checked silk tie, the perfect counterpart to Ava's outfit. In his lapel was pinned a miniature white carnation.

Sitting at a table with their friends, Sinatra and Gardner looked like the ideal couple and seemed to be having a good time over a selection of coffee and liqueurs—until Sam Giancana walked in with a gaggle of "boys." Delighted, Frank jumped to his feet. "Mooney, over here. C'mon, buddy boy," he said, "Join us. Look, Ava. It's Sam."

Immediately, Ava started to seethe.

"When Sam sat down, you could see the ice forming on the table. Ava's attitude was that chilly," said DiBella. "Sam was being Sam, you know, nice guy, slaps on the back, buying drinks. And Frank was grinning from ear to ear, like a Cheshire. But Ava was just staring at the two of them—until she finally got up."

"Excuse me, gentlemen," Ava said. Her tone was frosty. "There's a fellow over there I simply must see."

"Who the hell's that?" Frank wanted to know.

Ignoring her ex-husband, Ava sauntered over to a gentleman sitting at a table on the other side of the room and, without any encouragement, began flirting with him. She touched his arm and gently rubbed the back of his neck as she spoke to him. The stranger looked the screen star over from top to toe appreciatively, probably wondering what he had done to have suddenly become so fortunate. He looked over at Frank and raised a glass of wine in his direction as if to say, "Here's to ya, sucker." The smug expression on his face conveyed the notion that he possessed something that Frank Sinatra—with all of his millions, all of his power, and with that terrific suit as well—did not: Ava Gardner's undivided attention.

Sinatra's face hardened.

Ava didn't stop there. She hoisted herself up onto the surprised guy's lap and giggled girlishly. Then she turned toward Frank, challenging him with steely green eyes to do something about her behavior. This was more than Frank could bear.

Frank got up, and when he did, he pushed his chair back with such force it fell over, and he went over to the stranger's table. According to three witnesses, he pushed Ava off the interloper's lap. She nearly fell to the floor. Then he pulled the stranger up by his collar, looked him straight in the eye, and in a voice loud enough to be heard over the music said, "You're lucky I don't kill you with my bare hands, you idiot. Who the fuck do you think you are? Are you *crazy*? You want to *die*? Because I'm the guy to make that happen, you chump." When Frank finally released his grip, Ava's new friend fell to the floor.

Then Frank grabbed Ava by the arm and, ignoring her loud protestations, dragged her back to his table. With an abrupt shove, he pushed her into a chair. (One observer said that it was as if a scene from Sinatra's song "Luck Be a Lady" was being played out in front of witnesses: "A lady doesn't leave her escort. / It isn't fair. / It isn't nice.")

"Ava hated being manhandled like that," said DiBella. "She got back up and said, 'How dare you? I'm going.' Frank, standing behind her, pushed her back down by her shoulders and said, 'Like hell you are. Sit the fuck back down, Ava.' The next thing everyone knew, they were into it, cussing and fighting.

"As they fought, Sam kept instigating matters, saying things under his breath to Frank like 'You ain't gonna let her get away with *that*, are you?' and at one point, 'Man, now she has *really* crossed the line.' "

Suddenly, in one swift movement, Ava doused Frank with Sam's gin and tonic.

"What the fuck was *that* for?" Frank said, astonished.

"He had to have been humiliated," said DiBella. "To have this dame throw a drink in his face in front of Sam Giancana, well, that was bad. That was real bad. Frank grabbed her, and at first I could have sworn he was gonna smack her but good," said DiBella. "We all held our breaths. Instead, he started pleading with her."

"Apologize to Sam, Ava," Frank said, trying to control his temper. "Apologize to me, too. You know that ain't right, what you did with that guy over there and what you just did to me. What's wrong with you?"

Ava turned to Sam and stared at him for a moment with narrow, cold eyes. She didn't say a word. Then she broke free of Frank's grip and left the room.

Sam laughed riotously. "Buddy boy, you need to straighten that broad out," he told Frank. "She's got no respect for you. I ain't never seen anything like that. That was *classic*. You hear me? Classic."

Frank Sinatra didn't say a word for the rest of the night. He was clearly embarrassed and disgusted—with Ava Gardner and probably with himself as well.

The next day, Ava moved out of Frank's apartment. She was out of his life again—but not for long.

By the end of 1963, speculation about Frank Sinatra's ties with the underworld continued. Frank continued socializing with "the boys"; as a result, his name can be found on hundreds of FBI surveillance documents throughout the period. Some of the documents are fairly damning, and it would appear that Frank was often on the fringe of what would or could be considered illegal activity. However, Los Angeles County sheriff Peter Pitchess said thirty-two years later (in 1995): "I have probably spent more time investigating Frank Sinatra than any other man or organization. First, because I was active in the intelligence section of the FBI when I was an agent, then as sheriff; then because Mr. Sinatra is my personal friend and I had to find out to protect my career. And let me tell you something: You might as well go home, because you're not going to be able to confirm any of those things."

How Frank Sinatra managed to stay on the right side of the law is a mystery even to people who know him best. "Either he was extremely shrewd and never got caught," said one close associate, "or he was extremely shrewd and managed not to do anything wrong." However, in mid-1963, the odds seemed to catch up to him. What started out as a small, inconsequential dispute between a girl singer and her road manager—one that did not even involve Frank Sinatra—ended up costing him his gaming license and almost severed his relationship with Sam Giancana.

It was said by those inside Sinatra's camp at this time that Giancana had become a secret co-owner of the elaborately appointed Cal-Neva Lodge in Lake Tahoe, along with Frank, Dean Martin, Hank Sanicola, and Paul "Skinny" D'Amato (once described by the chief counsel of Congress's Assassination Committee as "a New Jersey gangster").

According to FBI documents, Sam Giancana had gone to visit his girlfriend Phyllis McGuire while the McGuire sisters were appearing at Cal-Neva for a singing engagement. As one of the twelve governing chieftains of the Cosa Nostra, Giancana was *persona non grata* in the eyes of the Nevada gaming officials, who were attempting to ensure that no criminals were even remotely connected with the state's huge gambling industry. The FBI had issued a "Las Vegas Black Book" containing the names of the eleven known criminals not permitted in Nevada casinos. While it was not a criminal offense to permit one of the men listed in the Black Book on the premises, doing so could result in the loss of the casino's operating license.

Since Giancana was not allowed in any Lake Tahoe or Las Vegas casino, he was hiding out in Cottage 50, a lovely suite, overlooking the lake, assigned to Phyllis McGuire. At night, he and his "boys" would drink and gamble and have a little fun with the ladies. During the day, Sam would keep a low profile. Nobody was really discreet, however. (An FBI document states: "Giancana sojourned in Chalet Fifty at the Cal-Neva Lodge at various times between July 17 and July 28, 1963, with the knowledge and consent of the licensee [Sinatra].") When the Nevada State Gaming Control Board learned that Sam was on the premises, Sam was unfazed. "So fucking what?" he said.

"Frank wasn't happy, though," said Andrew Wyatt, a former Lake Tahoe police investigator who at the time was working for the Nevada gaming board. "I heard that he and Sam had a fight about it. Frank didn't want to take the heat for Sam's presence just so he and his girlfriend, Phyllis, could hole up in Chalet 50. Frank wanted Sam to leave, to get the hell away from Cal-Neva before people started asking questions. He knew he was tailed by the FBI; he knew this was trouble. But you didn't tell Sam Giancana what to do. So Frank just had to deal with it. Sam said he would leave in a few days. Frank just had to take his chances that nothing would happen. But his luck ran out."

One evening, Victor LaCroix Collins, the McGuire Sisters' road manager, got into a scuffle with Phyllis in the dining room about something so silly as to not even be memorable. Their verbal discussion suddenly turned physical, and before anyone knew what was happening, Victor and Phyllis were shoving each other around. Hearing the shrieks of the other two McGuire Sisters—Christine and Dotty—Sam came bounding into the room, saw what was happening, and with a sharp left hook, decked the road manager. Then LaCroix—either the bravest man in show business or the dumbest—retaliated with his own fists, and before long he and Sam Giancana were rolling on the floor, throwing punches at each other. Phyllis McGuire and Victor LaCroix say that when Frank heard what was going on, he ran into the room and pulled the two men apart. Then Sam stormed out of the dining room, infuriated with Frank for breaking up the fight. (In 1981, Frank would insist he was not present at the fight, that he was in Las Vegas.)

Just another night in Frank Sinatra's life, or so it seemed at the time. Afterward, according to a source close to Giancana, Sinatra and Giancana went for a walk on the property surrounding Chalet 50, and as the two gazed up at a starless sky, Frank said, "Tomorrow you're leaving here. Right?" Sam shrugged his shoulders. "Sure, why not? I caused enough trouble." The two had a good laugh. (Again, Sinatra has insisted he was not with Sam Giancana at Cal-Neva.)

Sam's departure would be one day too late. A month later, when the Licensing Control Board of Nevada learned that a fight had occurred at Sinatra's establishment and that Sam Giancana had been involved in it, trouble started brewing. Frank was working at the Sands in Vegas at the time when he was asked to meet with the Nevada State Gaming Control Board. Commissioner Edward Olsen asked a lot of questions; Frank didn't give many answers. He did say that he'd run into Sam Giancana at Cal-Neva but that it was a brief meeting, which was hedging the truth. He also said he didn't know of any fight that had occurred, which was not true. And he said that he had never invited Sam to the lodge, which was true. When reminded that he could lose his license if he allowed Sam on the premises of Cal-Neva, Frank promised that he would not see Giancana in Nevada, "but I'm gonna see him elsewhere if I want to, and I want to," Frank said. "This is a way of life. This is a friend of mine. I won't be told who I can see and who I can't see."

Just when Frank thought he was probably in the clear and that the Sam Giancana–Victor LeCroix bout would be forgotten, it was learned by licensing officials that the entire incident was witnessed by one of Frank's Cal-Neva employees. That employee was called in to answer questions about the incident before the Licensing Control Board of Nevada. However, when the employee failed to show up, news reports contended that Edward Olsen had speculated that perhaps Frank had intimidated the employee.

When Frank read these stories, he was furious. He insisted that he did no such thing. "The guy didn't show up because he took off, scared to testify. Don't ask me why," Frank said. "I didn't have nothing to do with it. How dare he blame me?"

Frank Sinatra had a few volatile meetings with Olsen about that article and about the investigation in general. Olsen wanted official meetings with Frank; Frank wanted "off the record" conversations. There was a meeting in which Frank asked Olsen to put off any investigation until after the summer season was over—a few more weeks. (Cal-Neva was not doing well, and Frank wanted to get as much as he could out of the summer season, because by November—as was Cal-Neva's practice—the casino would be open only on weekends.) Olsen told him he didn't care about the state of Sinatra's business. As the discussions continued, Frank became more irate. Then, in a final telephone call, Frank let him have it after Olsen threatened him with a subpoena. "You're not in the same class with me," Frank hissed at him. "So don't fuck with me. And you can tell that to your fucking board and that fucking commission, too."

Apparently, Olsen was the wrong man to threaten. The next day, he filed an eight-page complaint against Frank saying he used "vile, intemperate, base and indecent language" in their conversation. That night, gaming control investigators showed up at Cal-Neva. Frank threw them out. The gaming board then stepped up its investigation of Frank, filing official charges against him and threatening to revoke his license for allowing Giancana to be at Cal-Neva in the first place. Subpoenas were served on just about everyone who knew Frank, Sam, Phyllis, and the rest. Even poor Christine and Dotty McGuire said, "We told Phyllis that Sam was going to be trouble, and now look! We're ruined."

Questions would be asked about Giancana's financial involvement in Cal-Neva, Frank's relationship with Sam, Sam's with Phyllis, and any other relationship even remotely connected to Cal-Neva. Frank wasn't happy about any of it. He certainly didn't enjoy answering questions, especially under oath, nor did he want his friends to be forced to answer them, either.

Police investigator Andrew Wyatt recalled: "The word was that Frank was going to lose his gambling license over this stupid business, all of which was caused by a silly fight between a road manager and a blond girl singer. The investigation got nasty, people started asking too many questions."

In September 1963 the Nevada State Gaming Control Board filed charges against Frank Sinatra for having entertained Sam Giancana—

who was described in the complaint as being "fifty-four years of age, one of the twelve overlords of American crime and one of the rulers of the Cosa Nostra"—at Cal-Neva. The complaint went on to note that "Sinatra has maintained and continued social association with Giancana, well knowing his unsavory and notorious reputation, and has openly stated he intends to continue such association in defiance of Nevada gaming regulations."

Now Frank would be compelled to officially address the allegations and further involve Sam in the matter as well. This was more trouble than it was worth for Frank. He was also concerned about how this snowballing investigation would affect his relationship with John F. Kennedy, and he didn't want to further jeopardize his relationship with the president. So, on October 10, he announced that he would give up his gaming license and Cal-Neva. Along with it would go his 9 percent interest in the Sands casino in Las Vegas.

That hurt. Frank had purchased a 9 percent share of the Vegas resort for $50,000. In a few years, his share's worth had swollen to a hefty $500,000, and the projected income was in the many, many millions. The total of Frank's gaming interests—Cal Neva and the Sands—was estimated at $3.5 million. Giving up such a lucrative business venture simply because the lead singer of the McGuire Sisters had had a little tiff with her road manager—which had been interrupted by a gangster Frank didn't even want at his establishment in the first place—infuriated Sinatra. But give it up he did.

"No useful purpose would be served by my devoting my time and energies convincing the Nevada gaming officials that I should be part of their gambling industry," Frank said in a statement. Then, in a goodwill gesture, Frank said he hoped that the casinos he was abandoning would continue to thrive, "because they provide wonderful opportunities for established and new performers to present their talents to the public."

That same day, the gaming commission formally revoked his license and moved to divest Frank of his $3.5 million investment in the Sands and in Cal-Neva. He was given until January 9 to sell off his interests in the two casinos.

Frank sold all of his casino holdings to Warner Studios—for just a million dollars, as it turned out—in exchange for a lucrative deal there for his own film-production company. Then Frank issued a statement saying he was giving up the gaming business because he now had a new production deal with Warners and wanted to focus on making movies instead.

In other words, Frank told the Nevada State Gaming Control Board, "You can't fire me. I quit."

"Bastards," Frank said of the control board officials to one of his confidants. "All of the money I brought into this industry—millions and millions of bucks—for them to treat me like this. Just fuck them."

Phyllis McGuire, who, it would seem, was inadvertently responsible for the fracas that led to all of this trouble, says in retrospect, "Frank was so rude to the gaming board that it aggravated the situation. It could have been worked out if Frank hadn't been so verbal. He called the gaming chairman a goddamn cripple."

"He was arrogant and hostile to everyone involved," Dorothy Kilgallen wrote at the time, "so they were understandably hostile in return. After all, they do represent law and order."

This incident at Cal-Neva also had a long-lasting affect on two of Frank's relationships, with Hank Sanicola and Sam Giancana.

Sanicola was unhappy about Frank's ongoing relationship with Giancana. The two had worked hard over the years building the Sinatra empire—Sanicola even had $300,000 invested in Cal-Neva—and he simply could not accept the fact that Frank was willing to jeopardize it for a mobster. The two had a rancorous fight about Cal-Neva in an automobile while driving through the desert from Palm Springs to Las Vegas. Frank blew up, insisted on buying Sanicola out of all of their joint partnerships (including the one they held in Sinatra's Park Lane Films), and gave Sanicola the rights to five of his music-publishing companies—Barton, Saga, Sands, Tamarisk, Marivale—worth anywhere from $1 to $4 million, and then kicked him out of the car, right in the middle of the hot desert.

As difficult as it may be to believe, considering their long, fruitful friendship, Frank Sinatra never spoke to Hank Sanicola again. Jilly Rizzo, who had been a pal for years, became Frank's new "best bud."

Sinatra's other friends were astonished that he would end the valuable relationship with Sanicola, his *paisano.* However, Frank felt as he always did about these matters: "My life goes on no matter who comes and who goes." For his part, though, Hank Sanicola was said to be devastated by the way he was dispatched. He had devoted decades to Sinatra; they'd known each other since the forties, when Sanicola started unofficially managing Sinatra during the Rustic Cabin days. He had seen Sinatra cut off many friends without giving them a second thought; he probably never dreamed he'd one day be one of them. (He died a little more than ten years after the split, in October 1974.)

As for Sam Giancana, he thought Frank had been a fool for blowing up in the meeting with Olsen. "This whole thing could have been avoided if Sinatra had kept his cool," he said.

"Sam lost a bundle because he was a secret part owner of Cal-Neva, and the whole thing went belly-up," says Tommy DiBella. "So, for a while there, Sam didn't want anything to do with Frank. And I know that Frank was pissed at Sam, because, as he put it, 'that fucker shouldn't have been there in the first place. Look at the trouble he caused. This is *his* fault.

Not mine.' It wasn't the same buddy-buddy relationship between Frank and Sam, not after Cal-Neva, that's for sure."

Nicholas D'Amato, a former member of the Philadelphia mob (no relation to Paul "Skinny" D'Amato) adds: "Frank was lucky he was who he was, because if he was anyone else—anyone not so famous—I believe that Sam would have seriously hurt him over all of that Cal-Neva business, star or no star. I remember that someone bought Sam a Sinatra album as a present at this time, and when he took the gift wrap off the record and saw it was one of Frank's, he broke it over his knee and said, 'I fucking wish this was Frank Sinatra's back.'"

To this day, despite overwhelming evidence to the contrary—stacks of FBI surveillance reports and numerous interviews with witnesses, including Phyllis McGuire—the official word from the Sinatra camp is that Sam Giancana was not invited to Cal-Neva by Frank Sinatra, nor was he even there in July 1963, nor did the gaming commission go so far as to actually revoke Frank's license. In Nancy Sinatra's official biography of her father, *Frank Sinatra—An American Legend*, the Sinatra family attorney, Mickey Rudin, is quoted as saying, "We were prepared to prove that [Frank Sinatra] had not invited Sam Giancana and that, in fact, he (Giancana) had not stayed at Cal-Neva Lodge. There was never a finding that he [Sinatra] would lose his license, and there was never a finding that he had invited Sam Giancana to Cal-Neva Lodge."

Of course, the Sinatra family's denials seem to fly in the face of reams of newspaper accounts to the contrary, not to mention official documents from the commission regarding the investigation. It should also be noted that it would have been difficult to uncover any of the "findings" Mickey Rudin speaks of, since Sinatra never did address the charges that had been brought against him by the gaming commission, nor did he ever answer any questions under oath. Clearly, the Sinatras choose to exercise a family prerogative and remember this piece of history their own way.

CHAPTER 28

L isten, I want to talk about your drinking," Frank Sinatra said, pulling Dean Martin aside.

"What's the matter?" Dean asked, slurring his speech. "Did I miss a round?"

The small crowd laughed.

"C'mon, let's have a drink, boys," Dean suggested.

"You *are* drinking," Sammy Davis reminded him.

"What? Is that *my* hand?"

More laughter.

"Actually, I'm gonna stop drinking tomorrow," Dean offered after taking a sip.

"Well, good for you, buddy boy," Frank said, patting him on his back.

"That's right," Dean continued proudly. "Starting tomorrow, I'm just gonna freeze it and eat it like a popsicle."

It was late September 1963. The occasion was a private party in the fabled Polo Lounge of the old Mission Revival–style Beverly Hills Hotel, on prestigious Sunset Boulevard in Beverly Hills, California. Frank Sinatra, Dean Martin, and Sammy Davis were making a public appearance for a charity. No songs—just stage patter, audience questions, and autographs.

This was the place where Hollywood's *glitterati* communed, where international celebrities came for a sip of the bubbly or a touch of beluga caviar. More myths, legends, tall tales, and grand gossip about the private lives and sex quirks of movie stars were born at the Polo Lounge than most people in Hollywood today can even remember. Charles Chaplin, Glora Swanson, Rudolph Valentino, Greta Garbo, Elizabeth Taylor, Marilyn Monroe—all of them, and so many others, not only stayed at the 253-room hotel but also ate food and got drunk in the pink-and-green-decorated Polo Lounge, where the booths all had (and still have) telephones so that theatrical agents can be quickly summoned in case a big deal has to be struck.

The Polo Lounge was, and still is, divided into two rooms, plus an outdoor-patio area. Frank, Dean, and Sammy were performing in the room with the bar for about two hundred people. In the other room, filled with about a hundred others, sat three young men at a corner table. They weren't celebrities, not yet, anyway. However, they had a plan in mind that, if it worked, would most certainly make them famous.

"See, Sinatra ain't so big and bad," twenty-three-year-old Barry Worthington Keenan told his pals, Joseph (Joe) Clyde Amsler and John Irwin. "What'd I tell ya? I just wanted to remind you of that. That's why I brought you guys here. I wanted you to remember that he's just a man, just like you and me. No big deal."

Amsler and Irwin, both a bit starstruck, nodded their heads as they stared at Frank Sinatra and his performing pals.

Amsler, twenty-three, was a semipro boxer, a scuba diver, and a drifter; Irwin, forty-two, a former underwater-demolition-team expert and a World War II–decorated hero.

291

"Just like you and me," Irwin said as he gazed intently at Sinatra. "Just like you and me," he repeated.

"So look," Keenan, a crew-cut blond, pushed ahead. "Do you guys think you can do it?"

"Kidnapping, man, I don't know," Amsler said, sipping his drink. "That's a pretty big deal, don't cha think?"

"No, man, it's not a big deal," Keenan insisted. "I'm telling you. I've got the whole thing worked out. I've been thinking about this for a long time. We *know* the Sinatras, Joe," he reminded Amsler. "And what I don't know from going to school with Nancy, I learned at the library. Man, I've been researching this thing for months. The plan is all written down," he added, pointing to a pad.

Keenan then explained that he had spent a week in the Palm Springs library researching Frank Sinatra's background and personality. He had also gone to the Los Angeles library and researched kidnappings from biblical times to the present day.

"See, where they always go wrong," Keenan told his friends, "is that they get caught when they pick up the ransom. If we get past that point, man, we'll be okay. Not only that, but the FBI's policy is that they won't interfere with a ransom pickup as long as they don't know the disposition of the victim.

"If we pull this off," he continued, "we'll be able to live like the movie stars who hang out here," Keenan said, motioning to their Polo Lounge surroundings. "It's symbolic, us being here."

The audience laughed at another of the Rat Pack's gags, but by this time, Keenan, Amsler, and Irwin weren't paying attention. Instead, Keenan continued trying to convince his friends to join him in the kidnapping of Frank Sinatra's son, Frank Sinatra Jr.

Frank Sinatra Jr.—Frank junior or Frankie, as he was sometimes called by family and friends—always had a deep love for music; he appreciated it, studied it, understood it academically, and enjoyed it. Unfortunately for him, he chose to make it his life's vocation; he wanted to follow in his dad's footsteps and be a singer. So he dropped out of the University of Southern California and soon found himself singing with the remnants of the so-called Tommy Dorsey band, comprised of whoever was left of the original group, along with a few replacements.

Had he been a doctor, an attorney, an accountant—*anything* but a singer—perhaps his life would have been different. In any of those professions his name might have been a blessing, an asset. However, as a singer, he was destined for constant—and often unfair—comparison to his father, "the Voice." Just as his own "old man" had done, Frank senior wanted his son to go to college. "Get your degree and then go into show business," he told him. But Frank junior dropped out because he so desperately wanted to be in "the business." He started working part-time at Dad's Reprise Records and Essex Productions but yearned to get up onstage and make a name for himself.

Frank junior always felt that Frank left a lot to be desired as a father; his parents split when he was four. Because his father was gone most of the time, his communication with him was often strained. Frank junior was sent off to a boarding school when he was a teenager because his dad didn't like his friends. In time, he would resent not being allowed to stay at home with his mother and sisters.

Doug Prestine, a childhood friend of Frank Sinatra Jr.'s, once recalled, "I still remember when we were walking home from school one day and, completely out of context, Frankie turned to me and said, 'You don't know how lucky you are to have a real father.' Even though we were only about thirteen at the time, I knew that that statement was significant; I just didn't know what to say to him. Big Frank would come around when he was in town or for a special occasion, like Thanksgiving, but then he'd be gone for months at a time. He called a lot, but that wasn't enough for the kids. At least it wasn't enough for Frankie."

At Christmastime, Nancy and Tina were given stacks of presents, all beautifully wrapped, from their father. Frank junior was lucky to receive just a few presents, and nothing extravagant. "It was so pathetic," said Rona Barrett, who, as a friend of Nancy junior's, spent one Christmas with the family. "The girls got furs and diamond bracelets and cashmere sweaters and silk blouses and loads of $100 shoes. I'd say each of their piles was worth at least $15,000, but Frankie didn't get more than $500 worth of gifts. I felt really sorry for him."

In time, Frank junior would become bookish and quiet, much more his mother's son than his father's. He was intellectual and not at all "hip." However, he was a brilliant musician; he played piano, did his own musical arrangements, wrote lyrics, and talked about the art form as if it were second nature. His peers had long hair, wore bell-bottoms and Nehru jackets, and sang the praises of the Beatles. Not Frank junior. He was conservative, wore suits and ties like his father's, and loathed the Beatles and any other musician connected to the rock-and-roll era.

In fact, Frank junior's disdain for rock and roll never diminished. In 1997, he said, "Originally what we call rock and roll was nothing more than an attempt of very bad white performers to sound like black rhythm-and-blues performers. They did their best to emulate; they did their best to paraphrase. And that started what later became rock and roll.

"When I was a kid in the sixth grade and first learned how to dance with a girl, we had a record called 'Shake, Rattle and Roll' [by Bill Haley and the Comets]. 'Get out in that kitchen and rattle them pots and pans.' It was all about mundane things. Then came the invasion from across the ocean, and suddenly we're hearing things like 'I get high with a little help from my friends,' You know who my friends are, don't you? Those funny little pills. That was when the content of the music began to become diseased. You'll forgive me," he concluded, "but I have a jaundiced view of that time. I hated the entire decade."

At this time, December 1963, Frank junior was just beginning to embark on his own career. Three months earlier, on September 12, the nineteen-year-old had made his professional singing debut at the Royal Box of the Americana Hotel in New York. He was slim, handsome, sported a conservative haircut, and looked debonair in a tuxedo—pretty much the way one might expect Frank Sinatra's son to appear. The audience was filled with celebrities, friends of his father's, and curious media types. It was a terrific opening, and during it, Frank junior exuded a great deal of self-confidence and vocal proficiency. When attempts to coax him back onstage for an encore were unsuccessful, a comedian in the audience said, "He's just like his old man. He's already left with a broad."

Frank missed his son's opening night because he didn't want to steal attention away from him during his big moment. He attended another performance later in the week. Of his son, he said, "The kid sings better than I did at his age."

Not all of Frank junior's engagements would be as prestigious as his grand New York opening, however. In December 1963, Frank junior found himself working as a prototypical lounge lizard in Lake Tahoe, and it was there that the fates of Frank Sinatra Jr. and Barry Keenan would intersect.

Thirty-four years later, in the same Polo Lounge in which he, Joe Amsler, and John Irwin planned to abduct the son of the most popular singer in the country, fifty-seven-year-old Barry Keenan gave to this writer his first interview regarding the kidnapping and the events leading up to it. Keenan, an amiable person, is a real estate developer today. He was once the youngest member of the Pacific Stock Exchange in Los Angeles. He had received his securities license on his twenty-first birthday. His father was a prominent stockbroker with his own firm, Keenan and Company, operating from downtown Los Angeles.

Keenan's middle-class existence in West Los Angeles was rocked by a 1960 automobile accident in which he suffered debilitating back injuries. Three years later, he was depressed, in chronic pain, addicted to drugs, and desperate because he was nearly out of his supply of Percodan. Indeed, narcotic addiction and alcohol abuse had led to his downfall. His parents were disappointed in him; he owed them and close friends money. At the age of twenty-three, he recalled, he was "a washed-up stockbroker." His thinking clouded by drugs, he was anxious to find a solution to his financial predicament and also to get enough money to feed his addiction. After considering the notion of robbing a bank, he decided that such a venture would be too risky. Selling drugs? He didn't have the street savvy for such an undertaking, he decided. "But I knew you could get a lot of money for kidnapping somebody who was rich."

In a mad, hazy state, he made a list of potential victims, the wealthy youngsters with whom he had gone to school in Los Angeles. He settled on Tony Hope, Bob Hope's son.

"But after thinking about him for a few days I discounted him because Bob Hope had done so much for our country, with the USO tours and so forth," said Keenan. "I felt it would be un-American to kidnap his son. I might have been planning a kidnapping," he recalled, clearly recognizing the absurdity of his words, "but I still thought of myself as a solid citizen. I also thought of Chris Crosby, Bing's son. We had palled around together for a while. But it didn't seem right to do that to Bing. Somehow he seemed too fragile to me. I didn't think he could handle it.

"But Frank Sinatra, I thought, now *there's* a tough guy," Keenan remembered reasoning. "He could definitely take the stress of having his son kidnapped. Plus, I had seen him walk over the parents of some of the kids at my school who were TV and film producers, so I rationalized that I didn't care too much about him because he clearly didn't care about anybody else. However, I wanted to make sure that Nancy senior and the girls didn't have a traumatic experience, so I planned a short kidnapping, just twenty-four hours."

A devout Catholic, Barry Keenan went to church weekly to pray for guidance in his nefarious endeavor. His agreement with his maker was that the caper he was planning had to be for the Sinatra's "highest good" as well as for his own; otherwise, "it would be wrong to do it.

"I knew that the father and son were estranged," he remembered, "that father didn't approve of Junior's lifestyle, they weren't close, he was away at boarding school. He was always put down by his sisters, who got all of the attention.

"I knew all of this from having been over at Nancy's house," he explained. "She was my friend from grade school all the way to University High in West L.A.. We had gone to the same schools for twelve years together, and for six of them we were in the same classroom together. We graduated together. My best friend, Dave Stephens, dated her in the sixth, seventh, and eight grades. My mom would take Nancy and Dave places, and Nancy confided in my mom about little problems they were having."

As a friend of Nancy junior's, Keenan had been to the Sinatra home on several occasions. He had met Frank junior, but the four-years-of-age difference kept them from being close friends. He also saw Frank senior at the home occasionally, and recognized that "he was a pretty hard-boiled guy when he wanted to be." He noticed that Frank idolized his daughter Nancy and wanted the high school boys to stay away from her. Still, he took a bunch of youngsters, including Keenan, on a school junket, all of them crammed into an Eldorado sedan, with Frank driving.

"I thought that a good kidnapping would only serve the Sinatras by bringing father and son together," Keenan recalled. "Also, Senior was in a little trouble for entertaining the Mafia at Cal-Neva Lodge, and I thought, Well, this would take the heat off of him. Plus, it may bring him and his ex-wife, Nancy, closer together."

As two months passed, the kidnappers finalized plans for the abduction. It was decided that Junior would be abducted during an engagement at the Cocoanut Grove at the Ambassador Hotel on November 22, 1963. Keenan had a strong alibi for that day—except for the actual abduction period—because he intended to be at a UCLA football game the next day and be seen by hundreds of people there. That morning, the kidnapping was canceled when John F. Kennedy was assassinated in Dallas. "No matter what you were doing that day, your plans were changed," said Barry Keenan.

The news of John F. Kennedy's assassination struck Frank Sinatra, as it did the rest of the world, like a thunderbolt. Frank was in a cemetery filming *Robin Hood and the 7 Hoods* for Warners when he heard about it. He wanted to go to the funeral, for he still felt a kinship to Kennedy despite the murky history that had evolved in recent years. However, at this time, Sinatra rarely attended such ceremonies. He explained that he simply could not stand the morbidity.

He regretted many of the things that had occurred in recent years having to do with the President: the way Sammy Davis had been treated by the Kennedys; how Peter Lawford was forced to take the "fall" for JFK's Palm Springs visit (thereby ending his relationship with Frank); the embarrassment Kennedy had caused him by refusing to take his telephone calls; the manner in which Sam Giancana and some of Frank's other underworld friends had been so hotly pursued by the Kennedys, thereby causing him also to be placed under constant surveillance.

However, there were good times with Jack, and he couldn't forget them. They shared certain intimacies, and at times they actually were buddies. The inaugural party in 1961 was a night Sinatra would never forget, and Kennedy's words of praise that evening had meant a great deal to him.

"Poor Jackie," Frank said to one associate after returning from church, where he had gone to pray. "What's this country coming to? What's this world coming to?" After Sinatra finished the cemetery location shots for his film, he went to Palm Springs, where he stayed in seclusion for three days, canceling a benefit concert for Martin Luther King Jr. in Santa Monica (with Frank junior and the Count Basie Band.)

* * *

The clock was ticking.

Unbeknownst to Frank Sinatra, his only son's safety was in jeopardy. His kidnappers had hoped to abduct him in November, but the Kennedy assassination had quashed those plans. They then hoped to nab him at a singing job at the Arizona State Fair in early December; however, the logistics for that abduction didn't work out.

By this time, Keenan's pal, Joe Amsler, was beginning to have second thoughts about the entire scheme; it seemed that he was about to back out. He had dated Nancy Sinatra on several occasions and now thought it would perhaps be in poor taste to kidnap her brother. In order to keep him and John Irwin interested in the plot, Keenan began giving both of them fifty- and one-hundred-dollar bills. This money was coming from Dean Torrence, a rock-and-roll star—of Jan and Dean, one of the top recording groups in the country. Torrence, who went to school with Keenan and Nancy Sinatra, financed the kidnapping "a few thousand dollars at a time," according to Barry Keenan.

Keenan knew he had to act fast in order to keep Amsler's services. He learned that Frank junior would be appearing at Harrah's Lake Tahoe casino in Nevada with Sam Donahue and what was left of Tommy Dorsey's band. Telling Amsler that they would both be working for a construction company in Tahoe, he managed to get his friend to Nevada before he broke the news to him: Frank Sinatra junior was in town, and they were going to get him. Keenan then telephoned Reprise Records to find out where Frank junior was staying during the engagement, and whoever answered the telephone actually divulged the information that the entertainer was sleeping at Harrah's two-story South Lodge (where owner Bill Harrah put up all his entertainers), in Room 417. The lodge was across the parking lot, about a hundred yards from the casino.

On the snowy Sunday evening of December 8, 1963, at about 9:30 P.M., Barry Keenan, wearing a brown ski parka, made his move. With Joe Amsler outside the room on the lodge's landing between the first and second story and John Irwin in Los Angeles (where he was told to wait for further instructions), Barry Keenan knocked on the door to Room 417.

Inside, Frank junior had just finished eating a chicken dinner with John Foss, a twenty-six-year-old trumpet player with the Dorsey band. Sinatra junior, in his underwear and freshly shaved for the ten o'clock performance, was killing time before putting on his tuxedo.

"I knocked," Keenan remembered. "Someone said, 'Who is it?' I said, 'Room service. I have a package for you.' Junior, I think, said 'Come in.' I walked into the room, and it appeared that I was delivering a liquor order to him, because I had a wine box with me. It was actually filled with pinecones. I put the box on the table.

"Then I tried to whip the gun out, a long-barreled blue steel .38 revolver. I couldn't get it out of my pocket, though, I was that nervous. I actually had to struggle with it. When I did get it out, I pointed it at Junior. 'Don't make any noise and nobody'll get hurt,' I told him. Then I repeated it, 'Don't make any noise and nobody'll get hurt,' like a stuck record.

"I knew Junior was a gun collector," recalled Keenan. "He was always away at boarding school, so Nancy and I would go into his room just to see what was in there, snooping, I guess, and he had all kinds of guns in there. Gun aficionados know when they're looking at an empty or loaded weapon. So I knew that if I didn't have a loaded gun, he would have known it; therefore, I made sure it was loaded.

"Joe [Amsler] walked in at that point. He was in a state of shock, as was I. This was the real thing. It was really happening. It was as if I was in a director's chair, looking down at a film as it was being made."

Frank recently said, "When someone under the pretense of delivering a Christmas package screws a .38 in your ear, it gets your undivided attention, and you become conscious of many things. The first thing that struck me was that I needed to change my shorts."

" 'Where's the money?' I demanded to know," Barry Keenan recalled. "We were completely out of money, and we needed to rob Junior before we could kidnap him because we didn't have enough gas to get to the hideaway house in Los Angeles. It turned out Sinatra only had twenty dollars and some change. Foss had no money at all. It was enough to get us to L.A., though."

"Okay, we'd better take one of you guys with us," Keenan said. He pointed to Frank junior. "You. You're coming with us."

"But I'm in my underwear," Junior protested.

"Then get dressed because you're coming with us."

"I taped up John Foss with adhesive tape," remembered Barry Keenan. "Joe [Amsler] was freaking out by this time. So I had the gun on Joe, telling *him* what to do, to calm down, put a strip of adhesive across Foss's mouth, put a blindfold on Frank."

After taking both men's wallets, Keenan and Amsler forced Frank junior into the cold night at gunpoint, his hands bound behind his back. He was now wearing gray slacks, brown shoes without socks, a dark blue windbreaker over a T-shirt, and was blindfolded with a sleep mask. The temperature was twenty-five degrees, and there was a heavy snowfall—two inches within an hour. Upon leaving, Barry Keenan shouted at Frank's constrained companion, "Keep your trap shut for ten minutes or we'll kill your friend. *We mean business.* If we don't make Sacramento, your pal is dead." Then Keenan turned around, came back into the room, and ripped the telephone cord from the wall.

With Joe Amsler in the passenger seat, Sinatra in the back, and Keenan at the wheel, they drove off in his 1963 Chevrolet Impala in a full-blown blizzard. Their destination: Los Angeles, 425 miles away.

"I was impressed by Junior's coolheadedness," said Keenan. "He was scared, but cool all the way. I wondered what was going on in his mind.

"I knew it wouldn't be long before there would be major police confusion. So I told Junior (we always referred to him as 'Junior' when we talked about him and 'Frank' when we talked *to* him): 'Frank, somebody is likely to die tonight, and there's no need for it to have to be you. You gotta play like you're drunk and passed out in the car if we get pulled over. If you say anything, there's gonna be gunplay.' He said, 'You don't have to worry about me. I'll play along.' He was a coconspirator of sorts after about the first ten minutes.

" 'Somebody might recognize this ring,' he said, taking off his "FS" signet ring, 'so here.' He gave it to us to show that he was going to play along. He was helping us to save his own butt.

"I said, 'Okay, Frank, what I need you to do is take a couple of swigs of whiskey, and take these sleeping pills, so that if we get pulled over you'll look drunk.' He did what he was told.

"I did not tell him it was a kidnapping, however. I told him it was a robbery and that he was just a hostage. I acted like it was a holdup gone awry, and he believed it. We told him we were taking him to San Fransisco and that we were gonna let him loose there, even though we were actually headed to Los Angeles."

John Foss, the man left behind by the kidnappers, freed himself and ran to the front desk in the lobby, where the receptionist sat, thumbing through a magazine. "Call the police," he shouted. "Frank Sinatra Jr. has been kidnapped." The operator called Gene Evans, one of Bill Harrah's assistants, who telephoned the Douglas County sheriff's substation at Zephry Cove, five miles away in Nevada. By 10:20 P.M. the hotel was swarming with police officials and state troopers. It fell upon Frank junior's manager, Tino Barzie, who was staying in the room next to Sinatra's, to call Frank senior. Afraid of Sinatra's reaction, and knowing his reputation for taking out his temper on the bearer of bad news, he called Nancy senior instead.

Nancy was having dinner at her home in Bel-Air with Hollywood reporter Rona Barrett when the telephone call came.

"Good Lord, Rona," Nancy said, holding her hand over the telephone. "They've kidnapped Frank junior!"

Frank senior was in Palm Springs when he got the call from his ex-wife. He was frantic. "Oh, my God. I can't believe it," he reportedly said. "Oh, no. Oh, no. Oh, no."

Chartering a plane, he flew to Reno, Nevada, where he met William Raggio, Washoe County's district attorney (and an old friend of Frank's), in the owner's private three-room suite on the sixth floor of the Mapes Hotel. He had wanted to go straight to Lake Tahoe but was unable to do so due to the blizzard. Arriving in Reno after two-fifteen in the morning, he was distressed to find that his plane was greeted by reporters and photographers. The news was out.

"I got no comment to make," Frank said. "Just get away from me, you bums."

Sinatra and Raggio were joined at the Mapes Hotel by four FBI agents, Sinatra attorney Mickey Rudin, publicist Jim Mahoney, Jilly Rizzo, Jack Entratter, and Dean Elson, special agent in charge of the FBI in Nevada.

Sinatra called John Foss in Lake Tahoe. "Did they say anything about a ransom?" he wanted to know. "I mean, what the hell is this?'

Foss, still shaken, said that no ransom was mentioned. "It coulda been me, Frank," he said. "I don't think they knew they were kidnaping your kid specifically. It was random."

"Yeah, right," Frank said, unconvinced.

The party spent the next sixteen hours waiting for a call from the kidnappers. Frank sat right next to the phone with not a wink of sleep, chain-smoking, scared. "Why don't the bastards call?" he wanted to know. He was understandably impatient. "What do we do? *What do we do?*"

Frank's nemesis, Bobby Kennedy, called. The two spoke for about five minutes, and suddenly Bobby was an ally who promised to do what he could to spearhead the FBI's investigation. Immediately following Bobby's call, Sam Giancana called. What could he do to help? "Nothing," Frank said abruptly. "Please. Don't do a damn thing. Let the FBI handle this."

"Frank knew which side of his bread was buttered," said Tommy DiBella, Sam Giancana's friend. "Sam wanted to do his own investigation, break some heads, do whatever he had to do to get Frank's kid back. But Frank didn't want him to intrude. This was serious business to Frank, and in the end he knew that it had to be handled in the right way, the legal way, not Giancana's way. Sam was hurt, very hurt. He already had bad feelings toward Frank because of the Cal-Neva mess, but he was willing to put them aside for this emergency. Then, when Frank rejected his assistance, Sam was pissed."

When Frank and Sam hung up, Sinatra reportedly said to one of the agents, "My God. I can't breathe. I'm dying here. I'm dying, man. They're gonna kill my son, the way they did Bobby's brother, Jack. *They're gonna kill my fucking son.* If they touch him, I swear to God, I'll tear those bastards limb from limb."

White House press secretary Pierre Salinger called, as did California governor Edmund G. Brown.

FBI agent Dean Elson later said, "Sinatra would have gone anywhere, paid any amount, risked everything; all he wanted was his son back alive."

"You know how emotional he is," said his publicist Jim Mahoney. "I finally got him to force some food down."

300

Meanwhile, kidnapper Barry Keenan had his own problems.

Roadblocks had gone up along the entire Lake Tahoe perimeter, which was under heavy police guard. A check was being made of every car entering or leaving the state.

"About an hour out of town," he said, "we came around a sweeping turn to U.S. 50 and Highway 395, and there was a roadblock way down the hill, about five hundred feet away."

Keenan pulled over and got out of the car, acting as if he were about to take the snow chains off his tires, his mind racing all the while as he tried to determine how to proceed. Meanwhile, a police car began to approach. Keenan ordered Amsler to "scram!" realizing that the authorities would be looking for three people. Amsler, at full gait, ran off into the heavy snowfall and head-on into a fence post and knocked himself unconscious.

As Keenan began taking off the snow chains, the officer pointed a shotgun at him and demanded to know what he was doing on the road at that time of evening, in a blizzard. Then he shined a flashlight in Frank Sinatra Jr.'s face, but he didn't recognize him. Sinatra, drugged but conscious, said nothing. (Keenan had removed the blindfold and the tape from his hands.) The officer then got back into his patrol car and proceeded to the roadblock.

After Keenan got the chains off the car, he hollered out for Amsler, who was about fifty feet down the mountainside and just regaining consciousness. When Amsler climbed back up the hill, Keenan ordered him into the trunk of the car, realizing that they would have a better chance getting past the roadblock if there were only two people visible in the automobile.

Keenan got back into the driver's seat and began heading toward the roadblock, proceeding cautiously. He hoped the authorities would let him pass through. They didn't. Instead, they flagged him down.

Stopped at the roadblock, Keenan rolled down the power window of the car on the driver's side; in an instant, a police officer shoved a shotgun in the opening.

"But we've *already* been searched,' Keenan protested.

"Well, boy, we're gonna search you again."

"I knew then that it was over," Barry Keenan remembered. "I knew that if they opened the trunk and found Joe in there, they would blow him away. Just as I was about to tell the cop that there was somebody in the trunk and not to shoot him, the first officer who had seen us came over and said, 'Oh, just let 'em go. I've already checked them. They're okay.' "

"Okay, boy," said the other wary officer, "next time you come to a roadblock, you'd better stop, hear me?"

"Asshole," Frank junior muttered under his breath at the cop.

As Keenan drove off, Barry Keenan breathed a sigh of relief and swallowed a couple more pills.

Back at the Mapes Hotel, J. Edgar Hoover telephoned Frank Sinatra, and in an effort to make sure that Frank didn't give any statements to the press, told him, "Just keep your mouth shut. Don't talk to anyone but law officers." (Sinatra was terrified; that's probably why J. Edgar Hoover got away with telling him to say nothing.)

In Lake Tahoe the FBI gave lie-detector tests to John Foss and Tino Barzie.

"Is this kidnapping a hoax?" they were asked.

"No, it's not," they both answered.

"Sinatra is ready to make a deal with the kidnappers," his publicist announced, "and no questions asked."

"There are fears for the life of the young Sinatra," said Sheriff Carlson to the reporters who had swarmed over the Mapes Hotel. "There always is in every kidnapping."

Despite Hoover's admonishment, Frank issued a personal statement: "They know that I would give the world for my son. And it's true. But they haven't asked for money. He wasn't dressed too warmly, and if they have him out in the cold, what chance does he have?"

CHAPTER 29

"Frank Sinatra's son has been kidnapped," intoned the radio announcer. "And, now, let's hear a little of that 'Old Black Magic' on this 'Sinatra Spectacular' as we await word on young Frankie's fate."

"Man, that is so typical of the media," Barry Keenan remembered Frank junior as having said. "Look at how they're exploiting this goddamn thing."

As Keenan drove along Route 395 in his 1963 Chevrolet Impala headed toward Los Angeles, his kidnapping victim sat in place in the backseat (his blindfold back in place and hands taped behind his back) and began griping about what he was hearing on the car radio.

"I can't believe that they're using this thing to get people to tune into this radio broadcast," Frank junior complained.

"I know, man. Neither can I," Joe Amsler said. He and young Frank had actually bonded.

"My father's been putting up with this shit for years," said Frank. "The press is always fucking exaggerating. Now look at them, saying I've been *kidnapped.* They're capitalizing on the Sinatra name, playing his music to attract listeners to the story, and then not even getting the story straight. Jesus Christ, don't they know a hostage situation when they see one."*

Keenan and Amsler said nothing.

"You know what?" Frank continued. "I'm sure I can manage now, you guys, if you just drop me off here. We must be near Sacramento by now." He still thought they were headed toward San Fransisco.

"No way, Frank. You're staying with us," said Keenan. "The weather. You'll freeze out there. Wait till we get to San Fransisco. It'll be better for you. You can trust us."

Nineteen hours passed.

"We finally got back to Los Angeles, to the hideout house at 8143 Mason Avenue in the San Fernando Valley, and by this time Joe wanted to call the whole thing off," said Barry Keenan. "But I was amazed we had gotten this far, and I figured that we might as well see how far we could go. I had to keep Joe medicated just to keep him from blowing the whistle. Now it seemed I had kidnapped two people, Junior and Joe Amsler.

" 'We're going to go to prison for the rest of our lives,' I told Joe. 'Our only chance is to get the money and get the hell out of here.' My fear wasn't that Junior would escape. No, it was that Joe would use his superior strength and overpower me and be gone—with Junior.

"We had no concept of the heinousness of the crime we were committing," Keenan said. "We had no idea the hysteria we caused, that there were six thousand agents in the FBI, half assigned to the Kennedy assassination and half assigned to us, that Sinatra was on the phone with Bobby Kennedy and Sam Giancana, that we were at the center of a scandal that had gripped the nation.

"Junior had been very cooperative until we got to Los Angeles and I confessed to him that this was *not* just a robbery and he was *not* a hostage but that he had, in fact, been kidnapped and we were in Los Angeles. He got very angry, very upset that I had lied to him. He said, 'I've done everything you guys asked me to do.' I didn't know how to handle him getting mad at us, he had been such a nice guy. Then he refused to give

---

* Frank Sinatra Jr. does not remember being quite as unaffected about radio reports of the kidnapping. In fact, he recently said, "I can't begin to describe what it feels like when you're held captive by armed men who have a fondness for radios so that you hear your own eulogy tearfully spoken on the news by your friends back home."

me the phone number to his Dad so that John [Irwin] could call and get the ransom money."

"As soon as you give me that number, Frank, we can get this thing over with," Keenan tried to reason.

"No. Fuck you," Frank junior said contemptuously. "I'm not cooperating anymore. Go ahead, shoot me. Go ahead. I fucking dare you. *Shoot me.*"

Instead, Keenan shoved Frank into a back bedroom of the house and padlocked the door. Then he remembered that Sinatra senior wasn't at his Los Angeles home, anyway. The constant news reports he had heard on the car radio indicated that he was at the Mapes Hotel in Reno. Keenan got that telephone number from directory assistance, and the next day, John Irwin, who had the harshest, most adult sounding voice, which is why he was given this assignment, made the call.

At 4:45 P.M. the phone rang in Frank's suite rang.

"Is this Frank Sinatra?"

"Speaking," said Frank.

"It doesn't sound like Frank Sinatra," John Irwin said.

"Well, it is," Frank replied, anxiously.

"Can you be available at nine A.M. tomorrow?" Irwin asked.

"Yes, I can," Sinatra answered.

"Okay. Your son is in good shape. Don't worry about him."

The following morning, the kidnappers let Frank talk to his son on the telephone for just a moment (while the FBI taped the telephone conversation):

"Hello, Dad."

"Frank junior?"

"Yeah."

"How are you, son?"

"Alright."

"Are you warm enough?"

No response.

"You on the other end of the phone there?" Sinatra senior said. "You on the other end of the phone there?

"Yeah," Irwin said.

"You want to talk to me about making a deal?" Frank offered. "You want to resolve this thing?"

"Yeah, I do," Irwin responded. "But I can't do it now, Frank."

"Why not?"

"Gotta wait till around two o'clock."

"Well, do you have any idea what you want?"

"Oh, naturally we want money," Irwin said.

"Well, just tell me how much you want."

"Well, I can't tell you that now."

"I don't understand why you can't give me an idea so we can begin to get some stuff ready for you," Sinatra pressed on.

"Well, that's what I'm afraid of," Irwin said. "I don't want you to have too much time to get ready."

"Well, hey, I gotta have some time."

"I know, but you see— Don't rile me," Irwin warned. "You're making me nervous. I'll call you back about two o'clock."

"Well, can you call before that?" Sinatra asked, his voice sounding desperate.

"I don't think so. I gotta hang up now."

"Hey, can I talk to Frankie again?" Frank said.

There was a dial tone.

"Frank was shaken when he hung that phone up, let me tell you," said John Parker, another FBI agent (now retired) who worked on the case. "I was right there, in the room. I saw him break down. 'I just want my kid back,' he said emotionally. 'That's all I want. Give me back my kid.' I don't think anyone had ever seen Sinatra like this. Everybody just sort of looked at him, not knowing what to do. I mean, do you comfort him or leave him alone?

"When I saw all of this, that's when I started thinking, Man, this guy's got no mobster connections. This guy's got no underworld ties. 'Cause if he did, Jesus Christ, that woulda been the time to use 'em, wouldn't it have been?"

Finally, another call came from John Irwin with the odd demand of $240,000. "That's exactly what I've decided we needed."

"What are you talking about?" Sinatra said, baffled. "I'll give you an even million, nice and clean and easy."

"We don't need that much," John Irwin said politely. "We're not gonna take advantage of you, Mr. Sinatra. We need $240,000."

"By this time, Junior was calmed down," said Barry Keenan. "He and Joe Amsler were cracking up, telling each other dirty stories. He said to us, 'You know what? I hope you guys get away with this. You have a lot of nerve.' "

Frank Sinatra telephoned his friend Al Hart, president of City National, a Beverly Hills bank, and asked him to make the necessary arrangements; each and every bill would be photographed by the FBI. Then, because the FBI sensed that his son was now in Los Angeles, Sinatra flew back to the city and waited for another call at his first wife's home at 700 Nimes Road in Bel-Air, which by now was surrounded by reporters and photographers.

There was a great deal of front-page speculation as to why the Sinatra heir had been kidnapped. To most reporters, the motive seemed obvious: money. Others felt that Sinatra must have angered some underworld figure. As one put it, "Now it was Sinatra's turn to pay." Twenty-six FBI

305

agents and over a hundred local police were on the case. This was big news, comparing in scope and attention to the notorious 1932 Lindbergh baby kidnapping, and at the center of it were three hapless young men who, in essence, were very barely pulling off a prank.

The next day, December 11, Frank and FBI agent Jerome Crowe were to deliver the money: $239,985. (Fifteen dollars of the ransom money had been used to buy a fifty-six dollar valise in which the money was delivered.)

Sinatra and Crowe were then sent on a proverbial wild-goose chase: first to Los Angeles International Airport, then to a gas station, then to another gas station, where they were told they would find two parked school buses, and that they should leave the valise between the buses. They were promised that Frank junior would be released hours after the money was dropped off. As they delivered the money, a team of FBI agents "shadowed" the drop-off point in a Good Humor truck and several taxicabs.

Barry Keenan picked up the money. But in the process he lost his coconspirator, Joe Amsler, who took off in the middle of collecting the ransom because he thought he had seen an FBI agent lurking about the site. When Keenan called John Irwin from a pay telephone to tell him that he had a black valise filled with Sinatra's money but didn't know what had happened to Joe Amsler, Irwin became suspicious. He suspected that Keenan had "iced" Amsler to get rid of a witness to the "Kidnapping of the Century." Indeed, by this time—Tuesday—dissension had broken out among the kidnappers, and it seemed that Frank junior was the last thing on any of their minds. No one had slept in three days, and everyone except Frank junior was almost incoherent, on drugs.

"Junior was now highly irate that we had caused his family all this trouble," said Barry Keenan. "He was sick of us. He wanted to be set free. This was not the fun we thought it was going to be. John [Irwin] and Frank had bonded, and John wanted to set Frank free. He thought maybe I had gone crazy and killed Joe [Amsler], and he didn't want to take any chances."

"So, without me knowing it, he called Frank senior and told him that he was dropping his son off and to pick him up."

At two in the morning, four hours after the money payout, John Irwin called Sinatra.

"Something has gone wrong," Irwin said.

Sinatra immediately became frantic. "What do you mean, something has gone wrong?" he shouted into the phone. "We did every goddamn thing you said. Now where's my son?"

"No, not with you," Irwin said. "Something has gone wrong here. So I just dropped your son off at the San Diego Freeway and Mullholand. I wish to hell I hadn't gotten into it, but it's too late to get out. I'm sorry."

Frank hung up on Irwin, and turning to Nancy, he announced, "I'm getting our son. I'm bringing him home."

He and Nancy hugged.

His daughter Tina sobbed. "I'm gonna get him," Frank promised her as he held her tightly. "Don't worry."

Then Frank got into his car—headlights out in order to evade reporters—and drove to the drop-off point, the overpass at Mulholland, on the San Diego Freeway.

Meanwhile, Barry Keenan returned to the hideout. "When I got back to the hideout with the ransom and found that John and Junior were both gone and I had already lost Joe, I just burst into tears," he remembered. "None of this had worked out. I had the money, but I had lost the kidnap victim and both of my partners. And it was very important to my plan that *I* have the opportunity to let Junior go. I didn't want to get caught and not have Junior. I wanted everyone to know I had good intentions. This had turned into a comedy of errors.

"I freaked out, got into my car, and started looking for Frank junior," recalled Barry Keenan. "As I'm out there looking for him, who do I pass on the road? Frank senior and an FBI agent, doing the same thing, *looking for junior*. My heart stopped as they just passed me by."

Barry Keenan couldn't find Junior.

Neither could Frank Sinatra.

The fifteen-minute drive back to Nancy's house must have been unbearably long for Sinatra, who did not have his son with him. "I cried the whole way back," he later confided in one friend. "I cried, man. I was losing it. I couldn't even drive the fucking car. *I was losing it.* I thought, Jesus Christ, they took the money, and they killed Frankie. They murdered my son."

When he walked through the back door of Nancy's home without his boy, his ex-wife almost fainted from sheer despair. Frank collapsed into a chair, tilted his head back, and stared into space.

"Do you know what Dad's face looked like?" Tina later told her sister, Nancy, who was in New Orleans at the time with her husband, Tommy Sands. (Sands was appearing at the Hotel Roosevelt there.) "I've never seen a face like that."

"What now?" Frank demanded to know. He was exhausted.

"We were double-crossed," he said, shaking his head in disbelief. "How the fuck do you like that. They got the dough, and they got Frankie. I acted in good faith. *I acted in good faith.* A deal is a fucking deal.

"Call Bobby Kennedy," he barked at one of the FBI agents. "Call Hoover. Jesus Christ, call the president, I don't care. *Wake up the fucking president.* Somebody *do* something."

Then, according to FBI agent John Parker, Sinatra looked up to the ceiling and said in a tortured voice, "God, look, don't take it out on

Frankie, okay? I'm the one. I'm the jerk. Punish *me*. Not Frankie. That's what you're doing, anyway. Punishing me, ain't you? Taking it out on me."

"In five more minutes, he said, he was going to have to call Sam [Giancana]," said John Parker. " 'If I have to handle it that way, then I got no choice,' he said. 'I don't want to do it. I don't want to get the boys involved in this, because someone's gonna get hurt if I do, and I don't want to take a chance on it being Frankie. But what can I do?' "

While Frank was deciding whether or not to call on Giancana for help, the doorbell rang. An FBI agent answered as Nancy senior followed. A man in a uniform who appeared to be a security guard stood blank-faced in the doorway.

"Mrs. Sinatra," he said, "I have your boy in the trunk of my car. And he's all right."

Nancy just stood in the doorway, her mouth wide open.

Frank came to the door.

"What's going on? What's going on?"

"Mr. Sinatra, I have your boy in the trunk of my car."

Frank must have thought his son was dead.

"Get him out, get him out," he said frantically. "Get him out. *Get him out.*"

Everyone in the house raced out to the car; the trunk was opened, and Frank junior got out. Nancy became hysterical at the sight of her son. "Hi, Ma," he said as they embraced, "Don't cry. It's over." Then he turned to his father. "Dad, I'm sorry."

"For what?" Frank said. "Jesus Christ. For what?"

A tearful Sinatra embraced his son, then backed away to let his mother hold him again. As he stood in the doorway, Frank Sinatra seemed older—much older—than his forty-eight years. In all, his son had been held captive for a frightening fifty-four hours.

As it was later learned, when set free, Frank junior walked two miles to Roscomare Road in Bel-Air rather than wait at the drop-off point. He hadn't been told that his father was going to be coming for him.

As cars drove by, Frank junior would jump behind bushes, scared that the kidnappers had changed their minds and would come back for him. He was eventually found by Bel-Air patrol guard George C. Jones. Frank had a sleep mask hanging from his neck. It had been decided that he would hide in the trunk to avoid being detected and then immediately photographed by the throng of media outside the house.

"Virtually everything I had outlined in my plan of operation in terms of how the Sinatras would be affected had worked," observed Barry Keenan in retrospect. "Father and son were hugging. Divorced parents were reunited in the moment. And the public now viewed Sinatra in a sympathetic light rather than as a hoodlum. They had a big celebration party that night. It couldn't have worked better if they had paid me to do it, which, by the way, they hadn't."

The next few days were hectic: Phone calls to and from Dolly Sinatra to keep her apprised of how her grandson was faring. Another from Robert F. Kennedy to make sure everything was okay. Sam Giancana called to express his relief, and also his disappointment that Frank hadn't availed himself of Sam's services. The FBI interviewed Sinatra junior, who told them, "I think they were a bunch of amateurs. The one guy looked familiar to me. They were more scared than I was. Another guy gave up the whole thing, chickened out, and got me out of there before the first guy [Keenan] came back."

When George C. Jones returned to work the day after he dropped off Frank junior at his parents' home, he found a note asking him to return to the Sinatra estate. When he got there, he was greeted by one of Sinatra's aides, who handed him an envelope. There appeared to be money in it, so Jones did not immediately open it.

"I moved over to the edge of the living room, and Mr. Sinatra saw me," recalled Jones. "He got up, came over, and we shook hands. I said, 'Mr. Sinatra, I feel I shouldn't take anything from you. I feel this is some kind of reward or something.' He said, 'You go right ahead and take it. And have a fine Christmas.'"

When Jones got back to his office, he opened the envelope. In it were ten crisp one-hundred-dollar bills.

Two days later, on December 14, Frank received a telephone call from J. Edgar Hoover. The kidnappers were in custody.

It has been written in past accounts of the kidnapping that the reason the perpetrators were caught was because of the many details Frank junior was able to remember of the kidnapping and what the men discussed among themselves during the abduction. However, while those details might have provided the FBI with some direction, Joe Amsler's brother, a purchasing agent for the Imperial Beach, California, school district, turned him in, thus solving the case. Amsler's brother, James, called in his tip to the FBI while his brother was sleeping. Amsler was arrested within the hour.

"John and I were hiding out in Culver City at a friend's home," recalled Barry Keenan. "We were going to just lay low there. Our priority was to buy our families Christmas presents with all of this loot we now had and then invest the money in the stock market and pay back Frank Sinatra with proceeds from the investment. But I knew it was over when I heard on the radio that Joe had been arrested in Imperial Beach, California [in the San Diego area]. Then, at Amsler's direction, the authorities found the hideout house [in Canoga Park, California, about twenty miles away from Beverly Hills]. I was going to burn it down, as John [Irwin] had suggested, so that there would be no evidence. But I wasn't sure that the little old lady who had rented it to me had insurance on it. I was concerned that if I burned her house down, it would leave her without an income."

Keenan was arrested walking into his girlfriend's parents' house in La Canada, California. He said that fifteen FBI agents showed up to arrest him. They beat him up, forcing him to tell where he had hidden Sinatra's money.

"Just before I was arrested, I had given my ex-wife several thousand dollars to buy some furniture," he remembered. "And I must say, to Sinatra's credit, that when he found out about that, he asked the FBI not to take the furniture that she had purchased with his money. Sinatra said, 'Christ, just let her keep the furniture.'"

If anything, the kidnapping of Frank Sinatra Jr. proved to a lot of people that his father wasn't as protected and reliant on the Mafia as had long been suspected. It would seem that his family was just as vulnerable to stalkers and kidnapers as any other celebrity's.

There was no retaliation against the kidnappers, says Barry Keenan. However, according to Sam Giancana's friend Tommy DiBella, "Giancana did offer to take care of those guys in Sam's special way, but Sinatra said not to touch them. He knew that if anything ever happened to those kidnappers, the finger of guilt would be pointed straight at him, and he was already in enough trouble because of Cal-Neva. Plus, I know that Frank Sinatra would never have wanted to be so indebted to Sam Giancana."

To this day, many people—reporters, fans, interested parties who remember the ordeal as it unfolded—wonder if the kidnapping was a publicity stunt orchestrated by either father, son, or both. Some have even proffered the theory that Frank junior set it up and that his father didn't know—and maybe still doesn't.

At the trial in late February 1964 in Los Angelses' U.S. District Court, the kidnappers' attorneys—Charles L. Crouch (representing Barry Keenan), Gladys Towles Root (for John Irwin), and George A. Forde, and Morris Lavine(for Joe Amsler)—argued that the whole event had been staged by Sinatra for the purposes of publicity, "an advertising scheme." In her opening statement, John Irwin's attorney, Root said, "The apple doesn't fall far from the tree, and Frankie junior just wanted to make the ladies swoon like Papa. Frankie told my client, 'The ladies used to swoon over my father, then some wise publicity agent took that on and made my father an international star.'"

Joe Amsler's attorney, George A. Forde, continued: "The kidnapping headlines are doing the same thing for Frank Sinatra's son. There is a vacant seat here for a fourth defendant, a financier who finanaced this whole thing." Realizing that Forde was referring to him, Frank Sinatra glared at him.

"How that evolved was that I was in jail, lonely and desperate," remembered Barry Keenan. "I feel guilty because of the pain I had caused my parents and because of the way I had coaxed my friends to get involved in this scheme. And one of the attorneys—not my own—came in one night and said to me, 'Look, if this was a publicity stunt and you are able to tell us that it was a publicity stunt, then that would be a very strong defense. Since I was the ringleader, I was the one who had to make the statement.

"By that time I had sobered up, and I realized we were all in a heap of trouble. I slept on it. The next morning, I came out with this lie about the kidnapping being a publicity stunt, and that's all my attorneys needed to hear. It became our defense. I'm not proud of it. It was a lousy thing to do to the Sinatras. But I did it, I'm sorry to say."

During the trial, circumstances and events were revealed that seemed suspicious to some observers and bolstered the defense's claim of an "advertising scheme." Much of Frank junior's testimony seemed to actually assist the defense: that at the beginning of the abduction he told his kidnapers, "You guys don't have to worry about me, I'll help you in every way possible"; that he voluntarily took drugs in order to become drowsy and appear drunk if spotted by any police officer; that he gave his signet ring to his abductors so that he would not be recognized; that he did not summon help when the police officer shone a flashlight in his eyes at the roadblock, and had shaken hands with his captives and said, "I know you won't believe this, but I hope you guys get away with this. You guys got guts." He had also said, "Well, it's sure too bad we couldn't have met under different circumstances." Moreover, he never once tried to escape and had personally guided Joe Amsler to a spot where he was dropped off.

When asked why he was so cooperative, Frank's testimony was succinct: "Because I didn't want to get killed."

Gladys Root hammered away at Frank junior. "Well, this doesn't make sense, sir," she said sarcastically. "Why didn't you just tell the police officer when he shone the flashlight in your face that you were the man they were looking for? Why didn't you signal him, at least? Why didn't you *do something?*"

Frank junior responded testily, "Because Mrs. Root, the number-one man [Keenan] stated that when we came to the roadblock, there was going to be some shooting. I did not want a sudden and idiotic move to cause this man, who was stupid enough to kidnap me, to voluntarily blow the brains out of this officer."

Mrs. Root smiled. "Indeed," she observed snidely. Then she turned to the jury. "The truth is that you would have wrecked your little kidnap plot, which you arranged, and it would not have been successful."

Frank junior jumped from his seat and shouted at her, "*That is not true.*"

Today Barry Keenan reflects: "Most people don't understand that there's usually a bonding between the kidnapping victim and his captors. In a sense, Frank was a victim turned coconspirator in a matter of hours.

"Junior went out of his way at the trial to make his testimony as honest and as fair as possible, and it actually showed Joe in a favorable light. He liked Joe and said nice things about both Joe and John, that they were good people who had made a mistake. He didn't like me because I had lied to him and told him he was a hostage rather than a kidnap victim. He was a person of extraordinary high character during that period of time.

"During the first two hours of his testimony, it was as if he was a defense witness the way he was supporting us," said Barry Keenan. "Then they had a break, and he was different, because his attorneys probably told him he was being too nice to us."

By the time the kidnapper's defense lawyers called Frank junior to the stand a second time, he had become more aggressive. He was the victim, he argued. "The seeds of doubt have been sown on my integrity and guts and will stay with me for the rest of my life," he said angrily. Federal judge William G. East excused him from further questioning.

Finally, the judge addressed the jury, telling them, "I must comment that there is no direct evidence in this case by Frank Sinatra Jr. or persons on his behalf that prearrangements were made for his abduction."

It was never revealed at the trial that Barry Keenan had been a friend of the Sinatra family's and had been at their home.

"That was intentional," said Keenan. "As much as I wanted to get off by saying it was a publicity stunt, I didn't want to add fuel to the fire, because I knew that what I was doing was wrong. I realized that if I were to admit that I had been a family friend, that would have ended it. It would have looked like a conspiracy on the Sinatras' part.

"At one point, the FBI actually asked me why I used a real gun if I didn't plan to hurt Junior, and I said because I knew that Junior was a gun aficionado. And they said, 'How do you know that?' and I told them the whole story, how I was a friend of the family's. But they decided not to bring it out at the trial because they knew it would make things worse for the Sinatras. They wanted to get a conviction. They had a ten-page signed statement from me, and despite that, it looked like the conviction was going to get away from them if they let it be known that the Sinatras knew me, so they covered it up.

"Since I did not testify at my own trial and refused to cooperate with the other guys' attorneys when they wanted to bring up the relationship with the family, it just never came out. My own attorney, Charles L. Crouch, absolutely refused to push the conspiracy theory because he simply didn't believe it. One motion after another and all matter of legal diversion kept my friendship with the Sinatras out of the trial. It's never been known until now."

After deliberating for six hours and fifty-three minutes, the jury found all three defendants guilty. Neither Sinatra was in court when the verdict was read. Frank senior was returning from Tokyo on business. Junior was in London, performing.

As the active kidnappers, Joe Amsler and Barry Keenan were sentenced to life in prison, plus seventy-five years, which was the maximum sentence they could have received. John Irwin got sixteen years and eight months for conspiracy. All three had psychiatric-diversion sentences and as a result were sent to the Medical Center for Federal Prisoners, in Springfield, Missouri. There they underwent four months of psychiatric evaluation.*

"The report that came back was that I was legally insane and that I had duped Joe into the kidnapping," Keenan said. "They said we had not intended to harm Junior. For a probation report, they interviewed family and friends and determined that we were nice kids. They kept trying to make John the fall guy because he was older and should have known better. After all of that, our life sentences were reduced to twenty-five years, a fairly light sentence for that crime. All the rules were different in those days. John and Joe kept their appeals going, and that's really how we got out."

According to Barry Keenan, as presiding judge East reviewed case files, preparing to send them to the appellate court for Amsler's and Irwin's appeals, he found that Sinatra's attorneys had tampered with a key report. He found the original draft of a letter that was sent to the court from the medical facility which noted that Keenan was legally insane at the time of the kidnapping and should be diverted to psychiatric counseling as opposed to being sent to prison. He also noticed a doctored copy, which had been submitted to the court by Sinatra's attorneys.

Keenan said, "The prosecution had manipulated the report and sent it back rewritten, changing the wording to make it less favorable to us. They changed the executive summary and the conclusions so that it wouldn't give the judge a reason to give us probation. And the judge got so incensed with what they had done that he censured the prosecuting attorneys and reduced my sentence to twelve years."

In the end, Keenan would spend only four and a half years behind bars; his two partners spent three and a half years. Keenan was released in 1968.

---

* Dean Torrence of "Jan and Dean," who was financing the operation with hundred-dollar bills, was indicted as a coconspirator. "It would never happen today, but they decided not to indict him in the interest of justice because he was a rock star," said Barry Keenan.

"I often tell people that I'm the luckiest kidnapper in the world. I should have never seen the streets. And in today's world I never would see the street."

While in prison, he wrote a letter to Frank Sinatra to apologize for what he had done. Eighteen months after he was released, he wrote another letter to Sinatra requesting his permission to publish a book about the kidnapping which would have put to rest the lie that it had been a publicity stunt. Mickey Rudin, Sinatra's attorney, wrote back to Keenan to say that Sinatra would never give permission for such a thing.

In the late sixties a concerted effort was made to get Sinatra to change his mind and let the story be told. Television producer Burt Sugarman was interested in doing a movie about the ordeal, but Sinatra would not budge.

Despite the verdict, speculation as to what really happened ran rampant until the London Independent Television News used the subject as a topic of discussion and claimed that the kidnapping was a hoax. Frank senior sued and eventually collected a sizable amount of money, which he gave to charity.

After that, not many reporters were eager to investigate the matter further. However, that didn't mean they didn't have opinions about it.

Frank would not let it rest. He deeply resented the accusation that his son was a liar.

"Sam [Giancana] continually egged him on about all of this," said Tommy DiBella. " 'You gonna let people think that these lies about your son are true? You gonna let those bastards who planted that seed in people's heads get away with this? You gotta handle this,' he told Frank. 'Or let me handle it for you.' "

Sam felt that Frank should retaliate against the attorneys who represented the kidnappers. In his mind, they were as bad as the kidnappers themselves simply because they defended them. Frank decided that Sam had a point. If it wasn't for those attorneys, he reasoned, no one would have begun believing that the kidnapping was a setup.

"I'll do it my way," he reportedly told Giancana. "No monkey business. No help from the boys. We'll take the bastards to court and fuck with 'em a little. That'll teach them a lesson. I got all the money in the world to spend on this. I ain't done with them."

Indeed, at a press conference after the kidnapping Frank junior said threateningly, "My father will take care of anyone who thinks that this kidnapping is a hoax."

"Sinatra was angrier at our lawyers because of the publicity-stunt angle than he was at us for kidnaping his son," said Barry Keenan.

In fact, Frank did manage to exact a measure of revenge on two of the attorneys, Gladys Towles Root and George A. Forde (but not on Barry

314

Keenan's lawyer, Charles L. Crouch, who refused to promote the conspiracy theory).

In July 1964, Sinatra pressed to have the two attorneys charged with unethical conduct, including conspiracy, corruption, perjury, and obstruction of justice. Outside the courtroom on the day they were arraigned, the pair of lawyers charged that the indictments resulted from Frank Sinatra Sr.'s effort to "clear the reputation of his son for having participated in a kidnapping that was a hoax and publicity stunt." Both attorneys said they were "shocked and bewildered" by the charges and that they had done nothing during the trial but represent their clients by presenting a defense case. "I feel sorry for anyone that vindictive," Gladys Root said of Frank Sinatra Sr. "I have always believed in the power of truth, and truth will be the winner in this case."

For the next couple of months, Root and Forde were deluged with telephone calls from attorneys all over the country rallying to their defense. "If a person can be indicted because a plaintiff is unhappy about the way he or she has represented a defendant, then I don't know what to say about the system," Root said later.

In the end, it was decided that there was no merit to any of the allegations against these attorneys. All of the charges were dismissed before they reached trial stage.

In a 1979 interview with writer George Carpozi, Gladys Root, who is now deceased, said, "I most certainly still do believe this whole thing was a hoax. The whole scheme was concocted among the defendants and Frank Sinatra Jr. No question in my mind about that."

Today fifty-seven-year-old Barry Keenan—who orchestrated the kidnapping of Frank Sinatra Jr.—lectures at treatment centers for alcohol and drug abuse. "I found redemption in my life when I stopped drinking and using drugs, which happened when I found the Twelve Step Program. I was the luckiest criminal in the world, no doubt about it."

To this day, many people think that the kidnaping was a hoax despite Sinatra's best efforts to prove otherwise.

"In my heart of hearts," wrote Rona Barrett in her book *Miss Rona*, "I always felt Frank junior had staged his own kidnapping. Not for money. Not for publicity. But for the attention of his father. All of his life he'd had to compete with Nancy for that—and he lost."

James Wright, butler to Edie Goetz (L. B. Mayer's daughter and a good friend of the Sinatras'), recalled, "When I worked for the Goetzes, it was clear that Frank senior didn't really care for his son. He ignored him at parties, treated him poorly. The rumor going around the Goetz household was that Frank junior had staged his kidnaping and that Frank senior didn't know about it but then found out. And Frank junior's actions had caused a rift in their relationship. It was a feeling that most people in the household had. The Goetzes and the Sinatras were close friends, and

315

if this was a rumor in *their* household, it's easy to see why it was so popular a story among people who didn't even know the Sinatras."

Barry Keenan maintains: "If I have any remorse other than the harm I did to my friends who I induced into kidnapping Frank, I'm sorry that he got this bad rap. For him to have lived with this stigma all of these years is a shame. That defense was perpetrated by me and our attorneys to confuse the jury and get us off the hook, plain and simple. It didn't work. The media, of course, ate it up. It's stuck, to this day."

Barry Keenan has actually seen Frank Sinatra Jr. since that fateful evening in 1963. "I still run into him once in a while in Beverly Hills," he said. "But, needless to say, he's a little nervous about being friendly. We don't shake hands."

His childhood friend Nancy Sinatra no longer acknowledges that she ever had a relationship with Barry Keenan. "She's still upset that I kidnapped her kid brother," he concludes. "Guess you can't blame her for that"

And the final word from Frank Sinatra Jr.: "Seeing the faces of both my parents when the ordeal was finally over, it seemed to me that they had aged ten years. I sometimes wonder if Dad has ever really recovered from the experience. I'm sure my mother hasn't."

CHAPTER 30

Like any father, Frank Sinatra was deeply affected by his son's kidnapping. The year 1963 was mercifully coming to an end, and as it did, Frank promised that he would make some behavioral changes in the coming year. "I'm grateful to the man upstairs," he said in one interview. "I really am. I owe him one, you know? I mean, for saving my son's life. I'm going to try to be a better man. I could do some things differently, you know? I mean, I could, well . . ." He was at a loss for words. Then he smiled at the interviewer and affected a "Kingfish" (from "Amos n' Andy") accent: "It ain't gonna be easy, lemme tell ya, but I'm gonna try, anyway."

"He's not a religious person," Sammy Davis once said of Frank. "But the kidnapping, man, that made him take another look at faith. He thought that maybe he had made some mistakes in his past, maybe he had to pay for them, and that maybe that's what the kidnapping was . . . a wake-up call, you know? I mean, it wasn't like the whole thing went down and then everyone just went on with their lives unaffected afterward. Frank junior—he never got over it, I don't think. And neither did the old man."

During the holiday season of 1963, Frank Sinatra received a note from the former first lady, Jacqueline Kennedy, dated December 31, 1963:

I do want to thank you for the enchanting pin you sent me for Christmas. You have always been so thoughtful.

The only happy thing that seems to have happened at the end of this year is the way your son was brought safely back to you. Please know I am so deeply happy about that.

With my appreciation—the very deepest—for all you did for Jack and for believing in him from the beginning.

She signed it, simply, "Jackie."

Sinatra could not help but be moved. To think that the former first lady would take the time to write to him in the midst of what she was going through at that time, with the death of her infant and murder of her husband, was mind-boggling even to him. He knew that there was no love lost between them; Jacqueline had never much liked Frank. However, he admired the fact that she was able to put aside any animosity at this difficult time in both their lives.

He was glad 1963 was over. It had been a difficult year.

Frank junior went on with his life and career but carried a gun with him everywhere he went for many years. He would never forget what happened to him and became much more suspicious. For years, he suffered from nightmares. To some observers, it seemed that he blamed his father for what had happened. Thus far, it seemed that his dad's success not only had kept him from being an entertainer in his own right but also had almost cost him his life. He did what he could to get ahead in show business, but he would find that being Frank Sinatra's son was always more of a hindrance than an advantage.

Still, Frank junior was his father's biggest fan; he would lock himself in his bedroom and listen to his dad's records for hours at a time. It was as if the music were all Frank junior had of his "old man"; clearly, he didn't have much of his attention.

In time, by osmosis, Frank junior began to sound a great deal like his father. As years went by, however, he would undergo an artistic metamorphosis and become much more than just a pale imitation of an icon. He would actually develop his own distinctive style; he could really *swing*. He has a beautiful voice, a lovely sense of phrasing, and innate taste. (As a performer, however, he has never projected his father's charisma or magic. He does have serenity, however, and is self-assured.)

There's nothing wrong, for instance, with Frank junior's 1971 *Spice* album. In fact, the title track, which he wrote, has Frank junior's easy, yet precise, vocal phrasing and Nelson Riddle's fantastic orchestral arrangement. You can listen to this song a hundred times and never get tired of it. He does remind you of his father, as did a lot of singers who honed their craft after Sinatra became popular, among them the great Steve Lawrence and certainly Bobby Darin, who sounded about as close to Sinatra as possible without actually being an imitation.

The fact is that Frank Sinatra Sr. had so reinvented the popular singing style that most male vocalists at least *tried* to imitate him, if not his voice, then certainly his phrasing, the way he "talked" through a song. Even Sammy Davis sounded like Frank Sinatra when he first started out. At one point, Sinatra actually had a talk with Sammy and told him that he should develop his own style if he really wanted to be successful in the entertainment business, which, of course, Sammy did.

"Musically, my father only gave us one piece of advice," Nancy Sinatra recently stated. " 'Stay away from what I do.' I stayed away. My brother didn't, God bless him. He's been swimming upstream the whole time."

If one really *listens* to Frank junior, however, and feels compelled to draw comparisons to other singers, again, it's the *phrasing* that is suggestive of the senior Sinatra, not the voice itself.

With each recording over the years, Frank junior would hone his own style, even if the presentation did seem to pay unintentional homage to the old man. However, most people wouldn't seem to notice, or care, that Junior was trying to carve out his own niche. For the most part, audiences would pay money to see him perform only because of his ancestral connection to a legend. That he always included some of his dad's songs in his act probably didn't help him establish his own persona, but in that true Sinatra tradition of wanting to please a crowd, he was acutely aware of what his audiences really wanted to hear.*

In January 1964, Frank Sinatra Sr. recorded the patriotic *America I Hear You Singing* album with Bing Crosby and Fred Waring and His Pennsylvanians. On January 27 and 28, Frank recorded the album *Frank Sinatra Sings Days of Wine and Roses, Moon River and Other Academy Award Winners.* With the *Days of Wine and Roses* album, Sinatra kept up with the times. He quietly, and seamlessly, moved from concept albums into collections of covers of current hit records by other artists and other single-type material.

While not considered by Sinatra purists to be a memorable album, *Wine and Roses* did include the truly lovely "The Way You Look Tonight,"

* Frank junior would also hint at some acting ability—many scenes but not many lines—with his performance as Sammy Davis's trumpeting protégé in the 1966 film *A Man Called Adam.* The movie, which starred Davis as a trumpet player, was a serious film with overtones of racial violence and protest. Frank junior is beaten by southern racists in a climactic moment. The film also starred Peter Lawford and Cicely Tyson.

as arranged by Nelson Riddle. Sinatra fans consider it one of many Sinatra classics. Indeed, his performance is sublime. Originally performed by Fred Astaire in the 1936 film *Swing Time*, "The Way You Look Tonight" went on to be Astaire's biggest hit record (number one for six weeks) and received the Academy Award for Best Song in 1936. Frank first recorded this one back in 1943. In 1989 he performed it in a hugely popular Michelob beer commercial, lip-synching the 1964 version and giving it a new life.

In February, Frank Sinatra and Dean Martin appeared together on a Bing Crosby television special. (By this time, Bing was a Reprise recording artist; indeed, Frank was corraling the best in the business, such as Rosemary Clooney, Jo Stafford, Keely Smith, and Dean Martin, though, with the exception of Martin, few were able to sustain a career at Reprise.) In April, the trio—Frank, Dean, and Bing—recorded the soundtrack album for *Robin and the 7 Hoods*. Then, on April 27, Frank was off to Hawaii to begin work on the film *None But the Brave* for Warner Bros., his debut as a director (Nancy's husband, Tommy Sands, also appeared in this antiwar film.)

In *Frank Sinatra—An American Legend*, Nancy recalls that her dad almost drowned while in Hawaii when he attempted to rescue Ruth Koch (producer Howard Koch's wife) after she was swept away by the undertow during a swim. (Mrs. Koch was brought safely back to shore by a wave while Frank was on his way out to get her.) "He struggled against the surf for thirty-five minutes," she wrote, until he was finally rescued by fire lieutenant George Keawe, who later said, "In another five minutes he would have been gone. His face was turning blue."

It is interesting that Nancy credits Keawe with saving Frank's life when it is well known among Sinatra's inner circle—and has been reported countless times in the media—that actor, producer, and close friend of Sinatra's, Brad Dexter, actually rescued Frank. "[When I reached him], Frankie was whispering with a sort of incredible wonder, 'I'm drowning,'" recalled Dexter. "He couldn't see anything. I've seen people drown, and they lose their eyesight and go blind—and he was completely white."

Dexter is really the one who pulled Frank to safety. Frank could barely bring himself to thank Dexter, however. He never liked it when it appeared that he was indebted to the people who worked for him or were associated with him in any way, for that matter, unless they were either presidential candidates or mobsters. Instead, he told Dexter, "My family thanks you." Sinatra later had a falling-out with Dexter over the film *The Naked Runner*, which he had produced, and Dexter was banished from Sinatra's kingdom, although they had been friends for many years. Later, when someone asked Frank how Brad was, Frank responded, "Brad who?" This may explain why Nancy decided not to give credit to him for saving her dad's life in the official Sinatra history.

At the time, Frank and Joey Bishop were estranged. No one, including Joey himself, seems to remember what caused the problem between them. However, Bishop sent Sinatra a telegram after he heard of the near drowning: "You must have forgotten who you were. You could have walked on the water."

"I got a call from him the next day like nothing had happened between us," Bishop remembered.

None but the Brave finished its principal photography by June. "It's an antiwar story that deals with a group of Americans and a group of Japanese stranded together on a Pacific Island during the war," Sinatra explained. "I tried to show that when men do not have to fight, there is a community of interests."

Of Sinatra's work as a director, *Los Angeles Times* critic Kevin Thomas noted: "Sinatra's style is straightfoward and understated. It is to his credit that he tackled a serious subject on his first try when he could have taken the easy way out with another gathering of the Clan." When released later in the year, the movie did well at the box office.

On June 9, Frank was back in a studio in Los Angeles recording the excellent *It Might as Well Be Swing* album, arranged by Quincy Jones and featuring the Count Basie band. If you only have one Sinatra album in your collection, this has got to be it, because it includes one of his most memorable performances, "The Best Is Yet to Come." With his impeccable voice and unique phrasing, Sinatra bit into the song as if it were his last meal. And the remarkable Count Basie orchestra pressed the music onward—insistently, persistently. Music has never sounded this good; it's clear that all—singer, musicians, producers, and arrangers—were having the time of their lives.

On June 27, 1964 , Warner Bros. released *Robin and the 7 Hoods*, the film that gave birth to the Sinatra classic "My Kind of Town," the musical tribute to Chicago that went on to become one of Frank's trademark songs. The movie was a satire on the old Robin Hood fable and starred Rat Packers Dean Martin and Sammy Davis, with Bing Crosby. It was a dreadful film. None of the Rat Pack movies, including *Sergeant's 3*, were any good, actually. They were just Sinatra and his friends having fun and spending a fortune on filmmaking to do so.

A month later, on July 13, Frank celebrated the twenty-fifth anniversary of the first time he stood in a recording studio with Harry James and sang "From the Bottom of My Heart" for the Brunswick label. It had been twenty-five years of music, performances, and images, so many of which had helped shape our American culture, all of it mixing with the rhythm of America's heartbeat, becoming the soundtrack to so many of our lives.

And to paraphrase an appropriate song title, for Frank Sinatra, the best *was* indeed yet to come.

In August and September 1965, forty-nine-year-old Frank Sinatra was in Italy filming the location shots for his next film, *Von Ryan's Express*, in which he played an American army colonel imprisoned during World War II in an Italian POW camp. At the same time Frank was there, in August, Ava Gardner, now forty-two, was also in Italy filming the John Huston–directed, Dino De Laurentiis–produced epic *The Bible*.

Ava had not been too enthused about the role of Sarah in the film; the movie seemed too massive a project to her, and she wasn't interested in working that hard at this time in her life. Plus, the script by Christopher Fry was so complicated and the language so contrived that she didn't feel she would be able to memorize all of her lines, at least not without a great deal of effort and concentration.

It had been De Laurentiis's idea to cast opera star Maria Callas in the role, but John Huston—who shared the same business manager as Ava, Jess Morgan—wanted Ava. She reluctantly agreed because she so implicitly trusted Huston's opinion and felt he was the only good director with whom she had ever worked after they did *Night of the Iguana* together in 1964. Ava would later tell Rex Reed that she hated the role of the barren Sarah, who nobly insists that her husband, Abraham, take another woman in order to sire a son, but if that's true, one would never know it judging from her multilayered, sensitive performance.

The European press made much of the fact that the former "Battling Sinatras" were in the same city at the same time, Ava at the Grand Hotel and Frank—with thirty-two pieces of luggage, four bodyguards, and the rest of his entourage—in an eighteen-room villa, leased for him by 20th Century–Fox, surrounded by a ten-foot wall. The expensive property had ten water fountains, indoor and outdoor swimming pools, stables, a heliport, and all of the other accoutrements to which Sinatra had become so accustomed. Italian photographers, anxious to get a photograph of Frank and Ava together, pooled their resources and offered him 160,000 lira if he would arrange a picture session with his ex-wife. Frank made a counteroffer: he would double the money if he could take a few free swings at some of the local paparazzi. No deal was struck.

Ava's costar in her film—Abraham to her Sarah—was the actor George C. Scott, thirty-seven years old, six feet tall, powerful, and broad-shouldered. Known to be an intense genius of an actor, he was also a volatile, difficult man. In fact, he had many of the same personality traits as Sinatra: a brooding presence, friendly and generous when he wanted to be but temperamental and even violent if angered. Like Sinatra, he also drank too much. So did Ava, and so, it would seem, did everyone else connected with these people. Today they would probably be considered alcoholics. None of them—Ava, George, Frank, and most of their friends—could get through the day without more liquor in their system than most people could tolerate in a week.

Ava was mesmerized by George. A woman of experience, she knew she was playing a dangerous game by becoming sexually involved with him, another married man [to actress Colleen Dewhurst, whom he married twice]. Still, she couldn't help herself—even though she knew that Dewhurst was also in Italy—and commenced having an affair with Scott, repeating past behavior that, it could be argued, had never served her well. Fred Sidewater, Dino De Laurentiis's assistant, recalled, "Scott was crazy about her from the beginning. And I mean crazy. He was hopelessly in love with her, and she was not in love with him."

Immediately, George C. Scott became possessive and jealous of the fiery, tempestuous Ava. For instance, the mere mention of Frank Sinatra's name would set him off. And as she did with Frank, Ava was certain she could also tame this wild beast of a man. But this time she could not, as she learned when the cast went to a hotel in Avezzano, a small town in the Abruzzi mountains, to film exterior shots. After a day's work, the two had dinner and then drank as much as they could take and still make it back to the hotel. Once there, they became embroiled in a heated argument—the kind Ava was accustomed to having with Frank Sinatra in the past, only worse.

"The problem with George C. Scott, as Ava soon learned," said her good friend Esther Williams, "was that he apparently hit people when he got drunk. He hit Ava. It was terrible, just awful."

Incensed at whatever she had said to him, Scott smacked Ava across the face and then began pummeling her with punches. There was nothing she could do to protect herself; he had overpowered her and would not stop beating her. Bloodied, she somehow managed to escape to her own room, certain—as she would later recall—that she had crossed a line with Scott and that her life was now in danger. The next day, when Ava showed up on the set black and blue, the crew treated Scott with disdain. Even though she refused to say who had beaten her, it seemed clear. Everyone with whom she was working so loved her, they felt that for Scott to have done this to Ava was unforgivable.

Scott apologized profusely to Ava for his reprehensible behavior, as most batterers do after the fact.

However, never the most prudent of women, Ava made matters worse for herself by openly having sex with others on the set, including Fred Sidewater. "One day I took some papers to her tent in the Abruzzi for her to sign," he remembered. "She said, 'Oh, let's go to bed now and I'll sign the papers later.' So we did, she signed the papers, and I left."

This kind of outrageous behavior only served to further infuriate Scott and inflame his jealousy. It also caused many observers to wonder if perhaps Ava Gardner had a death wish.

Somehow—no one seems to remember exactly how—Frank Sinatra found out about what was going on behind the scenes of the set of *The Bible*. After a day's shoot, he showed up at Ava's door and demanded to know the details.

"She was afraid to tell him," said her friend Lucille Wellman, "because she knew, as sure as she ever knew anything in her life, that Frank Sinatra would kill, absolutely *kill*, George C. Scott. Can you imagine the rage he felt seeing Ava so beat up that they could barely cover the bruises with heavy makeup to get through the day's shooting? She told me that he cried, actually sobbed, when he saw her, he was so devastated by it. My understanding is that she did not tell him Scott had beaten her. She told him she had been mugged. He didn't believe her."

"If there's one guy I don't tolerate, it's a guy who mistreats women," Frank would say in an interview with *Photoplay* in 1965. "They are the real bullies in this life, and what they need is a real working over by a man their own size."

According to what Ava told Lucille Wellman, Frank did what he could to help.

"Quit this goddamn picture now," he begged Ava. "I'm begging you. Or let me take care of that motherfucker. I'll break his arms. He'll never hit another woman again."

"No, Francis," Ava insisted. "Please, you'll just make it worse. I can take care of myself. If you want to help me, you'll leave now. *Please.* "

"She wanted him out of there," said Lucille Wellman, "because she believed that if Scott found him there with her, he would take it out on her later and really do her in. Frank left, heartbroken. The next day, as I recall it, the cast moved to Sicily."

It was in Sicily that Ava started noticing what she remembered as "three very tough looking guys just hanging around the set. They had nothing to do with the film crew; they were just there. As we were in Sicily, I naturally thought, I never knew mafiosi were so interested in the Bible. . . ."

"Frank had sent three of his men to shadow Ava and report back to him everything that was going on," remembered Jim Whiting, Jilly Rizzo's friend. "I remember it like it was yesterday. Jilly said, 'Frank wants Scott to make one wrong move so he can have him executed.' "

One night in Sicily, Ava, George, and an assistant of hers had dinner in a lovely restaurant on top of a rolling hill in Taormina. As they sat down, Ava noticed the same three burly gentlemen she'd been seeing around the set being seated at a table across the room. After an argument broke out between Ava and George over their spaghetti dinners, she ended the evening and angrily stormed out. He followed her. Outside the restaurant, the tension between the two began to escalate. Ava, not one to be cowed by anyone, was right in his face, screaming at him. It looked as if Scott were about to punch her when, seemingly out of nowhere, her beefy guardian angels swooped down onto the scene. One took Scott's left arm, another took his right, and the third followed as they dragged him down the street. Without saying a word, they hustled him along to a waiting automobile and drove off into the night, leaving Ava with her mouth agape. She fell to her knees, sobbing with relief.

Ava decided, and later wrote in her memoirs, that these men must have been hired by John Huston to keep a watchful eye on her. However, in the back of her mind, she must have known that Sinatra was responsible. The next day, Scott came back to the set, subdued but, she said, not physically injured, at least not that anyone could detect. That same day, Ava flew back to Rome and drove an hour to Frank's villa, which was situated outside the city.

"She needed to be with him," said Lucille Wellman. "She told me later that he was wonderful to her. She never asked him about the bodyguards. For some reason, she didn't want to have it be openly acknowledged that he was taking care of her. They were together at the villa, but they were not intimate."

"She stayed at the villa for a couple of days," said Frank's assistant Brad Dexter. "I came over one night to have dinner with them. She was lovely. Frank was still trying to revive the relationship, but she had started to hit the bottle and it was painful for Frank to see the woman he adored destroying herself with booze."

Frank was disappointed in Ava. She was doing the one thing he never tolerated from a woman: She was being weak. He wondered how she could allow herself to be beaten by any man and go back for more. He also noticed that she was looking haggard and drawn, and Frank knew it was the result of her alcohol use. As much as he enjoyed it himself, he felt that Ava's addiction to it was out of control.

By mid-September, Frank was off to Spain with the crew of *Von Ryan's Express*, and Ava, finished with *The Bible*, went on to London, where she stayed at the Savoy Hotel. George C. Scott followed her there, convinced her that the violence that had occurred between them would never happen again, and then asked her to join him for a romantic dinner. For some reason, Ava believed him and went. "She could be the most foolish woman," said her friend Lucille Wellman. "It excited her to flirt with danger."

Over dinner, as had always happened, she and Scott began to argue. Soon she fled the restaurant and went back to her hotel. Moments later, Scott broke down her door, held a jagged broken bottle to her terrified assistant's throat, and demanded to know where Ava was. She was locked in the bathroom, shaking with fear for her life. She managed to escape through a transom and took refuge with friends across the hall. Scott, infuriated, trashed Ava's room and then his own before he was finally arrested, charged with drunken and disorderly conduct, and forced to spend the night in jail.

Ava said later that she escaped the Savoy without injuries that night, but others remember it differently.

John Huston once recalled to Ava's biographer Charles Higham: "Not only did he [Scott] attack her at the Savoy, but he struck her and damn near broke her jaw. She was black and blue. She was so terrorized, she was hysterical. I have the greatest admiration for him [Scott] as an actor and the greatest contempt for him as a man."

Ava's friend, writer Nunnally Johnson, added, "Her agent was to take her to the plane the next morning. He said she was afraid she wouldn't make it, she was so shattered by her experience with Scott. She was disheveled; she looked terrible."

A short time later, Ava—who said that she believed she'd never see George C. Scott again—was staying at the Beverly Hills Hotel, home of the legendary Polo Lounge. At one A.M., Scott broke into her room.

"I was terrified out of my mind at the sight of this huge, completely drunk, almost insane man," she once remembered. Scott told her that if he couldn't have her, he would kill her. Then he beat her, brutally smashing her face with his fists. John Huston said that Scott "molested" Ava that evening.

Luckily, Gregory Peck's wife, Veronique, telephoned Ava, who managed to get to the phone in the middle of the beating. Without Ava even having to tell her what was occurring, she seemed to know and sent Ava's doctor, William Smith, to the hotel. He sedated Scott with an injection and then telephoned Ava's sister, Bappie, who arrived shortly after and took Ava away from the hotel, but not before reaching for a fire poker with which to stab Scott in a moment of insanity brought about by seeing her beloved sister having been beaten to a pulp. As Ava convinced Bappie to put down the poker, Scott fled through the same smashed back door by which he had entered. (Later, Ava would learn that she had suffered a detached retina in the fracas.)

Ava's business manager, Jess Morgan, shook his head sadly when he recalled the incident at the Beverly Hills Hotel. "He beat her. How he could do it, I don't know. But he did it. Anyone who knew and loved Ava wanted this to end once and for all."

"Bappie called Frank Sinatra," said Lucille Wellman, "and told him the whole story. He was very upset about it. He kept saying that he couldn't understand why Ava had allowed this to happen, but what he didn't realize was that she had been physically abused by many of the men in her life, all the way back to Howard Hughes, who used to hit her. This was not the first time. It was just the first time Frank fully understood it. He was a violent man himself, but he would never have done that to Ava, never."

Bappie took Ava to Frank's home; he had just gotten back from Europe himself, having completed filming of *Von Ryan's Express*. She stayed there for some time. He helped her. He healed her. He loved her.

Then, according to a number of sources, Sinatra had George C. Scott taken care of, though people seem to disagree about just how he did that.

"The way I heard it, Frank paid Scott a little visit," said Jim Whiting. "Jilly said that Frank and four other guys went to Scott's home and beat the crap out of him. He said that, at gunpoint, Sinatra had Scott begging for mercy, that he made Scott get down on his knees and beg for forgiveness. And that Frank told Scott that if he ever got near Ava again, he would kill him."

"That's not what I heard," Esther Williams recalled. "I know he took care of it, all right. But he sent some people to 'talk' to George C. rather than do it himself. I don't know who said what or who did what to whom. All I know is that George C. was out of Ava's life after that. Permanently. She never saw him again."

Not quite. Sadly, it would seem that Ava Gardner could not stay away from George C. Scott.

In November 1971, Ava took a job in Tucson, Arizona, playing nineteenth-century theatrical star Lillie Langtry in the film *The Life and Times of Judge Roy Bean*, starring Paul Newman. Her role was just a cameo, and some wondered why she bothered to take it. However, as it would turn out, George C. Scott was also in Arizona, making another movie.

Fearing what might happen to her, Ava's director did what he could to keep Scott from her, but the two managed secret meetings just the same. "George and I kept ducking under the guards," Ava once recalled, laughing. When the director found out that Ava had been surreptitiously seeing Scott, he was furious with her for being so foolhardy. That director was John Huston.

In September 1964, Frank took a break from the filming of *Von Ryan's Express*. He spent the month relaxing with his pals on the French Riviera. He was back in the studio on October 3 with Nelson Riddle recording "Dear Heart" and a few other songs for the *Academy Awards* album before beginning a monthlong production schedule of interior shooting at 20th Century–Fox for *Express*.

A young blond waif, one of the stars of the new *Peyton Place* television show, had begun loitering about the movie set, eyeing Sinatra. When he first saw her, she was wearing a white nightgown from the wardrobe of her show. She was enchanting. Reed thin, with pale skin and luminous blue eyes, she was, at once, child-like and seductive. At just five feet five inches and weighing only ninety-eight pounds, she had the figure of a young boy. Still, though, she had what Frank would later describe as "something you just can't describe, some kinda female magic." Frank couldn't help but wonder about her. He tapped her on the shoulder.

"How old are ya, kid?" he asked her.

"That's hardly a question to ask a lady," the young woman responded. Then she flicked her long blond hair coquettishly from one side to the other and said, "I'm nineteen."

"I was hers instantly," Frank recalled to one pal. "I loved that hair, man. The hair's what got me."

Maria de Lourdes Villiers Farrow—Mia—was the third of seven children, and was born on February 9, 1945, in Beverly Hills, to actress Maureen O'Sullivan and her husband, director John Farrow.

"She was always starstruck and loved Hollywood," said Theresa Lomax, who attended Marymount High School with Farrow in Beverly Hills and now lives in Santa Monica. "She loved show business, collected fan magazines, cut out pictures of her favorite stars and pasted them onto her locker. One of her best friends was Liza Minnelli, and she was proud of that; I believe they went to nursery school together. She would often talk about Liza—what they would do together, how close they were. She often told of the time Ava Gardner came to visit and how she treated her as an equal, not as a child. She and Bette Davis were friends, she had bragged.

"She would regale us with these stories, I think, because she wanted to be noticed, recognized," Lomax observed. "She exaggerated a lot of her tales, I believed. She had quite an imagination, actually. She once told me that she remembered being born, every detail of it."

Indeed, Mia's home life as a youngster was an unusual one in that she and her siblings lived in a nursery—with its own kitchen—that was separate from the main house. Maureen, who worked as a successful actress in films throughout Mia's adolescence, had explained that Mia's father enjoyed peace and quiet when he got home from his work on the movie set (no easy feat with seven children) and "didn't like everything messed up." The children, therefore, were basically raised by nannies, trotted out in their expensive "Sunday best" when the rich and famous of the entertainment industry visited and then sent back to the nursery at the end of the evening.

In retrospect, though, Farrow never criticizes her parents for her upbringing. "There was a magical element to it," she says. "We lived in beautiful homes, our gardens were beautiful, even the nannies dressed beautifully. Beautiful birthday parties, and we had beautiful clothes. And people spoke well and thought well of each other in those days in Hollywood. We had problems, too, growing up, but I think my parents were successful at raising us because all of my brothers and sisters are wonderful. But any problems we had were because we were living in such an unrealistic environment; we didn't have a clear idea of what the world really was."

"It seemed at an early age that she was practically destined for some kind of stardom," said Lomax. "Her parents were famous, her godmother was [gossip columnist] Louella Parsons, and her godfather was [director] George Cukor. She once told me that her grandmother had been told by a psychic that her firstborn granddaughter would become distinguished. Mia wanted to prove the psychic right, but she was always worried. She was insecure. She wanted to make something of her life. But what that would be, she didn't know. Making a simple decision—well, that was not Mia."

As a youngster, Mia created fantasy characters and friends, perhaps because she felt that she was being overlooked by her family. One, named Mildred, practically became an obsession of the youngster's. Her mother was concerned, so much so that when the family took a cruise, she used that vacation as an opportunity to eradicate her daughter's fantasy character. She told Mia that Mildred had drowned after having fallen over the side of the ship. The six-year-old became hysterical but eventually accepted the fact that her playmate was gone. By eight years of age, she was an insomniac. (As an adult, she would say that she only needed four hours of sleep a night.)

A year later, she contracted polio. Before she left for Cedars of Lebanon Hospital in Los Angeles, the sensitive youngster wrapped all of her toys as gifts and presented them to her brothers and sisters. After she left the house, all of the toys—and the rest of her belongings—were burned by one of the maids because they were thought to be contagious. (Mia eventually recovered from the disease, with only a residual and permanent weakness in one arm.)

Mia Farrow attended a Catholic boarding school in London as well as schools in Madrid and Beverly Hills. Upon graduation from Marymount, she left Los Angeles and headed east to New York to become an actress. In short order, she found herself appearing in the off-Broadway production of *The Importance of Being Earnest*, replacing Carrie Nye (later Mrs. Dick Cavett). She signed a contract with 20th Century–Fox and appeared in a film (replacing Britt Eklund in *Guns at Batasi*). Troubles on the home front, though, kept her temporarily preoccupied. Her father, a talented man who unfortunately was also a womanizer with a penchant for liquor, died in 1963 of a heart attack at the age of fifty-three. This loss was difficult for the entire family; apparently, all of his children had certain issues regarding their father and his lack of affection. Now none of those problems would be resolved.

Mia's mother, Maureen, also had a difficult time coping after losing her husband of twenty-five years, though he was not faithful to her during their marriage. She accepted a job on the *Today* show as cohost opposite

Hugh Downs, a job she regretted ever having taken. Broadcasting was not her forte; her eventual departure from the show opened the door for someone who really was suited for it: her replacement, Barbara Walters.

Meanwhile, Mia began work on *Peyton Place* in August 1964.* As the pensive and brooding heroine Allison MacKenzie, she became very popular when the program debuted in the fall of 1964. Though the show would go on to become one of the biggest series of its time, she still felt undirected in her life. Did she really want to act in a soap opera about real-life romances? She'd never even had a serious relationship; she was still a virgin. Confused much of the time, she was often lost in her own thoughts, wondering about her future not only as an actress but as a woman. In truth, though, she was probably no more confused than any other young girl of her time, navigating difficult shoals to adulthood.

She was young, with her whole life ahead of her. She just wanted things to work out. She decided it wasn't too much to ask for.

CHAPTER 31

In October 1964, Mia Farrow was relaxing on the 20th Century–Fox lot, wearing a nightgown from her show, and accidentally found herself wandering on the set of *Von Ryan's Express*. She was embarrassed by the fact that she had almost ruined a scene by getting into the shot. Farrow, always a most disarming, self-deprecating woman, described to Oprah Winfrey in a television interview her first meeting with Sinatra. She, of course, knew he was famous, but she wasn't a fan. She had no Sinatra albums; she listened to the Beatles. Her parents never listened to Sinatra, either; they played Gregorian chants. Still, she was struck by his charisma.

"I was such a klutz, and he was so cool, I couldn't imagine why he'd want to even know me. He asked me to come over and sit down. As I sat, I had this shoulder bag, and everything spilled from it, all over the floor in front of Frank Sinatra and between his feet and under his chair. And I just kept saying, 'I'm sorry, I'm sorry, I'm sorry,' as he was picking things up. This old green doughnut had fallen out, and I was just horrified. My cat food. My Chapstick. My retainer [removable dental brace]." She laughed at the horror of it all. "It was real embarrassing.

---

* This soap opera, the first of the genre to be aired in prime time, was based on the bestselling novel by Grace Metalious, which was also the source for the blockbuster film starring Lana Turner in 1957.

"I thought the only thing I could do now is get out of here and with any shred of dignity that might remain," she remembered, laughing. "And as I stood up to leave, his eyes met mine, and my heart stopped, you know? Everything came together. I was just so alive in that moment, whole parts of me that I had never used before."

As he walked her to the door, Frank invited her on a date to a private screening of his first directorial effort, *None But the Brave*, in a Warner Bros. screening room. During the film, he held her hand. Afterward, he asked her if she would go to Palm Springs with him (with Brad Dexter and Billy Daniels, the cinematographer). "I'd never been anywhere with anybody," she recalled. "I never even had a date before. So going to Palm Springs with somebody—I couldn't even get my mind around it. He wanted me to leave right then and there. How could I possibly do that? And I just remember babbling how I didn't have any of my stuff, my pajamas. My retainer. My cat. So I didn't go that night. He sent his plane [a Lear Jet] for me the next morning. And I just lost any semblance of sanity I had left with this man when he sent his plane for me and my cat."

Her friend Theresa Lomax said, "Their love affair began on that weekend. She was head over heels, thought he was fantastic. The age difference [almost thirty years] didn't matter to her. It was as if he was as much a father figure as a lover. He definitely gave her the kind of love and attention that she never got from her dad, a man whom she adored, but from afar. She was a virgin before her encounter with Frank in Palm Springs, so this was very special."

Mia wrote in her memoirs, *What Falls Away*, that she was swept off her feet not only by Frank's charm but by the opulence of his Palm Springs home, which she described as "casual, modern, with a lot of Chinese things and plenty of light. With obvious pride he showed me a room where John Fitzgerald Kennedy had slept and the brass placque behind it. One whole side of the living room and bar was glass, with a sliding door that opened to a large patio, and beyond that was an oval swimming pool. He explained to me that recently he had moved the pool because it had been too near the house. I made what I hoped were understanding noises, but after seeing the two octagonal guest houses at either end of the pool, each with two bedrooms and four bathrooms, and the helicopter pad, I was well along in being utterly overwhelmed."

Mia also remembered that there were many photographs of Ava Gardner about the house and that when he spoke of her it was with such pain that she was glad when he changed the subject. She decided not to mention the fact that her father, John Farrow, had an affair with Ava (in 1953, while they filmed *Ride, Vaquero*). Ava and Frank were still married at the time; that was the year Sinatra slashed his wrists in Jimmy Van Heusen's New York apartment.

Frank and Mia began dating regularly.

"He was so attractive," Mia said in retrospect. "I mean, wasn't he just so attractive?" she asked, smiling at the memory. "He was just so . . . so . . ." And then she said the one word that probably best sums up Frank Sinatra: ". . . *cool.*"

Later, she added, "I was just swept off my feet. There was no rhyme or reason why he fell for me. I was a nitwit. I pretty much was. But he was—is—swell. He's just terrific."

Sheila Graham was the first gossip columnist to break the news of a possible romance, in her column on November 30, when she reported that she had been at the taping of *Peyton Place* and noticed that Farrow had received telephone calls from Sinatra. "I can still hear Mia telling me breathlessly in the 20th Century–Fox commissary, 'I've just had a call from the man I love,' " Sheila Graham once recalled. "I had heard some rumors and queried, 'Frank Sinatra?' 'Yes.' It was a clear, confident affirmative." (As she followed up on the story with regular romance updates, Frank became incensed with Graham and told one of his press people, "Shut that dame up. Jesus Christ. Tell her to give the kid [Mia] a break. Her life is gonna be shot to shit if this dame doesn't give it up.")

"Frank stormed at Mia for talking to a reporter, especially this one," said Sheila Graham. "He had not liked me since I telegraphed his obnoxiousness to the press during the divorce from Ava Gardner, pushing reporters around and smashing or threatening to smash the cameras of photographers."

" 'You Make Me Feel So Young,' one of Frank's signature songs, really sums up the way it was with Mia at the beginning," said Nancy Sinatra Jr.

Frank would later tell friends that his intimacy with Mia was passionate. It was as if all of the sex with other women before her were really just practice sessions for Mia. Frank had also said that with Mia he did not suffer from premature ejaculation, a pesky problem that had just begun to bother him about a year before he met her and one over which he had agonized. But with Mia, for some reason, it was not a problem.

Mia felt that she didn't have much to offer Frank, so she gave him everything she had in terms of attention and devotion. She was inexperienced at first, but as she learned to satisfy Frank, she used the knowledge to her advantage.

She would overdo it, making their intimate encounters seem more thrilling for her than they actually were, carrying on in such a way as to make Frank Sinatra—a forty-eight-year-old man—believe he was still the greatest lover in the world. If anything, the way Sinatra felt he pleased Mia, a young virgin, gave him a self-confidence that made him more appealing, not only to her but to everyone around him.

"They were dynamite together, and Frank was nuts about her from the very beginning," said Jim Whiting. "They had long talks. They shared so many intimacies. To downplay what they had together, to just brush it off as an old man trying to recapture his youth with a young girl, really doesn't do it justice."

"I'd never seen him more happy or caring," Frank's daughter Tina remembered. "He was, I think, the father figure Mia never had. Sometimes Mia and I—she was only two years my senior—would take him to the Daisy, a Beverly Hills nightclub, and we would get him to dance. Those were great, fun times."

Mia was into mysticism and yoga. Frank's friends thought she was wacky, sort of spacey. She said she was friendly with Salvador Dali. She smoked dope and talked about the joys of LSD. ("I think LSD is invaluable. LSD opens up another forty percent of our minds. This can be quite dangerous for those who are not equipped emotionally to enter the huge abyss of a wide-open mind.")

She was a flower child, a hippie, from another generation. She would spend hours chanting *mantras* and combing her hair, and Frank loved watching her do just that because, as he told his buddies, he was fascinated by that long, sexy blond mane of hers. She nicknamed him "Charlie," and he called her "Angel Face," sometimes "Baby Face." He tried to teach her to play golf. It was hopeless. He tried to teach her to shoot a gun, in the desert; he felt she should carry one with her at all times. That, too, was hopeless. He took the gun away from her because he knew she would accidentally shoot herself.

Everyone knew that Frank was going to marry Mia. It was just in the air, "they" said.

She was nineteen. He was forty-eight. What could they possibly have seen in each other? Indeed, Frank's and Mia's friends were mystified by their developing romance. Who can fully explain the reasons why love grows between two people, but considering their personalities, it's not difficult to understand the attraction.

Mia Farrow was vulnerable, fair-minded, and innocent. She saw life in simple terms and believed that at the core of each human being was pure goodness. Indeed, she possessed qualities Frank had sometimes longed for. He had become annoyed at himself, at times, for making certain mean-spirited comments during arguments, words that would tend to inflame situations and make matters worse. For instance, deep down he knew that he—not Phyllis McGuire, Sam Giancana, or anyone else for that matter—was really responsible for the ruination of Cal-Neva.

He was a hothead; he'd always been one—everyone knew that—and his temper had gotten him into plenty of trouble in the past. "I'm Italian" he would say by way of feeble explanation. "It's just the way you are when you're Italian." However, in his private moments and sometimes even in front of casual friends, Frank would chastise himself for his temperamental behavior, saying, "When am I ever gonna learn?" Indeed, the older he got, the more bored with his temperament—and with the fallout it would bring to his life—he had become. He was also beginning to wonder about spiritual repercussions; he'd said that he thought he was being punished when Frank junior was kidnapped, and he vowed to be nicer. He was about to turn fifty. It was time for a change. In other words, there was a good guy buried deep inside of Frank Sinatra, and it was time for him to stand up and be counted. Perhaps Frank thought Mia Farrow could help. Perhaps he sensed that some of her generosity, her benevolence, might influence his own behavior in a positive way.

Frank would note in an interview with Walter Cronkite later in the year, "I've always admired people who are gentle and have great patience. And, apparently, what I've done is I've aped these people and begun to follow down that kind of line."

For her part, Mia discovered qualities in Frank that she felt were missing in herself. He was strong and defiant. She often felt weak, vulnerable. He was powerful, decisive. When had she ever made a decision with which she was happy? He was supremely self-confident; what seemed like a lifetime of success had imbued him with an air of self-assurance the magnitude of which boggled Mia's mind. She felt like a bumbling fool most of the time. Oh, to walk into a roomful of strangers and actually be comfortable in her own skin. It seemed like more than she could ever hope for. It simply had never occurred. But for Frank it was a way of life.

Also, Frank Sinatra was older, a father figure in many ways. The fact remained that she had never had the opportunity to work out some of the problems that existed between herself and her own father. He had been distant toward her. She never felt that she had his attention or his love. Not really. Frank was as paternal toward her as he was romantic, and he *was* romantic. He was also witty and charming. It was difficult for her to resist a long-term relationship with Sinatra. And why should she?

Reaching him was not easy, though, Mia soon realized. After the relationship with Ava ended, Frank built an emotional wall of protection around himself. His most recent romances had been superficial; no woman had been allowed to penetrate his armor. If anything, though, his evasiveness made him more seductive to Mia. She welcomed the challenge of breaking down his defenses, especially when—as they became closer—she saw how successful she was at it.

"We're going to get married, I just know we are," Mia told Jacqueline Park, an actress and former girlfriend of Jack L. Warner's . " 'This is my destiny, and there is nothing I can do about it.' I thought at the time that she was seeking a replacement for her dad."

There was a problem, though, that was much bigger than the age difference, and that was Mia's career. Frank had made it known to his friends and family that he would never marry another actress after Ava Gardner. He simply did not want to share a wife with show business. "If I would marry again, it would have to be somebody out of show business," he told one reporter for *Life* magazine, "or who will get out of show business. I feel that I'm a fairly good provider. All I ask is that my wife look after me, and I'll see that she is looked after."

"Mia and Frank started having heated discussions about her career early on," said one friend. "This was to be a problem. All of Frank's friends knew it. At first, we all thought she would just give up her career because she was told to. But then, when she didn't, we realized that this was one headstrong girl who was going to give Frank a little more trouble than he expected."

Mia needed her career. It made her feel special and gave her a sense of purpose. She had no intention of staying at home, at the beck and call of her spouse. Indeed, it would seem that—at least in some ways—she was a liberated woman at a time when that notion was just beginning to become politically correct. She realized—and told friends—that if she married Frank Sinatra, he would want her to abandon her career, and she simply was not prepared to do that. "I like being what I am," she said. "Wanting the career is as much a part of me as my mind and heart."

That Mia did not immediately agree to give up her career, that she had a streak of determined independence, somehow made her more intriguing to Frank—at least at first. He told friends that he would let her have "her little hobby" for a while but that if they ever got married, she would simply have to give it up. "It ain't like she's gonna have a whole lot of choice," Frank said.

As the relationship blossomed, photographers snapped pictures of them together everywhere they went in public. Movie magazines began trumpeting headlines about the controversial relationship and the tantalizing possibility of marriage. Frank threw a twentieth-birthday party for her at Chasen's, even though she asked him not to. "I don't want to call attention to my age," she explained. Two hundred of Frank's famous friends attended, but something was wrong with Mia.

She was completely uncomfortable and acted like an outsider at her own party. These weren't her friends. Some of them—the older celebrities—were her mom's and dad's, but they weren't hers. Hers were hippies, and she wouldn't think of exposing them to Frank, not yet, anyway. Sinatra came over to her during the festivities and, according to witnesses, said, "Lighten up, baby, have some fun." Mia replied, "I can't. They're all staring at me. They're all waiting to see me make a fool of myself. I can't stand it. They think my nails look bad because I bite them." With that, Frank embraced her, holding her tight, for a long time. He whispered something in her ear. She smiled. They kissed tenderly. It was a warm, touching moment.

Later in the week, though, Mia Farrow got just a dose of the flip side of life in Sinatra's world.

Swifty Lazar hosted a party at his Los Angeles home and invited Frank and Mia. He also invited Lauren Bacall, knowing full well that Lauren and Frank had not said two words to each other since that dreadful telephone conversation six years earlier when Frank suggested that the two of them "not see each other for a while," thereby cruelly ending their engagement. (Lazar, who at least had a hand in the breakup of the Sinatra-Bacall engagement, since he confirmed to Louella Parsons that the ill-fated nuptials were to take place, was quite the prankster, it would seem. Either that or he was getting back at Frank for, so many years ago, setting a fire in the backseat of his Rolls-Royce when he gave Sinatra, Dean Martin, and Judy Garland a ride in it.)

Mia waited for Frank at Lazar's home while he was delayed at a television taping. When he finally arrived, he was in a foul mood; the taping had not gone well, he hated doing television shows, he told anyone who would listen, and he was in no mood for a party.

Then, when he noticed Lauren Bacall, he seemed immediately uncomfortable. After a few too many drinks, Frank began a heated argument with Swifty Lazar.

"You! You're the one responsible for what happened between her and me," Sinatra said, pointing at the startled Lauren Bacall. Then Frank suddenly pulled the tablecloth out from under the buffet, sending plates of food and glasses of wine flying everywhere and the guests, for whom the goodies were intended, running for cover.

"You're the one, Swifty," Frank said as he grabbed a horror-stricken Mia Farrow by the arm and dragged her out of the room. "You're the one responsible!"

Mia never forgot that night. She had no idea what it was about until she asked mutual friends and couldn't believe her ears when it was explained to her. "Did you *really* break up with Lauren Bacall and not tell her about it?" she asked Frank. He told Mia that whatever happened was none of her business and that he "did it for Betty's own good."

"Mia was stunned by the whole thing," her friend Edie Goetz said. " 'That doesn't sound like the Frank Sinatra I know,' she said. 'He must have been a different man. He would never do such a thing to me. *Never.*' "

It was 1965, the year of Motown and of the Beatles—rhythm and blues and the Liverpool sound—as well as youthful, folk protest songs by artists such as Bob Dylan. Music had changed dramatically, and at this point the youth set had little time for Elvis Presley, let alone Frank Sinatra. But Frank always had an audience, especially in Las Vegas. In fact, the prior year had ended with Frank playing the Sands Hotel. The two-week engagement was a complete sellout. With Frank sharing the bill with the Count Basie Orchestra, conducted by Quincy Jones, the reviews were terrific.

Sinatra still seemed to have his place as an American icon with an older audience. His record buyers had grown older with him, and they were still loyal and supportive of everything he did: recordings, films, and concerts. In fact, in the summer of 1965, Frank embarked on a six-city concert tour, which was promoted as Frank Sinatra and Company with Count Basie and his band, marking the first time Frank had toured with a band in twenty years. (Mia wanted to accompany him on the road, but she became ill and had to stay behind.)

The tour was a smashing success: At the Forest Hills Music Festival, he earned $125,000 for three nights. The tour grossed $600,000, breaking box-office records at each stop along the way. His performance at the Newport Jazz Festival on the Fourth of July set records, even though there was much discussion among music critics as to whether or not Sinatra should be allowed to perform at the festival, since he wasn't considered by most to be a jazz singer. Jazz singer or not, *Variety* noted that Frank brought something unique to the festival: "glamour, showmanship and his own brand of casual hip." The trade publication noted that Frank received a huge ovation and that he was "worth every penny" of the $40,000 he earned for his hour-long performance. (Frank arrived by helicopter behind the stage and made his exit the same way.) Indeed, he may have been forty-nine, but as far as his audiences were concerned as the tour moved through Chicago, Detroit, and Baltimore, he was still in his prime.

A couple of days after the tour was over, Frank's hands—along with his signature—were immortalized in cement at Grauman's Chinese Theater. Daughters Nancy and Tina accompanied him to the ceremony. *None but the Brave* had been released to critical raves. Another film, *Marriage on the Rocks* (with Deborah Kerr and Dean Martin), also featured Nancy Sinatra as Frank's daughter.

This was not a good year for Nancy Sinatra. While working on the movie, her marriage broke up. She had married former teenage idol Tommy Sands five years earlier (on September 11, 1960). Now Sands wanted out. She has said she was stunned; she thought they had a good marriage.

Being married to Nancy was not easy for Tommy. Friends say he could never live up to her expectations; she wanted him to be her father. Frank did what he could to make it worse. He continued to lavish upon Nancy expensive gifts, just as he had always done, presents that her own husband could never have afforded—like a $10,000 leopard coat—which made Nancy happy but Tommy insecure.

"She had looked for another Frank Sinatra to be her man," wrote Hollywood reporter Rona Barrett in her memoirs *Miss Rona.* "Anyone who had the opportunity to see Nancy and Big Frank together, especially as she matured, would quietly walk away with a funny, gnawing feeling: If they weren't father and daughter, they could certainly pass for lovers. . . ." (Frank never forgave Rona for that statement and often lambasted her from the stage, as was his custom when he was angry at members of the media.)

Barrett also recalled a story she had been told: A friend was in the kitchen when Frank entered. The friend asked Frank, 'So what do you think of your prospective son-in-law?" Frank said, "He's okay. Too bad he doesn't have any balls, though."

It would take years for Nancy junior to recover from the divorce. Like mother like daughter.

"Her divorce nearly destroyed her," recalled Rona Barrett. "I never watched a human being suffer so deeply and so painfully as Nancy did when her marriage to Tommy ended. She fell apart. Doctors were called in. She became a living vegetable. No one could communicate with her. She was like a pathetic baby, suffering from some disease for which there was no cure. I ached for her."

Nancy Sinatra once recalled, "In my mother's bed, crying and feeling sorry for myself, I thought it was the end of the world. Dad came in and he said, 'I know you're sad. I know you're unhappy. And I know you're miserable. But I can only tell you that it will pass and that I'm glad you're not alone. You have me and Mom and your sister and brother. I had to go through it alone.' " Nancy assumed he was talking about the breakup of his marriage to Ava Gardner.

Frank was never happy with the way Tommy handled the breakup of his marriage to Nancy, and a lot of people in show business were well aware of Sinatra's displeasure. He hated seeing his daughter suffer. To one close associate, he said, "When I get my hands on that asshole, his life will be over. Look what he's done to my kid. Just look at her."

While Frank never did anything to encourage it—none that anyone has ever been able to document, anyway—Tommy Sands's career took a nosedive when he and Nancy split. That the entire show-business community knew how Sands dumped Nancy and how angry Frank was about it seemed to be more than enough to kill Sands's career. "Tommy's days now became a living nightmare," said Barrett. "He eventually cracked up. I honestly cried on and off for a week when I saw him at Cedars of Lebanon Hospital."*

By August 1965, Frank Sinatra was exhausted, having just returned from Israel, where he filmed United Artists's *Cast a Giant Shadow* with Kirk Douglas. He needed some time off. So he chartered a 170-foot-long

---

* Tommy Sands eventually left show business and wound up in Hawaii selling real estate. Nancy Sinatra married producer Hugh Lambert on December 12, 1970, at St. Louis Catholic Church in Cathedral City, California. Theirs was a happy union. He died in 1985 of throat cancer at the age of fifty-five.

yacht, the *Southern Breeze*, and invited Mia to sail with him, along with nine other friends, including Rosalind Russell and Claudette Colbert and their husbands, Freddie Brisson and Joel Pressman. Mia and Frank flew into the New England area together on Frank's private jet to begin the vacation. So sure were the producers of *Peyton Place* that the rumors were true and that Mia was going to marry Sinatra and then demand an extended honeymoon that they wrote her out of the show for six weeks by putting her character in a coma. Indeed, as Sinatra and friends cruised New England waters, rumors abounded that a wedding to Farrow would either take place on that yacht or at one of its stopovers. The *New York Daily News* posed the question in its headline "Sinatra and Mia Sailing to Altar?" The *Journal-American* asked in its headline, "Are They, or Aren't They?"

"Within twenty-four hours, you couldn't see the ocean for the flotilla of paparazzi, and you couldn't hear yourself think for the helicopters," Mia remembered, "and you couldn't watch television without seeing yourself and hearing about how ancient Frank Sinatra was and how young I was. . . ."

Frank had planned occasional stops along the way for Mia to enjoy. He loved showing her new sights, sharing his success and good fortune with her. Feelings and emotions that he would never allow himself to expose in the real world—his fast-paced, contentious world of big bucks, big deals, and big problems—he began to share with Mia in their little fantasy world, where it was just the two of them in a crowd. He was tired of his career, he told her. He loved singing, but the politics of the business was wearing him down. He wished he could give it all up, but he was booked so many years in advance that he saw no end in sight. "The audience gives me life," he told her. "But my voice, my throat—I just can't do it anymore, Mia. I can't take the pressure of wondering if it's gonna hold up. When I think of all the people whose living depends on my goddamn throat, I wanna puke."

He wanted some peace in his life, he told her. "I just want to breathe," he said. "If I could just breathe."

He was also so sick of the paparazzi that had been trailing him for decades, he told her, that he was afraid that one day he would actually kill one of them. "I've come close a couple of times," he said.

Indeed, at each stop Frank and Mia were greeted by the photographers and reporters Frank had complained about, all wondering about the wedding. It was as much an annoyance as it had always been. Who could forget what he and Ava went through with the press? "I got no comment to make about any of it," Frank said at a Cape Cod stop. "I got a dozen chaperones on this cruise," he said. "I'm behaving myself, so get lost!"

Their fantasy cruise ended badly, though, when a twenty-three-year-old crewman, returning to the yacht from shore with a pal and two waitresses, drowned when his boat capsized on August 10. Frank and Mia were stunned, as were all of the guests. Because all of the news reports about the drowning focused on the fact that Frank and Mia were together on the cruise, Mia's mother began to think that the publicity her daughter was receiving was not good. She urged her by telephone to cut the cruise short. By this time, however, Frank had already decided that the fun had gone out of this vacation, and the trip was ended after a week, even though he had paid in advance for thirty days at $2,000 a day.

When the decision was made to end the cruise and set final anchor in the Hudson River, all of Frank's guests enjoyed a night on the town in Manhattan with Frank and Mia at the Aegean restaurant, then on to Jilly's for a nightcap, and then to Frank's penthouse overlooking the East River. (Sinatra sent a huge floral wreath to the funeral home on the day of the crewman's burial, as did Roz Russell.)

"It had been the most closely observed cruise since Cleopatra floated down the Nile to meet Mark Antony," noted *Time* magazine after the cruise ended and no nuptials had taken place.

"The only reason Mia was on that yacht was because she burned her eye while shooting *Peyton Place*," Maureen O'Sullivan somewhat feebly explained to the press. "One misconception is that Mia was on the yacht unchaperoned," she went on. "Why, all those guests were there, and they're all friends of mine; they would take care of her if she needed any taking care of—which she didn't."

Sinatra was only four years younger than Maureen O'Sullivan, so she wasn't happy about the pairing. However, she would later say that she sensed that if she dared tell Mia how to handle this older man's attentions, Mia would rebel and run off with him. So she didn't say much to Mia about it at all.

Meanwhile, Frank's mother, Dolly, had her own concerns. She insisted to anyone who would listen that Frank was really just trying to help Mia launch her career. "How many times has he helped somebody to the top?" she asked one reporter. "That is what he is doing." (Actually, her explanation of her son's relationship was based on what Frank had told her prior to his becoming intimate with Mia. He explained to her that he was interested in Mia appearing as his daughter in a film.) She maintained that her son would never marry Mia Farrow. After all, two of Frank's children (Nancy and Frank) were older than Farrow.

Dolly's approval meant the world to Frank, and so while he and Mia were on the East Coast, he took the opportunity to introduce Mia to his mother. The couple went to Fort Lee, New Jersey, one evening for one of Dolly's home-cooked Italian meals.

Mia won Dolly over that night. Dolly was prepared to hate her. But Mia was so innocent, and she seemed so needy, that Sinatra's mom couldn't resist the urge to mother her. Frank loved the fact that his mother had suddenly become so instantly protective of Mia. Some felt Mia's greatest charm was that she made people want to hover over her and protect her from the world. In fact, as they were leaving the house, Dolly said to Frank, "You take care of her or I'll smack you." In other words, she approved of Mia.

However, a friend of Sinatra's said, "Dolly didn't want Frank to marry Mia, not because she didn't like the girl but because she knew it would end in divorce. 'The age thing, it's just too great,' she had said. 'Why get married? Why can't they just live together? I can't bear to see Frank go through with this one what he went through with that other one [Ava].' "

By October 1965, Mia Farrow was a big star, largely due to all of the commotion regarding her relationship with the Chairman of the Board (a nickname that stuck, supposedly conferred by acclaimed New York disc jockey William B. Williams). She was on the cover of October's *Look* magazine. Her asking fee per film had increased from about $12,000 to over $100,000 per picture, and she hadn't even appeared in one yet.

Of course, Frank's career was in high gear with the film *Assault on a Queen* (with screenplay by Rod Serling) and an appearance on the *Tonight Show* with Dean Martin, with Joey Bishop as guest host; and then followed more work in the recording studio on October 11, when he rerecorded the classics "Come Fly With Me" and "I'll Never Smile Again." The year also saw the release of the very cool *Sinatra '65* album, a compilation of some of his best songs of the last five years.

At the end of 1965, Reprise released one of Frank's finest recordings, the Grammy Award–winning, *September of My Years*. It would seem ironic that at a time when Frank's age—he would turn fifty in December—was such a topic of discussion because of his relationship to the much younger Mia, he would release an album which had the subject of aging as its theme, with songs such as the "September" title track, "Last Night When We Were Young," and "Hello, Young Lovers." Brilliantly arranged and conducted by Gordon Jenkins, each song was given a deeply personal, life-affirming performance by Sinatra. As Sinatra sang the lyrics of "How Old Am I" ("You kiss me and I'm young"), it wasn't difficult to imagine that he was singing of his relationship with Mia.

The centerpiece of this wonderful album, though, is Frank's rendition of the hauntingly reflective, autobiographical "It Was a Very Good Year," for which Frank was awarded a Grammy for Best Male Vocal Performance. In fact, the album won four Grammys: Best Arranger (Gordon Jenkins for "It Was a Very Good Year"), Album of the Year, and Best Album Notes.

Written in 1961, "It Was a Very Good Year" had been first performed as a folk song by the Kingston Trio. After Sinatra heard the song on the car radio, he knew he had to record it. (When Frank performed the song on his terrific television special *A Man and His Music* (November 24,

1965), he observed of it, "A lyric can be a lament, it can be an exclamation of joy, or a lyric can tell the sum and substance of a man's life."

"Mia loved that song so much," said a friend of hers. "In fact, she actually became a fan of Frank's with that song and the *September* album. She really had not paid much attention to him prior to it. She'd never seen any of his films until he took her to see *None But the Brave* early on in their relationship. She loved the fact that he was an older, experienced man and seemed proud enough of it to record a whole album about it. She thought it was honorable. She was swept off her feet by him. She found his maturity and his experience to be highly sensual."

Problems arose, though, as Nancy senior and Nancy junior began planning a party to celebrate Frank's fiftieth birthday. Should they invite Mia? Hundreds of Frank's closest friends and associates would be in attendance—"a veritable cream of Hollywood society" is how the *Journal-American* put it, "emphatically A and not B group people." But Nancy senior, who had worked for weeks to make this a wonderful evening for her ex-husband, simply felt that Mia's attendance would be inappropriate. "I absolutely won't have her there," she announced to the family during a planning meeting for the party. "I'm sorry," she said, clearly flustered by the mere thought of Frank's arriving on the arm of a twenty-year-old. "It's just too . . . too . . . *humiliating.*"

Frank was not sure how to proceed when his daughter Nancy told him of her mother's decision. Certainly he still cared about his first wife's feelings, but he knew that it would be unfair of him to leave Mia behind.

He presented his dilemma to Mia, according to intimates, and asked for her opinion. "What should I do? I'm in a real mess here," he told her. They were a couple, Frank reasoned. Perhaps they should discuss the situation in a mature, reasonable manner. But there was a problem with that logic: Mia Farrow was not a mature, reasonable person, not yet, anyway. Frank may have wanted to try for a meaningful dialogue about a personal quandary—rare for him, so it was clear that he was really trying—but Mia, who, at twenty, was just barely out of her teens, wanted only one thing: She wanted to go to the party.

"When Mia thought she wouldn't be going to the party, she was crushed," said a friend of hers. "She thought he was ashamed of their relationship. Her sadness quickly turned to anger. I heard that she threw an ashtray at him. It missed Frank by a hair. She told me later that he was so pissed, he punched a hole in the wall. 'Now look what you made me do!' he told Mia. 'Fine, now you really ain't goin' to the party. You made up my mind for me. Have it your way.' They fought, throwing things at one another. The angrier *she* got, the more turned on *he* got, and the next thing Mia knew, he was ripping off her clothes and making love to her on the floor. At least that's what she told me, and I believed her.

"You see, they had that kind of wild relationship where their big fights

341

always ended with them tumbling into bed," said Deidra Evans-Jackson, who knew Mia in the sixties, having been a friend of her sister's. "Jesus, Frank was getting ready to turn fifty, but this girl was turning him on like he was a teenager. How could he resist her?"

On the subject of women, Frank said at this time, "I've never met a man in my life who could give another man advice about women. I'm supposed to have a Ph.D. on the subject, but I've flunked more often than not. I'm very fond of women; I admire them. But like all men, I don't understand them. Sex? There's not enough quantity and certainly not enough quality. . . ."

At the same time as the Sinatra birthday party, a major publicity coup in honor of Frank was in the works at CBS-TV when its news division scheduled a tribute not only in honor of his birthday but also to commemorate his twenty-fifth anniversary in show business. Walter Cronkite was set to interview Frank at Sinatra's Palm Springs home. Prior to the interview, the network was instructed by Sinatra's attorney, Mickey Rudin, that Cronkite should not ask any questions about Farrow. Producer Don Hewitt, ostensibly speaking for the network, reportedly agreed that any such line of questioning would be deemed inappropriate. "Hey, if that's what Frank wants, that's what he'll get," said Hewitt. However, Walter Cronkite would not have his line of questioning dictated by any celebrity. Even though he was told not to do so, he did ask about Sinatra's romance with Farrow. It was an innocuous question and one that Frank dodged easily. Still, Sinatra was incensed by it.

Then Cronkite made an even bigger mistake. As Cronkite remembered many years later, "Don [Hewitt] leaned over and whispered to me not to forget to ask him about the Mafia. My question was simply how he responded to charges that he had Mafia connections. Sinatra's lips tightened to a tiny line. He gave me a piercing look through narrowing eyes."

"That's it," Frank announced angrily. He practically leapt out of his chair and stormed off to a bedroom, with Hewitt and Jilly Rizzo following. An argument ensued which, said Cronkite, "featured the great voice raised to a level seldom used in a concert hall. The only coherent phrase I picked up was a charge that Hewitt had promised that the Mafia questions would not be raised."

Frank came back to continue the interview and respond to the question the way he usually did: "I do meet all kinds of people in the world because of the natural habitat from day to day; in the theatrical world, nightclub world, in concerts, in restaurants, you meet all kinds of people. So there's really not much to be said about that, and I think the less said the better, because there's no answer. When I say no, it's no, and for some reason it keeps persisting, you see, and consequently I just refuse to discuss it because you can't make a dent anywhere."

"And he didn't care whether anyone believed that or not," said Cronkite.

Two weeks before the show was to be broadcast, Frank's attorney, Mickey Rudin, shot off a letter to CBS, charging the network with what can only be regarded as an ingenious and novel allegation: "breach of understanding."

In the end, CBS deleted references to Mia Farrow [though Frank mentioned "Miss Farrow" in telling of an anecdote] from the November 16, 1965, broadcast of *Sinatra*. The program was a well-produced, even-handed study of the man despite the sensational publicity that surrounded it (as a result of the network's making Rudin's missive public). Some interesting facts were revealed: Cronkite noted that Sinatra made $25 million while at Capitol and, as of the broadcast, $15 million at Reprise. He earned royalties of $60,000 a year from his recordings at Columbia. Frank Sinatra Enterprises brought in $4 million a year. "He uses his private jet like the average millionaire uses a limousine," said Cronkite. "There are no commercial airlines that would take Sinatra to the unlikely places he goes at the unlikely times he wants to go there."

Studio footage of Sinatra—tie loosened, standing before his sheet music and recording "It Was a Very Good Year"—was put to wonderful use; it was fascinating to watch him work, tailoring the song in his unique, self-assured way. The studio was filled with people, sitting in the studio on chairs in rapt attention as if watching a concert. In fact, Sinatra always had spectators in the studio, unlike practically every other artist in the business, who preferred to record in solitude. Sinatra's sessions were charged with electricity, an excitement that can only be generated by people watching as he made his music. On one side of the studio would be the orchestra, with Sinatra in the middle and his "audience" on the other side. (Incidentally, they did not applaud at the end of "takes." That would have ruined the session.) During the playback of the song when Sinatra, clearly delighted with the outcome, heard himself sing "When I was thirty-five, it was a very good year," he turned to one of the studio personnel, flashed a boyish grin, and said, *"Those* were the swingin' years."

Of contemporary pop music, Sinatra said, "The biggest complaint I have about a lot of the kids who sing today is that I can't understand what they're saying. If I could only understand some of the words, I might be interested in what they're doing. But there's no enunciation, no clarity of diction."

Cronkite noted that there had been, in the past, stories that Sinatra had struck several newsmen. "Not true," Frank said. "The only time I had any physical contact with a newspaper man was with a man [Lee Mortimer] who is now dead [he spat out the word dead], who said some pretty nasty things about me in a column for about two years, and they were all gross lies. He once said something to me in person; I reached the boiling point, and it was all over. Frankly, if he were alive and he said it again, I would do it again, because he was just that kind of a man."

Frank was still angry, however, even though everyone in his circle was thrilled by the respectful tone of the show (which held the distinction of being the only program to ever beat *The Fugitive* in its time slot). When Frank's publicist, Jim Mahoney, suggested that, as a goodwill measure, they send a note of thanks to Don Hewitt, Frank facetiously inquired, "Lemme ask you something? Can you send a fist through the mail?"

His friends weren't surprised by Frank's annoyance. To Sinatra, a deal is a deal. It wasn't so much the benign question about Mia that annoyed him as it was the lack of principle behind what had occurred. Indeed, Don Hewitt had promised no questions about Mia Farrow, and as far as Frank was concerned, Hewitt was speaking for the network, and the network did not honor its word. It didn't matter to him that the network couldn't control Walter Cronkite any more than it mattered that both the question and Frank's answer had been excised from the broadcast. Privately, to friends, Frank called both Hewitt and Cronkite every name in the book after that laudatory special was aired.

"What the fuck is the point of a deal if nobody bothers to honor it," he reportedly said. "Then people wonder why I am so supposedly goddamned difficult."

Frank was also annoyed at his daughter Nancy for a comment she made on the broadcast. Over a visual of Sinatra and many of his friends, including Liza Minnelli, Sammy Davis, and his first wife, Nancy, laughing, drinking, and having a good time at Jilly's in New York, Nancy said, "When you have a daddy, you kinda want him to be a daddy all the time. And sometimes when he's with his friends, they carry on like a bunch of kids. And it's great. They're having a marvelous time," she said. "But that bothers me."

Her comment was framed with a shot of Nancy looking sad and glum at the table of partying people. Jack O'Brien, TV critic for the *Journal-American*, observed, "Nancy's low-keyed whimper seemed somewhat embarrassing, plaintive, even poignant."

One happy result of the broadcast was that Hewitt included in it an excellent clip of Frank recording "It Was a Very Good Year." By this time, the *September of My Years* album had begun to slow in sales, but once the American viewing audience saw that memorable footage of Frank in the studio, the album's sales picked up. It remained on the charts for sixty-nine weeks, helped along the way by a terrific TV special NBC presented—a one-man Emmy award–winning show—on November 24th, *A Man and His Music*, in which he also performed the song.

Frank wrapped up November 1965 in the studio recording "moon songs" for the album *Moonlight Sinatra*: songs like "Moonlight Becomes You" and "Oh, You Crazy Moon."

Moonlight Sinatra, often overlooked, is one of Sinatra's shining achievements. The "Moon" idea for an album was not new, but typically, Sinatra had a completely different take on it. He and Nelson Riddle approached the album as a classical piece. The orchestrations shimmer, glimmer, and shine. Sinatra takes inherently sentimental songs and strips them of their sentimentality, contrasting the deep blue moonlight of the instruments with a squeaky-clean, forthright interpretation of the songs. Only he could take a cliché and make it utterly original.

At the end of the month, in the spirit of celebration, Reprise released a two-record set it also called *A Man and His Music*. Not a soundtrack from the special, this double album, narrated by Frank himself, is really a musical memoir with thirty-one songs and a comedy routine from the Summit. Nancy Sinatra has said, "If you buy only one Sinatra album, this is it."

The album was notable for the packaging. It was a double-fold album within a slipcase with a stamped metal foil cover inlay and a beautiful book accompanying it. It was remarkable for its day and for its influence on special-project record packaging thereafter. The book was impeccable in content and design and included a complete Sinatra recording history. Everything the man did reflected his care for completeness, detail, and quality. The price wasn't that high, but if you couldn't afford it, you could also purchase the double-fold album alone, in its own right a complete package. Sinatra thought of everything. The package went on to win a grammy for Album of the Year.

Frank's fiftieth-birthday dinner party, given for him by his first wife and his daughter Nancy, was scheduled to be held at the Trianon Room of the Beverly Wilshire Hotel on Sunday evening, December 12. Nancy senior apparently felt bad about her insistence that Mia Farrow not be present and telephoned Frank three days before the party to tell him that she was sorry for what she had said about Mia and that he could bring her if he wished. Frank appreciated Nancy's kind gesture and told Mia that she could accompany him if she still wanted to. Of course she was delighted and purchased a stunning blue chiffon gown for the occasion at an expensive Beverly Hills boutique.

But then, two days later, Frank junior telephoned his father and accused him of being a fool. He argued that Mia's presence would indeed embarrass his mother. "And how can you do that to her?" he wanted to know. Father and son exchanged furious words until finally Frank senior slammed the telephone down. Even after the kidnapping they didn't seem to understand each other.

Apparently, Frank senior now felt that Mia's presence would cause too much unpleasantness among his family members. He was really in a dilemma, since he had already told her she could accompany him. Could he discuss this situation with Mia and reach an adult decision? Probably not, at least based on what happened the last time he attempted to do just that. So he laid down the proverbial law and told Mia that he had changed his mind: She would not be going, after all.

Despite all of the behind-the-scenes squabbling, the party was a success, with 150 invited guests, including some who performed, such as Sammy Davis Jr., George Burns, Jack Benny, and Tony Bennett. Daughters Nancy and Tina had not only helped their mother plan the party, they also performed a loving sketch for their dad. Guests could see, though, that Frank was clearly preoccupied. It was obvious all evening. Later, it would be learned by Sinatra intimates that he felt guilty about leaving Mia behind.

Frank wanted to see Mia. He left the party early and drove to her apartment. When he walked in, he discovered a side of Mia that no doubt startled him. First of all, the apartment reeked of marijuana, and according to what Frank had told one source, "Mia was high as a kite." Perhaps even more disturbing, she had been so distraught about not being able to attend the party that she cut off all of her hair in a fit of fury. Frank was astonished.

"I can't believe she did that," he later told a friend. "That worries me. I don't know what to think about it. That's a pretty dramatic thing to do."

Mia was understandably disappointed, but she had really acted like a child. She threw a temper tantrum simply because she could not have her way, and in an act of sheer rebellion—or maybe to get attention—she lopped off the long, luxurious blond hair Frank loved so much. In other words, she showed *him.*

Mia's impulsive actions marked the first time Frank saw the depth of her immaturity, and he wasn't sure what to make of it. ("Now you can go out for Little League like the rest of the boys," he told her jokingly.) In the end, though, never one to really analyze a situation much, Frank decided to brush off Mia's tantrum and in a conciliatory gesture, he bought her an expensive diamond necklace.

Mia insisted in her 1997 autobiography, *What Falls Away,* that she cut her hair at the television studio in the makeup room because "of the horror of vanity" of her Catholic upbringing. "There must have been nothing going on in the world that week, because my haircut got an absurd amount of press coverage," she wrote. She also said that she did not cut it "to spite Frank."

However, Ryan O'Neal, who worked with Mia on *Peyton Place* said, "She didn't cut it at the studio. She came in with it already cut. *That* I remember. I don't know why she did it, but I heard she was mad at Frank. What can I say? I couldn't have cared less at the time, and I don't care now."

CHAPTER 32

The romance of Frank Sinatra and Mia Farrow continued through the holidays. They spent Thanksgiving together at friends; he gave her a solid-gold cigarette case as a Christmas gift, which he inscribed "Mia, Mia, With Love, From Francis." (Mia used the case to stash marijuana, even though Frank had said that he didn't want her smoking around him because, as he put it to one pal, "it makes her even wackier than she already is.")

They began spending all of their weekends together at Frank's home in the desert, which was still filled with pictures of Ava Gardner. They shared their hopes and dreams as well as their failings and despair with one another. This was not easy for Frank; his emotions after Ava were too raw to expose to anybody, but he trusted Mia with them just the same. She listened to stories of his anguish during and after his relationship with Ava, and she promised that she would never inflict such misery upon him. He believed her. He, in turn, vowed that he would always love and protect her. She believed him. For about three months, their life together was blissful. "I am so happy," Frank said at the time. "Finally."

But suddenly things went awry.

By the spring of 1966, Frank and Mia had been together for almost two years. However, when he went to London to film the movie *The Naked Runner*, their relationship became troubled. There was great speculation about why, but no one seemed to know the particulars at the time; no one but Frank and Mia, anyway.

"There was a lot of mystery about that," said Deidra Evans-Johnson, "and most people assumed that Frank called it off. Everyone was on a 'Poor Mia' kick. But the fact of the matter is that Mia had been the one to end it, around February of 1966, after a nasty argument with Frank."

What happened, according to Evans-Johnson, was that Mia had suggested that she and Frank live together first rather than marry immediately. These were the sixties; it was the thing to do. Marriage was considered by many young people as being passé. "At least don't do it until you really know the person," Mia told her friend.

However, Frank thought that living with Mia without the benefit of marriage was a dreadful idea. Indeed, the so-called generation gap reared its head as the two battled over whether or not cohabitation was acceptable. Finally, it came down to the real issue: Sinatra admitted that his family would be mortified and felt strongly that he had to consider their feelings.

Frank would later admit that he was still apprehensive about making a deeper commitment to Mia. After what had happened with Ava, could he possibly do it again with another woman? She had broken his heart and shattered him; it had taken him years to get over her. (To be honest, he would confess to some close friends, he really *wasn't* over her. He had simply learned to go on without her, but he thought of her every day.) So, although he carried himself with great assurance, in reality Frank was scared. Afraid of commitment, of love, and, certainly, marriage. However, he also had too much pride to admit all his fears to Mia, so he focused instead on familial concerns.

"You know what? I've had it with your family," Mia cried. "What about me? What about *my* feelings? What about if *I'm* upset."

Then Mia reportedly picked up a lamp and hurled it at Frank in a moment of anger. According to the story she told her friend, Frank ducked. The lamp missed him by about an inch. Infuriated by the close call, he went for her. He grabbed her by the throat with his left hand and lifted his right as if he were about to strike her.

"No, no, no," she shrieked. "I'm sorry, Frank. I'm sorry, Frank. I'm sorry, Frank."

Perhaps realizing he was out of control, Sinatra backed off.

Mia was scared by the notion that Sinatra might actually hit her. She asked him, "How could you do it, Frank? I love you so much; how could you even *think* to hit me. Now go. Please. I'm begging you."

"If I walk out this door," Frank warned her, "I'm walking out of your life."

"Then go," she demanded. "Just go!"

After Frank stormed out, Mia called one friend after another, sobbing. "My life is over. Nothing means anything anymore." Mia began dating other men—Michael Caine, Eddie Fisher, Mike Nichols—but she couldn't get Sinatra out of her mind.

For his part, Frank was contrite and regretted that matters had gotten so out of hand during the quarrel with Mia. He told friends that he had "fucked up, and now she won't have anything to do with me and my goddamn temper. When am I ever gonna learn? *When am I ever gonna learn?* How am I ever gonna find another dame like that?" Finally, though, in a determined effort to save face in front of his pals at Jilly's one night in New York, Frank puffed up his chest and said, "If she calls, fuck her. I ain't in." They could see the pain in his eyes, though. Try as he might, Frank couldn't hide the way he felt about Mia. "He really seems to love this one," Jilly said. "You can tell he don't mean it when he says, 'Fuck it.' You always know when he means it and when he don't."

That same night at Jilly's, a fan came over to Frank and began pestering him for an autograph. According to one eyewitness, Frank was in no mood to be bothered—he was gloomy over Mia—yet the fan was persistent. "C'mon, man, just an autograph. Don't be a jerk." At that, one of Sinatra's bodyguards, whom Frank referred to as the "Dago Secret Service," held up a coat jacket in front of the man while another guard apparently punched him in the stomach. "Now, *there's* your fuckin' autograph," the bodyguard said to the man, who was by now doubled over in pain.

"That's the kind of thing that happened around Frank all the time," said one of his former employees. "His reputation in the sixties was the worst. People were always getting hurt around him. He didn't endorse it, didn't authorize it, but didn't stop it, either. He was surrounded by hotheaded assholes who wanted to impress him, kiss up to him, by showing him how tough they were and what lengths they'd go to to protect him. But from what? From autograph seekers?

"They beat people up because they thought that was a compliment to Frank. 'See what I'll do to protect you, to make you happy?' Frank ate it all up. He thought they were being loyal, his goons, his idiotic Dago Secret Service, which was comprised of a bunch of losers who hung on to Frank because he was all they had in their lives. It was pathetic."

The split from Mia Farrow did not last long, only about three months, in fact. When Frank heard that she had just gotten back from Rome, where she had been visiting Elizabeth Taylor and Richard Burton with Mike Nichols (who directed *Who's Afraid of Virginia Woolf?*), he was worried. "That's not so good," he told one friend at Jilly's. "I think I'm gonna have to be the one to straighten this out with Mia. Can you believe that? Sinatra on his knees?"

"When the columnists, including myself, were printing that Mia and Frank were reconciling, an imp of doubt was always on my shoulder," said Sheila Graham. "because I knew how much Mia had punctured Frank's godlike image of himself. 'How much longer can he take it?' I asked frequently in my column and on the *Merv Griffin Show*."

Indeed, with Mia, Frank seemed to have met his match. While women were still falling over themselves for him, the one he truly wanted was the one who told him to "get lost." Like Ava before her, he couldn't dominate Mia, and he loved that about her. He telephoned Mia from Jilly's and tried to smooth things over with her. According to someone who overheard the conversation, Mia apparently asked Frank if he was sorry for what he'd done, because Frank, ever the sweet-talker, said, "Baby Face, lemme tell ya somethin'. I am so fuckin' sorry, you'd never fuckin' believe it. I miss you so fuckin' much. I love you, Mia. I do. I swear to God."

There was a pause. Mia had apparently said something nice to Frank, because his eyes started dancing and he smiled broadly.

Then he softly crooned into the phone, "The best is yet to come, and babe, won't it be fine . . ."

Mia Farrow was back in Frank Sinatra's life.

Frank began 1966 by booking another successful engagement at the Sands in Las Vegas with Count Basie and Quincy Jones. These shows were recorded and were to be released later in the year as a striking live album, *Sinatra at the Sands,* considered by many fans and critics to be a masterpiece because it does capture him as he really is, not cleaned up in the studio.

At this time—February 1966—Frank's daughter Nancy had her only number-one record with the unforgettable "These Boots Are Made for Walking." Nancy had been recording for five years on her dad's Reprise label before she finally struck gold with this one. In fact, she had recorded fifteen singles—such as "Cufflinks and a Tie Clip" and "Like I Do"—before she teamed up with writer-producer Lee Hazlewood for this hard-edged feminist song. "Boots" was a tough, no-nonsense lyric, and Nancy would later say that she had to dig deep to find that aspect of herself. (" 'Boots' was hard, and I'm as soft as they come.") But Hazlewood felt differently about her. "You're not a sweet, young thing," he told her. "You're not the virgin next door. You've been married and divorced. You're a grown woman. I know there's garbage in there somewhere."

"Her head changed after the divorce," Rona Barrett observed. "In trying to pull herself together, she found a career. It changed her, too. Her career gave her a sort of 'I'll show you' attitude. I have always felt it was 'I'll show you, Tommy Sands, what you really missed.' "

Nancy Sinatra still has a huge, loyal following. She has had a number of hits other than "Boots" (such as "How Does That Grab You, Darlin'?" "Sugar Town," and "Summer Wine" and "Jackson" as duets with Lee Hazlewood). While she started with somewhat limited ability and a narrow range, she was blessed with a pretty voice and assured intonation. As her producers turned any limitations into an undeniable style all her own, she recorded a number of albums, many of which are today cult classics. Her lesser-known sides, such as "The City Never Sleeps at Night," even show that she grew to be a persuasive vocalist of skill and attractiveness.

Nancy always felt that had she not chosen to become a wife and mother, she could have segued into a career in adult pop or standard pop similar to that of Linda Ronstadt. Though the public mainly knew her through hit singles and her "Boots" image, she would go on to do impressive shows in Las Vegas. In her films, such as *Speedway* (1968), with Elvis Presley, she demonstrated a relaxed presence; the camera loved her.

Rex Reed once wrote that "no matter what she does to herself with her father's money, she still looks like a pizza waitress," but she was far from it. Her album covers, particularly the lovely *Nancy*, show a truly sexy young woman. Her image, with long blond tresses and a clinging slip dress and patent leather go-go boots, is still striking today. She was—and remains—a classic beauty.

It was a good time for the Sinatras on the music charts, because on April 11, 1966, one of the classic Sinatra songs was recorded, the ever-so-romantic "Strangers in the Night." Frank's was the third number one for Reprise following Dean Martin's "Everybody Loves Somebody" and Nancy's "Boots."

"Strangers in the Night," with its tango rhythm, became Sinatra's biggest worldwide hit. It was the first single to replace the Beatles at the top of the charts on July 2, 1966, when it supplanted "Paperback Writer." (One look at the *Billboard* top five that week and it's clear that Frank was *the Man* among a bunch of upstart kids: the Beatles, Cyrkle ["Red Rubber Ball"], the Rolling Stones ["Paint It Black"], and Dusty Springfield ["You Don't Have to Say You Love Me."])

Reprise A & R executive Jimmy Bowen was responsible for finding "Strangers" for Frank when he heard a melody by German composer Bert Kaempfert and promised that if Kaempfert could write English lyrics, Sinatra would record them. Bobby Darin and Jack Jones had already recorded the song by the time Frank was ready to go into the studio with it. Three days before Jack Jones's version was to hit the streets, Jimmy Bowen telephoned arranger Ernie Freeman to tell him that Sinatra—not Darin—had to have the hit with this one and that he needed to come up with a classic arrangement. Three days later, on a Monday, Bowen and an orchestra were in the studio rehearsing by 5:00 P.M. By eight, Frank was behind the mike. An hour later, the session ended. Twenty-four hours later, the record hit the street, and radio stations were playing it. "You couldn't do that today if you had a million bucks on the line," Frank said in the mid-eighties. And as for Jack Jones's version? Not bad, but an also-ran.

Frank and Nelson Riddle cut the *Strangers in the Night* album in two days. (Is there anyone who was buying record albums in 1966 who doesn't have this one in his or her collection?)

Strangers is interesting in that it demonstrated that Sinatra was capable of doing almost any kind of album effectively. This clearly is a patched-together, hurried effort designed to capitalize on a hit single with songs which have no relation to each other. Yet it is utterly engaging and charming and, after all these years, eminently listenable.

The album was number one on *Billboard*'s charts and stayed there for seventy-three weeks. Frank would go on to win a Grammy for his performance of "Strangers in the Night," and Ernie Freeman won one for his arrangement.

While "Strangers in the Night" was the big hit, the follow-up is the enduring classic. "Summer Wind" (with lyrics by Johnny Mercer) is considered by most music critics and Sinatra aficionados one of Frank's best recordings. His laid-back vocal performance and Riddle's sultry arrangement (with jazz organ) found just the right groove, even if it didn't enjoy the commercial success of "Strangers in the Night." While "Summer Wind" was also recorded by Perry Como and Wayne Newton, it was Frank's rendition that really mattered to most listeners and disc jockeys.

In the summer of 1966, Frank faced another major problem brought about by his legendary temper. On June 5 and 6, Frank filmed a TV special at NBC in Burbank (*A Man and His Music, Part II*). Two days later, on June 8, Frank hosted a party at the Polo Lounge of the Beverly Hills Hotel in honor of Dean Martin's forty-ninth birthday. As usual, the Sinatra partygoers were a rowdy bunch and provided disruptive annoyance to anyone else who happened to be in the lounge that evening. Sitting at a nearby booth was Frederick R. Weisman, the president of Hunt's Foods, and Franklin H. Fox, a businessman from Boston. As raucous laughter and obscenities from the Sinatra party filled the room, Weisman leaned over to Frank and asked him to keep it down. He also mentioned that he felt that some of the remarks made by Frank's friends were offensive. Frank was annoyed by Weisman's intrusion. "Listen, buddy, you're out of line," he warned Weisman.

Angry words were exchanged, and Frank got up and stormed out of the room.

A few moments later, he returned. He and Weisman then became embroiled in a verbal argument, and depending on which version of the story from which eyewitness is to be believed, Frank either decked the man by throwing a telephone at his head (the Polo Lounge has telephones in many of the booths), or the man just fell over the cocktail table and hit his head. Whatever the case, an unconscious Weisman was taken away by ambulance.

This was more nasty business for Frank Sinatra.

For the next couple of days, Weisman remained in critical condition with a skull fracture; his prognosis was not good. The Los Angeles Police Department wanted to question Frank and embarrassed him by telling reporters he was "hiding out." He was actually in Palm Springs, and he telephoned the authorities from there to proclaim his innocence in the matter. When questioned by the authorities, Dean Martin waffled: He said he didn't see a thing.

352

According to those who know him well, Frank was truly desolate about what had occurred at the Polo Lounge. What had really occurred remained shadowy at best. However, Frank knew that he had handled himself in precisely the hotheaded way that he was trying to dispel from his life. He realized that if Weisman died, there would be serious trouble. It seemed to most people, though, that he was more concerned about his own fate than he was about the victim's. "Now I've gone and done it," Frank said, according to one friend. "I really fucked up. If this guy croaks, I'm fucking finished." Mia flew to Palm Springs to be at his side, and for two weeks Frank and a few other friends remained in the desert to wait out Weisman's fate.

When Mia Farrow—all sweet and innocent and understanding—tried to convince Frank that what had happened was "probably" not his fault, the two became embroiled in an argument over her use of the word "probably." Indeed, a problem had been developing between them in recent weeks, and it was graver than the question of his or her choice of words. Mia's saintly ways were beginning to irritate Frank. He was starting to realize—especially after the incident at the Polo Lounge—that he was never going to be as understanding, as reasonable, indeed as *sainted*, as Mia Farrow, and as a result, something terrible had started to occur: When he looked into her eyes, he didn't see in them what he aspired to be; instead, he saw what he was not. He saw his own inadequacies, and he didn't like that. So he began to lash out at her, to treat her badly. And *she* didn't like *that*.

"He was starting to be really mean to her," said Deborah Astair, an actress and friend of Farrow's at the time. "It was as if something had changed between them. Mia was confused, unhappy. The Polo Lounge matter was a defining point in their relationship, and what it defined was not good, not good at all."

Finally, when Frederick Weisman recovered enough to discuss what had happened with the police, he did not remember the incident itself because of partial amnesia. His family wanted to press criminal charges against Frank Sinatra but decided not to bother. There just wasn't enough evidence. The Los Angeles District Attorney's Office closed its investigation of the case on June 30, 1966. Frank celebrated by giving Mia an $85,000, nine-carat engagement ring (on July 4), which he had purchased at Rusar's jewelry store in Beverly Hills. Despite what he must have known was considerable tension between them, he decided to go ahead and marry her. Mia was ecstatic. At a formal dinner party to announce the engagement—hosted by Bill and Edie Goetz—she stood up in front of the guests and said of her upcoming nuptials, "Now I know why I was born."

"They certainly seemed an absolutely devoted couple," said Garson Kanin. "She doted on him, and he certainly loved her."

The next day, on July 5, Frank was off to London to begin filming *The Naked Runner.*

Mia telephoned her mother to tell her the good news, and Maureen O'Sullivan apparently decided to make the best of it, even though her intimates would say that she was worried that her daughter was rushing into marriage. "I couldn't be more delighted," she told the press. "I know they'll be very happy."

The wedding was to be kept a secret. Nancy senior didn't know about it, nor did her children or Mia's mother. The only people who knew were members of the press, who flocked to Las Vegas on July 19. Mia and Frank were wed in Jack Entratter's suite, but not before Frank placed a telephone call to Ava Gardner. It has been previously reported—and is really a part of the so-called Sinatra legend by now—that Frank had his valet George Jacobs call Gardner to break the news to her. While Jacobs may have called, Lucille Wellman, who was a close friend of Gardner's for years, recalls Gardner as having said that Frank also made a call.

"Ava said that she was watching television when the phone rang. It was Frank calling," said Wellman. "He was upset and nervous, she said, and told her that he was marrying Mia Farrow but that he hoped he wasn't making a big mistake. Ava told him to stop and think about what he was doing. He didn't sound like he was sure of his decision, and Ava wanted him to call off the ceremony. 'It's too late, baby.' He told her. 'The judge is standing right there. I gotta do it. The clock is tickin'.' "

Before he hung up, according to Wellman, Frank told Ava, "Tomorrow, when you read about all of this in the papers, remember that no matter how I feel about this young chick, I will always have a place in my heart for you. I still love you. I will always love you."

Ava told Wellman, "I just hung up the telephone, stunned beyond words. And then I cried. I cried for all that might have been. I cried for Frank. I cried for myself. I cried all night long for what might have been between us if we were just . . . different people."

The marriage ceremony, performed by Judge William Compton, lasted four minutes. Bill and Edie Goetz stood up for the couple. Entratter gave Mia away. Red Skelton was also present, even though his wife, Georgia, was in a Los Angeles hospital after "accidentally" shooting herself. (In her memoirs, Mia says that Skelton shot her.)

Mia was dressed simply in a short, sheer white dress with full caftan sleeves. It looked like the kind of informal dress a woman would wear for her second wedding, not her first. Her hair was cut as close to her head as Frank's. Actually—and without exaggeration—she looked like a thirteen-year-old boy in a dress. After a champagne toast with friends, Sinatra gave the press a photo opportunity in the hotel's Japanese garden.

"Still photographers and reporters only," announced a Sinatra aide. Frank wanted no footage taken by television crews because he wanted to break the news to his family before they had an opportunity to see it on television. He never did.

"Maybe you can be a happy man now," George Jacobs told Frank as the newlyweds boarded Frank's private jet, headed back to Palm Springs for their first night together as man and wife.

It was reported that Ava Gardner's comment on the wedding was "Ha! I always knew Frank would end up in bed with a boy."

"Well, that was Ava," observed her friend Lucille Wellman. "She said later that she had never said such a thing, I believe she did. That was her sense of humor. I know, though, that she wished the best for Frank, even though she did think he was making a mistake. She was worried about him. She always said, 'One day, he's just gonna blow himself up,' whatever that meant."

(In fact, Ava and Mia got along well when they were in each other's company. Once, Ava—a bit tipsy—grabbed Mia, embraced her tightly, and whispered urgently into in her ear, "You, my dear, are the child that Frank and I never had.")

Everyone in Frank's family was stunned by the sudden wedding; they heard about it from the press, not from Frank himself.

Twenty-two-year-old Frank junior—who was a year older than Mia—was performing at the KoKo Motel in Cocoa Beach, Florida, when reporter George Carpozi, hopeful of soliciting a comment from him, called him with the news of his father's marriage.

"You must be kidding," he gasped. "I don't believe it. When did it happen?"

After Carpozi explained the details, he asked why Sinatra senior had married so quickly—and quietly.

"I think you got the wrong party, pal," Frank junior said, annoyed. "I think you ought to confine questions like that to Frank Sinatra."

"Is this true love?" Carpozi said, pushing for information.

"How the hell am I supposed to know," Frank junior screamed into the telephone. "You got the wrong person, I told you. Go ask Frank Sinatra."

He was livid at having to find out that way. That night, before singing one of his father's numbers during his performance, he said, "I'm going to devote exactly five minutes to my father because, as he once confided in a moment of weakness, that's exactly how much time he devoted to me." (When Frank senior heard about his son's comment, he became teary-eyed, according to one associate. "He just hurts me over and over again," said Frank. "That's what he does. He hurts.")

Nancy senior, and Frank's two daughters—Nancy and Tina—were inconsolable. Friends said that they had dinner the night after Frank married and just resigned themselves to putting on a happy face for his sake. "After all," Nancy senior reportedly reasoned, "there's not much we can do about this now." To which Nancy junior quipped, "There wasn't much we could do about it—ever."

Frank's daughter Nancy took the news worse than anyone else in the family. She couldn't believe her father would marry someone so young, not only once again replacing her mother in his life but now her as well. When she worked on a movie called *The Wild Angels* (1966), a reporter overheard her saying, "If my father marries that girl, I'll never speak to him again."

She felt a sense of competition with Mia. Even though she and Mia would both write in subsequent books that they got along famously, the truth is that they did not for the first couple of years of Frank and Mia's courtship. After the marriage, they tolerated each other for Frank's sake. They finally would warm up to each other, when it appeared that the marriage was in trouble.

Frank's mother, Dolly, wasn't thrilled by the news, either. Frank telephoned her from New York, where he and Mia spent part of their honeymoon, to tell her.

"Dolly was mostly pissed that Frank called her after the fact," said the daughter of an old friend of Dolly's. "She told him, 'Jesus Christ, you son of a bitch you, *now* you tell me? After you've gone and done it? How could you do this to me, your own fucking mother!' "

Then, according to the friend, Dolly sobbed pitifully—Italian guilt, if you will—as Frank told her how sorry he was for not having told her sooner, how much he loved Mia, and how much she loved him as well. Certainly Dolly felt strongly that the marriage would not last, but she wanted nothing more than for her son finally to be happy. The friend says that Dolly told Frank that night, "No matter what people say, you gotta do what you gotta do. I'm your mother, goddamn it. Of course I'm happy for you."

Before they hung up, she invited her son and his new wife to her home for an Italian feast with all of her friends, his friends, and many Sinatra hangers-on as guests. Dolly Sinatra spent days preparing that meal— fetuccine, linguini, ravioli, scallopini, *scungilli*, meatballs, *braccioli*, anisette, and *cannoli*—the whole Italian works, saying, " 'This is gonna be the party my Frank and his new wife will remember years and years after I'm gone. This is gonna be the one.' My God, the depth of her love for Frank!"

Frank continued work on *The Naked Runner* in London, with Mia at his side on what was considered an extended honeymoon. On weekends they flew to the South of France for relaxation. It was a romantic time for them; an unspoken truce had been called, and there were no arguments at all. They were clearly very much in love, reported visitors to the set. Mia began to enjoy those rare moments when she had Frank to herself, and he started to like the idea of not having his Dago Secret Service as his

Frank as "Maggio," the role in *From Here to Eternity* for which he won an Academy Award. "One of the most dramatic comeback stories in entertainment history," said his daughter Nancy. (Photofest)

(Inset) "Sure, I've met frustration, discouragement, despair, and all those other cats," Sinatra said. "But I knew that sooner or later, something good was bound to happen to me." Here he poses with Walter Brennan and Mercedes McCambridge (*far left and right*) and fellow Academy Award winner Donna Reed, March 25, 1954. (Archive Photos)

Said John F. Kennedy, "Every night, before I go to bed, I pray to God that I don't wake up and read in the newspaper that Frank Sinatra has been arrested again, at least not until after I'm elected." Here Frank converses with President John F. Kennedy, with whom he had a complex relationship. Sinatra liked to consider Kennedy a pal, though the feeling didn't always seem to be mutual. (Paragon Photo Vaults)

Sinatra escorting Jacqueline Kennedy to the inaugural ball in 1961. She wasn't very fond of him and his Rat Pack buddies, and thought they were "uncouth." For this important evening, though, she put on a happy face. (Photofest)

"Go ahead, shoot me," Frank Sinatra Jr. told his kidnapers. "I dare you. *Shoot me!*" Here he is on January 12, 1964, in his first television appearance since his kidnapping, on the *Ed Sullivan Show*. (Paragon Photo Vaults)

Though Rex Reed said of Nancy Sinatra, "No matter what she does to herself with her father's money, she still looks like a pizza waitress," Nancy still proved herself a skilled entertainer and struck gold (in 1966) with "These Boots Are Made for Walking." (Retro-Photo)

Joey Bishop,

"It was such a shock," said Lauren Bacall of being jilted by Frank Sinatra in 1959 (the two are pictured here at Villa Capri restaurant in Hollywood). "I spent night after night in tears. My humiliation was indescribable." (Darlene Hammond)

"Talk about short engagements," Johnny Carson said of Frank's to dancer Juliet Prowse. "Frank's had longer engagements in Las Vegas." The whole thing was just a publicity stunt, even though neither ever admitted as much. (Archive Photos/Darlene Hammond)

"I ain't gonna jeopardize my relationship with the Kennedys for this punk mobster," Sinatra said of Sam Giancana. "Do I look like some kind of moron?" Here Phyllis McGuire poses with her boyfriend Sam Giancana circa 1960. (Paragon Photo Vaults/New York Public Library)

The Rat Pack in 1960, from left to right: Peter Lawford, Sammy Davis Jr., Sinatra, J and Dean Martin. (Archive Photos)

Frank and Joey Bishop onstage at the Sands in 1961, with Elizabeth Taylor and Marilyn Monroe in the audience. Frank and Marilyn were having an affair at this time. "Oh, my God, that Marilyn Monroe is a mess," Liz said that evening, "How she keeps her beauty, I'll never know. Now, me, *I* know how to hold *my* liquor." (AP/Wide World)

"I'll see you in your dreams," Marilyn told Frank a week before she died. Here they are at the Cal-Neva Lodge with Sinatra's friend "Wingie" Grover. Sinatra considered marrying Monroe, just to save her from herself, and might have done so if she hadn't met an untimely death in August 1962. This is the only known photograph of Monroe and Sinatra together. (Don Dondero)

Frank's one night with Jacqueline Onassis in September 1975 was all he would ever have. After Ethel Kennedy clued Jacqueline in on the fact that Sinatra had helped her husband, JFK, procure women back in the sixties, Jacqueline said, "I will never go out with him again. I can't believe how stupid I've been." (Archive Photos)

Frank Sinatra's wedding to Mia Farrow on June 19, 1966. Later, Frank's ex-wife, Ava Gardner, said to Mia, "You, my dear, are the child Frank and I never had." (Archive Photos)

Frank and Barbara Marx on June 2, 1976, about a month before their July wedding. "After Barbara saw the photos of Frank and Jacqueline together, she thought twice about breaking up with him," said Dinah Shore. (Retro-Photo)

On November 14, 1976, Frank received the Scopus Award from the American Friends of Hebrew University of Israel. Here, Frank is with the two women in his life, Dolly and Barbara, at the ceremony. Tragically, Dolly would be killed in a plane crash just months later en route to seeing her son perform in Las Vegas. (Paragon Photo Vaults)

Frank and "the boys" in 1976 at the Westchester Premiere Theater: top row: Paul Castellano, Gregory DePalma, Thomas Marson, Carlo Gambino, Jimmy Fratianno, Salvatore Spatola; bottom row: Joe Gambino, Richard Fusco. Afterward, Frank testified in a Nevada State Gaming Control Board hearing, "I didn't even know their names, let alone their backgrounds." (J. Randy Taraborrelli Collection)

On May 12, 1985, Frank received the Medal of Freedom from President Ronald Reagan. Frank and Nancy Reagan had a long friendship, and while it was reported that their "lunches" had turned intimate, he had actually acted as her "therapist" as she faced old age. (Paragon Photo Vaults)

"May you live to be one hundred," Frank used to say to his audiences, "and the last voice you hear be mine." Frank performed all the way up until February 1995. His songs, and his audiences, never let him down—even if his voice sometimes did. (DMI Photos) only company. She made him laugh; he wasn't lonely anymore. They were in bed, making love, by ten P.M. Frank would sleep through the night, and without downing a bottle of Jack Daniels, which was a departure for a man who had been an insomniac for years. Mia had such a calming effect on him, he wanted to be with her all the time, but he did have a film to make. If anything, it was a distraction.

Director Sidney Furie said of his work with Frank on *The Naked Runner*, a suspense drama in which he portrays an inadvertent assassin, "It was a difficult experience. Frank, I didn't feel, was focused on the film. He seemed to be distracted for some reason. I don't know if it had anything to do with Mia or not, and frankly I didn't want to know. It was none of my business."

At one point, Sinatra refused to continue working, saying that he wanted to go back to Palm Springs and that they should just finish the picture there. "I'm tired and so's Mia," he said. Sidney Furie, exasperated by the temperamental star's continual outbursts, quit the film, only to return shortly thereafter.

"I don't have anything bad to say about Frank Sinatra," he observed years later. "As an actor, he's the consummate professional. He's an extremely sensitive person. You have to put up with this kind of thing from sensitive people. You can't expect them to be sensitive as actors and not overly sensitive as people. I accepted Frank Sinatra, all of him, just to have the honor of being able to say that I worked with him, which I'm proud of."

While the production was in Denmark, Frank took some time off from the film to go to Los Angeles with Mia in order to perform in a benefit for Gov. Edmund "Pat" Brown at the Sports Arena. Brown, a Democrat seeking a third term, was running against former actor Ronald Reagan, who was making his first bid for public office. Everyone who knew Frank understood he felt only disdain for Ronald Reagan. He just didn't like his politics and thought that the only reason he was even a candidate was because no one would give the guy a job as an actor. "He despised Ronnie almost as much as Richard Nixon," Peter Lawford once said. By extension, Frank also had nothing kind to say about Nancy Reagan.

After the Los Angeles benefit, Frank produced another for Brown in San Francisco featuring Dean Martin and Joey Bishop. Frank had campaigned diligently for Brown, raising a great deal of money in the process. Still, in 1966, Reagan won the election.

"Son of a bitch," Frank raged to one former employee. "Can you believe that this asshole is going to be in office? I'm moving out of California, I swear it. Put the house on the market. Tell Mia to start packing."

Of course, Frank didn't move out of California just because Reagan was governor. He and Mia had just bought a home in Bel-Air. (They also added a tennis court, a two-bedroom bungalow, and a four-bedroom guest house to the Palm Springs estate.) After he cooled off, he decided to ignore the Reagans.

One day, Nancy Reagan called the Sinatra household to ask for Frank's participation in a benefit concert. Mia had been speaking to her for about a minute when Frank walked into the room. When he asked who was on the line, she wrote Nancy's name on a piece of paper and handed it to him. Without saying a word, Frank then took the phone from Mia's hand and, while Nancy Reagan was still talking, simply hung it up. Mia just looked at him with innocent saucer eyes.

In November 1966, Frank opened an engagement at the Sands in Las Vegas, his first since his marriage to Mia Farrow. Mia hated Las Vegas and found herself bored whenever she went there with Frank, who was usually off gambling while she and the wives and girlfriends of Frank's other friends watched. "The women, who didn't seem to mind being referred to as 'broads,' sat up straight with their legs crossed and little expectant smiles on their carefully made up faces," she remembered. "They sipped white wine, smoked and eyed the men, and laughed at every joke. A long time would pass before any of the women dared to speak; then, under the mainly male conversation, they talked about their cats or where they bought their clothes, but more than half an ear was always on the men, just in case. As hours passed, the women, neglected in their chairs, drooped—no longer listening, no longer laughing. Often I fell asleep with my head on my arms folded on the table."

On opening night, Frank and Mia had a terrible fight, said Monica Hallstead, a Los Angeles friend of Mia's. "She suspected that Frank was cheating on her. Things were going badly all of a sudden. It happened almost overnight. They had been so happy, then *bam!* this."

When Mia confronted Sinatra with her suspicions, he became angry and kicked in the television screen in the hotel room. Then he threw a chair through a window. Glass flew all about.

Actually, Mia had been perplexed by much of Frank's behavior ever since she got to know him better. For instance, he would often change his underwear at least ten times a day. This unnerved Mia, a woman who was always looking for the underlying psychological reason to everything people did. Analyzing Frank, she said, "He feels unclean, that's why he does that. Deep inside, he feels dirty. But it's not him, it's this dirty business he's in and these dirty friends he has and these dirty woman chasing after him all the time. It's not him."

"I kept thinking, They have it all wrong, they don't really know him," Mia would say of Frank. "They can't see the wounding tenderness that even he can't bear to acknowledge—except when he sings. Maybe if they

358

looked at the earliest photos of Frank, when he was a skinny kid singing in his big bow tie—if they really looked at that face, almost feminine in its beauty, they'd see exactly who it was that Frank Sinatra the tough guy has spent his life trying to protect."

Was Frank having an affair? His friends say that it doesn't seem likely, not at this juncture, anyway.

"He loved Mia," says one, "but what infuriated him about their relationship was that she was just so goddamn nice all of the time, and he was so goddamn mad all the time, it got to be a pain in the ass. At least with Ava, they had their anger in common, and maybe it even helped things. Who knows?"

That night, Frank introduced Mia from the audience. She stood up and received a huge ovation. What happened next is difficult to explain. Frank told the audience, "Yeah, I sure got married. Well, you see I had to. I finally found a broad I could cheat on. . . ."

An uncomfortable silence greeted Frank's "joke." Mia took a deep breath and then stared down at the table when she realized that all eyes were on her. She turned her face so no one would see her tears, but everywhere she turned there were people looking at her, pointing at her, laughing at her. *How could Frank have been so cruel?* she must have asked herself. She told Monica Hallstead later that she had never felt more humiliated.

"Jesus Christ, it was just a joke," Frank reportedly told her in his defense when she confronted him about what had happened. "What's the matter with you, Baby Face? You used to have such a great sense of humor."

"And you used to be such a nice man," Mia shot back, her eyes filling with tears.

"How much longer could Mia be happy with Frank's cluttered way of life, bored by his elderly friends and ill at ease with the uncouth drinking pals," Sheila Graham recalled. Graham remembered that Frank was gambling heavily in the casino at the Sands while Mia waited on the sidelines. Finally, bored, she touched his arm and said, "Let's go."

Frank blew up at her. "Look, don't tell me what to do," he said, raising his voice angrily. "Don't ever tell me what to do. Don't try to change me."

"After the bloom was off the rose, Frank was no longer on his best behavior," said Monica Hallstead. "It was as if he was trying to sabotage the relationship, force Mia out of his life, ruin things between them. Mia was confused. 'I love him,' she told me, 'but I'm starting to not like him very much. He's paranoid. He thinks everyone's out to get him. He's always so upset. Nothing I say matters. He hates me, he hates his fans, he hates the press. . . .' "

CHAPTER 33

On January 12, 1967, Mr. and Mrs. Frank Sinatra (who had been married a year and a half) hosted a sixty-fifth birthday party for Joe E. Lewis at the Eden Roc Hotel in Miami Beach. They seemed tremendously happy; Frank called Mia "my girl." According to Earl Wilson, Mia said she wouldn't be making any films for a while because "I don't wanna leave my fella." A few weeks later, though, Mia announced that she would soon be doing her first film, *A Dandy in Aspic.*

For the next few months, Mia tried to be a dutiful wife. Guests would visit the Palm Springs home, and while she tried to be gracious, basically she was a clumsy and inexperienced hostess. She wanted to frequent the Factory, a discotheque in Hollywood, and dance with young people, not be stuck in Palm Springs ("Graveyard for the Dead-and-Coming," as she put it) serving poorly mixed cocktails to people twice—even three times—her age. Always with Frank in Palm Springs were Bill and Edie Goetz—Louis B. Mayer's oldest daughter and a renowned socialite with an art collection worth more than $50 million; Jack Entratter, president of the Sands Hotel in Las Vegas, and his wife, Corinne. Rosalind Russell and her husband were ever-present, as were Claudette Colbert and Merle Oberon—people who were more the peers of Mia's mother than of Mia.

Mia was intensely interested in metaphysics and in gurus and swamis, all of which Frank thought of as "nuts." Once, a friend from India came to the house barefoot and handed him a flower. "That made him feel square for the first time in his life," Mia said. In fact, the more time they spent together, the less they seemed to have in common. Even their lovemaking, once passionate and exciting, had become routine. Some intimates say that had occurred before they had even married despite Frank's testosterone shots.

In the spring, Mia went to Europe to film *A Dandy in Aspic* with Laurence Harvey. Frank said that she could make one picture a year—if she was a good girl.

In April, Frank was appearing at the Fontainebleau in Miami and filming the movie *Tony Rome* at the same time. It was a tough schedule—in front of cameras by day and audiences at night. Mia and Frank spoke on the telephone three, sometimes four, times a day, and they seemed to be getting along, even though Frank whined about the situation to Sammy Davis, saying, "I need this like I need a hole in the head." Then, when Mia and Harvey posed for a photo session to publicize the film's production, trouble started.

Frank was walking offstage at the Fontainebleau in Miami when one of his goons handed him a newspaper article with one of the photos. The two looked, at least as far as Frank was concerned, just a little too cozy as they danced, her arms wrapped tightly around his neck. When he telephoned Mia in Europe from his dressing room, he was in a Sinatra rage. He didn't believe she was having an affair with Harvey, say his associates. He trusted Harvey; the two had become great friends when they appeared in *The Manchurian Candidate* a few years earlier.* However, Frank was incensed because he felt that her cozying up to him for photographers was disrespectful to him. "I am fucking *Frank Sinatra*," he reportedly told her. "How do you think it looks having my wife posing with that guy? Have some consideration for me, why don't you?"

Mia tried to tell Frank that the photos were taken solely for the purposes of "publicity"—certainly he knew about public-relations machinery—but Frank wasn't buying it. He was enraged. He wasn't thinking straight, and as he often did when irate and illogical, he said some things to her—and called her some appalling names—that he would very much regret. He'd apologize later, sincerely, but it didn't matter to Mia.

Frank was always of the opinion that when a person is angry, he should say everything he feels he needs to say and thereby, as he would put it, "get it all off your chest." He felt that this kind of communication was good for a relationship and that both parties should engage in it. However, Mia was much too sensitive for such candor, which, coming from Frank, would often be hurtful. She would never forget his words of anger. "They leave little scars, his words," she said. Indeed, long after the fight was over and Sinatra had moved on to other battles, Mia would still be smarting from what he had said to her in the heat of the argument.

Still, after she allowed him to scream at her for an hour, she boarded the next airplane out of London for Miami so that she could be with him and reassure herself that everything was all right between them. It wasn't. Although she had traveled halfway across the world to be with him, Sinatra treated her coldly. She returned to London, depressed and anxious about the state of their marriage.

---

* *The Manchurian Candidate* (1962), directed by John Frankenheimer and based on a Richard Condon novel, should not be overlooked. Two American GI's (Sinatra and Laurence Harvey) are captured by the Communists during the Korean War. Brainwashed and then released, they become embroiled in an assassination plot (orchestrated by Angela Lansbury, who plays Harvey's mother). A recent release of the movie on laser disc includes fascinating behind-the-scenes interviews with Frankenheimer and Sinatra.

*   *   *

On April 15, 1967, Nancy and Frank Sinatra had a number-one record with the catchy—albeit innocuous—title "Somethin' Stupid." The song was actually recorded at the end of sessions for the critically hailed album *Francis Albert Sinatra & Antonio Carlos Jobim* (the immensely popular Brazilian vocalist and composer) back in February 1967. "Somethin' Stupid" is the only father-daughter duet to ever go to the top of the charts. Lee Hazlewood found the song for Nancy, and when she played a demonstration tape of it for her father, he felt it would be a perfect duet song. It was coproduced by Frank's producer, Jimmy Bowen, and Nancy's, Hazlewood. The single was completed in just four takes. Some executives at Reprise were concerned that a father and daughter singing a love song to each other would seem odd. One voiced that opinion to Frank, who said, "C'mon. Forget it. The song is gonna be a hit." Mo Ostin, president of Reprise, was one of those who thought the song would bomb. He bet Frank two bucks on its quick demise. Needless to say, he lost the wager.

In May, Frank was selected by the Italian-American Anti-Defamation League to head a campaign organized to discourage prejudice against Italians by television network executives, who'd lately been depicting mobsters on television shows like *The Untouchables* with Italian names and images. A week later, Ralph Salerno, a former police officer and self-proclaimed expert on mob connections, wrote an article in the *New York Times* saying that Sinatra was hardly the type of man that the Anti-Defamation League needed on its side. Then Salerno listed what he believed were Sinatra's Mafia ties. "It was obvious that Mr. Salerno had not done his homework," Nancy Sinatra groused, "since my father had never been indicted for anything."

The year 1967 had not been a good one for Frank Sinatra, and it only got worse in September when he played the Sands (which had recently been purchased by Howard Hughes). Eleanor Roth, who was (President) Jack Entratter's assistant at the Sands, recalled that it was a Thursday morning when the executive vice president in charge of the casino, Carl Cohen, told him that the general manager, Edward Nigro, had decided to cut off Sinatra's credit at the casino. Apparently, according to Eleanor Roth, when Frank won at the tables, he took the chips. But when he lost, he didn't pay his debt. So Frank's credit was withdrawn, but "Jack Entratter didn't have the balls to tell Frank about the situation," Roth recalled.

In contrast to Roth's version, a different story emerges in a memo from Robert Maheu, Howard Hughes's top aide, to his boss, which said: "Carl Cohen stopped his credit after he had obtained thirty-thousand-plus in cash and had lost approximately fifty thousand dollars. Sinatra blew his top and [told me] that he was walking away from the Sands and would not finish his engagement." Maheu also explained to his boss that another reason Sinatra's credit had been cut off was because Frank was "running around the casino stating in a loud voice that you [Hughes] had plenty of money and that there was no reason why you should not share it with him since he had made the Sands the profitable institution it is."

For whatever reason, Frank's credit at the Sands was a thing of the past. He had prided himself on that line of credit. He loved the fact that he could saunter up to one of the tables with a "broad" on his arm and say, "Hey, Charley, shoot me some credit," and always get it. It made him feel like a big shot. In truth, he deserved that unlimited line of credit because, after all, he not only owned stock in the Sands but also had helped build the hotel's reputation by appearing there in successful engagements countless times in recent years. *No one* brought in business not only to that hotel but to the whole city like Frank Sinatra.

On Friday evening, Jack Swigert, Wally Schirra, Tom Stafford, Gene Cernan, Walt Cunningham, and Ron Evans—all Apollo astronauts—came to see Frank's show. Afterward, they joined Sinatra at the baccarat table. Frank asked for credit, as he did every night, and was rejected. He could hardly believe his ears. Says Roth, "He was humiliated in front of his heroes. That's when the shit hit the fan. Frank pulled all the wires out of the switchboard in the phone room and went for a ride in a golf cart with poor Mia."

"Suddenly, without any warning, he turned the golf cart around and pressed the gas pedal down as far as it would go; we were headed straight for the shiny plate-glass window," recalled Mia. "I knew it was pointless to say a word. In the final instant, we swerved and smashed sidelong into the window. I realized we were both unharmed. He was already out of the cart and striding into the casino as I trotted after him, clutching my little beaded evening purse. He threw some chairs in a heap and with his golden lighter he tried to set them on fire. When he couldn't get a fire started, he took my hand, and we walked out of the building."

Frank's actions infuriated Cohen, and the two of them had a showdown in the hotel's Garden Room restaurant the following Monday morning during which Cohen told Frank, "Fuck you."

That did it.

Frank hurled a fistful of chips into Cohen's face. Then he tilted the table and spilled drinks and food on Cohen's lap.

"You son of a bitch," Frank shouted at him.

With those words, Cohen punched Frank right in the jaw. Frank went down, the caps on his two front teeth dislodged.

A scuffle ensued, with Frank accidentally throwing a chair at a security guard—he *meant* to hit Cohen—which required that the guard have stitches.

Frank walked out on the rest of that engagement. It was a bad situation which generated a great deal of negative publicity for him.

That night, he telephoned Mia in Los Angeles to tell her what happened. "His speech was unclear," she recalled, "but I soon made out that there had been a fight; the caps had been punched clear off his teeth, some other guy had been hurt, headlines were sure to follow, and his dentist was on the way with new teeth. It didn't much matter what started the fight; they always had to do with his powerful Sicilian sense of propriety. He sounded bewildered and upset as he said he loved and needed me, and with my whole being I loved and needed him, too."

Later, when Mia asked for details about the incident and wondered how he had let it get so out of hand, he raged at her. "That's none of your damn business," he told her. More and more, Frank would look at Mia and be revolted by what he saw—in himself.

Frank also blamed Sands's boss Jack Entratter, who had been a close friend of Sinatra's for many years. Phyllis McGuire said, "After Carl Cohen punched him out and Frank left the Sands, Sinatra never spoke to Jack again. And Entratter lived next door to him in Palm Springs!"

Later, when Kirk Douglas asked Frank about this embarrassing incident in his life, Frank said with a grin, "Kirk, I learned one thing. Never fight a Jew in the desert."

It would be nearly a year and a half before Frank Sinatra would play Las Vegas again—at Caesars Palace (from November 26 to December 19, 1968).

When Mia Farrow returned from filming in Europe, a defining moment in the Sinatras' relationship occurred when she went out to a Los Angeles nightclub and ended up dancing with one of Frank's enemies.

Mia and Robert Kennedy had danced together at a fashion party at the Factory and were seen there by hundreds of people. When Frank heard about it—Mia told him when she got home—he became enraged.

First of all, Frank had bodyguards watching over her, as they did whenever she went out, which always infuriated Mia. She once told comedienne Judy Carne, "I can't shake these bodyguards long enough to even smoke a joint. They're watching every move I make." Frank was angry that they had allowed his wife to dance with Bobby, who was really responsible for his exclusion from the White House after Jack was elected. Those guards were fired immediately.

Secondly, Mia should have known better, Frank decided.

"What is my fucking wife doing dancing with Robert Kennedy?" he blew up at one of his aides the next day. The aide recalled that Frank was so incensed, "you could see the veins popping out of the sides of his forehead. He thought Mia did it on purpose just to spite him because she knew how much he despised Robert Kennedy. He was embarrassed, and he was hurt."

More than likely Frank Sinatra realized later that he should have stopped for a moment, taken a deep breath, and tried to figure the situation out in his head. But he couldn't do that at the time. He was just too *pissed off.* To understand his rage, one only has to recognize that loyalty means everything to Sinatra. He felt that Mia had to have been well aware of the fact that there was animosity between him and Robert Kennedy. For her to dance with with one of Frank's enemies, knowing all the while that the two would be photographed together, seemed to be an act of defiant disloyalty.

However, Mia's supporters would rise to her defense. How was she to know of the problems between Sinatra and Kennedy? Had he told her about them? Of course not. Had he confided in her about Sam Giancana, Cal-Neva, and Robert Kennedy's investigation of the underworld and how all of it had affected him? Certainly not. Why would he have done such a thing? To Frank, that was all old business and none of it was Mia's.

In truth, Mia's motives for dancing with Kennedy were purely adolescent. "I thought that when he saw that Bobby Kennedy liked dancing with me, maybe he would want me," naive Mia told Judy Carne much later. "I thought he'd be proud to have me. I never dreamed he'd be mad at me."

"Frank and Mia had a terrible, terrible fight about the Kennedy incident," said her Los Angeles friend Monica Hallstead. "He really let her have it. She was extremely upset and sorry she'd ever done it. She just didn't know what she was doing."

In the spring of 1967, Frank had the idea that he and his wife should appear together—much like Richard Burton and Elizabeth Taylor—in a movie called *The Detective,* a cop film based on the bestseller by Roderick Thorp. However, Mia wanted nothing to do with that picture, and she was adamant about it. "I've got to do things on my own," she explained to one reporter. "If I were his leading lady, too many people would think he just handed me the role." In the end, though, she agreed to do the movie, probably just to keep the peace with her husband. It was set to begin filming on October 16, 1967.

In the fall of 1967, however, Mia announced to Frank that she needed to delay work on *The Detective* because she was still in New York and not yet finished with the film she had decided to do first, *Rosemary's Baby,* based on the novel by Ira Levin. Roman Polanski was directing, and Mia was having a wonderful working experience, even though they were four weeks behind schedule. Frank told her to "screw that movie if they're going overtime" and to meet him in New York. (She was in California.) "A deal is a deal," he told her. "You know how I feel about that, Baby Face. *A deal is a deal.* Ankle the fuckin' film."

Of course, Mia refused to walk off the picture. Her father was a director; her mother, an actress. She had better manners than to leave a set in the middle of production unless it was a dire emergency. Moreover, she felt that Frank would ultimately respect her less if she were to do such a thing. Frank couldn't understand any of that; he'd walked off plenty of pictures when they went overtime. He'd just take a stack of pages out of the middle of the script, throw them on the floor in disgust, and tell the director, "There. Now we're on time. And I'm outta here."

When, in 1956, producer-director Stanley Kramer was running behind schedule with *The Pride and the Passion* in Spain, Frank just took off, telling him, "I've had it, buddy boy. I'm jumping out. So sue me."

Now he had lost all patience with Mia and with her film, which he'd said he didn't understand, anyway, because "it sounds like some kinda kinky devil shit to me." He was constantly on the telephone with Mia, berating her. He seemed to devote himself to making each day of her life miserable.

"It was too much for Mia," Sheila Graham remembered. "She was near collapse. On the set she wept constantly. She lost weight. For the scene outside the Time-Life Building in New York, she had to look tired and drawn, and she didn't need makeup. A woman in the crowd, noticing her condition, said loudly, 'Look what Frank Sinatra has done to that poor girl.' "

Frank telephoned the movie's producer, William Castle. "He was very pleasant about it but asked when Mia would be finished with *Rosemary's Baby*. I told him the truth, that we were behind in our schedule. Sinatra said, 'Well, I'm going to call off your picture. [He was saying that he was going to force Mia to leave, thereby shutting down the production.] I said, 'Frank, that's silly.' And Frank said, 'No, that's the way I feel. I've waited long enough.' "

Impatient, Frank began an affair with thirty-two-year-old blond actress Lee Remick, who had replaced Mia in *The Detective*. It didn't mean much to either of them. They were both lonely, and as usual, Sinatra rationalized that the relationship with Remick had nothing to do with his wife. Immediately, Frank did what he often did: He went overboard. He told Lee that his marriage to Mia was in trouble and that if things worked out the way he expected, the two of them [Sinatra and Remick] would "probably be married by this time next year." Remick began to panic. She telephoned friends asking what she should do and in the end decided that her best course of action would be to run, not walk, in the other direction.

"But how do I get out of this?" she asked one friend. "I'm afraid of what he'll do to me." In fact, Lee Remick was so scared to break it off with Sinatra in person that she wrote him a note, taped it to his front door, and then scampered down his driveway like a scared little rabbit. When Frank found it, he told Jilly Rizzo, "If this is how the dame breaks up with a guy, then I don't want her, anyway. She's got no guts." Sinatra called Remick on the telephone and began leaving such a blistering message with her answering service that the operator actually hung up on him in mid-profanity.

At a loss about what to do about Mia, Frank telephoned his aging mother, Dolly, to ask for advice.

Doris Sevanto said, "As I understood it, Frank called her in the middle of the night, as he often did. He was in a very disturbed state, saying that his marriage to Mia was over and that he wanted Dolly to know it before she read it in the papers. He said he didn't know what to do."

"What d'ya mean, you don't know what to do?" she asked, according to her friend. "Doesn't Mia make you happy now? You were so happy with her. What the hell happened?"

"I don't know what happened. I ain't happy anymore."

"Then you gotta do what you gotta do," Dolly reportedly said. "You gotta end it with her, Frank, and go on with your life. Now pull yourself together. Jesus Christ, how old are you? Fifty? Grow up, for chrissake!"

"But I love her, Ma."

"I know you love her. Now divorce her."

After Frank Sinatra talked to his mother, he apparently called Mickey Rudin and told him to file divorce papers. And, as Frank might have said, that was all she wrote where Mia was concerned.

"I didn't believe he would do it," she says today. "I didn't believe it would all lead to divorce."

She got her walking papers from Rudin on the set of *Rosemary's Baby*, the day before Thanksgiving. "The lawyer walked onto the set with his briefcase and put this stack of papers on the table. I said, 'What are those?' They were divorce papers, all written in the first person, with *me* asking for a divorce. I signed everything."

To even the most dispassionate observer, this seems like cruel behavior on Frank's part. He and Mia had never once discussed divorce, and suddenly she was signing the papers. To his friends, it was eerily reminiscent of the way Sinatra had treated Lauren Bacall. Even Mia was amazed when she learned in 1964 that Frank had so mistreated Lauren Bacall. Now he was doing it to her.

"Well, he's tough," Mia said with a smile of resignation twenty-eight years later. "He's pretty tough."

Mia was crushed by Frank's cruelty toward her. She once had so much respect for him that she wanted to emulate him. She now realized that the kind of power, arrogance, and seeming invulnerability Sinatra possessed and which she had longed to find within herself could be destructive if not used properly. Not only could it destroy a relationship; it could destroy a person. Now it was destroying her. "I had nothing I wanted to live for," she would later say. "Nothing. My life was over."

Marjorie Nassatier, an extra on *Rosemary's Baby*, recalls, "That was a dark day. Everyone knew that she had been served. You could hear her wailing in her trailer like a hurt animal. It was a sound I'll never forget."

"The day that Daddy and Mia separated, I was shooting a commercial," Nancy junior would remember. "I'd had a terrible dream the night before. I dreamt that Mia had been shot. The next morning, I tried to get Daddy. I called him at home. But I couldn't get him all day until about five-thirty. He told me what had happened. They had separated. They were just crushed, the two of them."

It looked like Christmas, 1967, was going to be a depressing one. Frank missed Mia. He was brokenhearted without her, he told people. He wasn't sleeping. He was letting himself go, biting everyone's head off, impossible to be around. "It was Ava all over again," said one of his former employees.

On a good day, dealing with Frank Sinatra was a challenge for some of his household staff. But when he was in a funk, the stakes were raised, and he was impossibly demanding. With the Christmas season upon him, he was lonely and unhappy. His daughter Nancy, who had struck up a friendship with Mia, suggested that he call her and invite her to the Palm Springs house for the annual holiday party on December 15, 1967.

When Frank telephoned Mia, she begged him to take her back. Her life would not even be worthwhile, she told him, unless he loved her. Frank was thrown by that sentiment. He had said similar words to Ava on many heart-wrenching occasions. The cycle of pain was repeating itself, and now—this time—he was the victimizer. "It doesn't feel good," he told his daughter Nancy. "For her to need me that much—it makes me feel sick, like I've been there."

Of course, Mia attended the Christmas party. As a gift, she gave her husband an authentic London taxi which she had purchased there while making *A Dandy in Aspic*. Rosalind Russell and her husband, Freddie Brisson, the Garson Kanins, and the Bennett Cerfs all applauded Mia's gift. Frank seemed confused by it, but Mia was oblivious to that.

"I never had such a marvelous time," she said later. "Frank was so relaxed and happy. I have never seen him so happy."

Mia and Frank carried on as if they were a happy couple during the party, so much so that some gossip columnists even reported that they had actually reconciled. They had not. For the next two weeks, Mia stayed with Frank in Palm Springs and even slept in the same bed. They were not intimate, but Mia held out hope that it might happen, especially since not once did they ever discuss Mickey Rudin's visit to the set of *Rosemary's Baby* or the divorce papers she had signed. He took her shopping to exclusive Palm Desert high-fashion boutiques, to lunch at the Ruby Dunes, and to dinner in quiet, candlelit restaurants. If he wasn't interested in her romantically, it certainly seemed to observers that he was leading her on.

After the New Year, 1968, broke, Frank went to Acapulco to visit actress Merle Oberon and her husband—alone. Mia was stunned. She couldn't imagine that he would go without her, not after the lovely time they had just shared.

While Sinatra was gone, Mia started once again spinning romantic fantasies about him. She needed him. She didn't remember *why* she needed him or what those qualities were in him that she had admired and hoped to emulate. So much had happened, and so much of it unpleasant. She just knew that she needed him, and that was all there was to it. She became so worked up, she ended up in Cedars of Lebanon Hospital. Her publicist reported that she underwent an unexpected tonsillectomy. Others whispered of a suicide attempt. Upset about the rumors, Mia summoned a reporter from, of all places, *Photoplay* magazine, a gossipy fan magazine, to her side for "an exclusive interview."

As to whether or not she and Frank had reconciled, Mia said, "Well, I've just come back from spending the holidays with him in Palm Springs. I spent more than two glorious and happy weeks with him. Don't you call *that* a reconciliation?"

How did it happen, the reporter asked, that Mia ended up in Palm Springs?

"I begged him to take me back," Mia answered bluntly, "at least for the holidays. For just another try. He told me that he had invited a lot of people to spend the holidays with him and that if I didn't mind a crowd, he would be happy to have me there. It was a fun crowd; two weeks of fun and games. I never had such a marvelous time. Frank was surrounded by the people he likes best, me included. And he was so relaxed and happy. I have never seen him so happy. Maybe the happiness of those two weeks had a good effect on our marriage. I hope so."

Gaunt and melancholy, Mia checked out of the hospital after a few days and went back to the mansion she and Frank shared in Los Angeles; she waited to see what would happen next. Mickey Rudin, Frank's attorney, knocked on the door the next morning and told her that she would have to leave. "Frank called me from Acapulco and told me that you can stay anywhere you want and he'll pay for it, but you can't be here when he returns. So I'm sorry, but you'll have to leave."

Robotlike, Mia gathered some belongings, put them in a small suitcase, walked out the front door, got into her Thunderbird, and drove to a nearby hotel, sobbing all the way.

Frank called during the second week in January. But it wasn't the call Mia had anticipated. He confessed that he couldn't get her off his mind but decided: "We're history, and we just gotta accept it." He told her she could have as big a financial settlement as she liked. However, Mia didn't want money. She wanted him. "Sorry, Baby Face," he told her melodramatically. "You can't have me. No woman can ever have me."

"Gosh, it was probably doomed from the get-go," Mia now says of their union. "We could only try."

The next day, a distraught Mia Farrow left for India to meditate with a swami.

And Frank Sinatra refused to come out of his bedroom.

Two years earlier, on his television special "*A Man and His Music, Part II,*" Frank Sinatra had said, "When you're sad, there's a song that does your crying for you. When the tension of daily life kinda ties knots in your spirit, why, a song can be your tranquilizer, your quiet pill." A nice sentiment, but not always the case. By the spring of 1968, Frank was so low, no song could raise his spirits. From March 3 to April 6, 1968, Sinatra worked double duty in Florida, filming *Lady in Cement* (the sequel to *Tony Rome*) by day and working at the Fontainebleau by night. It was a stressful schedule and, given the circumstances of his emotional breakup with Mia, more than he could handle. He was difficult on the set and temperamental onstage.

Indeed, nothing was right in his career because as far as Frank could see, nothing was right in his life. How could he have treated Mia that way, he asked friends. "This sweet kid, this lovely, lovely kid, and I just treated her like dirt," he complained to Dean Martin. The guilt and misery ate away at him until finally his body rebelled; he came down with a 104-degree fever and pneumonia.

Someone in Sinatra's camp called Mia Farrow to tell her that he was terribly ill "and he may not make it."

After the separation, Mia tried to move on with her life. She had said during her marriage that she wanted to study transcendental meditation (TM) with the Maharishi Mahesh Yogi; she'd been studying Zen Buddhism for years. Frank wasn't happy about her interest in TM because he thought she was somehow being recruited by the movement to promote it because of her ties to him.

When the Beatles began studying with the maharashi, it lent what many might argue was an unfair air of faddishness to the concept of transcendental meditation. Frank didn't take it seriously or want to be associated with it through his wife. But Mia was searching for something to fill her life and ease her pain. She was tired of feeling bewildered and helpless and determined to do something spiritual about it. Saying, "I want to find happiness at last," she went off to the Himalayas to meet with and study with the marahashi.

When she returned to the States, she was revitalized. She moved out of the Bel-Air house and said that she didn't want anything from Frank; she just wanted to be his friend. She kept the yellow Thunderbird he had purchased for her (he had told her it matched her hair color), the silver place settings, the jewels. But she was practically broke, and now she had eleven dogs and several cats to feed; she kept adopting animals, perhaps in the longing to fill some empty space in her heart.

Then she got a call from Jilly Rizzo telling her that Frank was ill and that she should make plans to be at his side. Suddenly, all of her hard-earned tranquillity went out the window.

She was frantic with worry because she thought Frank was on his deathbed. She kept calling Florida, but no one would put her through to Sinatra because, they explained, they thought the sound of her voice would upset him. She telephoned her mother, who tried to remind her of her uplifting experience with the maharashi. She suggested that she meditate and get through this crisis on her own. "You don't need to find Frank Sinatra," she said. "You need to find yourself."

(It seems that Maureen had become as metaphysical as her daughter. "I'm having regular swami classes every Thursday," she told Earl Wilson. "We have such a wonderful swami on West End Avenue, there is no reason for me to go to India.")

However, Mia apparently decided she would go to Florida.

When she got there, Frank's so-called Dago Secret Service made her miserable. All of Frank's hangers-on blamed Mia for the boss's condition, and so they wouldn't let her near him. They told her he was near death and couldn't see anyone, scaring the hell out of her. They also told her that the divorce was to blame. "And it's all your fault," they said.

Shaking with anxiety because of the horrible things she had done to Sinatra, she lit a joint with quivering hands and took a deep, *deep* hit, according to one witness. This was unusual behavior because Mia never smoked pot around anyone connected to her husband. Finally, one of Frank's top men felt sorry for her and pulled her aside to tell her that it wasn't as bad as she was being led to believe and that she should just go home. Appearing to be ravaged, with a frozen look in her eyes, Mia got on the next plane back to Los Angeles.

As soon as she was gone, someone in Frank's camp telephoned Ava Gardner to tell her that poor Frank was losing his battle with pneumonia. She'd better come to Florida immediately or she might never see him again, she was told. Reluctantly, considering all of Frank's previous machinations, she arrived the next day. It was as if the Master himself was orchestrating all of these attention-getting schemes.

One of Ava's business associates confided: "She walked right into Frank's room, took one look at him, and said, 'Jesus Christ, you're not dying, are you? Here we fucking go again. What the hell is *really* wrong with you? You got a cold or what? What am I doing here, anyway? Do you know what I had to go through to get here?' And on and on and on. She was furious.

"She thought he was faking again, that Mia was out of his life and now he was trying to make Ava feel sorry for poor little him. He got pissed at her reaction. He really was sick; he just wasn't on his deathbed. He started coughing and hacking, and he said, 'I'm sick, lady. This ain't like Lake Tahoe. Fuck you, anyway. Scram. Who the hell called you?' "

Ava left the next morning.

Then Nancy junior showed up. "He was sad. He was hurting," she has recalled. "But he expressed his concern for Mia. 'It will be harder for Mia to mend because of her age. When you get to be my age, you build a wall around yourself. You don't hurt as much as you used to.' "

Then someone else called Frank's parents, Dolly and Marty, and they arrived less than a week later.

"All I need is for Nancy senior to arrive and all the people close to me will have checked in," Frank said. Indeed, he was getting the attention he apparently needed. In about a week he was fine. "Everyone needs a little loving when they feel bad about themselves," Dolly later explained. "He's a little boy. He feels lonely." Indeed, it would seem to be true that a mother's love knows no bounds.

Sinatra's close friends Edie Goetz and her husband, Bill, entertained Sinatra often during this period to elevate his spirits. The Goetzes' butler, James Wright (who worked for them from 1967 to 1971 and would go on to work for Frank Sinatra in the late 1980s), remembered the night Sinatra dined at the Goetzes' home with Elizabeth Taylor and Richard Burton:

"Miss Taylor sat next to Bill Goetz, Mr. Burton sat next to Mrs. Goetz, and Sinatra was at the head of the table. Dinner was served, and of course Elizabeth was served first as the guest of honor. Then I'd go to Mrs. Goetz, the hostess, then Mr. Sinatra, then Mr. Burton and Mr. Goetz. When I went to serve Mr. Sinatra and Mr. Burton, I couldn't believe how nervous they both were in Miss Taylor's presence. They were a wreck, just a wreck. They were so upset, they could barely eat. Maybe, I thought, Sinatra had a brief fling with Elizabeth somewhere along the way and *that's* what this was about. I'd never seen two men more uncomfortable in each other's presence. Elizabeth was calm, cool, and collected, loving every minute of it and looking fabulous. The next morning, Mrs. Goetz said, 'Wasn't that tense last night? What do you think that was all about?' I said, 'I have no idea, ma'am.' "

Frank and Mia's divorce was finalized on August 19, 1968, in Juarez, Mexico. They had been married for thirteen months.

"I don't seem to be able to please him anymore," Mia told the court in her brief appearance. (Of course, Frank didn't show up.) Her maiden name was restored. She didn't take a dime from Sinatra, contrary to reports that she had agreed upon a $1 million settlement. As for the rumors that she had charged Frank with mental cruelty, she had her press people issue a statement: "Mia says firmly that no cruelty was involved." Frank got word of the divorce while he was taping a television special.

"My father hurt like hell," Nancy Sinatra has remembered. "Just like everybody else."

By the time of the divorce, *Rosemary's Baby* was released. It was a success, and Mia Farrow was a star in her own right. It didn't mean much to her, though. Not without her Charlie.*

CHAPTER 34

The mid-to-late sixties were a time of violence and discord that would not end with the decade. The Vietnam protests pitted young against old and rich against poor as men who could afford college were given deferments to avoid serving in the military. Racial tension fueled the fires of discontent. Watts had burned in 1965, followed two years later by riots in Newark and Detroit. Martin Luther King Jr., a man as resented by some whites as he was beloved by most blacks, was a new leader of the civil-rights movement.

As the 1960s came to a close, some of the more colorful personalities in Frank Sinatra's life began to vanish, starting with his longtime gangster friend Sam Giancana. The close relationship Frank enjoyed with Sam had been irreparably damaged after the Cal-Neva incident. For the loss of his prized gaming license, Frank Sinatra adamantly blamed Sam Giancana for having even been at Cal-Neva when, by law, he shouldn't have been. For his part, Giancana had decided that Sinatra was a "blowhard" who had handled officials that had been looking into the matter in the most irresponsible way possible, which was quite an assessment given its source. Sam was certainly not a man known for diplomacy in his own line of work.

* Frank and Mia remained friends, and Sinatra often assisted her in her career, even when she may not have known it. For instance, his longtime valet Bill Stapely insisted that Frank convinced producers to give Mia a major role (Daisy) in the film *The Great Gatsby*. Stapely said, "Frank told me, 'Mia wanted to do it without my help, but I decided to do it my way.' "

After the Kennedy assassination, there were rumblings among some of the younger up-and-coming hoods out of Chicago that Sam Giancana was, as they would have put it, "full of hot air." What were all those threats about, really? None of them seemed to amount to anything, especially the promise that he was going to bring down the Kennedys by sacrificing Marilyn Monroe at their throne.

"Some people were beginning to question Giancana's credibility," observed his friend Tommy DiBella. " 'What kind of mobster was this old guy, anyway?' That's what they were asking. It sounds comical, but it's true. 'Couldn't even manage a good plot to bring down the Kennedys.' He still handled day-to-day activities of the Chicago underworld, but some guys were thinking his time was over."

In May 1965 the Justice Department began further inquiries into underworld activities in Chicago. Though Giancana was granted immunity, he refused to testify before a grand jury assembled to investigate certain individuals. As a result, he was sentenced to a year in Cook County jail, a turn of events that simply amazed Frank Sinatra. He couldn't fathom that Sam Giancana was behind bars. He said, "Just when you think you've seen it all, you see Sam Giancana in the fuckin' slammer." (Giancana would remain in jail until Memorial Day, 1966.)

Because Sinatra never attempted to contact Giancana when he was incarcerated, Giancana's jail time spelled an end to their already unstable relationship. In fact, when he was released, Sam wanted nothing to do with Frank. He called Sinatra "old news," and that apathetic feeling seemed to be mutual. After his release, Sam Giancana went to Mexico amid whisperings that the Chicago "boys" had put him out to pasture, exiled him in order to get him out of the way so that a younger set of thugs could take over. However, his brother Chuck says that Sam had big business dealings in Mexico—"Billions to be made in Asia, Europe, the Middle East"—and that Sam planned to run the Chicago business from below the border. Whatever the case, Sam Giancana was quickly becoming a footnote in Frank Sinatra's history. The distance his move to Mexico created was put to good use by Sinatra, who told Joey Bishop, "I don't know. Maybe this is what I need to get this whole fucking gangster thing out of my system. What the hell was all *that* about, anyway?"

On the evening of June 5, 1968, Sen. Robert Kennedy was assassinated in Los Angeles at the Ambassador Hotel, where he was celebrating the South Dakota and California primary victories. He died the next day.

Frank Sinatra had always had mixed feelings about Bobby Kennedy, a man who had caused a significant amount of annoyance for him. The government surveillance of Sam Giancana, which was instigated by Kennedy, had become directed at Sinatra as well. Also, Frank never forgave Bobby for interfering with his brother Jack's plans to stay at the Sinatra estate in Palm Springs back in 1962. (It often took Frank years to forgive his closest friends. His enemies were seldom granted absolution.) It must have been difficult, though, for Sinatra to feel only disdain for Kennedy; after all, he had come through for Frank during the kidnapping of Frank junior. He was one of the first to call after the incident was reported, and he promised the FBI's full attention, or as much of it as could be given considering the recent JFK murder. Still, because so much convoluted history had occurred since that time, particularly between the Kennedys and Frank's friend and sometimes lover Marilyn Monroe, Frank must have found it difficult to be clear about his emotions after Bobby's death.

Prior to Bobby Kennedy's tragic death, Sinatra had already decided that he would rather support Vice President Hubert Humphrey for president. Even though Humphrey had excellent liberal credentials, most liberals turned their backs on him because he was part of an administration that had sent troops to Vietnam. Sinatra had always been a staunch Democrat, and it would be easy to say that the older he got, the more conservative he became. In some respects, that's true. But not only were Sinatra's politics as complex as the times, they were also fueled by his personal feelings. For instance, he felt that Robert Kennedy was not ready for the presidency and had said so publicly. But surely that opinion was influenced as much by Kennedy's politics as it was by the fact that Sinatra considered him an enemy.

Sinatra liked Humphrey personally and felt that he would eventually end the war in Vietnam if he were elected. The reason he had not spoken out against Vietnam, Sinatra reasoned, was because he didn't want to embarrass President Lyndon Johnson. Indeed, the war was not really a conservative-versus-liberal issue; both liberals and conservatives eventually came to oppose it. But because of Humphrey's affiliation with Johnson, most liberals were against him as well, including Sinatra's friends, such as Sammy Davis, Shirley MacLaine, Sammy Cahn, and other pals who had been in full support of Kennedy. Frank was really the only major star to support Hubert Humphrey.

In May 1968, Sinatra flew to Washington to attend a party for Humphrey hosted by columnist Drew Pearson in Georgetown. Frank was with his friend Allen Dorfman, a known associate of Jimmy Hoffa's. Afterward, Frank had dinner with Mrs. Jimmy Hoffa and Teamster vice president Harold Gibbons. While they all may have been friends, this was precisely the kind of poor judgment call that caused trouble for Sinatra with the media. A reporter from the *Washington Post* had already begun asking questions about the relationship among Dorfman, Sinatra, and Humphrey and whether it had to do with the possibility of Humphrey's pardoning Hoffa in exchange for Sinatra's endorsement.

Hubert Humphrey sneaked Sinatra into the White House one evening through a back entrance during this particular visit to Washington. Sinatra and Lyndon Johnson really had no interest in knowing each other, however. While Sinatra didn't like Johnson's politics, Johnson felt that Sinatra was probably the thug he'd always been rumored to be. As far as Sinatra was concerned, the sooner LBJ was out of office, the better.

In July and August 1968, Sinatra would embark on a stumping concert tour for Humphrey that would take him to Cleveland, Baltimore, Minneapolis, Detroit, and Philadelphia. At this same time, *Wall Street Journal* reporter Nicholas Gage wrote a scathing "expose" of Sinatra that attempted once again to link him to the Mafia—"and not just two-bit hoods, either, [but] the Mafia's elite"—using FBI contacts and certain documents from the bureau as evidence. As could be expected, Sinatra was enraged by the article. It was so inflammatory, in fact, that certain aides to Hubert Humphrey suggested that he had better not align himself with the singer. This was exactly what had happened in the early sixties, when Robert Kennedy had encouraged his brother to distance himself from Sinatra.

It got worse.

Washington lawyer Joseph L. Nellis, who had been on the Kefauver Committee and had interrogated Frank in 1951 about his Mafia connections, shot off a letter to Humphrey warning him of Sinatra's mobster ties. "It's true you need support from every segment of the population," he wrote, "but surely you would agree that you don't need support from the underworld, and Frank Sinatra is unquestionably connected with the underworld." In response to it and to similar missives from concerned politicians, Humphrey said he would not disavow Sinatra completely; however, he would proceed with caution.

Then Martin McNamara, former Assistant U.S. Attorney in Washington, contacted Henry Peterson, head of the Justice Department's organized-crime division, and charged that Sinatra was indebted to Sam Giancana, Paul [Skinny] D' Amato, and other mobsters "for having picked him out of the entertainment doldrums a few years back." Although there is no evidence to support such an allegation, Humphrey grew more concerned. He may have wondered what he had gotten himself into by associating himself in the public consciousness with the likes of Sinatra.

Suddenly, history was repeating itself. A set of occurrences similar to those that had taken place between Sinatra and Jack Kennedy were now materializing again: Humphrey would no longer take Sinatra's telephone calls, nor would he respond to his letters. Frank was on the outside, and he didn't like it one bit. In fact, the word in Washington was that he was poison to Humphrey, and maybe even to anyone else in the political arena. Sinatra finally did get through to Hubert Humphrey on the telephone and screamed at him, calling him "every name in the book," as one of his associates put it, "getting it all out of his system." He didn't know, however, that Humphrey had him on a speaker phone. Every politician and aide present in the room heard the tirade, after which Humphrey just hung up on Sinatra.

After that, Sinatra kept stumping for Hubert Humphrey, even though it seemed clear to most of those close to Humphrey that he didn't really want his help. It was as if Sinatra were saying, "Screw you, pal. I'm supporting you because I believe in you. And I'll get votes for you. Maybe this country is more important than the way you feel about me."

Sammy Davis said, "I know that Frank worked hard for Humphrey, giving him tips about public relations, makeup for TV, anything he could think of to assist Humphrey in his bid for office, voter-registration drives, advertisements in newspapers which he paid for out of his own pocket, the whole bit. He tabled the fact that Humphrey was a jerk to him. Good for Frank."

In the end, despite Frank's best efforts, Hubert Humphrey lost the presidential election in November. However, it was a close race; in fact, the closest in American history: Richard Nixon won by only 223,000 votes, 43 percent of the vote, beating Humphrey and the third-party (the American Party) candidate, segregationist George Wallace. Sinatra was dismayed by the loss and began to wonder if perhaps the pundits were correct and he was a political kiss of death. So did many others. In fact, comedic satirist Mort Sahl joked, "Once you get Sinatra on your side in politics, you're out of business."

At the end of 1968, Frank recorded the *Cycles* album (in November) with Don Costa arranging. "Cycles," with its melancholy, world-weary lyrics, is one of Sinatra's best autobiographical songs. It tells of an aging man's recognition that life is cyclical and that, as they say, bad things happen to good people ("So I'm down and so I'm out / and so are many others . . .") but that hope remains constant in all situations. It's one of his finest moments on vinyl, and his performance of this song on the television special *Francis Albert Sinatra Does His Thing*, while sitting casually on a stool, wearing a tux and smoking a cigarette, is unforgettable. ("Nobody would really explain to me exactly what my thing is supposed to be," he said in his monologue. "But it can't be all bad, baby, 'cause they're lettin' me do it on television.") The rest of *Cycles* is less momentous: Sinatra's renditions of contemporary songs such as "Little Green Apples," "Gentle on My Mind," and "By the Time I Get to Phoenix." Sinatra was never at his best when tackling songs from sixties-era writers and composers. He was already considered passé by much of that generation's youth, and his personalized interpretations of popular songs of the day sounded, for the most part, creaky and somewhat "square." He was best when he did songs that really meant something to him, like "Cycles."

Perhaps one of the more embarrassing moments of his television career occurred on November 25, 1968, when the sixties pop/R & B group the Fifth Dimension appeared as guests on the previously mentioned *Francis Albert Sinatra Does His Thing* special. The group wore outlandish, glittering outfits, typical of the era, and Frank joined them wearing the same kind of getup for a duet on their hit "Sweet Blindness." It was awful, not just the garish turquoise-and-silver costumes but the performance as well. The lyrics to this particular Laura Nyro song, about drinking "moonshine" and hoping Mom doesn't find out about it, clearly meant nothing to Sinatra.*

Again, whenever Sinatra tried to "fit in" and be "hep" in the "hip" sixties, disaster resulted, and he seemed to know it. "Don't look now, Francis Albert," he said after that number, "but your generation gap is showing." He acquitted himself beautifully with a stellar version of "Nice 'n Easy," surrounded by a lush orchestra, but he could have done without the Nehru jacket and love beads.

Ironically enough, in retrospect it's Sinatra's music that has stood the true test of time, not that of the sixties to which he couldn't quite adjust. Though still highly regarded, much of the music of the era doesn't hold up lyrically or musically.

Frank ended 1968 by recording what is probably his best-known song, "My Way," on December 30. The song was actually a French composition, with lyrics by Gilles Thibaut and music by Claude François Ravaux, originally entitled *"Comme d'Habitude"* (As Usual). Paul Anka, a former teen heartthrob and pop vocalist who had matured into a creditable songwriter, penned the English lyrics. In essence, the song tells of a man who, at the end of his life, looks back over it all and brags that he lived it the way he saw fit, regardless of who was affected by his actions. It's easy to be cynical about such a self-involved, self-righteous theme, but this actually *was* how Sinatra had conducted his life up to this point and how he would continue to do so.

Paul Anka recalled: "RCA Victor, the label I was with at the time, was quite perturbed that I didn't keep the song. But my assessment was 'Hey, I'm in my twenties. Here's a guy that's in his fifties who's got a lot more experience, and that's casting to the song the way an actor does to a play. Frank Sinatra was the right guy to do it. He did more for that song than I ever could have done."

Frank never liked "My Way." In fact, the first time he heard it, he said it was "kooky." "I loathe that song," he once observed. "I loathe it. A Paul Anka pop hit which became kind of a national anthem."

* "I remember that when we did that with Frank, we planned to do it twice, once for rehearsal and once for the actual taping," Florence LaRue of the Fifth Dimension recalled. "But at the rehearsal take, Frank said, 'That's it. That's good enough.' And we were outta there."

Indeed, "My Way" went on to become a *Sinatra* anthem. While the record would go on to become a hit for him when released in 1969, it never cracked the Top Ten, peaking at number 27. (In the United Kingdom, however, it was a huge success, on the charts for 122 weeks.) What was originally considered a pleasant and interesting record became legendary. One reason is that it was introduced by a legend, and as the years progressed, Sinatra continually found new values in the song.

The year 1969 sounded a sad note for Frank Sinatra when his father, Martin, who had retired after twenty-four years of service with the Fire Department, became critically ill with an aortic aneurysm. Marty's chronic asthma had developed into emphysema over the years, which made his prognosis all the more grave. Frank decided to send his father to Dr. Michael DeBakey, a celebrated cardiologist who had pioneered artificial-heart research and whom Sinatra greatly admired. In fact, over the years, Sinatra had paid hundreds of thousands of dollars for certain friends of his to have heart operations, performed by DeBakey at Methodist Hospital in Houston. Frank flew his parents to Houston to meet with the doctor on January 19 and then stayed there with his father in the hospital for the last five days of his life.

"To lose your father on an operating table or in an accident, that must be wrenching enough," Nancy Sinatra wrote in her book about her father. "But to be at his side, holding his hand, hearing him gasp for air . . . to watch him die. I cannot imagine the magnitude of that grief or the torture for both men . . . but they went through it together."

Frank was desolated by the loss of his father. Even though he and Marty had often had a contentious relationship, he loved him dearly. They had become close, particularly in the last ten years, as Frank, in his forties, began to appreciate Marty's quiet wisdom and serene approach to life.

The funeral mass was held at Fort Lee's Madonna Church; the burial, at Jersey City's Holy Name Cemetery. Celebrities swarmed the grounds. Sammy Davis wore a gaudy Nehru jacket and a fur coat, and the townsfolk caused a huge traffic jam to catch a look at the hearse and procession of twenty-five limousines as it made its way from the church to the cemetery. "Frank was pissed at his ma," said Joey D'Orazio, his childhood friend. "She had told too many people too many things about the details of the funeral, made too many announcements, and so the scene was madness. There were cops and firemen everywhere, and it was a circus, something I know Frank would never have wanted."

Dolly, distraught and always one with a flair for the dramatic—which is probably where her son got his—attempted to throw herself onto the casket at the cemetery as she sobbed, "Oh, no. Oh, no. Oh, no. It can't be true." Frank and Jilly held her back. Frank pleaded with the priest, Father Robert Perrella, to "hurry it up with the prayers" as his mother screamed out, "Marty, Marty, please don't leave me." The priest raced through the service as quickly as he could while everyone—strangers and friends alike—wailed, sobbed, and moaned loudly, all led by the widow's understandable outpouring of deeply felt emotion.

"It was a funeral like you've never seen before," said Diane Phipps, a fan who observed the Sinatras at the grave site. "It was like a movie, it was so dramatic. You could tell that Frank had had it up to *here* with his mother. There were bodyguards everywhere with walkie-talkies, and people were taking pictures, and there were television cameras and people running around with microphones, and Dolly was sort of the center of attention. She was like the star of the whole thing. I'm sure she was genuinely grieving, but my, the show she put on. Frank and two other guys had to practically drag her away from the grave site into a limousine."

Afterward, Frank felt strongly that Dolly should move to the West Coast so that he could care for her. She was adamantly against the idea, however. Her life was in New Jersey, she said, and she didn't want to change that now. She needed her close friends, especially after the death of her husband.

The son of a friend of hers from Fort Lee said, "My mother and Dolly spent a lot of time talking the pros and cons of moving to Los Angeles, and I understand that she was against it at first. But there was also a feeling that her life was really over in Fort Lee. She and Marty never had the kind of relationship where they *needed* each other, but without him there, she knew it would never be the same. I've read that she really did not want to move to the West Coast, but I don't believe that was the case after too long. She was the type of woman who was always moving, always growing. She wanted a new life, and Frank gave her that opportunity. He built her a huge [five-bedroom] house right next to his estate and staffed it with maids and butlers and servants to wait on her day and night. She must have loved that."*

At this same time, 1969, Frank's friend Bill Goetz died. Goetz had been one of the founders of 20th Century–Fox and was married to Louis B. Mayer's daughter, socialite Edie Goetz. The couple had been friendly with Sinatra for years; they stood up for Frank and Mia at their wedding, were very wealthy, and were said to have the best art collection in town. Frank began dating Edie, an attractive woman in her fifties who at the time looked a bit like Shirley MacLaine. Writer Dominck Dunne, who knew the Goetzes, has said of Edie, "She was always referred to as Hollywood royalty."

---

* In January 1971, the Martin Anthony Sinatra Medical Education Center was dedicated in Palm Springs. Frank had personally raised the funds for the medical building and dedicated it to his father.

"Oh, my, she was an elegant lady," remembered her butler, James Wright. "She and Frank got along well; she had such a crush on him. She would always primp and want to look her best whenever he came by. If she had a diamond tiara, she would have worn it. She would practically have palpitations at the thought of him. It was obvious how they felt about one another. He called her every single day."

One evening, while they were relaxing in Goetz's Holmby Hills home, Frank asked Edie how she would feel about the prospect of marriage. Perhaps she did not think he was serious, because her response was flippant and even hurtful. "Why, Frank," she said, aghast. "I could *never* marry you. You're nothing but a hoodlum." She laughed merrily, but Frank apparently did not appreciate her sense of humor, for their relationship cooled somewhat after that evening.

"He faded out," said Wright. "Never bothered about her again, as if she had suddenly dropped out of his world. Considering how many years they had been dear, dear friends, it was strange. She was very perplexed. After her death, when I went to work for Sinatra, I would often hear him talk badly about her, saying terrible, unfair things. He held a grudge, I suppose."

The year 1969 also saw the recording of two of Sinatra's lesser-known albums, *A Man Alone* (lyrics by Rod McKuen) and *Watertown* (lyrics by Bob Gaudio). To some fans, both albums seemed to be a mismatch of artist and material and added little luster to their catalogs of Sinatra material. To them, it was as if Sinatra were searching for a more youthful, contemporary sound but had failed. The attempts seemed incongruous with who he really was—a fifty-four-year old man regarded as one of the great talents of the time. However, both *A Man Alone* and *Watertown* won glowing reviews from the most highly regarded critics, who found them to be boldly original projects from a man who had long before established his artistic credentials and didn't have to exhibit daring anymore. As music literature, the albums far exceeded what the public was getting at the time.

Sinatra hated getting old. He hadn't paid much attention to the fact that he was aging until the end of the sixties, which is when he realized that his life was changing. Sexually, he wasn't as proficient as he had been, and a steady decrease in his sex drive, abated only briefly by the passion he had felt for Mia, concerned him greatly. He despised the toupees he felt forced to wear to cover his baldness. He had gotten a hair transplant; however, it didn't "take." He was gaining weight and blamed rich Italian foods for that, but dieting was out of the question. Clearly, he wasn't as desirable to most of the opposite sex as he had once been, and this, he said, was something he never thought would happen to him. Also, he was tired more often, as most people are as they age. He could no longer drink booze all night and then be able to function the next day, as he had done for years. His voice was weakening; years of smoking un-filtered Camel cigarettes had done great damage to it. Long ago, he had been diagnosed as a manic-depressive, but these days the episodes of depression were deeper; the highs, few and far between. When there were rumors—which were untrue—that he was being treated for cancer, he said, "I think I liked it better when they were saying I was a gangster. Now they're saying I'm dying."

Of late, another problem had surfaced: His right hand, the one in which he held the microphone, was bothering him. He thought, at first, it was arthritis, but it turned out to be Dupuytren's contracture, a shorten-ing of muscle tissue in the hand. "It hurts like hell," Frank complained. As a result of this problem, his hand was becoming twisted; eventually, he would have surgery (in 1970). This kind of physical ailment only served to remind him that "old age sucks. I don't want to get old," echoing the sentiments of probably most people in the world, even older people. "Maybe I should just retire. Maybe my time is up."

That he seemed to be facing his mortality not only as a man but as an entertainer was difficult for Frank to accept. He was used to feeling strong and invincible. In a sense, getting older was, for him, like dying slowly. He would be found staring at his reflection in the mirror, and when asked about it, he would say, "I'm watching myself get old, and I can't believe what I see." In truth, Sinatra still had many good years left. There would one day come a time when he would wish he was fifty some-thing again.

No matter his physical or emotional travails, however, Frank Sinatra still enjoyed performing. He loved to hear the roar of the crowd when-ever he opened his mouth in song; the thrill of a standing ovation still excited him. That kind of approval meant a great deal to him, especially as he became older. To know that he still had "it," whatever "it" was, mattered to him, as it always had.

CHAPTER 35

On February 17, 1970, fifty-four-year-old Frank Sinatra found himself doing what he most despised: answering questions under oath. The New Jersey State Commission on Investigation had served him with a subpoena, expecting him to answer questions about his connections to the underworld. He received the subpoena, explained his attorney, Mickey Rudin, "while on a boat that stopped in New Jersey. This seemed to be the lark of an investigator who had a subpoena with him, filled it out on the spot, added Sinatra's name and served him with it."

Incensed, Frank complained, "I'm tired of being considered an authority on organized crime." He then filed a lawsuit in federal court in hopes of not having to testify before the committee. However, his statements in the suit seemed rather unbelievable and did little to boost his level of credibility. "I do not have any knowledge of the extent to which organized crime functions in the state of New Jersey," he claimed, "or whether there is such a thing as 'organized crime.'" When Sinatra's suit was dismissed, he appealed to the U.S. Supreme Court. His appeal was rejected by a vote of 4–3. Still, Sinatra refused to testify until, finally, the commission threatened to jail him for contempt.

Sinatra's attorneys agreed to allow him to be questioned in a secret session in Trenton at midnight on February 17. The hope was that the veil of secrecy would prevent the media from reporting the event and turning it into a major news circus. Frank answered questions for a little more than an hour and repeatedly denied any association with any member of the underworld. In fact, he testified under oath that it had never been brought to his attention that Sam Giancana, one of his closest friends, had ever been connected to either the Cosa Nostra, the Mafia, or the so-called underworld. He added that he also was not familiar with Lucky Luciano's reputation as a member of the Cosa Nostra or the Mafia, and he also denied any knowledge of the backgrounds or professions of a number of other known mobsters. Finally:

Q: Do you know anyone who's a member of the mob?
A: No, sir.
Q: Do you know anyone who's a member of any organization that would come under the category of organized crime?
A: No, sir.

One can only speculate as to why Frank Sinatra was hedging during the inquiry. It would not take a rocket scientist to figure out that he certainly did know that Sam Giancana was a Mafia figure. Perhaps his attorneys had warned him that to admit as much would only serve to open the door to further inquiry and that a flat no would end the questioning.

Nevertheless, this kind of unbelievable testimony from Sinatra only served to provide more evidence, if any was needed, to bolster the cynic's opinion that Sinatra himself was a mobster. Otherwise, his detractors asked, why was he protecting a bunch of thugs? Were people to believe that Frank Sinatra, this worldly, tough, bad-boy Rat Packer, was completely naive about the fact that the "underworld" existed in New Jersey? Moreover, every person in America who cared to know realized that Sam

Giancana was a renowned underworld figure. Was the public expected to believe that Sinatra hadn't heard about that? His testimony was so completely preposterous, it did nothing to enhance Sinatra's image and everything to further damage it.

"For many years, every time some Italian names are involved in any inquiry, I get a subpoena," Sinatra angrily said afterward. "I appear. I am asked questions about scores of persons unknown to me based on rumors and events which have never happened. Then I am subjected to the type of publicity I do not desire and do not seek."

Unfortunately, the older he got, the more things stayed the same for Frank Sinatra. He simply did not *get* it. He acted as if he were not a public figure, as if he could safely keep company with unsavory characters and then apparently lie about all of it under oath. It was as if he were either incredibly stubborn or so insulated from the world of public opinion that he simply didn't understand or want to face the consequences of his actions. Arrogantly, he felt he could do anything he wanted to do simply because he was Frank Sinatra and that if members of the media questioned him about those actions, then they were once again persecuting him.

It could be argued that there is a way to behave as a celebrity if you don't want people to think you're a mobster: Don't socialize with them at all, and if you do, don't lie about it.

On July 9, 1970, Frank Sinatra, an avowed Democrat, made a surprise announcement. Much to the amazement of many observers, he decided to support Republican Ronald Reagan in his bid for a second term as governor of California (even though he would remain a registered Democrat). Ronald Reagan had begun his political career by becoming governor of California in 1966, campaigning for law and order. Liberal-minded Sinatra never liked Reagan, always thought he was stuffy and unimaginative. Because he had always been a liberal, his support of the more conservative Reagan seemed astonishing to most observers. However, Frank may have had an ulterior motive in that Reagan's opponent was Jesse Unruh, former speaker of the California Assembly, who had been a protégé of Bobby Kennedy's. It was thought by some pundits that Sinatra's support of Reagan was really his way of settling the score with Kennedy by getting "even" with his disciple, Unruh.

"I support the man, not the party anymore," Frank explained. "I'm not voting for a man just because he's a Democrat. If people don't like that, screw 'em." It would seem, though, that Sinatra was serious about his new policy of not voting for any specific party because his allegiances were all over the political map in 1970: He was also supporting Democrat Edmund "Jerry" Brown Jr. for secretary of state of California, and he made it clear that he would support Nixon's opponent in the next presidential election. He put his support behind Republican John Lindsay for mayor of New York and donated thousands of dollars to Republican Nelson Rockefeller's campaign for his second bid for governor of New York.

"I got a little cold about my team [the Democratic party] there for a while; it wasn't pleasing me," Sinatra explained to Larry King (in May 1988). "And I began to move around a little bit, and it's a wonderful thing to be able to do, switch from one party to another. We have the right to do that."

Most perplexing, however, to many Sinatra followers was the singer's sudden friendship with, and allegiance to, Vice President Spiro T. Agnew. Politicians didn't come more conservative than Agnew in 1970, and Sinatra's relationship with him made him appear, at least from a public-relations standpoint, about as "square" as Agnew, who was vehemently against student protesters, antiwar demonstrators, and "those damn hippies."

"It's the amorality," Frank said when asked why he felt this country was in trouble. "And so much restlessness. I guess we just got used to a way of life in my age bracket. Take the protestations, called for or uncalled for. I'm not against protestations if they're for a cause. But I don't like rebellion without a cause." This from a former Rat Packer who lived his life on the edge of revolt just for the hell of it? It would seem that Sinatra—not unlike a lot of his older fans—was perhaps losing touch with the free-spirited values of his youth. It happens to most people when they get older; they "just don't understand these damn kids." It's just that no one ever thought it would happen to Sinatra. Also, the faint air around Agnew of something not being quite right morally seemed to escape Sinatra.

"There was instant chemistry—personally and politically—between Sinatra and Agnew," recalled Peter Malatesta, an assistant of Agnew's who also happened to be a nephew of Bob Hope's, "and because of that we started spending a lot more time with Frank in Palm Springs. He treated the vice president like royalty, even named the guest house he had built for JFK after him and filled 'Agnew House' with specially monogrammed matches and stationery."

In September 1970 a problem in Las Vegas erupted that would cause Sinatra further damage in the media. On September 6, one of Sinatra's employees cashed in $7,500 worth of chips so that his boss could play blackjack. It caught the attention of an undercover IRS agent who at the time happened to be investigating the entertainment industry's relationship with the underworld. As had always been the case at every hotel Sinatra played, he had IOUs on record with the casino for large amounts of money that he had lost at the tables. These amounts were rarely deducted from his salary or ever paid back by his winnings. It was an unspoken courtesy. The hotel actually gave him money to gamble with and rarely got any of it back. Frank thought this little perk was fair business; after all, he would argue, he brought millions of dollars into the hotel and casino during his sold-out engagements. The more people who came to see him perform, the more who gambled in the casinos. In the end, everyone made more money as a result of his appearance, he would argue, so why not extend him the courtesy of $10,000 here and $10,000 there?

An argument over this very issue was what had caused the huge rift between Sinatra and the Sands Hotel, as a result of which his credit was cut off—which was why he was now playing Caesars Palace.

Apparently, a discussion between Frank Sinatra and the casino manager, Sanford Waterman, about Sinatra's IOUs became ugly when, according to reports, Sinatra called Waterman a "kike" and Waterman retaliated by calling him a "guinea." Waterman then pulled out a gun and pointed it at Frank's head.

"I hope you like that gun," Frank said calmly, "because you may have to eat it."

In a moment, Jilly Rizzo lunged at Waterman and wrestled the weapon away from him.

Frank then shook his head in amazement, laughed in Waterman's face, and said he'd never work at Caesars Palace again. He turned and walked away, trying to remain composed, though he would later admit to being very upset.

The press coverage that followed this particular melee did further damage to Sinatra's image during a year when it had already been blemished considerably. District Attorney George Franklin told the media that he wished to interrogate Frank because, in a parting shot to Waterman, Sinatra supposedly said, "The mob will take care of you." (The notion that Frank Sinatra would ever make such a threat to a casino owner in Las Vegas is absurd.) He said he wanted to ask Frank "about who owned the nightclubs where he sang, the early days, who started him on his way, and his friendships with the underworld."

This D.A. was clearly a man who, like a lot of people, had heard a great many titillating stories about Frank Sinatra over the years and was now trying to bring to the forefront once again the tired, old rumors about how the Tommy Dorsey contract was settled and how Sinatra got the role in *From Here to Eternity*. He also claimed that Waterman "still had finger marks on his throat where Sinatra grabbed him."

Frank had no choice but to offer some kind of public explanation. "There was no such argument about credit or for how much I was going to play," he said. "As a matter of fact, I just sat down at the blackjack table and hadn't even placed a bet, since the dealer was shuffling the cards. At that point, Waterman came over and said to the dealer, 'Don't deal to this man.' I got up and said. 'Put *your* name on the marquee and

I'll come to see what kind of business *you* do,' and I walked away. As for his injuries, I never touched him. And as for the remarks attributed to me relative to the mob, they're strictly out of a comic strip."

Frank also said he was finished with Las Vegas and that he would never go back. "I've suffered enough indignities."*

Today the Sinatra family's version of the conflict with Waterman is a bit vague: According to their account, Frank got the impression that someone in the Sinatra camp—they have not said who—was not being treated fairly in the casino. He went to Sandy Waterman's office, and harsh words were exchanged there. (Press reports—and Sinatra's original explanation—indicate that the altercation took place in front of witnesses at the blackjack table, not in Waterman's office. It would be understandable that the Sinatra family would want to alter that particular detail so as not to have it appear that Frank Sinatra would ever have allowed matters to get so out of hand in a public place. Later, Sinatra would go back to the original—true—story that the incident happened in front of strangers.) Waterman then pulled out the gun.

During the year when the New Jersey State Commission on Investigation had questioned Sinatra on his dealings with the underworld, to which he gave cagey, disingenuous answers, it really didn't matter what his story was regarding what had happened in Las Vegas at Caesars Palace. Much of the public firmly believed he had instigated the fight. This amounted to more bad public relations for Sinatra. It was one matter for young Frank to play the dangerous rebel in the forties, fifties, and even the sixties—picking fights with the press, ending up in the "pokey" for punching out a writer, becoming embroiled in fisticuffs at the Polo Lounge in Beverly Hills that put a man in a coma. Young, temperamental men often do those kinds of things, it can be argued; in fact, it sometimes enhances their public image if they're in show business and actually wish to appear defiant. However, for a mature man like Sinatra to find himself in that kind of situation was bad image making. If anything, it only served to make Frank Sinatra look like a defensive, cranky old guy with a bad temper who couldn't stay out of trouble.

He continued to be temperamental as the year went on. At the Fontainebleau in Miami Beach, he became enraged when an employee gave him a hot dog with ketchup on it. Since he doesn't like ketchup, he threw the hot dog at the employee and then for some inexplicable reason began heaving furniture out the window of his eighteenth-floor penthouse.

* After this fracas, Nancy Sinatra had her manager cancel a new and lucrative seven-year contract he had been negotiating for her with Caesars. Unfortunately, Frank was back at Caesars within a year, but Nancy, who was just trying to be loyal to her dad, had made her choice, and she was out. She could not get reinstated until many years later; she did not ask for help from her father in that regard and was not offered it.

People sunning below at the pool scattered as the tumbling furniture hit the deck and smashed into pieces. Afterward, Sinatra called the hotel's owner and demanded replacement furniture, which arrived within hours. Then Sinatra ordered a tray of expensive watches, ranging in price from a thousand dollars to five thousand, and offered them to the loyal and quick-thinking bodyguards who had alerted the guests at the pool to "watch out!"

One of his bodyguards at that time, 240-pound Andy "Banjo" Celantano, said, "Frank can be so kind he'll bring tears to your eyes and so mean you don't want to go near him. He can be the meanest guy in the world.

"The wildest I ever saw him was one night in a Miami club. Wherever Frank goes, he likes to sit in a high-backed chair, and there wasn't one at the table. Furious, he picked up chairs and threw them across the floor and demanded a high-back one. The manager ran up, and they started the wildest cursing at one another you ever heard. Frank went for the guy. Well, we knew the people we were dealing with were dangerous as hell and Frank could have gotten hurt bad. I managed to stop him and got him out, but all the time he was yelling at me, 'Stay away from me!' "

The irony, of course, is that while Frank Sinatra was aging on the outside, *inside* he was still the young, obstinate rebel with the same egotistical temperament and danger-seeking disposition he'd always had. That others now saw him differently— Well, as Sinatra would say, that was *their* problem, not his.

Or as he put it in an interview at around this time in his life, "If a guy hurts you and you got the feeling that you wanna hurt him back, you hurt him back. But if he helps you, you do the same."

CHAPTER 36

By March 1971, Frank Sinatra was fifty-five years old. The last couple of years had not been easy either personally or professionally. There had been a dreadful, critically-assailed movie—his fifty-fifth film—*Dirty Dingus Magee*, with George Kennedy and Lois Nettleton, a comedy-western in which he portrayed a swindling miscreant. There had also been a mediocre, poor-selling album, *Sinatra & Company,* side one of which was wonderful (it teamed him again with Rio-born Antonio Carlos Jobim, composer of many bossa-nova numbers, such as "The Girl From

Ipanema" and "One Note Samba"); side two was not up to par. (It showcased Sinatra doing his version of contemporary songs by John Denver and Peter, Paul and Mary—never a good idea.)

The problem with Sinatra doing contemporary material such as John Denver's "Leaving on a Jet Plane" and the Carpenters' "Close to You" was that, as an artist, he far outranged the music. So he was always plumbing for depths of meaning and opportunity for interpretation that just were not there. It wasn't that the composers and lyricists and songs were substandard; it was that the standards for songwriting had changed. Clarity was "in," while deep and complex meaning based on eternal truths of life was "out."

Over the years, the media had been tough on Frank Sinatra—in his view, anyway—and after forty years, he was tired of defending himself against persistent rumors of his association with mobsters. In addition, because he was performing around the world most of the year, he was worn out by his touring schedule. He didn't feel well, he told confidants. "I'm exhausted from the inside out," he said. "Will somebody please get me the hell off the road?"

His father's death had a profound effect on Frank in that it forced him to confront his own mortality and also to ponder his future. How much more time did he have? Was he happy? Had he ever really been anything more than—as he put it—not *un*happy?

He was lonesome; he had never gone so long without a meaningful romance. However, his glory days seemed to be behind him, at least where passion was concerned: Nancy and Ava and Marilyn and Mia and all the rest. Despite press reports that still tantalizingly linked him with an array of luscious celebrities, the truth was that he no longer even felt sexual. Those days seemed to be over. He missed them, longed for them, even.

When he looked back at his life now, he told certain confidants, he felt nothing but discontent. Had he done the one thing he promised himself he would never do? Had he, in fact, finally settled? For being a superstar? In fact, he was a phenomenal success, a well-known celebrity, a respected artist. At this stage of his life, he most certainly should have been proud of his achievements, not bored by them. But show business wasn't the same, anyway. Entertainers like Sinatra, Dean Martin, Sammy Davis, and Joey Bishop were considered squares by the money-spending youth of America. Las Vegas was their last bastion of complete, unconditional audience approval, and Frank had recently seen to it that he wouldn't be appearing there again, at least not in the near future. "He says it's the end of an era, and he's right," his daughter Nancy noted. "His kind of show-business era has ended."

By 1971, Frank Sinatra felt unwanted. Always dramatic at heart, he did what he thought would cause the biggest sensation around him. In March he announced that he was retiring from show business. As a result, he made the cover of *Life*, with the headline "Sinatra Says Good-by and Amen."

It now seems a wrong emphasis would be made if any biographer of Sinatra devoted much attention to his "retirement" concert on June 13, 1971, at the Los Angeles Music Center, considering that he would be back onstage at a fund-raiser for the Italian Civil Right League five months later. However, his "final" concert, a benefit for the Motion Picture and Television Relief Fund, raised $800,000. Many of his political and show-business friends came to see the last show, including Vice President and Mrs. Agnew, Governor and Mrs. Reagan, presidential adviser Henry Kissinger, Cary Grant, Jack Benny, Don Rickles, and Rosalind Russell, who introduced him to the audience.

"This assignment is not a happy one for me," Russell said. "Our friend has made a decision. His decision is not one we particularly like, because we like him. He's worked long and hard for us for thirty years with his head and his voice, and especially his heart."

His first wife, Nancy, was present at the fund-raiser, as were his children, Nancy, Frank junior, and Tina. Sinatra's performances of "All or Nothing at All," "I've Got You Under My Skin," "I'll Never Smile Again," "My Way," and "That's Life" provided a well-rounded program of songs that spanned thirty years of timelessly enjoyable music and inspired four rousing standing ovations. In the article for *Life*, Tommy Thompson wrote: "He had built his career, he said softly, on saloon songs. He would end quietly on such a song. He slipped from his words into 'Angel Eyes,' surely a song for the short hours. He ordered the stage dressed in darkness, a pin spot picking out his profile in silhouette. He lit a cigarette in mid-sentence and its smoke enveloped him. He came to the last line, 'Excuse me while I . . . disappear.' And he was gone. It was the single most stunning moment I have ever witnessed on stage."

So much media attention accompanied Sinatra's "retirement" that if he had any doubts about his appeal to the American public, they must have been dashed.

On November 25, 1971. Frank Sinatra played host for three days to Spiro Agnew and his family over Thanksgiving weekend. Sinatra and Agnew had forged a close friendship; in fact, Sinatra was determined to see Agnew president in 1976, and so when Nixon threatened to take him off the ticket in 1972, it was a letter-writing campaign orchestrated by Sinatra that kept him in the race. (The campaign had been financed by private contributions.)

Sinatra was a Nixon-Agnew man because of the former's stand on admitting China to the United Nations, a position that Frank agreed with and about which he had been vocal. Though he had been extremely critical of Nixon in the past, Sinatra would now become his strongest supporter, contributing $50,000 to his campaign for reelection in 1972.

"I don't happen to think you can kick eight hundred million Chinese under the rug and simply pretend they don't exist, because they do," he said. "If the UN is to be truly representative, then it must accept all the nations of the world. If it doesn't, then what the hell have you got? Not democracy—and certainly not world government."

Many of Frank's friends were angry with him for supporting Nixon and the Republican Party. One of the most outraged of Sinatra's inner circle was Mrs. Mickey Rudin, his attorney's wife, who wrote him a letter berating him for his choice, thereby putting the job of her husband—a longtime Sinatra loyalist—in jeopardy. Sinatra never spoke to her again.

Frank's outspoken daughter Tina was also upset about her father's support of Richard Nixon. "I hit the roof," she recalled. She had been diligently campaigning for George McGovern, and she and her father had a row about Nixon.

"It was the one time I was genuinely angry with my father," she recalled. "Here I was in the middle of everything [the campaign], totally involved, and this hit me. It was midnight. I hung up the phone and went down to Palm Springs. I was deeply hurt."

In the end, though, Sinatra would not be swayed, especially by one of his children.

For his part, Richard Nixon seemed fascinated by Sinatra. He appreciated the support and seemed amused by him whenever they were together.

Former Secret Service agent Marty Venker, who worked for Nixon, said, "One night the Nixons dined out in New York with Frank. As they were walking out of the restaurant, a teenage boy took their picture. Sinatra flew into a rage," Venker remembered. "He said to me, 'Take his camera.' I ignored him until he said, 'Look, you either take the kid out or *I'll* take the kid out.' I said, 'Listen, Frank. Just get in the car and settle down.' He shut up after that.

"In the car, Nixon said to me, 'That Frank's got a hell of a temper, doesn't he?' "

On July 18, 1972, Frank gave a concert for Vice President Agnew at Baltimore's Lyric Theater. That night, a U.S. marshal attempted to serve him with a subpoena to appear before the House Select Committee on Crime, which had been investigating the influence of organized crime on sports and horse racing. "It's always something," Frank groused, "always some goddamn investigation, and I'm in the middle of it." Democratic senator John Tunney intervened and prevented the embarrassment to Sinatra of being served in public.

The committee wanted to ask Sinatra questions about a $55,000 investment in Berkshire Downs in Hancock, Massachusetts, ten years earlier. Frank said he would answer any questions "by invitation, not demand." In addition to Sinatra, other investors in Berkshire Downs were, unfortunately, New England Mafia boss Raymond Patriarca and New York mobster Tommy Lucchese. However, there was no evidence of wrongdoing on his part, and Sinatra returned the investment profits when he learned the identity of his partners. He also handed over a file to the FBI that completely detailed his involvement in Berkshire Downs.

Sinatra's testimony before the committee on July 18, 1972, in Washington got off to a bad start when Sinatra, more irate than he usually was at these kinds of inquisitions, took exception to a published allegation by syndicate enforcer Joseph "the Baron" Barboza that Sinatra had provided a business front for Raymond Patriarca. When the article in question, which carried the headline "Witness Links Sinatra With Reputed Mafia Figure" was displayed by committee attorney Joseph Phillips during Sinatra's hearing, Sinatra was infuriated. "That's charming, isn't it," he said derisively. "That's charming. . . . This bum went running off at the mouth, and I resent it. I won't have it. I am not a second-class citizen," he said bitterly. "Let's get that straightened out."

The rest of the hearing was more of the same: direct questions from the committee about Sinatra's mobster friends that elicited evasive answers from him. He said under oath he had met Tommy Lucchese a few times during his performances at Skinny D'Amato's 500 Club in Atlantic City. However, when asked if he knew that Lucchese was a gangster, Sinatra snapped, "That's *his* problem. Not mine. Let's dispense with that kind of question."

In the end, when Raymond Patriarca, serving ten years for conspiracy to murder in the Atlanta Federal Penitentiary, was questioned by the committee and testified that he had never even met Frank Sinatra ("I seen him on television and at the moving pictures"), it was clear that Sinatra was the triumphant figure in the proceedings. Incensed about what the committee had put him through, however, Sinatra and New York journalist Pete Hamill collaborated on an op-ed piece that was published in the *New York Times* on July 24, 1972. "Over the years, I have acquired a certain fame and celebrity," the letter stated, "and that is one reason why so much gossip and speculation goes on about me. It happens to a lot of stars. But it is complicated in my case because my name ends in a vowel. There is a form of bigotry abroad in this land which allows otherwise decent people, including many liberals, to believe the most scurrilous tales if they are connected to an Italian-American name."

In November 1972 the Republican Party was victorious in forty-nine states; Nixon and Agnew were back in the White House.

By the end of 1972, Frank had become romantically involved with Eva Gabor, whom he had taken to Washington in May at the invitation of the

Republican Party. "Frank was crazy about her," said Jilly Rizzo's friend Jim Whiting. "She was a real pistol, would stand up to him, not let him get away with anything. Something strange went down between them. I don't know what it was, but she wasn't around long, at least not romantically."

The problem that arose between Sinatra and Gabor had to do with an incident that occurred when the two were having sexual relations, which for some reason didn't happen until they'd been dating for about six months. According to a source close to the Gabor family, Eva was not prepared for a man of Frank's size. When they had relations, she was injured and required medical attention. The next morning, she went to a hospital for treatment. After that, she was no longer interested in dating Frank Sinatra.

Eva's sister, Zsa Zsa, also had an unpleasant experience with Sinatra, back in the late fifties, after he and Ava Gardner were separated. According to Zsa Zsa, when she was invited to the Brentwood home of a friend for a cocktail party, Sinatra was her escort. Afterward, Frank and Zsa Zsa went to dinner at LaRue's on the Sunset Strip. When Sinatra took Gabor home, she says he refused to leave until she submitted to him. Apparently, he meant business, because he wouldn't go when she refused. Finally, according to Zsa Zsa, rather than have her young daughter wake up the next morning and see Sinatra's gold Cadillac in the driveway and think the worst of her mother, "I made love to Frank Sinatra so that he would leave, and from then on I hated him. And Frank knew it."

During 1972, Frank Sinatra also dated actresses Lois Nettleton, Hope Lange, and Victoria Principal, but none of those dalliances led to anything serious. Principal has said, "It was a happy time, his mellow period, after he'd retired and before he went back to show business. We were very discreet. Few people even knew about our relationship. But I will treasure the memory of those happy months we had together."

Jim Whiting said, "Jilly told me that Frank had slept with all three of them dames—Lois, Hope, and Victoria—but that none of them meant anything to him. One of them—and I ain't gonna say which—wanted to be tied up during the act. And Frank said, 'I'm too fuckin' old for this shit. I used to do that when I was a kid. Now, hell no, I ain't tying up no broads.' When she pulled a rope out of her purse, Frank took it and threw it out the window. Then he said, 'What you want is out there, baby. Go on and find it,' and he kicked her out of the house. He told Jilly, 'Dames today, they don't got no class, man. It ain't like it used to be.' "

At this time, Frank also began dating the gorgeous and blond Barbara Marx, who was married to Zeppo Marx of the Marx Brothers. The former Barbara Jane Blakeley was born in Bosworth, Missouri, on October 16, 1930. When she was ten, her parents moved to Wichita, Kansas, where they struggled through the Great Depression. Tall and thin, she was able to find work modeling for department stores and auto shows after she graduated from high school and moved to Long Beach, California, with her parents and sister. She won several local beauty contests before marrying Robert Harrison Oliver, described in press accounts as both "an executive with the Miss Universe pageant" and "a singer."

An enterprising young woman, at the age of twenty-one she opened a beauty school—the Barbara Blakeley School of Modeling and Charm—had a child [Bobby], and then divorced. After her marriage ended, she went to Las Vegas, where she became a showgirl at the Riviera Hotel, fulfilling a "secret yearning." She has said that she considered herself "one of the worst dancers in the history of Las Vegas." When Zeppo Marx wanted to meet the "beautiful blonde who was always just slightly out of step," they became attracted to one another and began their relationship.

Though Barbara was ambitious, her long-range goals were more of a personal nature than professional. She intended to marry someone wealthy enough to provide for her and her son. So that Zeppo wouldn't think she was interested only in his money, she would borrow furs and jewels (from California designer Mr. Blackwell, creator of the World's Ten Worst Dressed Women list) to give the impression that she was well off. "No one knew better than Barbara the power of illusion in catching and keeping a man," said Mr. Blackwell of the woman who was his lead model in 1959. "Barbara bluntly stated that she was absolutely determined to marry a man of means. Zeppo Marx was her target; she'd succeed in landing the comic or die trying. Since she had no intention of dying, Zeppo didn't know what hit him."

And of her skills as a model, Blackwell noted, "Barbara was a quick learner and quickly drank up the meticulous details all major models are required to master: the proper way to turn, to coo, to seduce, and still remain aloof. Her brilliant smile, sexy saunter, and golden-girl aura catapulted her into the latest flavor of the week."

Zeppo and Barbara were married in 1959; he was twenty-nine years her senior. Although he was living off a trust fund, there was not much ready cash. That did not prevent Barbara from shopping, charge cards in hand. Zeppo did look after her son, Bobby, who took his last name. Barbara's marriage enabled her to become a member of the Palm Springs Racquet Club and the Tamarisk Country Club, which was close to Marx's house and to Frank Sinatra's. Suddenly, she had money, position, and entrée, golfing with celebrities like Dinah Shore, who became one of her closest friends. In fact, her tennis skills were so good that she was often invited to Frank's to play with Spiro Agnew when he was Sinatra's guest.

"I had a sneaky suspicion I would hear little from her after her marriage," said Mr. Blackwell, "and I was right. She certainly didn't need to borrow jewelry anymore."

"I'd always been a fan of [Frank's] singing," Barbara said in 1988. "I'd always had all of his records. But I really didn't care about knowing him because of the press I'd read. It just wasn't a pretty picture."

Eventually, Frank and Barbara started an affair, though she was not yet divorced from her husband, Zeppo Marx. "I think anyone who met Frank Sinatra would have to have sparks," she once said in trying to explain the attraction to him while married to another man. "Because he *is* a flirt. That's just part of his makeup. And there's no way to avoid that flirtation. No *way*."

"I can't talk about Barbara's relationship with Frank," Dinah Shore said in an interview eighteen months before her death in February 1994. "I would never betray her by telling any secrets. However, I have always felt she was a good person, a strong, determined person who would do anything she could to give her son a good life. I believe she was married to Zeppo for ten years [it was actually thirteen] before she and Frank started dating. Her marriage to Zeppo was over by that time, really.

"She was perfect for Frank. He didn't want a woman in show business, and she wasn't. She's the type of woman who would do anything to support her husband's interests. That's what I've always admired about her. She's what I call a 'team player.' "

Perhaps part of Sinatra's hesitation where Barbara was concerned stemmed from the fact that his mother, Dolly, despised Barbara and did not make a secret of her disdain. The Sinatras' maid, Celia Pickell, confided: "Dolly would say horrible things to Barbara. She would say real loud, 'I don't want no whore coming into this family.' Then Barbara would go running out in tears. But there was nothing Frank could do about it. He'd say, 'Ah, Ma.' But that was it."

By all accounts, while they were dating, Barbara Marx was a genuinely cheerful, beautifully dressed, remarkably even-tempered lady. Whatever Frank wanted to do, she was ready for it. She would sit ringside at every one of his performances. She put up with his constant entourage.

Barbara Marx sued for divorce on December 27, 1972, ending a thirteen-year marriage, shortly before she accompanied Frank Sinatra to the Nixon presidential inaugural.

"In the beginning, if I recall, Frank didn't want to get married," said Dinah Shore. "He was so hurt by what had happened with Mia, Ava, and Nancy, he wasn't sure that he ever wanted to do that again. Barbara called me one day and said, 'I think I'm wasting my time with this guy. He sees no future for us. If it were up to him, we'd be dating for the next fifty years.' I told her that if she wanted to get married, perhaps she should set her sights on someone else, because I didn't think Frank was the man for her. Frank was sometimes coarse and hard; she was soft and easy. I didn't think it could work."

CHAPTER 37

Barbara Marx, Frank Sinatra's new belle, would get a taste of life with the so-called Chairman of the Board on January 19, 1973, when the two of them attended a party hosted by Louise Gore, the Republican National Committeewoman from Maryland, at the Fairfax Hotel in Washington. Maxine Cheshire, society columnist for the *Washington Post*, had been critical of the Sinatra-Agnew relationship in the past. A few months earlier, she had confronted Sinatra at an Agnew state dinner in Washington and asked point-blank, "Mr. Sinatra, do you think your alleged association with the Mafia will prove to be the same embarrassment to Vice President Agnew that it was to the Kennedy administration?"

Sinatra tried to act unfazed. "No," he said. "I don't worry about things like that." He was seething inside and would not forget her insolence.

Now, as he and Barbara were entering the Fairfax Hotel, the same reporter confronted him with more questions. Words were exchanged between Cheshire, Sinatra, and Marx, culminating in a tirade from Frank during which he raged at the wide-eyed reporter, "You're nothing but a two-dollar cunt. C-U-N-T. You know what that means, don't you? You've been laying down for two dollars all your life." Then Sinatra pulled a couple of bucks from his pocket and jammed them into the plastic cup Cheshire was holding.

Shock waves from Frank's outburst reverberated for weeks; news reports about the incident astonished even his most devoted fans. Nixon and Agnew were both angry with the singer for what he had said to Cheshire. "If he had attacked me as a reporter, I would have taken it," Cheshire noted. "But he attacked me as a woman."

Before a nightclub appearance soon after that incident, Frank's friend Peter Pitchess, former sheriff of Los Angeles County, took him to task for what he had said to Cheshire. He told Frank that he should have demonstrated more class and that he should apologize for his actions. Frank thought it over for a moment and agreed. "You're right," he said. "I *should* apologize." That night, he went onstage, and during a break between songs, he said, "Ladies and gentleman, I have an apology to make." Sinatra making an apology? The room fell silent. "I called Maxine Cheshire a two-dollar whore," he said. "I was wrong and I apologize." Then, after a beat, he added, "She's really just a one-dollar whore."

One would think that Barbara Marx, who didn't know Frank well yet, though she was probably learning about him quickly, would have gone running in another direction rather than want to pursue a relationship with him after what happened at the Fairfax. However, this was not the case. In fact, she was proud of what he'd done. "He should have socked her in the nose," Barbara said later. "I thought he was wonderful for the way he put her down. Henry Kissinger called the next day and said, 'Frank, you overpaid her.' "

Eileen Faith was a friend of Barbara Marx's at this time. The two met when she was married to Zeppo; Faith lived in Los Angeles. "Barbara was a lot like Frank in the sense that she would never hesitate telling someone what she thought. She always believed that people should stick up for themselves, which would cause her years and years of problems with Frank's children. She could be sweet as pie, but when pushed, she would turn on you with such anger that you'd be scared for your safety. She told me that Cheshire had been goading her, trying to embarrass her, asking questions about her relationship with Frank and inquiring, 'You *are* still married, aren't you?' Barbara was happy that Frank came to her defense. Actually, I think that the Cheshire incident actually brought them closer together; I really do."

In April 1973, Sinatra performed at a White House dinner for Giulio Andreotti, prime minister of Italy. It was a wide-ranging, heartfelt concert during which he sang ten songs, including "You Make Me Feel So Young," "Moonlight in Vermont," "I Have Dreamed," and "The House I Live In." What kind of retirement was this? After that wonderful show, Nixon went up to Sinatra and said, "What are you retired for? You really should sing." Frank had to agree.

Most observers began to feel that he announced his "retirement" to garner publicity and to gauge whether the public still cared about him. Clearly, a great many people did.

"When I was a kid in New Jersey," Sinatra said during that concert for the prime minister, "I thought it would be a great boot if I could get a glimpse of the mayor of Hoboken in a parade. Tonight I'm honored and privileged to be here. Today, after the rehearsal, I looked at the paintings of President and Mrs. Washington, and I thought about the modest, marvelous dignity of the presidency up through the years to now and our president. It makes me very proud of our country. Thank you, Mr. President, for inviting me."

Nixon responded, "Once in a while there is a moment when there is magic in the room—when a great performer, singer, and entertainer is able to capture us all. Frank Sinatra did that tonight."

397

"Lovely words, sir," Frank said. "See you very soon." He had tears in his eyes as the applause rang out.

On May 5, 1973, Sinatra became involved in a conflict with an insurance agent from Salt Lake City, Frank J. Weinstock, who would later sue the entertainer for $2.5 million, charging assault and battery. Weinstock claimed that Sinatra had ordered Jilly Rizzo and Jerry "the Crusher" Arvenitas to beat him in the men's room of the Trinidad Hotel's cocktail lounge. (In the subsequent trial, it was learned that "the Crusher" was using the alias Arvenitas. His real name is Armaniera.) Of course, Sinatra and Weinstock had completely different versions of what had occurred by the time the suit went to trial in September 1974.

Weinstock testified that when he was confronted by Frank and his "bodyguards," Rizzo and Armaniera, in the men's room, an argument ensued, after which Frank snapped his fingers and said, "Get him, boys." Then Weinstock was badly beaten by Sinatra's goons. Frank testified, not in court but in two sworn depositions, that Weinstock had tried to provoke a fight by using ethnic slurs. Frank said he put his finger on Weinstock's chest and said, "Call me Mr. Sinatra or Frank. Don't call me anything else." And then he walked out. In other words, if Weinstock got beat up after Frank left, he knew nothing about it and was not responsible for it.

"I have never in my life purposely provoked anybody into any fight with me," Sinatra said, "never, for the single reason that in my kind of life, I just could not win. Even if you win, you lose."

Armaniera testified that he broke up a fight between Weinstock and Rizzo after Sinatra left, and Rizzo testified that he did indeed "slap" Weinstock, with "an open hand," because Weinstock had called him a "guinea bastard."

"Sinatra don't need no protection," Rizzo testified. "He's man enough to stand up and defend himself in his own way, like any man should."

In the end, after six hours of deliberation, the jury ruled that Sinatra and Armaniera were not responsible for what had occurred but that Jilly Rizzo was liable. In fact, Rizzo was ordered to pay $101,000 ($1,000 in actual damages and $100,000 in punitive). The judge then overturned the jury's verdict, granting Rizzo a new trial. Instead, the parties settled out of court for far less than $100,000, which Frank paid out of his own pocket.

"I never question those stories," Tina Sinatra has said of her father's many scrapes with the public and the law. "If something flashes on the news, I just call him and say, 'Well, you've done it again,' and he'll tell me the real story, the one the public never hears, the way it really happened. Or he'll say, 'Ignore it,' or, 'Don't bother me, I'm busy.' When you're in the public domain, you're an easy target. When your own brother is kidnapped, as mine was, you have to wonder where people's heads are. They don't seem to realize that celebrities are human beings."

By June 1973, Frank Sinatra was back in the recording studio with producer-arranger Don Costa and arranger Gordon Jenkins. In four sessions, he recorded eleven songs, including "Send in the Clowns" and "Let Me Try Again," one of Sinatra's most enduring ballads and in many ways an appropriate title for his "comeback album." The album would be called *Ol' Blue Eyes Is Back* when finally issued in conjunction with a television special of the same name with Gene Kelly, airing on November 18, 1973.

Both the public and music critics joyfully welcomed *Ol' Blue Eyes Is Back.* Sinatra had been missed. There was no one like him. The album revealed him still at full power as an artist and a man of impeccable musical taste.

While Sinatra was beginning to resume his career, one of his close friends was preparing to end his.

On October 10, 1973, Vice President Spiro T. Agnew resigned, pleading *nolo contendere* to one count of income-tax evasion. With the Watergate investigations occurring at the same time, the Nixon-Agnew team was clearly in trouble. Agnew had also been charged with taking cash kickbacks from a Maryland contractor, bribery, and extortion. Frank did what he could to help, even dispatching his attorney Mickey Rudin to look into the Agnew matter. In the end, Sinatra—who had felt all along that Agnew should fight back—was disappointed when he resigned.

"As a citizen who loves America and as a good friend of Mr. Agnew's, this is indeed a sad day," he said. "Certainly I offer whatever sympathy and support my friend may need. It takes great courage to pursue the route he has chosen."

In the past, Sinatra's White House friends had many high-level meetings to determine whether it was in their best interest to be associated with a man as controversial as Frank. Now the tables seemed to be turned. Sinatra, Mickey Rudin, and the rest of his staff were wondering how Agnew's troubles would affect Sinatra's comeback plans. Frank was adamant that he would not desert Agnew, even going so far as to pay the $30,000 penalty on his tax debt and attempt to secure a publishing deal for his memoirs for $500,000 (a deal he was not able to make). Loyalty is an important ideal to Frank Sinatra; he never abandoned Spiro Agnew and continued to be his friend long after the former vice president fell from grace.

Fifty-eight-year-old Frank Sinatra started the new year back onstage at Caesars Palace in Las Vegas on January 25, 1974. He had vowed never to appear there again after Sanford Waterman pulled a gun on him in 1970. However, when Waterman was indicted for racketeering, Sinatra felt that he could now go back to Caesars for one of his "comeback" performances. He was happy to be performing in front of an enthusiastic Las Vegas audience. He said he "missed" the applause, even though he had performed a number of times since his "retirement." He told the Las Vegas audience, "When you get out of show business, it's a little dangerous, because all of a sudden you're out of touch." The audience accepted the notion that Frank had been "out of show business" even though he had actually never left at all. Still, the public seems to like a good comeback and will play along with it even if it makes no sense. Sinatra's subsequent ten-city tour (April 8–27) was a sellout success each stop along the way.

In May, Frank recorded five sessions for the album *Some Nice Things I've Missed*, produced by Don Costa, Jimmy Bowen, and Sonny Burke—a collection of contemporary pop songs that Sinatra attempted to personalize as his own. It was the kind of project that never worked well for him. Comparisons to the original rock-and-roll artists were inevitable, and Frank would always come out the loser except where his own diehard fans were concerned. For instance, few people wanted to hear "Sweet Caroline" by anyone but its originator, Neil Diamond. Sinatra did acquit himself nicely, though, with the ballad "If," written by David Gates of the group Bread. Frank used to perform the song in concert, joking, "Can you imagine me trying to tell my eighty-year-old mother that there's a group called Bread?" And to hear Sinatra trying to interpret Jim Croce's "Bad, Bad Leroy Brown" is to know the true meaning of "bad."

Again, *Some Nice Things I've Missed* was a case of a great singer and poetic interpreter trying to mine diamonds when they just weren't there in the music or lyrics of the contemporary songs. It's not that the songs were poor; rather, that popular music simply had changed.

By this time, Frank and Barbara were living together in his Palm Springs home, much to the chagrin of Frank's children—Nancy, Frank, and Tina—who felt strongly that Barbara was a gold digger. Making matters worse was Frank's mother, Dolly, who did whatever she could to destroy the relationship. She disliked Barbara tremendously because Barbara did nothing to attempt to win her over. Unlike Frank's other girlfriends and wives, Barbara simply didn't care about Dolly's opinion. She felt that Dolly had too much influence over Frank, and so Frank was forced to choose between his girlfriend and his mother. This tug-of-war continued while Barbara accompanied Frank on a tour of the Far East in July 1974. In the Orient their life together was serene. Dolly was thousands of miles away and not able to interfere.

A successful five-country tour through Europe followed, which ended with a disastrous trip to Australia, where Frank insulted the press corps, calling the men "a bunch of fags" and the women "broads and buck-and-a-half hookers." Some of the reporters were even roughed up by a couple of Frank's overzealous bodyguards. Clearly, the concept of "media relations" was still not one embraced by Sinatra. When he would not apologize for his remarks, the Stagehands Union refused to work, and the Waiters Union would not serve him food at his hotel. Transport Union workers wouldn't even refuel his Gulfstream jet so that he could leave the country. Finally, a joint statement was issued from Sinatra and the Australian Labor union that placated everyone who had been offended by Sinatra's remarks—with no direct apology from the man himself—just so that Sinatra could get out of the country after performing a nationally televised concert.

Barbara took no issue with Frank's controversial behavior in Australia. In fact, she encouraged it. When a press agent there insisted that Sinatra appear at a press conference, he almost did so until Barbara reminded him that he didn't have to do anything he didn't want to do. "It could be said that she had become a little instigator," said Eileen Faith, "and a coconspirator of sorts. Frank liked her spunk."

"They finally let Frank out of the country," Bob Hope joked, "right after the head of the union down there woke up one morning and saw a kangaroo's head on the next pillow."

"Frank called me," Don Rickles said. "He just declared war on Australia."

Upon their return to Palm Springs, the problems Dolly had with her son's relationship came to a head when Dolly and Barbara became embroiled in a shouting match on the telephone having to do with Frank's not calling Dolly while he was away. According to friends of Barbara, she told Dolly that Frank was a grown man and did not have to "call his mommy every day."

"Dolly swore that she would not visit Frank as long as Barbara was living at the house," said Dolly's old friend Doris Sevanto "She just hated her. Oh, my, it was terrible. She called me once and said, 'Doris, listen. I'm trying to think of a way to poison her without Frankie finding out I did it.' I said, 'Dolly, you must be joking.' And she said, 'No, I'm not. It's just a thought. Now, either help me figure this thing out, what kind of poison to use, or just hang up the goddamn phone. Now,' she began, 'here's my plan. . . .' I hung up before I could hear it."

The Sinatras' butler, Bill Stapely, revealed that "Dolly hated Barbara's guts and told me that she'd kill Barbara before she'd allow her son to marry 'that tramp.' When Dolly made that threat, her voice bristled with anger and hatred. I'm convinced she was serious. She told me that Barbara was nothing but a gold digger after Frank's money."

When Frank told Barbara that he had decided to lie to his mother and tell her that they had broken up "just to keep the peace," Barbara realized that she would never win this particular battle. After another row, she broke up with Sinatra, telling him, "Your precious mother can have

401

you." Somehow Frank managed to convince her not to leave the house until after his comeback concert—another one!—this one at Madison Square Garden on October 13, 1974, was televised. Sinatra was nervous about the venture—he never liked doing television specials—and wanted to lean on Barbara for emotional support. She had a way of calming him and had become important in his life. (The Garden concert, staged in a boxing ring and hosted by sportscaster Howard Cosell, was billed as "The Main Event." It would be broadcast around the world, followed by an album of the same name, which would be released in November.

Dinah Shore revealed: "I believe that Barbara fell for Frank instantly. She said that from the start she was sure about him. That he wasn't sure about her bothered her, as it did any woman. But she hung in there."

Laura Cruz, a former maid at the Sinatra home—she only worked for a brief time, replacing another woman, who was on sick leave—recalled that Barbara Sinatra had a difficult time winning over Sinatra's servants, cooks, butlers, groundskeepers, laundresses, and the others who worked at the estate. She tried to do so by commiserating with them at first, by trying to be a friend to each of them. However, that was hopeless. They didn't want her as a friend; they didn't want her as the madam of the house; they simply wanted her *out.* They preferred the way things had been with Mr. Sinatra prior to her arrival on the scene.

"I believe she had her own home in the desert, but she stayed with Mr. Sinatra for the most part, and so she was technically the lady of the house," said Cruz. "She was more extravagant. She wanted fresh flowers every day; she wanted special foods; she wanted things to be nicer, more glamorous, for herself but also, it seemed, for Mr. Sinatra.

"For instance, Mr. Sinatra was satisfied with Italian food every night," said Cruz. "Mrs. Marx was concerned about his health and said she wanted foods that were less fatty. I personally felt that she had his best interest at heart."

One day, in the kitchen, Barbara had an impromptu discussion with the chef about his putting ground beef into the spaghetti sauce. "You know, I think he gets enough red meat in other areas of his diet," she said nicely. "Why does he have to have it in the spaghetti sauce?" According to Cruz, Barbara's tone was not confrontational but, rather, conversational.

The edgy cook tersely explained, "Because he *likes* it that way, madam, with meat in it."

Trying to maintain her composure, Barbara said, "Well, I don't know what to make of that."

"It's called Bolognese, Mrs. *Marx. Bo-log-nese,*" the cook declared flippantly.

The manner in which the cook emphasized Barbara's last name was clearly his way of reminding her that she was not the mistress of the home—yet. And for him to emphasize the word *Bolognese* as if she'd never heard it before was more than she could tolerate from a household employee. In an instant, Barbara became enraged.

"I may be new around here," she bristled, her eyes flashing, "but if you think I'm some kind of pushover, you are very wrong." Taking the pot of spaghetti sauce off the range, she said, "I have had *many* servants in the past, and one thing I know to be true is that they do what they are told." She then poured the sauce into the sink. "Now, I hope I have made myself clear." The cook did not respond. Instead, he stood helplessly in front of the sink as Barbara flicked on the switch of the garbage disposal to make certain that all of the sauce would vanish. In the process, much of the red gravy had splashed on the kitchen counter and sink.

"Now, I have what I think is a very good idea," Barbara said as she grabbed a towel from a rack and threw it at the cook. *"Why don't you clean this goddamn mess up?"* Then she walked out of the kitchen, but not before one last parting shot. "And don't you ever, ever, use that tone with me again. You will learn to listen to direction or you'll be out of here."

After that, Barbara Marx had a meeting with the entire staff in the living room. According to Laura Cruz, Barbara hosted a tea with biscuits and scones for the chef, maids, gardeners, laundresses, and others who had never before enjoyed the luxury of actually being able to sit and socialize in the Sinatra living room.

"All I expect from each of you," Barbara said to the group of twelve, "is simple respect. I promise that you will get the same treatment from me that I get from you, good or bad. Do we have an agreement?"

Everyone nodded.

"Now, please, have another cup," she said as she went around the room, pouring tea for the servants.

"Well, after that, she had *everyone's* allegiance," Cruz said. "I thought, This is a wonderful, smart woman. She really took over the house, and Mr. Sinatra's life, in many ways, and not all of them bad. She made sure he got his rest, for instance. One day, Jilly Rizzo came over early in the morning, and Barbara kicked him out, telling him that Mr. Sinatra needed to sleep. When Mr. Sinatra woke up at about three, he was furious with her, and they had a huge fight. I heard every word. I couldn't help it. They fought right in front of me in the living room."

"Listen, you crazy broad," Frank hollered at Barbara, "you don't tell me who to see and who not to see."

"I'm not trying to do that, Frank," she said in her defense. "I'm just trying to say that you need your rest, and you'll never get it with all these people hanging around here all the time. This place is like a bus station. I'm sick of it, Frank, and you should be, too. You're not getting any younger, you know."

"These are my friends," Frank argued. "If I have to choose between

403

you and them, I choose them. Don't try to change me. You're right, I ain't gettin' any younger. And I'm too fucking old to change now. If you're sick of it then, fine, why don't you just get the hell out."

Barbara ran from the room in tears. Frank then turned to the maid, Laura Cruz, and said, "I'm awfully sorry you had to see that. You know, I hate scenes like that." Then he poured himself a glass of Jack Daniels and said of Barbara, under his breath but loud enough for Cruz to overhear, 'If that broad puts up with me, she's crazier than I am."

Another more frightening incident occurred when Frank and Barbara were in the South of France. Gratsiella Maiellano, a girlfriend of Pat DiCicco's, a friend of Frank's, reported that Frank became enraged with Barbara when she laughed at him because he was attracted to a French woman, bought her a drink, and spoke freely to her, only to learn later that she was a reporter working on a story about him. "It was in the lobby of the Hotel de Paris, and Frank told her to go to her room and shut up or else he would kill her," said Maiellano. "He slapped her across the face for laughing at him, and she could not come out of her hotel room for two days."

Nancy Wood-Furnell, a golfing friend of Dinah Shore's, recollected: "I saw Barbara and Frank go at it one day on the green. She was just as bad as he was, right in his face, screaming at him at the top of her lungs about one thing or another. They didn't care who saw them; they would often fight in public. She gave as good as she got. On this particular day, after a fight, she got into the golf cart and sped away, leaving Frank in the middle of the course under the hot sun. He was shouting at the top of his lungs, 'Get back here, you crazy bitch. Whatsa matter wit' you?'

"As he walked back to the clubhouse, she pulled up alongside him in the cart. He got in. They kissed. Then he got back out of the cart, went to the driver's side, lifted her out of the chair, and plopped her down, right on the grass. He got back in and drove off, leaving *her* out there, screaming, 'Get back here, you crazy bastard.' To be honest, there was something oddly romantic about it.

"Because of the people they are, they explode every once in a while at each other," Dinah Shore said. "And then, when they come back together, their relationship is that much better. They get everything out in the open, so there's none of that sulking. It's a nice, healthy thing for both of them."

Apparently, though, Barbara didn't wish to "put up" with Frank much longer and broke with him at the end of 1974. They weren't kids, she reasoned to her friends Cyd Charisse and Tony Martin over dinner at Gatsby's, and so she was tired of "shacking up." She wanted Sinatra to formally commit to her, and since he wouldn't do that, as far as she was concerned, the relationship was over.

CHAPTER 38

On the afternoon of June 20, 1975, Frank Sinatra awakened in his suite at Caesars Palace in Las Vegas. As usual, his opening-night performance had been a great success. In many ways, he felt that he truly did have "the world on a string," as the popular song went. Earlier in the year, he was awarded the prestigious Cecil B. DeMille Award by the Hollywood Foreign Press during the Golden Globes Awards ceremony. (He wasn't present for that honor, however; Nancy and Tina accepted the award.) He had just returned from a record-breaking European tour that included Paris, Vienna, Munich, and Frankfurt. True, it hadn't been smooth sailing where Barbara Marx was concerned, but that didn't seem to concern him. There were plenty of "broads" out there, he knew, and when the time was right, he'd settle down with one of them. He was almost sixty.

That afternoon, over an omelet breakfast with basil-flavored tomato sauce—brought to him by room service, same meal each day—Sinatra heard the news: Sam Giancana had been murdered in Chicago. Staff members of the Senate Select Committee on Intelligence had just arrived in the Windy City to question Giancana about his possible connection to the CIA's Castro assassination plot. "More of the same crapola" is how Tommy DiBella, Sam Giancana's friend in Philadelphia, put it. "Like Sam was gonna tell them one fucking thing."

Perhaps there were those in the Chicago underworld who feared what Giancana might say, or perhaps he just owed some felon a couple of hundred thousand dollars. From the melodramatic and compelling to the nonsensical and inconsequential, it was all the same in a mobster's chaos-filled life. Whatever the case, sixty-seven-year-old Giancana was found dead in his basement, shot with what appeared to be a silenced .22 caliber automatic once in the back of the head, once in the mouth, and five times under the chin. At his viewing, he lay in a bronze casket wearing a blue business suit and clutching a string of rosary beads. "I couldn't help thinking it was probably the first time he had held a rosary since he was a child," remembered his daughter, Antoinette Giancana.

Phyllis McGuire, his gorgeous blond girlfriend, showed up at the funeral on the arm of millionaire Mike Davis, owner of the Tiger Oil Company. "She was still very beautiful, almost spectacularly so," said Antoinette. "If she was hurt by his death, it wasn't apparent then."

"I heard that when Frank heard about Sam, he said, 'Too goddamn bad for him.' " said Tommy DiBella. " 'You live by the fucking sword, you die by the fucking sword.' Frank really had little to do with Sam Giancana for the last couple of years. So, he wasn't exactly torn up by Sam's death. Of course, he wouldn't have been caught dead himself at that funeral.

"Then, after Sam died, Johnny Roselli got it. He was butchered in Miami. They found the poor fucker all chopped up and crammed into an oil drum. Skinny D'Amato, the nicest guy in the world, went in '82, I believe, of a heart attack. I know Frank was broken up by his death. All these guys, connected to the underworld, were dropping like flies by the end of the seventies.

"None of the shit they did made a bit of difference in history, if you think about it, except Skinny, who made a big mark on Atlantic City entertainment life with his nightclub," said DiBella. "The rest were all full of big-talking schemes, murdering the innocent and not-so-innocent, setting people up so that their lives would be ruined, being big shots in a fucked-up business. Now, Frank Sinatra—at least this was a guy who did something with his life. The fact that he never really got in bed with any of those guys was the best thing he never did."

It hadn't worked out with Barbara Marx, and as far as Frank Sinatra was concerned, that was a shame but not the end of his world. Barbara was not his only interest at this time, anyway. He had been dating a number of women, among them thirty-three-year-old blond, blue-eyed Carol Lynley, an intelligent, elegant actress from the Bronx whom he had been seeing sporadically for about three years. (Lynley's real name is Carole Ann Jones; she changed it because she was afraid she would be confused with the actress Carolyn Jones.) Sinatra found her a refreshing change from many of the women he knew in that she didn't seem to want anything from him. Fascinated by his intellect and charm, she wasn't aggressive in her pursuit of him and seemed to simply enjoy spending quiet, romantic moments. Not the least bit starstruck—in fact, she had never even seen him perform in concert—to her he was just "Francis Albert."

"Of course, we had a romantic relationship," she said with a laugh when asked to define their relationship. "I would have been crazy not to have had one with him. To just be friends with Frank Sinatra? I'd have been a fool!

"I found him to be a spectacular guy," she recalled, "very intelligent, sensitive. I always called him Francis Albert, which is what his close friends called him. The man I knew was interested in art, literature, music. He explained various techniques he utilized when singing, and we spent a lot of time talking about his craft, though he was definitely not a man to sit around and ever listen to any of his own records."

However, Lynley, as convivial a date as she was, could not provide the romantic sparks Frank Sinatra was looking for at this time. If anything, his time with Barbara had seen the reemergence of the passionate Sinatra. It had been a while since he truly felt ardent about a woman, and with Barbara certain masculine urges had resurfaced in Sinatra that he had almost forgotten about. Barbara had awakened "young Frank," who had been fast asleep under older Frank's skin. Now, with a new sense of romantic wanderlust, Sinatra said that he felt "like a kid again." He told Jilly Rizzo that he sensed "a surprise" awaited him around the corner. Only in a life like Frank Sinatra's would that surprise turn out to be Jacqueline Onassis.

Jacqueline Onassis had always had mixed emotions about Frank Sinatra. She never wanted her first husband, the president, to socialize with him while they were in the White House because she felt that his underworld connections were fraught with potential problems for the two of them. However, she couldn't help but be charmed by Sinatra when he hosted the inaugural ball in January 1961. Still, even after that, she felt strongly that the Rat Pack bunch was simply too lowbrow to be a part of the White House inner circle and continually discouraged associating with Sinatra.

Although Jacqueline may not have known the extent of Jack's extramarital affairs, she could not possibly have been blind to all of it. Perhaps she pretended not to see because her beloved father, "Black Jack" Bouvier, had behaved the same way and she reasoned that it was normal. Or maybe she figured it was a trade-off for the power and adoration that came with being the president's wife.

After Jack was killed, Jacqueline's courage touched the nation. No matter that Lady Bird was the president's wife, many people still considered Jackie the first lady long after she left the White House. Her move to New York contributed to her legend as a mystery woman. She guarded her privacy ferociously and managed a Mona Lisa smile that revealed nothing.

Following a suitable period of mourning, she started dating—among others, Aristotle Onassis, a divorced Greek shipping magnate with two adult children. The public couldn't believe that Jacqueline would marry Ari, who was so obviously unsuitable. He was older and relatively unattractive—at least compared to the kind of man Jacqueline could have had—with business dealings that appeared suspicious to the U.S. government. The popular assumption was that Jacqueline had gone berserk with grief over the deaths of Jack and Bobby Kennedy and that this was what drove her into Onassis's arms. They wed on October 20, 1968. At the time, he was sixty-two; she was thirty-nine. The American public felt betrayed; apparently, their saint was all too human. When Onassis died on March 14, 1974, of pneumonia after an operation for gallstones, Jacqueline ended up with $26 million.

By 1975, Jacqueline Onassis was an editor at Viking Press. Sinatra hadn't seen her in a couple of years. Three years earlier, he had asked her to accompany him to a concert in Providence, Rhode Island. It marked the first time they had seen each other since the White House days. It didn't go well. Jacqueline was cold toward him, and Frank had said that he considered it a challenge to "warm that frigid bitch up a little."

During that visit, in 1972, Sinatra also hoped to get to know Aristotle Onassis. In fact, after the concert in Rhode Island, there was a small dinner party at the Onassises' apartment in New York to which Sinatra had been invited. For some inexplicable reason, Sinatra took it upon himself to have fettucine Alfredo, broccoli with oil and lemon, and sautéed veal loin (pounded paper-thin) delivered to the Onassis home earlier in the day from an expensive Italian restaurant, expecting that it would be served at dinner. Jacqueline told him when he arrived that the meal would be breaded pork chops with baked apples. That was acceptable, he said.

After observing Onassis's behavior during dinner, Frank no longer wanted anything to do with him. He was unimpressed because of the way Onassis treated his wife, Jacqueline. "He treats her like shit," said Frank. "She's a cold fish, but she *is* the former first lady. She deserves respect. She doesn't get it from him. He's an idiot, anyway."

In September 1975, when Jacqueline telephoned Frank in Palm Springs to ask for a meeting, he agreed to see her, though he couldn't imagine what it could be about. Since he planned to be in New York on September 8, 1975, for a two-week engagement with Ella Fitzgerald and Count Basie at the Uris Theatre, Sinatra asked her to accompany him on opening night.

"The more he thought about her over the years, the more he wondered about her," said Jim Whiting. " 'What the hell was it that kept us from getting together after all these years?' he said. 'She's one unique dame, strong, independent. I mean, she's really my type, you know?' he said. 'I've always had kind of a crush on her. I'm surprised I ain't done somethin' about it by now.' "

Though Frank wished to take Jacqueline to opening night at the Uris, she felt that the media that usually attends such occasions would turn such a date into a circus. She suggested that they go to a later show instead. So they made plans to meet on Wednesday night, September 17, 1975. She also finally explained that her interest in seeing him was to discuss the possibility of his writing his memoirs for Viking, which she would edit. Sinatra said he had no interest in such a project but would, at the very least, be willing to discuss it with her.

Twenty-two years later, in May 1997, Bill Stapely (Frank Sinatra's valet for eighteen years), recalled: "Jackie O. was a beautiful widow, and as everyone knew, she was desired by just about every man in the world. Frank was on top of that list. He really had a special attraction to Jackie. Because she was a woman he felt he wasn't supposed to mix with I think made her even more intriguing to him. In the past he'd always been sort of intimidated by the likes of, and by the upper crust of, society."

Actor Brad Dexter, who was also Frank's close friend for many years, recalled that in 1964, when the two of them were filming *Von Ryan's Express*, they went on a ten-day vacation cruise together. He said, "We went to Portofino and Santa Margherita and Rapallo and then came back. The most memorable moment was pulling up alongside Aristotle Onassis's yacht, the *Christina*, and seeing Jackie Kennedy, the president's widow, onboard. I pointed her out to Frank, saying that she was an attractive woman with a good background—the kind of woman he should be interested in. He looked over at her and shook his head. 'It would never work,' he said. 'Never.' I sensed that he felt Mrs. Kennedy was unobtainable to someone like him."

"At the time that Frank would get his big chance with Jackie, Barbara was living with him and pushing him to get married," added Bill Stapely. "Frank was resisting, and they were feuding about that. So it could be said that Jackie was just what the doctor ordered."

Stapely remembered that an excited Frank called his upcoming evening with Jacqueline "the most important date of his life. He actually said that it made him feel like a king when she agreed to go out with him."

Sinatra so enjoyed being back in New York; it made him feel young and brought back many good memories. He was in good spirits at this time despite what had occurred between him and Barbara, staying at Jilly's restaurant and bar until three in the morning, drinking vodka, eating Chinese food, and enjoying Manhattan's nightlife. "I gotta get outta here," he would finally say. "I gotta work tomorrow."

Two days before opening night, Sinatra telephoned Jacqueline, wondering if they could meet prior to the performance. Otherwise occupied, she said that she preferred to wait until the evening of the show. They made the necessary arrangements. Jilly Rizzo was to accompany her to the Uris Theatre. Afterward, she and Sinatra would attend a small party backstage before going on to dinner. Jim Whiting remembers: "Jilly told me that he had six dozen roses delivered to her apartment on the day of the opening with a card that read—and I know what it said because Jilly called in the order and he's the one who told me—'Thank you for being my date on this very special evening. Francis Albert.' "

Jilly Rizzo met Jacqueline at eight P.M. at her apartment in a plain black town car, and the two were driven to the Uris Theatre at Fiftieth and Broadway. The marquee read: Basie, Fitzgerald and Sinatra. (Frank had requested that he be billed third under "two real legends.") About two blocks from the Uris Theatre, Jilly Rizzo could see that a mob of photographers, members of the press, and the general public had gathered, anticipating their arrival. Much to Sinatra's chagrin, columnist Earl Wilson had gotten a tip that Mrs. Onassis would be Sinatra's guest, and he published it in the newspaper. Jilly would later say, "We musta been nuts thinking we could go through the front entrance, anyway."

The car drove around to the back of the theater, and Jilly quickly ushered Jacqueline through the stage-door entrance. They met Frank and Jacqueline's friends Peter and Cheray Duchin, in his dressing room, which was mobbed with well-wishers, fans, and photographers. After a drink, Jilly took Jacqueline and the Duchins to their fourth-row seats just as the show began and then returned backstage to tend to Frank's needs.

Jacqueline wasn't sure what to make of Frank Sinatra's concert. He was in marvelous voice; she had always appreciated his obvious talent. His onstage persona, though, was a bit too rough-edged for her taste, and to her way of thinking, he hadn't changed much; he was still crude. While onstage at the Uris Theatre, he mentioned that it was the first time he had played a legitimate house. "I've fooled around in a lot of illegitimate houses, though," he cracked. Making a crack about the name Uris, he said, "The Uris! I'll send you some penicillin and clear it right up." However, musically, he was in great form, as usual. Jacqueline and the Duchins joined in a rousing standing ovation after his performance.

Following the show, there was an intimate gathering backstage for friends and relatives of Frank's from the New Jersey area, including Joey D'Orazio, Frank's buddy from Hoboken, who hadn't seen him in about fifteen years.

"Frankie and I had lost touch," he recalled. "I had moved out of Hoboken and was living in Philly at that time. I drove into New York with my wife to see the show. The concert was terrific, and afterward I wrote my name down on a card and gave it to a security guard at the door. 'Take this back to Frank, will ya?' I said. 'Tell him I want to see him.' I was being a big shot, trying to impress my wife, who I believed in her heart secretly felt that I never even knew Frank Sinatra. We stood at the stage door for about fifteen minutes and were getting ready to leave when the guard came back and said, 'Mr. D'Orazio, Mr. Sinatra told me to tell you—Well, excuse me, sir, but he told me to tell you to get your fat ass back there.' "

The D'Orazios were escorted backstage, through a long maze of hallways and into Sinatra's dressing room. "Man, he came right at me and gave me a big bear hug," he recalled. "He had a grin on his face a mile wide and said, 'Joey, ya bum, ya. How the fuck are ya? Have a drink, man,' he said. 'Enjoy yourself. Mingle. This is the big time.'

"I was eating a stick of fried mozzarella, which they had on a table of Italian foods [salami, provolone, artichokes, mushrooms and peppers] backstage when I noticed that Frank was with this dame, her back to me. She was wearing a plain black pants suit kind of thing, nothing special. She turned around, and Jesus Christ! It was Jacqueline Onassis.

"Frank was hanging all over her. He looked happy as hell, and she had her arm around his waist and was sipping a drink—looked like a Coke—in a small plastic cup. She was giddy and girlish. She was more flirty than I ever imagined. At one point, Frank made a dumb joke and she said, 'Oh, Francis, that is just *so* funny,' you know, trying to flatter him. He ate it up. My wife said, 'Oh, my God, she's like a dizzy schoolgirl. That can't possibly be her, can it? Look how she's acting!' And I said, 'That *is* her.'

"We stood there for a while, just watching, and Frank was so busy, we eventually decided to take off. So I went over to him and said goodbye, hugged him, and said softly in his ear, 'You come a long way, Frankie boy, with your date here, I mean.'

"He grinned and whispered to me, 'I'm the luckiest guy in the world. There ain't never been anyone luckier than me.' "

After the backstage party, Frank took Jacqueline by the wrist, and with Jilly to his right, the three of them departed, shoulder to shoulder, through the crowd of spectators and photographers. Their car took them to the popular Club 21.

"When he walked in there with Jackie on his arm, he was in seventh heaven, and that's no exaggeration," said Bill Stapely, who was also there. "You could tell by the expression on his face. He was a little drunk, and he told me, 'She was first lady a dozen years ago, but look at her now, man, on my arm. Too much, isn't it?' "

"They made no effort to get the privacy of the second-floor dining room," Earl Wilson reported. "They had supper in the first-floor bar area. A couple of columnists—I was one of them—had tables on bar positions overlooking Sinatra and Jackie but saw nothing to report. It was clear, though, that sitting at this table with the Duchins was the most charismatic couple in the world."

Later, Frank and Jacqueline ended up in Frank's suite at the Waldorf Towers, where they spent the night together.

"Frank would never talk about it," said Jim Whiting. "Jilly asked him, 'So, hey, what was *that* like?' and Frank was just too much of a gentleman where Jackie was concerned to say. All I know is that they absolutely were intimate. That's for sure, because Frank said so years later.

"I was at a party at Steve Lawrence's, and we were all pretty drunk. It was late, and we were talking guy talk, you know, and Jilly asked Frank who the biggest conquests were in his life. Sinatra said that right on top of the list was Ava [Gardner], then Jackie [Onassis], then Lana [Turner]—he said about her, 'I was young, and she was an unbelievable catch for any guy my age'—then Marilyn, whom he called "one of the classiest, nicest dames I ever knew; just so screwed up it broke my heart.' So everyone said, 'Jackie? What are ya kiddin' me? How'd that go?' And Sinatra got quiet and said under his breath, 'I ain't talkin' about that.' "

"Frank is a classy man," Sammy Davis reminded this writer in 1989. "He wouldn't talk about shit like that. I know that that night with Jackie was special to him, but hell if I know what happened, and I would never ask. I think it made him feel young again to be around her, you know, the whole Camelot thing."

Whiting added of Sinatra, "To be honest, I think the thing with Jackie was one of the only times that he wouldn't brag about a conquest. I know he was head over heels for her after that night, or at least he thought he was. He just jumped right in, like Frank always did, going way too far, making a big deal outta something that probably wasn't."

Indeed, Frank told Bill Stapely, "I can't believe this thing between me and Jackie. She used to look down on me. But I think she's accepted me now."

Stapely said of his boss, "After a couple of drinks, he said, 'She loves me and I love her. So you know what? To hell with Barbara. I think I'll marry Jacqueline Kennedy Onassis. Wouldn't *that* be somethin'?' "

Obviously, the notion that Sinatra and Onassis could ever have married at that juncture was preposterous; they had only spent one full evening together. When asked if Sinatra was being facetious, Stapely responded, "He was serious. He definitely was not joking."

That Sinatra had made that statement perhaps wouldn't have been so surprising if one considers his history. He really hadn't changed much from the twenty-four-year-old man he was in October 1940 when he suddenly told his long-suffering wife, Nancy, that he was in love with Alora Gooding and wanted to be with her or when he announced to Nancy six years later, "Lana [Turner] and I are together now." In fact, Sinatra had often made impulsive declarations of commitment where none really existed.

Perhaps one couldn't blame Sinatra for dreaming, though, where Jacqueline Onassis was concerned. After all, she was one of the most sought after women in the world, and Sinatra had her to himself, if only for one night—which, as it would turn out, would be all he would ever get from her.

After New York, Frank was off to singing engagements in Philadelphia, Cleveland, and Chicago. He telephoned Jacqueline from each stop but never heard back from her. He sent her flowers but received no acknowledgment from her.

"Jackie refused to take or return Sinatra's telephone calls after that one date," said Bill Stapely. "Of course, this really made him furious. One night, he slammed the telephone down after trying to call her, and he said, 'Man, I swear she liked me the night we were together, and now look at her. She won't even take my fucking calls. Well, then, hey, fine with me,' he decided. 'Who the hell needs her, anyway?' "

On another occasion, said one person closely connected to Sinatra, when he attempted to telephone Jackie, Barbara—who had joined him on his tour by this time—walked into the room just in time to see him hurl a plate of zampetto (pig's feet) across the room, barely missing a hotel maid. Sinatra shouted, "What a pain in the ass she is!" Barbara thought he was talking about her and broke down in tears. He apologized profusely and said he was speaking of the maid.

It was a mystery to many of Sinatra's colleagues why Jacqueline Onassis suddenly turned cold toward him. However, one longtime friend of hers, who requested anonymity (because she is presently employed by Jacqueline's son, John), said, "I know exactly what happened. Jacqueline's former sister-in-law Ethel Kennedy saw the newspaper accounts of Jacqueline's date with Sinatra and telephoned her. She told her something along the lines of 'How could you go out with this man? This is the person who got women for Jack when you were in the White House. This is the man who introduced Jack to Judith Campbell. Are you crazy? Have you gone *mad*? What is wrong with you?'

"Jacqueline, for all of her sainted qualities, and she had many, was the most naive woman in some respects," observed her friend. "She said that she had absolutely no idea that Frank was involved in all of that terrible business in the White House. Obviously, she knew Sinatra was incorrigible, which is why she didn't want him around the White House, but she really did not know he had been Jack's pimp all those years ago. That never crossed her mind."

Three separate sources corroborated the above statement by John Kennedy Jr.'s employee, none of whom wished to be identified for fear of retaliation by either the Kennedys or the Sinatras. Apparently, Ethel Kennedy took Jacqueline Onassis back to the days of Camelot and reminded her of things she had either forgotten or never knew at all. "Marilyn [Monroe] and all that," said the source, "and incidentally, you never mentioned Marilyn to her, because she simply didn't want to know anything about any of that and would never engage in conversation about it, ever. In 1982, I asked her an innocent question about Marilyn—whether she liked a photo book [by James Spada] that Doubleday [where Jacqueline was working at the time as an editor] had published, and she said,

'She *was* beautiful, wasn't she? But I don't discuss anything related to her.' And then she abruptly hung up on me."

Ethel had worked Jacqueline into a fury about Sinatra, and before long, they both agreed that not only had Sinatra taken advantage of her naïveté; he had made a complete fool of her in the process.

According to Jacqueline's friend, she told Ethel, 'That son of a bitch owes me for all he put me through [during the White House years]. Of course I will never go out with him again. I can't believe how stupid I've been. In my world, Frank Sinatra no longer exists."

Sinatra was completely mystified by the way Jacqueline Onassis had so suddenly dismissed him. "What'd I do? *What'd I do?*" he kept asking colleagues. Finally, in what was viewed by some as the move of a desperate man, he sent Jacqueline a letter from Harrah's in Lake Tahoe [October 1975] saying that his daughter Nancy had been thinking of writing a book about him and that he would consider taking over the project himself if she—Jacqueline—would edit it. When Jacqueline didn't even take that juicy bait, Frank Sinatra knew he had been rejected.

"I gotta say, I'm really disappointed in that dame," Frank said at Harrah's. "I look at it like this: When you got a problem with someone, you should just tell the guy what the hell it is. Don't just cut the person out of your life." One wonders if he caught the irony of his statement, considering some of his past behavior with others. "We coulda talked about it," he said of Jacqueline, "whatever the hell was buggin' her."

In years to come, Jacqueline and Frank would see each other again at social functions, but at least according to well-informed sources, she never had another conversation with him, let alone a date. "Something happened between the two of them; that I can tell you," Sammy Davis said. "But what it was, I got no idea . . . 'cept it was big."

Despite his disillusionment about her, Sinatra refused to ever utter a negative word about Jacqueline Onassis, nor would he reveal to any of his friends—who would speak of him for a biography—any much-sought-after details of his one night with the former first lady.

Apparently, Ethel Kennedy wasn't the only woman concerned about the photos of Jacqueline and Frank that appeared in the press. Barbara was also upset. Her friends would later say that Onassis inadvertently brought Frank and Barbara back together again.

"Barbara saw the photo and, I believe, thought twice about breaking up with him after that," said Dinah Shore. "That is just my personal opinion. She did not discuss it with me. However, I know she didn't want to lose him. She loved him so, and by the way," Shore said, rolling her eyes, "I don't believe for a single second that Frank Sinatra and Jacqueline Onassis were ever intimate. I simply can't imagine such a thing."

Barbara telephoned Frank in New York, and they talked for hours, trying to work things out between them. He was lonely and tired of feeling that way. He may have known—it's difficult to determine, though—that he only had himself to blame for his loneliness, always on the lookout for the next big conquest and never focusing on any relationship long enough to establish a complete understanding and real bond with a woman. Sinatra agreed that Barbara should fly to New York to be with him for the rest of the Uris engagement. In fact, it would seem that even though he was fascinated by Jacqueline Onassis and wanted to know what had happened between them to cause her to act so coolly toward him, he already knew that he was going to marry Barbara Marx.

Carol Lynley was appearing on Broadway at the time, taking over for Sandy Duncan in *Absurd Person Singular* when Sinatra had Jilly Rizzo call her to invite her to his performance at the Uris Theatre. Carol—who was married when she was eighteen, divorced at twenty, and never remarried—said that she had been dating no one else for the last three years because, as she put it, "all of the other men were intimidated by the fact I was dating Frank, to tell you the truth." Since she had never seen Sinatra perform in concert, even though they had been dating for three years, she was excited about the invitation. She and a companion went to see the performance; Sinatra had arranged front-row, center seats. "He basically sang the whole show in my direction," she remembered. "What a thrill it was." Afterward, she and her friend ("who was not a date, just a pal") went backstage to see Sinatra and then went out to dinner with him. Over dinner, Frank asked Carol if he could escort her home.

He took her to her hotel-room door, and just as she was about to invite him in, he paused and said, "Carol, I must tell you something. I'm getting married. To Barbara."

She was a bit taken aback by his sudden announcement, she recalled. "But at least he had the decency to tell me personally after three years rather than have me read it in the papers."

Looking at her warmly, Sinatra said, "Is there anything you want?"

"I don't understand, Francis."

"Well, what can I *do* for you?" he asked. "What would make you happy?"

At a loss, she said that she had just had bookshelves built in her home and didn't have enough books to fill the space. Knowing that he was a voracious reader, she thought he might be able to give her some books. "Done," he said. The next day, Sinatra made an arrangement with Bennet Cerf, publisher of Random House. For the next five years, Carol Lynley received advance copies of every book published by that company, including every book published by the children's division, for her daughter, who was four at the time.

"I thought it was probably a very good idea for Francis and Barbara to marry," said Carol Lynley, who today is still a close friend of Frank's daughter Nancy. "They were closer in age than Francis and I. They were more compatible. She seemed to make him happy. I felt that he needed her."

After being rejected by Jacqueline Onassis and before settling down with Barbara, Sinatra, like a bachelor half his age, perhaps felt he had some "wild oats to sow." He went back to his past behavior with prostitutes. (Only Frank Sinatra would enjoy such a wide array of women, from a former first lady to a hooker, and just nights apart!) Bill Stapely had been instructed to get any woman who had spent the night with Frank out of his suite at the Waldorf Towers before eight A.M. but to be sure to give her a $600 "gift." (Sinatra wasn't exactly generous with the working girl.)

One morning soon after the Onassis rendezvous, Stapely walked into Sinatra's bedroom and found the singer passed out on his bed in his shorts, a naked blonde, on her side, facing him and pressed up against him, sleeping soundly. She had a small rose tattoo on her buttocks. She was what Stapely called "a newcomer."

"I gently shook her," he recalled. " 'Time to get up, missy. You must be off now. Come, come.' "

"Oh, no," she protested groggily as she awakened. Sinatra snored loudly next to her as she said, "You don't understand. Frank is taking me out tonight. We're going to dinner and then the 21 Club."

"I'm sorry, my dear, but there has been a change of plans," Stapely told her. "Now, please hurry along."

He turned his back as she arose and then dressed. Then he walked her to the elevator, presented her with her "gift," pushed the "down" button, and sent her on her way.

When Barbara arrived in New York, she and Frank found themselves drawn to one another in a way that surprised them. Was it love? For Barbara, it probably was. Frank would confess to being confused about matters of the heart; some say he still hadn't gotten over Ava Gardner, even though it had been almost twenty years since their relationship had ended. Indeed, if this man actually professed love for Jacqueline Onassis after spending only one night with her, it's not likely that he could be clear about his feelings for any woman. However, he did enjoy Barbara's company, and so she stayed with him for the rest of the tour, on to London, Tehran, and Israel. However, Frank never stopped trying to solve the puzzle of what had happened to his brief relationship with Jacqueline Onassis. In fact, he sent her a $25,000 diamond bracelet from London, in November 1975. When he returned to California, he found that the package bearing the gift had been returned unopened.

When Nancy Sinatra was preparing to write a book about her father, she contacted Jacqueline Kennedy Onassis for laudatory comments about him. She was amazed and irate when Jacqueline refused. "My father escorted, campaigned—he helped JFK in every way—and *this* is how Mrs. Onassis handles it?" she said to the *Los Angeles Times*. "The late John F. Kennedy was a very big part of my father's life. How dare she be that cruel?"

Sixty-year-old Frank Sinatra began January 1976 with an engagement at Caesars Palace, then on to Lake Tahoe. That month, renowned atheist Madalyn Murry O'Haire, of Austin, Texas, wrote to Sinatra asking if he would consider performing at a benefit for the American Atheist Convention in New York. If not, would he at least make a small donation? Sinatra's one-sentence reply to O'Haire: "I will not attend or perform or contribute to your Atheist Convention. Thank God."

In February, Sinatra taped a critically hailed television special with John Denver. It aired on March 29 on ABC.

By May, he had proposed to Barbara Marx and presented her with a $360,000, seventeen-carat diamond engagement ring. "Yes, it's true," Frank responded when asked by one reporter if he and Barbara were engaged, "but it's nobody's goddamned business."

Why had Frank decided to marry Barbara? One intimate said, "Frank told me, 'You know what? She ain't bad. She looks out for me. I'm gettin' older, and I need someone to do that; see that I eat right, look right, stuff like that.' When I asked him if he felt about her the way he felt about, say, Ava Gardner, Frank got sad. He shook his head and said, 'You can't go back. . . . That was then. I don't ever want to feel that way again about any woman. Look what it got me.' "

As he approached sixty, Frank Sinatra clearly preferred the tranquillity—such as it ever was in his life—of a sensible, calm relationship with Barbara Marx than he did the chaos of a passionate, head-over-heels romance with someone like Ava Gardner. For her part, Barbara was "mad about Frank," as Dinah Shore put it. "You can see the deep love in her eyes whenever she mentions his name. Fights or no fights, she loves him."

"Barbara was happy she had Frank in her life," said her friend Eileen Faith, "and she promised herself that she would make the marriage work. There were friends of hers who wondered if she was making a mistake. His temper was known by all. But you didn't dare mention that to Barbara, just as you wouldn't to any woman head over heels in love with someone. I was concerned about the fights, though. I witnessed some terrible rows, and I wondered what kind of marriage it would be."

Dolly was still against the union, so much so that Frank asked his attorney, Mickey Rudin, to break the news to her rather than have to face her himself. Dolly said she would never be able to accept Barbara.

Clearly, no one was good enough for her son, and there would never be anything Barbara could do to convince Dolly otherwise.

Worse for Frank, perhaps, was that his daughter Nancy was also adamantly opposed to having Barbara as a stepmother. Sinatra probably could have avoided hurting Nancy's feelings if he had told her in advance of the engagement. He didn't because he simply did not want to hear her complaints about Barbara, particularly the accusations that she was a "gold digger," which is what Nancy steadfastly maintained. Understandably, she also held on to the hope—of which there was, practically speaking, none—that her parents would reconcile.

Frank and Nancy senior had had a peaceful, cordial relationship for years, and Nancy was always present at every holiday at the Sinatra household, even after Barbara became Frank's constant companion. Daughter Nancy thought that perhaps there might be a chance for her parents to resume their marriage, even though they had been divorced for almost twenty years. Frank had other intentions, however. Unfortunately, Nancy, Tina, and Frankie junior heard the news from mutual friends before they did from their father, similar to the way they found out about his last marriage, to Mia Farrow.

Nancy could not stop crying when she learned of her father's intention. She vowed to not have anything to do with the ceremony, though she must have known in her heart that there was little chance she could keep such a promise. Her feelings for her father were so strong, she would have to find the strength and resolve to accept his choice of Barbara even if she did not agree with it.

Much of Nancy's distress came from the notion that her father's impending marriage to Barbara was hurting her mother, who, she believed, also hung on to some hope that she and Frank would reunite. But Nancy senior was no longer the weak, needy woman she was in the fifties. She had long ago accepted the fact that her romantic relationship with Frank was over, and she had no designs on him. She used to say, "All the women Frank has had, I'm the only one who gave him children. They can't take that away from me, now, can they?" It was really just Nancy junior who wanted her parents back together, more than even Tina or Frankie.

"Nancy was her father's protector after Mia," Dinah Shore observed. "She loved him so. And he had been alone for a long time, almost ten years. She was used to being the center of attention. Now she had to share that with Barbara. It wasn't easy."

Frank and Barbara made a public announcement that they would marry on October 10, 1976, at Kirk Douglas's home. Actually, they were planning a secret wedding that would take place in July. The 120 invited guests thought they were attending an engagement party, even though the invitations suggested that male guests wear neckties. Barbara even lied to Zeppo Marx when he asked her if a rumor he had heard about a July wedding was true; she said it was not. Zeppo was not invited, anyway.

The ceremony was held on July 11, 1976, at Sunnylands, the thousand-acre Palm Springs estate of Walter Annenberg, publisher of *TV Guide* and former ambassador to the Court of St. James's. Of course, despite Sinatra's best efforts, the press got wind of the impending nuptials but were made to wait outside the gates in the 115-degree heat.

Many of the 120 guests arrived by private planes at the Palm Springs airport, eight miles away. The guests included the Ronald Reagans, who interrupted their presidential campaign, Spiro Agnew, Sammy Davis Jr., the Gregory Pecks, Jimmy Van Heusen, Leo Durocher, and famed heart surgeon Dr. Michael DeBakey. Dolly was present—begrudgingly, no doubt—as were Nancy and Tina. Frank junior, did not attend because of a prior commitment, an East Coast singing engagement. Dinah Shore, Barbara's good friend, was also not invited. (It was reported that Frank did not like the way she had interviewed Spiro Agnew on her television program. This was not true, Dinah Shore said before her death. Frank still had not gotten over the fact that Dinah had tried to play matchmaker while Barbara and Frank were separated.)

Frank's best man was Freeman Gosden, who played Amos on the *Amos 'n' Andy* radio program. Bea Korshak, wife of Beverly Hills attorney Sidney Korshak, was the matron of honor. A *New York Times* reporter, noting the armed guards, considered it "security befitting an international summit conference."

The forty-six-year-old bride wore a Halston-designed beige chiffon wedding dress with a prominent jeweled brooch at the point of the off-center V-neck. She was escorted by her father. Frank, sixty, wore a beige silk-and-linen suit with a beige silk tie and a brown-and-beige handkerchief in his breast pocket. Prior to the ceremony, Frank took his daughters aside for a private moment. "I've really thought this through," he told them. "And yes, I've considered your mother. You know I'll always love her. But this is what I want now. This marriage is what I need in my life." Both women burst into tears. Indeed, the expression on Nancy's face in photographs that day tells the story of her complete and utter despair.

When Judge James H. Walsworth asked the bride if she "took" Frank for richer or poorer, Frank said with a grin, "Richer, *richer.*"

After the champagne reception, the guests rode in air-conditioned buses to dinner at Frank's house, just a few blocks away. On display were his gift to Barbara—a peacock blue Rolls-Royce—and hers to him—a gray Jaguar XJS. The newlywed Sinatras honeymooned with three other couples (the Morton Downeys, the Bill Greens, and the Paul Mannos).

"He turns every day into Christmas," Barbara said of her new husband. "It knocks me out. Maybe I appreciate it more because I didn't always have it."

CHAPTER 39

No one had been more influential in Sinatra's life than his mother, Dolly. From the time he was a boy, he had always revered her. While theirs was a combative mother-son relationship, it was built on love and trust. It had hurt him deeply that she refused to accept his new wife, Barbara, but he long ago had learned to accept his mother for who she was and her opinions for what they were worth. He often valued her advice and solicited it in times of crisis, as he did when he was confused as to how to handle his relationship with Mia Farrow. At other times, he would be forced to disregard Dolly's often-biased point of view. He had to live his life his way, after all.

As she got older, Dolly Sinatra became more of a challenge to those who loved her. Unlike some others who live to be in their eighties, she did not mellow with age. In fact, she became even more opinionated and obstreperous. However, because she was the Italian-American mother of an Italian-American son, respect was something she believed she deserved, and she received it in great abundance. Frank loved her deeply and would not have changed anything about her, even though he would constantly gripe to others that "this old woman is driving me crazy." His children felt the same way about Dolly. They, too, adored her, although she was constantly offering unsolicited opinions about their lives and mates.

After her husband, Marty, died, Dolly found herself lonely and wanting to be even more involved in her son's busy life and in the lives of his offspring. She was proud of Frank and thought of his success as her own. "She thinks she's the big hit," Frank said in an interview at this time. "She's fine. She lives next door to me in Palm Springs. If she was here with us now and she wanted to say something about me, she would refer to me as 'Frank Sinatra' while I'm sitting here. She wants to be sure that everyone knows who she's talking about."

Dolly's ever-present need to be at the center of everyone's life caused myriad problems for the Sinatras. Her natural bent was to meddle, and with nothing else to do it had practically became an obsession. It was understandable, though, that she would want to be involved in her son's life. She missed her husband, her life in Hoboken, the power she once wielded, her friends, and even her enemies.

Though her three grandchildren, Nancy, Frank, and Tina, filled much of the void, she began to feel a deep melancholy by the mid-seventies.

In August 1976, Dolly told Nancy that she sensed that she would not live much longer. Since her grandmother was in generally good health—though persistently swollen ankles had become a source of pain and annoyance—Nancy dismissed Dolly's morbid notion. She decided that she was simply fatigued and, as she knew Dolly was wont to do, feeling self-indulgent and self-pitying. Perhaps she just wanted more attention.

Dolly was still heartbroken that her "little bastard of a son" Frank had married "that horrible, horrible woman," as she called Barbara to anyone who would listen. That he would do such a thing, even though he knew that she was so adamantly opposed to it, made Dolly feel unwanted and unnecessary, which was certainly not the case. She and Nancy junior commiserated about the loss of Frank in both their lives, even though he really hadn't gone anywhere. Their despair over his love life and, it could be argued, his lack of attention had completely blinded them to his presence.

On Thursday, January 6, 1977, Frank Sinatra was scheduled to open in Las Vegas, again at Caesars Palace. Dolly, who enjoyed Las Vegas and thrilled to the sounds and sights of gambling machines, intended to be present for her son's opening. (In fact, she enjoyed gambling so much that Frank had a slot machine installed in her Palm Springs home. "When she loses, she doesn't worry about it," he said. "She just gets out the screwdriver.")

At five P.M., Dolly and a visiting widowed friend from New Jersey, Anna Carbone, boarded a twin-engine Lear Jet, which Frank had hired for her, at the Palm Springs airport for the twenty-minute flight to Las Vegas. Dolly's plan was to go directly from the airport to Caesars. Because of a storm in the Coachella Valley, visibility was poor. Perhaps the plane should never have taken off, because once it was airborne, visibility was zero. The pilot would have to rely on radar for the entire flight. Two minutes into the flight, ground control lost communication with the plane. It was due to land in Las Vegas at five-twenty.

Nancy senior received a telephone call from Mickey Rudin to tell her that he had just received a telephone call from Jet Avia, Ltd., the company that owned the Lear Jet. It was feared that Dolly's plane had smashed into the San Gorgonio Mountains. This seemed impossible to believe; Nancy senior became hysterical. She telephoned her daughter, Nancy, also in Los Angeles, and the two prayed for a last-minute miracle. "But we all knew it was over," Nancy junior said in retrospect. They telephoned Frank in Las Vegas with the horrible news.

Three hours later, Sinatra was onstage, somehow managing to perform for a full-house audience while a search crew was organized to look for his missing mother. "I know he did it for his mother," Nancy said of that concert. Sinatra received a standing ovation; no one in the audience had even a hint of the nightmare that was unfolding in his personal life.

"It was the most terrible night of his life," said Eileen Faith. "How he was able to go on, no one knew. There was that hope, that small ray of hope, that maybe, somehow, Dolly had escaped injury. It was impossible to comprehend her dying that way. She hardly ever flew, maybe a couple of times a year. No one could accept it. After the first show, Frank canceled the rest of the engagement and flew back to Palm Springs."

On Friday, the next morning, Frank asked his son and two daughters to drive to Palm Springs from Los Angeles to be with him and Barbara. When they arrived, after an emotional, panicked drive, they found their father in the Sinatra living room with a priest. As Frank tightly gripped a Bible, the priest performed a private Catholic service. On Saturday, the nightmare continued. No word. While Tina and Nancy desperately consulted psychic Peter Hurkos and Frank junior cried alone in a guest room, Frank senior went up in a Civil Air Patrol helicopter with a pilot, Don Landells, searching the snow-swept mountainside for his beloved mother. He didn't find her.

By the third day, Sunday, a cloud of hopelessness enveloped the Sinatra home as its occupants walked about in a daze, stunned by the reality of what had probably occurred. Even Barbara, who had had such a difficult relationship with Dolly, was inconsolable. At 11:25 P.M., Barbara got the telephone call. Wreckage from the Lear Jet had finally been found by pilot Don Landells, who had again gone out in search of it. It was split in two, the nose destroyed. The wings and tail had been torn from the aircraft. While the bodies of both pilots had disintegrated upon impact, other body parts were covered with bloody ice and snow.

Dolly Sinatra's colorful muumuu dress hung from a tree limb, whipping in the wind as if it were a flag set sail to assist in the search for her body.

Visions of Dolly, panicked and horror-stricken in her last moments, haunted the family when they gathered in the Sinatra living room; Frank was devastated. Mickey Rudin told him that Dolly was found strapped to her seat. Even though Frank probably knew in his heart that this was an unlikely scenario, he tried desperately to believe him.

It was learned later that the plane crashed into the 11,502-foot mountain—the same one that would later claim Dean Martin's son, Dino—at full takeoff speed of 375 mph as a result of a mix-up in communications from the control tower and bad weather conditions.

The funeral was at St. Louis Roman Catholic Church in Cathedral City, outside Palm Springs, on January 12, 1977. Dolly was buried at Desert Memorial Park, next to her husband, Marty, whose body, at her request, had earlier been exhumed in New Jersey and moved to Palm Springs. Dean Martin, Jimmy Van Heusen, Leo Durocher, Danny Thomas, Pat

Henry, and Jilly Rizzo were pallbearers. The Associated Press said that Sinatra's "eyes were unswerving from the casket covered with white lilies and pink roses."

Many of his intimates believe that Frank Sinatra never recovered from the emotional trauma and grief of his mother's sudden, tragic death.

"My father was devastated," recalled Frank junior. "The days that followed were the worst I had ever known. He said nothing for hours at a time. All of us who were nearby felt helpless to find any way to ease his agony. Back at home after that terrible hour at the graveside, I felt it best not to leave him alone. I sat with him and watched the tears roll one by one down his face."

"A lot of laughter has gone from his life," Nancy Sinatra wrote in her book *Frank Sinatra—My Father*. "Yet there still must be solace somehow in looking up at that mountain, so much more beautiful and lasting a memorial than any graveyard, and getting a peaceful feeling from living in the shadow of Grandma's mountain."

Making matters worse, shortly after Dolly's death, Barbara suggested that Frank have his marriage to Nancy annulled so that they could be married again in a Catholic ceremony. This idea caused a family war.

"The truth is that Frank became more religious after Dolly's death," said Dinah Shore. "I believe that Barbara, who was Protestant, wanted the annulment and a new Catholic ceremony because she thought Frank would consider it a present for Dolly. Dolly was devoutly Catholic. But, oh, the problems it caused. I have to say, Barbara must have regretted opening that can of worms. It drove a wedge between her and Nancy junior that I think is probably still there."

"Back in the thirties and forties in Hoboken, the Sinatras were not a religious family," said Joey D'Orazio. "Frank had his First Holy Communion, I remember, but the way I understood it, Dolly just wanted him in on that because she thought the ceremony was kinda grand. Actually, the only reason Frank was Catholic was because he inherited the faith from his parents, and they from theirs. Italians were God-fearing, though, even if they didn't go to church every Sunday. Frank once said it was something in the ingredients in spaghetti sauce that gave Italians a glimpse of heaven even if they didn't go to church.

"You'd never catch Dolly in church, either, except when she got older. I once asked Frank about that, and he said, 'Jesus, if my ma went to church, she'd try to change the whole goddamn thing. She'd have them doing different prayers, singing different songs. . . . They're better off without her, trust me.' I know that Dolly became more religious in her sixties, when she actually started giving money to church charities."

Her friend Doris Sevanto said, "She once told me that she had a dream that she and Frankie and Marty were standing at the golden gates of heaven and couldn't get in. In her dream she was shaking and rattling the gates until finally God came over and said, 'Who the hell's out there?' And she said, 'It's us, dear Lord, the Sinatras of Hoboken.' And God said, 'Who? Never heard of ya. Go away.' Then he went back to his business. After that, Dolly said, she started going to church. Over a twenty-year period, she tried to convince Frank to take his religion more seriously. But he didn't do so until after she died."

Indeed, his mother's death had spurred Frank Sinatra on to a deeper interest in Catholicism. In searching for some logic and reason behind the senseless tragedy that had occurred in his life, he turned to a faith he had never completely lost but had certainly ignored over the years.

Sinatra's marriage ceremonies to Ava Gardner and Mia Farrow had not been performed with Catholic rites, so they were not recognized as valid. However, the 1939 union with Nancy that had taken place at Our Lady of Sorrow Church in Jersey City was not only a legitimate marriage but, as far as the Catholic church was concerned, still binding in that the church does not recognize divorce. The Revised Code of Canon made it possible for Frank to annul that marriage, even though it had resulted in three children, and start over again with Barbara.

To remarry Barbara Marx Sinatra in a Catholic ceremony now seemed to Frank to be the most conscientious thing to do. Barbara was right; the idea had somehow eased Frank's suffering. He felt that this new religious ceremony—and Barbara's converting to Catholicism—would somehow make his mother happy in her afterlife. However, in truth, Dolly never expressed the slightest concern about the religious legitimacy of her son's marriage to Barbara. In fact, she was probably just as happy that the marriage *wasn't* recognized by the church. Her issues with Barbara certainly did not relate to spiritual matters.

Frank's children—Nancy in particular—were furious with both Frank and Barbara about the impending annulment. This course of action deeply hurt their mother, they felt, and it placed their own futures in doubt. Would this annulment somehow make them illegitimate in the eyes of the law? And how would that affect their inheritances? Millions were at stake. Did Barbara really have a master plan to take all of the Sinatra money for herself? Was she using the rules of the Catholic faith to her advantage in attaining that goal? Frank's three grown children were acting so completely irrational that Frank sent a priest to talk to them and convince them that the annulment had nothing to do with them or with their legal standing as Sinatra's heirs.

All of the attendant controversy and outrageous suspicions of Barbara's motivations did nothing to ingratiate Frank's children to her or her to them. "She was a woman who was simply trying to help her husband through a terrible grieving process," said her friend Eileen Faith, "but those Sinatra brats were so blinded by rage, they couldn't see that.

What a spoiled bunch they are, I'm telling you. Wealth and privilege have given them a lot of things, but common sense is not on the list."

Frank was granted the annulment in 1978. He and Barbara remarried in a private Catholic ceremony, and no public announcement was made. It wasn't until Sinatra was photographed receiving Communion in 1979 that the media began to question what was going on. Since there was no publicity surrounding the annulment, some members of the media assumed that Frank had paid off the Vatican to get him a quick entrée into Catholic legitimacy, not realizing that he had been working on this matter for some time. "Did Frank Make the Vatican an Offer It Couldn't Refuse?" asked the *Los Angeles Herald Examiner*. Privately, as one might imagine, Frank Sinatra seethed.

CHAPTER 40

Now in his sixties, Sinatra would be more active on the concert trail in the 1980s than would many entertainers half his age. In January 1980 he began the year by performing at Caesars Palace. (His contract at Caesars would have him performing there throughout the coming decade, always to standing room only.) Following the Vegas engagement, he went to Brazil, where he had never before appeared. Four sold-out shows at the Rio Palace in Rio de Janeiro preceded a huge turnout of 175,000 people at the Macarena Stadium, a soccer field. (The audience is listed in the *Guinness Book of World Records* as having been the largest ever assembled for a concert.) When he returned to the United States, he performed at another fund-raiser for Ronald Reagan, this one with Dean Martin at the Shrine Auditorium in Los Angeles. In March he began filming a movie, *The First Deadly Sin*, with Faye Dunaway.

Despite his advancing age, his schedule never slowed down; for Sinatra, it would seem there was always more to do, more to experience. Throughout the year, he performed at benefits for hospitals, research centers, the Red Cross (in Monaco, for Grace Kelly), the University of Nevada, and St. Jude's Ranch for Children. Later in the year, he would break a ninety-year record at Carnegie Hall when a two-week engagement there sold out in one day. When thirty-four-year-old Liza Minnelli couldn't perform at her December 1980 engagement at the Riviera Hotel in Las Vegas, Frank stepped in to take her place.

Sinatra's notorious battles with the media would also continue into the eighties. Unfortunate feuds with venerable women of the press, such as Liz Smith and Barbara Walters, did nothing to ingratiate him with those influential reporters or their audiences. Simply put, Sinatra still did not appreciate being criticized in the press, especially, it would seem, by women.

"Why doesn't this great big bully just shut up and sing?" an exasperated Liz Smith finally asked in her column. "Here is one of the finest talents of our time, a real legend both from his long career and his many good works for friends and for charity. Why does he have to keep ruining it all the time by stooping onstage to the petty throwing of cow chips?" (It should be mentioned that Liz and Frank later patched up any differences over a lunch and remained friendly thereafter.)

Regarding the critical press, Sinatra told Larry King in an interview at about this time, "I have never once disputed a critique about me. Never. Never, never, never. A man or woman doesn't like what I do, what can I do about it? So anybody who says I don't like critics is an idiot.

"The majority of the time they [critics] have been good to me. The ones who were nasty were people who sent a surrogate to cover the show. I'm never sure they even saw the show. Those kind of guys—I say if they weren't critics they'd be snipers on the roof with a rifle.

"But editorially speaking, the so-called serious, fine journalists in the world today—they don't impress me. They're vitriolic. They don't even criticize; they just inject poison. Most times they should be more constructive. Do it carefully. I avoid them. I will not do anything to help them in their job unless I know they are a decent person that I know didn't hurt me or anybody else I know.

"For instance, this kid did a nice piece on me for *Time* magazine," Frank added. "When the article came out, it was pretty much what I said, but the last line said, 'I can sing any son of a bitch off the stage today,' and I looked at that and said I never said that. I called him and said, 'I never said that; what's that?' and he said one of the editors said the article was too bland and they added that last line. If it's in print and I deny it, they can say, Oh, yeah he said it, and I can't prove I didn't' "

Indeed, despite his age not much had changed for Frank when it came to his frustrations with the media.

By the end of 1980, Frank Sinatra was sixty-five-years old; Barbara surprised him with a country-and-western-styled birthday party for 250 people. He had issued his first studio album release since 1973, a three-record package called *Trilogy* that took a look at his past, present, and future through music. Disc one—Collectibles of the Early Years—included rerecordings of some Sinatra favorites, such as "The Song Is You" and "It Had to Be You," arranged by Billy May. Disc two—Some Very Good Years—featured Sinatra on contemporary numbers such as Neil Diamond's "Song Sung Blue" and the Beatles' "Something" (truly odd, with Sinatra singing "Stick around, Jack, and it will show . . ."). Disc three—Reflections on the Future in Three Tenses—featured new material, none of which most people really understood. It was arranged by Gordon Jenkins. In all, this Sonny Burke production was a monumental musical endeavor that involved five hundred musicians, and even Frank had to admit later that most people "just didn't get it," referring to disc three.

Trilogy is most noteworthy because Frank was willing to do something different with his music and thereby take a chance. Whereas other artists Sinatra's age were rerecording the same songs, Sinatra was marching ahead and trying new ideas, as he did on disc three. That third disc was regarded critically as a misfire, but a sincere one, just the same—a try, at least, at something provocative and important. It was to Sinatra's great credit that he was still on the trail of new conquests. That the album was such a sensational sales success is amazing, but what remains significant is its artistic intent.

Trilogy sold well, went to number one on the charts, and received six Grammy Award nominations. Its success was ironic, considering the fact that executives at the record label, Reprise, didn't even want to release it. "There was a reticence to record him," remembered his son, Frank junior. "When the Trilogy tape was brought by its producer—the late Sonny Burke—to Reprise Records, which Sinatra himself had formed in 1960 [but which was now under different management], they said, 'We're not sure we want to record Frank Sinatra.' The reason was the rise of rock and roll, which repulsed him [Frank senior] the way it repulsed me," said Frank junior.

From *Trilogy* came another of Frank Sinatra's signature songs, the extremely commercial "Theme From New York, New York," arranged by Don Costa on disc two. Originally from the Martin Scorsese box-office musical disaster *New York, New York*, starring Liza Minnelli, the song was a minor hit for Minnelli. Sinatra first began performing it in concert in 1978 as an opening number at Radio City Music Hall, and in months to come he would tailor the song to his own taste, transforming it into a more dramatic interpretation not only vocally but musically before finally recording it on September 19, 1979, with a superior, brassy, big-band Don Costa arrangement.

"Theme from New York, New York" was a huge hit for Sinatra and erased any fears Reprise may have had about Sinatra's enduring appeal. Combined with the success of *Trilogy*, it marked Sinatra's biggest record-selling bonanza in a decade. The song became Sinatra's closing number and was a guaranteed showstopper every time, especially—and obviously so—when he performed it in New York. In his book *Sinatra! The Song Is You*, Will Friedwald put it best: "As sung by Minnelli, it's just your average show tune. In the hands—or tonsils, rather—of Sinatra, it exemplifies the

427

anger and the optimism, the ambition and the aggression, the hostility and the energy, the excitement and the excrement that is New York. And that is also Sinatra.''

Sinatra would follow *Trilogy* with another album in 1981, *She Shot Me Down*. By this time, Sinatra's voice had become an almost completely different sound—huskier, older, sometimes richer, sometimes creaky, sometimes melodic, sometimes off-key. His impeccable phrasing and elocution shone through, however, and as a result, *She Shot Me Down* remains the definitive album—artistically and thematically—of Sinatra's maturity.

Many who have followed Sinatra's life and career have said that they wept when they first heard the album *She Shot Me Down*. Certainly one reason was that Gordon Jenkins had turned out arrangements so affecting and eternal that they stirred the deepest longings in listeners' hearts. This was "Gordy's" last work with Sinatra, or with any artist, for he had already been diagnosed with ALS (amyotrophic lateral sclerosis) and had lost the use of his tongue. Now, more than ever, the music spoke for him.

Another reason for tears was that Sinatra, who long ago should have given up recording, had turned out an album as deep, moving, and revelatory as any he had produced before, with such songs as "Hey Look, No Crying," "Monday Morning Quarterback," and especially, a medley of "The Gal That Got Away" and "It Never Entered My Mind." Moreover, Sinatra was still growing and evolving as an artist, still putting his life experience into his work.

Heard today, *She Shot Me Down* remains simply heart-stopping in its depth of emotion. It reached forty-two on the *Billboard* charts, which not only annoyed Sinatra's followers but the man himself, who had already grown cynical where the music industry—and his place in it—was concerned.

At the age of sixty-five, Frank Sinatra again began taking stock of his life and career. How, he wondered, would he be remembered? As one of the great voices of the twentieth century? A cultural icon? Friend of presidents? Civil Rights and political activist? An altruistic man who had raised millions for charities? Certainly each of those descriptions seemed a comfortable fit. However, Sinatra realized that one perception of him endured after all of these years, and it was the one that galled him most: "Friend of the mob." How had he allowed this identification with the underworld to continually tarnish his image?

To his way of thinking, his reputation as a man on the fringe of legitimacy had always been unfair. He didn't seem to understand that the public's notion of him as a friend of the Mafia was, in part, his own doing. The glaring lack of judgment he had so often demonstrated when it came to the people with whom he socialized had caught up with him over the years, spoiling his reputation. Instead, he continued to blame the press for reporting details of those associations.

Of course, the media often *were* unfair to Sinatra; articles about him and "the gang" were sensational. However, as far as the public is concerned, Frank would have been well advised to have exercised more caution about those darker relationships. If he had done that, there would not have been anything to report, even inaccurately.

For instance, in the summer of 1978 there had been a great deal of negative publicity generated by the accusation that Frank Sinatra had somehow been involved in skimming funds from the Westchester Premier Theater in Tarrytown, New York. Frank had performed at the theater in April 1976 and was paid $800,000 for the engagement, the most he had ever been paid for singing in a venue of that size. It had been rumored, though, that the Mafia had financed the establishment. If true, it was not Sinatra's concern. As long as he was paid for his work, he didn't care who bankrolled the theater; neither did Steve Lawrence and Eydie Gormé, Diana Ross, or any of the others who performed there.

Frank performed at the theater again in September 1976 and then a final time in September 1977 (with Dean Martin) when the establishment was on the brink of bankruptcy, after having generated $5.3 million. All of that money, it was rumored, was going *somewhere,* and if it wasn't going back into the theater, it was probably finding its way into the coffers of the mobsters who had financed "the joint," one of whom was rumored to be Carlo Gambino, head of a powerful, influential crime family in New York, who reputedly had helped finance the theater with $100,000 on the understanding that Sinatra would be signed to perform there.

The problem for Sinatra began during his first engagement at the Premier when a contingent of known gangsters—including Carlo Gambino, Greg DePalma, Jimmy Fratianno, Paul Castellano, Joseph Gambino, and Richard Fusco—came backstage on April 11, 1976, after a performance. True to form, Frank allowed himself to be photographed with these characters. It could be argued that he had no choice. Perhaps it would have been impolite to refuse to allow his picture to be taken with these fans, even if they were all Mafia kingpins, especially since mob chieftain Carlo Gambino was with his granddaughter, whose name is Sinatra!

However, in the world of show business it's a fact that a celebrity can always figure out a way to avoid having his photo taken if he really wants to. Someone like Sinatra, who was surrounded by bodyguards, assistants, and others whose job it was to insulate him from the public when necessary, would most certainly be able to find a discreet way to avoid posing for a picture with a bunch of gangsters, especially since these kinds of photos had been used against him in the past.

"Unfortunately, they got into the hands of the press," Mickey Rudin explained of the photos of Sinatra and the mobsters. As if it were not practically *guaranteed* to occur considering the subjects of the impromptu photo session. One picture would later end up a large two-page spread in *Life,* January 1979. The photos were introduced into evidence when certain individuals were accused of bankruptcy fraud in connection with the Westchester Premier Theater. Sinatra was not subpoenaed to testify in the matter. However, the press did make much of Sinatra's connection to the theater and to Gambino and the rest of the men in the photograph. Others who did testify—such as Jimmy Fratianno—insisted that Sinatra was involved in raising money for the mob and in skimming profits from the Westchester Premier Theater. Since Fratianno was a mobster informant who had been granted immunity by the government for his testimony, he wasn't exactly a credible witness. The case ended in a mistrial, with some of the principals being tried separately later and ending up in jail and Sinatra's image being further tarnished.

Frank Sinatra was getting older; he knew that his days on this earth were numbered. He recognized his own mortality, and he had to accept it, as much as he detested the notion of dying. He had campaigned tirelessly for Ronald Reagan in the 1980 presidential campaign, had raised more than $250,000 in fund-raisers, attended the Republican Convention in Detroit, where Reagan received the nomination, and when Reagan was elected, was even named chairman of the inaugural gala, held on January 19, 1981, at the Capitol Center in Maryland.

Even though he was now a close friend of the president's—Reagan would even appoint him to the President's Committee on the Arts and Humanities—when asked about Frank's alleged ties to the mob, Ronald Reagan could only offer rather weakly, "We've heard those things about Frank for years. We just hope none of them are true."

Was that the best the president of the United States could do in defense of Frank Sinatra? *Hope* it wasn't true? Sinatra knew that he had to finally address some of the more enduring questions about his character. His legacy had always mattered to him, which is why he had devoted so much care and attention to the music he would leave behind. That he was thought by many to be of ill repute was a perception he wanted to change. Therefore, after he received the Humanitarian of the Year Award at the Century Plaza Hotel from Variety Clubs International on April 24, 1980, Sinatra decided to finally do something about having shaken hands with the "boys" on more than one occasion.

In 1980, Frank Sinatra applied for a Nevada gambling license. He had lost his original license in 1963 when Sam Giancana became embroiled in a fight with Phyllis McGuire's road manager at Sinatra's Cal-Neva Lodge, a skirmish that—according to witnesses—Sinatra broke up. By law, Giancana was not even supposed to be on the premises, and as the result of an intense investigation, Sinatra gave up his license just before it was to be revoked. Now he wanted it back. However, in order to get it, he would have to submit to a full investigation of his life by the Nevada Gaming Control Board.

According to the Nevada statutes regarding the approval of a gaming license, such a license can only be approved for "a person of good character, honesty and integrity, a person whose prior activities, criminal record, if any, reputation, habits and associations do not pose a threat to the public interest." To Sinatra, it was worth the gamble to prove that he was such a person. Not only did he want that license, he wanted the record to be cleaned up where his alleged affiliations with the Mafia were concerned.

Most observers agreed that Sinatra would be granted the gaming license he so desired regardless of testimony offered at the hearings; he, too, was closely aligned to the Reagans and to other political figures and had raised too much money for charity, especially in recent years, for the investigation to go against him. The Nevada Gaming Commission did not have subpoena power and therefore could not compel certain known underworld players and Frank's associates, like Judith Campbell Exner, to testify. The committee was assisted by Sinatra attorney Mickey Rudin in locating those people Sinatra and Rudin felt could best vouch for his good character, such as Ava Gardner and Nancy Sinatra Sr. It seemed to most people in Sinatra's circle, and in the media, that the investigation, which would ultimately cost Sinatra $500,000, and the subsequent hearings were a sham.

Frank Sinatra would give his testimony on February 11, 1981, in Las Vegas's city council chambers. He was accompanied by his wife, Barbara, various attorneys and publicists, and Jilly Rizzo. Earlier in the day, Frank's close friend Sheriff Peter Pitchess, of Los Angeles County, testified that "if Mr. Sinatra is a member of the Mafia, then I am the godfather." A Catholic priest and Sinatra family friend Father Herbert Ward testified that Frank "gave glory to God." While CNN cameras broadcast the proceedings live, Gregory Peck, Kirk Douglas, and Bob Hope, in sworn affidavits, testified to Frank's generosity and benevolent spirit. *Las Vegas Sun* publisher Hank Greenspun insisted that the incident that caused Sinatra's license to be revoked in 1963 was "nothing more than a shouting match" between Frank and Ed Olsen, chairman of the Nevada Gaming Board, now deceased. Mickey Rudin said that the FBI had always been "out to get" Sinatra and pointed out—accurately—that much of the "information" in their official files on Sinatra was rumor and innuendo masquerading as fact.

Finally, the pièce de résistance: Frank Sinatra's sworn testimony. It would be viewed by his critics as a five-and-a-half-hour-long revision of history. His supporters thought of it as Frank's opportunity to once and for all address for the first time in public many of the controversies in his life. Either way one looked at it, it was a great show. Sinatra, wearing a suit and black thick-rimmed glasses and with notes, documents, and other legal records at the ready, testified that Sam Giancana never had a financial interest in the Cal-Neva Lodge and that "I never invited Mr. Giancana to come to Cal-Neva Lodge, and I never entertained him and I never saw him" on that night in 1963—or any other night, for that matter—that had caused him to have his license revoked. He further testified that Giancana had never been to Cal-Neva at any other time.

When it was pointed out at the hearing that his testimony was in direct conflict with that of Phyllis McGuire's [on January 27, 1981] to the committee that Sam Giancana was there for the first three to five days of her engagement with her sisters and that Sinatra was not only present but that he had broken up a fight between McGuire and her road manager, Victor La Croix (who, inexplicably, was not called to testify), Sinatra seemed unfazed. He insisted that he wasn't even in Nevada, but rather in Los Angeles, when that fight broke out. When asked if he was now changing his story because eighteen years earlier, in 1963, he had told Ed Olsen that Giancana *actually* was at Cal-Neva, Frank explained, "I might have said it. I was frustrated. I was angry. I might have said anything. But if I said it, I didn't mean it." He also testified that he could not recall how he met Sam Giancana.

Mickey Rudin testified about the night in question in 1963: "He [Sinatra] went back and forth several times [to Cal-Neva from Los Angeles]. I would have to tell you it was my recollection that he was not there [when Giancana was present], and I would also have to tell you that I don't have that much confidence in my recollection. Maybe I fixed in my mind that he wasn't there and that's now the story.

"I do know he [Sinatra] didn't invite him [Giancana] and both of us were upset that he was there," Rudin further testified. "I don't know if he [Sinatra] sent up word or I sent word to tell the man [Giancana] to leave or if I was even on the premises.

"I'm a little confused about it, but I do know that neither one of us invited him, and we were unhappy about his being there."

Frank testified that he thought he remembered Mickey Rudin telling Giancana to leave the premises, but Rudin said he didn't recall having done that. Rudin also said that the reason Sinatra gave up his gaming license in Nevada was because "Jack Warner (of Warner Bros., with whom Sinatra had a number of pending deals) said he wanted Sinatra out of Nevada and that his being in Nevada would be a problem for Warner."

Frank also testified that he wasn't aware of any connection between Sam Giancana and the Villa Venice nightclub in Chicago, that Giancana had never asked him to perform at the club, and that it was "just possible" that he saw Giancana while performing there.

Sinatra's final word on Sam Giancana: "I never had anything to do with him business-wise and rarely, *rarely*, socially. No connection whatso-ever."

Sam's daughter, Antoinette Giancana—also, inexplicably, not called to testify—was incensed by Sinatra's testimony, saying later that she and her father were at the Villa Venice every night Sinatra performed there and that her father and Frank hugged each time they saw one another. Phyllis McGuire was also angry with Sinatra for disavowing his relationship with her boyfriend, Sam Giancana. "Frank adored the man and then, after his death, turned on him and denied their friendship just to get that damn license," she said later. "All the proof of Frank's friendship with Sam is in the FBI files. It's all there. Everything."

There was also some intriguing testimony regarding Frank's trip to Havana in 1947, in which Frank said his purpose in going was not to meet with any underworld characters, such as Lucky Luciano, but rather "to find sunshine." In response to the allegation—which seemed to have been first made by Lee Mortimer—that Sinatra brought $2 million to Havana in an attaché case, Frank said, "If you can find me an attaché case that holds two million dollars, I will *give* you the two million dollars." Sinatra further testified that he had no idea why his name and address were in Luciano's possession when the gangster was once searched by Italian officials. And as to the allegation that his early career was financed by mobsters, Sinatra had only two words: "It's ridiculous."

Regarding the photograph of Frank Sinatra and the group of mobsters that visited him backstage at the Westchester Premier Theater—described by one committee member as "a who's who and what's what in the area of organized crime"—Frank explained, "I was asked by one of the members of the theater—he told me Mr. Gambino had arrived with his grand-daughter, whose name happened to be Sinatra . . . and they'd like to take a picture. I said, 'Fine.' They came in and they took a picture of the little girl, and before I realized what happened, there were approximately eight or nine men standing around me, and several other snapshots were made. That is the whole incident that took place." Of the gentlemen in the picture, Sinatra said, "I didn't even know their names, let alone their backgrounds."

Afterward, to demonstrate the kinds of photographs that are often taken backstage, Sinatra showed a scrapbook of photographs of himself with Gregory Peck and the prime minister of Israel; with Anwar Sadat and his wife, Barbara; and with inspectors of the San Francisco Police Department, who, Sinatra said, looked like "unsavory guys. If you look at this picture without my telling you [who they are], it's frightening." In effect, he was saying that if these inspectors looked like mobsters, there was no way he could tell backstage who was a hoodlum and who was not.

The one time Sinatra seemed to lose his composure occurred when he was asked about the volatile incident that took place in 1967 between him and Caesars Palace casino manager Carl Cohen, when Cohen cut off his credit and embarrassed him in front of the Apollo astronauts. Frank had been so upset by Cohen's actions, he took Mia on a terror ride in a golf cart and then confronted Cohen about his actions. He then ended up getting punched in the face when he called Cohen a "kike."

When asked what had really happened, Sinatra snapped, "That was a personal incident, just between the two of us, between two fellas. I'd rather not discuss that. It was something I think has nothing to do with the Sands, Las Vegas, or anyplace." The committee members seemed stunned by Sinatra's heated response. Frank added, "A dislike was formed between two people, and there was a scuffle."

Sinatra had so intimidated the committee by seeming so annoyed at them for bringing up Cohen that no one dared pursue the line of inquiry. When the subject was quickly changed, it appeared clear to most observers that Sinatra was in charge of the proceedings.

As to the incident at Caesars Palace in the early seventies, when casino manager Sanford Waterman pulled a gun on Sinatra, Frank continued to testify rather defensively. "I came off the stage and went up to Waterman, who was in the pit. I asked for some credit, and he gave me a rough time. I thought maybe he was going senile or something because he had never spoken to me like that before. He put a gun in my rib and said, 'You're never gonna hurt me.' If we hadn't stopped the people from wanting to take his head off, he would have been hurt very badly that night. We actually saved his life and got him into an office. Because when the people saw him with a pistol in his hand . . . I just whacked his hand and got rid of it. I nearly shook myself to death two minutes later when I realized what happened."

Of the Kennedys, Frank said that he never attempted to intercede on behalf of Sam Giancana with either John or Robert Kennedy. (Actually, though, he didn't explain that he had asked Peter Lawford to do that business for him and Lawford had failed. Then, later, he lied to Giancana and said that he had, in fact, spoken to Robert Kennedy. He said he had written Sam's name on a piece of paper and said to Kennedy, "This is my buddy. This is what I want you to know, Bob.")

Mickey Rudin turned over what he described as "fourteen pounds" of FBI files which Sinatra and Rudin obtained under the Freedom of Information Act. Anyone who has ever seen these files, which comprise thirty years of investigation into Sinatra's life by the FBI, can attest to the fact that they are, at first glance, incomprehensible. It takes months of work to decipher them, with so many sections and names blackened out to protect certain parties. In the end, they can only be used as a road map for further inquiry. They most certainly cannot be used to draw conclusions, because so much of the material found in them is based on hearsay, gossip, and rumor.

However, perhaps because of their daunting volume, it seemed that the committee apparently did not bother to go through them all. They probably reasoned that they knew everything they needed to know about Frank Sinatra—a man who has had more words published about him than any other figure in the history of popular entertainment—just based on his press coverage. As a result, the committee was powerless to pin down Frank Sinatra on important details or challenge him on any lapses of memory, if, in fact, anyone was interested in doing that.

Stephen Webb, a former FBI agent, explained: "Years had passed, and Sinatra picked the right time to do this little dance with the Las Vegas officials. Too many people were dead, and too much water had gone under the ol' bridge. No one cared as much as they might have in the 1950s, and to have to read all of those documents, well, forget it. I was one of the guys assigned to go over the paperwork before it was handed over, and I saw for myself what a complete mess it was. I didn't know what Sinatra was guilty of, and frankly I didn't care. However, reviewing the boxes of papers that were to be sent to the committee did nothing to illuminate anything for me. It was one big mess."

As expected, at the end of the five-and-a-half-hour testimony, Nevada Gaming Control Board chairman Richard Bunker moved that Frank Sinatra be recommended to the Nevada Gaming Control Commission for a six-month license; the other three commissioners who had interrogated Sinatra agreed. Then, on February 19, 1981, Frank appeared before the Gaming Control Commission and answered more questions for about an hour and a half, again saying that he has never had any association with members of organized crime. The commission then gave Frank his gaming license, and without the six-month limitation. Sinatra felt vindicated.

In retrospect, what can be made of Sinatra's sworn testimony? It would seem that much of it was in direct conflict with the memories of people who, over the years, have been close to him. With many of the principal players—such as Sam Giancana, Ed Olsen, the Kennedys—deceased, it was not difficult for Sinatra to rewrite his relationships with them if, in fact, that's what he intended to do. It would certainly seem, at least from all available evidence, that Sinatra was not telling the whole truth during the hearings. In fact, even the authorized Sinatra television miniseries produced by his daughter Tina (which would not air until ten years later, in 1991) portrayed a close relationship between Sinatra and Giancana.

That Frank Sinatra hedged on certain issues and seemed to actually be untruthful about others called his credibility into question as far as many members of the press and public were concerned. However, Sinatra had a bigger picture in mind, one that loomed larger than the gaming license for which he had applied and one that perhaps mattered to him more than the beliefs of people who would be dead and buried in years to come. He knew that in the court of public opinion, many were certain he was guilty of fraternizing and doing business with mobsters, and he wanted that perception changed. With this testimony, Sinatra was clearly attempting to clean up the historical record about him for future generations; he never wanted it to remain as the final word that he had lost his license in 1963 because of his association with Sam Giancana or that he was a friend of the underworld's.

Sinatra may or may not have told the entire truth during those 1981 hearings before the gaming commission, but he finally had read into the official record what he and his family wanted history to reflect about him. In doing so, he had protected his legacy, which, in the end, may actually have been Frank Sinatra's intention.

CHAPTER 41

When he was being investigated for the approval of his gaming license, Frank Sinatra submitted President Ronald Reagan's and Nancy Reagan's names to the Nevada committee as character references. He must have known that the committee would not call upon the Reagans for such a reference, but their names gave the list of references submitted by his attorney Mickey Rudin a certain impressive distinction. Reagan also provided a letter of recommendation to the commission, calling Sinatra "an honorable person, completely loyal and honest." Frank's use of the Reagan name for this purpose did not sit well, however, with some of Reagan's supporters.

Former FBI agent Clarence Newton said, "I called Ed Meese the minute I heard the news and told him that Frank Sinatra's closeness to Reagan was going to do nothing but bode ill because the guy's been controlled by hoodlums for years. Meese said, 'But he's never been indicted.' I said, 'Oh, Christ, Ed, you sound like a defense attorney, not a prosecutor.' I tried to warn them, but Sinatra was giving them a hell of a lot of money at the time from doing benefits, so what I had to say fell on deaf ears."

Former FBI agent Stephen Webb said, "As I understand it, the Reagans made it clear not only that were they willing to be used as character references but that they would actually testify before the committee if necessary. Nancy, in particular, wanted to do anything she could. She seemed to have a crush on Frank, which many people in Washington knew. She would do whatever was necessary to help him and force Ronnie to cooperate if he was inclined not to do so."

Webb continued: "I also understand that Nancy said, 'I wish I could clear *my* name this way. Some of the things that have been said about me are just as unfair.' But my information has it that Sinatra decided not to impose on the Reagans to testify. He didn't want to trouble them, and also I don't think he wanted it to look as if he was calling in the big guns for help. However, if the committee decided to ask for the Reagans, then he would have appreciated their making an appearance on his behalf. They were not asked, however, so it was all moot."

People in Frank Sinatra's circle had been whispering about his relationship with the first lady, Nancy Reagan, for years. Back in the 1960s, Frank Sinatra had nothing but contempt for her. "A dumb broad with fat ankles who can't act" is an assessment of Mrs. Reagan attributed to Sinatra in various accounts of his life and hers. He felt that she had somehow bullied her husband into politics. However, his opinion of her changed in the 1970s.

When Sinatra supported Ronald Reagan for governor, he became better acquainted with Nancy Reagan and found her to be a charming, effervescent person. After having in-depth conversations with her, he believed she was misunderstood by much of the public and the press, which thought she was cold and heartless, and in that respect he felt they had much in common.

Nancy Reagan suffered a great deal of ridicule from the press during the 1980 presidential campaign; it did not abate when she became first lady. It started with "the gaze," the constantly adoring look she fixed on her husband whenever he was speaking, no matter what he was saying or how many times she had heard the words before. While former first lady Rosalynn Carter dressed in practical polyester, Nancy Reagan was the epitome of haute couture. Whatever she wore was always attributed to one designer or another; red was her signature color. Her light brown, blond-streaked hair was always flawlessly in place. Her jewelry was elegant, tasteful. She was so thin, at times she looked anorexic.

Once in the White House, everything she did was scrutinized. Her friends were too rich. She was described as being too stingy, too demanding, too cold, too calculating, too imperious. She was portrayed as both the iron hand in the velvet glove and Marie Antoinette.

"She's had such a bum rap," Frank told Larry King during a radio interview. "The china was a terrible, terrible misrepresentation. [Mrs. Reagan was accused of spending over $200,000 in tax dollars on 220 expensive place settings.] She didn't buy it with tax money. It was given to the White House, and what's wrong with having pretty china in the White House? What's wrong with having a White House that is the most wonderful building in the world? Nothing wrong with that at all. She got a bad going over by the press, which doesn't surprise me."

In January 1981, when Frank Sinatra hosted the Reagan inaugural gala, which had raised more than $5 million for the president's $10 million inaugural (the most expensive in history), he sang the song "Nancy" (with the laughing face) to Mrs. Reagan. Special lyrics were added to the song, which made it "Nancy with the Reagan Face." Sinatra's delivery was so touching and intimate, it raised some eyebrows.

Close friends of Nancy Reagan's were well aware of her interest in Frank Sinatra, but viewed it as nothing more than a crush. Said one, "I know that Nancy fancied him. She once told me that he was the most attractive man she'd ever known, including Ronnie. So, it was definitely a flirtation on Nancy's part."

Ronald Reagan was not happy about Nancy's fascination with Sinatra, not because he was jealous but rather because he felt that his wife was being somewhat juvenile. He felt that a "teen-age crush" was beneath her, and it annoyed him. Nancy Reagan played Frank Sinatra's music constantly, especially—claim her friends—"Strangers in the Night." Exasperated, Ronald Reagan would tell her, "Enough with that goddamn record. If I hear it one more time, I'm going to throw it out the window. Put on someone else, Nancy. *Please.*"

"Nancy and Frank—whom she called Francis Albert—would talk on the telephone from all over the world. How Barbara allowed that, I don't know," said one former White House secretary who still lives in Washington, D.C., and who says she is still "in constant communication" with the Reagans. "When he got his gaming license back, I know that Nancy was on the phone with him as soon as she heard the news.

"I know that when Frank got that license, Mrs. Reagan was giddy as a schoolgirl about it. She said to the president, 'Isn't this great news?' and he said in a very deadpan manner, 'Yes, dear, I'm sure it is.'"

One particular photograph of Nancy and Frank taken at Ronnie's seventieth birthday party (on February 6, 1981) caused a small sensation among those in the Reagan camp. The two were pictured dancing together at the festivities, with Ronald Reagan attempting to cut in on the dance. The expression on the president's face as he notices his wife in Sinatra's embrace has been described by some as "amused," and "perplexed" by others. Nancy Reagan looks to be in the throes of romance . . . with Frank Sinatra.

When Michael Deaver saw the photograph in the paper the next day, he stormed into the office of the chief White House photographer, Michael Evans. "You dumb son of a bitch," he shouted. "You goddamn stupid idiot. Why did you release a picture of the first lady with Frank Sinatra, of all people? You know damn well that he is mobbed up to the eyeballs. You know about his Mafia connections. What the hell is wrong with you?"

Nancy Reagan was so taken with Frank Sinatra that, says the former White House secretary, "she actually had that photo of them dancing together in her wallet, with Ronnie cut out of the picture. I saw it myself. She opened her purse to get a business card out of her wallet. When she did, a small dog-eared photo of the two of them fell out, and she quickly put it back into her purse.

"I would never have dared to ask her about it. I did think it was a bit unusual for the first lady to be carrying around a wallet-sized photograph of herself dancing with Frank Sinatra—and with the president cut out of it."

When Kitty Kelley's Nancy Reagan biography was published in 1991, she made much of what she called "private lunches" enjoyed by the first lady and Frank Sinatra, implying that the two of them were having sex in the White House.

Kelley's insinuation of a sexual relationship between Sinatra and Mrs. Reagan is, at least according to people who know them best, misguided. Frank Sinatra was on the President's Committee for the Arts and Humanities, so he had good reason to be at the White House. Mrs. Reagan depended on him to organize much of the White House entertainment and Sinatra even had a new lighting and sound system installed in the White House to enhance the performances there.

What was actually going on between Sinatra and Reagan, according to informed sources, is that Nancy was having a difficult time accepting the aging process, and Frank was helping her get through it. He was her therapist, not her lover.

"She was turning sixty, and most unhappy about it," said one woman who knew Nancy Reagan well during her White House days and became even closer friends with her after she moved to the west coast after her husband's presidency. "It was an issue for her. She and Frank started having long discussions about her problem when he came to be with her after Ronnie was shot [in March 1981]. He had canceled an engagement [actually, Sinatra canceled only the last night of his stint at Caesars Palace] to be with her. She broke down during one of their many quiet times together and confessed to him that she was turning sixty and was sad about it. She said she wished to remain young, but of course that was impossible.

"She told me that Frank had said that he, too, had a terrible time turning that age. He had told her, 'There's nothing worse than being an old swinger. I can't stand it. I hate that I'm getting old.' He said that when he looked into the mirror, he saw his father's face on his body. It sickened him."

Getting old is a fear second only to death for most celebrities. As hard as they try to convince the world that they welcome their golden years, many in the public eye battle hard to retain their youth. For them, the passage of time brings with it an undeniable truth: Their "product" is spoiling.

According to her friends, Nancy Reagan told Frank Sinatra that all the hours she spent in front of a mirror applying makeup for a White House photo session had become agonizing to her. No amount of foundation could hide the fact that there were wrinkles and lines. She would study her face nightly, sometimes for as long as an hour, slathering on creams and gels, doing facial exercises, finally strapping an elastic bandage under her chin to "tighten" it. Nancy saw the beautiful woman she knew herself to be disappearing. She felt defeated and mourned the loss of her youth. Frank could relate to Nancy's hopelessness about aging.

Frank Sinatra had said, when he turned fifty years old, that looking into the mirror was actually a devastating experience for him. He told one colleague in Las Vegas, "I feel so goddamn young inside. Whose body is this, anyway? It ain't mine, that's for damn sure." That he hated turning fifty seemed like a cliché to Sinatra, which made it even worse for him. He never wanted to think of himself as a cliché. By the time he turned sixty, he had accepted the inevitable: He was getting old. However, he did not like it, nor would he discuss it with many people, not even his wife, Barbara. Nancy Reagan, however, was someone who had— for whatever reason—taken Sinatra into her confidence about her own problems with aging, and vice versa.

Ronald Reagan apparently had little time for Nancy's anxiety about the aging process. As president of the United States, he was a busy man. What did he care that his wife was having this particular crisis? Aging had never bothered him. Wisely, he thought of it as a natural process and didn't want to hear Nancy constantly whining about it. However, she and Frank spent hours talking about this subject—about their own mortality, the problems they faced growing old, and the strain it was on their public images. It would seem that *that's* what those "private lunches" were about.

"I remember that in May [7] 1981, Sinatra sang at a luncheon for Mrs. Reagan at the Congressional Club in Washington," said the former White House secretary. "She was so giddy that he was going to be there that she changed her outfit six times; I believe just to impress him. She said, 'Francis Albert is coming to see me, and I'm damn well going to look *at least* sixty for him, not eighty—which is how I feel these days.' "

Frank Sinatra was present at Nancy's sixtieth birthday party (on July 5,

1981) in Washington. (Mrs. Reagan's birth certificate says that she was born on July 6, 1921 in New York City, though she altered the date to 1923 when she became an actress in Hollywood.) A week after the party, she telephoned Sinatra and they commiserated about aging. During that conversation, Frank referred to the youth of America as "freaks of the week," which Nancy enjoyed tremendously.

According to what Frank said later, he also confided in Nancy that when he turned sixty he began shaving four times a day just to prevent gray hair from showing in his beard. He hated the toupees he had to wear, he told her. Also, he had had the scars on his neck (left by the doctor's forceps when he was born) removed by Australian plastic surgeon Dr. Rudi Unterthiner. However, that did not make him appear much younger. Finally, he decided, "I don't care anymore. I'm sixty. I hate it. So, fuck it. I just have to accept it." He, then, decided to stop bemoaning the natural aging process, and simply continue to live his life to the fullest.

Finally, according to one of Nancy's friends from Beverly Hills, Marian Long-Deveaux, "After Frank told her that, Nancy used to say the same thing, though I don't think she meant it: 'I don't care anymore. I'm sixty. I hate it. So, darn it'—she changed the word fuck to darn—'I just have to accept it.' It was as if she was trying to convince herself of it. Then, she would begin to once again despair, 'I'm an old crone, aren't I?' and call Frank Sinatra for reassurance, which he always provided."

"If they had sex, well, good for them," said another of Nancy Reagan's friends with a laugh. "However, I would doubt that she would have been able to get away with having an affair in the White House. It wasn't the most private place in the world, after all. However, besides that small detail, why not? Just because they were older?

"I know that Nancy was still active sexually with Ronnie; she was a vibrant, exciting woman even at that age. I don't know about Frank's virility—I wouldn't know about such a thing—but to think that they would not engage in physical intimacies because of their age is discriminatory thinking. However, this would be something Nancy would never have discussed with me, or anyone else for that matter. So it would all have to be pure conjecture. I do not believe, though, she would ever cheat on Ronnie. She adored him too much."

Jilly Rizzo's friend Jim Whiting said of Sinatra, "Let me tell you this, and I'm not trying to be mean-minded or indelicate, just factual. By 1981, Frank Sinatra was not getting it on with Nancy Reagan or with anyone else on the planet. He was about sixty-six, and he had had all the sex any man could want. He had been impotent for at least the last five years because of all the booze he'd soaked into his system for most of his life. His doctors had warned him of this possibility, but he wouldn't listen.

"It [the impotency] started in the 1960s, really. It was a problem throughout the seventies, and by the eighties, forget about it. . . . Frank wasn't having sex. Period. And he didn't care. It wasn't like this thing bothered him anymore, as it had when he was in his fifties. He accepted it. He said, 'Man, I can fantasize about all the dames I had in the past, and dream about them, because I remember each and every one of them. Ava,' he would say, 'now that was great sex. If it's over, the hell with it. I had my day. I did it all.' "

Frank and Barbara had been sleeping in separate bedrooms since 1979, three years after they were married. In fact, the Sinatras added another bedroom to their home just for Frank so that Barbara could have the master bedroom. "Frank liked to sleep late; Barbara wanted to be up early. Frank wanted to go bed late, and she wanted to be in bed early," said Jim Whiting. "So they had the room added to the house for him. The fact that they were separated at night, though, also made Frank feel better about the impotency, I think, because he didn't have to perform for her. I had the impression, though, that she didn't care about sex, either. These were older folks, settling into their lives."

"Theirs really was an intimate, important friendship," said a close friend of Nancy Reagan's, of Nancy's relationship with Frank. "I know that Barbara Sinatra was jealous of Nancy Reagan, and perhaps she should have been. I have friends who are close to Barbara, and they have told me that Frank never shared intimacies with his wife, that their relationship was a bit cold and distant. I believe that for whatever reason Nancy Reagan and Frank Sinatra had those so-called lunches, it was enriching for both of them. Nancy would often complain that it was not easy for her to find friends, companionship."

During their lunches together Frank introduced Nancy to *macedonia,* an Italian fruit cup of melons, cherries, nectarines, and peaches, all flavored with white wine and maraschino liqueur. "Frank found them in an Italian deli outside of Washington. He knew where every Italian deli was in the country," said Jim Whiting. "A couple of those desserts and poor Nancy would be three sheets to the wind."

"She has a great sense of humor and giggles, and she's just great," Frank said of Nancy Reagan. "It's just that the whole world can't sit down with her over a cup of tea to see what she's like."

Early in 1982, Nancy Reagan sent one Beverly Hills friend a record that Frank had produced for a campaign for Foster Grandparents* she was spearheading at the time. With the disc, she enclosed a note. "This is a new record Francis Albert did just for me. I am so proud. What girl wouldn't be?"

* On December 5, 1981, Frank recorded "To Love a Child" written by Joe Raposo and arranged by Don Costa, for Nancy Reagan's Foster Grandparents program.

CHAPTER 42

By 1982, Frank Sinatra's relationship with his wife, Barbara, was strained at best. It had never been an easygoing, completely loving marriage, and most observers felt that it most certainly would have ended had Sinatra been younger and more interested in the notion of philandering. "If I were a younger man, I'd get a divorce and remarry," he told Bill Stapely. Then he added sadly, "But I'm not a younger man . . ."

The two fought, often in public, before stunned, alarmed witnesses. They called each other terrible names while engaged in these arguments, and unlike in his volatile relationships in the past—such as the one with Ava Gardner—to some observers there didn't seem to be a foundation of romantic love between them on which they could fall back. At least to observers, they seemed to dislike one another a great deal. Bill Stapely said that he witnessed many fights between the couple, "an average of about one a week during the first twelve years of their marriage. Frank was never proud of himself for blowing his top with her," said Stapely, "so after every fight, he rewarded her with a costly gift, sometimes jewels, other times cars or cash."

An ongoing dispute between the Sinatras related to Frank's drinking. By 1982, Barbara felt that it would be in the best interest of his health if he stopped.* He refused. When working in Las Vegas or in Atlantic City, where there were casinos, Frank would stay up all night long, drinking and gambling. Even at his advanced age, he couldn't settle down; he wanted to act like a youngster. His behavior infuriated Barbara. She felt that he was not only damaging his health but his voice as well.

Indeed, by the 1980s, the Sinatra voice was all but ruined, ravaged not only by the aging process but by his careless lifestyle as well. There were times when he could approximate certain nuances of his former singing style, but those occasions were rare. He tried to quit smoking sometime in the early 1980s—cold turkey. That brief break in a sixty-year habit had

---

* Comic Roseanne tells this true story: "I was invited to his house one time with one of my ex-husbands [Tom Arnold]. And Frank asked my ex-husband to have a drink with him at the bar. And my ex-husband pointed at me and said, 'She made me stop drinking.' And Frank said, 'There's not a broad on earth that can make *me* quit drinking.' And I said, 'Well, I guess you've never been with a *really big* broad.' "

been in an effort to save his voice. However, he would still sneak a smoke on occasion.

Sinatra realized that his audiences were no longer coming to his shows to hear a great voice, anyway, though for many the hope lingered that they might. Rather, they were hoping to reclaim, if only for two hours, a lost part of their pasts, the part that was Sinatra. His presence was still overwhelming; he had such great command of the stage. His self-confidence never seemed to waver even if his voice often did. Theaters which had been filled to capacity with tens of thousands of anxious, excited people would be completely hushed—not so much as the sound of a cough or sneeze to be heard—as Sinatra performed his familiar, sad saloon songs. He still approached songs like "Angel Eyes" with the concentration and insight of an actor breathing life into a role onstage.

Still, after all these years, he was nervous before going onstage, as he told Larry King in May 1988.

"I swear on my mother's soul, the first four or five seconds, I tremble every time I take that step and walk from the wings onto the stage," he said. "I keep thinking to myself, When I go for the first sounds that I have to make, will they be there? I'm terrified for about four seconds, and then it goes away. I can't explain it. I've always had it, all the time. Will you remember the lyrics? Is your tie right? Will you use your hands right? Will you look pleasant to this audience?

"You've got to be on the ball from the minute you step out into that spotlight. You've got to know what you're doing every second on that stage; otherwise, the act goes right into the bathroom. Good night."

Under the circumstances—that he must have known he was slipping—imagine the courage it must have taken for Sinatra to walk onto a stage every night. He mustered it, and he did it.

He may not have been able to sing as he once did, but as Greg Sandow said in reviewing one of his concerts for the *Los Angeles Herald Examiner* in 1988, "He triumphed over his condition, shaping his songs—not with voice so much as with sheer force of intention—as decisively as ever." Indeed, Sinatra still heard the music in his head. As he got older, his greatest frustration would be that he could hear the notes reverberate in his mind, he just couldn't sing them. It was as it always ends up being: the old man's body not responding to the commands of the young man inside fighting to get out. Still, he communicated like no one else, if not the notes, definitely the message behind them.

Some critics—and even fans—did not want to see Frank Sinatra onstage in his late sixties and early seventies, even if he was still a great communicator, because often he wasn't such a great singer. However, Sinatra seemed determined to demonstrate by his actions that there was nothing wrong with aging. In his private moments, he would admit, he was frightened by the prospect. However, he would not stop working. To stop, he believed, would mean a sure death.

As his son, Frank junior, who would act as conductor of many of his father's shows in the 1980s, put it, "My old man's not just a star. He's American history. If he misses a note here or there, so what? Who can do what they used to be able to do? The public relates to that. He's a legend."

The word "legend" is used a great deal when people attempt to define Frank Sinatra's influence on our culture. However, Frank has never thought much of the moniker. Once, when Larry King asked him what it was like to be a "legend," Sinatra dismissed the notion. "I don't know what a legend means. I really don't quite understand," he said. "I'm not a stupid man, but the definition of legend is so broad, I don't know what it means. King Arthur was a legend, Franklin Roosevelt was a legend, and this guy, that guy . . . What does it mean? It's longevity. I think if you're around long enough people become aware, your name comes up in conversation, people write about you, they talk about you. Your name comes up. . . ."

His fourth wife, Barbara, had not been there for most of Frank Sinatra's reckless life—the years of drinking and partying in Las Vegas with the Rat Pack, the wild women, the excesses of superstardom. As Frank aged and became more cantankerous, she had to deal with the aftermath of his former lifestyle, which was not always easy.

"I can't explain it," said one of Barbara's close friends. "I was at their home one evening when they were going at it. He was impossible, just a difficult old goat used to having everything his own way. He called her an old bitch. She called him a bastard. She was always threatening to leave, and he was always promising to help her pack. She thought he fancied himself a king, and to be honest, he did. He was exasperating as he got older, a real dictator, always ordering people to get out of a room, banishing them from parties, showing his disapproval in outrageous, immature ways. He would throw things, have temper tantrums. Poor Barbara. I think she had a dreadful marriage, but she was devoted to him."

Billy Stapely said, "Once, as I looked on, they started arguing in a hotel suite, and Frank flew into a rage. He picked up an ashtray and flung it at Barbara. It whisked by her head and exploded into a hundred pieces against the wall. Frank then threw his cigarettes and lighter at her, hitting her on the leg. Next, he picked up a telephone and threw it at her. Luckily, the cord pulled the phone up short before it reached her.

"Barbara yelled, 'Frank, stop it, you fool. You're going to hurt me.' Frank surveyed the mess he'd made, then stomped off to his bedroom, slamming the door behind him." Stapely added, "I don't think he ever really hurt her. I never saw any bruises."

The Sinatras almost got into it on a television interview with gossip columnist "Suzy" (Aileen Mehle). For just a few tense moments, they revealed the kind of bickering that might have escalated into an argument if it hadn't been taking place on camera. Barbara started it by saying that Frank's "general opinion of the press is probably not the highest."

"I think you should clarify that," he told her, clearly annoyed. "Certain members of the press I have trouble with, and I wouldn't want them for friends if I lived to be a thousand years old."

"Of course, Aileen is, does, represent the press," Barbara said, trying to make a point.

Frank dismissed her with a wave of his hand and continued his thought. "But those who are my friends are my friends in the press. The ones that are my enemies I don't want as a friend."

"My point," Barbara cut in, now herself annoyed, "is that your loyalty to a friend is almost unequaled." It appeared that she was paying her husband a compliment, but she clearly did not like the dismissive tone he was using with her.

He cut her off again. "Yes, but it goes both ways. If it's true, it works both ways; otherwise, it can't possibly exist."

What he said seemed unclear. But Barbara apparently thought it best to end this line of discussion. "That's true," she said demurely.

From all accounts, it would seem that the Sinatras did not have the ideal marriage. However, they remained together despite whatever problems they were experiencing. It could be said that the former Barbara Marx had a full-time job being Frank Sinatra's wife. She always had to look her poised and elegant best; in the 1980s, she would spend a fortune on excruciatingly painful plastic surgeries—liposuction, eye tucks, face lifts—not only because she is vain (admittedly, there is an element of narcissism involved when any older person spends so much money in an effort to appear younger) but because she believes that a man of Frank Sinatra's distinction *should* have an attractive, engaging wife.

Barbara's penchant for plastic surgery might also be indicative of a lack of self-esteem, which, if true, she certainly had in common with Frank's first wife, Nancy. Always anxious to lose weight so that Sinatra would love her, Nancy also had her teeth capped and did what she could to make herself appear beautiful for him so that he would stay with her, which, of course, never worked. If plastic surgery had been more readily available in the forties, there's little doubt that Nancy, and probably Ava Gardner as well (and maybe even Mia Farrow, who also had an inferiority complex in the sixties), would have had such surgeries. Ironically, Sinatra never asked any of his wives to alter their appearance, thought the idea of such surgery was ludicrous, and apparently didn't understand why any woman would want to put herself through what he called "such bullshit."

A hairstylist, manicurist, and makeup artist comes to the Sinatra home on a regular basis to tend to Barbara. She stays physically active as a golfer, tennis player, and horseback rider.

As Frank's wife, Barbara must always be well dressed in the latest fashions, practically dripping with expensive jewels, whenever they are in public together. A woman of her position must have knowledge of nearly every aspect of social protocol, because the Sinatras are constantly entertaining, and being entertained by, important and fussy dignitaries. Not only that, but she has the responsibility of understanding and—if possible—diplomatically controlling the volatile temper and wild mood swings of an aging, difficult, and often egotistical superstar. Despite the pressure and anxiety that must be inherent in her life as the wife of one of the most famous, beloved men in the world, she is poised, charming, and charismatic whenever she is seen in public.

For years she worked for her husband's causes, and she is also still active in the Barbara Sinatra Children's Center at the Eisenhower Medical Center in Palm Springs, which opened on October 31, 1986, and treats young victims of child abuse. Frank has never been allowed to spend time at the center despite his contributions to it in excess of a million dollars. Molesting fathers often come in for treatment, and Barbara is afraid of her husband's reaction to them.

"My husband's from a totally different school," she once admitted in 1988. "He wants to break their legs. He wants to round up all the men and break their legs." He said, 'You can talk to them all you want, but let *me* teach them and they'll never do it again. If you put them in a hospital for a year, when they come out, they're not going to do that.' So he's not allowed in there."

In many respects, Barbara Sinatra is a remarkable woman, but she is also a controlling person who—as far as many of Frank's associates are concerned, and even his children, for that matter—has attempted to monopolize every one of her husband's waking moments. However, she is his wife. Perhaps it is her prerogative to at least try to have him all to herself.

Frank and Barbara's marriage continued to be difficult for Frank's three children, particularly for Nancy, who became concerned when Frank and Barbara began talking about legally adopting Barbara's grown son, Bob, from her marriage to Zeppo Marx. Nancy would say later that she was not happy about the notion that someone could actually become a "Sinatra" by adoption.

"I couldn't help feeling that to be a Sinatra kid, you had to pay your dues, had to go through the tough times with the business and the press and the personal crises," she wrote in her book *Frank Sinatra—My Father.* "To be a Sinatra, you needed a history that carried a mix of pain and prominence. A bit second rate of me, perhaps. Everybody has troubles, but someone just can't step in and take over. It doesn't work."

Nancy says that she was not worried about the distribution of wealth after her father's death, but that seems somewhat unlikely. Surely she must have been at least somewhat concerned that a relative newcomer would receive, at her affluent father's death, more money than he—in her mind, anyway—would be entitled to. These are thoughts that are often not discussed openly because they tend to make a person seem greedy and petty; however, in a wealthy family, they are realistic concerns just the same.

One of Barbara's friends remembers: "Barbara and Nancy had a screaming fight about Bobby. It was awful. Barbara said, 'There's enough money to go around, Nancy. Stop being so goddamn stingy. How much money do you need, anyway? You have millions, don't you?' Nancy was furious with her and tried to enlist her father's aid, but his position was always clear. 'You're a Sinatra, so buck up and stop your whining. She's my wife.' "

Bill Stapely said, "In 1988, Barbara talked Frank into changing the deeds on their two homes, one in Beverly Hills and the other in Rancho Mirage. So she'll get a bigger inheritance upon his death. Before the changes, Frank's three children were due to inherit half of each home. But now Barbara will get both houses all by herself, and the kids won't get so much as a doorknob or shingle."

Though Nancy and her sister, Tina, and brother, Frank, will no doubt have no financial worries after their father's death (they will inherit all of his record royalties, while Barbara will receive most of the property), perhaps they won't be as wealthy as some might expect. "I'm not a princess and I'm not an heiress," Nancy said frankly. In fact, as recently as a few years ago, she had to ask her mother for a loan because she didn't have enough money to support her two children. "He [Sinatra] didn't set up trust funds for my brother, sister, and me," she admitted. "He figured we'd handle things on our own and instead gave it [money] to people who were in need of it. He took very good care of my mother always and still does."

Nancy and Barbara would continue to have a strained relationship throughout the eighties. Whereas Nancy is emotional, it would seem that Barbara is practical. When she told Nancy, "Just because we're related doesn't mean we have to be friends," Nancy became offended. "I suppose that's true enough," she said later of Barbara's pointed observation, "especially if it's a relationship through marriage rather than blood. Get comments like that, though, and you know where you stand. I think she's a street fighter. Fortunately, I don't have to see her very often."

In truth, it could be argued that as far as Nancy Sinatra is concerned, no woman would be good enough for her father—except for Nancy's mother.

* * *

For Frank Sinatra, the years 1982 and 1983 would be consumed by sold-out performances in clubs and concert halls around the world, benefit shows for charities, award presentations for humanitarian efforts, and, of course, recordings. His daughter Nancy accompanied him for much of the 1982 tour, beginning with an engagement at Caesars Palace in March. She had suffered some career reversals in recent years as a result of having to put her ambitions aside to raise her two children. Sinatra offered to take her on the road with him for a year in hopes that positive notices would help revive her career once again. Like her father, she proved to be a hard worker and consummate performer. (The critic for the *Las Vegas Sun* noted, "Nancy Sinatra is not only gorgeous, she has more vocal ability than she'd ever been credited for having. The audience thoroughly enjoyed her.")

Throughout the tour Frank treated Nancy as he would any other opening act. They may have had warm moments offstage, but they rarely discussed business. Instead, she would receive disconcerting notes from him via his employees: "The closing number is too long; cut it." "Change the second song." "Too much talk between songs." This was typical behavior from the inaccessible Frank Sinatra. In fact, during the many years Frank junior conducted his father's orchestra, he would often not know that he and his "old man" were leaving town on a tour until the last minute.

"Usually, it's about three in the morning. I'll get a phone call from somebody in the office, in Florida, saying, 'There'll be a plane ticket tomorrow. Get ready. Get the book in order. We're going out.' You never know with him [Frank senior]. There's no way to even make a prediction. All of a sudden, he'll decide, 'Well, we've got to do this.' I turn on the fax machine. A travel itinerary will come through."

Later in March 1982, Frank and Perry Como performed at the White House during a state dinner honoring President Sandro Pertini of Italy. A few days later, Sinatra teamed with Bob Hope for a tribute to Grace Kelly in Philadelphia. Then, in April, he and Don Costa produced a wonderful album for singer Sylvia Syms, *Syms by Sinatra*, in New York. More concert dates followed in the spring; then he hosted a Friars Club tribute to Cary Grant. Caesars Palace in Las Vegas followed, then on to the Universal Amphitheatre in Los Angeles, a vacation in Monaco with Princess Grace and Prince Rainier in the summer (the last time he would see his good friend "Gracie" before her fatal automobile accident less than a month later) and a benefit at Carnegie Hall with Buddy Rich when he returned.

At sixty-seven years of age, Sinatra had not slowed down even the slightest bit; the schedule for 1983 was just as demanding. "I don't know how to stop doing things," he said in an interview at this time. "I gotta do *something.*"

Tragically, Frank's brilliant arranger Don Costa died in January 1983.

It was a difficult personal loss for Sinatra; Costa had arranged many of Sinatra's best recordings, and while they did not always get along, the two shared intimacies in the recording studio that would mean much to Frank. In some ways, his arrangers, producers, and musicians were the ones to really see Frank's true emotions—when he would translate into song whatever he was feeling at the time or what he recalled having felt years before.

Engagements in Atlantic City, Las Vegas, and Los Angeles preceded Frank's cameo in *Cannonball Run II*, with Sammy Davis, Dean Martin, and Shirley MacLaine. The hope was to recapture some of the madness from the Rat Pack's sixties adventures. Burt Reynolds was along for the ride because of his box-office drawing power.

"It was a disgrace, of course," Shirley MacLaine said of the film, and even she is mystified as to why she took a role in this silly movie after her brilliant Academy Award performance in *Terms of Endearment*. "Frank only worked half a day, and that was too long for him. He did one take and left. It looked like he had never been there at all.

"Dean had deteriorated. He seemed withered, drawn, with a grayish pallor. I noticed he put five spoons of sugar in each cup of coffee. I chided him for it and said he'd better quit. The next day, he emptied a five-pound bag of sugar inside my trailer."

In November, Sinatra and a host of stars participated in the Variety Clubs All-Star Party honoring Frank at NBC in Burbank. As with past honorees, during the special, it was announced that Sinatra's many benefit concerts over the years for the Variety Clubs International charity had enabled the building of a wing at Seattle Children's Orthopedic Hospital, which is called the Sinatra Family Children's Unit for the Chronically Ill.

The year 1983 ended with Frank celebrating his sixty-eighth birthday, but not before being honored in December with the prestigious Kennedy Center Honors for Lifetime Achievement. The Sinatra family attended a dinner hosted by Secretary of State George Shultz and a White House reception hosted by President and Mrs. Reagan before the awards ceremony at the Kennedy Center. Other honorees that year included Katherine Dunham, Elia Kazan, Virgil Thomson, and Jimmy Stewart. "There's not the remotest possibility," said Gene Kelly during the taping of the presentation for a television special, "that he will have a successor."

As he sat in the presidential box, Frank Sinatra, the elder statesman of show business, seemed older, more feeble, that evening than he ever had in the past. Even his daughter Nancy couldn't help but notice: "I kept thinking, He looks older. God. He suddenly looks older. Every time I turned to look, he seemed to age another ten years." For a loving daughter whose world had always revolved around her father—her hero—it was a mind-numbing, almost paralyzing, experience. She never could have imagined that her heart could ache so much in the midst of such a gala occasion. The realization of his aging hit her like a bolt from the blue. How much time did he have left? How could she survive without him? How could any of them?

That particular evening in Washington at the Kennedy Center had been extraordinary for Frank Sinatra for many reasons. Foremost, he had been truly successful in cleaning his record. Back In 1981, after the Nevada Gaming Commission restored Frank Sinatra's gaming license, he had felt completely vindicated. He had cleared the slate, as far as he was concerned, anyway, and had written into the historical record his point of view regarding many of the controversies of his life. Most of the principals were deceased; Frank's version would have to suffice.

Practically everything of a relevant nature had been discussed during those hearings—his Mafia connections, his gambling habits, his finances; however, mercifully, some matters were not brought up, such as Dolly's illegal activities in Hoboken.

Frank had never gotten over his mother's death; quite simply, he never would. Nothing had ever been the same for him after she was killed in that plane crash in January 1977. It seemed that everything he did had a bit less importance in his life without her to share in it with him. He treasured her memory.

Dolly Sinatra's activities as an abortionist and her resulting arrests were secrets that had been closely guarded by the Sinatra family for years out of respect for her as well as for her world-famous son. In fact, it's been said by those in the Sinatra inner circle that family members rarely even discussed these matters among themselves, preferring to just forget about them and remember Dolly in a happier light.

It's not that the Sinatras were so opposed to abortion. In fact, when Frank's daughter Nancy became pregnant at the age of nineteen, her mother took her to have the pregnancy terminated. "In those days, you didn't sleep with anyone before marriage, and you never had an abortion," Nancy remembered. "I explained my reasons, and my mother understood. She never once made me feel guilty. Neither did my father. They simply didn't want me to get hurt."

These were private matters, however, not discussed freely over coffee and *biscotti*. Many of the more distant Sinatra relatives weren't even aware that Dolly Sinatra had ever been arrested for performing abortions, which is, perhaps, as it should have been.

By 1983, though, all of that was about to change. At that time, sixty-seven-year-old Frank Sinatra realized that he was about to have a problem involving one of the few women in his life he would not be able to control: perky and petite but ever so dauntless and determined biographer Kitty Kelley. Kelley, who had written controversial and successful biographies about Jacqueline Onassis and Elizabeth Taylor, was now researching a book about Sinatra. At first, he didn't care. Other books had been written about him in the past. He knew that it went with the terri-tory. "How bad could this one be?" he asked. "They all say the same goddamn boring things, anyway."

However, when Sinatra began receiving telephone calls from friends in Hoboken telling him that Kelley had been asking certain townsfolk about Dolly's illegal activities, he became worried.

"What the hell is Kelley doing that for?" he asked one friend from Hoboken. "Why is she asking about my mother? What's *she* got to do with anything?"

"Frank, she's gonna write it all, man," reported the friend. "The whole fuckin' thing, the abortions, the arrest. Man, *she's talked to people,* Frankie, people your mother helped out. This ain't good."

"Jesus. You gotta be kidding me," Frank said incredulously. "She found people my mother helped out? I mean, I can't believe that dizzy broad would do that. I seen her on TV. She ain't that sharp, man."

Frank immediately called a meeting with his longtime attorney Milton "Mickey" Rudin (now a senior member of the Beverly Hills law firm of Rudin, Richman & Appel) and some other business associates at his home in Los Angeles. As they began to talk, one of the cooks brought out a tray of *crostini*—oven-toasted sandwiches layered with mozzarella, *pro-sciutto,* and anchovies.

"Look, this can't happen," Frank said. "What can we do?"

Rudin, who had represented Sinatra in many disputes with the media over the last forty years, told him, simply, that there wasn't much they could do about Kelley's book, at least not until it was published. Accord-ing to a witness to the meeting, Frank's spirits fell. "This is bad," he said. "Real bad. This kind of thing hurts me; it hurts my kids, my grandkids, not to mention my mother's memory. Maybe she won't write it. You think?" Frank tried to be hopeful. "Maybe she'll just let it go about the abortions. I mean, I got plenty in my own life to write about. Maybe she'll do the decent thing."

No one at the meeting held out much hope in regard to Kitty Kelley's sense of propriety where Sinatra's mother was concerned. Certainly this was uncharted terrain for Frank Sinatra: He had advance warning that something was taking place that could hurt him and his family, and there was nothing he could do about it. He wasn't about to accept such a situation. So a number of meetings were held at his home during the next few months with his legal staff, headed by Rudin, and other employ-ees to determine how to proceed in what became known as "the Kitty Kelley matter."

"Look, scare her off," Frank demanded during one meeting. "I don't care how you do it. Get rid of her. Pay her. Give her money," he sug-gested to one of his staff members. "She'll take money, the greedy broad. I know she'll take money. That's what this is all about, anyway. Give her a

452

million bucks. Who cares? If it works, it's worth it. The abortion stuff can't come out."

Sinatra was told that if it were ever revealed that Kelley was offered money, it would appear to others that Sinatra was attempting to hide something. And it was further agreed that Kitty Kelley herself would probably leak any offer of hush-money to the media.

"Well, call her, then," Frank said, pacing the room. "Reason with her. I mean, she's got a mother, doesn't she? She'll listen to reason.

"Wait. No," he said, having a second thought. "Forget that. *I'll* call her. *I'll* talk to her. *I'll* reason with her. What's her number? She'll probably have a fuckin' heart attack and keel over when she hears my voice, anyway. Then for sure there'll be no book."

Another of the attorneys advised Sinatra that if he were to call Kitty Kelley, she would be able to promote her book by saying that she had "an exclusive interview" with him, thereby lending the project an air of credibility.

By now, a frustrated Sinatra's breathing was so labored, one person in the room would later say that he feared "the old man" would have a heart attack. "You sue her, Mickey." Frank instructed Rudin. "Hear me? Sue her greedy, parasitical ass. That's the only answer."

Rudin wasn't sure of the wisdom of any such lawsuit. Perhaps he remembered the last time Sinatra brought a lawsuit against a biographer. In fact, it had made Sinatra look a bit ridiculous when, in 1976, he sued New York columnist Earl Wilson and publisher Macmillan for a million dollars over Wilson's flattering book *Sinatra*. The charge was not libel or slander. Frank came up with another complaint: "The book is boring and uninteresting," he charged in the suit.

Frank also claimed that Wilson's book was unfair competition to the book he himself might one day write. Moreover, he charged that some of what Wilson wrote wasn't true. However, as to those parts he claimed were false, he said that if it was ever proved at trial that they *were* true, it would only be because Frank had told Earl Wilson these things in the first place and in that case the statements were then supposedly protected by "a common-law copyright" because Sinatra hadn't wanted the statements to be published when he made them to Wilson. Certainly this was one of the more unusual lawsuits ever brought against a writer.

By now, at the meeting, Frank was trembling over the Kitty Kelley problem. An aide brought him a shot of Jack Daniels, and Sinatra threw it back. He sat down and tried to calm himself.

"You gotta understand that my mother was the most important thing in my life," Frank explained to the concerned people in the meeting after he composed himself. "And this woman thinks she can just ruin my mother's reputation, write anything she wants to write? Fuck, no. We gotta try," he said flatly. "We gotta at least try . . . for Ma's sake."

"Plus, it's really bad public relations, Frank," someone in the room piped up.

Sinatra glared at the guy who made that observation. Clearly, this strategy meeting was not about "public relations."

"You know what? I oughta punch you right in the face for saying that to me," Sinatra threatened. "To bring it down to that. Public-fucking-relations. Whatsa matter with you? Don't even go dere." (Frank still says that when someone in his view goes too far.)

It was decided that Sinatra would file a lawsuit against Kitty Kelley and her publisher, Bantam, prior to publication of the book in hopes of preventing it from going forward. To justify the action, Sinatra claimed that he owned his own story and, moreover, that Kelley was misrepresenting herself as Sinatra's "official biographer." (She claimed that she did no such thing.) The action was filed in Los Angeles Superior Court on September 21, 1983. Writers groups, such as the National Writers Union, came to Kelley's defense, fearing that if Sinatra prevailed, the result would have a chilling effect on freedom of the press. Sinatra dropped that lawsuit in 1984. To most observers, it seemed without merit, anyway.

Even Kitty Kelley was not aware of Sinatra's true concerns about her book. He couldn't have cared less about the rest of her research or about anything she would write about him. He felt that he had corrected any "misconceptions" during the Las Vegas hearings, anyway. He simply wished to preserve the memory of his mother. That was his main objective. He would wait with great apprehension for Kitty Kelley's book and hold out hope that what she reported would not be as devastating as he believed it would be.

CHAPTER 43

At the end of 1983, Frank got the news about Peter Lawford.

He had died at Cedars-Sinai Medical Center in Los Angeles on December 24 after having suffered terribly from liver and kidney problems. Just sixty-one, he was cremated on Christmas Day, heavily in debt and with no assets. His ashes were entombed just yards from Marilyn Monroe's at Westwood Village Mortuary. (Five years later, with his funeral expenses still unpaid, his wife, Patricia Seaton Lawford, got the notice that his ashes were being evicted. After picking them up from the mortuary, she scattered the dust into the Pacific Ocean while photographers from the *National Enquirer* took pictures.)

Frank had no comment to make about Peter Lawford's death publicly or, it would seem, otherwise. He hadn't spoken to Peter since that day over twenty years earlier when he kicked him out of his home, and his life, simply because Lawford had delivered the news that John F. Kennedy would not be staying at the Sinatra home. One associate of Sinatra's says that when the singer heard of Lawford's death, "he shook his head sadly, made the sign of the cross, and then went back to his dinner of ravioli stuffed with meat and spinach, which he ate while watching *Jeopardy!* on television."

The year 1984 would continue in the same vein of accomplishment for Frank Sinatra—concerts, benefits, award shows, telethons, trips abroad, etc.

In April and May he recorded the truly mediocre *L.A. Is My Lady* album, produced by Quincy Jones, an album Frank has never been fond of because he felt they didn't spend enough time choosing material for it. This was less an album than a collection of this and that song. In the end, people would buy it because it was a Sinatra album but not because it was a very good one.

At the end of the year he and Barbara had dinner at the White House with the Reagans.

"I don't feel sixty-nine," he told Larry King in an interview. "I feel physically in good shape. I work out as much as I like to. Sometimes I overdo it and get sore muscles, but then that's cured. Barbara and I walk a great deal. No jogging. A doctor told me that anybody over forty who jogs is fooling himself. I swim. I punch a sandbag. I skip rope. If you wanna try something that'll knock you out, try skipping rope."

Frank still tried to turn back the hands of time, but those efforts were not successful. "He had some work done on his face in 1985," said one of his closest associates. "He had his neck tightened, I know that, by Dr. Rudi Unterthiner. And another failed hair transplant. He wanted to have his eyes done, but Barbara vetoed that. She was afraid it would change his face. He was getting older, and because he really wasn't taking care of his health—he'd eat anything he wanted, drank like a fish. Well, you could see it in his face."*

By 1985, Frank and Barbara Sinatra seemed like a couple who should reconsider their matrimonial bond. The frequency and severity of their conflicts had been building for some time. Many of Sinatra's associates remembered one unpleasant scene at Bally's in Las Vegas. Frank, Jilly Rizzo, and several others were drinking, gambling, and losing money when Barbara spotted her husband. He was crouched over the craps table

---

* "He's had three face-lifts since 1979, because his muscle tone is not as good as most people's," said Australian-born Dr. Rudi Unterthiner. "I know because I worked on them."

with a cigarette hanging from his lips. He removed it for a moment as he downed the last few drops of his vodka and soda.

"Don't you think you've had enough to drink?" Barbara asked.

Frank rolled his eyes in her direction. "Listen, I'm working hard. Gimme a break. I'm relaxing."

"But you're losing all of the money you're making by working so hard," she said, trying to reason with him. "Between what you lose and what you give away, you'll never be able to stop working."

An ongoing quarrel between the Sinatras had to do with Frank's working so hard to maintain his lavish lifestyle and spending money about as quickly as he could make it. A point of contention in his marriage to Barbara had developed because Frank habitually gave his children— Nancy, Tina, and Frank—thousands of dollars in cash as gifts. Barbara felt that these offspring were old enough not to have to accept these kinds of gifts from their father.

"Dad used to shower us with gifts all the time, and that stopped," recalled Nancy Sinatra. "All of his gifting was now to his new wife. This sounds selfish. It wasn't the gifts; it was what they meant. It wasn't the lack of presents; it was the lack of his presence. When you tend to show love by giving presents and they stop, well, what is there to think? I felt I was losing him."

Frank's children also felt that Barbara was siphoning Sinatra's money. According to Sinatra intimates, he had purchased so much expensive jewelry for Barbara—gold chains, bracelets, diamond earrings, necklaces—that they filled a steel strong box two feet long, a foot wide, and eight inches deep.

"One day she asked me and the housekeeper to carry the box out of the house so she could put her prized possessions in a safe-deposit box," said Bill Stapely. "We were both grunting and groaning under the strain. That thing weighed a ton.

Also, Barbara Sinatra, like Ava Gardner years before her, was never fond of any of Frank's friends; she thought some of them were uncouth gangsters, and she wanted nothing to do with them. Others were simply immature in her view, and she felt that her husband acted like a juvenile whenever they were together, which is why Barbara's wrath turned on Jilly Rizzo during the Bally's confrontation. Barbara had barely gotten a word out about Frank's old friend when her husband blew up.

"Jilly is my friend, goddamnit," he shouted at her. "You know that, Barbara. And who he's with, they're friends of his, so they're friends of mine. Who the hell do you think you are, talking about my friends like that?"

The throng that had gathered fell silent.

"You're outta here," he hollered at his wife. "You get your bags packed, every one of 'em. I want you out of the suite before I go back in there. We're finished, Barbara. It's over." Aside from his heaving chest, Frank stood motionless. His eyes, darkened with rage, made it clear there was nothing more to say.

Barbara was speechless. She gathered herself as best she could, and after one deep breath she moved away from the crowd and toward the elevators. Frank went back to his gambling as Barbara returned to their suite.

She did as she was told; she packed her belongings and took the Sinatra plane to their Rancho Mirage home, outside Palm Springs.

"Frank came home two days later," said Bill Stapely. "For the next two weeks, there was an icy chill between them. I never heard them say a word to each other. After two weeks of this, Barbara packed some bags and moved out of the house. After she left, Frank told me, 'This marriage is over. I'm glad that broad is out of my life. She was driving me crazy.' "

Heartbroken, Barbara went to Europe after the fracas. She had endured enough, she decided, and had her attorney draw up divorce papers while she was gone.

To Frank, it made no sense to get divorced at their age. "What are we gonna do?" he asked her when she returned a month later. "Find other people? Who the hell is gonna put up with us, Barbara? Let's face it, baby. We're meant to be together. No one else will have us."

When Sinatra sincerely apologized, Barbara tore up the divorce papers. "What can I say?" she later said with a shrug. "I love him."

In May 1985, Frank Sinatra was presented with the Medal of Freedom by President Reagan. It was a proud day for him. There were clouds on the horizon, however. Advance publicity about Kitty Kelley's upcoming book indicated that she would delve into his history with mobsters in a way that had never been done before. Frank wasn't sure what she would uncover, but he was unhappy about the prospect. Also, in August 1985, Nancy Sinatra Jr.'s beloved husband, Hugh, died of cancer. He had been diagnosed back in August 1984, and the illness was a blow to the entire family. His marriage to Nancy was a strong, loving one, and so his death affected her deeply. Frank did what he could for her, but the depth of her pain was boundless. He felt he should cancel an engagement at the Golden Nugget in Las Vegas at the end of the month, but Nancy, ever her father's daughter, insisted that the show go on.

In December 1985 the seemingly impossible occurred: Frank Sinatra turned seventy years old. This fact was difficult for much of his public to accept. Bob Greene said it best in a column in the *Chicago Tribune* when he wrote, "The fact that Frank Sinatra is celebrating his 70th birthday this week is something that will cause many people to stop and think for a moment. Frank Sinatra—70 years old. It has less to do with Sinatra than with the rest of us. If Sinatra is 70, what has happened to us?" Indeed, it would seem that as Frank faced his mortality, much of his public was forced to do the same. He had been a part of our lives for so long, it was difficult, even painful, to watch him grow old, mostly because it reminded us that he was not alone.*

Twenty years earlier, in 1966, Frank Sinatra, his daughter Nancy, wife, Mia, and publisher Bennett Cerf were having a meal at Trader Vic's in Beverly Hills, and they began talking about some of the negative reports regarding Frank and Mia's recent marriage. Cerf said, "You should write a book about your father, Nancy, and tell the true story once and for all." Mia agreed. Frank said nothing, but Nancy would later recall that from the expression on his face she knew he wanted her to do it.

Now, in 1986, it seemed as if the time had come for Nancy to write that book, especially given the onslaught of bad publicity Kitty Kelley's tome was sure to generate when published, which was scheduled for September 1986. Nancy's book, *Frank Sinatra—My Father* was a thorough—though decidedly and understandably biased—book published by Doubleday in the fall of 1985. The family hoped that it perhaps would take some of the sting out of what was to come from Kelley. (Nancy, however, did not mention anything about her grandmother's ever having been arrested for performing abortions. The family probably decided to take the chance that neither would Kelley, therefore preserving the secret.)

When Kitty Kelley's *His Way* biography of Sinatra was finally published in October 1986, it was worse than Frank and the Sinatra family could ever have imagined. Indeed, Kitty Kelley held back no details of Dolly Sinatra's history. The Sinatra family's secret about Dolly was out for all to know and to scrutinize. In retrospect, it is rather surprising that it didn't happen sooner. Certainly many press people were well aware of Dolly's activities as an abortionist, but out of respect for—and perhaps even fear of reprisal by—Sinatra, they refrained from writing about them.

Of course, there was much that Frank objected to in Kelley's book. That was to be expected; no celebrity is ever happy about the results when an author writes about his life. Indeed, some of what Kitty Kelley wrote seemed suspect. For instance, she wrote that Sinatra arranged for Elizabeth Taylor to abort a pregnancy by him "at the end of her unhappy marriage to Michael Wilding" without providing a date, a hospital, a source, or any other data to support her story, which by all accounts seems to be untrue. However, Frank would just have to accept that tale and the book's other controversies as simply the price of fame. The Sina-

* A couple of months before his birthday, his good friend and arranger Nelson Riddle passed away of a liver ailment at the age of sixty-four (on October 6). The two had had a few disagreements in recent years, but they were still close; Riddle accompanied Sinatra to a dinner celebrating Reagan's reelection in January 1985. They made fourteen classic albums together.

tras would have their "say" in *another* book by Nancy (*Frank Sinatra—An American Legend,* really her first book, *Frank Sinatra—My Father,* but with an update and hundreds of photographs) and an authorized television miniseries produced by Tina Sinatra in 1994. The way Kitty Kelley portrayed Dolly's activities as "a mother who kills babies," though, infuriated Frank.

"If I ever see that broad, I swear I won't be able to control myself," Frank said of Kelley. "How can you write that about a guy's mother?"

In fact, the entire Sinatra family was crushed by Kelley's portrayal of Dolly. It was as if a dark cloud had descended upon the Sinatra fold when the book debuted at the number-one position on the *New York Times* bestseller list on October 12, 1986. When Sinatra turned the television set on one day and saw Kelley talking about his mother's arrest, he became so agitated that his family thought he would have to be treated at a hospital for an anxiety attack.

One relative said, "I saw him sitting in a room in the dark watching a videotape of this woman on a talk show, chirping happily about what she learned about Dolly. He was crying in his booze. Just shaking his head, saying, 'I'm sorry, Ma. I really am. Look what this broad is doin' here. Can you fuckin' believe it?' "

One former employee remembers the night Frank almost talked to Kelley on a television call-in program.

"I take issue with a lot of what's in it," he said of the book to the segment producer who was screening callers for the broadcast. "But I just want to ask one simple question: Does this dopey broad have a mother? That's all I wanna know. Does she or does she not have a mother? And if so, then how can she write that stuff about mine? That's it. That's the whole enchilada. That's all I gotta know."

The producer, who must have been excited by the prospects of such an on-air confrontation, put Frank on hold. As he was waiting on the line for a commercial break to end, Barbara Sinatra walked into the room and asked him what he was doing. When he told her, Barbara exclaimed, "Oh, my God."

She ran to the phone and disconnected the call. "Will you please stop it?" she said to her husband. "Don't give her the satisfaction of calling her, and on national television! Get a hold of yourself, Frank."

"I believe that book made him ill," said his daughter Tina. Frank was hospitalized (November 9–16), at Eisenhower Medical Center in Palm Springs a month after the book was published, suffering from acute diverticulitis, which is usually caused by poor diet resulting in a form of constipation that causes abscesses in the intestine. He had been performing at the Golden Nugget Casino in Atlantic City when he became ill.

His opening act, Tom Dreeson, recalled the show Frank performed the night before he had to be flown out of New Jersey and back to Los

Angeles. "I had been opening for Frank for three years, and that night he showed he really is Mr. Showbiz. There was absolutely no way the audience knew he was suffering excruciating pain. Frank's a very private person, and there's no way he would ever let an audience know there was something wrong. He left in a private jet the next afternoon, and by ten that night he was in the hospital being prepped for surgery."

His doctor, Dr. Alan Altman, said that Sinatra had to have a twelve-foot section of intestine removed during a delicate seven-and-a-half-hour operation. Frank was greatly distressed by the operation. It was another indication that he was getting old. Bill Stapely remembered visiting him in the hospital. Frank had tears in his eyes. "I was surprised," he said. "I'd never seen Frank cry before."

When Sinatra saw his employee looking at him, he turned his head away and buried it in the pillow. Stapely reached out and took his boss's hand and squeezed it.

Frank, always a proud man, yanked his hand away. "Get away from me," he hollered at Stapely. "I don't need you. Just get away." Stapely stayed at his side and squeezed his hand a few moments longer as Sinatra drifted to sleep.

"I had a lot of surgery; they had to cut up my tummy pretty badly," Frank recalled of the operation. "It was an intestinal infection that began to spread throughout my stomach and bowel and so forth. I was close to buying it [dying]. If I hadn't come back from the trip I was on, I woulda bought it. They woulda had flowers and a big band behind the casket."

As a result of the operation, he would have to wear a colostomy bag for about a month and a half, until his intestines healed, which, for Sinatra, was a humiliating experience. When he went back into the hospital for a third operation—this one, presumably, to reverse the colostomy—he told Bill Stapely that he wanted him to accompany him into the operating room. "And if those doctors don't get this thing right, I want you to take a gun and shoot the bastards." When Stapely saw Sinatra later in the recovery room, Sinatra asked him, "Are the doctors still alive?" The two shared a warm smile as Frank, still under the effects of the anesthesia, went back to sleep.

"I think Kitty Kelley taxed his life," Tina Sinatra observed, "and for that I will never forgive her."

"He was a bear during that time," said a family friend. "He hated the bag because it made him feel old. The whole thing was a nightmare."

" 'Grandma—she doesn't care, Pop,' his daughter Nancy told him. 'She's in a better place now, anyway. She wouldn't want you to go through all of this. Try to forget it.' But Frank—he couldn't forget. 'I'll get even with that broad,' he said. 'It may take me a few years, but I'll do it.' "

After he was back on the road, a fan presented him with Kelley's biography and asked him to autograph it. Frank got a mad-dog look in his eyes, grabbed the book, and smacked the guy on the shoulder with it so hard, it looked almost as if he might have dislocated it. Then he threw the book at the fan and said, "If you spent money on that trash, I hope you choke on it, ya fuckin' bum." Later, Frank said, "Fucking idiot should know better. Like I'm gonna sign it. I shoulda shoved it up his ass; that's what I *shoulda* done."

Many of Frank's friends wanted to speak out about what they believed were inaccuracies in Kelley's book, but Frank decided not to allow it. He said later that he realized the book would have been less anticipated and ultimately less successful had he not drawn attention to it by filing a lawsuit against its author.

"My father issued a gag order and forbade any of us to say anything public about this situation," Nancy Sinatra later said. "We nearly strangled on our pain and anger."

Over the next few months, the word quickly spread that Frank Sinatra was furious with Kitty Kelley because of what she wrote about Dolly and that perhaps because of his alleged Mafia connections Kelley had good reason to be worried about her safety. Kitty was duly concerned. If it had been any other celebrity, she probably would not have cared as much. However, it was Sinatra. His image, his reputation, his persona, are formidable, threatening at times. Most people are not anxious to antagonize him.

Kitty Kelley telephoned former Washington, D.C., police inspector Joseph W. Shimon and asked, "Do you think Frank Sinatra will break my legs for what I wrote about his mother?"

"You can say anything about an Italian," he told her, "but you don't attack his mother."

Shimon told Kelley that he had no idea what Sinatra would do to her, if anything at all. "But I don't think you should ever stop looking over your shoulder, Kitty. You never know what can happen. . . ."

"Do you really think he'll harm me?"

"How can I know?" he answered. "All I can tell you is that you wrote things about his mother that you shouldn't have. Italians sometimes take years to retaliate.

"You just have to be careful. There are trashy people in his crowd. These trashy people worship the ground he walks on, and they have long memories."

Kitty Kelley called another friend and said, "Oh, no. Frank Sinatra is going to kill me because I wrote about his mother. I'm dead. What do I do?"

The friend said, "Run, Kitty. That's what you do. Till the day you die, run."

"People in Hoboken were getting phone calls from Sinatra's friends in

Los Angeles," said Salvatore Donato, who lived in Hoboken at the time and was an acquaintance of the Sinatras'. "They were nosing around, trying to find out who talked to this woman and why.

"A friend of mine called me up and said, 'Jesus Christ, I talked to that reporter. Now Frank's gonna be mad at *me*? I shoulda kept my mouth shut about his mother. But I didn't say nothing about the abortions. I swear it. I swear it on the Bible!' Frank's image, it's unbelievable. He's as feared as he is loved, like Dolly was, to be honest," Donato remembered.

Some of those who had talked to Kitty Kelley about Sinatra's mother were even contacted personally by the man himself.

"I'm in my kitchen one day eating a pepper-and-egg sandwich and the phone rings," said Debra Stredella, who did not speak to Kitty Kelley for her book, since she no longer lived in the Hoboken area. "The voice on the other end says, 'Hello. This is Frank Sinatra.' I swear to God, I almost died.

"He says to me, 'Mrs DiMaio—that was my married name then—you don't know me, but my mother was a friend of your grandmother's.' I was speechless. Oh, my God, I thought. Why is Frank Sinatra calling *me*? How did he ever find me? I'm not even in the book. I didn't say nothing to him. I couldn't. I was shaking inside.

"And he went on: 'All I want to say to you is that if anyone ever calls you to talk about my mother in the future, please don't do it, if not out of respect for me, then for her. In fact, refer anyone who calls to my office.' And he gave me a telephone number in Los Angeles.

"I managed to say, 'But Mr. Sinatra, I didn't talk to that writer. I swear.'

"'Call me Frank,' he suggested. 'I know you didn't talk to her. But we're calling just for future reference.'

"And I thought, Oh my God, what did he do, make a list of all the women his mother ever operated on, and their descendants, too? Was such a thing even possible? It seemed so far-fetched. Then, I thought, What am I talking about? This is *Frank Sinatra*. Anything's possible.'

"I said, 'Mr. Sinatra, your mother was a wonderful woman. She helped my mom during a hard time, and my family will always be grateful.'"

"He said, 'Thank you. Thank you for saying that. I appreciate hearing that. I loved her very much.'"

"He sounded so downhearted. Then he said goodbye and hung up. I had to sit down before I fainted. I actually started hyperventilating. I was so nervous, excited, scared, happy, everything. . . ."

"No one wants to upset Sinatra in these parts," said a Hoboken resident. "He's a town hero. After the book, there was a lot of talk about 'Frank's gonna hurt this Kelley dame. She's gonna be swimmin' with da fishes.' Like Frank would do anything to her. Certainly he would have been the prime suspect if anything ever happened to Kitty Kelley. She was probably the safest person in the whole world."

Joseph Shimon offered to contact his well-connected friend Ed Becker, the former vice president of the Riviera Hotel and Casino in Las Vegas, to find out what he might know of Frank Sinatra's intentions. Becker, who had known Sinatra since 1956, telephoned Kitty Kelley.

"She was concerned that Frank Sinatra would never give up seeking some kind of revenge on her," he recalled. "But I told her flat-out, 'Kitty, he doesn't even give you a thought. What do you think of that? Moreover, Barbara wouldn't allow him to do anything to you. And the way I see it, the only thing he's probably annoyed about is what you did to his mother.' "

Frank Sinatra would get over "the Kitty Kelley matter" in time. However, he would neither forget nor forgive. Years later, he told a sold-out concert audience in Phoenix, "I hope the next time she [Kelley] crosses the street four blind guys come along driving cars. If Kelley were a man, somebody would be whacking her out every fifteen minutes."

He also said to Larry King [in May 1988], "I hope that she had a lot of fun with the money she made by writing a lot of crap, which really was all it—or most of it—was, anyway."

When asked if he was hurt by the book, Frank adopted his Sinatra tough-guy persona and said, "Naah, it really didn't sting me that much. I've been whacked around before. And I came through pretty good. I worried about my family a lot. They never said a word. They never mentioned it. We never discussed it. My friends were angry. They said, 'That so-and-so.' I said, 'Forget about it. In six months time, nobody will ever remember what she wrote about. And she can't do it again.' "

For Frank Sinatra, the rest of 1986 was a blur of concert dates—the Golden Nugget in Atlantic City; Carnegie Hall in New York—and personal appearances. He opened at the refurbished Chicago Theater in September to a huge reception. "This is about chicks leaving you in crummy hotel rooms where you drink whiskey for four or five days," he said while introducing the song "One for My Baby" in Chicago. "You can ask Eddie Fisher. He'll tell you the whole goddamn thing. She [Elizabeth Taylor] left him. But then she got fat, so who cares?"

"In 1986, he raised $1 million for the Desert Hospital in Palm Springs with a $1,500-a-plate benefit," Bill Stapely recalled. "Frank arranged everything, including the guest list, the food, and the entertainment. He even waited on tables. Then, after he was done serving dinner, he slipped out of his waiter's clothes and into his tux to sing for his guests."

In an odd way, the success of Kitty Kelley's book *His Way* demonstrated that Frank Sinatra was still a popular figure in pop culture as he turned seventy-one. Certainly he and his family were mortified by the tremendous sales, but would they have been happier had it been a dismal failure? What would that have said about the public's interest in Sinatra's life and career?

As it was, Frank Sinatra worked throughout the rest of the year and throughout 1987 as well, trying not to give a second thought to the book. No doubt that's the way Dolly would have wanted it.

CHAPTER 44

As performers and personalities, Frank Sinatra, Dean Martin, and Sammy Davis had been linked in the public consciousness for over twenty-five years. By 1987, although older, they were still active as entertainers despite a myriad of physical and emotional problems that had beset all three. In October 1986, they were together in Palm Springs doing benefit performances for the Barbara Sinatra Children's Center at Eisenhower Medical Center (in Rancho Mirage) when it occurred to Sammy that the three men should work together again. They still had that instant rapport; all three had remained friends, though there were long stretches in the last twenty-five years when they didn't see each other. Why not find a project that would team them up?

There was practically no possibility that they could do another film, like *Oceans Eleven*, together. By the end of 1986, Frank was seventy-one, Dean was sixty-nine, and Sammy was sixty-one. Roles for men of that age were rare. Perhaps they could have created their own projects, but no studio would finance it because it was believed that there simply wasn't an audience for films starring men of their age. Instead, Sammy suggested that they perform together at Bally's in Las Vegas, where all three were presently under contract. Frank, always one to push an idea to its outer limits, had another suggestion: a full-fledged concert tour.

Frank said he wanted to further consider the possibilities and that the three should meet again in the near future to finalize some plans. Sammy, who always enjoyed performing and had such a great affinity for Frank, was excited about the prospects. Dean was not.

By October 1987, Dean Martin was a changed man. It had only been six months since the death of his handsome, thirty-five-year-old son, Dean Paul, whose air force Phantom jet crashed at 500 mph into the same San Gorgonio Mountains, near San Bernadino, that had claimed Dolly Sinatra's plane in 1977. When his son died, it was as if the light went out in Dean Martin's world. So overwhelming was his sense of grief, he immedi-

464

ately began to sink into a pit of self-destruction. Even though he tried to continue working—he was onstage at Bally's in Las Vegas in front of fourteen hundred people just eight days after the funeral—his will to live was all but extinguished. In subsequent months, his health deteriorated, and his drinking habits spun out of control. All of his friends were concerned about him, but none more than Frank and Sammy. Both men had sons they treasured; they could only imagine the desolation Dean felt but were powerless to do anything about it.

In fact, Frank had a special place in his heart for Dean's son, Dino. In 1965 thirteen-year-old Dino formed a singing group with two friends, Desiderio (Desi) Arnaz IV (son of Lucille Ball and Desi Arnaz) and Billy Hinsche. Sinatra was at Dean's home one afternoon when he heard the trio rehearsing in an upstairs bedroom. He thought they sounded pretty good, signed them to Reprise, and then teamed them up with Lee Hazlewood (who was also Nancy Sinatra's producer). As "Dino, Desi, and Billy," the youngsters had some hit records for Reprise, including "I'm a Fool" and "Not the Lovin' Kind." Sinatra always felt a certain pride for having "discovered" the act.

"Dean would never talk about it," Sammy once said of Dean's reaction to his son's death. "We tried, you know? But the thing was, none of us were into serious discussions. You know? We were the kind of guys who tried to be there for each other, but we weren't into this baring-your-soul crap. Dean would have been too embarrassed to say how he felt. It was rare for any of us to . . ."

"I would run into him from time to time after his son's death," singer-composer Paul Anka said. "And he would say, 'I'm just waiting to die, pal. Just waiting to die.'"

Two days after the first discussion among Frank, Sammy, and Dean about the possibility of a tour, Frank called Sammy.

"Smokey, let's do it," Frank said eagerly. "It will be hard work, but it could be exciting. And I think it would be great for Dean. Get him out. For that alone, it would be worth doing."

A few weeks later, the men had another meeting at Frank's Beverly Hills home. Over coffee, Italian rum cake, and *biscotti*, Frank told them that he now realized that an idea he had shared with them, of traveling by train, was impractical. The combined entourages, musicians, and technical crew of all three entertainers would amount to eighty-one people. Because it would take a week to travel between cities, feeding and housing that many employees would be a costly endeavor. "We'll have to fly," Frank decided. "I'll use my plane, and we can charter another G-2 for you guys." Frank said that he believed the three of them could sell enough tickets to fill auditoriums that seated as many as twenty thousand.

Dean was skeptical. "You really think we can draw that much?" he asked.

"Well, if they're not going to come and see us," Sammy answered, "then there is no show business."

"I didn't want to do it. Hell no, I didn't," Dean Martin would explain years later, sitting in La Famiglia restaurant in Beverly Hills. "Who the hell needed it? We were old. I was done. My best days were behind me. I was working here, working there, you know, just to keep myself going, somethin' to do. But this? I knew that this was gonna be a lot of work. But how could I say no to those guys? I couldn't do it. I had to go on. I didn't want to let Frank and Sam down. In my heart, though, I knew it was the biggest mistake of my life."

In December 1987, Frank, Dean, and Sammy held a news conference at Chasen's restaurant in Beverly Hills to announce the tour. Wearing tuxedos, the three men met at Frank's home, talked over what they were going to say over a breakfast of spinach omelets (zucchini for Sammy), and were then driven to the restaurant together in a black stretch limousine. They were met at Chasen's by an unruly battery of reporters. This was news. The Rat Pack was reuniting, and the wire services, newspapers, television networks, and foreign press were all present for the official announcement. American Express was sponsoring the tour; HBO would be televising one of the performances as a special. The three men took their place in front of the dais.

"Ladies and gentlemen, we thank you for coming here today," Sammy began.

Dean cut in: "Is there any way we can call the whole thing off." Everyone laughed. "I wasn't joking," Dean said later, shaking his head. "I looked out at those guys, and I thought to myself, What a fucking joke. What do they expect from us now? I hated the attention. I didn't even want to be there. I thought Frank shoulda' just done it alone."

For the most part, the press conference went well. The guys heckled each other in much the same way as they did in the sixties, as they would during the upcoming concerts. It was clear that they had the same irreverent sense of humor, even though Dean was clearly uneasy.

When someone from the sea of reporters asked if the reunion would be an annual event, Sinatra quipped, "Look, Sammy is sixty-two, and he's the kid. I'm seventy-two, and Dean is seventy. At our ages, the only annual event you hope for is your birthday."

Then another writer, this one from the foreign press, asked Frank, "What about that book that woman wrote about you?" Frank must have expected a question about Kitty Kelley, still, the look on his face was one of exasperation. "That's not a question for here," he said curtly. "This is about the tour."

When someone mentioned the Rat Pack, Frank cut the writer off by saying that the moniker was "a stupid phrase." The tour would be billed as the "Together Again Tour."

Each of the twenty-nine city stops along the well-publicized tour sold out well in advance of the concert dates. Frank was relieved. He had wanted to remain optimistic about the ticket sales, but he feared the worst. "I'm considered an over-the-hill performer at my age," he said in an interview at around this time. "There's no doubt about it. I think in the industry I'm considered over the hill."

Buoyed by the good news, Frank telephoned Sammy and said, "The accountants say you should come out of this thing with from six to eight million dollars." It looked good for all three men, another beginning or maybe a glorious finish.

"Frank designed the tour so that we'd make four years' salary in one," Sammy later explained. "I wanted to retire before, but I couldn't afford it and continue living the kind of lifestyle I want to live. That's the hard part. If I feel like buying my wife a $40,000 necklace, I want to buy it."

Rehearsals began at the Ren Mar Studios a few weeks later, where an elevated, square-shaped duplicate of the stage they would be using was erected. The forty-piece orchestra had been organized using New York musicians under the guidance of conductor Morty Stevens.

Frank and Sammy were used to entertaining "in the round," with audiences surrounding them instead of just in front of them, but Dean was not. He seemed uncomfortable, unfocused. "I'm gettin' dizzy," he kept saying as he roamed the stage. It was at these early rehearsals that Sinatra and Davis realized that there might be a problem in the offing.

Joseph Wilson, who once worked as a sound technician at Ren Mar Studios, remembered the early rehearsals. "Frank was awesome. He sang like he was performing in front of a huge audience. I am a big Sinatra fan, and for me this was a thrill. His presence, man, in a black satin bomber jacket with a baseball cap, lumbering along on that makeshift stage, singing 'Mack the Knife,' was incredible. This old guy looked like a champion in front of that orchestra.

"Then Sammy did some numbers, 'What Kind of Fool Am I,' 'Candy Man.' I knew Sam well. He had a new hip, he told me. They'd just operated on him shortly before this time. Still, he looked good. He sang well, like a man half his age. He was the best, vocally, of the three.

"Then Dean started singing 'Volare,' and well, that was sad. He didn't even know the words. We even had a TelePrompTer there, but he wasn't looking at it. He just sat on a stool and halfheartedly sang this thing and as he did, you could see Frank looking at him with an expression on his face that said: Oh, fuck. This ain't gonna work. He did a couple more things, 'That's Amore' I think, and then he just stopped in mid-song and walked offstage. He kind of crumpled into a chair, lit a cigarette, and started hacking."

Frank went over to Dean, slapped him on the back, and said, "That really sucked, what ya did up there. Worst goddamn thing I ever heard."

467

Dean grinned and said, "No shit."

"You know, we got TelePromTers these days," Frank said, ignoring his comment. "You don't gotta know the words."

"Yeah, but you gotta know how to read," Dean said, tossing off the line as if he were in front of an audience.

Frank rolled his eyes, shook his head, and walked over to Sammy. The two went into a conspiratorial huddle.

After that rehearsal, Joseph Wilson pulled Sammy aside and asked about Dean. "What's up with him, man? He looks bad."

Sammy let out a long sigh. "This tragedy with his kid, it's killing him. What the fuck can we do? Jesus, this is bad. Real bad. Goddamnit, why'd this have to happen to Dino? Why? It's so goddamn unfair."

"You think he'll last on this tour."

"Fuck, man, I'll be amazed if he lasts through the rehearsals," Sammy said.

Wilson handed Sammy his silk jacket, which was emblazoned on the back with the words "Michael Jackson—Bad Tour."

"But I pray to God he does," Sammy said, putting on the coat. "Jesus, I don't know what we're gonna do if he doesn't. Frank told me last night that maybe we shouldn't be pushing Dean like this, and maybe he's right. I don't know. . . ."

Years later, Dean said, "I stunk. I think they were using new arrangements. I didn't have time to rehearse. I liked to rehearse on my own, not in front of people. Take my tapes home, you know."

One popular misconception about Dean Martin is that he would not rehearse prior to his popular long-running television show the *Dean Martin Show,* which ran for nine years, from 1965 to 1974, often ranking in the Top Fifteen. "The truth is that he *did* rehearse, but he did it at home," said his longtime manager Mort Viner. "He'd take his cassette tapes and music and script home and rehearse, and when he got to the studio, he knew it. Everyone else—crew and guests—were there five days a week. Dean came in on the last day for a quick rehearsal and then taping. You never heard any performer say, 'Gee, we only had one rehearsal, and Dean didn't know it.' They were always amazed at how Dean knew everything, because they thought he was just learning it the day he came in. He already knew it."

"Frank and Sam were ready to replace me after the first rehearsals; I knew that," Dean recalled years later. "I didn't know who they could get, though. I couldn't think of anyone old enough."

During that first rehearsal, Sinatra not only saw that there could be a problem with Dean, but also realized that out of forty musicians hired by the contractor—the man who organized the band—only three were black: lead trumpet, drummer, and bass.

"What the fuck is this snow-white orchestra you got here," Frank asked the contractor. "That stinks."

"But Frank, it's too late to change 'em."

"Bullshit," Frank said, upset. "I want at least thirty percent black musicians. Change 'em."

"That's expensive, Frank," the contractor said.

"Pay what we have to. Fix it!" Frank said. "Now, let's go eat."

Fifteen black musicians were eventually hired.

About a month before the tour was to begin, Frank decided to sell his private jet. He, Dean, and Sam would travel on a rented, thirteen-passenger Gulfstream jet. The forty musicians and fifty crew members would travel to each city on buses.

The first date was at the Oakland Coliseum on March 13, 1988. There were signs of divisiveness among the three Rat Packers when they landed in Oakland. The plane taxied to a deserted area of the runway, where they were met by security guards. Then Sinatra and Davis got into a stretch black Lincoln, while Martin went his own way to the Hyatt Regency, where the three were staying, in a beige stretch Cadillac.

Dean remembered: "There was something cold about Frank, you know? I didn't want to be around him. I felt like he thought I was a *putz*. I don't know. Sam? Well, he was Frank's sidekick. I was out of my league, man. I'd rather be playin' my own joint, doin' my own act, be my own boss. I didn't want Sinatra givin' me orders. Fuck that. I was grown. This wasn't 1960. I was grown back then, too, but . . ." His voice trailed off. "Frank just likes to have it his way, you know. His kind of food, his kind of car, his kind of living. I'm simpler. I didn't need all that crap."

With the Oakland house sold out—sixteen thousand seats—the show was a complete success. Each singer would have a solo set, and then they would join together for a lengthy medley of their hits as a swinging finale. The medley started with special-material lyrics for "Side by Side." (We're making a barrel of money, / that's why we're feeling so sunny, / just traveling along, / singing a song, / side by side.")

Dean held up well throughout his part of the act. His self-effacing, easygoing charm remained intact despite his uneasiness with his surroundings. He sang laid-back versions of his own special-material songs, such as "Pennies From Heaven" ("When it rains, it always rains, bourbon from heaven") and "When You're Smiling" ("When you're drinking, you get stinking . . . and the whole world smiles at you"), with finger-snapping ease. He had been performing these numbers for decades with little alteration.

As part of his act, Dean would often take a long drag from his ever-present cigarette, flick it onto the stage floor, and then plug his ears with his index fingers as if in anticipation of an explosion. The gag usually got laughs. During his performance in Oakland, however, he inexplicably flicked the cigarette into the audience. When he put his index fingers into his ears, the audience members laughed, as they always did, though many observers wondered if anyone had been burned.

The three finished the show to a standing ovation.

Afterward, backstage, Frank Sinatra raged at Dean Martin, according to eyewitnesses. "They had just gotten offstage, and Frank grabbed Dean by the arm and pulled him into the dressing room, saying, 'You come with me,' " said a member of the tour's road crew. "Sam followed."

"What the fuck was *that* about?" Sinatra demanded to know.

"Huh?" Dean asked, out of breath. He seemed not to know what Frank was talking about.

"That thing with the cigarette butt into the audience?" Frank said angrily. "What, are you crazy? You don't ever do that to an audience. You don't insult an audience like that. What the fuck is wrong with you, Dean?"

"Oh, fuck you, Frank," Dean said, exasperated. "Who the fuck cares? I'm tired. Gimme a break."

"Now c'mon, guys," Sammy jumped in, trying to stave off an argument. "Let's the three of us—"

"Let's nothin', Charley," Frank said, cutting him off. "Let's just fuckin' *nothin'*."

Then Frank stormed out of the dressing room. As he left, Dean said quietly, "Sorry, Frank. I'm just . . . sorry."

Years later, Dean Martin would remember this confrontation. "I was an asshole. You don't do that. Someone coulda got burned or somethin' and they woulda sued us for everything we made. It was bad. Frank was right. But I was humiliated. I was scared. I almost had to change my shorts, I was so scared that night. Fucked up. Just fucked up. Why'd I even go there? I don't even remember."

After the show in Oakland, Frank wanted to go out drinking and maybe find some "broads," just like in the old days. Dean was tired, however. He wanted to stay in the hotel room and watch TV. "When'd you get so goddamn old?" Frank wanted to know. Then he toppled over the chair in which Dean was sitting. Dean spilled out onto the floor. He wasn't happy. Later that night, over a late meal of spaghetti with clam sauce and Italian bread on the side (hard and crusty, the way Sinatra always liked it), he started in again on Dean.

"I wanna go out, Dean. C'mon, pal-y. You're making me feel old."

"You *are* old," Dean said.

At that, Frank took Dean's plate of spaghetti and dumped it on his head. Frank laughed uproariously, but Dean just stared at him with clam sauce dribbling off his face. Perhaps Frank was trying to remind Dean what their raucous days together had been like, maybe jolt him out of his grief, old-age dormancy, or whatever it was that had changed Dean. He probably would have been relieved if Dean had started flicking the dripping clam sauce at him. That's what Dean would have done in 1960. However, this was not 1960, and Dean didn't appreciate Frank's prank, whatever the reason for it. Dean *liked* being old.

"What the fuck is wrong with you?" Frank screamed at Dean. It was as if he couldn't stand to even be around Dean any longer, because this man now served only one purpose: He was a morbid reminder that the best was *not* yet to come, the glory days were over, and that old age was a bitch.

There was another engagement at the Pacific Coliseum in Vancouver and then one at the Seattle Center Coliseum in Seattle, Washington. Of Dean's performance, *Seattle Times* critic Patrick MacDonald wrote, "If his drunk act is an act, it's mighty believable. He was teetering through the show. He was an embarrassment."

It had been reported that Dean was distraught about the reviews in Seattle. Not so, says longtime manager Mort Viner. "Dean didn't read critics," he recalled. "He was perfectly happy with what he did in his career, whether critics got it or not."

The fellows were then scheduled to perform at the Chicago Theater (March 18–20). Sinatra was annoyed in Chicago because they were not able to have suites on the same floor of the Omni Ambassador Hotel when they checked in at two-thirty in the morning. So he arranged to have the three of them moved so that they could be together, but Dean had already unpacked and didn't want to move. By the time Sinatra and Martin were ready to leave for the show the next evening, tempers were frayed.

Despite any hard feelings the concert was a big success.

SAMMY (to Frank): Your pipes are as good as ever.
DEAN (to Frank, handing him a glass of booze): But I brought some Drano just in case.
SAMMY: You're still the Chairman of the Board, Frank.
DEAN: Yeah, you're the chairman and we're bored.

Rick Kogan of the *Chicago Tribune* called it "one of the most amazing evenings of entertainment that has ever taken place." Of Martin, Kogan noted, "He looks too fit to be the boozer of legend, still handsome around the edges, but determined to play the hooch habit to the hilt. . . . One wished for more singing and less boozy burlesque."

After the performance, Frank raged to Mort Viner that Dean wasn't performing up to par. Viner told Martin what Sinatra had said, and Martin said, "That's it. I'm quitting." Viner chartered a plane and arranged for him and Martin to fly back to Los Angeles, leaving Frank and Sammy to perform as a duet. Before they left, Dean said goodbye to Frank at the hotel.

471

"I said, 'Frank, I gotta go,'" Dean remembered. "And he looked at me and said, 'You son of a bitch you. If you didn't want to do this god-damn thing, why didn't you just say so? Now what the fuck are we s'posed to do?' I didn't have an answer. Frank hugged me. He kissed me on the cheek. Then he said, 'Get the fuck outta here, you bum. Go home.' And I left. It was as simple as that. No big deal."

After Dean left, Frank, Sammy, and Eliot Weisman, executive producer of the tour, had a meeting to determine how they would continue. Dean would have to be replaced. They thought of Shirley MacLaine or Steve and Eydie but settled on asking Liza Minnelli, if she was available. Still, Sammy hoped that Dean would return. Frank didn't.

Frank told Sammy, "That S.O.B. better check into some hospital some-where, because if he ruins this tour for all of us by giving us the bad rap that we couldn't get along, I'll strangle him with my own hands."

Sammy looked at Frank blankly, astonished by his friend's lack of sensi-tivity where Martin was concerned. Noticing Sammy's reaction, Frank stopped his own tirade.

"You're right, Charley," he said, seeming to read his mind. "It was too soon. Too soon after Dino. I shoulda known. I just shoulda known. A man loses his son, he ain't never the same. We can't blame Dean."

At that, Sammy remembered, he couldn't help himself. He just burst into tears.

"The stress of it, man—it was killing all of us," Sammy said. "I can't tell you how anguished I was about it, to see Dean like that. Part of me died on that tour."

When Dean returned to Los Angeles, he checked into Cedars [Cedars-Sinai Medical Center]. His publicist said he was sick with a kidney ail-ment.

A few months later, Frank Sinatra gave his version of the events leading to Dean Martin's departure from the tour to Larry King. "Dean Martin is a man who doesn't like to work; let me begin that way. I saw that he looked tired backstage the day before he went home. I said to him, 'What's the matter, are you all right?' He said, 'I'm tired. I'd like to go home.' I said, 'Well, we're nearly finished [with this leg of the tour]. You can go home after that. Meantime, Sammy is a bunch of rubber bands jumping around, saying, 'What [dates] can we add on to [the tour],' and I'm saying, 'No, we're not gonna add on to it.' The night he left after the performance, he said, 'I have to go home.' I said, 'Okay.' I kissed him on the cheek, I gave him a hug, and he went home.

"I felt badly he didn't finish, but you can't put a gun to his head. He just didn't want to do it."

As for the supposed kidney-ailment excuse, Sinatra said, "He had a kidney problem for, like, four years, and he never done anything about it.

So now it's beginning to really bite him a lot. But that didn't send him home. I believe he still feels badly he didn't finish.''

Frank telephoned Dean in Los Angeles to see how he was doing and to determine if he intended to rejoin the tour sometime in the future. Sinatra told Larry that they spoke. However, Dean had said that they did not, that he refused to take Sinatra's calls.

On March 22, 1988, Frank and Sammy went onstage for the first time during the tour without Dean at the Metro Center Arena in Bloomington, Minnesota.

"We just got through talking to Cedars-Sinai in Beverly Hills,'' Sammy said to the packed house before he sang his first song, "Here I'll Stay.'' He continued: "Mr. Martin is improving. They haven't got any final word, and he's got to go through some more tests. But Frank and I wanted to come here to do this show because that's first of all the tradition of what show business is all about, the family continues. And that's what Dean would have wanted us to do in any event. This one we're dedicating to our man. . . .''

It had been too soon to change any of the orchestrations, so Frank and Sammy had no choice but to perform Dean's songs during the twenty-minute medley that concluded the act. Sammy did an excellent imitation of Martin when he sang Martin's hit "Memories Are Made of This,'' while Sinatra threw off "Volare'' as an afterthought but sounded terrific on Martin's "Oh Marie.'' The two received a standing ovation. Still, it was a sad show. Without Dean, the whole point of the tour—reuniting the Rat Pack—was lost. When Liza Minnelli joined the tour, replacing Martin, in April 1988, it was renamed "The Ultimate Event,'' and it went on to rave reviews for the rest of the year.

Then, on April 28, Dean Martin opened his solo act at Bally's Grand in Las Vegas. "Frank sent me a kidney,'' he joked, referring to the ailment that supposedly ended the Together Again Tour, "but I don't know whose it was.''

In 1989, Sinatra's touring schedule was full, with dates costarring Sammy Davis and Liza Minnelli all over the world. He also performed on his own, in his own show. Dallas, New Orleans, Miami, Las Vegas—all Sinatra stops along the way. Osaka, Japan; Melbourne, Australia; Rotterdam, Holland; Oslo, Norway; Munich, Germany; such a grueling schedule would have been exhausting to most young performers, but Frank Sinatra, at the age of seventy-three, seemed to thrive on it.

"But *why*?'' his longtime friend Esther Williams asked. "Why did he have to kill himself like that? Those heroic performances when he'd gained weight and lost his hair and Liza and Sammy would open the show and both of them were dynamos and poor Frank had to come out and top them. *Why*? Who's he doing it for? All I could think of, watching him

473

onstage with Sammy and Liza, was that he was raking in all of that money to leave to Tina, Frank junior, and Nancy and Barbara and the boy [Bob Marx]. I guess he thought he could do it, had the strength to do it. I have a little schnauzer, and you know what they say about the schnauzer? He looks in the mirror and he sees a Great Dane. Well, that's Frank when he looked into the mirror."

In each American city, Sinatra would catch up with old friends, mostly crusty ex-gangsters, over sumptuous *antipastos, insalatas,* and pastas. Shirley MacLaine, who would tour with Frank in 1992, remembered: "The eating was out of an old Coppola film. Almost always Italian and usually at a place outside of town, conveniently located for those running from authorities. There were nights I wished I had the audacity to bring a tape recorder . . . because of the subtle power plays that ebbed and flowed between him and these gangsters."

Shirley remembered that at the beginning of dinner Frank would usually be "deferential to the boys." By the time he'd finish his second martini, though, Frank would take charge. Looking with disdain at a bottle of wine which one of the old thugs had selected for the meal, Frank would say, "What the fuck is *this?*" Then, before Shirley knew what was happening, Frank was in complete charge as washed-up gangsters practically fell at his feet trying to please him. He was their Godfather.

To Frank, being on the road was the good life. His wife, Barbara, usually wasn't with him, which, say some, was one of the motivating reasons to tour in the first place. Even in his seventies, he couldn't squeeze enough passion out of life; he treated—or perhaps *mis*treated—his system with fatty Italian foods, sopping in heavy cream sauces, high-caloric desserts like cheesecakes with strawberries, plenty of Jack Daniels (sometimes vodka), $1,500 bottles of wine, and one Camel cigarette after another. Following a gut-busting dinner, there would always be after-dinner drinks at a piano bar until everyone in his party was completely sapped of energy, everyone but Frank. If he could have had sex—hell, yeah—he would have done that as well. He couldn't, though, so this seventy-three-year-old man would just crawl into bed at five in the morning, alone.

While on tour, the waking hours of every member of his crew and management were dedicated to anticipating the needs and whims of "the Old Man," which is what they called Sinatra. A twenty-three-page list of demands for backstage comforts—called a "technical rider"—accompanied Sinatra's one-night performance contract in the late eighties and into the nineties. According to the rider, in Frank's dressing room were to be twelve rolls of cherry Life Savers, three cans of Campbell's chicken and rice soup, and two egg-salad sandwiches. A backup plate of two chicken-salad and/or two turkey sandwiches with lettuce and tomato (mustard on the side) was also to be provided in case Frank wasn't hungry for egg salad.

A carton of unfiltered Camel cigarettes was to be on his dressing table, with the cellophane already taken off. The boxes were to remain unopened. Two bars of Ivory soap, with added moisturizer, six boxes of Kleenex, and six linen napkins were also to be included. Also in the contract, the most important aspect, perhaps, the liquor order: a bottle each of Absolut vodka, Jack Daniels, Chivas Regal scotch, Courvoisier cognac, and Beefeater gin. For mixers, six bottles of Evian water, two dozen sodas (75 percent of which were to be of the diet variety); and six eight-to-ten-ounce glasses.

Compared to some stars' demands—Diana Ross likes to have the entire dressing room and backstage area redecorated in "earth tone" fabrics just for a one-nighter—Sinatra's rider was not unreasonable, considering his star status. However, the absence of any of the items called for in the deal would sometimes cause big problems for the offending promoter.

Whether or not "the Old Man" was in a good mood could affect the lives of many dozens of people. Like the song, when he was smiling, the whole world smiled with him. But when he was crying, he brought out the rain, and in torrents, over anxious employees, who would run for shelter. (Frank even used the phrase "I think it's gonna rain" to mean that there was about to be a problem.)

A tirade could be the result of the smallest detail that had been inadvertently left unattended to: Two coffee beans or four in a glass of *sambucca* instead of the requisite three (for good luck) could cause Sinatra to hurl the drink against the wall. Paradoxically, for all his talent and onstage presence, there was still a darkness about Sinatra in public. Once, in Las Vegas, a waiter standing at attention near him ducked just in time as Sinatra sent a plate of golden fried swordfish airborne because it was slightly burned on one side. In Cleveland, another waiter slipped and fell on eggplant *parmigiana*, which Frank had thrown to the floor because the eggplant was "too goddamn tough." He then ordered a plate of veal in lemon-and-wine sauce. "When I brought it out to him," the waiter remembered, "I was such a nervous wreck, he looked at me and said, 'Look at you, you fink. You're so goddamn scared of me, you're making me lose my fucking appetite. Get outta here!' And I thought, *this* is Frank Sinatra?"

Indeed, that was Frank Sinatra, temperamental as ever but now old and cantankerous as well. Who was going to stand up to him?

Sammy Davis Jr. had been having trouble with his voice throughout 1989, and during the summer in Europe he was experiencing some pain. When he got home at the end of the summer, he went to see his doctor. The news was bad. Throat cancer.

None of his friends wanted to accept the fact that Sammy Davis was gravely ill, least of all Sinatra. The next few months were painful ones, physically for Davis, emotionally for everyone who loved him. It was possible to remove the tumor surgically, but that would prevent Sammy from ever singing again. He said he would rather die than not be able to sing. He chose radiation—a slow, agonizing death.

A television special paying tribute to Sammy Davis's sixty years in show business was taped at the Shrine Auditorium in November 1989. Of course, Frank attended. So did Dean. (It was difficult for some observers to determine who looked in poorer health: Dean or Sammy.) After the special, Sammy deteriorated rapidly, much to Frank's dismay.

"Frank Sinatra was ripped apart that Dad was dying," Sammy's daughter, Tracey Davis, said. "I'll never forget it. Frank would come over to the house and spend a few minutes with Dad. He was a different man when he emerged later: fallen, stunned, head bowed, jaw set. He wouldn't look at anyone, just fade through the glass doors to the circular driveway and pace around in a sobbing daze. I wanted so to comfort him but held back a little, respecting his privacy. Frank didn't want me or anyone else to see him crying."

On January 25, 1990, Frank Sinatra received more devastating news. Ava Gardner had died a day earlier in London, at sixty-seven, of pneumonia.

Some of her friends felt that Ava had not aged well. For a movie star who so valued her appearance, it must have been difficult for her to have to deal with the loss of her beauty, but she did by the mid-eighties. Too much liquor had ravaged her body, as it did that of everyone who had overindulged in the fifties. Her face was lined, puffy. Physically, by the time she was sixty, she was but a dim memory of her former self. "I made it on my looks," she said in an interview a year before her death. "What else did I have to offer? I was never really an actress."

Even though Ava Gardner was no longer a glamour girl, she never lost her blunt wit, her plucky sense of humor, or her charismatic personality. She had stopped making movies years earlier, and she didn't seem to miss Hollywood at all. She had a pet Welsh Corgi named Morgan, with whom she enjoyed a love-hate relationship: She loved him, he hated her, yet he could not share her with anyone. When guests would call, he would become so obstreperous, the visit would have to be cut short so that Ava, his mistress, could tend to his needs.

Sinatra never abandoned any of the women with whom he was truly in love: Nancy senior, Mia Farrow, Ava Gardner, and even Marilyn Monroe, though he may not have actually been in love with her, would all attest to his loyalty long after their romances with him were over.*

---

* When Mia was in the midst of her well-publicized problems with Woody Allen and her daughter Soon-Yi Previn, Frank telephoned her to ask her if she'd like him to

476

"Their fondness for each other was lifelong," said Tina Sinatra of her father and Ava Gardner, "and my father continued to look after her until the day she died."

When Nancy Sinatra was preparing to write her book *Sinatra—My Father*, she sent a letter to Ava Gardner asking for quotes and comments "from all of those who had close contact" with him. Ava was not amused. "Close contact?" she said angrily. "Doesn't she remember that I *married* him?" Ava at first said that she refused to respond, but later she said, "I told her sorry, but no, thanks."

A popular misconception about Ava in her last years is that she had fallen on financial hard times and that Sinatra was supporting her. Her business manager, Jess Morgan, who was certainly in a position to know about her finances, said, "Frank was supportive of Ava, but he was not supporting her. She had plenty of capital, was in sound financial condition, and lived on her assets. She wasn't superrich. However, she didn't need any money from anybody."

Ava's flat was in a converted nineteenth-century town house that faced London's Hyde Park. It was tastefully appointed with expensive antiques—such as an early-nineteenth-century French giltwood barometer, an Italian girandole and a Chinese enamel hanging lantern—decorative paintings, and plush furnishings. She lived with her longtime housekeeper, Carmen Vargas, and died in her canopied Chippendale bed.

"Yes, Frank did give her money, but it wasn't something she asked for, or needed, but something he volunteered. There was an existing tie between these two people that he liked to keep going, and she did as well."

"I do think Ava was still in love with Frank," Morgan observed, "and that nobody could live up to the image she had of him. In her mind she had glamorized him and their time together. Do I think she could have lived with him? Of course not. Could he live with her? Definitely not."

That Sinatra continued to send Ava Gardner money was a point of contention between him and his present wife, Barbara. In fact, she didn't even know he was sending Ava money until she picked up a telephone extension one day and heard Ava thanking Frank for his generosity. Barbara simply didn't understand, and the two had a loud disagreement about his devotion to Ava. "When you signed those divorce papers," she told him, "well, *that* should have been the end of it."

"Ava told me that she called the Sinatra home once and Barbara answered," said Lucille Wellman. "She said that Barbara was rude to her

---

send someone to New York to break Allen's legs. She declined his offer. Then, according to an associate of Frank's, he called Woody Allen and told him, "I don't know what the hell is going on back there, but I got my eye on you, and I just wanted you to know it." Frank slammed the phone down before Allen could respond.

and said, 'Frank is busy. He'll have to call you back . . . someday.' Ava ended up slamming the phone down.

"She later told me, 'You know, I need to have a good talk with Francis about that one [Barbara]. She may think she's the queen. But I sat on that throne long before she did. *I* was royalty before she was even a fucking Las Vegas showgirl.' Ava still had a sense of humor, almost until the end.

"One thing, though, that always bothered her was that Frank had a lovely statue of her on his Palm Springs property as "the Barefoot Contessa." When Barbara moved in, she had the statute removed. Ava thought that was petty."

Jess Morgan recalled: "She came down with pneumonia in January 1988, I believe. She had a doctor here that she liked, Dr. William Smith, who was also my doctor. [Smith rescued her that time at the Beverly Hills Hotel when she was beaten badly by George C. Scott.] We, in my office, arranged to get her here to see him. We had to charter a private plane because she was too ill to fly commercial.

"I got a telephone call from Mickey Rudin telling me that Frank wanted to help. I said, 'Terrific,' and I called Ava and told her he was giving her some money to use for medical expenses, and the chartering of the plane, if we chose to use it that way. The Italian in him, the gentlemen in him, always wanted to feel that he was taking care of her."

Jess Morgan refused to say how much money Frank offered (others have said it was $50,000), and his face reddened when asked Ava's reaction to this demonstration of generosity.

"Let's just say that she appreciated it," he said, "but she thought it could have been a bigger gesture. She didn't think it was enough. She had given him the best years of her life, after all," Morgan said, smiling. "So, yes, she had a caustic comeback which I did not convey to Mickey Rudin. But that was just Ava, her way of being sarcastic."

"I understand that Barbara would not allow Frank to visit Ava in the hospital once she got to L.A.," said Ava's friend Lucille Wellman. "Ava wanted to see him badly, but that's where Barbara drew the line, I guess. That didn't stop Frank. Ava said she woke up one morning, and there he was, standing at the foot of her bed, smiling."

While at St. John's Hospital, Ava suffered a stroke.

"Emotionally and physically she was affected by the stroke, which paralyzed her left side," said Jess Morgan. "For a woman like Ava, always so alive and full of life, this was hard. It was shocking to her that this had happened. She didn't know how to deal with it, and she retreated. She withdrew from everybody."

"After the stroke, I had a difficult time staying in touch with Ava on the phone," said Lucille Wellman. "So I went to visit her maybe six months before she died. I noticed she kept a framed photo of herself and Frank, kissing, on a table next to her bed. There were no other reminders of her former life in Hollywood, not a single memento, except for that picture. She said her 'old man' spoke to her on the phone at least once every couple of weeks. She would just come alive whenever she spoke of him. But she was lonely; she longed for the past."

Her longtime friend actress Esther Williams said, "Debbie Reynolds called me at two-thiry in the morning and said, 'I think we should get on a plane and go see Ava. I know she's lonely, and I know she's there all by herself and depressed, and we should go and cheer her up.' And I said, 'But what if she won't see us and we've flown all the way to London. What do we do? Throw rocks at her window to get her to come down and open the door?' With Ava, at the end, you never knew if she would see you. Debbie said, 'Oh, you're no fun. I'll have to go myself.' She didn't."

Mickey Rudin telephoned Frank, who was in New York at the time, to give him the bad news about Ava's death. A member of his staff recalled: "The tears just kept coming. Mr. Sinatra sat in the chair, bawling. It must have been at least ten minutes. He just kept saying over and over, to no one in particular, 'I should have gone to see her. I should have been there for her.'"

Ava's funeral, attended by about fifty friends, was held under rainy morning skies at the small Sunset Memorial Park—a small cemetery bordered by a trailer-home park—in Smithfield, North Carolina, on January 29. "She was no saint," intoned the Reverend Francis C. Bradshaw, "but her relatives talked about her authenticity, her genuineness, her wanting to be strictly who she was." Another memorial was held in Hollywood for her show-business acquaintances.

Three thousand townsfolk stood outside the cemetery hoping for a glimpse of a celebrity, maybe even Sinatra himself. However, Frank could not bring himself to attend either service. He sent a large wreath of pink and lavender flowers to Smithville that bore a simple message: "With my love, Francis."

"The last time I spoke to her was a week before she died, and it must have been three in the morning," Stewart Granger once remembered. "She was drinking again. She called and said, 'Dah-ling, it's Ava.' And I said, 'I know it's Ava, darling.' And she said, 'You know what I'm doing? I'm watching *Bhowani Junction*. Weren't we beautiful?' she asked. 'Weren't we just *beautiful?*' And I said, 'Darling, you're still beautiful.' And that was the last time I spoke to her."

"When I visited her before her death," recalled Lucille Wellman, "Ava said to me, 'I feel like it was just yesterday when I was giving Francis hell. Goddamnit, I loved that bastard, and I still do. Where did the time go?' she asked me. 'I just always thought we would have more time.'"

CHAPTER 45

The 1990s would prove to be more challenging than any other period in Frank Sinatra's life. Truly, these would be the years that would test his mettle. Sinatra still had the ambition and drive of a young man, but the reality was that by January 1990 he was seventy-four years old. Still, he refused to slow down. Why should he? He was still able to work; in fact, his touring schedule between 1991 and the end of 1994 was an astonishing one. He entertained practically every week, traveling, performing, singing for enthusiastic audiences around the world, and certainly not because he needed the money. (In 1991, Forbes listed his worth at $26 million, but that seems astonishingly low to those who know him best.) The schedule couldn't have been easy for a man his age. However, for Frank it was easier than dying. It was as if he were running from death, city to city, country to country. "If I stop working," he told associates, "I know I'll be next."

The unabashed adulation, approval, and appreciation demonstrated by his audiences seemed to imbue him with life and even the strength to stave off the inevitable. The need for love, or perhaps vindication, now seemed to be Frank Sinatra's guiding force.

Loyalty had always been important to him. He expected it from everyone, even the nameless, faceless people beyond the footlights. Like his songs, they never let him down, never abandoned or betrayed him, and their devotion was as intoxicating to him as Jack Daniels. He wasn't ready to give it up. Not yet. "Thank you for letting me sing for you," he would say to his audiences. That wasn't an empty sentiment. He meant it, because he knew he was one of the fortunate ones. After all, just a luck of the draw would make it Sammy's turn to cash in his chips rather than his own.

Sammy Davis lost his eight-month-long battle with cancer on May 16, 1990, at the age of sixty-four. His death was almost more than Frank Sinatra could bear, coming so soon after Ava's. They had had their differences; there were times when Frank wouldn't even speak to Sammy. But they had been such integral parts of each other's lives for more than forty years, they thought of each other as brothers.

"Mr. Sinatra kept his reaction to Sammy's death to himself," said

James Wright, his former butler. "When he was well, Sammy would come into the kitchen and hug the servants, he was so wonderful. After his death, Mr. Sinatra was quiet, very quiet. I think he would take his emotions out on Barbara in these little battles they would have at night; that's when it would all come out."

Friends couldn't help but remember the night in the 1940s when Sammy Davis was turned away when he went to see Sinatra—who, at the time, was his idol—perform at the Copacabana simply because of the color of his skin. It was a humiliation to which Sammy had become accustomed. The next night, Frank demanded that Davis be allowed to enter the establishment. Then, against his better judgment, Sammy went back, walked into the Copa's show room, and was shown a table—in the back of the room. (Sinatra then sent two of his pals to sit with Davis so that he would not have to sit back there alone.) Years later, Sinatra would buy a home for Sammy in Beverly Hills just so that the neighborhood would be integrated and Davis would be the one to start the trend.

Davis and Sinatra only had two major rifts in their long relationship. The first, which occurred in February 1959, was the result of a radio interview Davis gave in Chicago. "I love Frank and he was kindest man in the world to me when I lost my eye and wanted to kill myself. But there are many things that he does that there are no excuses for," Sammy told the commentator, Jack Eigen. "Talent is not an excuse for bad manners. I don't care if you are the most talented person in the world. It does not give you the right to step on people and treat them rotten. This is what he does occasionally."

Then, when Davis was asked who he thought was the top singer in the country, he replied that he thought it was he.

"Bigger than Sinatra?" he was asked.

"Oh, yeah," he replied flippantly.

Sinatra was extremely unhappy about Davis's observations. Frank simply could not understand why Sammy would be so critical of him, especially considering how close they were and how supportive Sinatra had been of Davis, both personally and professionally, over the years. Rather than speak to him about it, though, Frank did what he usually did in situations such as this one, when, in his view, a loved one let him down or betrayed him. He disappeared from Sammy's life; rather, he made sure that Sammy disapppeared from his.

Dean Martin once quipped, "It's Frank's world. We're just lucky enough to be able to live in it." Overnight, Sammy's luck ran out because of what he said on the air; he was no longer living in Frank's world. No more singing engagements together, no more good times, no more shared dames, or as Sinatra would put it, "No more *nothin'*."

"You wanna talk destroyed," Milt Ebbins once said. "Sammy Davis cried from morning to night. He came to see us when Peter [Lawford] was at the Copacabana. He said, 'I can't get Frank on the phone. Can't you guys do something?' Peter told him, 'I talked to Frank, but he won't budge.' "

Sammy Davis discussed many things in his three autobiographies in the years before his death in 1988, but the split with Sinatra was not a topic he chose to revisit.

"It was a bad time for me, man," he said in an interview with this writer to promote his memoirs, *Why Me?* "But, hey, that's how Frank was. If a friend disappointed him, didn't rally around him, as it were, did something that upset him, that was it. See ya later, pal-y. *Adios, amigo.* A lot of people were barred from Sinatra's life because of things Frank heard that they did that they didn't even do!

"For a guy who never liked people to believe what they heard about him, he was sometimes a little too quick to believe things said about other people and what they had supposedly said about him," said Sammy. "In my case, man, it was a fucking joke I had made about being better than him. Who's better than Sinatra? Nobody. Frank got a tape, took it seriously, and cut me out of a film. [1959's *Never So Few*, a war film with Sinatra, Gina Lollobrigida, and in the role intended for Davis, Steve McQueen.] I was sorry, so sorry."

"Sammy never did the picture, never got any money [for it]," said Milt Ebbins. "He could have sued because he had a contract, but he didn't dare. You don't sue Frank Sinatra."

After a few months, Frank finally gave in to Sammy's pleas and invited him to dinner at his home. While slurping mussels from shells, they talked about what had happened; Sammy tried to explain his position. Years later, he remembered that Frank mopped up the leftover broth in his plate with Italian bread and said, "Charley, don't ever let me down again. You gotta promise me." Sammy promised. Then, his mouth stuffed with garlic-scented bread, Frank took a deep breath, stretched his arms upward, and concluded, "*Aaaah.* This is the life, ain't it, pal-y?"

Sammy had to agree.

Their friendship was strong for many years, but then, in the 1970s, another rift developed between Sinatra and Davis. As did Frank, Sammy had a difficult time with aging. When he turned fifty, he found his own way of dealing with that particular midlife crisis: He turned to cocaine. Later, he would admit that the early- to mid-seventies would be nothing but a blur to him because of all the drugs and liquor—his drink of choice was vodka; his drug, cocaine—in which he had indulged. In the 1989 interview to promote *Why Me?* Sammy remembered that he was performing in Las Vegas when he ran into Frank's good friend Jilly Rizzo.

"How's Francis," Sammy asked. "What the hell's up? Why's he avoiding me?"

Jilly responded, "Well, Sam, you and me, we been friends a long time. I hate to tell you this, but the reason you ain't heard from Frank is because he's hacked off [angry]. He hears that you're into that coke crap. He told me, 'Look, if Sammy's into drugs, then I don't want to be around him. And I don't want him around me. That's just the way it's gotta be.' ''

Sammy was taken aback for a moment. Recovering, he said, "Well, hey, fuck him then, Jilly. I'm grown. I don't need Frank Sinatra to hold my hand in this life. It's not like the old days."

"Sure, Sam," Jilly said. "I just thought you should know, that's all. See ya, pal."

The two shook hands and parted company.

Sammy would recall: "I was trying to act like a big shot with Jilly, but I was dying inside. I loved Frank Sinatra. To know that he was pissed off at me, well, that was tough. I also knew that he probably sent Jilly to tell me that he was angry. That'd be like Frank.

"This was a hard time. Man, getting old in show business—it ain't easy," Sammy continued. "You fall into certain traps trying to keep your youth, trying to be hip. I was doing coke, drinking, trying out Satanism, into pornography. In fact, we used to rent out the Pussycat Theater, no shit, and go there to watch porno movies. I'd have all of Hollywood out there, had them picked up in limousines—Shirley MacLaine, Steve and Eydie, Lucille Ball—and we'd all sit in this theater and watch movies like *Deep Throat*. Can you imagine this? Lucy sittin' there watchin' Linda [Lovelace] give a man a blow job. She said afterward, 'I didn't know a woman could open her mouth so wide. To me, *that* was the big surprise.' I mean, it was wild. I ain't kiddin', either.

"But that was just good fun. I was into other shit that was destructive, like coke. Now, Frank, he never did drugs. Frank's drug was wild women. Safer but no less dangerous, I used to tell him."

In the next three years, Frank and Sammy only saw each other occasionally at cocktail parties, and even then it was just a curt hello and goodbye between them. "I missed my friend," said Sammy. "But I'd just go home, do some more coke, and be fine. 'I'd said, Yeah, well screw Sinatra if he can't let me live my own life. Least I got my cocaine.' ''

Then, at the end of the three-year mark, Sammy was performing at Caesars Palace in Las Vegas, with Frank following him there with an engagement. Their wives, Altovise and Barbara, decided to arrange for a reunion dinner.

"I didn't want to go," Sammy remembered. "But we were getting older. Years were going by. What a waste."

At dinner in the Caesars Palace dining room—which Frank Sinatra had closed to the public for this reconciliation meal—the four slipped into a red leather booth. After pleasantries, as Sam recalled it, Frank tapped him on the shoulder and motioned him to another booth. They excused themselves for a private moment.

"Charley, how can you do it?" Frank wanted to know as soon as they sat down again.

"Do what, Frank?" Sammy asked, trying to act innocent.

"Sam, I am so fucking disappointed in you," Frank began, ignoring Sammy's act. "What's with this coke shit? How can you do this? That stuff is destroying you. Look at you. You look like shit."

"Hey . . ." Sam began, protesting.

"Fuck you, Sam. Let me finish," Frank continued. "You're breaking my heart. Can't you see that. You know how hard it's been for me not having you around? But watching you kill yourself is worse. You've always been a gasser [the best] in this business. Stop with the coke. End it now. Promise me."

"I . . . I . . ." Sammy was speechless.

"You and I, we never lied to each other," Frank said. "If you can look me in the eye right now and tell me you'll never do this drug again, I'll believe you. So look me in the eye, Sam. Tell me what I want to hear."

Sammy grabbed a cloth napkin from the table and wiped away tears. "I'll give it up, Frank," he said, looking at his friend squarely. "I'm done. No more coke. I promise."

Sammy Davis Jr. kept his promise.

During 1990, Frank and Barbara Sinatra's head butler was James Wright. (Wright, who worked for Sinatra's friends Edie and Bill Goetz from 1968 to 1971, had been hired by Sinatra in 1989.) Wright was the only employee of the Sinatras' who actually lived in their home with them.

"This was a sad time for Mr. Sinatra," said Wright. "He'd lost an awful lot of friends in show business. It tormented him. My sense was that he was unhappy. He would often lament about the loss of Dean [Martin] as a friend. He missed him a great deal. He wanted to be closer to Dean Martin, but for some reason, that was impossible. Mr. Sinatra wished it could have been different.

"Healthwise, he had his ups and downs, but he was more up than down at this time. Just old age. By 1989, I did feel he was losing his memory—a lot of people did—but nothing was ever said about it. I was their only driver at the time and had been there about a year when I opened the door of the car for them and Mr. Sinatra looked at me and then looked at Barbara and said, 'Who's he?' She said, patiently, 'Why, he's our driver, dear.' And he said, 'Oh,' and got into the car."

James Wright described the day-to-day life in the Sinatra household at this time, when Frank was in his mid-seventies.

"His bedroom was very plain; nothing fancy at all," he said. "The carpet was orange, his favorite color. He had one chair, bed, nightstand, a big-screen TV, his closets, and that was it. There were some photographs in his room of his mother and of Barbara and his kids. He had blackout drapes, a heavy material so that absolutely no light would get through. I never heard music. He never played his own records, ever."

The Sinatra couple's bedrooms were separated by an adjoining bathroom, which Frank used. On the other side of Barbara's room was her own private bath.

"Her bedroom had a king-size bed, big-screen TV, a dresser; to be honest, there was nothing glamorous about her bedroom, either," Wright said. "Barbara was an elegant woman, though, quite attractive. She was not jovial; rather, she was serious. You never saw her in a dressing gown, ever. Every hair was always in place; she looked immaculate from morning to night, a striking woman in every way."

Frank was never up early in the morning; he didn't rise until 2:30 P.M. When he would venture forth from his bedroom after awakening, he would never have his toupee on; he wasn't sensitive about his baldness. He would not get dressed right away, and if he had no specific plans for the day, he wouldn't get dressed at all, choosing to stay in his pajamas. He didn't have many business meetings by 1990. If there were any, Barbara would tend to them herself, with her personal secretary, LaDonna Webb-Keaton.

"Mr. Sinatra would have his breakfast in the living room in his pajamas and dressing gown," said Wright. "He always started with half a grapefruit, then pancakes, sometimes scrambled eggs or French toast, sometimes fried eggs. He would always have bacon. We would make sure his two cavalier King Charles spaniels were in the living room when he would wake up in the afternoon. He would sit with them and be lovey-dovey before breakfast."

By the time Frank rose, Barbara had already eaten breakfast and lunch. She'd be off enjoying her day with her secretary. Frank would spend his afternoon lounging by the pool, reading newspapers or speaking on the telephone with friends. In the early evening, he would watch the television game show *Jeopardy!* and then *Wheel of Fortune*. He never missed either program.

At eight o' clock, dinner was served, which was usually when the fireworks were launched in the Sinatra household.

Because Frank was not an early riser, Barbara was responsible for arranging dinners with the chef. However, since she never told Frank in advance what they would be eating, the same argument would ensue every night.

"He wasn't much for fancy foods," said James Wright. "He would prefer to have Italian food every night. Mr. Sinatra loves pasta. He knows his sauces; he knows Italian food. He likes his pasta *al dente*, the correct Italian way. Never overcooked. 'Oh, can you imagine overcooking pasta for him? He would throw it out the bloody window.' "

Making matters more complicated, though, was that Barbara did not like her pasta cooked *al dente*; rather, she liked it chewy. Eventually, the cook learned that in order to keep the peace, it was best to boil two separate batches of pasta.

James Wright's predecessor in the household, Bill Stapely, remembered: "Cooking for Frank Sinatra was a nightmare. He could have feasted on the world's finest gourmet foods, but he insisted on cardboard cuisine—macaroni and cheese from the box, Oreo cookies, Aunt Jemima pancakes—and toasted-cheese sandwiches. He loved to spoon pork and beans right out of the can and eat them."

"Mrs. Sinatra was more fussy," said James Wright, "which is why he would get upset at dinnertime.

"The chef would make a meal, I would serve it, and Mr. Sinatra would throw a bloody tantrum because he didn't want that particular kind of food that evening. He would push it away from the table, almost onto the floor, and say, 'I don't want it. I'm not going to eat this crap.' Then he would push the chair away from the table, go into his room, and slam the door. And poor Mrs. Sinatra would be left at the table, tears streaming down her face. Sometimes, I must admit, I felt genuinely sorry for her. I would think to myself, Oh, Mrs. Sinatra, *please*, why don't you just *tell* him what you are going to serve rather than go through this ordeal every evening?' She wanted to show her authority over him, I suppose, but it was always a disaster."

After dinner, Barbara would get up from the table, go to her room, watch television, and then retire for the evening. Frank would go to his art studio and stay there until four or five in the morning, painting. Ordinarily, he did not drink when he was alone, only when entertaining.

"At about midnight, I would go into the kitchen, and there he would be," remembered James Wright. "And I'd say, 'Can I help you, Mr. Sinatra?' And he'd be standing there in a fog and would answer, 'You know what? I don't even remember what I came in here for.' It was for the jar of pickled pigs feet, of course, which he would eat every night. (We had to keep pickled pigs feet and pickled eggs in the refrigerator for him at all times.) He had already taken the jar out of the refrigerator, and it was on the counter. Or he'd have his glasses on, and he'd say, 'I wonder where my glasses are?' Common, old-age things. I must say, in all sincerity, I got on very well with him. He was quite nice to me, quite a gentleman, amiable."

During football season, Frank and Barbara had an agreement whereby they had their Monday evenings to themselves. Frank would go to a restaurant in Palm Springs with his buddies, while Barbara would have six ladies, Palm Springs friends—no show-business celebrities—over for bridge and a Mexican dinner that would be served at the counter of the bar, with Margaritas for all. It was an informal weekly gathering; paper napkins were used rather than cloth. The guests were always gone by the time Frank returned home, which was one of the stipulations of their agreement.

Occasionally during the week, Frank and Barbara Sinatra would leave their Rancho Mirage estate for a function. About an hour before departure time, a hairdresser would come to the house to arrange and comb Frank's toupee on his head.

"I remember one night Mrs. Sinatra asked me to drive them to an expensive restaurant in Palm Springs where there was to be a gathering of celebrities," said Wright. "I dropped them off and waited in the car. At ten-thirty, the party broke up, and the Sinatras came out of the restaurant. I brought the car right up to the restaurant door. They said goodbye to their friends and got into the backseat, and it seemed that they had had a good time.

"On the way home, however, Mr. Sinatra was upset. He said to Mrs. Sinatra, 'Don't you ever, *ever*, sit me next to Dinah Shore again. You're lucky I didn't get up and walk out. I never want to eat dinner with her, that no-talent person, again, ever. Do you hear me, Barbara?' Barbara just sat there, silent. Obviously, Mr. Sinatra was not fond of Dinah Shore."

In fact, Frank Sinatra had a long history with Dinah Shore. Both were with Columbia Records in the forties, appeared on numerous radio broadcasts together, and were friends at that time. In the early sixties, Sinatra produced what was probably Dinah Shore's best recording session, "I'm Gonna Wash That Man Right Out of My Hair," for an album of songs from the musical *South Pacific*, all sung by Reprise artists. Their relationship soured, though, in the seventies, when Sinatra suspected that she had used her considerable influence as Barbara's friend to instigate a breakup of the couple prior to their marriage, for Barbara's own good. Sinatra was also unhappy about an interview Shore did with Spiro Agnew on her television program because he thought she made Agnew sound vapid and superficial. However, since Dinah was a longtime friend and frequent golf partner of Barbara's, Frank had to put up with her, anyway.

Sinatra also disliked Bob Hope, whom he had known for decades but considered to be a "cheapskate," often saying that the entertainer "still had the first dime he ever made." Even though they lived just miles from each other in Palm Springs, the Hopes and Sinatras rarely, if ever, socialized.*

---

* Actually, the rift between Hope and Sinatra can be traced to the late forties, when Frank became annoyed with Bob for having become romantically involved with Sinatra's ex-girlfriend Marilyn Maxwell. Sinatra might have been able to accept the relationship if Hope had not tried to rub it in his face by sending Frank a photograph of himself and Maxwell arm in arm and bearing the simple inscription "Sucker!" That gesture ended Sinatra's friendship with Hope, though they would make many public appearances together over the years.

However, the Sinatra household came to life when the couple entertained other guests, which was at least once a month and sometimes more often than that. Ordinarily, the household staff would consist of James Wright, "Vie," Sinatra's trusted personal maid, who has been with him for years ("a wonderful, wonderful lady. She must be in her seventies," said Wright),* a chef, and two "laundry ladies." For dinner parties, the Sinatras would often hire additional help, sometimes as many as twenty-five workers, to cook food and otherwise prepare the home for dinner parties.

The guest list—usually there would be forty people—would read like a "Who's Who of Show Business," James Wright said. "Everybody came to visit," he remembered. "The Gregory Pecks, the Chuck Connors, Merv Griffin, Robert Wagner and Jill St. John, Steve and Eydie, Roger Moore, Barbara's son, Bobby, of course Nancy, Frank junior, Tina. One person I did not care for who came often was Gary Morton [Lucille Ball's husband]. He'd talk badly about Lucy. Why talk about her when she's dead? I wondered. Nancy senior never came to the house," said James Wright. "He went to visit her because she didn't get along with Barbara. When he would go to visit Nancy, Barbara would stay behind and simmer."

At the parties, Frank and Frank junior would sit at the bar for hours drinking Jack Daniels and talking about music that would be used for upcoming concert appearances. "That was the relationship I saw between them, professional," James Wright said. "As far as a close father-and-son relationship, I didn't see that. They shook hands, never hugged.

"Mr. Sinatra's attention was always directed to his daughter Nancy, the light of his life, and her children, whom he adored. He would have had the grandchildren there every day, but Barbara wouldn't allow that."

Frank Sinatra's music was rarely played at these gatherings.

"I can't stand that," Frank said to Bill Boggs in an interview on WNYW in New York when asked whether he listens to his own music. "If I'm out visiting someone, I say to them, 'If you play my records, I'm going home.' Because often I was a little impatient in making a record, and I said, 'That's it, press it, print it.' And there was one little note in it that isn't right. And every time I hear that record, it comes back to me. If I'm in my car listening to the radio, I cringe before the note comes on, and I think to myself, Why didn't we do it one more time? Just one more time."

His wife, Barbara, was just as exacting about dining etiquette as Frank was about his music. The Sinatras' Palm Springs dining room was deco-

* Of Sinatra's personal maid, Vie, James Wright added, "Mr. Sinatra bought a house for her in Palm Springs, sent her kids through college, and gave her anything she wanted in this world to reward her for her loyalty. She was the only person in whom he would confide, and she was at his beck-and-call twenty-four hours a day. For Christmas, he would give her at least $10,000.

rated in an Oriental motif, with six large, round tables. Ten people would be seated at each table. "One thing I am particular about are my tables," Mrs. Barbara Sinatra told her staff before one party. "I like the guests to be surprised and impressed by the glamour of the tables when they see them." Drinking glasses, plates, knives, and forks in the right placement on the table, as well as candles and flowers—fresh roses brought in every day—perfectly centered, were all important details to Barbara.

"Guests would never see the dining room until that big moment of grand presentation," said James Wright, whose party (and even daily) uniform consisted of black trousers, white shirt, black tie, and black jacket. "I would then announce to Mrs. Sinatra, 'Dinner is served, madam,' and open my set of double doors, while someone on the other side of the room would open the other set. The guests would then file in. I would stand behind Mrs. Sinatra's chair, because she was the hostess, and pull it out for her. After she was seated, I would go to each lady and seat her while the gentlemen stood by. Then, after each lady was seated, the men would finally sit down. It was quite formal.

"At every dinner, there was always a pasta dish, chicken, potatoes, broccoli, pork. Barbara liked pork," James Wright said. "But there was never anything spectacular served. It was just plain down-to-earth food, such as what regular folks would have."

After dinner, the guests would get up from their tables and mingle for about a half hour. The ladies would then go into one room and enjoy coffee, and the men would proceed to another for cigarettes and drinks.

After about an hour, Barbara would announce that a movie was ready to be viewed, and the party would noisily adjourn to the home's theater room. (A day prior to the festivities, Barbara's secretary would have movie reels shipped in from Hollywood film studios. Frank Sinatra's movies were never viewed; rather, the guests delighted in first-run features.)

"The theater was huge, with a bar, a ladies' and gents' room, a long settee, a divider upon which was placed a variety of candies and snacks," James Wright recalled. "The room had individual armchairs and small tables for each person. We had to have popcorn ready for the guests, which was served in plastic bowler hats, set out on the tables in advance."

Frank would never go into the theater with the other guests; rather, he preferred to either go to his art studio and paint or to his "train room."

Sinatra had always been fascinated by toy trains. He once said, "At Christmas, when I was a kid, I'd leave Hoboken and take a four-cent ferry ride and a five-cent train and head for the New York stores. I'd stand and look at the train displays for three to four hours. I wanted a train set so badly. One day, my mother pawned her fox fur piece to buy my first train set, a windup engine and oval truck. I was old enough [age eleven] to understand the sacrifice she made."

Frank had an elaborate room built in his Palm Springs estate to house an enormous train collection. There were two hundred and fifty expensive model trains on an eighteen-by-thirty-foot train station. The layout was based on the same Lionel train showrooms Sinatra used to visit as a youngster in New York. Along the track was a model of his Hoboken neighborhood, an Old West town, a New Orleans riverboat, and a billboard announcing a sold-out Sinatra concert. No kids' toys, these were expensive models; a locomotive bore his initials (FAS) in diamonds. He had a crystal replica of the 1025 Chattanooga Choo Choo.

While his friends watched movies, Frank would do what he always did in his train room: clean the tracks, oil the engines, change the cars, and stare at the trains for hours as they moved along the tracks.

James Wright said, "Barbara would say, 'Darling, aren't you coming in to see the movie?' And he'd say, 'No. I'm not fucking going in there. I don't want to see the movie. Please, just leave me alone.' He'd stay out. He was sloshed, you see, by this time, anyway. He'd go into the train room, drink, and smoke Camels."

Finally, the guests would leave, often never even having the opportunity to say goodbye to Frank Sinatra.

Unlike the household of many celebrities, the atmosphere in the Sinatra home was not chaotic. It was orderly and predictable. Occasionally, however, a dramatic incident would occur.

"One terrible incident," Wright said, "was when Mr. Sinatra's dog was killed. He had two King Charles spaniels, and one was killed when it got out of the property and was run over by a hit-and-run driver on Frank Sinatra Drive, the four-lane highway outside the Sinatras' home. Mr. Sinatra was devastated about it and placed an advertisement in the local newspaper to try to find out who did it. He never did find out. He was just walking around the house, miserable. He loved those dogs. He always wanted them to sleep in the kitchen, but Mrs. Sinatra wouldn't allow that. She would always put them in the yard."

James Wright's job with the Sinatras ended after two years.

"The Sinatras were going to Las Vegas," he remembered. "I drove them to the Palm Springs airport, where they had their own jet. I got out, took them right up to the pilot, made sure the luggage got onto the plane safely.

"Then, just before she got onto the plane, Mrs. Sinatra gave me her hand and said, 'Thank you, James, that was very, very nice.' I thought that was unusual. I had taken them to the airport many times before and she never shook my hand like that.

"I went back to the house and said to [secretary] LaDonna Webb-Keaton, 'Well, they're off,' and she said to me, 'James, I have to tell you something. Mrs. Sinatra is going to let you go. We're not going to need you.' It was a shock. I had no warning. They gave no reason.

"They left for Las Vegas on Thursday, and I had to be out of the house by the time they got back on Sunday. I had no place to go; I had to check into a hotel.

"However, to tell you the truth, that is absolutely the correct way to let an employee go. It's done through the secretary. It's never done through the madam or sir. They gave me the appropriate severance pay, and more. I was exhausted, anyway. It was like running a twenty-four-hour bloody hotel."

In 1990, the Frank Sinatra Diamond Jubilee Tour began, with Steve Lawrence and Eydie Gorme, at the Meadowlands Arena in East Rutherford, New Jersey. It would continue through 1991, playing to sold-out houses.

Whenever Frank and his friends went out on the town, he liked to have his limousine accompanied by four motorcycle policeman—sirens blaring, lights flashing. It seemed preposterous to most observers, especially since Sinatra and company wouldn't hit the town until well after midnight. The streets would be empty except for the police motorcade that escorted the Sinatra contingent to whatever restaurant had been selected—which would remain open after hours for Frank's party—waking up everyone who happened to live along the route. As usual, waiters would snap to attention as the Sinatra party invaded the eating establishment.

By 1991, the performances were becoming more difficult for Frank. His memory was fading quickly. On some nights, he couldn't remember Eydie's last name. There were other nights when he couldn't remember her first.

The four TelePrompTers at the edge of the stage, which scrolled the lyrics to all of Frank's songs, had become more difficult for him to read because of cataracts in both eyes. Without the TelePrompTers, though, he would simply not remember the lyrics. This memory loss was becoming embarrassing not only for Frank but for his fans, who felt sympathy for him. Still, Sinatra went on and generated hysteria at each stop along the way. Sometimes he was brilliant onstage. At other times, he was not. But it was clear from the way he performed the songs that they still somehow enriched him. Through them—those "wonderful, wonderful songs," as he called them—Sinatra not only manifested a sensitivity that he had never been able to fully express in his personal life but also a sense of identity and dignity at a time when many of his older friends were beginning to lose theirs.

His son, Frank junior, who conducted the large orchestra, would attempt to focus on his job with the music. However, on some nights he would obviously be concerned by his father's shaky performance as the old man's troubled, smoky voice would lose power in the middle of a simple song like "Strangers in the Night." "It's as if the kid is hoping the

491

old man doesn't just keel over in the middle of 'My Way,' " noted one cynical critic. A lengthy medley of songs with Steve and Eydie at the end of each performance was a welcome relief for both Sinatras, senior and junior.

Obviously seasoned professionals in their own right, Steve and Eydie could always rise to the occasion and handle any misstep that might occur. They were always concerned for his dignity, and if they noticed that Sinatra was drifting, they would gently take him by the arms and move him with them, gracefully bringing him back to alertness. If he forgot any lyrics, they would softly sing them from behind him, spurring his memory, filling in the lost stanzas, urging him on. Certainly he never had truer friends than Steve Lawrence and Eydie Gorme.

Most Sinatra intimates agree, however, that Frank Sinatra would not have been performing at all at the end of the 1980s and into the 1990s if not for his son, Frank junior. Junior compensated for many of his father's vocal shortcomings by rearranging certain orchestrations to make the singing of them easier. Most important, he offered moral support when his fatigued father most needed it. He remembered: "I'd say to him, 'Listen, champ, you're too old an athlete to give up now.' Those are the exact words I said. 'You must not give up until the time comes that deep down inside yourself you know it's right. Until that time, do not be influenced by external forces; you're too old to quit. Now get in there and fight.' At night, when he'd be onstage and he'd get tired, I'd give him this," Frank junior said, showing a clenched fist. "Now get in there and fight."

If Frank senior was grateful, he didn't always show it. Quite the contrary. He was sometimes unkind to his son. He even berated him from time to time in front of audiences, saying that the reason he hired him was "because the kid needed a job."

A particularly unsettling incident stands out in the minds of Sinatra associates. One evening, Frank senior was about to sing "One for My Baby" when he turned to Junior and asked him if he knew the lyrics. Of course Frank junior knew the lyrics; he knows the lyrics to every song his father ever recorded, ever sang, and probably has every *thought* about singing. His in-depth knowledge of music—from classical to pop—is extraordinary.

"Then you sing it and I'll wave my arms for the orchestra," Frank said to his son.

Junior took the microphone from his father, walked to center stage, and without even a hint of apprehension, performed the melancholy, lonely-hearts number, which is one of his father's most memorable signature songs. "And he sang his ass off," said one musician present that evening. "He tore it up." His voice was strong and commanding. He sounded a bit like his father, albeit a younger, more vibrant version.

492

Frank Sinatra of the 1950s. The audience was struck by his splendid performance and cheered wildly afterward.

With a nod to his son, Frank senior nonchalantly took the microphone back, sat on a stool under a blue light, and lit a cigarette. He took a drink. Then, as the applause died down, he said, "Now I'll show you how it's *supposed* to be done." With that, the Old Man sang the song again in a rendering that was superior—if not vocally, certainly emotionally—and because he is the recognized "master," even more enthusiastically received. The audience stood and roared its approval. Frank junior had no choice but to bow to his father, which is exactly what he did. To most observers, this seemed an unkind thing for Frank senior to do, setting his son up, only to knock him down in order to demonstrate who was the better and more appreciated talent, as if his son hadn't lived his entire life with that knowledge.

Despite his father's occasional boorishness, Frank Sinatra Jr. was there for him when, as one friend of his put it, "the chips weren't just down, they almost didn't exist." As an adult, Frank junior is nothing like his father ever was. He's not charismatic. He's dull. He's pedantic. He's round, stoop-shouldered and wears glasses.

"He put up with his father's crap because that's what an Italian son does, whether he's Joe Blow in some small town dealing with his annoying father who wants him to fix his car for him or he's Frank junior dealing with his father, the great star. It's all the same," said one of the musicians in Frank junior's band. "People think he's angry, but he's not. He's used to it. He's used to not being thought of as the best, only second best."

"Frank told me once when we were young in Hoboken that if he ever had a kid, he would have a better relationship with him than he had with his own father," remembered Joey D'Orazio, Frank's friend from the old neighborhood. "I know that it must break his heart to realize that never happened. Frank never seemed proud of Frank junior, just as his father never really seemed proud of him. That kind of thing tends to repeat among fathers and sons, I guess. I always thought Junior was a sweet kid. If his father hadn't been a star, he would have been one. He had the chops, but his old man never encouraged him. Unlike Frank senior, Junior didn't have what it takes that causes people to make it no matter what."

A loner, Frank junior never married; he has one son, Michael, born on March 1, 1987. The boy's mother, Pat Fisher, was a secretary at Sinatra Enterprises and is a longtime friend of the family's. Two other women have also claimed to have had illegitimate children by Frank junior, but Fisher's is the only child he and the family has recognized as a true Sinatra. In 1994, Frank junior enjoyed a brief, highly publicized flirtation with the so-called Hollywood Madam, Heidi Fleiss, which amounted to nothing and was never serious. The family has always hoped he would settle into a meaningful relationship, but it fears, as his sister Nancy has put it, "that Frank doesn't feel worthy."

"He is buried away behind a profound defense," wrote Jonathan Schwartz of Frank junior in an *Esquire* magazine article (May 1995). "Suspicions abound—somewhere in there he must be alert for yet more wounding afflictions. If he could weep for weeks, he would finish unresolved. His loneliness is palpable."

(In 1996, Frank Sinatra Jr. recorded *As I Remember It.* Released by Angel Records, it is a fascinating collection of songs and spoken verses that pay homage to his father's music and career. "It is the most important work he has ever done," noted the *Chicago Tribune.*)

By the end of 1991, Frank Sinatra was still drinking more alcohol than men half his age could ever tolerate. He was told by his doctor that he would have to wear a hearing aid in his left ear, and the prospect frustrated and exasperated him. Before a November 1991 engagement at the Sands Hotel, another unfortunate public scene took place in New York at the Waldorf-Astoria, in Sir Harry's bar. Frank, Jilly Rizzo, and Steve Lawrence were having a drink at about five in the evening. Frank, who was already intoxicated, went to the bar, ordered a straight-up whiskey, and then took a seat on a couch with his friends. A fan who had noticed the group walked over and asked Frank for an autograph. "Don't you see I'm on my own time here," Frank shouted at him. "You asshole. What's wrong with you?"

The fan apparently then said something to Frank that the singer didn't like. Sinatra lunged at him. Lawrence and Jilly held him back as the terrified fan ran off. A hotel security guard then used the house phone to call Barbara Sinatra in an upstairs suite. It only got worse when Barbara finally appeared.

"You trying to kill yourself?" she asked her husband. "Is that what you're trying to do?"

"Oh, no, here we go again. You get away from me," Frank hollered at Barbara. "I'll drink when I want, what I want."

"But Frank, the doctors said—" she began, trying to reason with him.

"To hell with the doctors," Frank shouted at her. Then he turned to Jilly Rizzo, and in a clear effort to defy Barbara, he said, "Get me another drink." Instead, Jilly convinced Frank to calm down. Then he helped him out of the bar, to the hotel elevators, and up to his room. Frank could always count on Jilly, his closest friend.

In May 1992 tragedy struck when Jilly Rizzo was killed in an automobile accident on the night of his seventy-fifth birthday.

Jilly's friend Jim Whiting remembers: "He wasn't even in his own car. He was in a Jag [Jaguar] that belonged to a neighbor of his girlfriend's. He was hit by a drunk driver, and the car just exploded into flames. He couldn't get out. The doors were automatically locked. It was a horrible way to go. Frank's road manager, Tony Oppedisano, broke the news to Barbara. Frank took it badly. He sank to his knees when they told him. They had to sedate him, he was so devastated. He locked himself in his room and stayed there for five days."

Frank and Jilly had met in 1959 in Miami Beach and immediately struck up a friendship. Rizzo, a former bartender, opened Jilly's in the sixties, in New York. A popular bar and hangout for many celebrities, Jilly's was also the place to go for Chinese food. Inside was a piano bar, where Judy Garland would often pass the time. Whenever Sinatra came to New York, his fans knew that Jilly's was the place to be for "Sinatra watching." This was his favorite hangout; he even mentioned it in ad-libs to some of his songs, such as "Me and My Shadow" (with Sammy Davis Jr.) and "Mrs. Robinson." After Frank and Hank Sanicola ended their relationship in 1963, Jilly Rizzo became Sinatra's closest ally. He was one of the few people who really understood Sinatra's moods, his anxieties, his lifestyle. He knew all of Frank Sinatra's secrets. They couldn't have been closer if they were related.

"Jilly used to come to the house every day at eleven, before Mr. Sinatra had even risen," said James Evans, the Sinatras' butler. "The first thing Mr. Sinatra wanted to know when he woke up was 'Where's Jilly? Is Jilly here? Get him in here.' I would say, 'He's in the kitchen, Mr. Sinatra.' And he would say, 'Bring him in here, that bum.' Jilly used to call him 'Sinat.' Sometimes Jilly would be gone by the time he'd wake up, and Mr. Sinatra would be miserable about that."

As difficult as it was for him, Frank went to Jilly's funeral at the St. Louis Church in Cathedral City, California. He was a pallbearer. His face was ashen and haggard; he seemed almost stricken as he and the other pallbearers carried the mahogany casket. Betty Jean Kelly, Jilly Rizzo's girlfriend, recalled: "It absolutely broke my heart to see how much Frank was suffering. He and Jilly adored each other. There was such a look of agony in Frank's eyes, it was hard to bear."

Frank sobbed uncontrollably during the recessional hymn "Amazing Grace."

Four days later, Frank's good friend singer Sylvia Syms died of an apparent heart attack in New York at the age of seventy-three. He had to leave for a European tour in a couple of weeks, and he considered canceling it. So much tragedy had occurred, he didn't know if he would be able to perform. However, he decided to go. As it turned out, the tour was a disaster; audience response was weak, and reviews were poor. His heart simply wasn't in it.

In November 1992, CBS aired a television miniseries based on Frank Sinatra's life entitled *Sinatra*. With his blessing, Frank's forty-four-year-old daughter Tina (who had been an actress for a short time before working as an agent and then a producer) was executive producer.

After Kitty Kelley's 1986 biography received so much attention, Frank wanted to write an autobiography to "set the record straight." Tina explained: "Though he knew he could fill volumes, he said, 'The biggest part of my life would be missing. My music. My songs. You couldn't hear my songs in a book.' " It was then decided to produce a miniseries, which would be nine years in the making.

The four-hour-long program spanned the years 1920–1974, ending with Frank's return to the stage at Madison Square Garden after his "retirement." Originally, the script was for a ten-hour-long miniseries. Certainly it would have had to be at least that long to do Frank's life complete justice. As it was, at four hours, it could be nothing but superficial in some respects, with some sketchily drawn characters. However, the performances were first-rate, particularly Philip Casnoff's emotionally involving portrayal of Frank Sinatra. "I went to Dad and said, 'I can't find anyone with the essence of the street who could aspire to your social polish.' And he said, 'Then find someone who has the polish and rough him down.' "

Philip Casnoff, who starred in *Chess* and *Shogun* on Broadway, was chosen after 250 performers had auditioned. A singer himself, for the miniseries he lip-synched Sinatra's songs, singing live—but unmiked—to the records. "That was the one area where maybe I was the most Frank-like in my approach to it," he said, laughing. "If they wanted to move along, I said, 'We can't go on. We have to do this again. It has to be perfect or it's not going to fly.'

"Onstage, Sinatra was more available to himself emotionally than in almost any other place in his life. He was really open when he was out there in front of an audience. He didn't just sing. There was always something else going on behind the songs, which I wanted to capture."

To prepare for the role, Philip Casnoff viewed all of Sinatra's movies, because, as he said, "due to the kind of actor he was, regardless of who he was playing in a film, some part of himself would emerge. Then I got ahold of some of his old variety shows and studied them. I also read the two books, the laudatory one and the trash one, the one from Nancy [Sinatra] and the one from Kitty Kelley. I also went to Hoboken and talked to people there, which helped a great deal.

"I wasn't going to imitate him, but I tried to emulate him," said the actor. "I studied little things, like the way he smokes, how he takes a cigarette out of a box and the way he holds it. And the way he held his hands when he sang, the way he moved his body, and the way he walked—all of that was important. I tend to walk with my feet going out, and one thing Tina [Sinatra] was always saying on the set was 'Keep your feet straight!'

"I was lucky enough that Frank Sinatra wasn't an icon in my personal life," said Casnoff, who was thirty-six when he essayed the role. "He was my parents' icon more than mine. So I wasn't daunted by the project. It would have been harder for me to play Jim Morrison than for me to play Frank Sinatra."

Much to the surprise of many critics, the miniseries did not avoid the various controversies in and around Frank Sinatra's life. Unlike Nancy Sinatra's two books about her father, the program admitted to Dolly's activities as an abortionist (referred to as "illegal operations" in the network's press kit for the program). In a powerful scene, Dolly (portrayed by Olympia Dukakis) and Frank (Casnoff) argue about her tarnished reputation in Hoboken after the first arrest.

Sinatra's relationship with Sam Giancana (played by Rod Steiger) was also portrayed in the miniseries, as was his friendship with other gangsters. ("It doesn't matter anymore, does it?" Frank said when asked in 1992 about his mob connections. "Most of the guys I knew, or met, are dead.") His volatile affair with Ava Gardner (Marcia Gay Harden) also received considerable attention.

"He's such a private man," Tina Sinatra observed. "My father will never write a book, so this is it. This is his life."

Tina Sinatra's miniseries about her beloved father was the truth about his life; certainly not *all* of the truth, but much of it.*

Philip Casnoff has met Frank Sinatra only once, on the set before they started production.

"I was a little nervous, but I was told that he was a little nervous, too," he remembered. "And he was real nice to me. Based on nothing but what his daughter had told him about me, he said, 'You're gonna do a great job, kid.' I was standing behind him posing for the picture, and he said, 'It's okay, you can put your hand on my shoulder. Go 'head.' I would liked to have had the chance to talk to him some more. I understand that to really get to know him, you have to sit down and have a couple drinks with him. I still hope to one day." Sinatra did not visit the set during production.

"Apparently he was very moved by the piece when he saw a tape of it," said Casnoff. "He didn't talk to anyone for about twenty-four hours afterward. It was hard for him to watch his divorce. All the stuff about Nancy and Ava—that was very difficult for him. Afterward, he and Tina sent me a beautiful gift, a nineteenth-century silver humidor with his signature and hers and an inscription. I treasure it."

* * *

* It was odd to some observers that there was no mention of the kidnapping of Frank junior. Casnoff says that the event was in an original draft but was cut because of time constraints.

In early 1993, Frank's friend lyricist Sammy Cahn passed away. Frank attended his funeral on January 22. For a man who had never liked attending funerals—and he once refused to do so—these sad occasions seemed to be more frequent. Cahn's death affected Sinatra deeply. Theirs was one of the most successful singer-songwriter relationships in the history of popular music. "Come Fly With Me," "Come Dance With Me," "Hey, Jealous Lover," "Time After Time," "Three Coins in the Fountain," and the Emmy Award–winning "Love and Marriage" were all Cahn classics.

Frank told some intimates that he felt his music career was over with the death of Cahn, but 1993 would be the year he would find himself back on top of the charts with his first studio album in ten years, *Duets*. Produced by Phil Ramone and coproduced by Hank Cattaneo, thirteen of Sinatra's better known songs were recorded as duets with popular singers of the day. The repertoire included "I've Got the World on a String" (with Liza Minnelli), "New York, New York" (with Tony Bennett), "Witchcraft" (with Anita Baker), and "I've Got a Crush on You" (with Barbra Streisand).

"There were a lot of people who didn't believe it could be done and that he would change his mind or walk away from it," said producer Phil Ramone. "I mean, right until the minute before he actually sang, he said to me, 'This better work.' And I said, 'It's gonna work.' And he said 'It'd *better* work.' I thought to myself, Oh, okay. I got it. The pressure's here. We'd better make it work."

It seemed to most observers that Sinatra really didn't want to take on this project and that he was just doing it to be amiable. "Why am I doing this?" he asked coproducer Hank Cattaneo in frustration. "Why am I recording all of these songs again?" During the sessions at Capitol in Hollywood, he sounded surprisingly strong and compelling for a man his age, or even one half his age. Or as one music journalist asked, "Is Sinatra half the singer he was in 1942 or 1956? Actually, he's about three-fifths the singer he was—but that still makes him about twice the singer anyone else is." Certainly his performance on "One for My Baby" (One for the Road) ranks among the best of his career, if not vocally, then emotionally.

Respected Sinatra historian and journalist David McClintick attended the session and wrote about it for *Vanity Fair*. "Accompanied only by his pianist and a few strings, Sinatra sings the song through once. [When] he concluded, there is just a slight catch in his voice, as if he's nearly overcome with emotion. The studio and control room are silent. Then the entire orchestra stands and applauds. . . . The lion is still roaring, still irrepressible, still feisty, still difficult and still the most potent singer of songs who ever lived."

In one night alone, July 1, 1993, McClintick remembered, Sinatra recorded nine songs. Some artists are fortunate to finish three songs in a session, but most just do one.

Although the album appealed to a wide audience—and as a result of its success, some of Sinatra's most enthusiastic supporters were now under thirty—longtime Sinatra aficionados are divided in their opinions of the *Duets* recording. Was this really a Frank Sinatra album? Or just studio wizardry? One might have been able to overlook the fact that Sinatra was never in the studio with any of his duet partners had it not been so well publicized that the singers never had any contact with Frank. Either they recorded their parts subsequently in the same studio or actually phoned in their parts using a digital system that had been developed by George Lucas's Skywalker Sound.

This knowledge did not enhance the listening experience for many fans and critics. For instance, it sounded odd to hear artists like Aretha Franklin and Barbra Streisand mention Frank's name in the middle of their songs ("What Now My Love," and "I've Got a Crush on You," respectively) knowing that they were standing alone at a microphone in a darkened recording studio just listening to his vocal stylings on their headphones. Sinatra recorded an overdub to "I've Got a Crush on You," replacing the word "baby" with "Barbra" in order to personalize the number as Streisand had in her performance. But Frank sang his overdub into a digital tape recorder in his dressing room just prior to a concert in Chicago.

Barbra Streisand was so excited about recording her part of "I've Got a Crush on You," she brought with her, for inspiration, a dog-eared copy of a note Frank had written her almost thirty years earlier when he saw her performance in *Funny Girl*. Sinatra had arranged for her to be greeted by a huge floral display, along with a handwritten note from him, when she got to the recording studio. She had the letter she brought with her photocopied and enclosed it along with another note to thank Sinatra for the flowers. That was about as close as she got to the Voice. When his part of the song was melded into hers, it *sounded* as if they had recorded the song together. However, the listeners knew they hadn't. Therefore, some-how the listening experience is tainted. In the past, one of the hallmarks of Sinatra's recordings had always been their honesty and emotional integrity. This one was fake.

The album was a big success, however, selling millions of copies and soaring to the number-one spot on the *Billboard* chart, a testament to the continued interest in Frank Sinatra's work among record buyers. In fact, this was Sinatra's most successful album ever. Indeed, it had been a smart move, teaming Sinatra with young, contemporary artists, because it gave the project a broad, commercial appeal.

A follow-up album, *Duets II,* was issued a year later, using the same technology, with duets on songs such as "Embraceable You" (Lena

Horne), "Where or When" (Steve Lawrence and Eydie Gorme), and "Luck Be a Lady" (Chrissie Hynde, horribly miscast and sounding like Edith Piaf). This was an even less engaging package than its predecessor. For many, the only reason to purchase *Duets II*, other than to hear a seventy-nine-year-old Sinatra still sounding full-bodied and vibrant on at least most of the songs, is to hear the duet with his son, Frank junior, on "My Kind of Town." Just as did the first album, *Duets II* received generally favorable reviews and sold millions of copies.*

In 1994, Frank Sinatra was awarded a Legend Award for Lifetime Achievement at the Grammy Awards presentation at Radio City Music Hall in New York City. Pop group U2's leader, Bono (who had appeared on the *Duets* album on "I've Got You Under My Skin" and in a video with Frank for the song), presented the award after introducing Frank with quirky and nonsensical comments. "Rock-'n'-roll people love Frank Sinatra because Frank Sinatra has got what we want: swagger and attitude. He's big on attitude, serious attitude. Bad attitude. Frank's the Chairman of the Bad. Rock 'n' roll plays at being tough, but this guy's . . . Well, he's the Boss, the Boss of Bosses, the Man, Big Daddy. The Big Bang of Pop. I'm not gonna mess with him—are you?" It probably would have been a more respectful and certainly more appropriate speech if, during it, Bono had focused on Sinatra the singer and explained his essence.

As Frank appeared onstage to a standing ovation, he paused for a long moment, taking in the young faces looking back at him. The man who had been vilified by the press for his "bad attitude" was now the hero of an entire generation, who found that attitude to be refreshing, a symbol of a man in control.

Frank spoke thoughtfully and introspectively about New Yorkers, his love for Barbara, the backstage booze, about not being asked to perform. In truth, he was rambling. But this was his special night; he was clearly overwhelmed by his own strong emotions at being so honored. After about three minutes, someone (widely rumored to be Sinatra's press agent, Susan Reynolds) decided to pull the plug on the Old Man.

Pierre Cosette, executive producer of the broadcast, said, "Sinatra's people were saying, 'Get him off, get him off now. He can't remember what he was going to say.' "

Thus, without warning, the band began to play, and Frank was simply forced to stop speaking. His staff was trying to protect his image. No one

---

* In the spring of 1997, another Sinatra album was released, *Frank Sinatra With the Red Norvo Quintet, Live in Australia, 1959*. The live recording of a performance in Melbourne received glowing reviews, and though the sound quality was abysmal, many observers feel that this record displays Sinatra at his jazz best. It hit number three on the jazz charts, a testament to Sinatra's enduring popularity.

wanted him to appear to be old, mixed-up. To the viewing audience, however, what happened looked rude, insulting, and disrespectful.

Cut off in mid-sentence? By one of his own employees? Frank Sinatra?

There was a time in the not-so-distant past when no one—let alone someone on his own payroll—would have dared cut off "the Chairman of the Board," when the sheer power of his presence would have kept such interlopers at a respectful distance, even when he appeared to be stumbling. But now it was as if "they" recognized a certain vulnerability. They were circling, moving in. And the hardest part of it all was that the Old Man in the center didn't seem to know what was going on.*

CHAPTER 46

"Frank was ready to retire after the Grammy incident," said one of his longtime associates. "He's too smart. He knew that he wasn't one hundred percent that night. He knew that he couldn't do it anymore. He said, 'I'm gettin' out while the gettin' is good. Fuck this.' "

A week later, on March 6, a moment occurred onstage that underscored any concerns about Sinatra's health that may have been caused by the faltering Grammy speech. Sinatra was onstage at the Mosque in Richmond, Virginia; the performance was a strong one. Despite two cataract surgeries in 1993, he was still unable to read the TelePrompTer. His voice was stiff and raspy. His pitch was unsteady. Still, he was in good humor. He apologized for all of the standards. "There's no new music," he explained. "The guys who wrote these songs, they got so fat with bread, they went to live in the mountains, those rat bastards. They got drunk or died, or something . . . so we go on."

Halfway through an uncertain delivery of "My Way," he began to feel dizzy. He had been cranky throughout the performance, complaining about the warm temperature, and was annoyed that his son had removed his whiskey tumbler from the stage. During the song, he turned to Frank junior to ask for a chair. Then Frank noticed a stool behind him and began to sit down. He touched the corner of the stool before slowly sinking to the floor, hitting the stage with a thud. The microphone fell

---

* A year later, Grammy officials had the terrific idea of having Sinatra open the show with his back to the camera. He would turn to face the audience, step up to the mike, and say, "Now, as I was saying . . ." After a brief monologue, he would perform "New York, New York." However, the Sinatra camp vetoed the idea.

from his hand and made a loud noise when it hit the floor. An audible gasp came from the stunned audience of thirty-seven hundred.

One ringside, longtime Sinatra fan—Marjorie Hyde—remembered: "My heart stopped when he fell, right on his face. He looked dead. The music continued playing, and there was chaos onstage for a moment as people started running over to him. They turned him over, took off his tie, unbuttoned his top shirt button. Frank junior took his pulse and said, 'He's alive. He's still alive.' ["This took ten years off my life," Frank junior later recalled.]

"They were about to carry him out when he came to [he was unconscious for about ten minutes] and stood up. Someone brought out a wheelchair, and he got in it. As they were wheeling him offstage, he waved to the audience and blew us a kiss to let us know he was all right. It was a terribly frightening moment, and the relief people felt when he waved— Well, everyone stood and cheered. The whole thing was a nightmare. I knew then that Frank should not have been onstage. I cried all the way home."

As soon as Nancy heard that her father had collapsed, she knew what was wrong with him. She immediately telephoned the emergency room of the Medical College of Virginia, where Frank had been taken, and told the doctors that she believed he was suffering from a potassium deficiency caused by the drugs he was taking for high blood pressure and that he had probably been dehydrated by the stage lights, which caused him to faint. Because Nancy happened to be taking the same medication, she knew of its effects. She was correct in her instant diagnosis.

Frank was embarrassed about what had occurred. After a three-hour stay at the hospital, his doctors wanted to keep him for observation, but Sinatra vetoed that notion—he flew back to Palm Springs in a private plane. Doctors diagnosed that the collapse was probably the result of "overheating," and he may also have been slightly dehydrated after perspiring heavily through the performance.

He was back onstage in a couple of weeks. But from this point on, nothing would ever be the same. There was an almost palpable sense of fear, felt not only by the musicians onstage but members of the audiences who had read or heard about what had occurred in Virginia, that Sinatra would collapse again and that this time it would be more serious. For the first time, as Frank Sinatra was about to turn eighty, his family and close associates began to think that perhaps he should retire. He had already made that decision, however. He knew he was failing. His vision, his hearing, his voice, were all going, and there was nothing he could do about it.

"This may be the last time we will be together," he told an audience of more than five thousand at Radio City Music Hall in April 1994. Sinatra would continue to perform throughout the rest of 1994, fulfilling commitments all the way up to his seventy-ninth birthday in December.

On Saturday, February 25, 1995, Sinatra gave what would turn out to be his final performance at Marriott's Desert Springs Resort & Spa for a private party of about twelve hundred on the last day of the Frank Sinatra Desert Classic golf tournament. For five songs, Sinatra was young again. First he did "I've Got the World on a String," "Fly Me to the Moon," and then "Where or When," which writer Jonathan Schwartz reported was "performed by a forty-five-year-old man. It is everything Sinatra wishes to convey. It is a ballad with tempo that gathers rhythmic steam and explodes at its conclusion. Its last long line, the 'where or when' is sustained to the last drop of the high E-flat, not repeated for lack of breath." Then "My Kind of Town"—his voice young and agile—and a standing ovation.

"You mean it's time to go home," Frank said, laughing, as the applause died down.

Finally, an encore, a now-ironic "The Best Is Yet to Come," which capped an excellent performance of surprising force. The show was so eloquently executed, some observers were reminded of Noël Coward's oft-quoted remark about Frank Sinatra: "Never once a breach of taste, never once a wrong move."

Sinatra's road manager, Tony Oppedisano, said, "It was a jubilant evening, reaching for notes and holding them. It was a phenomenal, phenomenal show. He was fantastic and made mincemeat out of the critics."

"When are you going to learn to swing?" his wife Barbara jokingly asked him as they entered the limousine that whisked them from the Marriott back to their home at 70588 Frank Sinatra Drive in Rancho Mirage.

After that show, Sinatra was elated. That youthful part of him that had always wanted more, more, *more*, now wanted even more. He felt that the audience's reaction to his performance was so enthusiastic and that he was in such excellent voice for a man his age that surely he had another couple of years left in him. He had also been proud of some shows just prior to this one. "I ain't quittin'," he announced. "Just takin' some time off, that's all."

The Sinatra family humored him. Frank junior agreed that, following a short rest, he and the Old Man would go back out again "and kick some ass." However, everyone knew that this was not meant to be. It was over.

"One after another, they're droppin' like flies," Frank Sinatra had said of his friends.

At the end of 1995, Dean Martin died at the age of seventy-eight. The reported cause of death was acute respiratory failure brought on by emphysema. Dean's devoted ex-wife, Jeanne (from whom he had been divorced since 1973 after twenty-three years of marriage), was at his side until the end. "He had quit smoking two or three years before he died," Mort Viner recalled, "but it wasn't soon enough."

After Dean's death, Frank sank into a deep depression. For him, it was as if many of the key players in his life were being toppled one by one: Ava, Sammy, Jilly, Dean. "I'm next," he told friends at Matteo's restaurant in Beverly Hills. "I ain't scared, either. How can I be? Every-fucking-body I ever knew is already over *dere*."

It has been often published that Frank and Dean did not speak for three years after that night in Chicago in 1988 when Dean walked out on the Rat Pack reunion tour and that a reconciliation took place just before Dean's death. "When Dean pulled out of the tour, yeah, it caused a rift in his relationship with Sinatra, but it was over within two weeks, and it never surfaced again," says Mort Viner. "That's where everybody went astray in the media after the tour ended. There was no problem between them in any way, shape, or form. So when they talk about a reconciliation, they're wrong, because there was never a need for one."

"Dean was never at the house, though," said James Wright. "Never at any of the parties. Sammy was around a lot, not Dean."

However, Mort Viner says that Dean and Frank spoke regularly prior to Dean's death. They saw each other on the occasion of Dean's birthday in June and, said Viner, once again just weeks before Dean died, when he and Frank had dinner. It's said by Frank's friends that he knew this would be the last time he'd ever see Dean.

"He calls me up," Dean said at La Famiglia restaurant six months before his death. As he picked at his dessert of *macedonia* (Italian fruit cup), he added, "We shoot the shit, you know. Two old guys. Frank wants to talk over old times. Only problem is, I don't remember the old times. I can't even remember the new times." He wasn't joking. Or was he? At the end, with Dean, one could never be sure.

Sinatra tried to attend Dean's funeral at Westwood Village Memorial Park. He broke down in tears while getting dressed. "I'm sorry," he cried, according to one former employee. "I want to do this goddamn thing, but I don't know if I have the strength to get through it." His family felt it would be better for his health if he did not attend. Barbara attended in his stead.

"He stayed in bed for two days after the funeral," Barbara Sinatra said. "He was broken up about it; he really was."

"That really hurt him," said Frank junior of his father's reaction to Dean's death. "That really did not go down too good. That was very bad. It was like he lost his brother. I mean, they were together—or at least talking on the phone—three or four times a week. Oh, my God, the two of them were Peck's Bad Boys all through the years."

In a prepared statement Frank said, "Too many times I've been asked to say something about friends who are gone. This is one of the hardest.

Dean was my brother—not through blood but through choice. Our friendship has traveled down many roads over the years, and there will always be a special place in my heart and soul for Dean. He has been like the air I breathe—always there, always close by."

Six months before his death, Dean Martin told this writer, "When I go, Frank and Joey [Bishop] will be the only two left. Then, I guess they'll be next and we'll all be together again. And *god damn it*," he exclaimed, clapping his hands, "we're all gonna have some fun then."

Earlier in the year, Frank's fifty-four-year-old daughter, Nancy Sinatra, raised eyebrows when she posed for the cover of *Playboy*'s May issue and was featured in a nude layout inside. These unclothed photographs of Nancy were difficult for many people to accept, her family and fans included. Perhaps the scandalous nature of the pictures should not have been a surprise, however. After all, the Sinatras have never embraced a clean-cut, wholesome image. Frank has always been thought of as a dangerous, dark person by many; Frank junior's kidnapping continues to be a source of great speculation; and Nancy's career was largely based on a sex-kitten, seductive image.

In 1995 she was attempting to infuse new life into her recording career (an excellent album, *One More Time*, was about to be issued), and in her view *Playboy* was an excellent vehicle for—exposure. The pictures were not discreet. Originally, she planned to just be topless, but in the end she displayed everything. "Once you get involved, it seemed stupid to be shy," she told *Variety*'s Army Archerd.

Nancy has said that her father did not take issue with her determination to show off her body for the magazine as long as she got more money than she had been offered. (She was offered $50,000; he told her to ask for $75,000.) "There's a certain price tag for the Sinatra name," she said he told her. "It's not just your name. It's mine."

"What possessed her to do this?" Barbara asked one friend of hers when she saw the layout. "When Frank sees this, I'm afraid he's going to have a heart attack. What an insensitive, crazy thing for her to do. But you know something?" Barbara asked, inspecting every inch of every photo. "I never knew she had such a fantastic body. Do you think she's had plastic surgery?" The friend said she had no idea. "Well, she certainly wouldn't tell *me* if she did," Barbara said. She added that she was astonished at how well Nancy, as she put it, "cleaned up."

"Everyone was amazed at how gorgeous she was in the photos," said James Wright. "I remember the first time I met her, in 1989, at the Beverly Hills home. I saw this woman sitting at the bar with a scarf around her head and a hat on top of that and a great big coat. I said to someone else, 'I thought Nancy was supposed to be coming tonight.' And he said,

'That's her over there.' And I said, '*That's* Nancy Sinatra. Why, it can't be? She looks like a bloody old woman.' I couldn't believe it. She looked awful, just awful. She looked a wreck. But she obviously could pull herself together based on the *Playboy* photos."

Frank junior was astonished, say Sinatra intimates, that his sister would pose unclothed. Sister Tina was "totally supportive." Nancy senior refused to look at the pictures and, according to some, still has not seen them.

Nancy wanted to show the photos to her father before his wife had the opportunity to do so. "Frank was pissed off," said an associate still involved with the Sinatras as of this writing. "He's an old-fashioned Italian American with a great deal of dignity. How's he gonna be happy seeing his daughter's breasts and you-know-what laid out for all the world in a national magazine. I understand he said, 'Look, get that outta my face,' when she showed it to him. 'You think I wanna see *that?*' Nancy was proud of it. But she couldn't have done it ten years ago. He woulda killed her. He was weak, old, tired. . . . He didn't have the energy to get as upset as he would have in the past. She was lucky."

"May you live to be one hundred and the last voice you hear be mine," Frank Sinatra used to say at the end of some of his performances.

On December 12, 1995, Sinatra turned eighty years old. He had finally reconciled himself to the fact that he would no longer be performing. "I'll never sing again in public," he told Larry King. "because those days are just gone. But I'm very, very happy."

Frank enjoyed his time off, spending a few nights a week at Matteo's in Westwood, his favorite restaurant. Said Larry Culler, the maître d', who has known Sinatra for twenty-five years, "He has a private booth in the main dining room anytime he wants it. It's close to the back door, so he can slide in and out without being hassled. I always say to the waiters, 'Don't let anyone near him,' just trying to protect him. But a lot of times, he'd say, 'Aw, just let that gal through. She wants an autograph.'

"We always have vinegar peppers for Frank. Matty [the owner] has them flown in from Italy just for Sinatra. Some of his favorite foods aren't on the menu, but we get them for him. He likes veal *Milanese*, salami, usually without the garlic, in the last year. He drinks vodka, Jack Daniels, sometimes red wine. Likes his expresso glass not filled all the way to the top."

Meanwhile, at home, Frank had become much more eccentric and demanding. For instance, he had always had an aversion to strong perfumes. In fact, as a young man, he usually insisted that his women wear only a light scent, if any at all. The older Sinatra expanded his dislikes to include not only strong perfumes but also fish, Mexican food, lamb, and even garlic, which, as an ingredient in many of his favorite Italian dishes, had once been a passion. None of those foods were served in the household. Also, Aramis cologne, Elizabeth Taylor's Passion perfume, and any body odors were the source of irritation to Sinatra.

His head butler was asked to discreetly sniff all guests before they entered the Sinatra home in order to subtly detect any aroma he knew Sinatra would find offensive. If he detected any such smell, he would ask the person to follow him to another wing of the home. There the butler would explain Frank's problem and ask the guest to wash off the offending smell in a nearby bathroom. Guests always complied.

As he aged, Sinatra also became more concerned about his appearance, as do most people, especially celebrities in the public eye. While he didn't care if he was seen without his toupee at home, when he was in public, he wanted it to be as natural looking as possible. To that end, his butler would wash his four (sometimes six) toupees in Woolite not only after one was actually worn but also if it was tried on and then discarded because it didn't fit properly. While on the road, Sinatra would have as many as a dozen toupees with him; sometimes he would wear as many as six different ones a day, depending on how much he would perspire that day. He most certainly would not wear the same one for two shows a night. At the end of the day, all toupees worn that day would be washed and hung side by side on the shower curtain bar to dry. "The bathroom looked like a trophy room for an Indian scalping party," said one of the butlers, Bill Stapely, who had this assignment.

A stickler for cleanliness, as he got older, showers took as long as three hours. He would become upset if he found lint on his silk black socks; and his boots—with half-inch lifts in each—had to be polished to perfection, because he felt they should shine under the stage lights.

About a month prior to his birthday, a television special was taped at the Shrine Auditorium to celebrate the event. It had been Barbara Sinatra's and producer and longtime family friend George Schlatter's idea to put together a show, the proceeds of which would go to AIDS Project Los Angeles and the Barbara Sinatra Children's Center. Frank wanted nothing to do with this special. In fact, when he attended a similar tribute to Sammy Davis, he was said to have told his manager, Eliot Weisman, "Don't you ever do this kind of bullshit tribute thing for me."

Barbara, who'd become even more protective of her husband as she and he got older—so much so that she even began screening his every telephone call and preventing even close friends from talking to him—was determined that her husband should participate in the affair, even though what he really wanted was to go off with his pals on his eightieth birthday and get drunk. Nancy, Tina, and Frank junior also wanted nothing to do with the special; they had no participation in it. If anything, the show was just another stumbling block in their long, difficult relationship with their ambitious stepmother.

A maid, who still works in Sinatra's Beverly Hills home today from time to time remembered: "I know that Mr. and Mrs. Sinatra had terrible screaming battles about the TV show. He didn't want to go; he thought it would be an embarrassment. During one battle about it, he took a plate and smashed it against a wall, proving to me that he still had some life in him. He said, 'Goddamn it, Barbara. I ain't goin'. I hate this kind of thing. *You* go. *You* have a good time. Tell everyone I said thanks but I was too sick to show up. I ain't goin'.' Then he asked the cook to open a can of pork and beans for him.''

Barbara forced Frank to have dinner with Bruce Springsteen and Bob Dylan, who were scheduled to participate in the event, a couple of days before the show; they came to the house and fawned over Frank for two hours. Barbara had reasoned that if Sinatra saw how excited younger entertainers (like Springsteen and Dylan) would be in his presence, he would become enthused about the show. Steve Lawrence and Eydie Gorme were also present for what had to have been the oddest dinner party ever assembled in a Beverly Hills home.

The evening was a great success. Frank, Bruce, and Bob got completely drunk on Jack Daniels. Sinatra had a wonderful time with his new friends. Barbara seethed and spent most of her time complaining to Steve and Eydie that her husband drinks too much. After a dessert of cheesecake with raspberries, the singers gathered around the piano and sang such songs as "All or Nothing at All" and "It Had to Be You" while Sinatra watched, amused and bleary-eyed.

"What great guys," Frank said of Bruce Springsteen and Bob Dylan. "We should have those two over more often. Forget Steve and Eydie. I'm sick of 'em. Let's have Dylan and Springsteen over once a month."

"Over my dead body," Barbara groused.

Frank's instincts about the television special *Sinatra: 80 Years My Way*, which aired on December 14, 1995, were accurate. As he predicted, much of it truly was an embarrassment. With entertainment such as choreographer Paula Abdul performing a dance routine to "Luck Be a Lady," rap trio Salt-N-Peppa singing their rap song "Whatta Man" as a preposterous tribute to Frank, rock-and-roll sensation Hootie and the Blowfish singing "The Lady Is a Tramp," and pop singer Seal singing "I've Got You Under My Skin," most Sinatra aficionados were hard-pressed to understand what any of this madness really had to do with Frank Sinatra. A tribute by acerbic Roseanne, comparing herself to Sinatra, left many observers asking the question "Why?" It was a farce whose only advantage was that it raised a million dollars for the two charities. If not for the wonderful Steve Lawrence and Eydie Gorme singing a medley of Sinatra songs with Vic Damone and an appearance by Tony Bennett, the evening would have been a total loss.

Sinatra, though, seemed to have a reasonably good time once he got to the Shrine. Though he seemed puzzled by much of the entertainment, especially the Salt-N-Peppa number, he was genuinely touched by other performances, such as Patti LaBelle's bizarre rendering of "The House I Live In." At the end of the show, during the finale, he went up onto the stage from the audience to sing the last two notes of "The Theme From New York, New York" with the disparate array of performers.

He sounded better than all of them. He also looked well. For the broadcast, he wore a $2,500 hairpiece—each synthetic hair in several shades of silver gray sewn on individually, which took two months—a gift from New York hairdresser Joseph Paris, who had tended to Sinatra's toupees since 1980 (when he made his first Sinatra hairpiece for Frank's film *The First Deadly Sin*).

After the taping, Frank and Barbara, Gregory and Veronique Peck, Steve Lawrence and Eydie Gorme, and Robert Wagner and Jill St. John had drinks together in a private dining room of the Four Seasons Hotel and tried to convince themselves that the special had been a success.

After the broadcast on December 14, another battle between the Sinatra offspring and their stepmother, Barbara, broke out when she arranged a dinner at producer George Schlatter's home on Frank's actual birthday. (It was actually scheduled to take place at L'Orangerie restaurant in West Hollywood but was moved to the Schlatters' home when the media found out about it.)

Noticeably absent were all three of Frank's children, Nancy, Frank junior, and Tina. Not only was Barbara angry with them for not supporting her in her efforts with the birthday television broadcast (which may account for their not being seated at the table with her and Frank), but she was also having a disagreement with them about the rerelease of certain Sinatra songs.

It would seem that Nancy Sinatra is primarily responsible for decisions on the reissuing of her father's music on Columbia, Capitol, and Reprise. Sometimes she reluctantly agrees to allow previously unreleased material to be issued, but she is adamantly opposed to the release of alternate takes of Sinatra sessions. And she bristles at the thought of the burgeoning bootleg market that thrives on such material, which she calls "illegal shit." The family makes no money from the sale of bootleg material.

Nancy had originally hoped that the family would celebrate Frank's milestone birthday with a quiet family dinner attended by his first wife, Nancy, her children, and his grandchildren. But because of all the dissension between Barbara and Frank's daughters, that was not to be.

Six months later, Frank and Barbara renewed their wedding vows on their twentieth anniversary, July 11, 1996, at Our Lady of Malibu Church. It had been Barbara's idea; Frank went along with it. It was said by those inside the Sinatra camp that seventy-year-old Barbara felt such disrespect aimed at her by Sinatra's children that she wanted to renew her vows to her husband in order to put into proper perspective her place in the family. This would be her and Frank's third wedding ceremony, the first having been in Palm Springs and the second, also in Palm Springs, after Frank's marriage to Nancy was annulled. While Frank junior attended the ceremony, his sisters, Nancy and Tina, did not.

Things were so tense between Barbara and Frank's daughters, it was best they didn't attend. Frankly, Barbara didn't want them there, anyway. Frank has been in the middle of this war between the women in his life for years. He's old and tired of it, but he also feels a sense of devotion to his wife, even more so recently.

Frank has appreciated the way Barbara has taken care of him during these last years of illnesses—the sleepless nights, the tears, the anguish she's gone through where he's concerned. He's been touched by it. Loyalty has always been a paramount concern in his life, and Barbara has more than proved hers over a twenty-year period. In return, Sinatra usually supports her in any family disagreements, much to his children's utter chagrin.

Frank asked Nancy and Tina not to come to the wedding ceremony unless they could promise to act as if they were happy and also show due respect to Barbara. They said they couldn't; neither is that good an actress. In their view, Barbara has done quite a bit to hurt their feelings over the years, and they've reciprocated in their own way—ignoring her, acting as if she's not a family member, an outsider even, after twenty years. In their hearts, it would seem, they feel that if a person is not born a Sinatra and is not Nancy [senior], then that person is *never* a Sinatra. Frank Sinatra, though, insists that if his children love him as they say they do, then they should continue to make an effort to get along with his wife, at least while he's still alive. It's an internal family problem that has existed, with little change, for years and, say his intimates, one of Frank Sinatra's greatest heartaches in his old age.

CHAPTER 47

By January 1997, Francis Albert Sinatra was eighty-one years old. Peter, Sammy, and Dean were gone.

The Kennedys—John and Robert and Jacqueline—all gone. Sam Giancana, also gone.

Ava, Lana, Marilyn, Juliet. Shooting stars, here for just a moment, and then—gone.

George Burns, Gene Kelly, Claudette Colbert, close friends, all gone in the last year.

Poor Jilly.

Dolly and Marty, gone.

And everyone who was left was getting on in years.

"With each passing, I think my father loses a tiny piece of his spirit," observed his twice-divorced daughter Tina.

"I haven't spoken to my father much lately, because he has really been withdrawn since Dean died," admitted Frank junior, who hadn't talked to Frank senior in a month. "And then there's the other thing. The inner, the deeper-set, problem that goes beyond poignancy. There's the actual state of depression; the fact of knowing that we're just getting old now.

"Emotionally, he's down," said Frank junior. "He's a little bit heart-sick. He sees a lot of his friends are getting old and dying, and it hurts him."

"I've been in touch with the family," Shirley MacLaine said, "and I have to respect their wishes." She paused, then added quietly, "He's failing."

Like many people when they near the end of their lives, Frank Sinatra has had an opportunity to reflect upon his long life, and in doing so he has realized that he does have some regrets. Apparently, Frank is sorry about some of the things that have occurred during his lifetime. For instance, associates say that he has never completely reconciled in his heart the matter of Peter Lawford. One business associate says that he heard Sinatra say, "I shouldn't have done that to Peter. Why was I such an ass?" He also seems to regret having left Nancy so many years ago, for Ava—but he has regretted that for years. "I was an idiot," he once told Jilly. "How could I have hurt Nancy that way?" Indeed, it would seem he has some regrets, but as the song goes, they probably really are too few to mention.

Earlier in the year, Frank and Barbara put the Rancho Mirage estate, which Frank had owned since 1954, on the market. (It would sell for $4.9 million.) Barbara decided that their party days were behind them and that it was time to begin a quieter life in both their $5.2-million, four-bedroom, six-bathroom Beverly Hills mansion and their $6 million beach-front Malibu home. Frank didn't seem to have much to say about the matter.

Barbara also decided that they should sell many of their prized posses-sions in an auction at Christie's rather than try to squeeze everything from the desert estate into the other two homes. So the 1976 Jaguar XJS that Barbara gave to Frank as a wedding present went to a retired real-estate developer in Delaware for $79,500. Frank's Bosendorfer black lacquer grand piano went for $51,750. Their glass-and-brass mailbox sold for $13,800. A white-and-blue golf cart—with the driver's side bearing the inscription "Ol' Blue Eyes" and the passenger side reading "Lady Blue Eyes"—which featured a built-in stereo system, went for $20,700. A statue of John Wayne, a gift from the Duke, went for $7,475. It was sad; Sinatra's children—especially Nancy—grew angrier as much of their inheritance was sold off, piece by piece. In all, Frank and Barbara earned $2 million from the auction.

Nancy, his first wife, who has never remarried, was now seventy-nine years old. Still devoted, she kept jars of Frank's favorite spaghetti sauce in her refrigerator at all times in case he ever wanted her home cooking. She would make eggplant *parmigiana*—her special recipe—and have it delivered to Frank by a limousine service. Frank enjoyed eating the eggplant in the morning with English muffins. Nancy and Barbara maintain a friendly relationship. "I'm just too old to get in the middle of it," Nancy said. "She takes good care of Frank. She's his wife. She deserves respect."

Though surrounded by love—even though his children were still at war with his wife—this was a difficult time for Frank Sinatra.

Tina Sinatra said in 1993, "As much as we would like to see Dad not work so hard, we also know that singing is his life force. For him to stop before he's ready might kill him." Frank felt the same way. Now it was as if everyone's greatest fear was coming to pass. Without the adulation and approval Sinatra craved to feed his soul, it began to wither. Without his music, he lost the will to go on. His body began to break down. While he was once a young man trapped in an old man's body, by the end of 1996, at the age of eighty-one, he was simply feeling old. Still, he would not give up. When his daughter Nancy asked him what he wanted for his eighty-first birthday, Sinatra said succinctly, "Another birthday."

Three hospital visits—one in November 1996 (which was also the month Sinatra made what would turn out to be his last public appearance, at the Carousel Ball Benefit in Los Angeles) and two in January 1997—would make newspaper headlines and television reports around the world.

In November, Sinatra (registered at Cedars under the name "Albert Francis") beat pneumonia in the lining of his left lung. Daughter Nancy credited the remarkable strength of his lungs for the recovery; all of that swimming to gain breath control some fifty years ago apparently continued to pay off.

On January 8, 1997, Sinatra called his family together in his private room on the eighth floor at Cedars-Sinai Hospital and told them that he feared he had little time left. He had some regrets, he said. He wished he had been a better father, a better husband. Nancy was too upset to comment. "Nonsense," Tina said as she brushed away his tears.

Frank wanted to smoke out in the hospital hallway, but Tina told him he would upset the other patients. So he lit a Camel and smoked it in bed. "He's not used to doing things not in his own way," Nancy said.

Even though it appeared to most observers that Sinatra was on his deathbed—magazines and newspapers prepared his obituaries and waited for the sad announcement—he rebounded, checked himself out of the hospital, and as soon as he got home, had a cigarette and a glass of Jack Daniels, loving every last sip.

At the end of April 1997, Congress voted to give Frank Sinatra a Congressional Gold Medal, which had been sponsored by New York Democratic representative José E. Serrano (with a push by Sen. Alfonse D'Amato [R-N.Y.]), who first heard English listening to Sinatra as a two-year-old in Mayaguez, Puerto Rico. The timing was right for such an honor in that there was a prevailing national nostalgia for a cultural icon who seemed to be nearing the end of his life.

Not many people in the media seemed opposed to the idea. However, a woman from Sinatra's past did step forward to log strenuous objections: Kitty Kelley. Much to the family's dismay, Kelley appeared on some television programs, and even wrote an editorial for *Newsweek*, voicing her opinion that Sinatra should not be so honored, citing his past association with organized crime. "I suggest [that] Congress simply give Ol'Blue Eyes a round of applause befitting any great showman. But save the gold for the giants," she wrote, further infuriating the Sinatra family. Kelley's objections meant little; Congress voted for Sinatra's medal, anyway. However, her reappearance in Frank Sinatra's life only served to remind the family that she was still out there, watching "like a stalker," Barbara said. "Why won't she just go away?"

Whether Sinatra would be able to personally accept the honor from President Bill Clinton remained to be seen; he was an extremely sick man by the summer of 1997.*

"I think he's wishing he were about twenty years younger," Nancy said. "But then, so am I. Aren't we all?

"I don't know if he'd sell his soul to the devil, but he would certainly try to make a deal to get more time," she concluded. "He ain't goin' easily."

During his life, it had always been "all or nothing at all" for Frank Sinatra. Unfortunately, it would seem that that credo would also charac-

---

* The first Congressional Gold Medal was issued to George Washington by the Continental Congress in 1787. One of the oldest awards in the country, it predates even the Constitution; the 320 past honorees include Robert Frost, Bob Hope, Thomas Edison, John Wayne, Louis L'Amour, H. Norman Schwarzkopf, and Colin Powell. "It's more than just an honor from his country as far as I'm concerned," said Frank's daughter Nancy. "It's like the country saying, 'Okay, Frank, we know the truth, and we love you.'"

terize his many illnesses. A pinched nerve. A heart attack. Cancer. Kidney problems. Bladder ailments. A touch of Alzheimer's, even. He has them all; Sinatra could never die in an anticlimactic way. "You gotta love livin'," he once said. "Dyin' is a pain in the ass." Now, more than ever, he must believe that those words are true.

Reams could be written about Frank Sinatra's various afflictions, doctors' visits, and hospital stays. About the way he has steadfastly refused to allow information about his condition to be released to the public; ever the showman, he insists upon being remembered as he was, not as he is. About the irrepressible fighting spirit, so personal to Sinatra, that has kept him alive long after all the medical prognoses. About his family, shattered by the reality that the Old Man's time with them is now most certainly limited.

The fear. The sadness. The desperation. The hope that tomorrow he will be healthy, again, kicking ass, being Sinatra, *the Man*. The sadness when tomorrow comes and he's not.

But Frank Sinatra has never been about death; he's been about life. Prattling on with details of a myriad of infirmities does nothing to illuminate his life and career except, perhaps, to underscore the startling realization that Frank Sinatra is not immortal. While his life was unique in every way, his slow, painful decline has not been.

Even at the end, however, in his last concerts, there was no separating the singer from the emotion and the meaning of the songs he sang. He continued to work and lead a productive, artistic life far beyond the point at which most ordinary mortals stop trying. His recorded music will stand as his legacy, just as he always knew it would. Certainly it will always serve as a true testament to the artistry, the pathos, the life that was Frank Sinatra's, a man who had everything, lost it all, got it back, and then let nothing ever again stand in the way of his living a full, passionate existence.

One of the most powerful Americans of Italian descent ever, Sinatra is a true study in paradoxes. He could be arrogant, rude, temperamental, and cruel one day and generous, kind, and completely selfless the next. Throughout it all, his ability as a vocalist and interpreter of lyrics remains indisputable. It has never been difficult to separate the notoriety from that talent, and through his great ability as a performer he found an absolution that might not have been granted otherwise.

In the winter of 1965, Walter Cronkite asked Frank Sinatra, who was about to turn fifty years old, how he would like to be remembered. What he said then, over thirty years ago, still seems a perfect representation of the man:

"I think I would like to be remembered as a man who brought an innovation to popular singing, a peculiar, unique fashion that I wish one of these days somebody would learn to do so it doesn't die where it is. I would like to be remembered as a man who had a wonderful time living his life and who had good friends, a fine family, and I don't think I could ask for anything more than that, actually. I think that would do it."

Though his public wants him to go on forever, he obviously can't. Eventually, the passion has to end. It always does. But for Sinatra—and for many of us as well—it was nothing if not one hell of a ride.

SOURCES AND NOTES

While the following notes are by no means comprehensive, they are intended to at least give the reader a general overview of my research.

Over a five-year period, 425 people were interviewed for this work, either by myself or by my researcher, Cathy Griffin. Whenever practical, I have provided sources within the body of the text. Some who were not quoted directly in the text provided observations that helped me better understand Sinatra and his life and career.

Some of the books and newspaper and magazine articles that I consulted are included below; however, there are simply too many to be listed in their entirety.

Obviously, I viewed innumerable hours of Sinatra's television programs, television specials, concerts, press conferences, documentaries (as well as those relating to Dean Martin, Sammy Davis, Peter Lawford, and other principal players in this story), and also hundreds of hours of radio interviews and other broadcasts in which Sinatra took part or of which he was the subject. It would be impractical to list them all here.

Frank Sinatra has many fan clubs, but two in particular are amazingly well organized and informative: the Sinatra Society of America (headed by Charles Pignon, a longtime trusted friend of the Sinatras) and the International Sinatra Society (directed by thorough Sinatra historians Mary and Dustin Doctor in memory of the late Gary L. Doctor, who compiled Citadel Press's excellent *Sinatra Scrapbook*). Through their newsletters and other forums, including invaluable Internet Web sites, I was able to confirm important details and add color to certain sections of this book. I also obtained historically important videotapes and recordings from the International Sinatra Society. Mr. Sinatra is fortunate to have these two fan clubs so devoted to preserving his legend and reputation.

In writing about a person as powerful and as influential as Frank Sinatra and about the Sinatra family, a biographer is bound to find that many sources with valuable information prefer not to be named in the text. This is understandable. Throughout my career, I have maintained that for a person to jeopardize a long-standing, important relationship for the sake of a book is a purely personal choice. Because I so appreciate the assistance of many people close to Sinatra over the years who gave of their time and energy for this project, I will respect their wish for anonymity. Those who could be named are named in these notes. Also, some sources are named in the text but asked specifically not to be named in the book's acknowledgments so as not to have their contributions singled out and held up to scrutiny by the Sinatra family. Of course, I've respected their wishes as well.

1915–39

"Unbelievable! I don't believe that there's another person writing a book about Sinatra," said Nancy Sinatra Sr., to my researcher, Cathy Griffin, on May 30, 1997. "Nobody ever gets it right, and it's just exhausting to me," she said. "However, I wish the author well with it, anyway. Maybe this one will make some sense." Laughing, she added, "I just hope he does a good job, for *his* sake."

I would like to thank Mrs. Sinatra for her limited participation, for clarifying certain points of which I was uncertain and for shedding light on other areas. A dignified, positive-thinking woman, she is not anxious to discuss the past, which is why I appreciate her time even more.

"I refuse to say anything bad about anybody, anyway, or anyhow," she said when pushed about one particularly painful memory, "because I have been hurt too many times through the years. Recently, I was asked something about Ava Gardner and I said, 'Look. It's just too late. It doesn't matter to me anymore, and it shouldn't matter to anyone else. I'm eighty years old, and I'm just not going to get into that anymore, *ever*.' And if people want to know how I feel, then tell them that, because that's how I feel. I don't mean to be rude, but this is my life, and I have a right to feel as I do about it. Don't you agree?"

I feel that Mrs. Sinatra's candid comments speak volumes for the way she has decided to deal with her life's history, and I admire her point of view.

Over the last five years, I spent many hours in Hoboken, New Jersey, where a number of people opened their homes—and their scrapbooks—to me as they remembered young Frank. I am indebted to so many people who lived in Hoboken when the Sinatras did—many of whom live elsewhere today—and also to the sons, daughters, grandsons, and granddaughters of people who were friendly with Dolly and Marty Sinatra and whose memories of them—as relayed to them by their ancestors—remain intact. I was impressed by their affection for the Sinatras and appreciate their trust.

I utilized the Park Avenue Library in Hoboken to glean details of Hoboken's history as well as the Sinatra family's. My appreciation to all of its staff for their assistance. Regarding Hoboken's history, I also utilized *The Hoboken of Yesterday* by George Long; *The Italians* by Luigi Barzini; *Gritty Cities* by Mary Procter and Bill Matuszeki; *Beyond the Melting Pot* by Nathan Glazer and Daniel P. Moynihan; *Halo Over Hoboken* by John Perkins Fiel; and *The Changing Nature of Irish-Italian Relations* by Joseph A. Varacalli.

My thanks to Tina Donato for her insight and for taking me to all of the pertinent Sinatra sites in Hoboken, allowing me to enjoy the atmosphere and ambience and to get a sense of what it must have been like for Sinatra and his family in the thirties and forties. Doris Sevanto, who no longer lives in Hoboken but took the time (and incurred the expense) of returning there after twenty-five years to assist me, was invaluable to my research. I am grateful for her amazing memory, good cheer, and hospitality. Thanks are due those who submitted to interviews, including Tony Martin, Tom Gianetti, Rocco Gianetti, Thomas LaGreca, Debra Stradella, Delilah Lawford, Tom Raskin, and Salvatore Donato. Thanks also to Lisa's Italian Deli on Park Avenue in Hoboken.

My special thanks to Joseph D'Orazio, a friend who was close not only to Sinatra but to Hank Sanicola and Emmanuel "Manie" Sachs. He and I became pals during the course of my five years of research, and I thank him for so many hours of interviews. "Joey Boy" is one of a kind.

I was deeply saddened by the recent death of Nancy Venturi, who, even though she was quite ill, spent hours sharing vivid memories of young Frank. I will miss her.

Thanks to the staff of the Hudson County Courthouse for its assistance in locating certain arrest records and other court documents relating to Sinatra's arrest on morals charges vital to my research. My thanks also to the staff of the Hudson County Records Bureau. I also reviewed editions of the *Hudson Dispatch* to confirm other details.

Throughout this book, I culled quotes from many published and televised interviews with Mr. Sinatra as well as from radio broadcasts. Most helpful to the early years was "He Can't Read a Note But He's Dethroning Bing" (*Newsweek*, March 22, 1943);

"Sweet Dreams and Dynamite" by Jack Long (*American Magazine*, September 1943); "The Voice" (*Newsweek*, December 20, 1943); "Phenomenon, Parts 1 and II" by E. J. Kahn, Jr. (*New Yorker*, 1946); "Star Spangled Octopus" by David G. Wittels (*Saturday Evening Post*, 1946); "The Nine Lives of Frank Sinatra" by Adela Rogers St. John (*Cosmopolitan*, 1956); "When Ol' Blue Eyes Was Red" by Jon Wiener (*New Republic*, 1986); "Here's Why Sinatra Is a Camp" by David Hinkley (*Daily News*, (March 13, 1994); "Sinatra Means a Jumping Jilly" by Gay Talese (*New York Times* Company, 1965); "Frank Sinatra Had a Cold" by Gay Talese (*Esquire*, April 1966); "Lauren Bacall—"Be Open To Whatever Happens" by Dotson Rader (*Parade*, May 18, 1997); and *Dark Victory—Ronald Reagan, MCA and the Mob* by Dan E. Moldea.

Frank Sinatra gave a lecture at Yale Law School in May 1986 for the Zion Lecture Series. The transcript of this lecture proved an excellent source of information.

I also referred to "The Un-American Activities in California—the (California) Senate Fact-Finding Committee on Un-American Activities, Third, Fourth and Fifth Reports" (Sacramento, California, 1947), which is on file at the Margaret Herrick Library of the Academy of Motion Picture Arts and Sciences.

I reviewed the personal papers and files of columnist Sidney Skolsky and the files of the Production Code Administration, also on file at the Margaret Herrick Library.

Nancy Sinatra's two books, *Frank Sinatra—My Father* and *Frank Sinatra—An American Legend*, were both helpful in forming a time line. I was careful to independently verify her material, however, and found that her work is accurate. Where points of view differ as to the Sinatra family's opinion on certain issues and the views of others, I attempted to present both sides. I also studied the authorized television miniseries *Sinatra*, produced by Frank's daughter Tina, to glean details of the official family viewpoint and studied the narration by Frank junior of his oral history and musical study of his father, *As I Remember It.*

I also made judicious use of Kitty Kelley's Sinatra biography, *His Way*, in order to establish a framework of Sinatra's life but was certain to independently verify information from her research before incorporating any of it into my own.

I also referred to *Sinatra—The Song Is You* by Will Friedwald and *Sinatra 101—The 101 Best Recordings and the Stories Behind Them* by Ed O'Brien and Robert Wilson, as well as *Sinatra: The Man and His Music, The Recording Artistry of Francis Albert Sinatra* by Ed O'Brien and Scott P. Sayers. These three books are the best of the lot where Sinatra's music is concerned and should most certainly be included in the library of any Sinatra enthusiast. Since any complete Sinatra discography would take a book in itself to publish, I recommend that anyone interested in such a listing refer to the above three books for an intelligent examination of the music, if not a discography. I also made use of *Legend—Frank Sinatra and the American Dream*, an excellent compilation of articles about Sinatra edited by Ethlie Ann Vare.

At the Library of Congress, I reviewed tapes of the "Major Bowes and His Original Amateur Hour" programs with the Hoboken Four, including Sinatra's first appearance (September 8, 1935); the *Fred Allen Show* (May 2, 1937); and Sinatra's farewell appearance with Dorsey (September 9, 1942). Vital to my research was a booklet called "The Music of Frank Sinatra," written by respected and thorough Sinatra historian Charles Granata. This booklet includes "Frank Sinatra—An A to Z Discography," which is a listing of every song Sinatra has released commercially, in alphabetical order, with writers, producers, arrangers, and recording dates. This partial discography is not credited, but I suspect it was compiled by Granata in association with Nancy Sinatra. I also utilized *The Sinatrafile (Parts 1, 2 and 3; 1977, 1978, 1980)* by John Ridgeway.

My thanks to Jess Morgan, Ava Gardner's business manager for nearly thirty years, for his assistance and memories of Miss Gardner, which were invaluable to me. My interview with Morgan was most appreciated.

My appreciation to Esther Williams (Sinatra's costar in *Take Me Out to the Ball Game*) for her time, astute observations about Ava Gardner and Lana Turner as they related to Sinatra, and for so many years of entertainment. Hopefully, one day Miss Williams will write her memoirs, for that book would surely be a bestseller.

My appreciation to Joey Bishop for allowing himself to be interviewed three times and for his boundless energy and memories interspersed throughout this book, particularly in those sections about the Rat Pack.

As the former editor in chief of *Soul* magazine, I had the opportunity to interview Sammy Davis Jr. on several occasions over the years, in 1976, 1980, 1984, and 1989. I utilized many of Davis's memories about Sinatra in this work. I have re-created certain conversations between Davis and Sinatra, based on his excellent memory, particularly from my interview with him on February 1, 1989. Mr. Davis was a kind and generous man who is deeply missed. I also referred to his autobiographies *Yes I Can!, Hollywood in a Suitcase*, and *Why Me?*

I had the good fortune of interviewing the late Jule Styne at the Mayflower Hotel in New York in 1988 for a new edition of my book *Carol Burnett—Laughing Till It Hurts*, and I utilized many of his comments about Sinatra from that interview. The talented production director Joe Layton introduced me to Styne when Layton and Gary Halvoroson directed "A Tribute to Jule Styne" at the St. James Theater that year. Layton is also much missed.

My thanks to Patti Demarest for the interviews she granted me regarding her early memories of Nancy Sinatra, Sr. in Jersey City, New Jersey. Thanks also to Ted Hechtman for his assistance and his invaluable recollections and for the many hours we spent poring over his old appointment and date books.

Thanks to certain friends and family members of Lee Mortimer, who requested anonymity because of what they feared might be reprisals against them from the Sinatras. After so many years, it is true that the Sinatras are still—and perhaps justifiably so—angry about much of what Lee Mortimer wrote about Frank in the fifties and sixties and whatever participation he had in the FBI's ongoing investigation of Sinatra. It says a great deal about the public's perception of the Sinatra family's influence, though, that anyone would ever think they would retaliate against people who were, or are, associated with the Mortimers, even after all of these decades. It's simply not true; however, I respect their concerns.

Thanks to Betty Wilkin and Josephine Barbone for allowing me to go through photo scrapbooks and for making themselves available to answer my endless questions.

I also had access to an oral history taped by Dick Moran, which he still one day hopes to have published. Mr. Moran allowed me to utilize many work-related papers and original drafts of press releases, which are fascinating and enlightening as to the relationship Sinatra had with George Evans in the forties and fifties.

Of all of the Sinatra biographies published over the years, two were particularly helpful to my research and are recommended by this author for their insightful approach: *Sinatra* by Earl Wilson (1967) and *Sinatra—Twentieth-Century Romantic* by Arnold Shaw (1969).

Many of Earl Wilson's notes, memos, and correspondence can be found at the Lincoln Center Library of the Performing Arts. I utilized a great many of them throughout my book, and I thank the staff of the Lincoln Center Library for all of its assistance throughout the years of research on this project.

Dorothy Kilgallen's husband, Richard Kollmar, donated seventy of his wife's scrapbooks to the Lincoln Center Library of the Performing Arts. They are filled with her articles, columns, unpublished notes, and other material which she personally accumulated over her lifetime, including her rough drafts of her "exposé" "The Real Frank Sinatra Story." Much about Sinatra and her relationship with him can be found in her papers, and I reviewed them all thoroughly as part of my research.

Thanks also to the staffs of the New York Public Library, the Beverly Hills Library, the Glendale Central Public Library, and the Brand Library Art and Music Center.

I viewed every film Sinatra ever made to determine which were important to my particular needs and which were not. I also reviewed all of the press clippings, press kits, and other studio-related material, biographies, and other releases for each of Sinatra's films, all of which are on file at the Margaret Herrick Library. I also viewed and culled certain quotes from *Frank Sinatra—Relive the Magic*, a video history of Sinatra, and viewed many episodes of *The Frank Sinatra Show* for background purposes, as well as episodes from other Sinatra series, television specials, and miscellaneous appearances.

I reviewed hundreds of FBI documents which were released under the Freedom of Information Act. My thanks to Tommy DiBella for helping to make them available to me.

Thanks to William Godfrey, Dick Moran, Ida Banks, Mack Millar, Beatrice Lowry, William Merriman, Marilyn Lewis, Shirley Jones, Terrence Gibb, Ethel Anniston, and Jeanne Carmen for interviews.

Lucille Wellman and Mary LaSalle-Thomas are two gracious, generous women who were both friends of Ava Gardner's. They spent hours with me, individually and together, and helped me re-create moments in the Sinatra-Gardner relationship based on what Gardner told them. They also shared with me much correspondence from Ava, sent by her when she was married to Sinatra, which practically acted as a diary of their relationship and helped to finally clear up inaccuracies that had been published in other books. I am so grateful for their help and trust, as I am for the assistance of Gardner's friend Nancy LaPierre.

I also referred to Ava Gardner's autobiography, *Ava—My Story*, as well as Lana Turner's *The Lady, the Legend, the Truth;* Lauren Bacall's *By Myself;* Sammy Cahn's *I Should Care*, and Tony Curtis's *Tony Curtis—The Autobiography*. Also, *Ava* by Charles Higham; *Ava Gardner* by John Daniells; *Kim Novak—Reluctant Goddess* by Peter Harry Brown; *Lana—The Public and Private Lives of Miss Turner* by Joe Morella and Edward Z. Epstein; *The Private Diary of My Life With Lana* by Eric Root; *Always Lana* by Taylor Pero and Jeff Rovin; *Sinatra and His Rat Pack* by Richard Gehman; *Frank Sinatra: Is This Man Mafia?* by George Carpozi; *Frankie: The Life and Loves of Frank Sinatra* by Don Dwiggins; *Sinatra* by Tony Sciacca; *The Big Bands* by George T. Simon; and *For Once in My Life* by Connie Haines. *The Frank Sinatra Reader*, edited by Steve Petkov and Leonard Mustazza, is an excellent compendium of Sinatra features, which I also utilized. I also referred to *The Sinatra Celebrity Cookbook* by Barbara, Frank, and Friends; *Sinatra* by Robin Douglas Home; *B.S., I Love You* by Milton Berle; *The Great American Popular Singers* by Henry Pleasants; *The Frank Sinatra Scrapbook* by Richard Peters; *The Revised Compleat Sinatra* by Albert I. Lonstein; *Sinatra: An Exhaustive Treatise* by Albert I. Lonstein; *Frank Sinatra* by John Howlett; *Yesterdays: Popular Song in America* by Charles Hamm; *Music in the New World* by Charles Hamm; *Sinatra* by Frank Alan; *Tommy and Jimmy: The Dorsey Years* by Herb Sanford; *Dr. Burns's Prescription for Happiness* by George Burns; *Kilgallen* by Lee Israel; *Rainbow—The Stormy Life of Judy Garland* by Christopher Finch; *The Other Side of the Rainbow With Judy Garland on the Dawn Patrol* by Mel Torme;

Judy by Gerold Frank; *Weep No More My Lady* by Mickey Deans and Ann Pinchot; *Brando for Breakfast* by Abba Kashfi Brando and E. P. Stein; *Sammy Davis Jr.—The Candyman: His Life and Times* (L.F.P, Inc., 1990); "Tips on Popular Singing" by Frank Sinatra and John Quinlan (Embassy Music Corporation, 1941); "So Long Sammy" by Marjorie Rosen for *People* (May 28, 1990).

Hedda Hopper's personal notes and unpublished material are housed in the Margaret Herrick Library of the Academy of Motion Picture Arts and Sciences. I utilized many of her papers throughout this book, especially those having to do with Sinatra's suicide attempts. Most helpful were her unpublished notes relating to her story in *Photoplay* (May 1947), "What's Wrong With Frankie?" I also reviewed her copious notes from over thirty interviews she conducted with Sinatra through the years. Any biographer would be grateful for such a find, and I must thank the Margaret Herrick Library for making all of this material available to me and the estate of Hedda Hopper for having the vision to donate it. I also referred to *Hedda and Louella* by George Eells.

I also had access to a complete library of *Photoplay* and *Look* magazines from the fifties of a generous person who wishes to remain anonymous, which was beneficial to my research, particularly the three-part series on Sinatra *Look* published in the summer of 1957. Thanks, also, to that same benefactor, who gave me access to hundreds of notes and transcripts from Louella Parsons having to do with Sinatra, Dean Martin, Sammy Davis, and Joey Bishop.

I consulted the transcript of Joseph Nellis's questioning of Frank Sinatra on March 1, 1951. I also reviewed numerous court documents relating to the separation, and the October 1951 divorce, of Frank Sinatra and Nancy Sinatra.

I interviewed the late Fred Zinnemann (who died on March 14, 1997) on the telephone in June 1995. He was gracious enough to respond in his own hand to a list of questions I sent to him regarding *From Here to Eternity* and his observations of Sinatra. At his direction, I also utilized his private papers in the Fred Zinnemann Collection at the Margaret Herrick Library of the Academy of Motion Picture Arts and Sciences. Of course, I also referred to *The Godfather* by Mario Puzo and also his memoirs, *The Godfather Papers*, as well as *Monty—A Biography of Montgomery Clift* by Robert LaGuardia and *Montgomery Clift* by Patricia Bosworth; *Adventures in the Screen Trade* by William Goldman; and *Uncle Frank: The Biography of Frank Costello* by Leonard Katz.

I utilized tapes of Cathy Griffin's many hours of interviews with the late, famed hairstylist Sydney Guilaroff for his memories of Ava Gardner and Frank Sinatra. Miss Griffin was the author of Guilaroff's memoirs, *Crowning Glory*.

I also had access to Cathy Griffin's taped interviews with the late private investigator Fred Otash for background material regarding the Wrong Door Raid as well as the *Confidential* magazine report in February 1957 and many court documents relating to that particular case. I also reviewed notes and other unpublished material from the *Los Angeles Examiner*'s file on the "raid" and on subsequent hearings.

I examined the Stanley Kramer Collection in the Special Collections Department of the UCLA Library, from which were culled Kramer's comments.

Maryanne Reed allowed me access to her complete collection of Sinatra memorabilia, most of which was culled from the files of the newspaper *Hollywood Citizen News* and the *Woman's Home Companion*, both of which are now defunct. This material was invaluable to me in that it provided many leads and also included the unpublished notes and interviews of reporters who were covering Sinatra for the *News* and *Companion* in the fifties. I listened to and utilized in this work thirty-five previously unpublished taped interviews and conversations with Sinatra intimates, including George Evans, Hank Sanicola, Jimmy Van Heusen, Sammy Cahn, Jule Styne, Jack Entratter,

521

Edie Goetz, Axel Stordahl, Sammy Davis, Marilyn Maxwell, as well as employees of Lana Turner's and Ava Gardner's, all of which Ms. Reed generously had transferred from reel-to-reel format to cassette for my convenience. I am so grateful to her for her assistance. I am also grateful to Isabella Taves for her diligence in keeping such excellent notes for her stories on Sinatra in 1956.

1960–79

I interviewed Dean Martin at Lafamiglia restaurant in Beverly Hills on June 24, 1994. His comments about Sinatra are found throughout this book.

"Frank's an okay guy," Dean told me. "No one understands him because they try to figure him out. You can't figure out Frank, so don't bother trying to do that in your book. You just gotta accept him. He never thought about a thing he ever did. He just did it. He just lived his life, like me, like all of us. Singin', workin', havin' a good time, taking our raps. He coulda' been nicer, though," Dean added, thoughtfully. "We all coulda' been nicer, especially to each other, and to the dames, too. Especially to the dames."

When in doubt, because Mr. Martin's memory was sometimes cloudy, I independently confirmed what he told me during the two-hour conversation.

"Don't be so quick to jump to conclusions," he warned me when I brought up the subject of Frank and his underworld ties. "Nothing about Frank Sinatra is what you think it is. Remember that, kid."

My thanks to Barry Keenan, who gave me his first interviews about the Frank Sinatra kidnapping. Mr. Keenan demonstrated by his experience that a man can turn his life around and be a success in this world no matter what crazy thing he did in his youth. His vivid memory was invaluable in reconstructing the events that led up to his kidnapping of Sinatra junior.

No one could write about the Rat Pack without reviewing their films *Ocean's 11*, *4 for Texas*, *Robin and the Seven Hoods*, and *Sergeants 3*. I also reviewed the Rat Pack's concert at the Museum of Television and Radio in Beverly Hills, California, and again, Joey Bishop's memories were helpful, as were Sammy Davis's. I also listened to a number of unreleased Rat Pack concerts on audiotape and viewed and studied an unreleased videotape of a concert by Sinatra, Davis, and Martin at the Sands Hotel in 1963.

My thanks to Bud Gundaker, a longtime family friend who made available to me a taped interview with Paul "Skinny" D'Amato, which proved invaluable to my research. Mr. Gundaker made available a number of Sinatra interviews as well. I so appreciate his assistance.

My thanks to Mike Santoni for allowing me to listen to his tape-recorded observations of Sam Giancana and other characters from that time period. Mr. Santoni is working on a book about Giancana, and I appreciate his assistance.

Thanks to Thomas DiBella, whom I interviewed on seventeen different occasions. His insight into Sam Giancana's relationship with Frank Sinatra proved invaluable. He also made available to me a transcript of the federal wiretap from December 6, 1961, referred to in the text, as well as a number of transcripts involving Johnny Formosa and also many taped conversations among himself, Sam Giancana, and Johnny Roselli (which he is hoping to one day publish in book form).

Thanks also to Nicholas D'Amato for providing information I was able to use for background purposes throughout this work concerning "Lucky" Luciano, Carlos Marcello, and Jimmy Hoffa.

I interviewed two former members of the Secret Service who requested anonymity. I also interviewed four FBI agents who requested the same, one of whom kept a comprehensive scrapbook about the relationships among Sinatra, Giancana, and the Kennedys that was most helpful.

My time at the John F. Kennedy Library in Boston was well spent, and I thank its gracious staff.

I consulted Sam Giancana's Justice Department file, obtained through the Freedom of Information Act, as well as transcripts of federal wiretaps and Justice Department files on John F. Kennedy.

Thomas Calabrino made available to me the Justice Department's February 1962 report on organized crime, and other important documents relating to the department's investigation of organized crime and how it related to Frank Sinatra, including documents dated September 27, 1962, and October 1962, having to do with Giancana and Phyllis McGuire. He also allowed me to peruse Joe Fischetti's FBI files.

Calabrino made available to me a copy of the Justice Department's FBI report, "Francis Albert Sinatra a/k/a Frank Sinatra," which I examined.

I also referred to *The Luciano Story* by Feder and Joeston; *The Green Felt Jungle* by Ovid Demaris; *The Lucky Luciano Inheritance* by David Hannah; *Lucky Luciano—His Amazing Trial and Wild Witnesses* by Hickman Powell; *The Last Testament of Lucky Luciano* by Martin A. Gosch and Richard Hammer; and *Mogul of the Mob* by Dan Eisenberg and Meyer Lansky Landau; also, "The Last Act of Judith Exner" by Gerri Hirshey in *Vanity Fair* (April 1990) and "The Private Lives of Mia Farrow" by Betsy Israel for *Mirabella* (March 1997).

My appreciation to Don Dandero, an AP photographer working at the Cal-Neva Lodge during the Sinatra-Monroe years, who also covered the Sinatra junior kidnapping in Reno. Mr. Dondero was most helpful in giving me leads and ideas; also, one of his photos appears in this book.

My appreciation also to Darlene Hammond, who took many wonderful photos of Sinatra in the forties and fifties and shared her memories (and pictures) with me. Some of her work appears in this book.

My thanks to Charles Casillo, who helped me understand Marilyn Monroe's psychology, and also my deep appreciation to Marilyn Monroe historian James Haspiel and to Marilyn Monroe fan club president Greg Shriner.

I owe a debt of gratitude to Donald Spoto, the bestselling author of *Marilyn Monroe—The Biography* for his having donated his interview tapes for that project to the Margaret Herrick Library of the Academy of Motion Picture Arts and Sciences. His donation made it possible for me to obtain previously unpublished quotes from Sinatra's attorney, Milton (Mickey) Rudin; Marilyn Monroe's publicist, Patricia Newcomb; Peter Lawford's close business associate Milt Ebbins; and Lawford's longtime friend Joseph Naar.

I also consulted the following books: *Marilyn* by Donald Spoto; *Goddess—The Secret Lives of Marilyn Monroe* by Anthony Summers; *Marilyn Monroe* by Maurice Zolotow; *Conversations With Marilyn* by W. J. Weatherby; *The Masters Way to Beauty* by George Masters; *The Decline and Fall of the Love Goddess* by Patrick Agan; *The Agony of Marilyn Monroe* by George Carpozi; *Marilyn Monroe* by Norman Mailer; *My Story* by Marilyn Monroe; *Monroe—Her Life in Pictures* by James Spada with George Zeno; *Marilyn: The Tragic Venus* by Edwin P. Hoyt; *The Marilyn Monroe Story* by Joe Franklin and Laurie Palmer; *Marilyn—The Last Take* by Peter Harry Brown and Patte B. Barham; *The Secret Happiness of Marilyn Monroe* by James E. Dougherty; *The Mysterious Death of Marilyn Monroe* by James A. Hudson; *The Marilyn Conspiracy* by Milo Speriglio; *The Curious Death of Marilyn Monroe* by Robert F. Slatzer; *Marilyn Monroe—An Uncensored Biography* by Maurice Zolotow; *Norma Jean* by Fred Laurence Guiles. I also used with caution *Marilyn Monroe Confidential* by Lena Pepitone and William Stadem, and I reviewed a tape of her appearances on the *Mike Douglas Show* and the *Joan Rivers Show*.

I utilized *The Encyclopedia of Hollywood* by Scott Siegel and Barbara Siegel; *My Lucky Stars* by Shirley MacLaine; *Dino—Living High in the Dirty Business of Dreams* by Nick Tosches and *Peter Lawford—The Man Who Kept the Secrets* by James Spada (two important works for anyone who ever appreciated Mr. Martin and Mr. Lawford). I also referred to *Jackie Oh!* by Kitty Kelley; *The Making of the President* by Theodore S. White; *The Kennedys—Dynasty and Disaster 1848–1984* by John H. Davis; *The Other Mrs. Kennedy* by Jerry Oppenheimer; *With Kennedy* by Pierre Salinger; *Jacqueline Kennedy Onassis: A Portrait of Her Private Years* by David Lester; *The Joan Kennedy Story—Living With the Kennedys* by Marcia Chellis; *The Kennedys: An American Drama* by Peter Collier and David Horowitz; *JFK—The Man and the Myth* by Victory Lasky; *Jacqueline Kennedy Onassis* by Lester David; *My Life With Jacqueline Kennedy* by Mary Barelli Gallagher; *The Kennedy Women* by Pearl S. Buck; *A Woman Named Jackie* by C. David Heymann; *My Story* by Judith Exner, as told to Ovid Demaris; "The Exner Files" by Liz Smith for *Vanity Fair* (January 1997); *Double Cross—The Explosive Inside Story of the Mobster Who Controlled America* by Sam and Chuck Giancana; *The Boardwalk Jungle* by Paul "Skinny" D'Amato, as told to Ovid Demaris; *Mafia Princess* by Antoinette Giancana and Thomas C. Renner; *Vinnie Teresa's Mafia* by Vincent Teresa (with Thomas Renner); *Wall Street Swindler* by Michael Hillman and Thomas C. Renner; *Johnny, We Hardly Knew Ye* by Kenneth O'Donnell and David E. Powers; *Crime in America* by Estes Kefauver; *Mickey Cohen: Mobster* by Ed Reid; *Bugsy* by George Carpozi; and *The Don: The Life and Death of Sam Giancana* by William Brashler.

Also, *Debbie: My Life* by Debbie Reynolds; *Richard Burton—A Life* by Melvyn Bragg; *Eddie Fisher—My Life, My Loves* by Eddie Fisher; *Las Vegas Is My Beat* by Ralph Pearl; *The Fifty-Year Decline and Fall of Hollywood* by Ezra Goodman; *Revelations From the Memphis Mafia* by Alanna Nash; *Bogie and Me* by Verita Thompson and Donald Shepherd; and "We Might Call This the Politics of Fantasy" by Frank Sinatra (*New York Times*, July 24, 1972).

Sid Mark has been hosting the preeminent radio show about Sinatra, "Sounds of Sinatra," for forty-two years, and I utilized transcripts of many of his interviews over the years with the Sinatra family as well as with Sinatra's producers and arrangers.

I also reviewed the television program *Turning Point*'s profile on Sinatra ("The Man Behind the Legend," December 12, 1996) as well as *20/20*'s interview with Judith Campbell Exner.

And I thank Liz Smith for certain tips and advice to my researcher, Cathy Griffin.

Hundreds of articles were made reference to, but most helpful was Sinatra's own, "Is This Really His Life?" by Claudia Puig for the *Los Angeles Times* (July 26, 1992); "Me and My Music," *Life*, April 23, 1965.

My thanks to Jimmy Whiting for ten hours of interviews regarding Jilly Rizzo, Frank Sinatra, and Marilyn Monroe. I so appreciate his help and access to his personal notes and records. Please note that the name "Jimmy Whiting" is a pseudonym which he chose to protect his identity. It is the only pseudonym in this book.

Thanks also to Beatrice King for her insights into Sinatra's relationship with Juliet Prowse. Jim McClintick, Marty Lacker, Lamar Fike, Joe Langford, Paula DeLeon, Andrew Wyatt, Mickey Song, and Evelyn Moriarity were also all interviewed.

I referred to *Peter Lawford—The Man Who Kept the Secrets* by James Spada and *The Peter Lawford Story* by Patricia Seaton Lawford. Also, I utilized the *Playboy* interview with Sinatra, February 1963.

I reviewed Edward A. Olsen's Oral History, on file at the University of Nevada in Reno, which was helpful as concerns the Cal-Neva incident.

I also referred to numerous Los Angeles District Court documents—in particular, Frank Sinatra Jr.'s testimony in court during his February 1964 kidnapping trial—and newspaper and magazine accounts. Also, some of Frank Sinatra Jr.'s comments are from the popular Sid Marks weekly radio program devoted to his father, Frank Sinatra. I also utilized the book *Miss Rona* by Rona Barrett.

I referred to FBI transcripts of conversations between Sinatra and the kidnappers; thanks also to former FBI agent John Parker for his time and patience.

I also referred to court documents and newspaper accounts regarding legal action taken by Sinatra against Charles Kraft, Morris Levine, and Gladys Root. George Carpozi's book *Is This Man Mafia?* was also helpful. And I utilized my interview with James Wright, Sinatra's valet, and with Sammy Davis. Nancy Sinatra's book *Frank Sinatra—An American Legend*, was also referenced.

During interviews for this book, Jim Whiting, Esther Williams, Lucille Wellman, and Jess Morgan provided details for the violent George C. Scott/Ava Gardner/Frank Sinatra incidents. I also referred to Ava Gardner's memoirs, *Ava—My Story* and Sydney Guilaroff's memoirs, *Crowning Glory*. John Huston's and Nunnally Johnson's comments are culled from Charles Higham's *Ava.* I also reviewed *An Open Book* by John Huston.

My thanks to Theresa Lomax for all of the hours of interviews relating to the Frank-Mia years.

I also referred to, and used quotes from, transcripts of Mia Farrow's television appearances on *20/20, Today* and the *Oprah Winfrey Show* in 1997, to promote her memoir *What Falls Away* (which I also consulted).

I consulted *The Life of Mia* by Edward Epstein and Joe Morella. I utilized the files of Sheila Graham from the Academy of Motion Picture Arts and Sciences.

I referred to and am grateful for my interviews with Deidra Evans-Jackson, Doris Sevanto, Monica Hallstead.

Comments from Sidney Furie are also from my interview with him regarding, primarily, *Call Her Miss Ross* in 1985.

I viewed the November 16, 1965, CBS-TV Walter Cronkite interview with Sinatra (and I thank Maryanne Mastrodanto for providing me with same) and referred to Jack O'Brien's comments about it in the *Journal-American*. I referred to numerous published accounts of Sinatra's conflict with Frederick R. Weisman and consulted police reports about the incident.

I referred to published reports regarding the fracas between Sinatra and Carl Cohen at the Sands, to the Howard Hughes files at the Academy of Motion Picture Arts and Sciences, and also to Nancy Sinatra's two books as well as Mia Farrow's memoirs. I also consulted *Confessions of a Hollywood Columnist* by Sheila Graham and my interviews with Marjorie Nassatier, Florene LaRue, and Diane Phipps.

Other important books and miscellaneous material consulted include *Sinatra: His Life and Times* by Fred Dellar; *Frank Sinatra—A Photobiograohy* by George Bishop; *The Films of Frank Sinatra* by Gene Ringgold and Clifford McCarty; *Frank Sinatra* by Anthony Scaduto; *The Sinatra Scrapbook* by Gary L. Doctor; *Sinatra—The Entertainer* by Arnold Shaw; *Sinatra—A Celebration* by Stan Britt; *Sinatra* by Ray Coleman; *Sinatra* by Robin Douglas-Home; *Sinatra—The Pictorial Biography* by Lew Irwin; Sinatra's monologues from *Sinatra—A Man and His Music* (Reprise Records); "So Frank Is Seventy-Five" by William Kennedy (from *Frank Sinatra—The Reprise Collection*); "The Legacy" by Nancy Sinatra and "The Capitol Years" by Pete Kline (from *Frank Sinatra—The Capitol Years*); *The Industry* by Saul David; *Report on Blacklisting* by John Cogley; *American Entertainment* by Joseph Csida and June Bundy Csida; *The Encyclopedia of Jazz* by Leonard Feather; *Elizabeth Taylor—The Last Star* by Kitty Kelley; *Miss Peggy Lee—An Autobiography* by Peggy Lee; *Shelley—Also Known as Shirley* by Shelley Winters; *Marilyn Beck's Hollywood* by Marilyn Beck; *Grace* by James Spada; *Grace* by Robert Lacey; *The Billboard Book of Number-One Hits* by Fred Bronson; *If I Knew Then* by Debbie Reynolds with Bob Thomas; *The Complete Directory to Prime-Time Network TV Shows 1946–Present* by Tim Brooks and Earle Marsh; *The Last Mafioso* by Ovid Demaris; *Natalie Wood—A Biography in Pictures* by Christopher Nickens; *Brando—A Biography in Photographs* by Christopher Nickens; *Brando* by Peter Manso; and *Iacocca* by Lee Iacocca with William Novak.

Probably the best article about Ava Gardner was written by Rex Reed and published in his book *Do You Sleep in the Nude?* In it Ava is quoted as saying, "Ha! I always knew that Frank would end up in bed with a boy." She denied having made the statement later, but most of her close friends believe that she did say it.

Thanks also to Mary Jenkins for her time and patience and for the interview she gave me in memory of her mother, Choral.

I consulted copious court documents relating to the New Jersey State Commission on Investigation and Sinatra's testimony on February 17, 1970, and also conducted three interviews with one of the investigators, who asked for anonymity.

I reviewed documents and transcripts relating to the House of Representatives Select Committee on Crime Hearings on July 18, 1972, and Sinatra's testimony regarding Berkshire Downs. I also reviewed the *Congressional Record*.

I consulted an abundant amount of court papers and transcripts and trial and court records from *Weinstock* v. *Sinatra et al.* regarding the incident among Frank, Jilly Rizzo, Jerry Arvenitas, and Salt Lake City businessman Frank J. Weinstock at the Trinidad Hotel.

I reviewed copious documents and legal paperwork relating to the Westchester Premiere Theater case, including transcripts of depositions and wiretaps. I interviewed three attorneys connected with the case, all of whom asked for anonymity.

Throughout the book, I relied on Larry King's television interview with Sinatra (May 1988) for certain quotes.

I also consulted news reports of the conflict between Sinatra and Sanford Waterman and spoke to a number of people involved with Waterman at the time about the fracas, none of whom wished to be named in this book but all of whom provided details not only about this specific incident but about Sinatra's general relationship with Caesars.

Of course, there were many hundreds of published articles reviewed about Sinatra's "retirement," some of which were incorporated into the text. The best, of course, is the feature by Tommy Thompson for *Life*. I also had access to Robert L. Rose's drafts and transcripts relating to his articles about Sinatra for the *Chicago Daily News* in 1976.

I also made reference to "Protecting Sinatra Against the Big Beef Story" by Christopher Buckley for *New York* (1971); "My Father, Frank Sinatra" by Tina Sinatra as told to Jane Ardmore for *McCall's* (December 1973); "Sinatra: An American Classic" by Rosalind Russell for the *Ladies Home Journal*; "Frank Sinatra: He Still Does It His Way" by Mark Sufrin for *Saga* (November 1974); "Sinatra: Still Got the World on a String" by Michael Watts for *Melody Maker* (November 9, 1974); "Kennedy Never Cut Sinatra Ties" by Jack Nelson for the *Los Angeles Times* (January 19, 1976); and "The New Mrs. Sinatra" by Ron Home for the *Ladies Home Journal* (October 1976).

I referred to *Once in a Lifetime* by Zsa Zsa Gabor with Wendy Leigh; *Rags to Bitches* by Mr. Blackwell; *The Show Business Nobody Knows* by Earl Wilson; *Sammy Davis—My Father* by Tracey Davis; and *Life With Jackie* by Irving Mansfield and Jean Libman Block.

I utilized Paul Comption's radio interviews with Sinatra on KGIL in San Fransisco on June 5, 1970, and December 30, 1973. I also viewed *Suzy Visits the Sinatras* (May 25, 1977).

During the five years I lived in Palm Springs (1989–94) I had the pleasure of Dinah Shore's company on several occasions. She was an extraordinary, giving person, and I interviewed her three times. Comments included in this book are from an interview she gave me in the spring of 1992 during the Dinah Shore Golf Classic that year.

Thanks also to Eileen Faith, Nancy Wood-Furnell, Laura Cruz, and Carol Lynley for their insights during interviews for this work.

I obtained a bootleg copy of Sinatra's performance at the White House dinner for Giulio Andreotti and consulted it for this work for quotes from that evening.

My researcher Jim Mitteager interviewed Sinatra's valet of eighteen years, Bill Stapely, on May 28, 1997, for the comments regarding Sinatra and Jacqueline Onassis.

1980–97

My thanks to Mort Viner, Dean Martin's friend and manager of over thirty years, for his assistance in clearing up certain inaccuracies about Martin, Sinatra, and others.

Again, Ava Gardner's manager of thirty years, Jess Morgan, was tremendously helpful in providing insights into Sinatra's continued relationship with Miss Gardner. And thanks again to Lucille Wellman, Esther Williams, and James Wright.

I reviewed a videotape of the press conference Sinatra, Martin, and Davis held in December 1987 at Chasen's. I personally attended the first date of the "Together Again Tour" with Frank, Dean, and Sammy at the Oakland Coliseum on March 13, 1988. I also obtained a bootleg copy of the Sinatra-Davis concert on March 22, 1988, their first without Martin.

I am also indebted to the staff of the Department of Special Collections of the University of Southern California, which provided me with much material, including Lew Irwin's excellent 1981 "Earth News" radio interview with Sinatra.

I reviewed videotapes of testimony at the Nevada Gaming Control Board's hearings regarding Sinatra's application for a gaming license in February 1981 as well as copious FBI notes, documents, and transcripts relating to the hearings. Thanks also to Stephen Webb and Clarence Newton.

I had access to *The News of the World* files on Frank Sinatra in London, England, which I used judiciously. More than anything, they provided me with leads and the names of sources to verify information.

Thanks go to Philip Casnoff for his memories of portraying Sinatra in the family's authorized miniseries, which I studied—and enjoyed.

I interviewed a number of former White House staff members who requested anonymity.

Many published accounts were consulted, but most helpful were "The Majestic Artistry of Frank Sinatra" by Mikal Gilmore for *Rolling Stone* (September 18, 1980); "Doing It Her Way" by Nikki Finke for the *Los Angeles Times* (February 28, 1988); "A Perfect Singer Since He Began the Beguine" by Harry Connick Jr. for the *New York Times* (1990); "Under My Skin," by William Kennedy for the *New York Times Magazine*, October 7, 1990: "Frankly, My Dear" by Michael Roberts for *Westword* (December 5–11, 1990); "Are You Ready, Boots? Start Talkin' " by Jeff Tamarkin for *Goldmine*, (March 22, 1991); "Sinatra's Doubleplay" by David McClintick for *Vanity Fair* (December 1993); "Secrets of Sinatra—Inside Tales of His Life and Career" by Budd Schulberg for *New Choice for Retirement Living* (1993); "Frank Sinatra Jr. is Worth Six Buddy Grecos" by Tom Junod (*GQ,* January 1994); "Frank and the Fox Pack" by Julie Baumgold for *Esquire* (March 1994); "Sinatra's Last Audition" by Jonathan Schwartz for *Esquire* (May 1995); "The Voice of America" by Will Friedwald and Jennifer Kaylin for *Remember* (November 1994); "The Boots Are Back" by Steve Pond for *Playboy* (May 1995); "A Gold Medal for Ol' Blue Eyes" by Kitty Kelley for *Newsweek* (October 2, 1995); and "Frank Analysis" by Gregory Cerios for *People* (December 18, 1995).

Thanks to Debra Stradella, Joseph Wilson, Marjorie Hyde, Larry Culler (maître'd'

527

at Matteo's), and my anonymous friend in the Sinatra camp who provided me with a copy of Frank's performance contract. Thanks to Steve Stoliar, Groucho Marx's secretary and archivist and the author of *Raised Eyebrows: My Years Inside Groucho's House*. I also reviewed Sinatra's radio interviews with Sid Mark (April 28, 1984) and Jonathan Schwartz (on WNEW, 1988).

Again, thanks to Maryann Mastodonato for providing me with a copy of Bill Boggs's WNYW interview with Sinatra.

Thanks to Amanda Bridges, Tina Roth, Felicia Sands, and Betty Monroe for all of their notes, personal papers, and other documents relating to Frank Sinatra's later years.

Thanks also to George Carpozi, whose unusual—but useful—book, *Kitty Kelley— The Unauthorized Biography*, proved helpful. I also referred to court documents relating to "Sinatra v. Kelley, et al." I reviewed *Reagan* by Lou Cannon and *Crime Confederation* by Salerno and Tomkins; and *Sinatra—An American Classic* by John Rockwell.

I must mention Ed Shirak Jr.'s book, *Our Way—In Honor of Frank Sinatra*, which is an account of Shirak's three-year journey to meet Mr. Sinatra. Shirak, who is from Hoboken, New Jersey, wrote passionately of his experiences relating to Sinatra and to the people who knew him in the early days of his life. I found his work fascinating and invaluable to my own research.

Finally, I made use of the Sands Hotel Papers throughout *Sinatra: Behind the Legend*. These papers include many interoffice memos (some of which were utilized in this work) as well as newspaper clippings, photographs, negatives, brochures, press releases, audiotapes, news clips, interview transcriptions, and correspondence, all of it stored in forty-nine boxes. The papers were donated to the James R. Dickinson Library of the University of Nevada Las Vegas in December 1980 by the Sands Hotel through the office of Al Guzman, director of publicity and advertising. The collection comprises essentially the files of Al Freeman, director of advertising and promotion for the Sands Hotel from 1952 until his death at the age of forty-eight in 1972. My thanks to Peter Michel, head of special collections of the Dickinson Library, for his assistance with this material.

ACKNOWLEDGMENTS

Sinatra would not have been possible without the assistance of many people and institutions. First acknowledgment must go to my editor, Hillel Black, for this is our third collaboration; Mr. Black also edited my books *Call Her Miss Ross* and *Michael Jackson—The Magic and the Madness*. Somehow, he always manages to elicit my best work, and I appreciate his dedication, assistance, and encouragement.

Paula Agronick Reuben has been invaluable to me for many years, guiding my way through my previous books, and now through *Sinatra*. I would like to thank her for her dependable professionalism and staunch loyalty.

Warmest thanks to Cathy Griffin for conducting scores of interviews for this book and, in particular, for using her private investigative skills to locate people who have never before been interviewed for a Sinatra biography. Obviously, considering the span of Sinatra's life and career, we had the opportunity to interview a wide variety of sources. We purposely decided to focus on those who had not previously told their stories. Of course, these people were not always easy to locate, and I am so appreciative of Miss Griffin for her perseverance and tenacity.

Without a keen-eyed copy editor, a book does suffer. I had the best in Frank Lavena, and I thank him for his insightfulness. Thanks also to Renata Somogyi Butera for her excellent production supervision. And thank you, Gregory K. Wilkin, for such an imaginative and striking book jacket design.

And, of course, my thanks to Steven Schragis, Bruce Bender, Meryl Earl, Gary Fitzgerald, Gordon Allen, and all of those at Carol Publishing Group who have been in my corner.

I owe a debt of gratitude to Wayne Brasler of the University of Chicago, who read this book in manuscript form a number of times in order to verify information relating to Sinatra's musical career. In fact, Mr. Brasler has read all seven of my books in advance in order to render a much-valued opinion, and I have appreciated his assistance over the years.

Thanks also to John Drayman, the consummate Sinatra historian, and a good friend of mine, who also read this book numerous times prior to its publication. He and I engaged in many discussions about how to present this work in a fair and balanced manner. I am grateful to him for his vision.

Al Kramer, a trusted friend and writing colleague for years, also read the manuscript in its early stages in order to keep me on track. Thanks, Al, for sharing your wisdom.

During the final weeks of production I was fortunate to have the assistance of author, editor, and Hollywood historian Jim Pinkston. His eye for detail and knowledge of the golden age of the movies proved an enormous help. He swooped in at the last minute and fine-tuned many details just in the nick of time. I am so grateful to him for his contributions, which proved invaluable and enhanced this book in many ways. Thanks, Jim.

Thanks to Maryann Mastrodonato, who is much more than a Sinatra fan in that she is devoted to protecting his legacy and interested in seeing the facts of his life presented accurately. Miss Mastrodonato provided many videotapes of Sinatra interviews over the years, material from which is published in these pages for the first time.

Special thanks to Carlo Mastrodonato for the final photograph of Mr. Sinatra in the color section of this book.

Without a loyal team of representatives, an author usually finds himself sitting at home writing books no one ever reads. I thank mine: James Jimenez, Esq., of Gilchrist & Rutter; Melvin Wulf, Esq.; Ken Deakins, Rae Goldreich, and Terina Hanuscin, of Duitch, Franklin and Company; and Laurie Feigenbaum, of Laurie Feigenbaum and Associates. Bart Andrews has always been a trusted adviser, and I thank him for years of dedication. Thanks also to Glenda Tenucci and Angelica Fuentes.

My thanks to James Spada, author of *Peter Lawford—The Man Who Kept the Secrets*, for sharing contacts, telephone numbers, and ideas with me.

Special thanks to all of those who assisted me in tangible and intangible ways, including Richard Tyler Jordan, Dan Sterchele, Ray Trim, Jeff Hare, RuPaul, David Bruner, George Solomon, Lisa Reiner, Sven Paardekooper, Billy Barnes, Rev. Marlene Morris, Rev. Roger Aldi, Lydia Boyle, Sonja Kravchuk, Barbara Cowan, Chuck Dransfield, Randall Friesen, Scherrie Payne, Lynda Laurence, Cindy Birdsong, Paul and Diane Orleman, Dan Verona, Kevin Norwood, Carl Feuerbacher, Scott Haefs, Kate McGregor-Stewart, Louise Booth, Barbara Ormsby, Charles Casillo, Rick Starr, Cheryl Arutt, Dan and Stephanie King, John Passantino, Linda DeStefano, Ken Bostic, Mr. and Mrs. Joseph Tumolo, Daniel Tumolo, Steven Viens, Riva Dryan, Lisa Lew, Reed Sparling, Marilyn and Anthony Caruselle, Jim Kane, Christopher DeAnde,

Jackie Percher, Bill Hoffman, Danny Duran, Kiki Talbot, Jeffery Bowman and Michael Reid-Rodriguiez.

My appreciation to Roby Gayle Gidley for years of spiritual and emotional support.

Special thanks to Stephen Gregory, who helped make this book, and everything else, possible.

Thanks to my family Roz and Bill Barnett, Rock and Rose Taraborrelli, Rocky and Vincent and, also, Arnold Taraborrelli. Special thanks to my father, Rocco, who has always been my inspiration.

Finally, this book is dedicated to my mother, Rose Marie, who passed away on August 9, 1996. Through my years of planning, developing, researching, and writing this book, she believed that Sinatra was the right subject for me, and she urged me to complete it. As always, she was right. I miss her.

INDEX